Indian Economy

Indian Economy

Volume III

K.R. Gupta

ATLANTIC
PUBLISHERS & DISTRIBUTORS (P) LTD

Published by

ATLANTIC

PUBLISHERS & DISTRIBUTORS (P) LTD

7/22, Ansari Road, Darya Ganj,
New Delhi-110002
Phones : +91-11-40775252, 23273880, 23275880, 23280451
Fax : +91-11-23285873
Web : www.atlanticbooks.com
E-mail : orders@atlanticbooks.com

Branch Office
5, Nallathambi Street, Wallajah Road,
Chennai-600002
Phones : +91-44-64611085, 32413319
E-mail : chennai@atlanticbooks.com

Printed in India at Nice Printing Press, A-33/3A, Site-IV, Industrial Area, Sahibabad, Ghaziabad, U.P.

Preface

Indian economy has come a long way since India's Independence in 1947. Although the major problems of poverty, unemployment, unequal distribution of wealth, and inadequate infrastructure still continue to persist, the fact cannot be denied that a rapid development is being made in many important areas. Some landmark policy decisions like delicensing, and prudent monetary and fiscal measures taken by the government, have put the economy on a higher growth path. In fact, the country's annual GDP growth has been quite remarkable since the initiation of economic reforms in the 1990s.

The book *Indian Economy* in three volumes is an attempt to assess all the key indicators of Indian economy from academic point of view. Volume 1 of the book provides a detailed overview of Indian economy, also giving the economic history of India, features of Indian economy, and India's demography. The major sectors like Agriculture and Industry have also been discussed, besides India's Public Finance. Volume 2 studies the structure of Indian economy and attempts to answer the key questions such as whether to go for mechanization across various sectors, which may aggravate unemployment situation, or to adopt labour-intensive methods of production, which are slow; whether to pursue disinvestment of Public Sector Undertakings (PSUs), which according to some experts tantamounts to giving away in private hands, enterprises established with public money, or to grow sluggishly; whether to encourage foreign multinational companies (MNCs) to establish their business in India, or to keep the economy insulated from foreign competition, etc.

This, volume 3 of the book studies in depth the financial system and structure of Indian economy. The entire banking and finance network, including indigenous and foreign banks, non-banking financial companies (NBFCs), Reserve Bank of India (RBI)—its regulatory and credit functions as well as monetary management, reorganization of banking structure, Indian money market, special financial institutions, merchant banking, venture capital funds, stock exchanges in India, central and state financial corporations, among other things, have been discussed in detail.

Monetary policy is a crucial weapon in the hands of the central bank as its efficacy is important in achieving the goals of growth, inflation control or price stability, fiscal stability, exchange rate stability and promotion of foreign exchange reserves. The basic objective of any central bank of a nation is to maintain sound monetary system. The term monetary management involves four major issues: price stability, control over money supply, control over money stock in the light of reserve money creation due to RBI credit to government, and rationalization of administered interest rate. Therefore, an exclusive chapter has been devoted to prices and monetary management in India, giving a brief historical background, position after 1990s and the latest trends, focusing on inflation management, covering food inflation, prices of non-administered petroleum products, housing price index, etc. Anti-inflationary measures taken by the government, of monetary, fiscal as well as administrative variety, have been discussed. Latest trends in monetary aggregates, including reserve money, narrow money and broad money, have also been analysed.

Like USA and Canada, India too adopted a federal system of government. In this structure, states collect certain taxes as assigned to them, the amount of which is used by the states themselves for running their governments besides for the development of the states. Transfer of resources is the main feature of present financial system in India. Thus, the financial relations between the centre and the states have been studied in an exclusive chapter explaining various pertinent issues like distribution and allocation of central revenue, including income tax, excise duty, estate duty, etc. Grants-in-aid, loans to states, debt reliefs, etc. have also been discussed. Besides, various finance commissions right upto the Thirteenth Finance Commission—constituted to make recommendations for the period 2010-15—have been examined in detail.

One of the objectives of India's national policies is to bring about a balanced development of all sections of people. It is therefore necessary to provide subsidies on some type of goods and services, for example, food subsidies to the poor, fertilizer subsidies to farmers and LPG subsidies to households. However, these subsidies are a heavy burden on the nation's exchequer. There is an ongoing debate whether subsidies should continue, be reduced or stopped altogether, with strong arguments for each proposition. An assessment of government subsidies has been made, describing their types, magnitude, impact and relative advantages and disadvantages.

A study of various constituents of currency system such as currency notes in circulation, the volume of money supply, money aggregates, reserve money and money stock is necessary to understand the impact of their variations in society on the overall functioning of the economy. The same has therefore been provided in detail, alongwith a discussion of related issues like exchange value of rupee vis-à-vis US dollar, exchange controls, full convertibility of rupee on current account, India's foreign exchange reserves, management of these reserves as well as legal framework and policies governing the reserves.

The strength, resilience and stability of a country's external sector are reflected by various indicators. These include a steady increase in reserves, moderate levels of current account deficit, changing composition of capital inflows, flexibility in exchange rates, sustainable external debt levels with elongated maturity profile and an increase in capital flows. All these, along with the net trade balance and all other payments and receipts present a complete picture of economy.

A format which presents the development of external sector is called balance of payments (BoPs). India's balance of payments has been discussed to get an overall view of the development in the external sector, covering recent trends, position of India's current account, in both merchandise and invisibles, and capital account. Major causes of balance of payments deficits have been discussed and measures to mitigate their adverse impacts suggested.

Black money, also known as 'unaccounted economy', 'illegal economy' and 'subterranean economy' is a big menace and a cause of confrontation between our legitimate and illegitimate sectors. It creates roadblocks in the path of achieving the social objectives of establishing a welfare state as enshrined in India's Constitution. Various estimates of black money in India, its impact on economy and society at large, how the huge amount of black money has been generated, the major causes of corruption in India, and measures to control black money, including tax reforms, removal of unnecessary controls, etc. have been discussed under 'The Parallel Economy in India'.

About 70 per cent of India's population lives in rural areas. However, rural India is increasingly becoming a diversified market with a strong demand for credit to buy agricultural inputs like seeds, farm implements, pesticides and other purposes like health care, education, housing, etc. Organization of rural credit has been taken up, focusing on the importance of credit delivery mechanism in rural finance and highlighting the new initiatives for agricultural sector, like Kisan Credit Card, Crop Insurance, Microfinance, Self-Help Groups, etc.

A special feature of this book is the inclusion of important Tables giving latest, and in some cases, also historical data on various parameters relating to Indian economy. The text has been supplemented with up-to-date information of facts, figures, policies, schemes, programmes and reviews. Various authentic sources like surveys, reports and sites have been consulted to gather relevant information, and they have been duly acknowledged in the text. I take this opportunity to thank the ministries, institutions, organizations and sites on whose data, etc. ideas and analyses have been developed in this book.

The book will help the economists, government executives, parliamentarians and legislators to frame effective economic policies. It will prove beneficial to the students and teachers of economics at graduation and postgraduation levels. Those preparing for competitive examinations like Civil Services will find this book useful. To those having an interest in Indian economy, particularly its financial structure, this book will provide for a stimulating and richly rewarding reading.

K.R. GUPTA

Contents

Indian Financial System—I: Commerical Banking

1

BANKING/FINANCE NETWORK

Earlier, there used to be specific finance institutions such as co-operative societies and industrial banks, mainly for agriculture and industries respectively. These were later followed by commercial banking system with the existence of commercial banks for all purposes. Funds are now collected from public and the same are passed on to borrowers of all segments responsible for stabilising the economy of the country. This banking system has so far been gladly accepted and patronised by the people who are getting the money at a very reasonable interest rate in comparison to heavy rate of interest charged by private moneylenders, namely *marwaries* and *banias*, etc. Any person or a private firm receiving deposits and lending money through *hundis* is an indigenous banker as per Indian Central Banking Enquiry Committee, 1931. Finance is provided by the indigenous bankers for various purposes to the traders and industries against the mortgage of houses, land or any kind of property apart from undertaking all types of banking operations.

Funds are needed not only by individuals and business houses but also by the government for various purposes. A factory owner needs funds to buy the machinery besides paying wages to his workers. A trader needs funds for buying and stocking goods in his godown. A farmer needs finance for buying seeds and manure, etc. for cultivation for a short-term of one year or so. An exporter needs money to buy raw materials to execute his orders in time. Even the government requires monetary resources to meet its expenditure on goods, services and for the implementation of the several projects and programmes for the welfare and betterment of the life of people. All such procedures do involve commercial banking transactions. Leaving aside commercial aspect of banking, the banks provide services to the individuals for safety of their hard earned-money and the secured lockers for their valuables.

Structurally, the financial system deals with finance pertaining to industry, agriculture, development and government expenditure. The Indian financial system also helps insurance companies, mutual funds, investment funds and institutions promoting savings among the public. Banking system plays a vital role while the new issues of stocks and shares are floated in the market. Money is collected from the investors and passed on to the companies.

Capital formation is one of the main functions of Indian financial system which mobilises the savings and properly distributes the same among the end-users of funds. The capital formation reflects the economic development, and the financial system is also termed as financial market. To achieve rapid economic growth and social objectives, the banks perform various functions. Banks have major role in various development works. Banking system is the backbone of a nation as it is instrumental in bring about the progress of society. Banks have worked tremendously by providing various types of facilities to people with small income and interestingly their money is further financed for the development of their area itself. Banks pass on the adequate funds to the government for procurement of foodgrains for public distribution and implementation of integrated rural development programmes. Banks have done a splendid job by opening branches in the rural and backward areas, thereby reducing inequalities between rural and urban regions.

As regards the composition of the Indian financial system, it comprises Indian money market in which funds are borrowed and lent for a short-term and Indian capital market, being the other case in which the same is done for medium and long term. Organised and unorganized are the two sectors classified in Indian money market. Commercial banks including private, public and foreign banks come under organised sector.

Unorganised sector covers indigenous banks and non-banking financial companies. Organised sector is broadly classified into the Reserve Bank of India, the central bank of the country, commercial banks and the co-operative banks. Reserve Bank of India is so called because it keeps cash reserves of scheduled banks and has supreme monetary power to control the entire banking system.

Another classification of banks in our country is scheduled and non-scheduled banks under Reserve Bank of India Act, 1934. Scheduled banks are those enlisted in the Second Schedule of RBI Act, 1934. Such banks have a paid-up capital and reserves of an aggregate value of not less than Rs. 5 lacs satisfying RBI that their affairs are carried out in the interest of their depositors. All commercial banks Indian and foreign, regional, rural and state co-operative banks are termed as scheduled banks. All commercial banks are profit-oriented whereas co-operative banks are based on co-operative principle of no profit-no loss. Non-scheduled banks are those which have not been included in the Second Schedule of RBI Act, 1934.

The Indian Capital Market

The Indian capital market pertains to the borrowing and lending on medium and long term. The demand for such capital normally comes from private as well as public sector manufacturing units, trading houses, the transporters and in many cases for the agricultural purposes. Eventually, the central and the state governments too raise adequate amount from the capital market. Supply of funds for the capital market comes from individuals and corporates through banks, insurance companies, public provident funds and several specific agencies. Government, semi-government and industrial securities besides financial institutions and non-banking financial companies are main classifications of Indian capital market, out of which government and semi-government securities carry fixed interest rates. The Indian capital market is also categorized as primary market covering new issues, and the secondary market for the old shares and debentures of the existing companies. The Indian capital market is an attractive market for the foreign institutional investors who are investing huge amount as per guidelines of the Indian government, thereby improving global image of Indian capital market. Such investments are made by foreigners as they are getting more profit and benefits in comparison to other stock markets of the world.

Indigenous Banks

Talking of Vedic era from the ancient days, the indigenous banking had been organised in the form of family business. However, during British rule, there was a decline of indigenous banks though they continue to exist even in the present times. In spite of severe competition of modern regular commercial banks today, these indigenous banks are efficiently carrying out their transactions and sometimes exceed business of scheduled banks. Like money-lenders, indigenous banks have a variety of clients including small farmers and the borrowers of the villages. Small amount is given on the verbal promises and loan of large amount on promissory notes or against mortgage of crops, etc. Heavy interest rate is charged and no doubt, the loan becomes a burden on borrowers which often continues from generation to generation.

These indigenous banks find place in the system due to some reasons such as: (i) where the modern banking is not adequate, (ii) where funds are provided on risk basis which is the basic requirement of small business, and (iii) where they extend more credit for various purposes as compared to modern banks. Moreover, operations of indigenous banks are simple and flexible, free from several formalities and consequent delays of modern banks. Their services are personalized coupled with promptness. These banks provide business of good return in the form of *hundis* to the commercial banks which in turn proves helpful in enhancing the scope of bill market in the country. Hence, these agencies with productive activities were declared useful by the Banking Commission (1972). These indigenous bankers employ their own capital and in some exceptional cases they do accept some deposits from friends and relatives. They give loan against all kinds of securities. According to the Committee on Finance for the Private Sector—the Shroff

Committee, 1954, between 75 to 90 per cent of the total internal trade of the country was being financed by the indigenous bankers.

Indigenous Bankers and the RBI

In the year 1931 when Reserve Bank of India was created, the Central Banking Enquiry Committee desired that the organised and unorganised sectors of Indian money market should be united besides linking of indigenous bankers with RBI. The Committee emphasised and also recommended that the *hundi* used by the indigenous bankers would get through as a regular official banking transaction provided the indigenous bankers stop trading and commission business, switch over to western type of accounting, develop banking activities of deposit side having their accounts audited by the certified accountants and submit the necessary statements to the RBI periodically, for this RBI promised them all the privileges and benefits enjoyed by the scheduled banks. The indigenous bankers did not accept the offers made to them stating that the privileges offered by RBI were not enough to compensate for the loss of their non-banking business. They were not prepared to give up their trading and commission business expressing their desire to remain confined to the banking business only. In view of this, the scheme suggested by RBI to bring indigenous bankers under its governing failed.

In the year 1954, Shroff Committee made a recommendation that RBI should encourage the rediscounting of the *hundis* of the indigenous bankers by RBI through the scheduled banks. Such proposals for the linking of the indigenous bankers with RBI and the organised Indian money market were put forward, among others, by the Bombay Shroff Association and the Banking Commission (1972).

Indigenous Bankers and Non-Banking Financial Companies

It is seen that there has been tremendous development in the banking sector comprising commercial banks as well as indigenous bankers. The indigenous bankers continue to play a prominent role in rural and urban areas mainly because of the risk they take. They gladly finance the small productive sectors and are also doing sizeable turnover by providing commercial banks with *hundis*. Gradually, the indigenous bankers are adopting the proper banking system and converting themselves into the non-banking financial companies.

Banking Progress in India since 1969

During the pre-independence period, the Indian banking system was in the grip of crisis with frequent failures of banks but later, after the independence, during second half of the 20th century, the Indian banking system remarkably progressed mainly due to the efficient planning, rapid economic growth, fast flow of money, control and proper regulation by the Reserve Bank of India followed by nationalisation of banks in July 1969.

In early fifties, there were more than 400 commercial banks but later due to mergers and acquisitions of small banks with big banks, the number of banks declined. In the early sixties, there were more than 250 small non-scheduled commercial banks but the number declined to four after the mergers in the beginning of eighties.

Nationalisation of Banks

Dynamic decision of nationalisation of 14 banks was taken by the late Prime Minister of India, Mrs. Indira Gandhi in July 1969 prior to which the banks were being run by the capitalists and industrialists who used to divert the money of public to their projects and in funding activities which were not national priorities, with the result that agriculture remained backward and industry made little progress.

Since there was no proper economic development of the nation due to lack of interest shown by the commercial banks, nationalisation of banks was inevitable. In the year 1980 again, government took over another six commercial banks taking the number of nationalised banks to 20. These are in addition to the State Bank of India and associate banks which were earlier taken over in the year 1955.

Expansion of Branch Network

Earlier, before the nationalisation of banks, there used to be the branches in big cities but later, after nationalisation, there was superb expansion of branches in rural areas and urban regions as well. Nationalisation of banks resulted into integration of organised and non-organised money markets in our country. Because of various loans given by banks on lower rates of interest, there was rapid progress towards opening of substantial number of branches. After nationalisation of banks, branch network splendidly rose at a rate of more than 800 per cent which so far has not been witnessed by any other country.

FUNCTIONS OF BANKS

Deposit Mobilisation

After nationalisation of banks, the number of branches increased rapidly thereby substantially accelerating the rate of growth of deposit mobilization. Banking system has vastly contributed to the saving habit of people coupled with planned economic development which has resulted into a trend of increase in deposits reaching the tune of more than 32 times after the nationalisation and expansion of branches till early nineties. Deposits would add up as the unbanked areas start getting banking services.

Factors for Rapid Deposit Growth

There are numerous factors which directly affect the rapid deposit growth such as prevailing financial conditions in the country and these environments tend to be favourable with aggressive expansion of branches of banks. Various schemes are floated and implemented through banks to mobilise the deposits in rural as well as urban areas. A good amount of deposits are collected on the basis of policies announced from time to time. People get attracted for the high rates of interest offered by the banks and put more money in the banks for investment. NRIs are also tempted for lucrative investments which generate sizeable deposits and simultaneously fetch adequate amount of foreign exchange.

Over and above, cash reserve ratio plays a significant role to boost the deposits which improve the economic development. Smaller the cash reserve ratio, the greater is the chance of multiplying the deposits. Earlier the Cash Reserve Ratio (CRR) and the Statutory Liquidity Ratio (SLR) were of the order of 3 per cent and 25 per cent when the bank used to get enough deposits required. But later both CRR and SLR were increased gradually with the result the banks were to maintain large cash reserves. Hence, the lending of banks was restricted and correspondingly the deposits declined. With the implementation of Narasimham Committee recommendations in 1992, both CRR and SLR were reduced by RBI, thereby increasing reserves with banking system and expanding bank deposits further. Though the commercial banks have been facing tough competition from mutual funds, housing banks, leasing and investment companies apart from the financial institutions which offer higher interest rates, still the commercial banks are doing a commendable job of maintaining expected growth rate. Besides domestic business gesture, the deposit growth gets indirect impact of global conditions. Recently, due to US subprime crisis the world economy in spite of huge bailout packages, inducted, has been severely disturbed. Its adverse effect has been felt all over of the world.

Expansion of Bank Credit

Bank deposits and bank credits are co-related. Banks have to meet the credit requirements of trade, industry and agriculture units. Hence, with the expansion of bank deposits there has to be proportionate increase in bank credits. It has been noticed that there has been remarkable increase in the bank credit to the tune of more than 20 per cent per year which has been mainly due to large reduction of CRR and SLR, increased food credit and procurement operations, more demand for credit of PSU and export, liberal RBI money policy reducing rates of interest and progressive expansion in bank lending for industry and other sectors. This principle applies in getting bank credit. The influential industrialists, businessmen and capitalists manage to get the maximum possible bank credit. They somehow please the concerned bank personnel and get their credit limits enhanced whereas it becomes very hard for small business units and the farmers to get the bank credit in spite of nationalisation of banks. Only for namesake, small portion of funds is passed on to the small scale establishments and farmers for agriculture.

Development-oriented Banking

Fundamentally, there has been long close association of trade and industry with the banking system. In olden days, the banks used to finance textile sector only covering jute which was traditional industry at that time. But with lapse of time, we could see banking finance catering to the needs of almost all segments of business. Banks are now providing long-term loans to factories for buying raw material, replacing old machinery with new one and paying wages to the workers. The traders are availing banking help to buy their items and stocking those in their godowns. Doctors are encouraged by the banks to set up their nursing homes and hospitals. Engineers get loans from banks to conduct research on new products followed by their commercialization. Farmers get loans from banks for buying seeds, manure, tractors and tools for agriculture. Commercial banks are equally responsible for the development of rural areas. Various schemes are announced by the government for the weaker sections for which banks come forward for extending the finance. Gradually, banks are trying to fill up the gap between rural and urban masses.

Priority Sector Lending of Banks

Before nationalisation of banks, the agriculture sector and small business units were ignored because the commercial banks during that period were owned by big business giants who were not keen in the development of such units. They passed on the responsibility of same to the co-operative credit societies and co-operative banks. This was the main cause of failure of planning of agriculture and due to the same reason small industrial units too did not grow. Immediately after the nationalisation, the commercial banks were specifically directed to the financing of priority sectors of agriculture, small industry, business units and operators of transport. Later, more sectors were added, like professional self-employed persons, retail trade of any kind, education, housing loans for weaker sections and other loans. Neglect of priority sector lending was one of the causes for nationalisation of the top 14 banks in 1969.

In the year 1980, RBI issued the following directives to the banks as regards priority sector lending:

(i) Priority sector advances should constitute 40 per cent of aggregate bank credit.

(ii) Out of priority sector advances, at least 40 per cent should be provided to agriculture.

(iii) Direct advances to the weaker sections in agriculture and allied activities in rural areas should form at least 50 per cent of the total direct lending to agriculture.

(iv) Bank credit to rural artisans, village craftsmen and cottage industries should at least be 12.5 per cent of the total advances to small scale industries.

(v) About 12 per cent of bank credit should go to exporters.

All the commercial banks welcomed the move to increase priority sector lending. Soon, there was rapid progress as per the directions of RBI amidst some problems faced by the commercial banks.

Problems of Priority Sector Lending

After initial positive response, some of the problems of priority sector lending listed below were felt:

(i) The banks were nervous to go for a target of 40 per cent which resulted into indiscriminate lending. Besides there was pressure on them to lend to weaker sections.

(ii) Profitability was severely affected because banks could not monitor and keep watch on recovery of small loans.

(iii) Till 1992 under CRR 15 per cent and SLR provisions 38.5 per cent banks were forced to keep a high proportion of 53.5 per cent in liquid reserves. Hence, they had 46.5 per cent of deposit resources for loans and advances out of which banks were to allocate 40 per cent as loans to the priority sector. The result was that other sectors were neglected and banks suffered loss because for priority sector, lending was done at a very low, concessional rate of interest.

(iv) There was no uniformity in the bank lending to the priority sector. In backward states it was low and so to achieve target of 40 per cent for the country as a whole, banks were stepping up loans to the priority sector in more of advanced states thereby adversely disturb the regional balance in the country.

Priority Sector Lending and IBA Panel

The Narasimham Committee (1991) on the financial system was against the continuance of the priority sector lending and made recommendations as under:

(i) The priority sector should be refined;

(ii) It should be fixed at 10 per cent of the aggregate bank credit;

(iii) It should be reviewed after a period of three years; and

(iv) It should be completely phased out gradually.

The Government of India did not accept the above recommendations of Narasimham Committee on priority lending. However, the panel of bankers constituted by Indian Banks' Association (IBA) suggested to the Narasimham Committee on Banking Sector Reforms (1998) that the present priority sector credit limit of 40 per cent of net bank credit should be slashed to 10 per cent for the following three reasons:

(i) Operating expense for small loans was very high due to deployment of large number of field staff.

(ii) Recovery process was very low in agriculture and small scale sector.

(iii) Quality of assets was bad as there were too many risk factors.

The panel of bankers of IBA also suggested redefining the priority sector as follows:

(i) Priority sector lendings should be restricted only to the core sector and all other loans should be left to the commercial judgement of banks.

(ii) Banks should also be involved in the selection process of beneficiaries in all government sponsored schemes.

(iii) The government should extend subsidies directly to the banks instead of routing them through intermediaries.

Social Banking: Employment and Poverty Alleviation Programmes

Banks are not only meant for commercial purposes but also have a prominent role in building social image of the country. Various schemes are announced by the government for the welfare of the weaker sections so as to provide them employment and for their socio-economic betterment. Banks provide finance for such schemes at a low concessional rate of interest because of which banks in return get low profitability but they do it somehow to fulfil their social commitment.

From April 1972, Differential Rates of Interest (DRI) scheme was introduced by the Government of India under which the loan was given to the weaker sections at the rate of 4 per cent even without security but who could improve their economic conditions through financial assistance from public sector banks. Initially, the scheme was covering more than 150 districts and later the same was extended to the entire country. The scheme was a grand success with number of accounts crossing over four millions and amount advanced rose to the tune of about 800 crores mark within a span of about two decades. But with lapse of time the number of accounts started declining as the banks could not trace the real deserving cases because of pressure imposed upon them to step up such lending.

Integrated Rural Development Programme

This programme was assigned for correcting the imbalances in rural economy and bringing an overall prosperity to the poor people of villages. In early nineties, banks had distributed about 1200 crores as loans to nearly 3 million beneficiaries covering Scheduled Castes/Tribes and women. Following three schemes were introduced by Government of India and implemented through the commercial banks:

(i) Prime Minister's Rozgar Yojana for Educated Unemployed Youth.

(ii) Scheme for Urban Micro Enterprises.

(iii) Bank credit to minority communities.

In the year 1996, a new scheme was launched, namely Prime Minister's Integrated Urban Poverty Eradication Programme so as to remove urban poverty in four years. The scheme was tried for 400 urban centres covering urban poor living below urban poverty line. But since there was more flow of people from rural to urban areas, the number of urban poor was on the rise and hence the scheme became almost impracticable. Government keeps on floating various schemes but because of rampant corruption in our country, the desired amount actually does not reach the right beneficiaries, with the result most schemes do not work for the purposes meant for.

Diversification in Banking

Sometimes it becomes a little difficult for the banks to survive only on traditional banking which they have been doing since 1969. Hence, Government of India issued guidelines to the banks under Section 6 of the Banking Regulation Act, 1949 giving them the green signal to diversify the functions described below:

Merchant Banking and Underwriting

Commercial banks have now set up merchant banking divisions and are also underwriting new issues particularly preference shares and debentures. Earlier such services were provided to some companies but later offer has been made to a wider variety of clients. This is a specialised field of banking and no doubt has good potential of profitability in comparison to the conventional banking.

Mutual Funds

Some of the banks have got the permission to float subsidiaries as mutual funds. At one time Unit Trust of India had monopoly and now of course, even this fund has a lot of competition from others.

Retail Banking

Many commercial banks are taking keen interest in retail banking pertaining to loans for the purchase of durables like refrigerators, televisions, air conditioners, cars, motor cycles, computers, educational loans and credit cards, etc. and educational loans. Retail banking with back-up of commercial banking plays a vital role in economic development. Loans are normally given for a short period whereas housing loan lasts for longer periods.

ATMs—Automated Teller Machines

ATMs are very common these days and almost all the banks have diversified into this kind of banking. It is easy, low cost and very convenient. An ATM occupies small space and is operatable all the twenty-four hours throughout the year. Every bank has tie-ups with other banks with the result one can withdraw the money from ATMs of other banks too with a little service charges in some cases. It eliminates manpower and works as profitable banking. It has been very well patronised by the public in totality.

Anywhere Banking

It is very popular and nowadays very common banking liked by people. Most of the branches of the bank are synchronised through computer. This system of banking was introduced by foreign banks and later was adopted by the public sector banks. Under this system of banking, a customer having account in one branch of the bank can operate in other branches of the bank in the same city or even other cities. All the branches of the bank are at par for him. No need of carrying heavy cash. Simply carry the cheque book. Even the passbook is updated from all branches and money or cash can also be deposited likewise.

Internet Banking

With the growing upgraded technology, use of internet has been increasing fast. Transactions are being carried on online, which has really brought remarkable changes in the system and pattern of banking. It saves substantial time which otherwise is wasted in going to bank. In this kind of banking, every customer is allotted a unique personal identification number (PIN) for online dealings. Keeping in view the frauds and cheating cases, the RBI has issued guidelines on internet banking such as risks involved, technology, security standards, legal implications besides regulatory and supervisory concerns of RBI.

Venture Capital Funds

Government of India has issued the guidelines and procedures for establishing Venture Capital Funds to provide equity capital so as to attempt commercial application of indigenous technology to the domestic conditions. Management structure, size, investment of the fund and other details are prescribed.

Factoring

It is a device by virtue of which book debts are quickly realised through outright sale of accounts receivable to a financial intermediary or a bank's subsidiary called the factor. Banks have been permitted to take up factoring by floating subsidiaries which has already been accepted by RBI. Indian commercial banks have shown rapid progress and transformed themselves beyond recognition. Banks may float many more subsidiaries to take up new activities.

Profitability of Banks in India

Table 1.1 indicates net profits of various banks for the year 2006-07 followed by enhanced profit for the year 2007-08 in all the cases Public Sector Banks show net profit of Rs. 20,152 crores and Rs. 26,592 crores for the year 2006-07 and 2007-08 respectively. Similarly, scheduled commercial banks show net profit of Rs. 31,203 crores and Rs. 42,726 cores for the year 2006-07 and 2007-08 respectively.

Various schemes are announced by the government as well as banks themselves to attract their clients for some or other commercial activities. In case you want to apply for a draw of flat, you need not pay the initial sizable amount and in lieu of that you have to pay only the interest amount. People's burden

Table 1.1: Working Results of Scheduled Commercial Banks

Items	Public sector		Foreign banks		Old pvt. sector banks		New pvt. banks		All SCB sector banks	
	2006-07	2007-08	2006-07	2007-08	2006-07	2007-08	2006-07	2007-08	2006-07	2007-08
(Rs. Crore)										
A. Income	187869	245941	24968	34947	13042	16799	48837	71200	274716	368886
(i) Interest income	164185	214025	17924	24417	11474	14694	38092	56435	231675	309570
(ii) Other income	23684	31916	7044	10530	1568	2104	10745	14765	43041	59315
B. Expenditure	167717	219349	20382	28335	11920	14821	43494	63656	243514	326160
(i) Interest expended	101960	148902	7603	10604	7055	9960	25802	38535	142420	208001
(ii) Intermediation cost (operating expenses)	43255	46598	7745	10355	2967	3234	12353	17033	66319	77220
(iii) Provisions and contingenies	22503	23849	5034	7376	1899	1627	5339	8087	34775	40939
C. Operating profit	63407	73190	12330	16967	4089	5212	17696	24578	97522	119946
D. Net profit (A-B)	20152	26592	4585	6612	1122	1978	5343	7544	31203	42726
E. Net interest income (spread)	62225	65123	10320	13813	4420	4734	12291	17900	89255	101570
F. Total assets	2440166	3022237	274392	364099	160562	194555	584842	745594	3459962	4326486
G. Net income (Aii+E)	85909	97038	17364	24343	5988	6839	23035	32665	132296	160885
(As per cent of total assets)										
A. Income	7.70	8.14	9.10	9.60	8.12	8.63	8.35	9.55	7.94	8.53
(i) Interest income	6.73	7.08	6.53	6.71	7.15	7.55	6.51	7.57	6.70	7.16
(ii) Other income	0.97	1.06	2.57	2.89	0.98	1.08	1.84	1.98	1.24	1.37
B. Expenditure	6.87	7.26	7.43	7.78	7.42	7.62	7.44	8.54	7.04	7.54
(i) Interest expended	4.18	4.93	2.77	2.91	4.39	5.12	4.41	5.17	4.12	4.81
(ii) Intermediation cost	1.77	1.54	2.82	2.84	1.85	1.66	2.11	2.28	1.92	1.78
(iii) Provisions and contingenies	0.92	0.79	1.83	2.03	1.18	0.84	0.91	1.08	1.01	0.95
C. Operating profit	2.60	2.42	4.49	4.66	2.55	2.68	3.03	3.30	2.82	2.77
D. Net profit (A-B)	0.83	0.88	1.67	1.82	0.70	1.02	0.91	1.01	0.90	0.99
E. Net interest income (spread)	2.55	2.15	3.76	3.79	2.75	2.43	2.10	2.40	2.58	2.35
Memo item										
1. Operating expenses as per cent of net income	50.35	48.02	44.60	42.54	49.55	47.29	53.63	52.15	50.13	48.00

Source: RBI

is reduced and at the same time banks too earn substantially. Likewise banks in India have shown rapid progress after the nationalisation.

Causes for Low Profitability of Public Sector Banks

Main causes for low profitability of PSBs are the declining interest income and rising cost of operation. On compulsion from government for extending loan to priority sectors, the profitability has diminished. On the other hand, the uneconomic branch expansion, unnecessary recruitment of employees, inefficiency of staff, low productivity, vagabond expenditure, too much of spending on entertainment and arranging parties pose problem of rising cost of operation to run the banking. Apart from all these things there were mega scams by Harshad Mehta, Ketan Parkash and several others which do weaken the banks and reduce their profitability as well.

Suggestions for Improvement of Profitability

Narasimham Committee suggested the following guidelines to improve the profitability:

(i) The setting up of Assets Reconstruction Fund to take overall doubtful debts.

(ii) SLR to be reduced to 25 per cent of total deposits over a period and likewise, CRR to be reduced to 3 to 5 per cent of the total deposits of the banks. This would leave more funds with the banks for profitable deployment.

(iii) Market interest rates to be offered to the banks by the government for government and semi-government securities coming under SLR arrangements.

(iv) Banks to get more freedom to fix minimum lending rates of interest.

(v) Priority sector lending to be reduced to 10 per cent instead of the 40 per cent of the total bank credit.

(vi) All concessional rates of interest to be removed.

(vii) Banks should go for new sources of funds, for example, Certificates of Deposits (CDs) which could bring in additional funds for the banks which in turn could lend the amount to the corporate sector at profitable rates of interest.

(viii) Banks should increasingly go for 365 days treasury bills which carry higher rates of interest.

(ix) Branch expansion to be carried out strictly on commercial principles and the banks be permitted to snap branches among themselves.

(x) Diversification of banking activities.

There are numerous reasons for low profitability of banks, the major reason being the political interference as the politicians get the funds diverted to the sectors of their choice in particular to weaker sections to seek their votes to win the elections. According to Narasimham Committee (1991), "The deterioration in the financial health of the system has reached a point where, unless remedial measures are taken soon, it could further erode the real value of and return on the savings entrusted to them and even an adverse impact on depositor and investor confidence."

NPAs and SARFAESI Act, 2002

Big corporates somehow manage to get the loan from public sector banks as well as financial institutions like IFCI and IDBI. Due to some reason they are not prepared to repay the borrowed amounts. So the accumulation of non-performing assets (NPAs), consisting of loans and advances given to corporates, result into low profitability because in such cases banks too find themselves helpless to recover the amount. Hence, the Government of India enacted Securitization and Reconstruction of Financial Assets and Enforcement of Security Interest Act, 2002—briefly known as SARFAESI Act. It was done so as to enable banks to realise their dues without the intervention of courts and tribunals. The Act enabled the setting up of Asset Management Companies to acquire NPAs of any bank or financial agency by issuing debentures, bonds or any other security. As per the Act, the company which is the second creditor gets entitled to serve notice to the borrower to discharge his liabilities within two months. Failing this, the second creditor will be entitled to take possession of the secured assets, take over the management of the assets and to appoint any person to manage the secured assets. Borrowers have the option of appealing to the Debts Tribunal after depositing 75 per cent of the amount claimed by the second creditor. The latter is also entitled to enforce any security interest created in his favour without the intervention of courts or tribunals. After the enactment of SARFAESI Act, 2002 there was decline in the gross NPAs. Accordingly, in April 2003, the RBI had issued guidelines and directions for the registration and operations of asset reconstruction/securitization companies.

RECOMMENDATIONS AND SUGGESTIONS ON BANKING

Narasimham Committee (1991) on Banking System in India

Ever since the nationalisation of banks in 1969, there has been a remarkable growth in expansion of banking network, deposit mobilization, implementation of various schemes and quality of work improvement. But later, decline in profitability was observed and the noticeable deterioration was felt in the services the banks rendered, may be due to some constraints imposed upon them resulting into reduced productivity and efficiency in the entire banking system. Under such circumstances, a high level committee was set up by the Government of India for a solution. Mr. M. Narasimham, former Governor of Reserve Bank of India, was appointed as Chairman to examine all aspects of the banking system.

Fundamental approach of the committee was to strengthen the financial system with the desired market orientation, to streamline the working patterns and procedure so as to increase the productivity and efficiency all around. Further, Narasimham Committee (1991) pointed out that the government directed investment and credit programmes are the two major causes besides the solvency, health and efficiency of the institutions should be central to effective financial reform.

Problems and Constraints of the Banking System: Government Directed Investment

Basic principle of sound banking is to maintain proper liquid assets in the form of cash, gold and unencumbered approved securities, i.e. government securities and government guaranteed securities equal to not less than 25 per cent of their total demand and time deposit liabilities. This requirement is known as Statutory Liquidity Ratio—SLR. RBI raised this ratio from 25 to 30 per cent in November 1972 and further gradually to 38.5 per cent by 1991 due to two reasons stated below:

(i) A higher SLR forced commercial banks to maintain a larger proportion of their funds in government securities and government guaranteed securities of public sector financial institutions which seems to reduce the capacity of commercial banks to grant loans and advances to business and industry.

(ii) A higher SLR diverted bank funds away from loans and advances to industry and trade, to investment in government securities. This was said to have an anti-inflationary effect.

The Narasimham Committee (1991) argued that the high SLR adversely affected profitability of the banks because the rate of interest received by banks on government securities was less than the market-related rates of interest. Besides, with higher SLR, the amount of funds left with banks for allocation to the productive economic sectors like agriculture, industry and trade was reduced. The Narasimham Committee characterized the high SLR as a tax on the banking system and also on the savings routed through banks.

Cash Reserve Ratio (CRR)

Under the Reserve Bank of India Act, 1934, every scheduled bank had to keep certain minimum cash reserves with RBI. Initially it was 5 per cent against demand deposits and 2 per cent against time deposits. Later in 1962, RBI varied CRR between 3 per cent to 15 per cent of total demand and time deposits. So taking SLR and CRR together, banks had to keep as much as 53.5 per cent of their aggregate deposits as cash balances with RBI or in government securities and securities of public sector financial institutions. The RBI paid interest at the rate of 3-5 per cent on the cash reserves kept by scheduled banks with it under CRR and at 5 per cent on incremental cash balances. Narasimham Committee (1991) found that the rate of interest received by the scheduled banks from the RBI for their eligible cash balances were below the rate which the scheduled banks had to pay to their depositors for one year deposits. Similarly, the rate of interest the banks received on government securities was much lower than the market rate. Hence, the reserve requirements imposed on the scheduled banks were like taxes which led to continuous loss in potential income of banks and in turn it adversely affected their profitability.

Government Directed Credit Programmes

After the nationalisation of banks in 1969, the Government of India directed the banks to extend the bank credit even in the unbanked rural areas to agriculture which was earlier a neglected sector as well as to other designated priority sectors. Later, the bank credit facility was extended to exports and food procurement operations with the result that directed credit programmes became grand success at the cost of deterioration in the quality of loans. Insufficient attention to qualitative aspects of lending consequently diminished banks' profitability. Moreover, the banks were asked to shift from security-oriented credit to purpose-oriented credit so that a link between technological upgradation in agriculture, small industry and availability of finance was established. But somehow this aspect could not come through.

Political and Administrative Interference

Government of India announced the nationalisation of banks in 1969 for the upliftment of weaker sections and priority sectors but due to misuse of power among the bank personnel, selected people of their choice are favoured for which their interest is taken care of. On the other hand, there is political pressure on administrative staff of banks to direct loans and bank credit to their supporters. In most of such cases borrowed money is not repaid, creating heavy burden on the banks and consequently resulting into low profitability. Hence, the sound banking is not established and the customers are deprived of quality of services. Loan melas were organised by some political parties for their own interest and favouring particular persons. Narasimham Committee (1991) on loan melas stated: "The intended socially oriented credit in the process, degenerated into irresponsible lending".

Subsidizing of Credit: Low Rate of Interest

Under SLR scheme at low rates of interest, banks could extend finance to the priority sector and no doubt government also managed the funds for its own use. This in fact amounted to subsidy on such loans which ultimately deprived other sectors of industry and trade for seeking loans at low rates of interest. Hence, to make for the loss incurred, banks were charging these sectors high rates of interest, thereby affecting the economic and industrial development of the country. People deposit their hard earned money in banks to get good return on their investment whereas the government keeps on directing the banks to finance the sectors at low rates of interest as desired by the ruling political party. According to the Narasimham Committee (1991), there was actually no need for interest subsidy which no doubt weakens the banking system. The policymakers in our country had neglected the fact that the institutional finance is certainly much cheaper than the source of money creditors and indigenous bankers. The Finance Ministry, which is the financial backbone of the government, has morally no right to waste the funds of public sector banks.

Mounting Expenditure of Banks

Commercial banks collect the money from people and pass on the funds to various sectors like industry, trade, export and agriculture, etc. Consequently, they show net profit after deducting the salaries of staff and other expenditures for their operations. Profitability can be increased by reducing the expenditures wherever possible. But it has been observed that in spite of substantial deposit mobilization and nicely extending the bank credits to lucrative stabilised sectors, the banks in some cases find it difficult to survive. The expenditures of banks have mounted to such a level that their commercial viability becomes very difficult in the present time of high competition.

On mounting expenditure of banks, the Narasimham Committee (1991) stated as under:

(i) There has been a phenomenal increase in branch banking without any relation to demonstrated need and potential viability.

(ii) The lines of command and control tended to weaken central office supervision, internal inspection and audit, and increased unreconciled inter-branch and inter-bank entries.

(iii) Rapid growth in number of staff and accelerated promotions led to deterioration in the quality of manpower, over-manning at all levels, etc.

(iv) The trade union had contributed increasingly to the restrictive practices regarding promotions, transfers, discipline and work culture, mechanisation and computerisation, etc. Remunerations and their upward revisions were not related to productivity of either individual banks or to the system. Inefficient customer service and declining labour productivity were the consequences.

(v) There was extension of bank credit to agriculture and small industry where the unit cost of administering the loans was high. Besides this type of credit was at low rates of interest as mentioned earlier.

Recommendations of the Narasimham Committee, 1991

The Narasimham Committee (1991) recommendations were aimed at:

(i) Ensuring a degree of operational flexibility;

(ii) Internal autonomy for the public sector banks in their decision-making process; and

(iii) Greater degree of professionalism in banking operations.

These recommendations have the basic approach that the public deposits the money with the banks so as to get the optimum benefit of it and the said amount is held by the banks in good faith. Banks utilise the public funds for various sectors for the desired economic development and fundamental growth as well as prosperity of the country. Banks have no right to use these funds for financing government's consumption expenditure.

On Directed Investment

Regarding SLR and CRR, the Narasimham Committee (1991) gave two main recommendations:

(i) *Statutory Liquidity Ratio—SLR*. It was recommended that the government should reduce the SLR from

38.5 per cent of net demand and time liabilities of banks to 25 per cent over next five years. A reduction in SLR levels would leave more funds with banks for allocation to agriculture, industry trade, etc. The committee further recommended that government borrowing rates should be progressively market related and that these higher rates would help banks to increase their income from their SLR investments.

(ii) *Cash Reserve Ratio—CRR.* The Committee recommended that the RBI should reduce its dependence on CRR and should rely on open market operations increasingly. The Committee further proposed as follows:

(a) CRR should be reduced progressively from 15 to 3-5 per cent; and

(b) RBI should pay interest on impounded deposits of banks above the basic minimum at a rate of interest equal to the level of banks' one year deposits.

These recommendations would reduce the amount of idle cash balances kept by the banks with RBI under CRR and release the amount for more productive and remunerative purposes. Besides, banks would also earn more income from the cash balances they keep with RBI.

On Directed Credit Programmes

The Narasimham Committee (1991) recommended that the directed credit programmes should be over and gradually stopped. Moreover, this system should not be a permanent affair. Priority sectors pertaining to agriculture, small industry and trade have already attained their optimum level of progress. Concessional interest rates should be discontinued as interest subsidy of 20 years was enough. However, the system of directed credit should support certain weak sections of the economy. So-called redefined priority sector should be fixed at 10 per cent of the aggregate bank credit and need to be reviewed every three years or so. The Committee further suggested that only weaker sections of the rural community such as marginal farmers, rural artisans, village and cottage industries as well as small sectors should be encouraged through directed credit programmes.

On the Structure of Interest Rates

The Narasimham Committee (1991) proposed that concessional rates of interest for priority sector besides controls and regulations on interest rates on lending and deposit rates of banks and the financial institutions on debentures and company deposits, etc. should be removed. The Committee further proposed that RBI should be the sole authority to simplify the structure of interest rates. Bank rate should be the anchor rate and all other interest rates should be closely linked to it.

On Structural Reorganisation of the Banking Structure

The Narasimham Committee (1991) proposed the reorganisation of banking structure so as to increase the efficiency in banking system by reducing the number of banks by way of mergers and acquisitions and suggested the broad pattern as under:

(i) Three or four large banks including the State Bank of India could become international in character and should possess the global status for the banking operations.

(ii) General or university banking should be engaged in the country with a network of 8 to 10 national banks.

(iii) Operations of local banks should be confined to a particular region.

(iv) Operations of rural banks including RRBs would be confined to rural areas only and that too for financing of agriculture and allied activities.

The Committee further proposed that there was enough network of banking and more of expansion of branches should be stopped. However, in some cases banks can open selected branches that too purely on the consideration of profitability. Moreover, the Committee wanted government not to nationalise more banks and should boost the private sector banking besides avoiding discrimination between public and private sector banks.

The Committee also recommended that the government should allow foreign banks to open branches or subsidiaries conforming to similar social obligations as the Indian banks. Joint ventures of these banks should encourage the merchant and investment banking as well as other updated techniques and forms of financial services.

OTHER RECOMMENDATIONS RELATING TO THE BANKING SYSTEM

Nationalised banks and Development Financial Institutions were suffering heavy losses because of sub-standard, doubtful and loss assets known as non-performing assets. Narasimham Committee recommended the setting up of the Assets Reconstruction Fund (ARF) to take over a portion of their bad and doubtful debts at a discount from the nationalised banks and financial institutions. Such an arrangement would gradually take away bad and doubtful debts from banks' balance sheets and recycle the funds realised into more productive uses.

The Committee suggested that the RBI should be the primary agency for the regulation of the banking system. The present system of dual control over banking system between RBI and the Banking Division of the Ministry of Finance should stop immediately. The Committee further proposed that every public sector bank should be free and autonomous so as to become competitive internally. The RBI should examine all the guidelines and directions issued to the banking system in the context of the independence and autonomy of banks. Moreover, the appointment of Chairman-cum-Managing Director in a bank should not be based on political considerations but on merited professionalism and highly dependable integrity judged by an independent panel of experts and not by the government.

The Narasimham Committee (1991) had no hesitation in directly blaming the Government of India for the kind of treatment given to the bank by Finance Ministry. The banks are misused by the Finance Ministry officials because of political pressure exerted. The banks management also has to listen to the trade union leaders who can speak anything and put any kind of allegations against any officer or personnel of the banks.

The Narasimham Committee (1991) made its recommendations for the rapid progress in respect of economic development and growth of the country as well as for the welfare and betterment of the bank employees.

Reform of the Banking Sector (1992-2005)

Economic development and growth are the significant issues of concern for the Indian economy. Several policies are announced from time to time on almost all the aspects such as industries, trade, agriculture, finance, etc. Gradually, government realised the weaknesses of the policies that had prevailed earlier. Initially, there were no significant reform measures, but since the beginning of nineties, many changes were made for the systematic sound planning system and efficient functioning of the banks. These have a positive impact on the banking sector which is the main strength of all segments of the commercial as well as social activities responsible for the streamlined stabilized economy.

Various political parties and also the trade unions staged protests to express their tough opposition for the major recommendations of Narasimham Committee (1991). In spite of all this, Government of India, without any hitch and hesitation started implementing the major recommendations in a straight forward manner:

(i) *Statutory Liquidity Ratio (SLR)*: On incremental net demand and time liabilities (DTL), SLR was reduced from 38.5 per cent to 25 per cent. SLR on outstanding net domestic demand and time liabilities was gradually reduced from 38.5 per cent to 25 per cent in October 1997. This was the minimum stipulated under section 24 of Banking Regulation Act, 1949.

(ii) *Cash Reserve Ratio (CRR)*: The incremental cash reserve ratio (ICRR) of 10 per cent was abolished. Reserve Bank of India, on the one hand, could reduce CRR immediately. RBI, however, gradually reduced CRR from 15 per cent to 5.5 per cent in December 2001 and that too when conditions softened and money growth started slowing down since 1995-96. Main reason of doing so was to release funds locked up with RBI for lending to the industrial and other sectors which were started by bank credit.

(iii) *Interest Rate Slabs*: These were gradually reduced from 20 to 2 by 1994-95. The main changes in interest rates since 1991-92 are as under:

(a) Interest rate on domestic term deposits has been decontrolled;

(b) The prime lending rate of SBI and most other banks on general advances of over rupees two lacs has been reduced;

(c) The rate of interest on bank loans above rupees two lacs has been fully decontrolled;

(d) The interest rates on deposits and on advances of all co-operative banks except urban co-operative banks have been deregulated.

Exploring healthy competition among the banks and also to increase their working efficiency was the purpose behind deregulation of interest rate on the high slab of bank advances thereby helping banks better adjust their lending rates to the trade record and risk perception with regard to their customers. So far the interest rates are concerned, scheduled commercial banks have the full liberty to fix the same on their deposits subject to minimum prescribed floor rates and maximum ceiling rates.

(iv) *Prudential Norms*: These were introduced by RBI in view of reformative process so that the supervision of banks becomes more effective in accordance with acceptable accounting practices of global level. Fundamentally, the main purpose of the prudential system of recognition of income, classification of assets and provisioning of bad debts is to ensure that the books of the commercial banks reflect their financial position. Prudential norms required banks to make 100 per cent provision for all non-performing assets—NPAs. Since the funding for this purpose was placed at

Rs. 10,000 crores, it was phased over two years. Banks had to make at 30 per cent provision against doubtful and bad debts during 1992-93 and balance 70 per cent in 1993-94.

(v) *Capital Adequacy Norms*: These were fixed at 8 per cent by RBI in April 1992 and banks had to comply with the same over a three-year period. By the end of March 1996 all the public sector banks had attained capital to risk weighted assets ratio of 8 per cent. The full norm of 8 per cent was also attained by foreign banks in India and by some Indian banks. Scheduled commercial banks were expected to make large provisions amounting to over Rs. 14,000 crores for bad and doubtful advances in their portfolio as per prudential guidelines and the new capital adequacy norms. As the resulting losses would erode the already inadequate capital of the banks, the viability and financial health of the banking system was sought to be protected by a capital contribution of Rs. 5,700 crores by the Union Government in the budget for 1993-94 and another Rs. 5,600 crores in the budget for 1994-95 for recapitalization of the less profitable nationalised banks. The recipient banks were required to draw up plans to become viable over a period of two to three years.

Based on the Basle Committee recommendations, a new capital framework was introduced for Indian scheduled commercial banks presenting two tiers of capital for the banks:

(a) Tier I or core capital, considered the most prudent and readily available support against unexpected losses includes paid-up capital, statutory reserves, share premium and capital reserve; and

(b) Tier II capital consisting of undisclosed reserves, fully paid-up cumulative perpetual preference shares, revaluation reserves, general provisions and loss reserves, etc.

Moreover, Tier II capital should not be more than 100 per cent of Tier I capital as it was so prescribed.

(vi) *Access to Capital Market*: To enable the nationalised banks to access the market for capital funds through public issues subject to the provision that the holding of the Central Government would not fall below 51 per cent of the paid up capital, the Government of India has amended the Banking Companies (Acquisition and Transfer of Undertakings) Act.

SBI was the first to raise funds through public issue of over Rs. 1,400 crores as equity and Rs. 1,000 crores as bonds. RBI shareholding of SBI is now 67 per cent as against 99 per cent earlier. The SBI Act has also been amended to allow 10 per cent noting rights to the shareholders. Gradually, other nationalised banks have also approached the capital market to raise the funds through public issues.

(vii) *Freedom of Operations*: All the scheduled commercial banks have been given full liberty to expand their activities like opening of new branches and upgradation of extension counters after obtaining capital adequacy norms and prudential accounting standards. They have also the freedom to wind up non-viable branches other than those in rural areas as well as to decide levels of holding of individual items of inventories and receivables after liberalising the bank lending norms.

(viii) *New Private Sector Banks*: The functioning of ten private sector banks has already begun. The said new banks are allowed to raise capital contribution from foreign institutional investors upto 20 per cent and from non-resident Indians (NRIs) upto 40 per cent. It is a part of expansion of private sector banks for better commercialized banking.

(ix) *Local Area Banks*: To mobilise rural savings and to channelise them into investment in local areas, the Government of India, during 1996-97 budget, announced the setting up of new private local banks

(LABs) subject to jurisdiction over three contiguous districts. In the year 1996, RBI had given its approval for setting up seven local area banks and out of these, the licences had been issued to five LABs which are in business in the states of Andhra Pradesh, Karnataka, Rajasthan, Punjab and Gujarat.

(x) *Supervision of Commercial Banks*: Any project or assignment, if undertaken or carried out with stage-wise supervision, the same would yield optimum productivity with best possible efficiency, but it was unfortunately not done by Government of India so far as the banking system was concerned. Eyes of our government opened after mega securities scam of year 1992. Then only supervision of commercial banks was tightened. Accordingly, RBI set up a Board of Financial Supervision with an advisory council under the chairmanship of the Governor to strengthen the supervisory and surveillance system of banks and financial institutions. To assist the Board of Financial Supervision and for supervision of commercial banks, the RBI also established, in December 1993, a new department known as Department of Supervision as an independent unit. Besides, the working group under Mr. S. Padmanabhan, set up to review the system of on site supervision of banks, recommended extensive changes in bank inspection which included target appraisal of major portfolios and control systems as well as a discriminatory approach to supervision and inspection that distinguished sound banks from problematic banks.

(xi) *Recovery of Debts*: Reducing loss is as good as gaining profit. Keeping in view this approach, the Government of India passed Recovery of Debts due to Banks and Financial Institutions Act, 1993 to facilitate and speed up the recovery of debts due to banks and financial institutions. Apart from an Appellate Tribunal set up in Mumbai, six Special Recovery Tribunals have been established at Kolkata, New Delhi, Jaipur, Ahmedabad, Bengaluru and Chennai for quicker recoveries of loan arrears within six months.

The reform was aimed to transform the highly regulated and directed public sector banking system into one characterized by openings, competition, prudential and supervisory discipline as a part of the banking reforms since 1992, based on the recommendations of Narasimham Committee (1991). In the Report on Trend and Progress of Banking in India 1992-93, RBI clearly states, "Commercial banks thus need to become conscious that they are entering a challenging environment and will have to redefine their position within the financial industry. New ways and methods will have to be determined in order to successfully respond to the new challenges, particularly the growing demands from customers for high quality service." This will necessitate commercial orientation of all banks particularly public sector banks and accordingly, they will have to provide better returns on the savings of the investors, adopt strategies to generate additional revenues, reduce emerging financial risks through the creation of new services, improve income-to-cost ratios and enhance operational effectiveness, apart from addressing aggressively to the problems of depressed profitability and high growing non-performing assets.

Committee on Banking Sector Reforms (1998)

To review the progress of banking sector reforms to date and chart a programme on financial sector reforms necessary to make Indian Financial System strong and globally competitive, the Finance Ministry of Government of India appointed Mr. Narasimham as Chairman of the Committee called as the Committee on Banking Sector Reforms. The Committee submitted its report to the government in April 1998. This report covers many issues such as bank mergers, creation of banks of international level, reformation of bank boards and restructuring bank legislation, etc. Main findings and recommendations of the Narasimham Committee on banking sector reforms (1998) are discussed below.

Need for a Stronger Banking System

The said Committee has made out a strong case to strengthen the entire banking system in the country particularly in context of Capital Account Convertibility (CAC) which involves large inflows and outflows of capital and consequent complications for exchange rate management and domestic liquidity. To overcome such problems our country needs a strong well-planned banking and financial system for which the Narasimham Committee (1998) recommended the merger of strong banks resulting into a multifold effect on industry. However, the Committee had indicated a word of caution that the merger of strong and weak banks may have a negative impact on the asset quality of the strong banks. The Committee suggested that two or three of large Indian banks be given global status. The then Finance Minister Mr. P. Chidambaram during 2004-05 advocated merger of public sector banks get the benefits of economies of scale.

Experiment with the Concept of Narrow Banking

The Narasimham Committee (1998) expressed serious concerns over rehabilitation of weak public sector banks which in some cases have mounted the accumulation of high percentage of non-paying assets to the tune of 20 per cent of the total assets. And accordingly, the said Committee suggested the concept of narrow banking to rehabilitate such weak banks. Narrow banking implies that the weak banks place their funds only in the short-term risk free assets. These banks attempt to watch their demand deposits by safe liquid assets. As per Committee's suggestive proposal, the issue of closure should be examined in case the concept of narrow banking is found to be applicable to rehabilitate weak banks.

Small, Local Banks

The Narasimham Committee (1998) argued that two or three banks of global status and eight to ten large national banks should sufficiently take care of the requirements of large and medium sized corporate sector. And larger of smaller enterprises, need larger local banks to cater to their requirements. Hence, the Committee suggested to set up small local banks to serve local trade, small industry and agriculture in cluster of districts. Simultaneously, these banks should have an effective rapport with large and international banks.

Capital Adequacy Ratio

The Narasimham Committee (1998) suggested that the government should consider raising the prescribed capital adequacy ratio to improve the internal strength of banks and to improve their risk absorption capacity. The Committee further suggested higher capital adequacy requirements for banks and setting up of an Asset Reconstruction Fund (ARF) to take over bad debt of the banks.

Public Ownership and Real Autonomy

The Narasimham Committee (1998) has argued that government ownership and management of banks does not enhance autonomy and flexibility in the working of public sector banks. For this, the Committee has recommended a review of the functions of boards so that the bank boards remain responsible for enhancing shareholder value through formulation of corporate strategy. The Committee has considered the issues of autonomous status for the Board for Financial Supervisor of RBI and the need to segregate regulatory and supervisory functions of RBI. The Committee expressed the need for RBI to keep an arm's length from those being regulated and hinted at the need for withdrawing RBI nominees from bank boards. The Committee stated: "Regulation should be concerned with laying down procedural and disclosure norms and sound procedures and ensure adherence to these and not get into the day-to-day management of banks."

Review and Update Banking Laws

The Narasimham Committee (1998) has suggested that our top priority should be to review and amend the provisions of RBI Act, Banking Regulation Act, State Bank of India Act and Bank Nationalisation Act, etc. so that these are in line with the current needs of the banking industry. Other recommendations of the Committee are related to the need of latest computerisation process in public sector banks, professionalising and depoliticising bank boards, reviewing of the recruitment procedures, training and remuneration policies, etc.

Evaluation of Narasimham Report (1998)

Some experts believe that it was too early and hasty to set up another committee within a span of less than ten years. Moreover, the recommendations of Narasimham Committee (1998) were only a little diversified in comparison to those of 1991. Considering a small impact of recommendations pertaining to more strong banks, review of capital adequacy norms and autonomy, the suggestions of Narasimham Committee (1998) were almost an action replay of Narasimham Committee (1991). So far as other issues are concerned, be it organisation, restructuring, freeing bank boards from day-to-day management and interference or segregating the regulatory and supervisory role of RBI, nothing was remarkably different from the previous Committee. In other words, it was unnecessary that Narasimham Committee of Banking Reforms (1998) was set up by the government. Earlier, Narasimham Committee (1991) had strongly recommended the closing down of Banking Division of Finance Ministry and it was further suggested that the banking system should be the responsibility of only one authority, i.e. RBI and the same was not acceptable to the Finance Ministry. It is quite obvious that the officials of Banking Division of Finance Ministry were just wasting time and money of the nation in setting up the committees frequently.

The Banking System and the Securities Scam of 1992

Different people work in different professions such as engineering, industry, trading, medicine, exports or any allied services, etc. Their main aim is to earn money which in fact is the medium to access the status of a person. Rich man has more money and poor person always struggles to earn money. It is wrong to say that the hard work pays more. A labourer works the hardest of all but he is the poorest person. Everybody, no doubt, runs after the money and the people are inclined to indulge in speculation to earn easy money. Way back to late eighties there was a spectular upward movement in the stock market due to liberalized policies pertaining to licensing procedures, fiscal measures, positive export-import trade and expansion of private sector, etc. announced by the successive governments. The upward surge of stock market got further momentum by Dr. Manmohan Singh's 1991-92 budget which was announced with a numerous market supportive policies. The rising trend of stock market continued superbly even after 1992-93 budget which was warmly welcomed by the business community. But later on, as an astonishment, it was known to be stock exchange boom with manipulation which was called securities scam. This mega securities scam of 1992 exposed the involvement of many speculative brokers who along with Harshad Mehta and some bank officials manipulated the banking system, to make huge amount by fraudulent transactions. The established rules, regulations and guidelines were severely violated resulting into one of the worst ever manipulated booms of stock market in India. Many people were ruined as a result of crashing of the market.

After thorough investigations, it was found that the serious weaknesses in internal control and on the part of bank employees led to huge losses to the banks and public as well. Reserve Bank of India set up the Janakiraman Committee to identify several types of irregularities in securities transactions which were adversely used to flush out the funds of banking system. The same are briefed as under:

(i) Purchases were made by banks and their subsidiaries without verifying the facts or in connivance. In some instruments the counter party was ostensibly another bank, but in reality the proceeds were directly or indirectly credited to the accounts of brokers.

(ii) Ready forward sale and purchase transactions were entered into either on their own or on clients' accounts by banks with brokers who used these funds for speculative activities.

(iii) Brokers in the stock exchanges were directly financed by banks by discounting bills not supported by genuine trade transactions.

(iv) Banks and other institutions showed large payments as call money to other banks. However, in the books of the receiving banks, there was no record of call money acceptances but instead, the amounts were credited to the accounts of individual brokers. On the due date, these alleged calls were repaid by payment out of the brokers' accounts in the name of other banks.

(v) Banks and other institutions rediscounted bills of exchange held by other banks and institutions but the proceeds and repayments were routed through brokers' accounts.

(vi) Sums received as inter-corporate deposits and under Portfolio Management Schemes (PMS) by merchant banking subsidiaries of public sector and other banks were passed on to brokers through ready forward deals.

Factors Responsible for Bank Irregularities

Janakiraman Committee scrutinized the environment in which the irregularities of banking system and securities scam of 1992 took place. Those are briefly taken up below:

Public Sector Undertakings (PSUs) and Search for High Returns

The public sector undertakings were on the look for avenues of profitable investment. They tried to take advantage of stock exchange market boom because they had huge short-term funds. They had restrictions to invest these funds in the call money market and on the other hand they were prohibited to invest in inter-corporate deposits as the same was considered risky.

Banks and Search for Profits

The banks burdened with CRR and SLR commitments on one side and social commitment of priority lending on the other, were faced with problem of low interest income and possible losses. Hence, they were looking for opportunities to make quick profits for which they had no other alternative but to improve the yield through trading in securities and mechanism of ready forward transactions.

Stock Exchange Boom and the Brokers

The stock exchange boom was splendidly on top and bulls desperately needed funds to finance their overbought positions. The banks who had funds could see that the only way to earn high returns was to finance stock brokers in booming market. And, thereafter, it was merciless crash of stock exchange boom when the government and RBI realised that the boom was not the result of public response to a favourable budget but it was just artificial manipulation by a few unscrupulous brokers with the support of bankers.

RESPONSE OF THE GOVERNMENT TO SECURITIES SCAM

The government obviously took the following immediate steps to recover the money of banks lost during fraudulent transactions and punish the persons responsible for the irregularities:

(i) A special court was appointed to try all matters relating to the securities scam and legislation was passed with powers to attach the assets of the notified persons involved in the scam.

(ii) A special judge of the Bombay High Court was appointed for trial of scam-related cases.

(iii) The government appointed a custodian for prompt disposal of the attached assets.

(iv) The Central Bureau of Investigation (CBI) was asked to take over investigation of all the frauds and underhand dealings.

(v) Because of the seriousness of the fraudulent transactions and the need for thorough examination of all aspects of the scam, a Joint Parliamentary Committee (JPC) was set up with Mr. Ram Niwas Mirdha as Chairman to enquire into the matter and to fix responsibility for making suggestions as regards future reforms of banking system.

Securities Scam and the Weakness of the Banking System

Smoothness gets disturbed when there is friction in the path, and the partnership of two persons gets disturbed or broken when the integrity of one partner becomes doubtful. In all such cases, the disturbance is caused by some force which is termed as weakness in one form or the other. In view of all this, the mega securities scam of 1992 occurred because of the weaknesses which transformed the mind of many bank officials owing to the greediness and temptative offers made by unscrupulous brokers and other persons who wanted to make huge amount with fraudulent operations. The scam reflected the deliberate criminal violation of rules and regulations with the intention of flushing out the money from the banks due to weaknesses listed below:

(i) Weaknesses in the internal control mechanism within the commercial banks themselves which led to the scam.

(ii) Weakness in the supervisory level. More effective internal control mechanism could have exposed the scam earlier. Reserve Bank of India proposed new Board of Financial Supervision under RBI to rectify this weakness.

(iii) Banks were under pressure because of Finance Ministry's directive to deploy bank resources at low rates of interest which was one of the main weaknesses of banking system responsible for the scam.

(iv) There were many difficulties and irregularities as reflected in running an overregulated financial system. Rigid control over interest rates was neither viable nor workable.

Accordingly, on the recommendations of Janakiraman Committee, the RBI took steps to improve internal control mechanisms in the banks and strengthen the supervisory system so as to prevent the recurrence of such problems in future. A number of structural reforms were worked out for a better banking system. But the common man is not convinced of such assurances of the committees formed for the scams, believing that these frauds take place because of the nexus between stock exchange brokers, unfaithful bank officials, weaknesses on the part of government supported by powerful influential politicians. Our government did not take any action against any high official.

The Governor of Reserve Bank of India, Finance Secretary, Banking Secretary of Finance Ministry and other senior officials of banks as well as Finance Ministry were not brought to book, nor even chargesheeted. They did not even realise their mistakes whereas keeping in view the mega scam they should have resigned of their own, morally. The CBI was not allowed to investigate on appropriate lines. The Joint Parliamentary Committee (JPC) did nothing and was of no use for the adversely affected small investors. Keeping in view other types of frauds, the Janakiraman Committee estimated that the extent of unreconciled amount was to the tune of Rs. 4,000 crores. And it was very clear that our government was just only interested in covering up the matter because top giants of the country were involved in the scam.

Ketan Parekh Scam, 2001

Mega securities scam of 1992 which was due to the consequences of fraudulent operations carried out by Harshad Mehta in conjunction with several brokers and senior bank officials could not make our government to take any action against RBI Governor, Finance Secretary or Banking Secretary of Finance Ministry. All were moving scot-free without any tension or hesitation. From this kind of attitude on the part of our government, there was every possibility of recurrence of fraudulent practices in the banking system in future. And it did happen almost a decade later in March 2001. Stock market scam with manipulation through the use of bank funds was repeated. This time it was Ketan Parekh and Medhavpura Urban Cooperative Bank as well as Bank of India in the year 2001. As usual practice, during scam Ketan Parekh misused funds of banks and probably those of the Unit Trust of India also to jack up prices of ten shares of his choice with an idea that he would manipulate the prices of the same to maximum possible level before booking profit. But somehow a group of brokers of Mumbai Stock Exchange came to know and brought down the prices of those shares to such an extent that the Sensex tumbled, resulting into a crash in all the stock markets throughout the country thereby ruining thousands of small brokers and causing losses to a large number of investors besides failure of several co-operative banks in the state of Gujarat. As in case of earlier scam of 1992, this time also Government of India appointed a Joint Parliamentary Committee (JPC) to enquire about the crash of stock market and fix responsibility, but as usual nothing came out. Talking of current status of stock market on 9 January 2008, the sensex soared to 21,206 and crashed to 7,690 in October 2008 with steep fall due to US subprime crisis which snowballed into a global crisis. This caused failure of many foreign banks and insolvency of many financial institutions in America and Europe. Again a lack of properly regulated financial system was responsible for such a situation. It is now increasing realised worldwide that the banking and financial system should be on a sound footing and governed by well laid out policies, rules and regulations.

Indian Financial System—II: Monetary and Capital Markets in India

2

THE COMPOSITION OF THE INDIAN MONEY MARKET

Money makes the mare go. We work for money. Money buys us most of the comforts. Everybody is after money. We will discuss here as to how the money moves in the forms of lending and borrowing. The Indian money market is for lending and borrowing the short-term funds the demand of which always comes from borrowers like individuals, companies and government itself. Commercial banks act like lenders as well as borrowers. The composition of the Indian money market is classified into three categories, viz. (i) organised banking sector, (ii) unorganised banking sector, and (iii) sub-markets which are sub-divided as call money market, bill market, 364-day bill market, Certificates of Deposits (CDs) and Commercial Paper (CPs). Bill market is sub-classified as commercial bills and treasury bills (90 days).

The organised sector is composed of Reserve Bank of India—the supreme monetary authority of country, State Bank of India and its associate banks, 20 nationalised banks and private sector banks—both Indian and foreign. The Indian money market consists of several sub-markets stated above, each one of which deals with a particular type of short-term credit. The unorganised sector comprises indigenous bankers and non-banking financial institutions.

Call Money Market

Call money market is an important sub-market of Indian money market which caters to very short-term funds, and all dealings are done very fast at short notice. Call market or overnight market and short notice market are two parts of call money market. Demand and supply of short-term funds decide the call money rates. The public sector banks account for 80 per cent of demand of borrowings and balance of 20 per cent goes to foreign and Indian private banks. About 80 per cent of short-term funds enter the call money market as lending from IDBI, LIC, GIC, etc., the non-banking financial institutions and the remaining 20 per cent supply is from banking system. Banks operate as lenders as well as borrowers. Since this call money market specialises in very short-term funds, the overall turnover of transactions is adequate and substantial.

Bill Market in India

Bill market is another main important sub-market of Indian money market in which short-term bills upto 90 days are bought and sold. This bill market is further classified as the commercial bill market and treasury bill market. Our market for commercial bills is not patronised and hence, it is not popular. Government of India raises short period funds through 91-day treasury bills as commonly known. Long back, Indian government had introduced 182-day treasury bills which were later converted into 364-day treasury bills. The Government of India also introduced the 14-day intermediate treasury bills in the year 1997.

The Indian Money Market and Reserve Bank of India

There occurs aggressive lending and borrowing in the Indian money market through private sector as well as public sector, through banks and non-banking financial institutions. There is fast moving of money at short notice but keeping in view all these, the RBI, which is the supreme monetary authority controlling the entire banking system and operations of the country, cannot be ignored. It is, no doubt, the leader of Indian money market. All the banks and financial institutions go as per the guidelines and procedures of RBI.

FEATURES AND DEFECTS OF THE INDIAN MONEY MARKET

(i) **Unorganised Money Market:** There exists a large number of indigenous bankers who are not competent enough to differentiate between short-term and long-term of financial lending and borrowing, nor do they know the purpose of the finance. RBI, tried its best to bring these indigenous bankers under its influence but with little success. There have been many non-banking financial companies which raise funds from general public but Reserve Bank of India has very limited control over them as these bankers and NBFCs are beyond organised money market. It has been seen that on the whole, the unorganised banking sector outnumbers the organised one. Hence, the problems and defects of Indian money market are known but not sorted out.

(ii) Lack of Integration: Another main defect of Indian money market is that it is divided into so many parts in the form of sub-classifications. Each class of banks such as SBI, private or foreign banks besides urban co-operative or indigenous banks is confined to working in a particular sphere of business and is independent of others. The coordination of various segments of Indian money market is not cordial. There is same position between the Indian banks and foreign banks.

Later, we could see that the Indian money market was gradually getting integrated since all segments had to follow the guidelines and procedures of Reserve Bank of India with the enactment of Banking Regulations Act, 1949 covering the lincensing, expansion of branches, share capital, kinds of loans offered and the advances given, etc. Theoretically, RBI inspects the books of scheduled commercial banks and monitors the banking sectors but it miserably failed while in cases of Harshad Mehta and Ketan Parekh scams in the years 1992 and 2001, respectively.

(iii) Diversity in Money Rates of Interest: One more defect of Indian money market is the existence of many rates of interest. Borrowing rates of government, lending rates of commercial banks, deposit rates of co-operative banks do not match. Because of this, simultaneously, no doubt, there is immobility of funds from one segment of Indian money market to another. Gradually, with the intervention of RBI, there is co-operation from all sections of Indian money market which are quickly adjusting to the changes of bank rate.

(iv) **Seasonal Stringency of Money:** It is not the public who celebrates the various seasons but even Reserve Bank of India does, and accordingly, there are varying characteristics of Indian money market so far as the rates of interest are concerned. High rates are charged in one part of the year and low rates in other part, depending upon the demand. RBI pumps more money in the market during busy season and withdraws the same in off season. From November to June, funds are required to move the crop yields from the villages to cities. This period fetches banks more rates of interest and from July to October, banks have lots of surplus funds on which the rates of interest are low. Banks therefore are also opportunists in present times and take the advantage of seasonal business to enjoy more profit.

(v) **Absence of the Bill Market:** Running of smooth organised money market demands a well-planned bill market whereas Indian money market lacks it. Hence, it is difficult to link up the various credit agencies in a proper way to RBI. It is also one of the main defects of money market. The commercial bill market or a discount market for short-term commercial bills could not be developed in India which is necessary for the country from the view of expanding credit as well as from the point of monetary policy. The commercial bills alongwith bank credit are an important source of finance for business and industry. Banks with surplus funds like to buy commercial or trade bills to earn good margin for a short period of three months. The RBI too gets benefit out of commercial bills for its open market operations. In the year 1970, New Bill Market Scheme was introduced by RBI under which genuine trade bills were rediscounted, but, somehow it could not persist for a long time as it was not developed as anticipated.

(vi) **Highly Volatile Call Money Market:** As discussed earlier, in the call money market, money is borrowed and lent for short-term funds. The rate of call money is determined by the virtue of demand and supply. But in spite of strict monitoring of the RBI to moderate the fluctuations, there is high volatility in rates of call money. Looking back to early nineties, the highest and lowest inter-bank call money rates in India were 70 per cent and 4 per cent per annum as against 6 per cent and 0.6 per cent after a span of about 15 years in the beginning of 21st century. The high rates are the reflection of the huge demand for short-term funds by the banking system, especially to meet the RBI requirement of minimum CRR. Overall, going through past facts and figures, it has been seen that RBI has limited success in terms of the volatility of the call money market in India which has been taken into account as a major defect of our call money market.

(vii) Lack of a Well Organised Banking System: It is a well-known fact that the absence of properly organised banking system has been adversely affecting Indian money market and it is considered as major defect of said market. Our banking system had no standard before nationalisation of banks in 1969. Thereafter, only the desired level of banking system of our country started picking up pertaining to expansion of bank network for the economic development in all respects. Prior to that there was slow movement of funds, different interest rates in different regions and inefficient pattern of working. Reserve Bank of India exercised its influence and control over the banking system after passing of the Banking Regulation Act, 1949 but even then scams of Harshad Mehta, Ketan Parekh as well as some frauds occurred.

(viii) Availability of Credit Instruments: Even after the nationalisation of banks in 1969 there was no availability of short time paper instruments till mid-eighties which has been a defect of Indian money market with the result that there were no specific dealers and brokers dealing in different types of paper instruments. Reserve Bank of India could introduce new paper instruments such as 182-day treasury bills which were later converted to 364-day treasury bills. Certificates of Deposits and Commercial Paper were introduced only after 1985-86. Non-availability of credit instruments in Indian money market was restricting the rapid economic development and re-distribution of income.

Indian Money Market—An Underdeveloped Money Market

In a money market, there is aggressive borrowing and lending of money for short term and at short notice but keeping in view the pace and facilities, the Indian money market is still considered as underdeveloped in comparison to other overseas money markets of England and America because of the following reasons:

(i) Indian money market lacks highly sophisticated organised banking system. The present technically upgraded banking is confined only to metropolitan cities and big towns. Rural areas are not yet connected to it.

(ii) Absence of adequate and regular supply of money market instruments such as the bills of exchange, treasury bills or short-term government bonds with the result the banks are not able to invest their funds for short-term gain. Hence, their surplus funds are not utilised properly. On the other hand, those who require short-term funds are unable to raise them from the market at competitive rates.

(iii) Between the government and the banking system there are no specific dealers of short-term assets who can act as intermediaries.

(iv) It does not consist of essential acceptance market and the commercial bill market.

(v) There are differences in the money rates in different sub-markets because of poor co-ordination between different sections of the Indian money market.

(vi) Earlier, the Indian money market was confined to domestic market only, but later substantial volume of foreign capital was captured. But this process was slow.

Reserve Bank of India and the Indian Money Market

There have been many defects in Indian money market, and thus, numerous difficulties came up which RBI tried to sort out but with limited success. Differences among different sections of the Indian market were removed. Those differences were pertaining to different rates of interest which existed at different places, different sections of money market and at different times besides monetary shortages which however were considerably reduced through open market operations. Simultaneously, RBI faces several difficulties while controlling the money market because in our country, a substantial volume of business is occupied by the indigenous bankers and non-banking financial companies whereas the RBI's influence of monitoring and stage-wise supervision is confined to the organised sector of Indian money market.

THE REFORM OF THE INDIAN MONEY MARKET (1986-2005)

As discussed above, Indian money market had some defects which were removed with the help of the guidelines and procedures introduced by RBI. Gradually, different sections of Indian money market could be knit together in the organised sector for which only RBI has the power. The main problem of Indian money market is the high volatility and the increase in call money rates. The Reserve Bank of India has taken some steps on the recommendations of the Sukhmoy Chakravarty Committee which reviewed the working of the monetary system, and the Narasimham Committee report (1991) on working of the financial system in India as regards the Indian money market. Some such steps are discussed below.

(i) **Relaxation of Interest Rate Regulations**: As a part of strict policy on interest rate control, RBI had the intensive monitoring and supervision towards deposit rates of banks and lending rates of banks and financial institutions. As per the recommendations of the Narasimham Committee in November 1991, the banking and financial institutions were told to determine and adopt market related rates of interest. Accordingly, the minimum lending rate of commercial banks and public sector development financial institutions declined from 18 per cent to 10.5 per cent in 2004-05. As per present interest rate regulations, RBI has reduced the bank rate from 10 per cent in 1990-91 to 6 per cent in 2004-05 due to improved liquidity position with the banking system and also because of the need to stimulate the economy. Besides, interest rates on domestic term deposits have been broadly decontrolled. Similarly, rates of interest on bank loans have been decontrolled and are determined by market forces.

(ii) **Introduction of New Instruments in Money Market:** Indian money market was considered as under-developed due to non-availability of short-term credit instruments. Earlier, our market had trading of only 91-day treasury bills, but later, on recommendations of Vaghul Working Group, RBI introduced new money market instruments such as 182-day treasury bills, 364-day treasury bills, longer maturity treasury bills, Certificates of Deposits, Commercial Paper and government securities, etc. With the traditional instrument of the 91-day treasury bill, Government of India raised funds from the market for short periods and the commercial banks invested their short-term funds in it. The 182-day treasury bills were variable interest bills. The yield of these long dated paper had become attractive for a highly liquid instrument. These were subsequently replaced by 364-day treasury bills which became an important instrument of government borrowing from the market and also in the sense that their yield is most reflective of market conditions.

In the year 1997, RBI introduced 14-day intermediate treasury bills to cater to the needs of state governments, foreign central banks and other bodies followed by a new category of 14-day treasury bills sold through auction to meet the cash management requirements of various sections of the economy. Government of India decided to sell 5-year and 10-year maturity on auction basis so as to develop dated securities as a monetary instrument with flexible yields to provide financial instruments to suit the expectations of investors and to meet government needs directly from the market.

Talking of repo market, it is now a regular feature of RBI's market operations. In case the banking system shows liquidity shortage and if the rate of interest is rising, then RBI comes forward to assist the banking system by repurchasing government securities. Commercial banks add to their liquidity enabling them to expand their credit to industry and trade when government securities are repurchased from the market and the payment is made to them by RBI. Earlier, repos were allowed in the central government treasury bills and dated securities created by converting some of the treasury bills, but later, the RBI allowed repo transactions in all government securities and treasury bills of all maturities. Recently, on 6 December 2008 as announced by RBI, the rate of repos is cut down to 6.5 per cent from 7.5 per cent while the cut-off rate for reserve repos is 5 per cent. These new rates came into force with effect from 8 December 2008. RBI lowered the repo rate, its short-term lending rate for the third time in less than two months by 100 basic points. This is its lowest level in two and a half years. Incidentally, 100 bps (basis points) make one percentage point. RBI has been enacting policy of repos and reserve repos to influence the volume of liquidity in the money market and in turn stabilize the short-term rate of interest or the call rates. This policy of RBI using repos and reverse repos is called the Liquidity Adjustment Facility (LAF) which is in force since the beginning of 21st century and no doubt has been a vital instrument of monetary policy.

Like the traditional term deposits, a Certificate of Deposit (CD) is a certificate issued by a bank to depositors of funds that remain with the bank for a particular period but the same are negotiable and tradeable in the short-term money markets. These CDs are important money market instruments. These were initially issued in multiples of Rs. 25 lacs, minimum value was reduced to Rs. 10 lac and to Rs. one lac as of present. Their maturity varied between three months and one year. In the year 1993, Industrial Development Bank of India (IDBI), Industrial Credit and Investment Corporation of India (ICICI), Industrial Finance Corporation of India (IFCI), The Industrial Reconstruction Bank of India, Small Industries Development Bank of India and Export-Import Bank of India were permitted to issue CDs with a maturity period of more than one year and upto three years. These are issued at a discount to the face value and the discount rate is freely determined according to market conditions. CDs are easily transferable after 45 days after the date of issue and later, they gained remarkable fame with the banks for raising resources at competitive rates of interest. Banks pay reasonably good rate of interest and hence the holders of CDs prefer to hold them till maturity. The stringent conditions in the money market induced banks to mobilise resources on a large scale through CDs and scheduled commercial banks have started picking up so since 2004-05.

The Commercial Paper (CP) is a short-term instrument of raising funds by corporates. It is essentially a sort of unsecured promissory note sold by the issuer to a banker or a security house. Commercial Paper is issued by companies with a net worth of Rs. 10 crores, later reduced to Rs. 5 crores subject to a minimum issue of Rs. 1 crore with maturity of CP ranging from 3 to 6 months. However, the maturity of this instrument is flexible and usually borrowers and lenders adopt the maturity of a CP as per their needs. Institutional investors also find CPs as an attractive outlet for their short-term funds. CPs are issued at a discount to face value and discount rate is freely determined. The purpose of introducing CP is to enable high level corporate borrowers to diversify their sources of short-term borrowing on one hand and provide an additional instrument to the banks and financial institutions in the money market on the other. Following the recommendations of the Vaghul Committee, CP was introduced in the Indian money market in January 1990. Banks are the principal holders of CPs and to some extent, lending to well rated companies through CPs was a substitute for direct bank credit to the companies. Due to many reasons, the CP did not become popular. Also there has been the fluctuation in the issue of CPs, depending upon liquidity conditions in the market.

COMPOSITION OF THE INDIAN CAPITAL MARKET

Money is money but it rolls in different forms in different stages of different ventures. If it is used for short-term market, it is called money market and in case the same is utilised for long term then it takes shape of market termed as capital market. The investment is made in physical resources such as infrastructure, machinery, stock of raw material or generating water sources, etc. so as to be used for the commercial production. Such investment constitutes the capital which is in fact the wealth to produce more of wealth.

Capital market in India is broadly classified into four categories such as: (i) Government Securities (gilt-edged market), (ii) Industrial or Corporate Securities Market, (iii) Development Financial Institutions, and (iv) Financial Intermediaries.

Long-term investment is made by the private manufacturing including even consumer goods industries which require substantial amount from the capital market besides the government needs largely for the purpose of economic development covering transport, irrigation, power, etc. Like all other markets, capital market is composed of borrowers and lenders. An ideal capital market, no doubt, provides adequate capital at the reasonable rate of return for any business which in turn gives yield sufficiently high so as to make borrowing justified and worthwhile.

The two main categories of Indian capital market are briefly discussed below.

(i) **Gilt-edged Market:** This market is so called because it means of best quality, in the sense that it deals in government securities or the securities guaranteed as to both principal and the interest part because the government cannot default, thereby making it risk-free. Main features of this market are:

(a) It refers to market for government and semi-government securities and that too backed by the Reserve Bank of India;

(b) The securities traded in this market are stable in value and are much sought after by banks and other institutions;

(c) Returns in this market are guaranteed. There is no uncertainty so far as the payment on time is concerned. Hence, it is free from speculation and manipulation of any kind whatsoever;

(d) The government securities are the most liquid debt investments;

(e) The transactions in government securities are of high value and each transaction runs into several crores of rupees;

(f) Many private sector mutual funds too prefer to enter this market in a considerable way because of risk-free returns guaranteed by the government securities and their high liquidity.

(ii) **Industrial or Corporate Securities Market:** Industrial or corporate securities market refers to a market in which securities like shares, bonds and debentures are bought and sold freely. It consists of the new issues through primary market and the stock exchange termed as secondary market. The public limited companies normally raise the funds through the primary market for setting up or expanding their business. Stock exchange or the secondary market deals with the securities already issued by the companies. Both the markets are equally important but the primary market somehow gets more weightage as it relates to the economic growth. However, it is not so easy a task for the primary market as it involves various formalities to be fulfilled and also to decide upon the appropriate timing and procedure of issue. The consultancy and assistance of underwriter, merchant banks or some special agencies are to be obtained to look after these aspects. The procedure of new issues starts with the invitation to general public through the prospectus indicating profile of the company and its financial position, etc. followed by private placing under which the shares are sold to individuals or institutions directly by making a private appeal to them resulting into substantial saving in cost of raising capital and finally by offering rights issue to the existing shareholders to a certain number of shares in proportion to the shares held by them.

On the other hand, the stock exchange or the secondary market is a highly sophisticated organised market for the purchase and sale of already listed securities. The Securities Contracts (Regulation) Act, 1956 defines a stock exchange as "an association, organisation or body of individuals, whether incorporated or not, established for the purpose of assisting, regulating and controlling business in buying, selling and dealing in securities." The quoting or listing of a particular security implies incorporating that security in the register of the stock exchange so that it can be bought and sold there. In the secondary market the daily turnover is extremely high sometimes leading to booming in market touching rupees one lac crores or above with high investment of foreign institutional investor (FIIs). Government earns substantial amount as revenue in the form of routine taxes. Brokers too earn adequately as brokerage. The optimum risk is always involved in the secondary market because of high volatility. It is aggressive market for the traders. It is also lucrative for long-term investments depending upon domestic and global conditions.

The Government Securities Market vs Industrial Securities Market

We have already discussed the important features of gilt-edged market which refers to government and semi-government securities backed by the Reserve Bank of India which plays a dominant role through its open market operations which are governed by the objectives of monetary stability and ensuring the success of government's borrowing programmes. There are no uncertainties as regards yield and payment. Hence, the risks of manipulation and speculation are eliminated. The investors in government securities are predominantly institutions which are often referred to as the captive market for the government. The transactions are of high value and sometimes a single transaction runs into hundreds of crores of rupees. In industrial corporate securities market there is no certainty of return and payment is not guaranteed. A lot of tension prevails because of speculation and manipulation. To get a better anticipated yield you have to foresee market conditions and rely on the performance of other companies which may or may not come out with the desired results. Frequent political changes and the global impact is always felt in primary as well as secondary security markets. There is the temptation of money and in fact that does come in your pocket and sometimes it takes away your all earnings. Government tries to control the stock market but in spite of strict supervision and stage-wise monitoring by Reserve Bank of India there have been mega securities scams with the involvement of Harshad Mehta in 1992, Ketan Parekh in 2001 followed by several frauds because of corrupt bank officials and brokers with corrupt mentality.

Indian Capital Market before Independence

Indian capital market before independence, no doubt, was underdeveloped. Growth of industrial securities was not upto the mark. A few securities could be seen for trading in the stock exchanges. There were many restrictions on the investors when they were forced to opt for investment in government securities and only a small part could be made in other shares or debentures. The British investors, even while sitting in India, used to trade on their London Stock Exchange. Mainly due to dominance of strict British rules and regulations, Indian capital market obviously could not grow in the absence of development finance institutions and financial intermediaries with the result corporate securities market could not flourish and was confined to hardly a level of professional trading.

The Indian Capital Market since Independence

After independence, especially after 1951, our capital market gradually came up significantly with splendid performance. To promote savings all types of rebates and tax reliefs now exist. Many boards and committees have been formed for the welfare and protection of the investors. Growth of joint stock companies and corporates indicates the rapid progress in sectors of industry and trade. Volume of capital market transactions has been picking up fast and increasing sharply. New financial instruments such as convertible debentures, 364-day treasury bills, Commercial Paper and Certificates of Deposits have been transacted. There has been tremendous growth in industrialisation which in turn has boosted the Indian capital market because almost every industry needs money from capital market. There has been superb acceleration in public borrowings for investment purposes which is also an indicator of rising capital market. Apart from various financial institutions there have been many financial intermediaries such as merchant banks, mutual funds, leasing companies, venture capital companies and others. The supply of funds has started coming from individual savers, corporate saving, banks, insurance companies, specialised financing agencies and provident funds so as to uplift the Indian capital market since independence. Besides gilt-edged market, there has been wonderful momentum in the industrial corporate securities market with the coming up of issues of many big companies followed by fast growing aggressive turnover of secondary market, generating substantial revenue for the government.

Special Financial Institutions and the Capital Market

Before independence, Reserve Bank of India had carried out intensive survey to set up regional as well as all India financial institutions. Efforts of RBI worked with positive attitude and accordingly after the independence, the Industrial Finance Corporation of India (IFCI) was established in 1948 to provide long-term finance to small and medium industrial units followed by ICICI (1955), IDBI (1964) and UTI (1964). LIC came up in 1956 to mobilize individual savings and invest part of the savings in the capital market. Many more specialised financial institutions were set up and are called public sector financial institutions which have been doing an excellent job in subscribing to the shares and debentures of new and old companies. LIC and UTI mobilise resources from public and forward them to capital market whereas the development financial institutions are engaged in financing private sector enterprises.

Government has taken initiatives to establish a wide variety of financial institutions on all India and state levels besides other specialised financial institutions. They are further classified into different categories according to their main activities and functions which have been described below:

1. *All India Development Finance Institutions (DFIs)*: Industrial Finance Corporation of India Ltd. (IFCI), Industrial Development Bank of India (IDBI), Small Industries Development Bank of India (SIDBI) and Industrial Investment Bank of India (IIBI). ICICI ceased to be a development financial institution after its merger in ICICI Bank w.e.f. 30 March 2002, whereas IDBI was converted into a bank on October 11, 2004.
2. *Specialised Financial Institutions*: Export-Import Bank (EXIM Bank), IFCI Venture Capital Funds [(IVCF), formerly RCTC Ltd.], ICICI Venture Ltd. (formerly ICICI Ltd.), Tourism Finance Corporation of India Ltd. (TFCI) and Infrastructure Development Finance Company Ltd. (IDFC).
3. *Investment Institutions*: These include Life Insurance Corporation of India (LIC), Unit Trust of India (UTI)

and General Insurance Corporation of India (GIC) and its four erstwhile subsidiaries.

4. ***Refinance Institutions***: National Housing Bank (NHB) and National Bank of Agriculture and Rural Development (NABARD).
5. ***State Level Institutions***: State Financial Corporations (SFCs) and State Industrial Development Corporates (SIDCs).
6. ***Other Financial Institutions***: Included in this category are Export Credit and Guarantee Corporation of India Ltd. (ECGC) and Deposit Insurance and Credit Guarantee Corporation (DICGC).

Commercial Banks and the Capital Market

Like financial institutions, commercial banks too play a vital role in the Indian capital market but the only difference is that their operations so far have been limited to government securities as regards sale and purchase of same. Contribution of industrial or corporate securities, i.e. shares and securities is very small. So far as the transactions of treasury bills, government securities and issue of Certificates of Deposits (CDs) are concerned, the commercial banks do have an active involvement and give considerable reflection in the capital market. Capital in some or the other way gets rolling through commercial banks which have been adequately participating in term lending through subsidiary to the shares and debentures of special financial institutions. The commercial banks are establishing a few financial subsidiaries such as merchant houses, mutual funds, venture capital companies and leasing companies, etc. to mobilise the resources for investment in industrial or corporate securities. The Reserve Bank of India is the supreme monetary authority to supervise the banking operations. So, more than 50 per cent of bank funds have to be invested in government securities under CRR and SLR provisions. Hence, commercial banks are always with the capital market.

NON-BANKING FINANCE COMPANIES (NBFCS)

Money is desired and required by all, may be for a personal use or any kind of business. Banks are approached because they give loan at a low rate of interest but for that a lot of formalities are to be completed and even after that the question of limit comes besides mode and time needed for the repayment. So, in most of the cases, more of loan is required than the sanctioned by one banks. Accordingly, some alternative is looked for. The borrower approaches some finance corporations, loan companies or finance companies, the so-called non-banking companies. These companies have small working capital of their own and collect deposits from their friends, relatives, or some local sources by paying them rate of interest a little more than they are getting from the banks. They lend their funds so collected to borrowers on higher rates of interest to the tune of 24 per cent to 36 per cent per annum or even more than that. Simultaneously, they charge considerable amount in the order of about 10 per cent of total loan given as processing fee or fill charges as it is commonly known. Over and above, these companies give loan to small sector besides purchasing or discounting *hundies*, taking up merchant banking, hire-purchase, leasing, etc. These companies are approached for the loan by those who are denied credit facilities by the banks. The attractive features of these NBFCs include simplified sanction procedures, promptness in processing, personalised attention given to the customers, attractive rates of interest offered on deposits, flexibility in repayment and availability of funds in emergency or at very short notice.

Non-banking finance companies perform the functions of inviting deposits from public and give loans, but these are not treated as banks, nor they come under the control and supervision of RBI. Hence, there is no minimum liquidity ratio or cash ratio, no specific ratio between their funds and deposits. There are various drawbacks of these NBFCs. The depositors of these companies always have a sense of fear and severe insecurity since the loans are further advanced to very risky business ventures at a very high rate of interest. Loans given for a short term are very easily renewed for a long period. Such borrowers normally become the defaulters and complications do arise to recover the funds from them. There is no interlink or communication of any kind among these different companies which makes it possible for a man to borrow from more than one of such companies. Finally, a word of caution! These NBFCs are not protected by the Deposit Insurance & Credit Gurantee Corporation (DICGC) or government in any form. So, the possiblity of loss always exists for the depositors.

Reserve Bank of India has classified the non-banking finance companies as NBFC, MBFC and MNBC. The NBFC in principal takes up finance business of receiving deposits from the public and making loan in any manner. They are also there in equipment leasing or financing, hire-purchase transactions, buying and selling of securities, etc. MBFC (Mutual Benefit Financial Company) is modified by the Central Government as a Nidhi Company under section 620A of the Companies Act, 1956. MNBC (Miscellaneous Non-Banking Company) manages, conducts and supervises chit funds. MBFCs and MNBCs are regulated by the Department of Company Affairs, Government of India and are not considered as NBFCs. According to the RBI, there are four Non-Banking Financial Companies as registered under section 451A of the RBI Act, 1934 amended in 1997, namely (i) Leasing Finance Companies, (ii) Hire Purchase Finance Companies, (iii) Loan Finance Companies and (iv) Investment Finance Companies. NBFCs are not governed by the provisions of the Banking Regulation Act, 1949.

Financial Position of NBFCs

With the exit of many NBFCs from deposit-taking business the total number of NBFCs-D (Deposit taking NBFCs) registered with the RBI declined from 13,014 at the end of June 2006 to 12,968 at the end June 2007. This trend continued and it further declined to 12,809 by 30 June 2008.

The number of NBFCs-D declined from 428 at the end of June 2006 to 401 at the end of June 2007. It again declined to 364 in 2008. Despite the significant decline in the number of reporting NBFCs-D, the assets, public deposits and net own funds of NBFCs increased by Rs. 12,549 crores, Rs. 2,074 crores and Rs. 795 crores respectively.

Table 2.1: Non-Banking Financial Companies Registered with RBI

End June	Number of registered (NBFCs)	NBFCs accepting public deposits
1999	7855	624
2000	8451	679
2001	13815	776
2002	14077	784
2003	13849	710
2004	13764	604
2005	13261	507
2006	13014	428
2007	12968	401
2008	12809	364

Source: RBI as published in Table 5.9 page 94 of *Economic Survey* 2007-2008.

During 2006-07, there was a turnaround in the financial performance of NBFCs largely on account of substantial increase in fund-based income (26.8 per cent) compared to an increase of 5.3 per cent during 2005-06. Fee based income, however, declined during the previous year. During 2006-07 income from this source declined by 7.6 per cent on top of the decline of 61.2 per cent in 2005-06. The overall income of NBFCs-D during 2006-07 increased by 25.7 per cent compared to the decline of 0.1 per cent during 2005-06.

The percentage increase of operating expenditure of NBFCs-D during 2006-07 was marginally higher at 33.9 per cent compared to 33.6 per cent during 2005-06. However, financial expenditure and other expenditure recorded substantial increases of 30.5 per cent and 22.3 per cent respectively during 2005-06. Net profit after tax declined by 6.7 per cent in 2006-07.

The asset quality of NBFCs-D continued to improve during 2006-07. Gross NPAs and net NPAs as percentage of gross advances of reporting NBFCs declined to 1.9 per cent and 0.4 per cent respectively at the end of March 2007 compared to 3.6 per cent and 0.5 per cent respectively at the end of March 2006.

Total number of NBFCs registered with the Reserve Bank of India, consisting of NBFCs-D, Residual Non-Banking Companies, Mutual Benefit Companies and Miscellaneous Non-Banking Companies (MNBCs) and Nidhi Companies declined from 12,968 at the end of June 2007 to 12,809 at the end of June 2008. The number of NBFCs-D has shown a steady decline to 364 at the end of June 2008, mainly due to the exit of many NBFCs from deposit taking activity as is evident from Table 2.1. Even though the public deposits declined in 2007-08 from the previous year, partly reflecting the decline in number of reporting NBFCs, total assets increased significantly by Rs. 23,019 crore (32.1 per cent), with net owned funds increasing by Rs. 3,974 crore (48.0 per cent) during the same period.

Capital adequacy ratio norms were made applicable to NBFCs in 1998. Accordingly, rated NBFCs were required to maintain a minimum capital (consisting of Tier I and Tier II capital) of 12 per cent (15 per cent in case of unrated deposit taking loan/investment companies) of the risk-weighted assets and of risk-adjusted value of off-balance sheet items. Total of Tier II capital cannot exceed 100 per cent of total Tier I capital at any point of time. There are a number of NBFCs, big and small, which do not report to Reserve Bank of India at all.

Legislative Control of NBFCs

There is no specific legislation governing the control and supervision of Non-Banking Financial Companies. These companies do accept deposits from public and lend further on higher rates of interest. They achieve substantial turnover thereby earning an adequate amount as net profit, but even then they don't have recognition of banks. Hence, they are not a part of banking system. Since they are of limited liability, NBFCs are governed by the Indian Companies Act, 1956 which does not describe much about a finance company. So far the deposits are concerned, NBFCs are governed by Non-Banking Financial Companies (Reserve Bank) Directions, 1997. Securities & Exchange Board of India controls only those NBFCs which are engaged in merchant banking and portfolio management services. Hence, the NBFCs have been vaguely working under various directives, guidelines and the procedures formulated from time to time.

In the year 1992, the RBI appointed Dr. A.C. Shah as Chairman of a working group to facilitate healthy streamlined growth of the NBFCs. The RBI accepted aforesaid group's recommendations and in the meantime, instead of accepting their industry's demand for a separate law for NBFCs, the government enacted the RBI (Amendment) Act, 1997 which confers appropriate powers on RBI for controlling the functioning of non-banking financial companies.

SALIENT FEATURES OF RBI AMENDMENT ACT, 1997

The Act defines a non-banking financial company (NBFC) as a financial institution or as non-banking institution which has, as its principal business, receiving deposits from public and making loan in any manner. The institutions engaged in agriculture or industrial activities are not covered by the definition of NBFCs. To bring NBFCs at par with commercial banks, the RBI prescribed the following standards and guidelines:

1. It is necessary to obtain registration certificate from RBI, the Net Owned Funds (NOF) should be Rs. 2 crores, which initially was only Rs. 25 lacs;
2. There is quantum of public deposits, and is fixed between 1.5 times to 4 times of NOF which can be received by an NBFC depending upon whether it is a loan and investment company or it is a leasing and hire-purchase company;
3. NBFCs have to invest at least 5 per cent of their assets in unencumbered approved securities;
4. Every NBFC has to create a reserve fund and transfer at least 20 per cent of its net profit every year to the reserve fund;
5. Prudential norms are fixed for those NBFCs which are raising public deposits. For instance, such NBFCs should maintain Capital to Risks Asset Ratio (CRAR) comprising Tiers I and II capital. It should be 12 per cent for leasing, hire-purchase finance companies,

15 per cent for loan and investment companies and 12 per cent for RNBCs;

6. RNBCs (Residuary Non-Banking Companies) are required to invest not less than 80 per cent of aggregate liabilities with the depositors in government securities, government guaranteed bonds, debentures, etc.;
7. All registered NBFCs should submit half yearly returns to the RBI at the end of March and September every year. As non-submission of periodic returns to the RBI was a common feature, RBI law imposes various penalties apart from cancellation of registration and permission of receiving deposits from public.

Future of Non-Banking Financial Companies

NBFCs are, no doubt, doing extremely well in the financial segment of our economy but the problem is that they are not working in an organised way because there is no control of the RBI or any body of government upon them. They would cease to show much turnover if they start working as per norms prescribed in any act due to series of formalities involved in the process. They work in freestyle aggressive manner and always prefer to be away from strict and complicated monitoring and intensive interference of any kind.

MERCHANT BANKING

After the nationalisation of banks in 1969, there has been tremendous improvement in the banking system resulting into the rapid progress as regards the economic development. In all the sectors, the banking had an important role. Gradually, the commercial banks started Merchant Banking Divisions which later turned into separate merchant banking subsidiaries. In association with foreign banks and money market institutions, some private financial service companies have set up a few merchant banks. Similarly, some individuals engaged in brokerage as well as financial advisory business also have made the same achievement. The Indian merchant banks do not undertake banking business such as deposit banking, lending and foreign exchange services. They do manage and underwrite new issues, advise corporate clients on fund raising besides other financial aspects.

The Securities and Exchange Board of India (SEBI) regulates all merchant banks on their activities and portfolios thereof whereas the RBI controls them whenever they raise deposits. The merchant bankers are under strict supervision of both the above authorities. Even the Narasimham Committee (1991) could see superb potential of merchant banking and had recommended the government to encourage the formation of joint ventures with the leading merchant and investment banks of international level.

LEASING AND HIRE PURCHASE COMPANIES

Whenever loan is required, normally banks are approached but keeping in view small or medium sized amount, the purchase is served by leasing companies which have flexibility for individual needs. These companies became popular and their financing method proved appropriate to acquire plant and machinery especially for small and medium enterprises. They are also engaged in hire and purchase system of working. In fact, a large number of leasing companies have been floated in recent time but most of them had to wind up because of mismanagement and under-capitalization. However, some of those are doing good business.

The Narasimham Committee recognized the importance and growing role of leasing and hire purchase companies. Accordingly, the Committee made recommendations that a minimum capital requirement should be stipulated, prudential norms and guidelines in respect of conduct of business should be laid down. Besides, supervision should be based on periodic returns by a unified supervisory authority.

MUTUAL FUNDS

Mutual Funds have proved to be most important among the latest capital market institutions of mobilizing resources since 1987-88 when the public sector banks were allowed to set up subsidiaries to undertake mutual fund business. We have four types of mutual funds—(i) Unit Trust of India, (ii) MF subsidiaries of public sector banks, (iii) MF subsidiaries of investment institutions like LIC and GIC, and (iv) Private sector mutual funds. Their main function is to mobilise the saving of the general public and invest in share market securities. They have attracted strong investor support and shown rapid progress. Consequently, some savings have been diverted from banks to mutual funds.

Regulation of Mutual Funds by SEBI

Securities and Exchange Board of India (SEBI) is the authority which lays down guidelines, supervises and regulates the working of the mutual funds. SEBI has introduced a uniform set of regulations governing the mutual funds in the country, known as SEBI (Mutual Fund Regulations, 1993). Some of the major regulations are mentioned below:

(i) Mutual funds have to be formed as trusts and managed by a separate Asset Management Company (AMC) and supervised by a board of trustees.

(ii) The AMC must have a minimum net worth of Rs. 6 crores of which the sponsors must contribute at least 40 per cent.

(iii) SEBI should approve the offer documents of schemes of mutual funds.

(iv) SEBI prescribes the minimum amounts to be raised by each scheme. A close-ended scheme should raise a minimum of Rs. 20 crores and open-ended scheme should raise a minimum of Rs. 50 crores. In case, the amount collected falls short by the prescribed minimum, the subscription amount must be refunded within a period of six weeks.

(v) The advertisement code prescribes norms for fair and truthful disclosure by the mutual funds in advertisements and publicity materials.

Growth of Mutual Funds

In the late eighties, several public sector banks and financial institutions were directed to set up mutual funds. Accordingly, savings were mobilised for investment in stock market securities.

Initially, in early nineties it was very difficult and hard enough to attract investors for the mutual funds since there were lucrative offers of investment at that time from leading housing finance company HDFC giving 14 per cent interest on fixed deposits and IDBI twin bond issue was available for 15.75 per cent return. Hence, the scheme of mutual funds almost failed with sluggish performance for many years. There was lack of confidence among the investors due to the stock market conditions.

In late nineties, however, there was gradual growth in the mutual fund sector with rising index of stock exchanges coupled with bright economic conditions followed by tax concessions given by the government thereby bringing back the confidence of investors but at that time the resources mobilised by mutual funds were adversely affected because of government's policy which created confusion as regards dividend declared, distributed and paid by companies besides debt-oriented schemes of mutual funds. Whereas in mid-nineties, many new mutual funds again come up with the entry of corporate giants like Reliance, SBI, Tatas and Birlas, etc. which made the schemes very attractive associated with improved liquidity and assurance of regular income to some extent which were also supported by the booming stock market. This could diversify many investors from banking system to mutual funds.

In the beginning of the 21st century, with Ketan Parekh scam, the stock market, no doubt, crashed leading to the emergence of a period of recession till mid-2003. The sector saw remarkable revival with the success of private sector mutual funds which account for 77 per cent of all assets under mutual fund management in March 2004 as compared to just 43 per cent in April 2002. During 2004-05 there was a steep fall in resource mobilization through mutual funds. It was as low as Rs. 3,015 crores. But later, gradually, the stock market index picked up nicely and aggressively touched 21,206 in January 2008 and thereafter dramatically fell to 7,690 in October 2008 due to US subprime and global financial crisis. This adversely impacted the confidence of investors for investment in mutual funds which ruined several small investors and brokers too. Hence, many analysts feel that the mutual fund industry as a whole is yet to be formulated keeping in view the extreme volatility in the stock market.

VENTURE CAPITAL FUNDS

Government of India has been proclaiming several schemes from time to time for war widows, unemployed educated youth, freedom fighters or senior citizens, etc. but at the same time attention is also paid to highly qualified technocrats with yeomen caliber and technical competence coupled with entrepreneurial expertise. They can emerge with flying colours if they are backed up with venture capital. There is significant scope for them and hence the venture capital financing is one of the most recent entrants into the capital market. As a part of it, importance is given to support new ideas including research and development of innovative, latest upgraded technologies. Venture capital is entering our country in a big way because of rapid progress in the Information Technology sector and other industries. The Narasimham Committee recommended that the government should review and amend the guidelines so as to widen the scope of eligibility criteria and impart a measure of flexibility to the operation of venture capital companies. The Committee further made recommendations for a reduction in tax on capital gains made by these companies and equality of tax treatment between venture capital companies and mutual funds.

In the year 1999-2000, the government launched the National Venture Fund for Software and IT Industry (NVFSIT), managed by Small Industries Development Bank of India (SIDBI) to provide funds for technical development for small and medium-sized industries. Under the chairmanship of Mr. K.B. Chandrasekhar, SEBI Committee on Venture Capital has recommended to facilitate the creation of a proof of risk capital to finance idea-based entrepreneurship with a disproportionate potential reward-to-cost ratio. The 2000-01 budget further liberalised the tax treatment of venture capital to serve as a strong boost for NRIs to invest some of their capital anywhere in the ventures. The Securities and Exchange Board of India is the authority regarding the registration and regulation of both domestic as well as overseas capital funds with stage-wise supervision and monitoring for best results.

OTHER FINANCIAL INTERMEDIARIES

Infrastructure Leasing and Financial Services Ltd. (IL&FS)

Infrastructure Leasing and Financial Services Ltd. (IL&FS) was established in the year 1988 to focus on leasing of equipment and infrastructure development. The company so formed specialises in structuring and financing important projects in the field of power and transportation besides identifying many infrastructure projects in association with state and central government agencies. During the past working of about two decades, IL&FS has made splendid progress in commercialization of infrastructural projects of various government agencies pertaining to roadways, power generation, telecommunications, water supply and transport system.

Simultaneously, the company has played a vital role in the merchant banking and in structuring the sale of marketable securities to project finance requirements of the corporate clients. Besides, it has also been actively engaged in money and gilt-edged markets for trading in government as well as semi-government securities, bonds of public sector undertakings, corporate debentures and units. Above IL&FS has proved its worth and has shown reasonably good performance in the projects handled.

The Credit Rating Information Services of India Ltd. (CRISIL)

To undertake the rating of fixed deposit programmes, convertible as well as non-convertible debentures and also credit assessment of companies, a credit agency, namely The Credit Rating Information Services of India Ltd. (CRISIL) was established in the year 1988. Debt instruments issued by public and private sector companies covering substantial volume of more than one lac crores were rated by CRISIL in a span of about eight years. CRISIL card could provide details regarding a company like the business it is engaged in, shareholding pattern, key management personnel, plant locations, equity share record, details of balance sheet, financial ratios and practices, main rivals of the field, main lenders, Directors' report, briefs and events of all types.

CRISIL had successfully rated Commercial Paper programmes and completed credit assessment of sizeable number of companies besides launching banking rating services and did a good job of rating debt instruments of nationalised as well as private sector banks. A warm word of appreciation was received from numerous clients in India and other countries like Indonesia, Malaysia, Israel, Sri Lanka and Pakistan who had desired the esteemed services of CRISIL to establish similar credit rating agencies for them. Followed by CRISIL, another credit agency Investment Information and Credit Rating Agency of India Ltd. (ICRA) was set up for rating debt instruments of both financial and manufacturing companies.

Stock Holding Corporation of India Ltd. (SHCIL)

Earlier, the transfers of shares and other type of securities involved a tedious paper work of large volume. To replace that, a new book entry with upgraded technology, a fast system was required. Stock Holding Corporation of India Ltd. (SHCIL) was formulated to provide the same. SHCIL has been sponsored by seven leading all India financial institutions, viz. IDBI, GIC, LIC, UTI, ICICI, IFCI and RBI. The corporation so established is also the trustee of LIC Mutual Fund and GIC Mutual Fund for holding and dealing with their securities. At present, the custodial services to UTI, LIC Mutual Fund, LIC, GIC and its subsidiaries are efficiently and effectively provided by SHCIL which has directive instructions from Government of India to cover all public sector banks and their subsidiaries besides mutual funds set up by the public financial institutions and public sector banks. However, the development financial institutions engaged in housing financing such as The Housing and Urban Development Corporation of India Ltd. (HUDCO). Housing Development Finance Corporation Ltd. (HDFC) and National Housing Bank (NHB)—a subsidiary of Reserve Bank of India are not covered by SHCIL which has, no doubt, done a tremendous job of eliminating voluminous paper work thereby increasing the overall efficiency and in turn the productivity in all respects.

STOCK EXCHANGES IN INDIA

Money is invested in shares, debentures or any other form of securities, of course, for a lucrative purpose. The investor puts his money as investment in shares of any company but whenever he wants the money back, he cannot get money back from the company. The shares so bought are traded on stock exchange which are routed through a broker. The stock market or so-called stock exchange is a place where stocks, shares or any other commitments or investments in any form are bought and sold. Hence, it is an important and essential institution of the capitalist system of economy for the smooth functioning of the corporate form of organisation. Here, a lot of speculation is involved coupled with high level of volatility and is ideally suited to secure large amount of capital from those who have surplus money besides the willingness to take the risk in investing in companies. Long-term fully paid investments sooner or later do pay. The investors need to have enough patience to make money safely from stock market. Time to time internal political conditions and global situation do play an important role as regards the fluctuations of the stock market. There are frequent ups and downs in the stock market. One should be prepared to bear the shocks to earn.

History of Stock Exchanges in India

Native Share Stock Brokers' Association organised and started first stock exchange in India which is known as Bombay Stock Exchange (BSE). Presently, it is the second biggest stock exchange in India next to National Stock Exchange (NSE) which started its trading operations from 30 June 1994. In the year 1995, the BSE ranked fifth in the world in terms of number of transactions. The National Stock Exchange has adopted fully automated screen based trading system which allows trading members to trade from their offices through a communication network. The Exchange has opened membership to a number of cities. Ahmedabad Stock Exchange came into existence in 1894 to deal in textile shares followed by Calcutta Stock Exchange which was started in 1908 to provide a market for shares of plantations and jute mills. The number of stock exchanges in the country rose remarkably to 21 in the year 1945 apart from several unorganised exchanges not enforced by law in any form. At present, BSE index is based on performance of 30 selected scrips on the basis of volume of their transactions while NSE is indicator of 50 scrips out of which 30 scrips of BSE are common. Additional 20 scrips are termed as contribution exclusively of NSE. Fifty shares of NSE are the indicator of Nifty which is the heart of stock market in India.

How Business is Transacted in a Stock Exchange

Firstly, the order is placed with a broker by the client. The broker passes on that order depending upon whether to buy or sell, to stock exchange on a bid price or current market price. Secondly, the order would be executed by the stock exchange as directed by the client. Thirdly, the broker sends a contract note to the client giving details of the transactions. Fourthly, the payment is to be made to the broker within a specified time if the shares are purchased and vice-versa. Broker would make the payment to the client of the securities sold.

Speculation and Stock Exchange

Speculation is basic fundamental issue of stock exchange. No stock market or exchange can operate without the speculation. Because of frequent buying and selling there is high volatility in upward and downward movement of most scrips. Whether you are investor or a trader, speculation cannot be eliminated. A long-term investor makes the full payment and relaxes to look forward for an anticipated profit. But the speculative measures do affect him thereby giving him tension and out of frustration he sells the securities in loss whereas patience could have paid good return. It all so happens because of panicky behaviour of the investor. Similarly, short-term investor books the profit or loss immediately and gets on one side. He is not in the market for a long time and watches the effects of speculation which is also based on manipulation as well. Manipulation is created by the traders by short selling also called blank selling which means that you are selling the securities even if you do not have delivery of the same. As soon as the rate comes down, you cover it or in other words, buy it to earn profit. Similarly, if the rate goes up you suffer loss.

Traders buy the lots of shares and the same are called as futures or future lot. Number of shares are different for different scrips. Here, full payment is not required to be paid. Only margin around 20 per cent is to be paid and you can trade for full value of shares. If the loss becomes more than margin then you are out of game. You can buy or sell the future lots and can carry the same upto last Thursday of the month which is the last day of settlement. You can, however, further carry forward to one more month by paying the loss amount. In future trading, turnover is more, risk is more and the investment is less.

Is Speculation Essential?

Speculation, no doubt, is essential for stock market and it becomes impossible to operate business of stock exchange without speculation. If there is no speculation, large volume of transactions cannot be achieved. Demand and supply of any share may not be equal in absence of speculation. If the demand is more than supply then the price of that share would shoot up. If supply is more, share prices will come down. Equilibrium of demand and supply is often promoted by the speculators to stabilize the prices.

More of speculation amounts to gambling which is attributed to manipulation which is caused by some brokers themselves or high profile capitalists to exploit small investors. The methods of manipulation are very well known to the government but no guidelines are formulated to curb the speculation and manipulation. On the contrary, in recent times, foreign institutional investors have been allowed short selling of shares in bulk quantities. More the speculation brings, more the turnover which generates more of revenue for the government in form of taxes. Hence, moderate speculation is not only inevitable but also necessary and desirable for the proper systematic working of stock exchange though it endangers the welfare of investors and community as a whole.

Major Defects in Trading in Stock Exchange in India

When trading of any kind of securities occurs, it gives rise to a number of problems and of course every problem has a solution provided the correct measures are taken by the stock exchanges followed by support from the governing authorities of government. Earlier, there was lack of integration because of which there were different prices and rates for different shares in different stock exchanges. That problem has been sorted out with only exception that Bombay Stock Exchange is operating separately whereas almost all other stock exchanges of India have been merged with the National Stock Exchange. Shares are classified into two groups, viz. Specified and Non-specified. To promote speculation, facilities like those of settlement period and carry forward are provided in case of specified shares. Speculation generates profit for the stock exchanges and brokers as well. Margins are imposed by the stock exchanges on speculative transactions which vary from share to share and the same is done entirely on the discretionary power of stock exchanges. These days because of high volatility of Sensex, sometimes extra volatile margin is also levied. Moreover, it has been seen that on the whole the interest of investors is not taken care of. Rules and regulations so formed are favourable to the stock exchanges or the brokers only. And the stock exchanges are not prepared to do anything for the welfare of the investors. Their tendency is always to exhaust pockets of small investors in particular and our government does not take any action against them.

Suggestions for Stock Exchange Reform

Since the establishment of stock exchanges, there have been numerous problems and weaknesses, the most of which were clubbed and sorted out with the setting up of National Stock Exchange in November 1992. The following changes were made in the working operation:

(i) The physical floor was replaced with computerized order matching with perfect price time priority;

(ii) NSE has a network of 2000 satellite terminals throughout the country which is larger than the capacity of the largest trading floors in the world;

(iii) It is not owned by brokers. It is a limited liability company where the brokers are merely franchisees. Hence, it is free from interference or pressure of brokers and is in a position to perform its regulatory and enforcement functions more effectively;

(iv) Traditional practices of unreliable fortnightly settlement cycle with the escape clause of badla were replaced by a strict weekly settlement cycle without badla. The improvements that accompanied this regime are:

(a) There is transperency—you can look comfortably at the rates on computer screen before placing an order;

(b) Anonymity—Electronic trading is entirely transparent and fool proof regarding the prices and quantities;

(c) Competition in brokerage industry—Because of NSE over a thousand new brokerage firms have entered the market thereby reducing the transaction costs by virtue of lower brokerages;

(d) Operational efficiency—Automation eliminated the weaknesses of manual trading; and

(v) Gains out Mumbai—Satellite based trading of NSE gave equal access to the trading floor from all the locations in India.

SEBI and Capital Market Reforms

The stock exchanges in the operations of trading could come across many weaknesses due to lack of transparency in procedures, insider trading or many other reasons. Hence, to regulate the capital market in a systematic streamlined manner, The Securities and Exchange Board of India (SEBI) was set up in 1988 which was given statutory recognition in 1992 on the recommendations of the Narasimham Committee. SEBI was empowered and authorised to oversee the working of stock exchanges besides mutual funds and merchant banking. SEBI, in consultation with the government has, no doubt, improved practices and brought transparency in the capital market for the benefit of investing public, besides bringing healthy development in the capital market. SEBI facilitates adequate mobilization of resources through the stock market. The aim of SEBI is to:

(a) Regulate the business transaction of stock as well as other securities markets;

(b) Regulate the working of stock brokers and other intermediaries associated with securities markets;

(c) Regulate the working of collective investment schemes including mutual funds;

(d) Regulate and promote self-regulating organisations;

(e) Prohibit fraudulent and unfair trade practices of securities market;

(f) Promote investors' education and training of intermediaries of securities market;

(g) Prevent insider trading in securities;

(h) Prevent substantial acquisition of shares and takeover of companies;

(i) Perform such functions and exercising such powers under, the provisions of the Capital Issues (Control) Act, 1947 and Securities Contracts (Regulation) Act, 1956 as may be delegated to it by the Central Government.

Primary Market Reforms in India

Various capital issues are floated in the market to raise the capital from the public with a code of advertisement which has been laid down to ensure that the advertisements are fair and do not contain statements which may mislead the investors. SEBI has been taking a number of measures to reform the primary market. The objective is to strengthen the standards of disclosure, introduce certain procedural norms for the issuers and intermediaries, remove the inadequacies and systemic deficiencies in the issue procedures. The issues also have to formulate a system of appointing SEBI representative to supervise the allotment process to minimise malpractices in allotment of oversubscribed issues and prudential norms laid down for rights issues, etc.

In the Prospectus which goes to public through press or otherwise, the companies issuing capital in primary market are required to mention all facts and the risk factors with their projects. They also have to give information as regards the basis of calculation of premium. Many companies also issue same shares in the private placement market which involves low cost of issuance. Such situation professionally arises due to stringent entry and disclosure norms for public issues. For reducing the cost of issue, SEBI has made the underwriting of issue optional in case the issue was not underwritten and able to collect 90 per cent of the amount offered to the public and accordingly, the whole amount collected would be refunded to the investors.

The minimum application size and also the proportion of each issue allowed for firm allotment to mutual funds has been raised. The guidelines governing sizeable acquisition of shares and takeovers lay down the conditions under which disclosures and mandatory public offers have to be made to the shareholders. Merchant banking also gets the cover of regulatory framework of SEBI. The companies inviting public issues have to deposit one per cent of issue amount subject to forfeiture if there is non-compliance of provisions of the listing agreement apart from non-despatch of refund orders and share certificates by registered post within the prescribed time.

To enable the shareholders to make comparisons between the promises made and the performance achieved, all the listed companies have to furnish annual statement to the stock exchanges as well as shareholders. Government has shown encouraging response for the investments in mutual funds and accordingly, many private mutual funds too have been permitted. All the mutual funds are allowed to apply for firm allotments in public issues, while government on the books shows its intention for the welfare and benefit of small investors. Strict guidelines are laid down for violation of the rules, regulations and procedures but even then malpractices do happen especially due to corrupt character of some brokers, bank officials and others.

Global Depository Receipts (GDRs)

Since early nineties, Indians were allowed to access international capital through Dollar and Euro equity shares. By launching GDR issues, they could raise more than 3.5 billion US dollars and more than 1 billion US dollars through launching of Euro convertible bonds. Government of India has largely liberalized the investment norms for NRIs and overseas corporate bodies to buy any securities without obtaining permission from Reserve Bank of India subject to certain prescribed limits. Otherwise, all foreign institutional investors are always encouraged for their investment in our stock market. They have been offered one time permanent registration with India with several benefits of trading. FIIs are very supportive to our stock markets and fetch substantial foreign exchange.

Secondary Market Reforms in India

Day-to-day trading pertaining to sale and purchase of securities is conducted on stock exchanges. Orders are routed by the clients through their brokers. Accordingly, under provisions of the Securities and Stock Exchange Board Act, 1992, SEBI started the process of registration of stock brokers and sub-brokers based on certain eligibility norms thereby making client-broker relationships more transparent. SEBI has been reviewing from, time to time, the traditional trading system in Indian stock markets such as simplifying procedures, achieving the transparency in orders executed. SEBI has issued directives to the stock exchanges to ensure that the contract notes are issued to the clients by brokers within 24 hours of the execution of the contract. Exchanges are to see that time limits for payment of sale proceeds and deliveries by brokers besides the payment of margins by clients to brokers are complied with. To ensure the fulfilment of deals in the market and for protection of investors, SEBI has introduced capital adequacy norms for brokers.

SEBI keeps a vigilant eye on insider trading under its provisions so as to preserve the integrity of stock market and also to inspire investor confidence in the stock market. Government of India has allowed foreign institutional investors like pension funds, mutual funds, investment trusts, asset or portfolio management companies, etc. to invest in the Indian capital market subject to their registration with SEBI. Because of bulk buying of FIIs the turnover of the stock touches high peaks. More turnover brings more revenue to the government but brings at the same time rising volatility in the index, especially when there is basket selling by FIIs at the time of periodical crash of market which is termed as cyclic correction.

Strengthening of SEBI

Government of India set up the Securities and Exchange Board of India in the year 1988 as a non-statutory body but later in January 1992 it was made a statutory body which had been mandated to create an environment to facilitate mobilization of adequate resources through the securities market and its efficient allocation, besides overall monitoring of working of the stock exchanges. SEBI did an excellent piece of work for smooth functioning of the stock market and at the same time interest of small investor was also covered besides formulating guidelines to invite foreign institutional investors for investment in our stock market. To perform still better, there was more strengthening of SEBI in January 1995 when the Government of India promulgated an ordinance to amend SEBI Act, 1992 so as to arm SEBI with additional powers for ensuring further improvement in the capital market and to enhance its ability for the protection of investors. Main features of this ordinance are as under:

(i) To enable SEBI to respond speedily to market conditions and to reinforce its autonomy, SEBI has been empowered to file complaints in courts and to notify its regulations without prior approval of the government;

(ii) SEBI is now provided with regulatory powers over companies in the issuance of capital, the transfer of securities and other related matters;

(iii) SEBI is now empowered to impose monetary penalities on capital market intermediaries and other participants for a listed range of violations. The amendment proposes to create adjudicating mechanism within SEBI for leaving penalities and also constitute a separate tribunal to deal with cases of appeal against orders of the adjudicating authority;

Earlier, the SEBI Act provided for the suspension and cancellation of registration and for the prosecution of intermediaries which led to the stoppage of business. The new system of monetary penalities constitutes an alternative mechanism for dealing with capital market violations;

(iv) While investigating irregularities in the capital market, SEBI is now given the power to summon the attendance of and call for documents from all categories of market intermediaries, including persons from the securities market. Likewise, SEBI has now the power to issue directions to all intermediaries and persons connected with securities markets with a view to protecting investors or secure the orderly development of the securities market.

SEBI has introduced a number of measures to reform Indian capital market in recent years by improving market efficiency, enhancing transparency and preventing unfair trade practices. It has, no doubt, succeeded to a considerable extent, in bringing up the Indian market to international level. The confidence of foreign institutional investors in the Indian securities market has increased considerably and now more than anticipated FIIs are registered with SEBI doing regular business with investment of high value. The Indian capital market is also getting integrated with global market, of course, in a limited way, through Euro issues.

The operations of the foreign institutional investors are governed by global strategies. Hence, external shocks can destabilise the Indian capital market at any time and therefore it is necessary to take adequate precautionary steps to avoid or prevent this possibility, or at least mitigate its adverse affects.

INSURANCE REFORMS

Once upon a time, Life Insurance Corporation of India had monopoly in the field of insurance having covered insurance policies pertaining to risk of life of people. LIC of course did flourishing business directly and indirectly through several agents and agencies. As the scope of insurance grew and keeping in view the huge potential, Government of India thought it better to govern insurance through some specific guidelines and regulations as in case of other fields. Accordingly, during 1999-2000, in the field of contractual savings there was passing of the Insurance Regulation and Development Authority (IRDA) Act which ended the monopoly of the government in the insurance sector. This act has the directives to promote the insurance in private sector including limited foreign equity and to utilise the funds of policyholders towards the development of social and infrastructure sectors. A number of private sector companies have been encouraged by government to enter insurance business. As on today there are several multinational companies in the aforesaid business.

CONSOLIDATED FDI POLICY

Foreign Direct Investment (FDI) is defined by the International Monetary Fund (IMF) as a category of cross border investment made by a resident in one economy (the direct investor) with the objective of establishing a 'lasting interest' in an enterprise (the direct investment enterprise) that is resident in an economy other than that of the direct investor. The motivation of the direct investor is a strategic long-term relationship with the direct investment enterprise to ensure the significant degree of influence by the direct investor in the management of the direct investment enterprise.

In the Indian context, 'FDI' means investment by non-resident entity/person resident outside India in the capital of the Indian company under Schedule 1 of FEM (Transfer or Issue of Security by a Person Resident outside India) Regulations 2000. It is the policy of the Government of India to attract and promote productive FDI from non-residents in activities which significantly contribute to industrialization and socio-economic development. In other words, FDI supplements the domestic capital and technology.

The Government of India from time to time comes up with new regulations and amendments/changes in the existing ones through order/allied rules, Press Notes, etc. The Department of Industrial Policy and Promotion (DIPP), Ministry of Commerce and Industry, Government of India makes policy pronouncements on FDI through Press Notes/Press Releases which are notified by the Reserve Bank of India. These notifications take effect from the date of issue of Press Notes/Press Releases. The regulatory framework over a period of time thus consists of Acts, Regulations, Press Notes, Press Releases, Clarifications, etc.

The Consolidated FDI policy issued on 31 March 2010 consolidates into one document all the prior policies/regulations on FDI which are contained in FEMA 1999, RBI Regulations under FEMA 1999 and Press Notes/Press Releases/Clarifications issued by DIPP and reflects the current 'policy framework' on FDI. It deals comprehensively with all aspects of FDI Policy which are covered under the various Press Notes/Press Releases/ Clarifications issued by DIPP. The Ministry has decided, from now on, to issue a consolidated circular every six months to update the FDI policy. Hence, the next consolidated circular will be issued on 30 September 2010.

The objective of the government is to promote foreign direct investment through a policy framework which is transparent, predictable, simple and clear and reduces regulatory burden. Since the legal edifice of FDI Policy Framework is built on notifications issued by RBI under FEMA, any changes notified by RBI from time to time have to be complied with and where there is a need/scope of interpretation, the relevant FEMA notification prevails.

Origin of Investment in India

A non-resident entity (other than a citizen of Pakistan or an entity incorporated in Pakistan) can invest in India, subject to the FDI Policy. A citizen of Bangladesh or an entity incorporated in Bangladesh can invest in India under the FDI Policy, only under the government route. NRIs resident in Nepal and Bhutan as well as citizens of Nepal and Bhutan are permitted to invest in the capital of Indian companies on repatriation basis, subject to the condition that the amount of consideration for such investment shall be paid only by way of inward remittance in free foreign exchange through normal banking channels.

Overseas Corporate Bodies (OCBs) have been derecognized as 'a class of Investors' in India with effect from September 16, 2003. Erstwhile OCBs which are incorporated outside India and are not under the adverse notice of RBI can make fresh investments under FDI Policy as incorporated non-resident entities, with the prior approval of Government of India if the investment is through government route; and with the prior approval of RBI if the investment is through automatic route.

The policy allows Foreign Institutional Investors (FIIs) to invest in the capital of an Indian company either under the FDI Scheme/Policy or the Portfolio Investment Scheme. Even when FIIs invest under the FDI Scheme/Policy 10 per cent individual limit and 24 per cent aggregate limit for FII investment would still be applicable. No person other than registered FII/NRI as per Schedules II and III of Foreign Exchange Management (Transfer or Issue of Security by a Person Resident Outside India) Regulations of FEMA 1999, can invest/trade in capital of Indian companies in the Indian Stock Exchanges directly, i.e. through brokers like a person resident in India.

However, a Foreign Venture Capital Investor (FVCI) may contribute up to 100 per cent of the capital of a Venture Capital Fund/Indian Venture Capital Undertaking and may also set up a domestic asset management company to manage the fund. All such investments are allowed under the automatic route subject to SEBI and RBI regulations and FDI Policy. FVCIs are also allowed to invest as non-resident entities in other companies subject to FDI Policy.

Types of Instruments

Indian companies can issue equity shares, fully, compulsorily and mandatorily convertible debentures, and fully, compulsorily and mandatorily convertible preference shares subject to pricing guidelines/valuation norms prescribed under FEMA Regulations. The pricing of the capital instruments are determined upfront at the time of issue of the instruments. Other types of preference shares/debentures, i.e. non-convertible, optionally convertible or partially convertible for issue of which funds have been received on or after May 1, 2007 are considered as debt. Since these instruments are denominated in rupees, the rupee interest rate is based on the swap equivalent of London Interbank Offered Rate (LIBOR) plus the spread as permissible for ECBs of corresponding maturity. Also, the inward remittance received by an Indian company vide issuance of Depository Receipts (DRs) and Foreign Currency Convertible Bonds (FCCBs) are treated as FDI and counted towards FDI.

Issue of Shares by Indian Companies under FCCB/ADR/GDR: Indian companies can raise foreign currency resources abroad through the issue of FCCB/DR (ADRs/GDRs), in accordance with the scheme for issue of Foreign Currency Convertible Bonds and Ordinary Shares (through Depository Receipt Mechanism) Scheme 1993 and guidelines issued by the Government of India thereunder from time to time. A company can issue ADRs/GDRs if it is eligible to issue shares to persons resident outside India under the FDI Policy. However, an Indian listed company, which is not eligible to raise funds from the Indian Capital Market including a company which has been restrained from accessing the securities market by the Securities and Exchange Board of India (SEBI) is not eligible to issue ADRs/GDRs.

There are no end-use restrictions except for a ban on deployment/investment of such funds in real estate or the stock market. There is no monetary limit up to which an Indian company can raise ADRs/GDRs. The ADR/GDR proceeds can be utilized for first stage acquisition of shares in the disinvestment process of Public Sector Undertakings/Enterprises and also in the mandatory second stage offer to the public in view of their strategic importance. However, erstwhile OCBs which are not eligible to invest in India and entities prohibited from buying, selling or dealing in securities by SEBI are not eligible to subscribe to ADRs/GDRs issued by Indian companies.

Two-way Fungibility Scheme: Under the limited two-way fungibility scheme, a stock broker in India, registered with SEBI, can purchase shares of an Indian company from the market for conversion into ADRs/GDRs based on instructions received from overseas investors. Re-issuance of ADRs/GDRs is permitted to the extent of ADRs/GDRs which have been redeemed into underlying shares and sold in the Indian market.

Sponsored ADR/GDR Issue: An Indian company can also sponsor an issue of ADR/GDR. Under this mechanism, the company offers its resident shareholders a choice to submit their shares back to the company so that on the basis of such shares, ADRs/GDRs can be issued abroad. The proceeds of the ADR/GDR issue are remitted back to India and distributed among the resident investors who had offered their Rupee denominated shares for conversion. These proceeds can be kept in Resident Foreign Currency (Domestic) accounts in India by the resident shareholders who have tendered such shares for conversion into ADRs/GDRs.

Eligibility of FDI in Resident Entities

Indian companies including those which are micro and small enterprises can issue capital against FDI. A Non-Resident Indian (NRI) or a Person of Indian Origin (PIO) resident outside India can invest by way of contribution to the capital of a firm or a proprietary concern in India on non-repatriation basis. For investments with repatriation benefits, NRIs/PIOs need to seek prior permission of Reserve Bank for investment in sole proprietorship concerns/partnership firms. The application is then decided in consultation with the Government of India. In case of investment by non-residents other than NRIs/PIO, an application needs to be made seeking prior approval of Reserve Bank for making investment by way of contribution to the capital of a firm or a proprietorship concern or any association of persons in India. However, an NRI or PIO is not allowed to invest in a firm or proprietorship concern engaged in any agricultural/plantation activity or real estate business (i.e. dealing in land and immovable property with a view to earning profit or earning income therefrom) or engaged in print media. Similarly, FDI in trusts other than Venture Capital Fund (VCF) is not permitted.

Calculation of Total Foreign Investment

Investment in Indian companies can be made both by non-resident as well as resident Indian entities. Any non-resident investment in an Indian company is direct foreign investment. Investment by resident Indian entities could again comprise of both resident and non-resident investment. Thus, an Indian company would have indirect foreign investment if the Indian investing company has foreign investment in it. The indirect investment can also be a cascading investment, i.e. through multi-layered structure.

For the purpose of computation of Indirect Foreign Investment, Foreign Investment in Indian company includes all types of foreign investments, i.e. FDI; investment by FIIs (holding as on March 31); NRIs; American Depository Receipts (ADRs); Gross Depository Receipts (GDRs); Foreign Currency Convertible Bonds (FCCBs); fully, compulsorily and mandatorily convertible preference shares; and fully, compulsorily and mandatorily convertible debentures regardless of whether the said investments have been made under Schedule 1, 2, 3 and 6 of FEMA (Transfer or Issue of Security by Persons Resident Outside India) Regulations.

Entry Routes for Investment

Investments can be made by non-residents in the shares; fully, compulsorily and mandatorily convertible debentures; or fully, compulsorily and mandatorily convertible preference shares of an Indian company; through two routes—the automatic route and the government route. Under the automatic route, the foreign investor or the Indian company does not require any approval from the RBI or Government of India for the investment. Under the government route, prior approval of the Government of India through Foreign Investment Promotion Board (FIPB) is required. Proposals for foreign investment under government route as laid down in the FDI policy from time to time are considered by the FIPB in Department of Economic Affairs (DEA), Ministry of Finance.

Caps on Investments

Investments can be made by non-residents in the capital of a resident entity only to the extent of the percentage of the total capital as permitted in the FDI Policy. While investment is prohibited in some sectors/activities, there are restrictions/

conditions/caps on the investment in certain other sectors/activities. FDI is prohibited in the following activities/sectors: (a) Retail Trading (except single brand product retailing); (b) Atomic Energy; (c) Lottery Business including government/private lottery, online lotteries, etc.; (d) Gambling and Betting including casinos etc.; (e) Business of Chit Fund; (f) Nidhi Company; (g) Trading in Transferable Development Rights (TDRs); (h) Real Estate Business or Construction of Farm Houses; and (i) Activities/sectors not opened to private sector investment. Besides foreign investment in any form, foreign technology collaboration in any form including licensing for franchise, trademark, brand name, management contract is also completely prohibited for Lottery Business and Gambling and Betting activities.

Conditions on Investment

In certain sectors/activities, investments by non-residents are permitted in the capital of a resident entity with entry conditions. These entry conditions, applicable for investment only by non-resident entities, include norms for minimum capitalization, lock-in period, etc. Besides the entry conditions on foreign investment, the investment/investors need to conform to all relevant sectoral laws, regulations, rules, etc. The national security/internal security related conditions as contained in relevant statutes also have to be complied with. Further, the regulations of the State Governments/Union Territories in relation to the subjects in their legislative domain also have to be complied with.

Downstream Investment by Indian Companies

The policy for downstream investment by Indian companies seeks to lay down and clarify about compliance with the Foreign Investment norms on entry route, conditionalities and sectoral caps. The 'guiding principle' is that downstream investment by companies 'owned' or 'controlled' by non-resident entities are required to follow the same norms as a foreign direct investment.

Approval Levels for Cases under Government Route

The Minister of Finance, who is in-charge of FIPB, considers the recommendations of FIPB on proposals with total foreign equity inflow of and below Rs. 1,200 crores. The recommendations of FIPB on proposals with total foreign equity inflow of more than Rs. 1,200 crores are placed for consideration of Cabinet Committee on Economic Affairs (CCEA). The FIPB Secretariat in DEA processes the recommendations of FIPB to obtain the approval of Minister of Finance and CCEA. The CCEA also considers the proposals that are referred to it by the FIPB/the Minister of Finance (in-charge of FIPB).

Cases which do not Require Fresh Approval

Companies may not require fresh prior approval for bringing in additional foreign investment into the same entity, if they had earlier obtained prior approval of FIPB/CCFI/CCEA for their initial foreign investment but subsequently such activities/ sectors have been placed under automatic route. Also, cases of entities whose activities had sectoral caps earlier and which had, accordingly, earlier obtained prior approval of FIPB/CCFI/ CCEA for their initial Foreign Investment but subsequently such caps were removed/increased and the activities placed under the automatic route need not take fresh approval provided that such additional investment alongwith the initial/original investment does not exceed the sectoral caps.

Indian Financial System—III: Development Banking and Financial Systems

3

INDUSTRIAL FINANCE CORPORATION OF INDIA (IFCI)

Necessity is the mother of invention; and soon after India's Independence there was urgency of industrial expansion. The Reserve Bank of India carried out intensive survey in the year 1945 to explore the possibilities of both all India and state level institutions for industrial finance. The era of development financing in India started with the establishment of the Industrial Finance Corporation of India (IFCI) in the year 1948. It, in fact, was necessary to set up such an institution as the small agencies were not able to finance large scale industries. The Industrial Finance Corporation of India, which was set up under a special act is authorised to issue bonds and debentures in the open market, to borrow foreign currency from the World Bank and other financial institutions besides accept deposits from public and also borrow from the RBI. The Industrial Development Bank of India (IDBI), scheduled banks, insurance companies, investment trusts and co-operative banks are among the shareholders of IFCI. Government of India took the responsibility of repayment of capital and at the same time guaranteed payment of a minimum annual period. With effect from 1 July 1993, the IFCI has become a public limited company and since then is known as Industrial Finance Corporation of India Ltd. Its objective is to provide medium- and long-term credit to industry.

After IFCI, several other all India financial institutions and other state level financial institutions were set up. Narasimham Committee (1991) called them Development Financial Institution (DFIs).

Functions of IFCI

Following are the main functions of IFCI:

(i) Granting loans/advances both in rupees and foreign currencies repayable within 25 years to industrial concerns and also subscribing to the debentures floated by them;

(ii) Guaranteeing loans floated in open market by industrial companies;

(iii) Underwriting of shares and debentures of the industrial concerns; and

(iv) Guaranteeing deferred payments in respect of imports of machinery, foreign currency loans raised from foreign institutions and rupee loans raised from scheduled banks or state co-operative banks by industrial concerns.

Initially, the IFCI was to provide finance to industrial concerns only in the private and co-operative sectors now it provides to both public and joint sector projects. IFCI finances new industrial projects as well as for expansion, renovation, modernisation or diversification of the existing ones including the purchase of plant and machinery, construction of factory building and purchase of land for the factory. IFCI also gives loans to the companies engaged in manufacturing, mining, shipping besides generation and distribution of electricity.

Lending Operations of the IFCI

In the beginning, IFCI was financing industrial concerns with an amount of moderate value but later, over the years, with rapid industrialisation, the amount required by industrial companies went on increasing, both in scope and size of industrial establishments. Accordingly, IFCI scrutinised the applications thoroughly before granting the loans, keeping in view the importance of the industry for the nation towards its economic growth, viability and the cost of the scheme for which the loan is sought, calibre and talent of management, the competence of technical personnel, adequacy of supply of raw material, quality of products manufactured, uplifting the image of the country suitability for exports to earn foreign exchange, and finally the nature of security offered which is normally in the form of fixed assets such as land, buildings, plant and machinery. The IFCI gets the reports of manufacturing from the borrowers periodically and carries out the inspections from time to time. Financial assistance sanctioned and disbursed by IFCI during 2006-07 was Rs. 1,050 crores and Rs. 550 crores respectively.

Working of the IFCI

After India's Independence there has been tremendous progress in the trade and industries giving rise to heavy demand of funds by the industrial sector in particular. Commercial banks were approached but they were not of much help to industrial concerns as banks were reluctant rather cautious as regards financing industries for medium and long term. Hence, almost all such requirements have been fulfilled and handled by the IFCI by giving top priority to sectors of national importance such as fertilizers, cement, paper, power generation, industrial machinery of heavy duty use and other projects.

The IFCI has set up Merchant Banking and Allied Services Department (MBAD) for capital restructuring, merger and acquisition, loan syndication with other financial institutions with guidance to the entrepreneurs in project formulation and raising resources for meeting project cost. Assistance is offered by IFCI for domestic as well as foreign loans besides underwriting of shares and debentures. A word of appreciation must go to IFCI for floating nice schemes pertaining to interest subsidy for women entrepreneurs, consultancy fee subsidy to small scale units for marketing assistance, modernizing tiny and ancillary units and controlling pollution. In the late eighties, the IFCI helped various industrial concerns in corporate and co-operative sectors by providing financial assistance through a scheme for equipment leasing and equipment procurement. The IFCI also formulated Risk Capital Foundation (RFC), now known as Venture Capital Funds Ltd. (IVCF), for promoting schemes regarding risk capital, technology promotion and venture capital.

Working of IFCI has solid backing of Industrial Development Bank of India, commercial banks, LIC and co-operative banks which account for its share capital. Apart from paid-up capital and reserves, major resources of the IFCI are bonds and debentures as well as borrowings from the government who has guaranteed its bonds and debentures for repayment of principal amount and payment of interest.

IFCI: A Sick Financial Unit

IFCI, no doubt, has played a vital role towards rapid progress of industrialisation accounting for the tremendous economic development of India. Looking at the growth of IFCI's capital and finance sanctioned and disbursed, its performance seems to be very impressive, but later, IFCI was plagued by the huge accumulation of non-performance assets (NPAs). For this reason, Government of India converted the IFCI into a public limited company in the year 1993 so as to approach the market to raise funds by way of equity and accordingly improve its loan sanctions as well as disbursements. But unfortunately, the IFCI has been adversely affected and burdened with heavy NPAs. In most of the cases, there have been defaulters and no action has been taken against them for the recovery of loan amount given.

Moreover, it has been alleged that it adopts discriminatory policy to the disadvantage of small- and medium-sized industrial units. The IFCI did hardly anything to eliminate regional imbalances and no justification was given as in the case of industrial concerns in Maharashtra, which got as much assistance as the ones located in five states of Assam, Orissa, Kerala, Rajasthan and Madhya Pradesh taken altogether. It is a known fact that the IFCI is really a sick financial unit since it miserably failed to exercise necessary control over the defaulting borrowers and in spite of government's full support for its rehabilitation in many ways. Under the policy of disinvestment of sick Public Sector Undertakings (PSUs) it has been announced several times that some part of government's stake in the IFCI will be sold to some private financial company or bank. But no progress has been made in this regard so for (2009-10).

STATE FINANCIAL CORPORATIONS

In the year 1948, Industrial Finance Corporation of India was established on all India level to cater to the financial needs of large public limited and co-operative sector. But small- and medium-sized industrial concerns were deprived of such an assistance of industrial finance. Accordingly, the State Financial Corporations Act was passed by Government of India on 28 September 1951 under which State Financial Corporations (SFCs) were set up. After the establishment of first SFC in Punjab in the year 1953, SFCs in other states were also set up. The SFCs are confined to operations in their respective states. The SFC can open offices at different places in the state depending upon the potential. The authorised capital of the SFC is fixed by State Government, five equal shares of which are taken by State Government, RBI, scheduled banks, co-operative banks and financial institutions like insurance companies, investment trusts or private parties as the case may be. Shares of SFC are guaranteed by the State Government. Like IFCI, SFC has a Board of Directors, Managing Director and the Executive Committee. Pattern of working of State Financial Corporations too is almost the same as that of the IFCI whereas scope of activities of a State Financial Corporation is wider than that of the IFCI.

Functions of the State Financial Corporations

State Financial Corporations have been established to provide financial assistance to small- and medium-sized industrial companies irrespective of their constitutional status such as public or private companies, co-operatives, partnerships or proprietary concerns. Main functional features of SFCs are:

(i) Grant of loans and advances to industrial concerns for a period of not more than 20 years;

(ii) Subscribing to debentures floated by industrial concerns repayable within a period of 20 years;

(iii) Guaranteeing loans raised by industrial concerns which are repayable within a period not exceeding 20 years and which are floated in the public market or from scheduled or co-operatives banks;

(iv) Underwriting the issue of stocks, shares, bonds and debentures by industrial concerns;

(v) Guaranteeing deferred payments for purchase of plant and machinery, etc. within India.

Apart from the above functions, SFC is permitted to act as an agent of State or Central governments, IDBI, IFCI or any other special industrial financing institution in respect of grant of loans or advances or subscription to bonds or debentures.

Differences between the State Financial Corporation and IFCI

The main differences between the State Financial Corporation (SFC) and IFCI are shown in Table 3.1.

Table 3.1: Difference between SFC and IFCI

Subject	SFC	IFCI
1. Amount of shares capital required	Between Rs. 50 lac and Rs. 5 crores	No limit
2. Percentage of shares permitted to allot to private parties	25%	Not permitted
3. Maximum period allowed for lending or guaranteeing or subscribing to debentures	20 years	25 years
4. Maximum amount of assistance which could be granted	Rs. 10 lac	Rs. 1 crore

Notwithstanding all the above points of difference, SFC and IFCI have similarities in many respects.

State Industrial Development Corporations (SIDCs)

For the industrial development and lending financial assistance to small entrepreneurs and helping backward classes, State Industrial Development Corporations have been established for promoting industrial development in their respective territories of states. Andhra Pradesh and Bihar were the first to set up SIDCs in the year 1960. As the name indicates, these SIDCs are wholly owned by the respective state governments. Their main functions include granting of assistance for financial needs, providing or helping for industrial sheds or plots, promoting as well as managing the industrial concerns, identifying project ideas, selecting and providing training to the entrepreneurs, assisting technically during project implementation, providing risk capital to entrepreneurs by way of equity participation and seed capital assistance, providing assistance in the form of direct investment loans, extending guarantee for loans and deferred payment underwriting and subscribing to the issue of shares, bonds and debentures. So, these State Industrial Development Corporations, percentage-wise, have outclassed the performance of many institutions, thereby accounting for the considerable economic development of their respective states and the country, in turn, as well. They are on rising trend since 1980-81.

INDUSTRIAL CREDIT AND INVESTMENT CORPORATION OF INDIA (ICICI)

After IFCI, which was established to provide financial assistance to public sector, Industrial Credit and Investment Corporation of India (ICICI) was the second all India Development Financial Institution (DFI) to be set up to look after the financial needs of private sector in India. The ICICI came into existence in January 1955 and commenced its business operations in March the same year with a distinguishing feature of extending underwriting facilities. In April 2002, ICICI was merged into ICICI bank and thereby ceased to be a Development Finance Institution.

The ICICI was registered under the Indian Companies Act with the aim of promoting rapid progress in industrialisation, encouraging new industries, expanding and modernising the existing industrial concerns, besides furnishing managerial aid and providing technical expertise so as to optimize the productivity, which in turn, generated large job opportunities.

The ICICI successfully helped the private sector industries by granting long or medium-term loans or through equity participation, guaranteeing loans from other private investment sources, participating in equity capital and in debentures as well as underwriting new issues of shares and debentures besides providing financial services such as deferred credit, leasing credit, instalment sale, asset credit and venture capital. Over a period of time the organised and well-planned financial assistance of ICICI had shown flourishing and rising trend pertaining to new industries in the backward regions. At the same time, the provision of foreign currency loans and advances enabled Indian industrial concerns to secure essential capital goods from foreign countries.

Initially, ICICI was set up to provide financial assistance to private sector and accordingly, bulk of loans were sanctioned by the corporation. Keeping in view the demand and enlarged scope, the activities of the institution were extended to joint, public and co-operative sectors having major contribution in non-traditional growth-oriented industries such as chemicals, petrochemicals, heavy engineering and metal products.

In the year 1983, the ICICI started the leasing operations providing leasing assistance to industries like textiles, engineering, chemicals, fertilizers, cement, sugar, etc. for computerisation, modernisation, replacement of old schemes, equipments required for energy conservation, export promotion, pollution control among other things. Also in partnership with professional understanding with IDBI and IFCI, ICICI provided loans to several industries for modernization and expansion.

The ICICI showed creditable performance in its Merchant Banking Division, providing yeoman services in areas relating to issue management through Prudential ICICI Mutual Fund. Another feather in the cap of ICICI was the setting up of subsidiary called ICICI Investors Services Ltd. and ICICI Banking Corporation Ltd. in the year 1994. ICICI also actively participated in setting up technical consultancy organisations in many states for weaker sections.

ICICI also promoted with success a number of concerns and institutions to provide credit ratings to the corporate sector, finance for transfer and upgradation of technology, technology information, assisted market-oriented R&D activity jointly undertaken by Indian and US companies, accelerated commercial energy funded by USAID besides introducing projects in collaboration with USAID on agricultural commercialization as well as environmental sciences and technologies.

In the year 1996, Shipping Credit and Investment Company of India Ltd., with specialisation of financing for acquisition of ships followed by diversification of the activities to a variety of other industries, was merged with ICICI.

THE INDUSTRIAL DEVELOPMENT BANK OF INDIA (IDBI)

Before the Industrial Development Bank of India (IDBI) there were several special financial institutions for providing financial assistance to industrial concerns. But later, keeping in view the scope and size of rapid industrialisation, there was the need for a central development banking institution for providing financial assistance and promoting rapid industrialisation with dynamic leadership. Accordingly, initially the IDBI was set up as a wholly owned subsidiary of the RBI in July 1964 and in February 1976 IDBI was made an autonomous institution and its ownership was passed from the RBI to Government of India. The IDBI as an apex organisation provided refinance against loans granted to industrial concerns by other Development Finance Institutions like IFCI, SFCs and rediscounted their machinery bills. Besides, it subscribed to the share capital and bond issues of IFCI, SFCs and the IIBI (Industrial Investment Bank of India). IDBI also acted as co-ordinator on all India level and thus it enjoyed a unique position in India's development financing system. However, IDBI was converted into a bank in October 2004.

Functions of IDBI

The Industrial Development Bank of India (IDBI) was established to meet the financial requirements of industrial concerns and its main features of functioning were:

(i) Direct financial assistance to industrial concerns which formed a major part of financial needs of the industry. Direct financial assistance was provided to industrial enterprises in the form of loans, underwriting and direct subscription to shares and debentures as well as guarantees. IDBI's direct assistance to industrial undertakings in the entire period of its existence accounted for about one third of its total assistance.

(ii) Indirect financial assistance to industries, which was a major part of IDBI's assistance, had been extended through some other financial institutions such as State Financial Corporations, State Industrial Development Corporations and commercial banks. The indirect financial assistance was provided in the form of refinance of industrial loans, rediscounting of bills, subscription to shares and bonds of financial institutions and seed capital assistance.

(iii) Special assistance of finance was provided to those industrial undertakings which otherwise were not able to secure financial help in normal course because of low rate of return. Such an assistance was given by Development Assistance Fund—a special fund created under the Industrial Development Bank of India Act, 1964. Providing special assistance to industrial concerns was not a regular practice of IDBI.

(iv) Foreign currency requirements which were raised by IDBI from international money markets and international funding organisations were made available to Indian industrial concerns. IDBI did not have any kind of restrictions imposed upon it for these kind of transactions related to foreign currency. IDBI had been taking maximum possible advantage of it which in turn accounted for the economic development of our country.

Assistance to Backward Areas

In the year 1969, IDBI had floated a special scheme of providing financial assistance to small- and medium-sized projects in the backward regions in softer terms with the concessional low rate of interest, long grace and repayment periods followed by several other liberalised schemes for weaker sections. And the non-financial measures aimed at helping potential entrepreneurs in identifying and formulating viable projects, technical assistance, etc. Along with providing financial assistance to industry, IDBI also included provision of training in project evaluation and development of entrepreneurship. Special survey was carried out by IDBI to study the industrial potential of no industry districts. Besides feasibility studies, project appraisals, industrial and market surveys, IDBI also formed a number of inter-institutional groups which provided a base for discussions on industrial development programmes. In spite of all this, in providing assistance to projects in backward areas and also to the small scale sector, the largest beneficiaries of assistance provided by IDBI were large industrial undertakings. The promotional and consultancy works were not assigned the same importance as financial assistance.

Being an apex institution, it had been assisting state financial corporations, IFCI and other companies related to field of financing with participation to supplement the refinance operations. Accordingly, Refinance Corporation of India was taken over by IDBI in November 1964 and it started providing refinance facilities to the industrial undertakings through member banks. IDBI also extended assistance of refinance of industrial loans to small-scale industries and small transporters through SFCs and commercial banks besides introducing a scheme to cover promissory notes to boost the sale of new trucks and jeeps because of which small road transport operators were benefited.

IDBI performed tremendously for the development of industries in the small sector by launching the National Equity Fund Scheme in the year 1988 for providing support in the nature of equity to tiny manufacturing industrial units. They were also rendered the services of highly experienced consultants with the setting up of a Voluntary Executive Corps Cell (VECC) besides establishing Small Industries Development Bank of India (SIDBI) under SIDBI Act in the year 1989 for administering, financing and developing small scale industries which was earlier done by Small Industries Development Fund and National Equity Fund.

Region-wise, of course, IDBI had been developing the industrial establishments and undertakings without any discrimination in offering financial assistance with the result that there had been a uniformity in the regional industrial development. From time to time, IDBI had been introducing soft loan schemes for providing financial assistance to industries pertaining to categories such as cement, cotton textiles, jute, sugar on low concessional rates for modernization as well as replacement and renovation of old plant and machinery to increase the efficiency and productivity. Such schemes were later implemented for the upgraded technology, export orientation, import substitution, energy saving, prevention of pollution, recycling of wastes and by-products so as to make industrial units technically comfortable for doing their job nicely. The schemes later gained momentum and became popular due to soft loan schemes for modernisation.

Keeping in view the outstanding routine performance of IDBI, Securities and Exchange Board of India (SEBI) permitted IDBI to diversify its activities in merchant banking simultaneously, for raising capital from the market. IDBI of course, came out with flying colours in first two years of its existence, managing over a hundred of issues and thereby mobilizing more than Rs. 12,000 crores from the market.

Restructuring of IDBI

IDBI initially showed good and effective performance having served as an apex association for medium- and long-term financing, but later it was felt that IDBI had not significantly boosted the development of industrialisation to the desired anticipated level due to its close association with the RBI with common board of directors. Besides, the governors and deputy governors were shirking responsibility entrusted to them making IDBI a slave of procedures. However, from February 1976 IDBI came out with remarkable results and splendid performance in all respects, particularly with rapid progress of industrialisation when Government of India delinked IDBI from Reserve Bank of India and made it as an autonomous corporation.

Narasimham Committee (1991) on IDBI

Since inception, IDBI was designated as an apex institution in the field of financing and it, of course, played a vital role in developing the organisational links with other development banks. IDBI, thus, was performing a double role consisting of direct financing like other DFIs and indirect financing through the system of refinance. Keeping in view this basic difference between IDBI and DFIs, the Narasimham Committee made a major recommendation that there should be competitive efficiency among banks and DFIs. Hence, all the term lending institutions like IFCI, ICICI, IDBI, etc. should compete for funds from the market and for providing lending facilities to the corporate borrowers. A precondition for bringing about such competitive efficiency was the restoration of "a level playing field" between different Development Financial Institutions. Accordingly, the Narasimham Committee, to facilitate this process, proposed that IDBI should give up its direct financing function so as to perform only apex promotional and refinancing role in respect of other institutions like IFCI, SFCs, SIDBI, etc. The Committee further recommended that the direct lending function should be entrusted to a separate finance company and it should be set up especially for this purpose. This recommendation of Narasimham Committee was rejected by the Government of India. Therefore, IDBI Act was accordingly amended with a view to restructuring IDBI's share capital and empowering IDBI to raise equity from the market. This decision on the part of Government of India proved its worth towards industrial growth of the country.

An Evaluation of IDBI

The Industrial Development Bank of India was designated as an apex organisation in the field of development finance and accordingly provided refinance loans granted to industrial concerns by other development finance institutions. IDBI did a wonderful job upto 2000-01 thereby achieving increase of loan sanctions from Rs. 1,280 crores in early eighties to Rs. 26,830 crores in 2000-01. Correspondingly, disbursements had come up from Rs. 1,010 crores to Rs. 17,480 crores during the same period.

Later, like other lending financial institutions, IDBI got the severe setback and a declining trend started. Its cumulative assistance sanctioned till end of March 2004 aggregated Rs. 2,23,524 crores which was a measure of the underdeveloped nature of the capital market and the difficulties which a large number of industrial firms encounter in raising funds from the market.

The amount of financial assistance disbursed by IDBI till the end of March 2004 from the date of establishment amounted to Rs. 1,75,572 crores. During 2006-07, assistance sanctioned and disbursed by IDBI stood at Rs. 19,776 crores and Rs. 14,533 crores respectively. It all happened because of heavy accumulation of NPAs as well as paucity of funds.

SMALL INDUSTRIES DEVELOPMENT BANK OF INDIA (SIDBI)

For ensuring smooth and larger flow of financial and non-financial assistance to small scale sector, during the budget of 1988-99, Government of India announced to establish Small Industries Development Bank of India (SIDBI) as a subsidiary of IDBI under a special act of Parliament in October 1989. Its operations commenced from April 1990. Union budget of 1998-99 proposed delinking of SIDBI from IDBI and transferring of IDBI shareholding in SFCs to SIDBI. With an initial paid-up capital of Rs. 250 crores which was subsequently raised to Rs. 450 crores, SIDBI started its working by taking over the outstanding portfolio of IDBI relating to small scale sector held under Small Industries Development Fund as on 31 March 1990 amounting to Rs. 4,200 crores.

Role of SIDBI

SIDBI is an important creative financial institution mandated to promote, finance and develop small-scale industries in the country with the co-ordination of existing such institutions thereby administering Small Industries Development Fund and National Equity Fund which was earlier done by IDBI. With the support of commercial banks and other financial institutions such as SFCs and SIDCs, etc., along with co-operative banks extends the required financial assistance to small-scale industrial units by its a wide network of branches throughout the country. Financial needs of around 900 institutions are professionally obliged by SIDBI.

Functions of SIDBI

To ensure larger flow of financial assistance, Government of India established Small Industries Development Bank of India. Its main functional features are to refinance loans and advances, discounting and rediscounting of bills, extension of seed capital/soft loans, granting direct assistance and refinancing of loans, providing services like factoring, leasing, etc. and extending financial support to State Small Industries Development Corporations.

SIDBI has to its credit an excellent record of performance which has been achieved by initiating steps for technological upgradation and modernisation of industrial units, expanding the marketing channel for promoting products of small industries in the market, creating more of job opportunities with promotion of employment-oriented industries, providing assistance to small-scale units through credit delivery system with the co-ordination and support of State Financial Corporations, State Industrial Development Corporations, commercial banks, co-operative banks and Regional Rural Banks (RRBs).

Progress and Growth of SIDBI

With the help of simplified procedures and liberalized terms of extending financial assistance, SIDBI has been able to get most of the schemes well-implemented accounting for the rapid progress of industrialisation. In fact, the operations of SIDBI have been very effective and are conducted in a systematic, streamlined manner.

A unique single window scheme (SWS) as launched by SIDBI was widely patronised and accepted so as to accelerate the proposals for rehabilitation, modernisation and technology upgradation of existing units. Besides, SIDBI has introduced equipment financing for assistance and provides refinance facilities under Automatic Refinance Scheme (ARS) upto limit of Rs. 50 lac. Retired workers of National Textile Corporation (NTC) were helped by SIDBI through its refinance scheme and similarly, entrepreneurs by a venture capital fund set up by SIDBI. Both direct and indirect assistance is extended by SIDBI, thereby emerging as a major source of contribution of finance for small-scale sector within a limited period. Till the end of March 2006, cumulative sanctions and disbursements were Rs. 1,15,561 crores and Rs. 78,808 crores respectively, while during 2006-07 sanctioned assistance was Rs. 11,184 crores and assistance worth Rs. 1,012 crore was disbursed.

INDUSTRIAL INVESTMENT BANK OF INDIA (IIBI)

There are some industrial units which have obsolete plant and machinery with poor management and consistent deterioration in economic position. These industrial units are called sick units. Government does not want to shut down these units to avoid retrenchment of workers which will result into large-scale unemployment of industrial labour. Accordingly, Government of India established the Industrial Reconstruction Corporation of India (IRCI) in the year 1971 for providing financial assistance to industrial sick units apart from providing the managerial and technical assistance required by them.

Industrial Reconstruction Corporation of India (IRCI) faced a lot of problems and difficulties to rehabilitate sick industrial units. Such a prolonged persistence on the part of IRCI made the government to issue a notification on 20 March 1985 to convert IRCI—which was a company registered under Indian Companies Act—into a statutory corporation to be called Industrial Reconstruction Bank of India (IRBI), which was later reconstituted into a new Development Financial Institution under the Companies Act, 1956 in March 1997 with sufficient flexible operations and functional autonomy. The entire assets and liabilities of IRBI were then transferred to a new company called Industrial Investment Bank of India (IIBI). Nothing concrete could be done towards the rehabilitation of sick industrial units whereas our Union Finance Ministry felt sick of reviewing the aforesaid institution from time to time. Assistance sanctioned by IIBI in 2003-04 was Rs. 2,412 crores while assistance disbursed was Rs. 2,252 crores. The operations of IIBI in the following years were negligible.

INVESTMENT INSTITUTIONS

The Unit Trust of India (UTI)

For the last more than four decades unit trusts have become popular because of investment in units is very attractive. A few advantages of unit trusts are diversified portfolio, talented professional management and high degree of liquidity. The unit trusts are open-ended investment trusts which means that these trusts can sell their units continuously in order to raise additional capital. They also repurchase their units to enable investors to liquidate their investment which is the main feature of units, which is known as redemption, as ensuring high degree of liquidity. The Unit Trust of India was formally established on 26 November 1963 under the Unit Trust Act and the sale of units started from 18 July 1964.

Initial capital of UTI amounting to rupees five crores was fully subscribed by Reserve Bank of India, Life Insurance Corporation of India, State Bank of India, scheduled banks and other financial institutions. The main aim of UTI is to motivate savings of low and medium income groups through its trust units for reasonable good return which along with initial capital is utilised for the economic development and rapid progress of industrialisation in the country. Initial capital along with proceeds of units is invested in industrial and corporate securities.

Operation of the Unit Trust

In the year 1965, about a year after UTI came into existence, the trend of operations was sluggish but later it gained momentum with mobilised funds to the tune of over, Rs. 70,000 crores in late nineties backed by over 25 million unit holders. The said amount was invested by UTI in more than 300 securities of reputed companies in different sectors for more than optimum gain coupled with safety of capital, besides extending loans to corporate sector.

Talking about the advantages of the units, the investment so made is safe, keeping in view the risk spread over a variety of securities of different categories, bringing stable and dignified income, and giving the benefit of several tax concessions, followed by high liquidity enabling an investor to encash them any time by selling units back to the trust.

An Assessment of the Unit Trust of India

Based on above cited advantages of investment in units, it proved as a boon for the development of Indian capital market and people started making substantial investment in Unit Trust of India. Being a public sector enterprise, public developed full confidence in UTI. Huge amount was mobilised from the market for investment in selected securities for maximum return. Keeping in view the dividends declared initiating with 7.62 per cent thereby rising to the tune of 26 per cent in 1993-94 maintaining consistency of 20 per cent thereof, fetched excellent response from investors of small and medium groups.

Starting September-October 1998, severe crisis developed in UTI because of serious problem in Unit Scheme 1964 with plunging BSE sensex on 5 October 1998 followed by deep depression and consequently market value of US-64 declined continuously day by day. Panic prevailed all around sounding the total collapse of US-64. Investors walked out of the scheme on large scale and it was a complete failure of UTI which took place due to mismanagement of Finance Ministry of Government of India. This is how the innocent public was cheated openly whose confidence could not be restored in spite of superb assurances from the politicians while seeking votes during the elections.

Causes for the Failure of UTI

UTI faced almost total collapse in the beginning of 21st century due to dirty politics of bureaucrats and the unscrupulous stock exchange brokers as well as business houses thereby ruining crores of small and medium group investors who have become habitual of bearing such scams in our country. Government does not do anything nor any action is taken against anybody except appointing various committees which by the time give decision or recommendations, another scam comes up. The sub scam is exposed depending upon politics of the time.

Main causes of failure of UTI were the highly doubtful integrity of some top officials of UTI and those of Finance Ministry as well as big business houses and stock exchange brokers with the result that UTI invested heavily in shares which later became worthless, extended loans to leading business houses and the same were not repaid, allowed brokers like Ketan Parekh to misuse the UTI funds. Besides, the Finance Ministry misled the public with wrong statements pertaining to ownership and management of UTI.

Accordingly, Government of India appointed an Expert Committee under the Chairmanship of Mr. Deepak Parekh to undertake a comprehensive review of the functioning of UTI and make recommendations to restore investor confidence. The Committee made many recommendations which included suggestions for converting US-64 into a net-asset-value drawn scheme over a period of three years. Simultaneously, two entities UTI-1 and UTI-2 were created. UTI-1 was given US-64 and all the assured return schemes, while UTI-2 was an unencumbered mutual fund now known as UTI Mutual Fund (UTIMF). This decision of splitting up of UTI into two parts was taken by the Cabinet Committee on Economic Affairs (CCEA) in its meeting held on 31 August 2002. UTI-1 is managed by a government appointed administrator where the responsibility rests with the government to cover any deficit and meet all other obligations annually. UTI could get a bailout package of Rs. 14,561 crores from the government during 2002-03 besides Rs. 6,000 crores for US-64 and Rs. 8,561 crores for other assured return schemes. On the other hand, UTI-2, comprising all NAV-based schemes is managed by Chairman of SEBI, registered Board of Trustees consisting of SBI, Bank of Baroda, Punjab National Bank, LIC.

Other Investment Institutions—LIC and GIC

Like Unit Trust of India, there are two other investment institutions—Life Insurance Corporation of India (LIC) and General Insurance Corporation of India (GIC)—which collect substantially large amount from the public. Out of the funds so collected, loans are executed to the corporate sector for long-term, and industrial securities are acquired from the market. Additional advantage of these two institutions is that they provide insurance cover and play powerful role of key operators in stock market, keeping in view their huge amount of mobilised funds. People have strong faith in these organisations for the secured return on their investment.

After the nationalisation of insurance business, about 250 private insurers were merged into Life Insurance Corporation of India which came into existence in the year 1956. LIC with its central office in Mumbai and seven zonal offices in big cities over a hundred divisional offices in important towns and over 2,000 branches has its effective operations throughout the country. LIC has over eight lac agents and is the largest field organisation of our country. During the year 2006-07, LIC sanctioned assistance worth Rs. 18,127 crores while Rs. 27,017 crores of the assistance was disbursed.

Prior to nationalisation of general insurance industry in 1971, there were more than a hundred Indian and foreign insurers operating in our country which were grouped later into four companies, namely National Insurance Company Ltd., New India Assurance Ltd., Oriental Insurance Company Ltd. and United India Insurance Company Ltd. These companies competing with one another and undertaking various categories of insurance business are the subsidiaries of General Insurance Corporation of India which was formed by the Central Government in November 1972. After the enactment of General Insurance Business (Nationalisation) Amendment Act, 2002, GIC got delinked from its above four subsidiaries. These four former subsidiaries are entrusted to carry general insurance business whereas GIC undertakes only refinance business. During 2006-07, GIC sanctioned assistance worth Rs. 624 crores while assistance disbursed amounted to Rs. 628 crores.

SPECIALISED FINANCIAL INSTITUTIONS

Apart from conventional financial institutions extending financial assistance to industrial concerns, there have been other specialized financial institutions too. Since mid-eighties, the transformation pertaining to structure of the financial sector has been on the rise. Accordingly, new institutions have been formed so as to serve the increasing financial needs of commerce and trade as regards venture capital, credit rating and leasing, etc. The major specialised financial institutions are briefly discussed below.

IFCI Venture Capital Funds (IVCF)

To provide both risk capital and technology finance under one roof to innovative entrepreneurs and technocrats for the technological ventures, in early 1975, IFCI sponsored the Risk

Capital Foundation (RCF) which was later converted into Risk Capital and Technology Corporation Ltd. (RCTC) in January 1988 to extend assistance to industrial sector through schemes related to risk capital, technology promotion and venture capital units. Technology finance is provided keeping in view the adequacy of sufficient creative technologies, products, processes, market services, energy conservation and upgradation of technology, besides meeting expenditures of consultants of national and international level as well as commercial R&D programmes.

On the basis of new technology of innovative calibre or new usages, RCTC has substantially sanctioned the assistance to numerous medium- and large-sized projects in the area of risk capital as well as under its Technology Finance and Development Scheme, whereas assistance is provided to companies regarding development and commercialization of upgraded technologies, introduction of new products and services, etc. under the venture capital unit schemes. RCTC was renamed as IFCI Venture Capital Funds Ltd. (IVCF) in the year 1998.

ICICI Venture Funds (Formerly TDICI)

In the recent years, keeping in view the rapid progress in terms of industrialisation and expansion of economic activities, some of the specialised financial institutions have been established. ICICI Venture Fund, formerly known as Technology Development and Information Company of India Ltd. (TDICI) was set up in 1988. It was renamed as ICICI Venture Fund in October 1998 which grants project finance to new technology ventures in the field of engineering, computers, drugs, biotechnology and non-conventional energy through venture capital funds—VECAUS I and VECAUS II schemes. This is now known as ICICI Venture Funds Management Co. Ltd.

Tourism Finance Corporation of India (TFCI)

Looking at rising potential of tourism in fetching sizeable foreign exchange, Government of India formed Tourism Finance Corporation of India (TFCI) which commenced its business activities from 1 February 1989. The said specialised financial corporation provided assistance to promote tourist growth and allied projects like amusement parks, ropeways, car rental services, sight-seeing buses and ferries for water transport. But our government does not carry out the survey before starting such a financial corporation which is not worthwhile. This kind of assistance can be managed more effectively in other forms at relatively low cost. There is no fun of conducting such costly experiments and so to say ultimately a common man is burdened directly or indirectly due to taxes and levies. Government officials simply sitting in air-conditioned offices give the orders without looking into the viability and consequences arising out of their decisions which they take. Main aim of government is to exhaust totally the allocation of funds sanctioned for particular projects even if those are not implemented as planned.

A NOTE ON THE EXPORT-IMPORT BANK OF INDIA (EXIM BANK)

To give relief to IDBI for its operations of international finance, besides providing financial assistance to exporters and importers, the Export and Import Bank of India, also called EXIM Bank was set up on 1 January 1982. It functions as principal financial institution for co-ordinating the working of other institutions engaged in financing of exports and imports of goods and services. Simultaneously, it provides refinance facilities to the commercial banks and financial institutions for carrying out the activities of import and/or export. EXIM Bank, besides having its paid-up capital, raises additional resources through borrowing from Government of India, RBI and the market by issuing bonds and debentures. It also borrows from other countries in the form of their currency. Assistance sanctioned and disbursed by EXIM Bank in 2006-07 was Rs. 31,760 crores and Rs. 23,773 crores respectively.

Functions of EXIM Bank

Main functions of EXIM Bank are to finance imports of goods, services, machinery to India and export to as well as joint ventures in other countries, providing loans to Indian parties for their participation in joint ventures in foreign countries apart from technical, administrative and financial assistance to parties related to import or export. EXIM Bank also undertakes merchant banking functions covering underwriting of securities related to import and export. The pre-shipment credit is given in case of export contract for capital goods by this bank. It also extends loans to commercial banks in India including export bills rediscounting scheme and refinance of export credit.

Funded Assistance

Among the functional features of EXIM Bank are financial assistance to Indian exporters to operate in international markets. These forms of lending are collectively called funded assistance programmes. Important projects which have received assistance from EXIM Bank pertain to textile machinery, chemicals, power generation, commercial vehicles, transport equipment, garments, etc. Areawise, South and South East Asia got sizeable share of EXIM Bank's assistance.

Non-funded Assistance

EXIM Bank participates with the commercial banks in India in issuance of guarantees in foreign currencies on behalf of Indian exporters in favour of overseas importers. This way of guarantees of various types is termed as non-funded assistance. In the year 1984, EXIM Bank introduced financing programme related to exports of specified transactions resulting in foreign exchange savings. Later, EXIM Bank effectively promoted Indian participation in projects funded by World Bank, Asian Development Bank and African Development Bank. In recent years, EXIM Bank has promoted exports through various schemes so as to offer rupee term finance for acquisition of equipment, helping Indian manufacturers to undertake strategic export marketing activities and providing integrated financing packages to manufacturer-exporters as well as export trading houses to implement vendor development plans.

PUBLIC SECTOR TERM-LENDING INSTITUTION: A CRITICAL EVALUATION

While we scrutinize the importance of working of financial institutions, the contribution of financial assistance extended by them to industrial concerns is quite impressive, especially during the last two decades. During 1961-62, total assistance sanctioned by the financial institutions was just Rs. 60.5 crores of which Rs. 29.8 crores were disbursed. With the coming up of IDBI in 1964, the total assistance sanctioned by all India financial institutions upto March 2004 aggregated Rs. 8,01,998 crores of which assistance worth Rs. 5,82,156 crores was disbursed.

Table 3.1: Loans by All India Financial Institutions

(Rs. Crores)

Items	April-March	
	2005-06	**2006-07**
A. Sanctions		
(a) DFI	12108	12479
(b) Investment Institutions	15558	18759
AIFIs (a+b)	27666	31238
B. Disbursements		
(a) DFI	9375	10799
(b) Investment Institutions	11771	27857
AIFIs (a+b)	21146	38656

Notes: (a) relates to IFCI, SIDBI, IIBI, IFCI Venture Capital Fund, ICICI Venture and TFCI.

(b) relates to LIC and GIC.

Source: Table 5.8 page 93 of *Economic Survey 2007-08.*

In the past few years, Development Financial Institutions had sluggish performance due to increase of non-performing assets while on the other hand the cost of raising funds has been rising, resulting into steep fall in their profitability. NPAs of some financial institutions have gone up to more than 30 per cent of net assets which is very high. Due to this, these institutions find it difficult to mobilise resources from capital market. Looking on the positive side with careful examination of the role of development finance in India after independence, we are in a position to say that both all India and state level development financial institutions have played a splendid role in promoting industrial development.

Loans sanctioned and disbursed by AIFIs improved during 2005-06 and 2006-07. Loans sanctioned during 2006-07 were 12.9 per cent higher (Rs. 31,238 crores), following 9.41 per cent increase (Rs. 27,666 crores) during 2005-06. Disbursement grew even more strongly during 2006-07 by 82.8 per cent (to Rs. 27,857 crores) on top of an increase of 38 per cent during 2005-06 to Rs. 21,146 crores. Keeping pace with the higher disbursements by AIFIs at the end of March 2007, their combined balance sheet registered an increase of 14.9 per cent compared to 8.2 per cent at the end of March 2006. Deposits with AIFIs increased by 51.5 per cent at the end of March 2007 compared to 8.7 per cent at the end of March 2006. Borrowings were also higher at 18.2 per cent at the end of March 2007 compared to 8.8 per cent at the end of March 2006. However, there was capital erosion by Rs. 543 crores in 2006-07, resulting in the reductions of the capital base to Rs. 4,888 crores. Nevertheless, AIFIs continued to have significantly higher capital adequacy ratio than the minimum stipulated norm of 9 per cent at the end of March 2007.

DFIs and the Corporate Sector

With the rising dependability of corporate sector, in view of financial needs, on DFIs, these institutions are responsible for a major share of corporate debt. By means of convertibility clause and through underwriting, there has been increasing share of DFIs in the equity of private sector. Along with LIC, GIC and UTI, their equity holdings in most major companies were considerable, often influencing mergers and acquisitions besides their important role in corporate takeovers, thereby reflecting the view of the government as to who should control the particular corporate unit.

Regarding the role of DFIs in corporate takeovers, the Narasimham Committee recommended that the DFIs should normally lend support to existing managements with proven record, beneficial to all concerned, except in those cases where the new management could be better. In all cases, the DFIs should exercise their individual professional judgements free of any pressures.

However, DFIs are now passing through a difficult time. They have developed a rigid attitude in their working which did not help them in the new environment in which they found new competitors. Since, at this juncture, government has withdrawn the protective shield from DFIs, the ownership of DFIs has diluted, concessional finance dried up, tax concessions stand withdrawn, access to captive clientele has reduced and lending-borrowing at market determined interest rates has become the worse.

Resources of DFIs

Initially, based on SLR mechanism, Development Financial Institutions had the priviledge to enjoy the concessional access to resources. Apart from that, they could easily mobilise the funds from the market with the support of government's guarantee. Though the lending rates of DFIs were low, yet considering the spread between the borrowing and ending rates as well as the total substantial turnover, the public sector financial institutions were able to earn reasonably good income.

With the lapse of time, conditions of business have entirely changed. There is a lot of competition in all the fields including financial sector. Pressure has developed through banks' SLR investments on the availability of privileged funds at concessional rates. Besides, there is intensive deregulation of interest rates. Hence, the DFIs have to move as per tough environments of the market raising the funds from capital market at market-related rates. They have to launch some different schemes which do not clash with the commercial banks so as to mobilise the savings of the household sector.

From the qualitative point of view, Development Financial Institutions in fact have to provide assistance to the new enterprises—small- and medium-sized industries of backward regions—in order to induce widespread industrial development and reduce regional disparity while the financial institutions granted major part of assistance to large industrial houses which are main defaulters for repayment of large loan amount. They are facing similar problem for the financial assistance extended in the developed states. All this has adversely impacted DFIs and resulted in their low profitability.

Weaknesses of DFIs

In the beginning, all the financial institutions designated as Development Financial Institutions gave a very impressive performance from the point of view of excellent financial assistance to the industrial concerns. As per the directives, DFIs had to offer substantial assistance to small- and medium-sized industries in backward areas of developed states but they passed on major part of their assistance to large industrial houses from where the repayment of loan amount does not come so easily. CRAR of IFCI was –27.9 per cent as at the end of March 2006. As far as cost of raising funds is concerned, it has been around 11 per cent for financial institutions as against only 8.5 per cent for banks. In view of such circumstances, DFIs suffered severe decline in profitability. Even IFCI and IDBI were badly affected. All this happened due to some weaknesses on the part of DFIs for their loan operations which are listed hereunder:

(i) Excessive and undesirable relaxation in the norms laid down by the financial institutions.

(ii) Financial assistance extended to projects which were practically not possible.

(iii) Entrepreneurs without technical competence were granted loans.

(iv) Defective processing procedures adopted by DFIs.

(v) Pressure from government for providing financial assistance to sick industrial units.

(vi) Absence of competition in operations of DFIs in financial transactions.

(vii) Liberalisation in recovery of loan amount, and no strict action against the defaulters.

(viii) DFIs offering consortium finance leaving limited choice for the borrowers for selecting an institution for financial requirement of their projects.

Recommendations of Narasimham Committee (1991) on DFIs

In the initial stages, Development Financial Institutions achieved targets for the desired industrial development, but later there was severe setback to DFIs due to several drawbacks inherent in the functioning of DFIs as discussed above. Accordingly, to overcome the problems and difficulties faced by

DFIs, the Narasimham Committee (1991) made the following major recommendations for DFIs:

(i) The ownership pattern of DFIs should be broad-based like that of the ICICI.

(ii) The government should ensure a measure of autonomy to the DFIs in matters of internal administration.

(iii) The chief executives of DFIs as in case of banks should be men of proven professional competence and should be selected on the recommendation of a panel of eminent persons.

(iv) The boards of DFIs should include representatives from the industrial sector.

(v) In the case of state level financial institutions, the link with the state governments should be broken and these institutions should be helped to work with improved efficiency, take up only that number of projects which they could efficiently follow up and recover their dues and approach the capital market for their funds.

(vi) The DFIs should raise their funds from the capital market at market-related rates. They should also mobilise the savings of the household sector without competing with the commercial banks.

(vii) Each DFI should be guided by professional appraisal of the technical and economic aspects of the project evaluation of the promoters, competence and integrity. Each DFI should have the sole responsibility in loan sanctions and should supervise its own loan implementation.

(viii) The present system of consortium funding should be given up. The cross-representation in each other's boards would not be necessary with the giving up of consortium funding.

(ix) The role and functions of IDBI should be changed. The IDBI should retain only its apex refinancing role and its direct lending function should be transferred to a separate institution which could be incorporated as a company.

(x) In the matter of corporate takeovers, DFIs should lend support to existing managements with proven record beneficial to all concerned except in those cases where the new management could be expected to do better. In all cases, the DFIs should exercise their individual professional judgements free of any extraneous pressures.

The Narasimham Committee further proposed that DFIs should adopt internationally accepted norms, restore capital adequacy, inject an element of competition in term-lending finance with a view to providing greater choice to the borrowers. The Committee had also recommended that commercial banks should be encouraged to extend term finance while the DFIs should start extending loans for short periods for working capital requirements.

Policy Reforms and DFIs

As discussed above, the Development Financial Institutions in the initial stage of their existence had shown remarkable progress in the field of industrialisation but their certain weaknesses resulted into their low profitability. Accordingly, a few of following reforms were initiated:

(i) So as to reduce dependence on SLR, the financial institutions have taken necessary steps to diversify their resource base and mobilise the funds from the domestic as well as international markets. IDBI raised capital by virtue of private placement while ICICI and SCICI did so through Euro issues from global capital markets. IFCI too came up with its first public issue raising over Rs. 600 crores as equity. Government of India empowered IDBI to raise equity from capital market.

(ii) Some DFIs were issued guidelines by the RBI on prudential norms similar to those prescribed for scheduled commercial banks. These norms were implemented by the DFIs so as to maintain financial health covering credit concentration, asset classification, income recognition, provisioning and balance sheet disclosure.

(iii) All the DFIs have been directed to diversify their business into areas other than extending financial assistance to industrial concerns. Accordingly, IDBI has expanded the scope of its Venture Capital Scheme to include a variety of projects, promoted Investor Services Ltd. to provide share registry services and acting as transfer agent as well as set up commercial bank, mutual fund and a stockbroking firm. Similarly, ICICI, IDBI, UTI and SIDBI have set up some or other ventures as part of their diversification for their alternative source of survival.

(iv) Interest rates have been uniformly rationalized keeping in view the progressive deregulation of interest rates. Ceiling on interest rate on debentures and bonds is removed and the floor rate of interest was lowered several times by RBI.

S.H. Khan Working Group on DFIs

Reserve Bank of India formulated a powerful working group headed by IDBI Chairman S.H. Khan to harmonise the role of Development Financial Institutions and banks. During April 1998, the report was submitted to RBI. The Khan Working Group made a recommendation that DFIs be allowed, over a period of time, to convert themselves into banks and that they be granted licences for this purpose.

Instead of considering only inter-bank mergers as recommended repeatedly by the Narasimham Committee (1991 and 1998), the Khan Working Group recommended the merger of one or more strong banks with DFIs, purely based on viability and profitability considerations. During the period of transition from development to commercial banking, the government should provide an appropriate level of financial support to enable DFIs to fulfil their development obligations.

Calling for speedy legal reforms, the Khan Working Group demanded that Debt Recovery of Banks and DFIs should be given top priority and that the 1993 Act of Recovery of Debt should be overhauled. The Working Group accepted the existence of regulatory discrepancies as between DFIs, and banks and called for measures to smoothen out these regulatory discrepancies. The group suggested that a super regulator be established to supervise and ensure uniformity in regulatory treatment. The Working Group called for a reduction of CRR of banks to international levels. Further, the Group recommended the complete abolition of Statutory Liquidity Ratio (SLR).

The Working Group also made some more important recommendations to make the process of movement from development banking to universal banking easy and smooth. For instance, direct lending and concessional lending to certain sectors should be replaced by specifically targeted subsidiaries to the sector. The Group called for modification in the definition of priority sector by excluding all infrastructure loans from the definition of bank credit, which was used in computing the 40 per cent priority sector target of banks.

The Group suggested that the stake of State Government in SFCs should be lowered below 50 per cent. Besides, IDBI shareholding of SFCs should be transferred to SIDBI and the ownership of SIDBI, in turn, should be transferred to RBI or to the Government of India. RBI accepted recommendation of Khan Working Group towards setting up of universal banking. The first universal bank has been set up by ICICI merging with ICICI Bank. Others would follow soon.

Reserve Bank of India and Monetary Management

4

Money market, capital market, financial system or any monetary transaction somehow ultimately come under Reserve Bank of India which is the central supreme monetary authority of our country. It was established as private shareholders' bank on 1 April 1935. This status was retained for about fourteen years. After Independence, there was remarkable development in all sectors and the banking system also expanded adequately. Accordingly, RBI was nationalised on January 1, 1949. Since then it has been actively engaged in building and improving financial infrastructure for development. Like other banks, RBI also performs almost all traditional central banking operations. RBI, in fact, was established on the pattern of Bank of England and it has been functioning almost on those lines. The activities of RBI are looked after by Central Board of Directors consisting of twenty members including Governor, four Deputy Governors, one official from Finance Ministry, ten government nominated directors and four directors for local boards with headquarters at Mumbai, Kolkata, Chennai and New Delhi. All the appointments of Reserve Bank of India are made by the Central Government and uniformity of working is maintained throughout the country.

FUNCTIONS OF THE RESERVE BANK OF INDIA

Reserve Bank of India has been authorised to function like Central Bank of the country as per the Reserve Bank of India Act, 1934. Its main functional features are mentioned hereunder:

Functions as India's Central Bank

(i) **Issue of Currency:** Like any other Central Bank, RBI has sole rights to issue currency notes under section 22 of Reserve

Bank of India Act. The RBI has been entrusted with the responsibility of adequate supply of currency to facilitate transactions of the government, banks and the public. RBI issues currency notes of all denominations other than one rupee coins and notes as well as subsidiary coins which are issued by the Central Government but the distribution of which is undertaken by RBI. There is a division of work between the Issue and Banking Department of RBI in respect of note issue. Issue Department issues currency notes as per the demand of the Banking Department for them. Accordingly, the Banking Department keeping in view the demand for currency notes has to transfer government or other approved securities to the Issue Department. As per the RBI (Amendment) Act, 1957, a minimum gold and foreign exchange reserve was to be of Rs. 200 crores. Value of gold was not to be at any time less than Rs. 115 crores. This is termed as the minimum reserve system and the same provision is adopted by RBI for issuing the currency notes.

(ii) Banker to Government: Reserve Bank of India provides useful services to the government as a banker, agent and adviser. It works as an agent for the Central Government and State Governments looking after their all financial transactions and banking operations on their behalf. It offers loans to them with credit of 90 days. To be on the safer side, it operates in the gilt-edged market so far as loan operations are concerned. RBI acts as an adviser to the government pertaining to monetary and fiscal policies.

Besides, RBI's advice is sought regarding financing pattern, resource mobilization, five-year plans and other credit related matters. In addition to financial transactions, the Bank acts as the agent of the government in respect of India's presence as a member of International Monetary Fund (IMF) and the International Bank for Reconstruction and Development (World Bank).

(iii) Banker's Bank and Lender of the Last Resort: Reserve Bank of India acts as a banker to other scheduled commercial banks and state co-operative banks. Hence, these banks are supposed to maintain a specified percentage of their deposits with RBI as per the turnover of transactions. RBI provides financial assistance to the banks in the form of discounting of eligible bills and loans as well as advances against approved securities. RBI also undertakes the periodical inspections of the banks and is always there to help them. In case of any problem, RBI comes to the rescue of the banks and serves as the lender of the last resort. So when the banks fail, they approach RBI for the assistance for their survival and for continuing their banking operations.

(iv) **Credit Control:** Reserve Bank of India has the power to use almost all quantitative and qualitative methods of credit control so as to influence the volume of credit created by banks. As per Banking Regulation Act, 1949, RBI is empowered to advise banks whether to give or not the credit to particular customer or any group of persons based on the nature of securities involved. RBI has been strict on these types of issues related to credit. RBI can call for the details of project or purpose for which credit is sought which may be followed by periodical inspections. RBI, in short, controls the credit operations of the banks regulating the quantity of credit and the rate at which it is made available. Selective control of credit is practised through specifying purposes for which credit is to be given and the margins to be maintained in respect of secured advances. Through the open market operations, RBI changes cash or reserve with the banks thereby affecting the credit capacity of banks.

(v) **Custodian of Foreign Exchange Reserves:** As a part of exchange management and control, RBI functions as the custodian of nation's foreign exchange reserves so as to stabilise the external value of rupee. After India became member of International Monetary Fund in 1946, the Reserve Bank of India has the responsibility of maintaining fixed exchange rates with all other member countries of IMF. Besides, RBI acts as the custodian of India's reserve of international currencies.

In the year 1947, exchange controls were enacted under Foreign Exchange Regulation Act (FERA) when its function of exchange management and control was looked after RBI. The act empowered the RBI to exercise control over foreign securities and payments besides transfer of currency, bullion, and securities to foreign nationals. This act was later replaced by the Foreign

Exchange Regulation Act, 1973 which was in force w.e.f. 1 January 1974. FERA provided that no unauthorised person would buy or sell foreign exchange. In the past years, FERA was amended several times and the same has now been replaced by Foreign Exchange Management Act (FEMA). In accordance with trade and exchange policies, the RBI has been instrumental in carrying out operations related to the foreign exchange.

Supervisory Functions

As we know, Reserve Bank is the supreme authority in the banking system of India. Apart from the conventional banking, RBI also has some non-monetary functions to be performed such as supervision and control over the commercial as well as co-operative banks so as to promote sound banking in country. RBI has been empowered to look after licensing, branch expansion, pattern of working, reconstruction, amalgamation and liquidation of the banks. Besides the above functions, RBI carries inspections of banks and gives directions to them for trouble-free working for the economic development of the country. Thus, RBI is performing functions of periodical monitoring of banks in order to promote banking facilities along with smooth functioning which, no doubt, account for well-planned development and prosperity of the nation.

Promotional Functions

Leaving aside traditional banking followed by strict control over working of banks, RBI also performs numerous functions related to development and promotional aspects such as expanding banking facilities in rural and semi-urban areas. A warm word of appreciation must go to RBI for helping to set up IFCI, SFC, Deposit Insurance Corporation, UTI, IDBI, Agricultural Refinance Corporation of India and the Industrial Reconstruction Corporation of India to promote saving habit, mobilise savings and provide industrial finance as well as agricultural finance. RBI had also established Agricultural Credit Department to extend agricultural credit. RBI has played an important role in co-operative credit movement and providing long-term finance to the farmers. Development of the institutional agricultural credit has been a major function of RBI since its inception. The National Bank for Agriculture and Rural

Development (NABARD) was set up on July 12, 1982 with half of its share capital provided by RBI. NABARD has taken over the entire working of Agricultural Refinance and Development Corporation (ARDC). As discussed, apart from being a controller of credit, the RBI also performs advisory function which has considerably helped in accelerating the development in the country. RBI also advises the government on general economic problems and other related issues which are of vital importance for the rapid progress in all respects.

CLASSIFICATION OF RBI'S FUNCTIONS

As discussed above, there are various functions performed by Reserve Bank of India. But its functional features mainly cater to two categories, namely monetary and non-monetary functions. Under the Banking Regulation Act, 1949, RBI has been empowered to promote sound banking related to licensing of banks, expansion of branch network, methods of working and liquidity of assets, etc. After Independence, RBI has shown impressive performance pertaining to industrial growth and agricultural development. RBI could not have justified its existence in India if it had confined its activities to the industrial sector and completely ignored agricultural sector, on the prosperity of which industrial development depended to a large extent. This function, therefore, has been significant. With the increase in importance of economic development at the national level, new demands were made on RBI and its functions increased steadily. Now many development and promotional functions are performed by RBI which were earlier considered outside the purview of the central bank. Moreover, *The RBI Bulletin*, a monthly publication, presents not only statistical and other information related to various sectors of economy, but also indicates results of important studies and investigations conducted on various aspects of developments by RBI.

MONETARY POLICY OF THE RESERVE BANK OF INDIA

Controlled Expansion (1951-72)

Reserve Bank of India being engaged in money matters, organises currency and credit and formulates monetary policy in order to achieve broad economic objectives of the country. Monetary policy, also termed as money and credit policy, concerns itself with the supply of money as also of credit to the economy. Main aim of the monetary policy is to raise national income, standard of living, reduce the inflationary pressure and ultimately accelerating the speed of the economic development in the country. The policy indicates the working of the economy specifying the measures that RBI intends to take regarding interest rates and inflation ensuring the price stability. In addition, the norms for the financial institutions, banks and finance companies are laid down in the policy. Economy, of course, has been expanded with the help of RBI by means of expansion of money and credit besides selective controls have been adopted to check the rise in prices.

RBI'S ANTI-INFLATIONARY MONETARY POLICY SINCE 1972

After Independence, economic growth had tendency to increase and it went on rising tremendously from 1969 onwards due to nationalisation of banks. But in the early seventies our economy started showing the downward trend and was indicating considerable inflationary pressure mainly because of frequent fluctuations in agricultural production, defective policies of government, global conditions, hike in oil prices and the Gulf War. RBI, accordingly, put restrictions on the expansion since 1972 and thereafter has been moving with credit restraint attitude.

OTHER OBJECTIVES OF MONETARY POLICY

Apart from traditional banking system and other conventional forms of working, sometimes keeping in view the adverse conditions of the market, RBI also has to look after and solve other problems which are, so to say, the additional objectives of RBI to be achieved in the interest of the nation. For example, in the mid-nineties RBI was constrained to enter the foreign exchange in a full fledged way to prevent heavy depreciation of rupee. Same performance was repeated in 1998 when RBI took several strict measures to check the steep fall of the rupee against the dollar. These were the short-term objectives and the same were attained with success to sustain the desired image globally.

CREDIT CONTROL

General Credit-Controls

Right from mid-fifties and particularly from the start of seventies, inflation has been on the rise and there is continuous increase in the prices which is the direct effect of government's increased expenditure financed through deficit spending. Inflationary rise in prices also accounts for shortfalls in production, hoarding and speculation in essential commodities. RBI has numerous ways, broadly called as weapons of control, classified into two forms—quantitative and qualitative methods to control credit flow. Their use has, however, varied from time to time depending upon the circumstances. Quantitative controls are related to volume of credit indirectly controlling inflationary and reverse pressures due to expansion and contraction of credit whereas credit controls which include bank rate, CRR, SLR and open market operations also play important role in controlling the mounting move of inflationary rise in prices.

(i) **Bank Rate:** It has been a principal instrument which RBI uses to check inflation. It is the rate at which RBI lends to the banking system which affects short-term as well as long-term rates and ultimately economic activity in the economy thereby influencing the international capital movements. Higher rates attract capital inflows. But the money market rates do not automatically adjust themselves to change in the bank rate. Similarly, the deposit rates and lending rates of banks are not related to the bank rate. Government of India and RBI review the guidelines and rules in order to make bank rate as an active instrument of monetary policy as in other economies.

(ii) **Cash Reserve Requirements (CRR):** CRR so-called Cash Reserve Ratio which is the ratio of a bank's cash holdings to its total deposit liabilities is another device to influence money supply. A higher ratio means that the amount of cash available for creating credit is reduced. Under RBI Act, 1934 every commercial bank has to keep certain minimum cash reserves with RBI. Pressure is always mounted on RBI to reduce CRR which leaves large cash reserves with banks enabling them to expand bank credit. Reducing CRR and expansion of bank credit for industry as well as trade is the main feature to stabilise the economy and accordingly RBI pursues its objective to reduce CRR to the maximum possible extent. The Narasimham Committee (1991) did not favour the use of CRR to combat inflationary pressures. In its opinion, a high CRR adversely affected bank profitability and thus pressured banks all the time to charge high interest rates in their commercial sector advances.

(iii) Statutory Liquidity Requirements (SLR): Besides the cash reserve requirements, commercial banks have to maintain liquid assets in the form of cash, gold or unencumbered approved securities equal to or not less than 25 per cent of their total demand and time deposit liabilities. This is termed as statutory liquidity ratio (SLR). The Banking Regulation (Amendment) Act, 1962 also empowers the RBI to raise the SLR upto 40 per cent if it is considered necessary to control liquidity. RBI has power to determine SLR for commercial banks w.e.f. 22 September 1990. SLR was raised to 38.5 per cent so as to reduce commercial banks' ability to create credit thereby easing inflationary pressures apart from picking larger resources available to the state.

The Narasimham Committee did not favour high SLR. In its opinion, the SLR had become an instrument in the hands of the government to mobilise resources in support of central and state budgets. Keeping in view the recommendations of the Narasimham Committee, the government decided to reduce SLR from 38.5 to 25 per cent from 10 October 1997 and at present also it is there on the same level which has been successful part of the financial sector reform.

OPEN MARKET OPERATIONS OF RBI

This is an important instrument of credit control. It was not used by RBI for many years and was developed much later. This tool was felt necessary when the bank rate policy was not effective and turned out to be weak instrument of monetary control. Because of the underdeveloped nature of the money market, bank rate changes could not matter much and hence open market operations were preferred and promoted. In our country, the gilt-edged market meant for government securities is very well developed and is strongly recommended for open market operations. In such highly favourable conditions of market, RBI Act authorises RBI to conduct purchase and sale operations in the government securities, treasury bills and other approved securities of risk free nature. RBI finds it safe for open market operations as institutional investors, banks and insurance companies are putting their funds in government securities. Through the open market operations, RBI changes the cash or reserve with the banks thereby affecting the credit capacity of banks. The sale of securities reduces reserves while purchase of securities increases them. In the former case, banks are forced to contract credit and in the latter case they get an opportunity to expand it.

SELECTIVE AND DIRECT CREDIT CONTROLS

India is a developing economy and several techniques are frequently adopted for the credit control which normally jeopardise the development efforts. In such cases, selective credit controls are introduced to check the misuse of borrowing facilities for specific purposes. RBI has the power to regulate credit to specific branches of economic activities through selective credit controls. Hence, by means of this practice, the speculation of essential commodities can be checked so as to prevent undue rise in prices because of hoarding.

RBI employs mainly three techniques of selective credit controls—determination of margin requirements for loans against certain securities, determination of maximum amount of advances or other financial assistance and charging of discriminatory interest rates on certain types of advances. Every care is taken by RBI that the bank credit for production and transportation as well as exports is not effected. Selective controls are focussed mainly on credit to traders involved in process of hoarding and speculation. Controls are selective as they are used to control and check the rising tendency of the prices of essential commodities of common use.

CREDIT AUTHORISATION SCHEME (CAS)

Reserve Bank of India had introduced Credit Authorisation Scheme (CAS) in November 1965, as a part of Selective Credit Control. As per this scheme, the commercial banks have to seek RBI's permission and authorization while sanctioning any credit amounting to Rs. 1 crore or above to a single customer. Keeping in view the rapid progress in all the sectors it was raised to Rs. 6 crore in April 1986. The commercial banks have strict instructions to investigate thoroughly the detailed data of the borrowing concerns so that the credit is provided according to their actual needs. There should not be any type of manipulation towards the under invoicing or over invoicing on the part of borrowers while they approach the bank for the required credit so as to meet the genuine demands without prior sanction of RBI. CAS was further liberalized in 1987 in the interest of nation for the enhanced economic development and growth. Finally, a bold step was taken by Reserve Bank of India and aforesaid Credit Authorisation Scheme (CAS) was abolished in October 1988 to accelerate the productivity.

CREDIT MONITORING ARRANGEMENT (CMA)

After Credit Authorisation Scheme (CAS), RBI floated a post-sanction scheme designated as Credit Monitoring Arrangement (CMA) according to which all sanctions of bank loans above Rs. 5 crore, to a single customer for working capital requirement and more than Rs. 2 crore, would be monitored and observed by banks ensuring basic financial discipline. Apart from selective credit controls, RBI may give directions to banks in general or otherwise as to the purpose for which loans may or may not be given. RBI stated, "The Selective Credit Control should not be assessed mainly in terms of their positive influence on prices since the latter primarily depends on the availability of supply of the relevant commodities relative to demand. The success of these controls is to be judged in a limited sphere, i.e. their impact on the pressure of demand originating from bank credit. In this sense, the measures should be deemed successful but for their operation it is likely that the price situation might have been somewhat worse." For more than four decades, Reserve Bank of India had extensively adopted the technique of margin requirements to check the hoarding of essential commodities for it causes artificial scarcities in the market and tends to raise prices.

AN EVALUATION OF THE MONETARY POLICY

Reserve Bank of India is extensively empowered to control the supply of money and credit. RBI had itself controlled expansion of economy and controlled inflationary pressure which had been two main objectives of monetary policy. RBI is adequately empowered to make use of devices of quantitative credit control like bank rate policy, CRR and open market operations. Monetary policy in India was formulated in the context of economic planning whose main objective was to speed up the economic growth in the country. The powers and devices of control available with RBI cover only organised banking sector such as commercial banks and co-operatives but the inflationary pressure mounts because of deficit of financing and shortage of goods. In this kind of situation, even RBI is helpless and does not have effective measure to control. It is all because of the fact that Reserve Bank of India does not have any power to control the non-banking financial companies and the indigenous bankers who form the major contribution for financing trade and industry. While we scrutinize the monetary policy it indicates partial success. There are some good achievements to its credit as well as some negative points termed as failures. The overall requirements of expanding economic activities have been sufficiently met with thereby providing the stipulated bank credit to the monetary policy to bring down the inflation adequately. Talking about the failures of monetary policy that has shown unsatisfactory results pertaining to expansion of money supply, giving rise to black market and speculation, apart from defective allocation of funds to many sectors. Moneylenders capture the agriculture and small industries which do not get institutional source of funds.

WORKING OF THE INDIAN MONETARY SYSTEM: THE CHAKRAVARTY COMMITTEE REPORT

After Independence, there has been noticeable improvement in development of economic growth in all the sectors with adequate mobilization of funds for the successful implementation of Five-Year Plans. So as to control inflationary trend of its rising nature, Reserve Bank of India appointed a committee in December 1982 with Professor Sukhmoy Chakravarty as Chairman to review the Indian monetary system. Accordingly, the Chakravarty Committee was asked to provide a review and recommend measures to make monetary policy more effective. The Committee dealt especially with the objectives of monetary policy, relation between monetary policy and fiscal policy, regulation of money supply, maintenance of price stability, interest rate policy and utilisation of credit. The Chakravarty Committee submitted its report in May 1985 after reviewing the structure and operation of the monetary system, evaluating various instruments of monetary and credit policies and assessing the interaction of monetary policy as well as public debt management.

THE STRUCTURE AND OPERATION OF THE MONETARY SYSTEM IN INDIA

The Chakravarty Committee made recommendations that the operation of monetary system should be consistent with plan priorities so that the process of mobilization of savings and utilization of these resources become socially purposive. But in spite of increased rate of savings, the public sector investment could not be financed as the rate of savings was not sufficient thereby giving rise to the inflationary pressures due to deficit financing. Hence, the Chakravarty Committee recommended to finance the Five-Year Plans in a non-inflationary way by virtue of tapping the savings of the public in a greater measure than in the past, raising higher savings from the public sector enterprises and improving efficiency in both revenue collection as well as in expenditure.

OBJECTIVES OF MONETARY POLICY: PRICE STABILITY

The Chakravarty Committee stressed the need to pursue price stability as the primary objective of the monetary policy. By the term price stability it does not mean that the prices would be same all the time nor it retains the constant price level. But it remains consistent with fixed percentage rise in the wholesale price index. Accordingly, Reserve Bank of India should control the expansion of reserve money and money supply while government should take the suitable measures to raise the output levels.

The Chakravarty Committee recognised the existence of violent fluctuations in agricultural production caused by weather conditions and the consequent difficulty in controlling inflationary pressures in India. Strong supply management measures were advocated by the committee. Simultaneously, demand management plays vital role with equal importance which cater for the demand for goods and services based on the volume of money and credit thereby necessitating the combined action coupled with the required co-ordination by the government and Reserve Bank of India related to the field of demand management and more effective use of credit.

MONETARY TARGETING

The Chakravarty Committee recommended the formulation of a monetary policy based on monetary target, keeping in view the inter-relationship between money, output and prices. As suggested by the Committee, the target for growth of money supply during given year in a broad sense should be in terms of a range based on anticipated growth in output in the light of the price situation. There should be advance announcement pertaining to the target range, modifications as well as the circumstances under which modifications are to be made.

The Chakravarty Committee further pointed out that the major cause of the substantial growth in money supply since 1970 was the rise in RBI credit to government which indicates that the rate of interest on government securities had been so low that neither the public nor banking, financial and other institutions willingly bought government securities or even the treasury bills. Hence, RBI loans and advances to the government became money.

Based on above facts, the Chakravarty Committee made recommendation that the RBI and the Central Government should come out with a policy as regards the regulations of RBI credit to the government so as to facilitate more of participation in government's borrowing programmes by the non-banking region of the public thereby reducing the growth in reserve money.

CHANGE IN THE DEFINITION OF BUDGETARY DEFICIT

Earlier, the increase in treasury bills outstanding were essentially taken by the central government as the budgetary deficit. But the treasury bills were partly absorbed by the public and all the treasury bills were not held by Reserve Bank of India. All the time, there was a lot of confusion in the fiscal operations as the budget deficit could not discriminate between the amount of bills absorbed by the public and the amount held by RBI. Moreover, the budgetary deficit did not indicate the support of RBI to the government in any form representing a rise in RBI credit to government with a proportionate impact on money supply. Accordingly, the Chakravarty Committee made a suggestion regarding a change in definition of budgetary deficit so that there could be clear distinction between revenue deficit, fiscal deficit and overall budgetary deficit.

INTEREST RATE POLICY

The structure of interest rate is entirely controlled by the concerned authorities under the general directives of the government. According to Chakravarty Committee, the present system of interest rates has unnecessarily become complicated and the modifications are required to be done for which the Committee has made some recommendations such as increasing the pool of financial savings, providing a reasonable return on savings of small savers, reinforcing anti-inflationary policies, providing credit at concessional rate of interest to the priority sectors and profitability of banks, etc.

To meet the credit requirements of the productive sectors, within prescribed limits, the committee suggested that the banks should be more at liberty to determine their lending rate which would too prevent excessive use of credit due to relatively low interest rates. The Committee was of the opinion that the concessional interest rates as redistributive device should be used in a very selective manner. For the interest rates pertaining to bank deposits the Committee suggested that they should be positive to encourage small savers. It highlighted the importance of providing bank credit in the form of loans and bills finance instead of cash credit as at present. The Committee also highlighted the disruptive effect on credit flows arising from payments to suppliers by large public and private sector units also by the government and recommended that the interest on delayed payments should be provided for in purchase contracts.

As per the opinion of the Committee, the problems associated with improving the effectiveness of the priority sector lending were principally in the area of organisational reorientation and effective communication and monitoring besides emphasizing the importance of strengthening the credit delivery system in the area of priority sector lending so that adequate and timely credit was made available to this sector.

RESTRUCTURING OF THE MONEY MARKET IN INDIA

The Committee was of the view that the money market in India should be restructured. In its opinion, in the restructured monetary system the treasury bills market, the call money market, the commercial bills market and the inter-corporate funds market should play an important role in the allocation of short-term resources. The Committee also recommended that RBI should adopt all the measures which are necessary to develop an efficient money market in the country.

Follow-up Action on the Recommendations

All the major recommendations made by the Chakravarty Committee were accepted by Government of India and also have been implemented. The Committee had stressed the need for developing aggregate monetary targets to ensure orderly monetary growth. The government has thus carried out such targets with the concurrence and consultation of RBI. The budget should indicate and give the reflection of increase in entire RBI credit to the government besides the narrowly defined figure of the budget deficit. All this has been accepted in totality by the government. The yields of the return on long-term government securities were increased and maturities reduced keeping in view the recommendations of the Committee. Moreover, according to proposal of the Committee, now treasury bills of 364 days maturity are being issued by the RBI. These instruments with flexible rates now enable banks to manage their liquidity better and help in evolving an active secondary market in short-term instruments.

ANNUAL POLICY STATEMENT FOR THE YEAR 2008-09

Box 4.1: Annual policy statement of the RBI (2008-09)

A: Annual policy statement for 2008-09, announced on April 29, 2008

- The bank rate kept unchanged at 6.0 per cent.
- The reverse-repo rate and repo rate kept unchanged at 6.00 per cent and 7.75 per cent respectively.
- The RBI retains the option to conduct overnight repo or longer term repo under the Liquidity Adjustment Facility (LAF) depending on market conditions and other relevant factors. The RBI will continue to use this flexibly including the right to accept or reject tender(s) under the LAF, wholly or partially, if deemed fit, so as to make efficient use of the LAF in daily liquidity management.
- Cash Reserve Ratio (CRR) of the scheduled banks increased to 8.25 per cent with effect from the fortnight beginning May 24, 2008.

B: Mid-term review of annual policy statement

- The bank rate kept unchanged at 6.0 per cent.
- The repo rate under LAF is kept unchanged at 8.0 per cent.
- The reverse-repo rate under the LAF kept unchanged at 6.0 per cent.
- RBI has the flexibility to conduct repo / reverse-repo auctions at a fixed rate or at variable rates as circumstances warrant.
- RBI retains the option to conduct overnight or longer term repo/reverse-repo under the LAF depending on

market conditions and other relevant factors. The RBI will continue to use this flexibility including the right to accept or reject tender(s) under the LAF, wholly or partially, if deemed fit, so as to make efficient use of LAF in daily liquidity management.

- The CRR kept unchanged at 6.5 per cent.

Annual Policy Statement at a Glance

Main points of annual policy statements are as follows:

(i) Reserve-repo rate and repo rate kept unchanged at 6 per cent and 7.75 per cent respectively.

(ii) Cash Reserve Ratio (CRR) hiked to 6.5 per cent earlier with effect from April 28, 2007, prevailing from 6.25 per cent.

(iii) Ceiling interest rate on NR(E) RA deposits reduced by 50 basis points to LIBOR/SWAP rates.

(iv) Ceiling interest rate on FCNR(B) deposits reduced by 50 basis points to LIBOR minus 75 basis points.

(v) Average cut-off yield on 182-day treasury bills to be used as a benchmark rate for floating rate bonds.

(vi) Overseas investment limit (total financial commitments) for Indian companies enhanced to 300 per cent of their net worth.

(vii) Listed Indian companies limit for portfolio investment abroad in listed overseas companies enhanced to 35 per cent of net worth.

(viii) Aggregate ceiling on overseas investment by mutual funds enhanced to US$ 4 billion from US$ 3 million.

(ix) Prepayment of External Commercial Borrowings (ECBs) without prior RBI approval increased to 400 million dollars.

(x) Limit for individuals for any permitted current or capital account transaction increased from 50,000 to 1,00,000 US dollars per financial year in the liberalized remittance scheme.

(xi) Risk weight on residential housing loans to individuals for loans upto Rs. 20 lacs reduced to 50 per cent as a temporary measure.

(xii) Ceiling rate of interest payable by NBFCs (other than RNBCs) on deposits raised by 150 basis points.

Mid-term View

(i) CRR increased by 50 basis points to reach 7.5 per cent effective from November 10, 2007.

(ii) Covering of "Short-sale" and "When issued" transactions to be permitted outside the Negotiated Dealing System-Order Matching (NDS-OM) System.

(iii) Reinstatement of the eligible limits under the past performance route for hedging facility to be permitted.

(iv) Oil companies to be permitted to hedge foreign exchange exposure by using overseas over-the-counter (OTC)/exchange traded derivatives upto a maximum of one year forward.

(v) Importers and exporters having foreign currency exposures to be allowed to write covered call and put options in both foreign currency/rupee and cross currency and receive premier.

Prices and Monetary Management

5

Monetary policy is a crucial weapon in the hands of the central bank as its efficacy is important in achieving the goals of growth, inflation control or price stability, fiscal stability, exchange rate stability and promotion of foreign exchange reserves. The basic objective of any central bank of a nation is to maintain sound monetary system. The term monetary management involves four major issues: price stability, control over money supply, control over money stock in the light of reserve money creation due to RBI credit to government, and rationalization of administered interest rate.

Monetary Management Prior to 1990s

Inflation targeting is an accepted goal of monetary policy in many nations, yet there are wide differences among them as regards the choice of inflation rate. It involves use of policy discretion by the central bank which logically results in the autonomy of the central bank. The pre-1990s time period was characterized by the following:

(a) Existence of a spectrum of interest rates with built-in elements of concessionality and cross subsidization to meet the priorities assigned to different sectors.

(b) Rate of return on government securities was fixed and was lower than market rates.

(c) Resolution of deposit rates and borrowing rates to maintain the cost of funds in relation to lending ratio.

(d) Unlimited accommodation through ad hoc treasury hills to meet budgetary deficits of the central government.

(e) Maintenance of high CRR and SLR of 15 per cent and 38.5 per cent respectively.

(f) Lack of depth in government securities market on account of application of lower than market coupons.

(g) Lack of depth and vibrancy in money market.

Position After 1990s

Since the advent of economic reforms, high trajectory growth and macroeconomic and financial stability seem to be the distinguishing features of India. After the economy was opened up and integrated with global financial sector, it seems to have developed the resilience, particularly in the wake of global shocks, the September 11 incident in US, border tensions, sanctions imposed after the nuclear tests, political uncertainties, the oil shock, the 26/11 Mumbai terror attack and even the worldwide economic meltdown.

In the present scenario, monetary policy is aimed at striking a fine balance between high growth rate and price stability. This obviously warrants an optimal allocation of financial resources to productive sectors of the economy as financial stability has gained greater significance after the economy was opened up. In 1998-99, the RBI adopted a multiple indicator approach, a shift from earlier, the earlier policy in which only the inflations was targeted.

This paradigm shift in monetary policy framework, consistent with structural changes, facilitated monetary transmission mechanism. The RBI took certain vital steps to integrate the Indian economy with the global economy. These included the development of money market, government securities market, and the foreign exchange market. It allowed market determined interest rates in the place of administrated rate of interest. The market biased monetary policy maintained a choice of instruments decisively from direct to more indirect measures. The reduction of SLR from 38.5 per cent (1992) of net demand and time liabilities to 25 per cent in 1997 and the CRR from 15 per cent to 4.5 per cent in 2003 were important steps. Another step was discontinuation of automatic monetization of fiscal deficit of the government since 1997 and freeing of RBI's balance sheet from the burden of exchange guarantees accumulated in the pre-reform era. The enactment of the Fiscal Responsibility and Budget Management (FRBM) Act (2003) strengthened the institutional mechanism, from 2006 onwards. Thus, the RBI is no longer required to subscribe to government securities in the primary market. At the recommendation of the Twelfth Finance Commission, the Central Government has stopped to raise resources on behalf of states governments, which now need to have direct access to mobilize their resources based on their financial health.

The overall stance of monetary policy is as follows:

(a) To reinforce the emphasis on price stability and well-anchored inflation expectations while ensuring a monetary and interest rates environment that supports export and investment demand in the economy so as to enable a continuation of the growth momentum.

(b) To emphasise credit quality and orderly conditions in financial markets for securing macroeconomic stability and in particular, financial stability while simultaneously pursuing greater credit penetration and financial inclusion.

(c) To respond swiftly with all possible measures as appropriate to the evolving global and domestic situation impinging on inflation expectations and the growth momentum.

In brief, between the pre-1990s and post-1990s, in the latter period the formulation and implementation of monetary policy has undergone a marked transformation. These changes encompass a shift in dependence from direct to indirect instruments of monetary control; a more transparent way of formulation and implementation, keeping up with time consistency; and recognition of the absence of trade-off between inflation and unemployment.

Inflation Management

The rate of inflation has a correlation with demand and supply equation. Hence, movements in the rate of inflation reflect changes in demand and supply conditions in the economy. Inflation management, therefore, involves controlling the demand situation as well as reining in inflationary expectations through various monetary measures. On the supply side, it would encompass various administrative and fiscal measures.

Trends in 2008-09

Monthly changes in headline inflation, year-on-year, measured in terms of the Wholesale Price Index (WPI) exhibited significant volatility during financial year 2008-09. Inflation figures showed high volatility and varied from 1.20 per cent in March 2009 to 12.82 per cent in August 2008. The volatility observed in the first half of 2008-09 was due to increasing international fuel and commodity prices which pushed WPI inflation to a high of 12.8 per cent. The subsequent decline in WPI inflation in the second half of 2008-09 was due to falling international fuel and commodity prices.

From September 2009 onwards WPI inflation has been rising at a very fast clip largely because of increase in the prices of food items, both primary and manufactured, and non-food agricultural items. Apprehensions of shortages in agricultural production due to a deficient southwest monsoon were mainly responsible for increasing inflation. Average food inflation which was 7.56 per cent during fiscal 2008-09 increased to 13.54 per cent in the period April to December 2009. Overall food inflation in December 2009 was 19.77 per cent. However, the overall WPI is expected to moderate and stabilize on account of the likely impact of several measures taken by the government to contain food price inflation.

Average Annual Trends in WPI Inflation

The years of relatively high average annual inflation of above 5.5 per cent since 2000 have been 2000-01, 2004-05 and 2008-09. All these were years of high fuel prices. The year 2004-05, however, also witnessed high inflation in manufactured products because of high growth in the gross domestic product (GDP) in this sector leading to high demand and high prices of raw materials such as basic metal alloys and metal products, non-metallic mineral products and machinery and machine tools. The year 2008-09 was, however, different from the earlier two years as high inflation was witnessed in all the three sectors primarily because of high international fuel and commodity prices including those of food items, reflective of gradual linking of the Indian economy with the world.

Table 5.1: Annual Average Inflation Rate Based WPI

(per cent)

Year	Primary articles	Fuel, power, light & lubri.	Manufactured products	All commodities
Weights (%)	**22.02**	**14.23**	**63.75**	**100.00**
2000-01	2.8	28.5	3.3	7.2
2001-02	3.6	8.9	1.8	3.6
2002-03	3.3	5.5	2.6	3.4
2003-04	4.3	6.4	5.7	5.5
2004-05	3.7	10.1	6.3	6.5
2005-06	2.9	9.5	3.1	4.4
2006-07	7.9	5.6	4.4	5.4
2007-08	7.6	0.9	5.0	4.7
2008-09	10.1	7.5	8.1	8.4
2008-09 (Apr.-Dec.)	**10.93**	**11.32**	**9.47**	**10.20**
2009-10 (Apr.-Dec.)[P]	**8.78**	**–6.35**	**1.77**	**1.63**

Source: Department of Industrial Policy and Promotion.

P: Provisional.

The year 2009-10 was totally out of sync with the trends seen in earlier years with overall average inflation until December 2009 being low at 1.63 per cent and average inflation in the primary and fuel groups being 8.78 per cent and –6.35 per cent respectively. The increase in overall inflation since September 2009 was primarily due to rise in prices of primary articles, particularly food items, due to a deficient monsoon and expectations of shortage. Lately, a rising trend in food prices was also observed in the global market, particularly in prices of sugar, palm oil, soyabean and tea.

Disaggregated Analysis of WPI Average Inflation

Each major group in the WPI commodity basket can be further disaggregated on the basis of use and analysed. Such analysis assumes importance in view of the fact that the phase of relatively high inflation in 2009-10 was concentrated in food items which is a subset of the primary group. There was a perceptible high food inflation, both in the primary and manufactured groups. Another apparent fact that emerges from the analysis is the relatively high inflation observed in the minerals group during the five years up to 2009-10.

Table 5.2: Annual Average Inflation by Major Heads in WPI

(per cent)

Commodities	Weight (%)	2004-05	2005-06	2006-07	2007-08	2008-09	2008-09 (Apr.-Dec.)	2009-10 (Apr.-Dec.)P
All Commodities	**100.00**	**6.48**	**4.43**	**5.42**	**4.66**	**8.39**	**10.20**	**1.63**
I. Primary Articles	**22.03**	**3.69**	**2.87**	**7.85**	**7.61**	**10.06**	**10.93**	**8.78**
A. Food Articles	15.40	2.70	4.83	7.78	5.46	8.02	7.57	13.31
B. Non-Food Articles	6.14	0.70	–4.48	5.14	12.64	11.17	14.24	0.43
C. Minerals	0.48	110.31	26.54	28.13	13.20	34.90	45.53	–5.51
II. Fuel, Power, Light & Lubricants	**14.23**	**10.14**	**9.49**	**5.61**	**0.93**	**7.46**	**11.32**	**–6.35**
A. Coal Mining	1.75	15.34	3.72	0.00	2.68	6.60	9.08	–0.91
B. Minerals Oils	6.99	15.17	13.93	7.87	0.95	11.08	17.17	–10.12
C. Electricity	5.48	1.73	4.07	3.15	0.48	1.06	1.40	–0.08
III. Manufactured Products	**63.75**	**6.26**	**3.07**	**4.43**	**4.97**	**8.09**	**9.47**	**1.77**
A. Food Products	11.54	4.98	1.09	3.22	4.27	10.04	10.59	15.49
B. Beverages, Tobacco & its Products	1.34	5.26	4.85	7.36	10.27	9.50	9.53	5.25
C. Textiles	9.80	3.04	–4.50	2.16	–0.98	5.95	4.96	4.18
D. Wood & Wood Products	0.17	0.06	8.41	6.01	4.65	8.34	8.30	1.62
E. Paper & Paper Products	2.04	0.75	2.23	6.83	1.84	4.38	4.23	1.04
F. Leather & Leather Products	1.02	5.99	7.13	–4.38	4.14	1.08	0.83	–0.99
G. Rubber & Plastic Products	2.39	–0.37	3.42	6.61	7.15	4.66	5.47	1.79
H. Chemicals & their Products	11.93	2.54	3.58	3.03	5.57	7.23	8.85	3.20
I. Non-Metallic Mineral Products	2.52	6.34	7.80	12.82	8.86	3.74	4.32	3.27
J. Basic Metal Alloys & Products	8.34	21.16	7.43	6.82	6.86	14.44	19.65	–12.67
K. Machinery & Machine Tools	8.36	5.65	5.14	5.56	7.07	4.74	5.44	–1.34
L. Transport Equipment & Parts	4.29	4.68	3.63	1.56	2.71	5.22	6.09	0.05

Source: Department of Industrial Policy and Promotion.

P: Provisional.

This indicates that there was a mismatch in demand-supply in the mining sector, fuelled by rise in international prices of minerals, and high growth rates achieved. Subsequently, the slowdown in domestic and international demand brought moderation in prices in this sector.

Food Inflation

Food index is computed by clubbing together the components of food articles in the primary articles group and manufactured food products in the manufactured products group. The overall weight of the composite food index in the WPI is 25.43 per cent, which comprises primary food articles with a weight of 15.40 per cent and manufactured food products with a weight of 10.03 per cent (after adjusting for oil cakes, weight = 1.42 per cent, and cattle feed, weight = 0.01 per cent).

A quarter-wise analysis of food inflation in the WPI series (Base Year 1993-94 = 100), during 1994-95 to 2009-10, reveals that before the spell of high food inflation in 2009-10, there were two earlier episodes—in the fourth quarter (Q4) of 1996-97 (13.6 per cent) and third quarter (Q3) of 1998-99 (17.1 per cent). The high inflation in 1996-97 was due to increase in prices of rice, wheat, gram, and fruits and vegetables. High fuel prices in the international market also contributed to the higher food prices as they led to an increase in transportation costs. The spike in food prices in 1998-99 was in the aftermath of implementation of the Fourth Pay Commission recommendations leading to a rise in the purchasing power of a large number of people, creating more demand in the market vis-à-vis supply. During 1998-99, high inflation was reported in the case of onions and potatoes among vegetables, pulses, rice and wheat. Among manufactured products high prices were reported in the case of edible oils but sugar prices were stable. The spell of high food inflation in 2009-10 was across the board for all food items except edible oils. Very high inflation was witnessed in the case of sugar, pulses, vegetables, fruits, and cereals.

Among other things observed are inflation measured in terms of the Consumer Price Indices (CPIs) remained higher than WPI inflation during November 2008 to December 2009. The divergence between the WPI and CPI (IW) reached its peak in July 2009 and has been declining since then. Food inflation based on WPI and CPIs has been rising since April 2009 and no significant divergence has been observed.

Main Drivers of Inflation

Besides the commodity-wise figures, the drivers of 2008-09 and 2009-10 inflation can also be understood by the weight contributions of different commodities to total inflation. In December 2009, thirty essential commodities with a weight of 17.63 per cent and annual inflation of 21.89 per cent contributed 51.88 per cent to overall inflation. Food combined (comprising primary and manufactured food) with a weight of 25.43 per cent and annual inflation of 19.77 per cent contributed 66.56 per cent towards overall inflation. Items which contributed significantly towards overall inflation in December 2009 were rice, wheat, pulses, vegetables and fruits, milk, fish and meat and tea in primary articles; non-administered mineral oils in the fuel group; and sugar/*gur* and oil cakes in manufactured products.

The first half of the financial year 2008-09 was marked by high wholesale price index (WPI)-based inflation, primarily due to the rise in global commodity and fuel prices. The subsequent global economic meltdown (starting September 2008) reversed the trend and WPI inflation slipped into negative territory during June to August 2009. This was due to sharp fall in demand and the resultant decline in commodity prices globally as well as the base effect.

As regards food inflation, the upswing noticed in the first quarter of 2008-09, continued during 2009-10 due to unfavourable south-west monsoon, the worst since 1972. The double-digit inflation in food articles witnessed in 2009-10 can also be ascribed to supply-side constraints. So, it is necessary to ensure that the monetary policy stance does not lead to pressure on prices. The RBI, therefore, initiated calibrated changes in rates to mop up the prevalent excess liquidity in the system through the second and third quarter reviews wherein increases in statutory liquidity ratio (SLR) and cash reserve ratio (CRR)

Table 5.3: Weighted Contribution and Inflation in WPI

(per cent)

	Weight	Weighted contribution			Inflation		
	(%)	Oct-09	Nov-09^{P}	Dec-09^{P}	Oct-09	Nov-09^{P}	Dec-09^{P}
All Commodities	**100.00**	**100.00**	**100.00**	**100.00**	**1.46**	**4.78**	**7.31**
Primary Articles	**22.02**	**137.15**	**58.39**	**48.23**	**8.67**	**11.84**	**14.88**
Food Combined	25.43	232.53	90.68	66.56	14.24	17.78	19.77
Food Articles	15.40	140.38	56.52	42.54	12.99	16.71	19.17
Food MP	10.03	92.14	34.16	24.02	16.68	19.88	20.93
Essential Commodities	17.63	209.39	75.00	51.88	18.53	21.15	21.89
Rice	2.45	21.48	6.19	3.99	14.29	12.95	12.33
Wheat	1.38	8.78	3.74	2.39	9.31	12.66	12.04
Pulses	0.60	11.44	5.04	3.95	25.08	35.22	41.58
Vegetables	1.46	7.67	5.98	7.28	7.06	16.92	39.22
Potatoes	0.26	17.60	5.60	3.70	98.60	101.58	123.85
Onions	0.09	2.03	0.70	0.42	33.10	32.41	27.41
Fruits	1.46	7.21	3.96	2.43	5.90	10.64	9.83
Milk	4.37	28.70	10.33	8.06	10.03	11.49	13.36
Eggs, Meat & Fish	2.21	36.96	14.55	9.03	23.37	29.75	27.16
Tea	0.16	0.29	0.43	0.37	2.96	15.30	21.45
Fuel and Power	**14.23**	**–100.02**	**–3.94**	**12.03**	**–6.66**	**–0.89**	**4.29**
Rest Mineral Oils	1.55	–66.59	6.46	13.77	–21.96	9.53	38.18
Manufactured Products	**63.75**	**60.11**	**46.10**	**39.46**	**1.60**	**3.99**	**5.17**
Food Products	11.54	117.69	51.30	36.33	17.33	24.70	26.40
Sugar	3.62	76.82	27.95	18.72	46.26	53.76	53.98
Gur	0.06	1.40	0.37	0.28	40.02	32.60	37.23
Oil Cakes	1.42	25.52	17.14	12.31	21.14	50.39	56.87

Source: Department of Industrial Policy and Promotion.

P: Provisions.

respectively were announced. It became necessary for the government to take suitable fiscal and administrative measures in order to contain the food price inflation and to prevent it from spilling over to generalised inflation.

The position in important food items in this regard is discussed below:

Sugar: Sugar production in India is cyclical in nature. Two to three years of high production are usually followed by two to three years of low production. The estimated area under sugarcane and sugarcane production fell significantly from the 2007-08 sugar crop year to 2009-10 sugar crop year. The estimated sugar production fell from 263 lakh tonnes in the 2007-08 sugar season to 146 lakh tonnes in the 2008-09 sugar season. Further, in years of shortage of sugarcane, the amount of cane available for crushing by sugar mills—termed drawl rate—is much lower with higher levels of diversion for other uses like production of *gur* and *khandsari* sugar.

In 2009-10 sugar season, the estimated production was 160 lakh tonnes, about two-thirds the demand of 230 lakh tonnes. Another factor that is adding to the tremendous pressure on sugar prices is the hardening of international sugar prices, based on expectations of large sugar imports by India.

Pulses: India has been a net importer of pulses. During 2005 to 2009, domestic production of pulses has been around 14-14.8 million tonnes while the demand is estimated at around 17-18 million tonnes. The gap between demand and supply is met by import of a variety of pulses from different countries depending upon their availability. Due to limited sources for different varieties of pulses, domestic prices fluctuate according to availability and prices in the international market. Kharif pulse production reached a peak in 2007-08 at 6.4 million tonnes and declined to 4.78 million tonnes in 2008-09. High inflation in pulses may be attributed to apprehensions of shortages.

Rice: The total production of rice in 2009-10 was estimated at 86.15 million tonnes compared to 99.15 million tonnes a year earlier. Lower production by about 12.93 million tonnes may be the reason for higher prices of rice.

Wheat: In rabi marketing season (RMS) 2009-10, a total of 25.38 million tonnes of wheat was procured as against 22.69 million tonnes in RMS 2008-09. Further, the area under wheat is estimated to increase by 1.71 lakh ha from 275.87 lakh ha in February 2009 to 277.58 lakh ha in February 2010. Expectation of a better wheat harvest is likely to moderate wheat prices.

Vegetables: Average WPI inflation in vegetables (weight: 1.46 per cent in the WPI) from April to December 2009 was more than 52 per cent, which was significantly higher than the 9 per cent recorded during the same period a year earlier. Month-on-month changes in the WPI index for vegetables displayed a relatively high increase in the months of April, June, July and November 2009. Potatoes, onions, tapioca, tomatoes, green peas

Table 5.4: WPI-based Domestic Year-on-Year Inflation

(per cent)

Period	Energy	Non-energy commodities	Agri-culture	Beverages	Food	Fats and oils	Grains	Other food	Raw materials	Timber	Other raw materials	Fertilizers	Materials and minerals
Jan. 2009	–1.70	6.81	9.79	8.91	9.37	0.60	11.25	32.73	9.98	10.05	0.19	8.38	9.54
Feb. 2009	–3.40	5.41	7.32	10.08	9.32	–3.01	13.14	25.52	1.76	7.69	–2.69	8.54	1.88
Mar. 2009	–6.00	3.17	5.14	9.34	8.07	–6.96	11.61	20.37	0.56	7.74	–12.90	5.43	–7.47
Apr. 2009	–5.69	3.21	6.71	5.88	10.14	–4.05	11.92	15.66	2.55	10.05	–16.35	4.03	–12.11
May 2009	–6.14	3.43	6.91	5.60	10.62	–2.14	14.14	36.27	1.86	3.57	–15.77	–0.60	–12.19
Jun. 2009	–12.53	2.32	7.74	5.99	11.13	–7.85	14.39	26.50	–2.20	0.25	–18.08	–1.46	–13.95
Jul. 2009	–10.37	2.29	9.03	5.45	12.36	–9.38	13.90	18.88	–5.18	0.25	–18.69	–3.19	–15.03
Aug. 2009	–9.26	2.44	9.08	5.14	12.98	–7.29	14.19	13.90	–4.22	0.25	–17.04	–3.03	–13.46
Sep. 2009	–8.18	2.91	9.08	4.75	13.75	–5.59	16.10	7.19	–3.57	0.25	–16.76	–2.68	–12.74
Oct. 2009	–6.66	3.75	9.35	4.75	14.67	–3.93	14.75	4.83	–0.66	0.25	–14.47	–2.28	–11.68
Nov. 2009P	–0.89	6.30	12.61	4.47	19.75	–1.38	16.46	12.50	1.17	0.25	–6.18	–2.03	–8.28
Dec. 2009P	4.29	8.09	16.01	5.29	21.94	0.18	16.86	16.30	5.62	0.25	–2.31	–3.52	–6.93

Source: Department of Industrial Policy and Promotion.

P: Provisions.

Note: Catagorisation of WPI items/groups as compared to items stock groups in the World Bank pink sheet. Used in Table 4.10 (Figures in brackets are items/groups in WPI basket): Energy (Fuel group); Non Energy Commodities (All commodities excluding energy); Agriculture (Food Articles and Non-Food Articles); Beverages (Beverages, Tobacco & Tobacco Products); Food (Food Articles and Food Products); Fats and Oils (Edible Oils, Butter and Ghee); Grains (Cereals and Pulses); Other Food (Other Food Articles); Raw Materials (Non-Food Articles and Minerals); Timber (Wood & Wood Products); Other Raw Materials (Naphtha and Basic Metals Alloys & Metals Products); Fertilizers (Fertilizers); Metals and Minerals (Basic Metals, Alloys & Metals Products and Minerals).

and brinjal were the highest contributors to the inflation in vegetables. The increase in vegetable prices could be attributed to the failure of monsoon followed by floods in some of the southern states.

Milk: The price of milk has increased in 2009-10 though there was no apparent shortage of milk in the market. One of the reasons for increase in inflation in milk and milk products could be inflation in coarse cereals and oil cakes, which are used as feed for animals.

Tea: There is shortfall in production of tea in India and other tea-producing countries. WPI-based domestic inflation in tea was 21 per cent in December 2009. The price of tea in the international market in December 2009 rose by about 55 per cent over the price in December 2008.

Non-administered Petro Products: The inflation in non-administered petroleum products is linked to international crude oil prices. WPI inflation in this group was negative in October 2009 and it moved to the positive zone from November 2009. Since its weighted contribution to overall inflation is much higher than its weight in the commodity basket, it becomes a commodity to watch. Average international crude oil prices increased from $ 44.11/ bbl in January-March 2009 to $ 75.5/bbl in October-December 2009. This contributed to increase in inflation in non-administered petroleum products.

World Food Inflation

A report on the food index published by the World Bank and WPI-based domestic food inflation reveals that since April 2008 world food prices reflected much higher volatility compared to the WPI food index. Further, in almost all commodity groups, a higher volatility was seen in the international market than in the Indian domestic market.

Private Final Consumption Expenditure

The Private Final Consumption Expenditure (PFCE) measures the average change over time in the price paid for all consumer purchases. In other words, the PFCE deflator measures changes in the cost of living. It is considered a more accurate

Table 5.5: Inflation in World Commodity Price Indices

(per cent)

Period	Energy	Non-energy commodities	Agri-culture	Beverages	Food	Fats and oils	Grains	Other food	Raw matrials	Timber	Other raw materials	Fertilizers	Materials and minerals
Jan. 2009	–45.48	–23.64	–16.56	3.41	–19.07	–33.25	–7.57	–0.79	–19.25	4.08	–33.60	14.39	–37.75
Feb. 2009	–51.58	–30.29	–23.60	–7.26	–26.35	–38.60	–20.59	–5.15	–23.94	–1.71	–37.50	–4.71	–42.46
Mar. 2009	–52.00	–34.12	–28.39	–13.24	–31.61	–43.36	–26.51	–11.64	–26.16	–6.28	–38.52	–26.80	–42.95
Apr. 2009	–52.87	–32.04	–25.79	–5.53	–29.51	–33.62	–36.31	–8.67	–24.11	–11.08	–32.60	–45.23	–38.33
May 2009	–52.31	–29.14	–22.00	–4.97	–24.33	–26.81	–31.51	–7.19	–23.27	–5.99	–33.79	–53.57	–34.49
Jun. 2009	–48.37	–31.14	–24.55	–7.92	–26.27	–30.98	–30.42	–8.66	–27.96	–9.27	–38.49	–55.93	–36.04
Jul. 2009	–52.48	–32.31	–26.17	–8.10	–28.90	–34.68	–33.02	–10.17	–27.35	–14.23	–34.92	–61.46	–34.86
Aug. 2009	–39.69	–22.70	–15.67	–0.06	–17.84	–17.95	–31.87	2.03	–17.86	–9.50	–22.76	–68.29	–21.27
Sep. 2009	–35.07	–19.00	–11.59	7.77	–14.17	–15.06	–31.78	12.90	–14.74	–9.44	–17.97	–68.09	–16.97
Oct. 2009	–6.15	0.74	9.13	32.28	5.40	10.90	–14.37	22.27	6.80	–7.18	18.25	–59.72	4.10
Nov. 2009	26.21	14.78	20.09	41.26	17.13	25.37	–0.02	25.65	16.77	–7.83	39.49	–52.05	23.12
Dec. 2009	55.23	27.65	28.22	37.30	23.49	34.59	5.02	29.63	36.25	–9.21	87.74	–41.70	42.79

Source: World Bank pink sheet.

measure of inflation than the CPI because it measures the price paid for all consumer purchases versus just a basket of goods.

Table 5.6: Annual Trends in PFCE Deflator, WPI, and CPI-IW Inflation

(per cent)

Year	PFCE deflator (Base: 2004-05)	WPI inflation (Base: 1993-94)	CPI-IW inflation (Base: 2001)
2005-06	3.2	4.4	4.4
2006-07	6.0	5.4	6.7
2007-08	3.6	4.7	6.2
2008-09 (QE)	7.0	8.4	9.1
2009-10 (AE)	6.4	1.6*	11.4*

Source: Department of Industrial Policy and Promotion, CSO and Labour Bureau.

QE—quick estimates; AE—advance estimates; *Average April-December

Annual inflation trends in PFCE deflator, based on new series of data released by the CSO with 2004-05 = 100, and its comparison with WPI and CPI-IW inflation, shows that PFCE-based inflation was at a lower level than CPI-IW inflation during 2005-06 to 2008-09.

Housing Price Index

The importance of the construction and real estate sector in creation of both physical and financial assets has been growing. The share of the construction sector in the GDP at constant prices (2004-05) has increased from 7.7 per cent in 2004-05 to 8.0 per cent in 2008-09. Similarly, the share of real estate, ownership of dwelling and business services (in the financial sector) in overall GDP has increased from 8.9 per cent in 2004-05 to 9.2 per cent in 2008-09. Both these sectors have grown at an average of 9.7 per cent (construction) and 9.6 per cent (real estate, ownership of dwelling and business services) during 2004-05 to 2008-09.

In 2007, the National Housing Bank (NHB) RESIDEX was launched in India as a maiden effort to capture the trend of price movements in residential property on a comprehensive scale. Initially, 2001 was taken as the base year for the NHB RESIDEX and price movements during the period 2001-05 were captured for five cities—Bengaluru, Bhopal, Delhi, Kolkata and Mumbai. Subsequently, based on data from the housing finance

Table 5.7: City-wise RESIDEX (Base 2007)

Cities	2007	2008 Jan.- June	2008 July- Dec.	2009 Jan.-June
Delhi	100	124	130	121
Bengaluru	100	73	76	58
Mumbai	100	112	117	124
Kolkata	100	114	140	159
Bhopal	100	139	151	139
Hyderabad	100	96	92	65
Faridabad	100	100	121	136
Patna	100	103	100	107
Ahmedabad	100	106	100	127
Chennai	100	104	95	120
Jaipur	100	119	115	71
Lucknow	100	103	102	104
Pune	100	101	97	103
Surat	100	101	98	111
Kochi	100	106	95	90

Source: National Housing Bank.

companies (HFCs) and National Council of Applied Economic Research (NCAER) the NHB RESIDEX was updated for two years, i.e. 2006 and 2007. Subsequently, the NHB RESIDEX was expanded to fifteen cities, namely Bengaluru, Bhopal, Delhi, Kolkata, Mumbai, Ahmedabad, Faridabad, Chennai, Kochi, Hyderabad, Jaipur, Patna, Lucknow, Pune and Surat. It was also updated up to December 2008 with 2007 as the new base year. From 2008, the NHB RESIDEX is being updated on half-yearly basis. In order to make NHB RESIDEX a truly national index, 63 cities that are under the Jawaharlal Nehru National Urban Renewal Mission (JNNURM) will be covered under the index.

In the 15 cities covered under the NHB RESIDEX (base 2007), the movement of prices of residential houses showed a mixed trend. During January-June 2008, out of 15 cities, residential housing prices showed an increasing trend in 12 cities, while 2 cities reported a declining trend and there was no change in case of one city. In the second half of 2008, nine cities reported a decline in prices and there was an increase in the case of six cities over the previous half-year figures. In the first half of 2009, however, there was some revival in housing prices over the previous half-year period with a higher price index reported in the case of nine cities, namely Ahmedabad (27 per cent), Chennai (26 per cent), Kolkata (14 per cent), Surat (13 per cent), Faridabad (12 per cent), Patna (7 per cent), Mumbai (6 per cent), Pune (6 per cent) and Lucknow (2 per cent). During the same period, the remaining six cities, namely Jaipur (–38 per cent), Hyderabad (–30 per cent), Bengaluru (–24 per cent), Bhopal (–8 per cent), Delhi (–7 per cent) and Kochi (–5 per cent) showed correction in prices. Three cities, namely Hyderabad, Jaipur and Kochi showed correction in prices both in the second half of 2008 and first half of 2009.

Anti-inflationary Measures

A number of short and medium-term measures were taken by the government to improve domestic availability of essential commodities and moderate inflation. The total stock of rice and wheat held by the Food Corporation of India (FCI) in January 2010 was 47.4 million tonnes comprising 24.3 million tonnes of rice and 23.1 million tonnes of wheat. Even after keeping the minimum buffer stock (8.2 million tonnes of wheat and 11.8 million tonnes of rice in January), there were enough foodgrains to intervene in the market to keep prices at a reasonable level. A strategic reserve of 5 million tonnes of wheat and rice was also created. This was in addition to the buffer stock held by the FCI every year. However, the Central Issue Price (CIP) for rice at Rs. 5.65 per kg for below poverty line (BPL) and Rs. 3 per kg for Antyodaya Anna Yojana (AAY) and wheat at Rs. 4.15 per kg for BPL and Rs. 2 per kg for AAY since July 2002 was also maintained to protect the interests of BPL families and AAY beneficiaries.

Some of the measures taken by the government to control inflation, especially food inflation were as follows:

Monetary Measures

The monetary policy stance for 2009-10 was, inter alia, to maintain a monetary and interest rate regime consistent with price stability and financial stability, and supportive of the growth process. The RBI in its Second Quarter Review of monetary policy on October 27, 2009 made a minor modification in the statutory liquidity ratio (SLR) and restored it to 25 per cent of net demand and time liabilities (NDTL) with effect from the fortnight beginning 7 November 2009. In the Third Quarter Review of the RBI's monetary policy on 29 January 2010, the CRR of scheduled banks was raised by 75 basis points from 5.0 per cent to 5.75 per cent of their NDTL in two stages.

Fiscal Measures

Import duties were reduced to zero for rice, wheat, pulses, edible oils (crude) and sugar, and for maize (under TRQ of 5 lakh tonnes per annum). Import duties on refined and hydrogenated oils and vegetable oils were reduced to 7.5 per cent. Import by sugar mills of raw sugar was allowed at zero duty under open general licence (OGL), which was again extended up to 31 December 2010. Import of white/refined sugar by STC/MMTC/PEC and NAFED up to 1 million tonnes by 1 August 2009 was allowed under OGL at zero duty, which was again extended up to 31 March 2010. Furthermore, the duty-free import of white/refined sugar under OGL was opened to other Central/State Government agencies and to private trade in addition to existing designated agencies. Levy obligation in respect of all imported raw sugar and white/refined sugar was also removed.

Administrative Measures

The following administrative measures were taken to keep inflation under control:

(i) Two million tonnes of wheat and one million tonnes of rice was allocated to states for distribution to retail consumers over and above normal public distribution system (PDS) allocation for the period October 2009 to March 2010.

(ii) One million tonnes of wheat was allocated for release by the FCI in the open market through OMSS for the period October 2009 to March 2010.

(iii) The National Agricultural Co-operative Marketing Federation (NAFED) was allocated 37,400 metric tonnes of wheat and 15,500 metric tonnes of rice for distribution through its outlets at the same rate at which allocations were made to state governments under OMSS (D).

(iv) The National Cooperative Consumers Federation (NCCF) was allocated 32,684 metric tonnes of wheat and 11,000 metric tonnes of rice for distribution through its outlets at the same rate at which allocations were made to state governments under OMSS (D).

(v) Export of non-basmati rice, edible oils and pulses (except kabuli chana) was banned.

(vi) No changes were effected in Tariff Rate Values of edible oils.

(vii) Stock limit orders were imposed in the case of paddy, rice, pulses, sugar, edible oils and edible oilseeds up to 30 September 2010. In order to discourage non-household sector consumers from stockpiling sugar and to ensure adequate availability of sugar in the open market for actual consumers, the Central Government issued a notification in August 2009 imposing stockholding limit on bulk consumers.

(viii) Minimum Export Price (MEP) was introduced to regulate exports of onion (averaging at $500 per tonne for January 2010) and basmati rice ($900 PMT).

(ix) Futures trading in rice, *urad* and *tur* suspended by the Forward Market Commission in the year 2007-08 was extended during 2009-10. Futures trading in sugar which was suspended w.e.f. 27.5.2009 was also extended up to 30 September 2010.

(x) Imported edible oils were distributed to States/UTs at a subsidy of Rs. 15/kg.

(xi) Public Sector Undertakings (namely STC, MMTC, and PEC) and NAFED were permitted to import and sell pulses under a scheme, and the losses, if any, up to

15 per cent were reimbursed by the government, to augment availability of pulses.

(xii) Imported pulses were distributed through PDS at a subsidy of Rs. 10 per kg to state governments.

(xiii) Sugar factories were permitted to sell processed raw sugar in the domestic market and fulfill export obligation on tonne to tonne basis.

(xiv) Proportion of sugar production requisitioned as levy sugar was increased from 10 to 20 per cent for 2009-10 sugar season to ensure adequate levy sugar supplies under PDS.

(xv) During 2009-10 sugar season, 19.34 lakh tonnes of raw sugar and 3.89 lakh tonnes of white/refined sugar were imported.

(xvi) Minimum Support Prices (MSPs) were systematically increased, leading to increased acreage, production, productivity and central procurement. For the marketing season of 2008-09, the MSP of wheat was increased to Rs. 1,080. For different grades of paddy, for kharif marketing season 2009-10, the MSP was increased to Rs. 950-980 per quintal with a bonus of Rs. 50 per quintal for all varieties.

Monetary Developments During 2009-10

The liquidity constraint that emerged consequent to the global financial crisis, led the RBI to maintain an accommodative monetary policy stance since September 2008. The slew of measures introduced after September 2008 to enhance the liquidity in the system included a series of downward revisions in policy rates covering repo rate, reverse repo rate, CRR and SLR, besides providing specified windows for accommodating distressed sectors. These measures had a salutary effect on the overall liquidity situation.

The monetary authority kept reviewing the emerging economic situation from time to time. Keeping in view the comfortable liquidity position, the SLR was restored to its earlier level of 25 per cent of NDTL with effect from 7 November

2009. A few sector-specific measures provided earlier by way of accommodative windows, whose utilization was lower than expected, were withdrawn in the Second Quarter Review of Monetary Policy 2009-10. In addition, in the Third Quarter Review of January 2010, the RBI raised the CRR from 5.0 per cent of NDTL to a level of 5.50 per cent, effective from the fortnight beginning 13 February 2010 and to 5.75 per cent, effective from the fortnight beginning 27 February 2010.

Trends in Monetary Aggregates

During 2009-10, the growth rates in reserve money (M_0) and narrow money (M_1) were higher as compared to the preceding year, while broad money (M_3) growth was lower. The moderation in growth of broad money was largely on account of the deceleration in growth of bank credit to the commercial sector.

Table 5.8: Movement of Select Monetary Parameters

(per cent)

Items	Growth rates (%)		Growth rates as on January 15, 2010			
			Financial-year basis		Year-on-year basis	
	2007-08	2008-09	2009-10	2008-09	2009-10	2008-09
M_0	30.9	6.4	3.8	–3.7	14.8	6.6
M_1	19.4	8.4	7.8	–1.1	18.2	8.6
M_3	21.4	18.6	10.8	12.8	16.5	19.1

Source: RBI.

Reserve Money (M_0)

Reserve money grew by 6.4 per cent in 2008-09 as compared to 30.9 per cent during 2007-08. During 2009-10, on financial-year basis, M_0 increased by 3.8 per cent (up to January 15, 2010), as against a decline of 3.7 per cent during the corresponding period of the preceding year.

Net Foreign Assets (NFA) of the RBI and Net Domestic Assets (NDA) are the two main drivers of reserve money. On a year-on-year basis, as on 15 January 2010, the NFA expanded by 4.1 per cent as against a 9.7 per cent increase in the previous year.

Net RBI credit to the Central Government increased by Rs. 29,638 crore during the financial year (up to 15 January

2010). This was mainly on account of unwinding of Market Stabilisation Scheme (MSS) balances and open market operations of the Reserve Bank, offset by increase in the cash balances of the Central Government and reverse repo operations. Increase in the net RBI credit to the Central Government, as on 15 January 2010, was Rs. 1,19,895 crore as against an increase of Rs. 1,27,184 crore during the corresponding period a year ago.

Narrow Money (M_1)

M_1 growth decelerated in the second half of 2008-09 and staged a recovery in 2009-10. It increased by 8.4 per cent in 2008-09 as compared to an expansion of 19.4 per cent during 2007-08. During 2009-10, M_1 increased by 7.8 per cent on a financial-year basis (up to 15 January 2010) as against a decline of 1.1 per cent during the corresponding period of the previous year. On year-on-year basis, as on 15 January 2010, M_1 growth accelerated to 18.2 per cent as compared to 8.6 per cent a year ago.

The components of narrow money are currency with the public and deposit money of the public. As on 15 January 2010, currency with the public expanded by 12.3 per cent over end-March 2009, as against an increase of 12.2 per cent during the corresponding period of the preceding year. The main element of the other components, namely demand deposits with banks, witnessed a modest increase of 3.1 per cent during the period up to 15 January 2010 as against a decline of 13.6 per cent during the corresponding period of the previous year. On year-on-year basis, as on 15 January 2010, the growth of currency with the public was marginally higher at 17.3 per cent as compared with 17.2 per cent on the corresponding date a year ago. During the same period, growth in demand deposits accelerated to 19.8 per cent as compared with a decline of 0.8 per cent a year earlier.

Broad Money (M_3)

Broad money (M_3) increased by 18.6 per cent during 2008-09. During the financial year 2009-10, up to January 15, 2010, the growth in M_3 was 10.8 per cent as compared to 12.8 per cent during the corresponding period of the previous year. On year-on-year basis, M_3 grew by 16.5 per cent as on 15 January 2010, as compared to 19.1 per cent on the corresponding date of the previous year.

The growth in M_3 was primarily reflected in the expansion in aggregate deposits during this period. Within aggregate deposits, time deposits registered a growth of 16.0 per cent as on 15 January 2010, as compared to 23.1 per cent on the corresponding date of the previous year. In 2009-10, there has been gradual deceleration in the growth of time deposits, with softening of interest rates, in contrast to the shift from demand to time deposits during the second half of 2008-09. On the other hand, demand deposits expanded by 19.8 per cent as on 15 January 2010, as compared to a decline of 0.8 per cent a year ago.

During 2009-10, the banking system's credit to the government was the major driver of growth in broad money, a trend that has persisted since the third quarter of 2008-09. The increase in government's borrowing programme to finance the expansionary fiscal response to the economic slowdown was the underlying reason. However, M_3 growth showed signs of deceleration after September 2009. This owes to the fact that being front loaded, the major part of the government borrowing was completed in the first half of the year. Among the sources of M_3, bank credit to the commercial sector, which had been decelerating since October 2008, showed a revival since November 2009.

Money Multiplier

During 2008-09, the rate of expansion of M_0 was lower than that of M_3. Accordingly, the ratio of M_3 to M_0 (money multiplier) showed an increase. In end-March 2009, this ratio was higher at 4.8 as compared to 4.3 in end-March 2008. During 2009-10, the increasing trend in the money multiplier continued, with reserve money registering a lower growth than broad money supply. As on 15 January 2010, the money multiplier was 5.4.

Movement in Other Monetary Indicators

During 2009-10, bank credit recorded an increase of 8.4 per cent (end-March, 2009—15 January 2010). As against this, bank deposits recorded an increase of 10.7 per cent during the same period. The lower expansion in credit relative to the expansion in deposits during 2009-10 resulted in a decline in the credit-deposit ratio. It fell from 72.4 in end-March 2009 to 70.92 on 15 January 2010. The investment-deposit ratio increased from 30.4 per cent in end-March 2009 to 32.53 on 15 January 2010 as scheduled commercial banks (SCBs) preferred to invest a larger share of their deposits in SLR securities. Commercial banks' holdings of SLR securities were 29.9 per cent of New Demand and Time Liabilities (NDTL) as on 15 January 2010 as against 28.1 per cent in end-March 2009 and 28.8 per cent a year earlier. This was consistently higher than the stipulated level of 24 per cent of NDTL with effect from 7 November 2008 and 25 per cent with effect from 7 November 2009.

Monetary deepening, as measured by the ratio of average M_3 to GDPMP (GDP at market prices), increased from 65.5 per cent in 2004-05 to 77.8 per cent in 2008-09. This could be attributed to the spread of banking services in the country and development of the financial sector. The monetization of the economy as measured by the ratio of average M_1 to GDP showed a marginally increasing trend during this period. In 2004-05, this ratio was 18.5 per cent, which increased to 20.4 per cent in 2008-09.

Liquidity Management

The monetary easing in the aftermath of the global financial crisis constituted the main theme of liquidity management during financial year 2009-10 with periodic fluctuations in cash balances of the Central Government providing temporary variations. The Reserve Bank continued its active policy of assuring liquidity during 2009-10 through Open Market Operations (OMO), Liquidity Adjustment Facility (LAF) and also unwinding (including desequestering) of balances under the Market Stabilization Scheme (MSS) to maintain appropriate liquidity in the system. As a result, liquidity conditions remained comfortable during 2009-10.

In its Annual Policy Statement 2009-10, the RBI reduced the LAF repo and reverse repo rates by 25 basis points effective

21 April 2009 to 4.75 per cent and 3.25 per cent respectively. In recognition of the easing liquidity conditions, the 14-day term repo facility was converted to a weekly facility effective 27 April 2009. The average daily net absorption under the LAF continued to remain over Rs. 1,20,000 crore during June 2009, notwithstanding advance tax collections around the middle of the month. This continued through July-August 2009 and the LAF absorption under reverse repo reached a peak of Rs. 1,68,215 crore in September 2009. Liquidity conditions continued to remain in surplus mode in October and November 2009 with average absorption under the LAF being around Rs. 1,00,000 crore. However, net LAF absorption declined by end-December mainly on account of advance tax outflows.

During 2009-10, liquidity was also facilitated through OMOs purchased aggregating Rs. 57,000 crore. Additionally, the decline in MSS balances and de-sequestering of around Rs. 28,000 crore provided liquidity of around Rs. 81,000 crore. Consistent with the changed tempo of forex inflows, the ceiling for the MSS which was Rs. 2,50,000 crore since November 2007 was scaled down to Rs. 50,000 crore in July 2009. The average weekly outstanding on account of the MSS reflected the situation as it steadily declined from a level of Rs. 75,146 crore in April 2009 to around Rs. 18,773 crore by November 2009.

Money Market

The money market remained by and large orderly during 2009-10, due to the prevailing surplus liquidity conditions. Call rate continued to hover around the reverse repo rate during first quarter of 2009-10 and averaged 3.2 per cent as compared to 4.2 per cent during the last quarter of 2008-09. During the second quarter of 2009-10, the call rate averaged 3.25 per cent. The average call rate was placed at 3.20 per cent during this period.

Interest rates in the collateralized segments of the money market—the market repo (outside the LAF) and the Collateralized Borrowing and Lending Obligation (CBLO)—also moderated in tandem with the behaviour of the call rate and remained below the call rate during 2009-10. The weighted average interest rate in the collateralized segment of the money market marginally increased from 2.4 per cent in the first quarter of 2009-10 to 2.7 per cent during the second quarter. During the third quarter of the year, it averaged 2.8 per cent. Transaction volumes in the CBLO and market repo segments remained at a relatively high level during 2009-10. Around 75 per cent of the lending in the collateralized segment was contributed by mutual funds, which reflected their enhanced lending capacity. The collateralized market remained the predominant segment of the money market and accounted for more than 80 per cent of its total volume.

Certificates of Deposit

With the persistence of surplus liquidity conditions, the fortnightly average issuance of Certificates of Deposit (CD) also remained high during most of 2009-10. The amount of outstanding CDs issued by Scheduled Commercial Banks (SCBs) increased from Rs. 1,92,867 crore in end-March 2009 to Rs. 2,43,584 crore as on 4 December 2009. The outstanding amount constituted 7.84 per cent (as on 4 December 2009) of aggregate deposits of CD-issuing banks with significant inter-bank variation. During April-December 4, 2009, the average issuance was of the order of Rs. 11,000 crore as compared to Rs. 6,131 crore during the corresponding period of the previous year. Most of the CDs issued were of more than six months duration. The weighted average discount rate declined from 7.53 per cent in end-March 2009 to 4.84 per cent as on 4 December 2009.

Commercial Paper

During 2009-10, the Commercial Paper (CP) market also picked up with the easing of liquidity conditions and the size of fortnightly issuance increased significantly. The outstanding amount of CP issued by corporates showed an increasing trend from Rs. 44,171 crore in end-March 2009 to Rs. 1,03,915 crore as in end-November 2009, marginally coming down to a level of Rs. 90,305 crore in end-December 2009.

Table 5.9: Activity in Money Market Segments

(Rupees crore)

Year/month	Average daily volume (one leg)						Commercial paper		Certificates of deposit	
	Call	Market repo	CBLO	Total	Money market rate* (per cent)	Term money	Out-standing	WADR (per cent)	Out standing	WADR (per cent)
Apr. 2008	9,758	14,966	38,828	63,552	5.31	374	37,584	8.85	1,50,865	8.49
May 2008	9,740	14,729	36,326	60,795	6.29	420	42,032	9.02	1,56,780	8.95
Jun. 2008	10,854	11,262	35,774	57,890	7.35	253	46,847	10.03	1,63,143	9.16
Jul. 2008	12,368	8,591	23,669	44,628	8.09	226	51,569	10.95	1,64,892	10.23
Aug. 2008	11,704	10,454	22,110	44,268	8.65	501	55,036	11.48	1,71,966	10.98
Sep. 2008	11,690	10,654	20,547	42,891	9.26	335	52,038	12.28	1,75,522	11.56
Oct. 2008	14,497	9,591	16,818	40,906	8.66	345	48,442	14.17	1,58,562	10.00
Nov. 2008	10,906	15,191	24,379	50,476	6.58	319	44,487	12.42	1,51,493	10.36
Dec. 2008	10,820	16,943	32,261	60,024	5.37	415	40,391	10.70	1,51,214	8.85
Jan. 2009	9,248	18,053	31,794	59,095	3.99	454	51,668	9.48	1,64,979	7.33
Feb. 2009	11,121	19,929	38,484	69,534	3.89	669	52,560	8.93	1,75,057	6.73
Mar. 2009	11,909	21,593	48,319	81,821	3.76	451	44,171	9.79	1,92,867	7.53
Apr. 2009	10,910	20,545	43,958	75,413	2.41	332	52,881	6.29	2,10,954	6.48
May 2009	9,518	22,449	48,505	80,472	2.34	338	60,740	5.75	2,18,437	6.20
Jun. 2009	8,960	21,694	53,553	84,207	2.69	335	68,721	5.00	2,21,491	4.90
Jul. 2009	7,197	20,254	46,501	73,952	2.83	389	79,582	4.71	2,40,395	4.96
Aug. 2009	7,569	23,305	57,099	87,973	2.62	461	83,026	5.05	2,32,522	4.91
Sep. 2009	8,059	27,978	62,388	98,425	2.73	381	79,228	5.04	2,16,691	5.30
Oct. 2009	7,888	23,444	58,313	89,645	2.70	225	98,835	5.06	2,27,227	4.70
Nov. 2009	6,758	22,529	54,875	84,162	2.87	191	1,03,915	5.17	2,45,101	4.86
Dec. 2009	6,651	20,500	55,338	82,489	2.91	289	—	—	2,43,584+	4.84+

Source: RBI.

+ As on December 4, 2009.

* Weighted average rate of call, market repo and CBLO.

WADR: Weighted average discount rate.

The weighted average discount rate (WADR) of CP declined from 9.79 per cent as in end-March 2009 to 4.71 per cent as in end-July 2009 and increased to 5.17 per cent in end-November 2009. The shares of 'manufacturing companies' and 'other financial institutions' in total outstanding CPs increased while the share of 'leasing and finance companies' declined. 'Manufacturing companies' accounted for 45 per cent of the share in end-November 2009.

Treasury Bills

Treasury Bills (TBs) issuances during 2009-10 were dynamically managed, keeping in view the emerging requirements of the government and the market conditions. The TBs issued for enhanced amounts in 2008-09 which became due for repayment both in the first and second quarters of 2009-10 were fully rolled over. The primary market yields for TBs of different tenors—91 days, 182 days and 364 days—remained by and large stable during 2009-10 as compared to the pattern observed in 2008-09.

In August 2009, a new short-term instrument, known as Cash Management Bill (CMB) was introduced to meet the temporary cash-flow mismatches of the government. CMBs are non-standard, discounted instruments issued for maturities of less than 91 days.

Central Government Borrowing

The Union Budget 2009-10 placed the net market borrowings requirement of the Central Government at Rs. 3,97,957 crore as against Rs. 2,42,316 crore raised during the previous year. Including repayments of Rs. 93,087 crore, gross market borrowing was estimated at Rs. 4,91,044 crore as compared to Rs. 3,18,550 crore raised in the previous year. The actual issuances during the first half of 2009-10 amounted to Rs. 2,95,000 crore as against issuances of Rs. 1,06,000 crore during the corresponding period of the previous year. The issuance calendar for dated securities released in September 2009 proposed to raise Rs. 1,23,000 crore during the second half of the year.

The gross borrowing requirement in 2009-10 was 54 per cent higher than in 2008-09. In order to carry out the borrowing programme in a non-disruptive manner, a number of steps were taken. First, the borrowing programme of the Central Government for 2009-10 was frontloaded as credit offtake by the private sector was low in the first half. Further, MSS securities of the order of Rs. 28,000 crore were de-sequestered. Besides, the Reserve Bank resorted to active liquidity management by way of unwinding of MSS securities and purchase of securities through a pre-announced OMO calendar. The unwinding of MSS securities through redemption was of the order of Rs. 42,000 crore during the first half of the year. As against the OMO announcement of Rs. 80,000 crore through the auction route for the first half of 2009-10, the actual purchases were Rs. 57,487 crore, the shortfall from the projected level being on account of easy liquidity conditions.

During 2009-10 (up to 15 January 2010), gross market borrowing raised through dated securities by the Central Government (excluding issuances under the MSS) was Rs. 3,93,000 crore (net Rs. 3,51,911 crore) as against Rs. 1,80,000 crore (net Rs. 1,35,972 crore) raised during the corresponding period of the previous year. This also included floating rate bonds amounting to Rs. 2,000 crore with a tenor of 11 years issued on 18 December 2009. Keeping in view market preferences, the weighted average maturity of dated securities issued during the year up to 15 January 2010 worked out lower at 11.17 years as compared to 14.62 years for issues during the corresponding period of the previous year. The weighted average yield of dated securities during 2009-10 (up to 15 January 2010) was lower at 7.22 per cent as compared to 8.15 per cent during the corresponding period of the previous year.

Yields on 10-Year Government Securities

The movement in yields in the 10-year G-Sec market may be categorized into three broad phases. During the first phase (April 2009), the yield on 10-year G-Sec declined from 7.01 per cent to 6.23 per cent between end-March and end-April 2009. This was due to substantial easing of liquidity conditions, decline in inflation rate, OMO purchase auctions and reduction in LAF policy interest rates.

During the second phase (May 2009-August 2009), the 10-year yields started rising following the increase in size of primary auctions (from Rs. 12,000 crore to Rs. 15,000 crore) as well as anticipation of overwhelming supplies in view of the large borrowing programme of the government. The 10-year yield rose to 7.17 per cent in end-September 2009 as compared to 6.23 per cent as in end-April 2009.

During the third phase (September-December 2009), the G-Sec yields traded in a broad range with a hardening bias. The yield declined on the back of the RBI's decision to hike SLR by 1 percentage point to 25 per cent in its Second Quarter Review of Annual Policy Statement for 2009-10. However, the G-Sec yield rose subsequently on account of a host of factors including absence of announcement of the OMO purchase auction calendar during the second half of the fiscal year 2009-10, and expectation by market participants that the policy rates might be raised due to increase in the inflation level. The 10-year G-Sec yield was at 7.72 per cent as on 12 January 2010 as compared to 7.17 per cent as in end-September 2009. However, the experts felt that increasing interest rates to curb inflation was not the right course of action as it would adversely impact the industry which is already struggling to recover from the after effects of economic slowdown.

State Government Borrowings

In the light of the policy measures to minimize the adverse impact of the global financial crisis, the Union Budget allowed the State Governments to borrow an additional 0.5 per cent of their Gross State Domestic Product (GSDP) up to a ceiling of 4 per cent of GSDP in 2009-10. Accordingly, the net market borrowings of the states were placed at Rs. 1,40,000 crore for 2009-10 (gross: Rs. 1,56,238 crore), compared to actual net market borrowings of Rs. 1,03,766 crore (gross: Rs. 1,18,138 crore) in 2008-09. During 2009-10 (up to 15 January 2010), the amount raised by State Governments aggregated to Rs. 1,05,937.71 crore as compared to Rs. 52,842.74 crore raised during the corresponding period last year. The weighted average yield of the auctions up to 15 January 2010 was 8.03 per cent as compared to 7.74 per cent during the corresponding period in 2008-09.

Monetary Policy Stance During 2009-10

Conditioned by the need for monetary policy to respond to the then slackening economic growth, the RBI's monetary policy stance during 2009-10 was aimed at providing a policy regime that would enable credit expansion at viable rates while preserving credit quality so as to support the return of the economy to a steady growth path. The Annual Policy Statement of the RBI for 2009-10 (issued on 21 April 2009) clearly indicated the continuance of the policy being followed since mid-September 2008 to minimize the impact of the global financial crisis on the domestic economy and restore the economy to a high growth path consistent with price and financial stability.

With the resolve to maintain a soft interest rate regime, the repo rate was further reduced from 5.00 per cent to 4.75 per cent with effect from 21 April 2009, while the reverse repo rate was reduced from 3.50 per cent to 3.25 per cent. There were no major changes in policy rates during 2009-10, except for restoration of the SLR to the earlier level of 25 per cent of NDTL (from 24 per cent) in November 2009 and an increase of 75 basis points in CRR effective February 2010.

Quarterly Reviews

The RBI's First Quarter Review of the Monetary Policy 2009-10 (28 July 2009) did not announce any revisions in policy rates. The Review, however, noted that there could be a reversal of the expansionary measures to anchor inflation expectations and subdue inflationary pressures, if so warranted.

The RBI's Second Quarter Review of Monetary Policy 2009-10 (27 October 2009) made an overall assessment of the economy and indicated that the stance of monetary policy for the remaining period of 2009-10 would be to

(i) Maintain a monetary and interest rate regime consistent with price stability and financial stability, and supportive of the growth process.

Table 5.10: Revision in Policy Rates

Sl.No.	Date	Repo rate	Reverse repo rate	CRR
1.	April 26, 2008	7.75	6.00	7.75
2.	May 10, 2008	7.75	6.00	8.00
3.	May 24, 2008	7.75	6.00	8.25
4.	June 12, 2008	8.00	6.00	8.25
5.	June 25, 2008	8.50	6.00	8.25
6.	July 5, 2008	8.50	6.00	8.50
7.	July 19, 2008	8.50	6.00	8.75
8.	August 30, 2008	9.0	6.0	9.0
9.	October 11, 2008	9.0	6.0	6.5
10.	October 20, 2008	8.0	6.0	6.5
11.	October 25, 2008	8.0	6.0	6.0
12.	November 3, 2008	7.5	6.0	6.0
13.	November 8, 2008	7.5	6.0	5.5
14.	December 6, 2008	6.5	5.0	5.5
2009				
15.	January 5, 2009	5.5	4.0	5.5
16.	January 17, 2009	5.5	4.0	5.5
17.	March 5, 2009	5.0	3.5	5.0
18.	April 21, 2009	4.75	3.25	5.0
2010				
19.	February 13, 2010	4.75	3.25	5.5
20.	February 27, 2010	5.00	3.50	5.75
21.	April 20, 2010	5.25	3.75	6.00

Source: RBI.

(ii) Keep a vigil on the trends in inflation and be prepared to respond swiftly and effectively through policy adjustments to stabilize inflation expectations.

(iii) Monitor the liquidity situation closely and manage it actively to ensure that credit demands of productive sectors are adequately met while also securing price and financial stability.

The Second Quarter Review recognized the dilemma that while growth drivers warranted a delayed exit from the accommodative policy regime, inflation concerns called for an early exit. The RBI noted that a premature exit from the accommodative stance could derail the growth, but a delayed exit could also potentially engender inflation expectations. Therefore, while keeping the bank, repo and reverse repo rates unchanged, it announced closure of some special liquidity support measures, which were not being fully utilized, besides restoring the SLR to the earlier level of 25 per cent of NDTL.

The measures adopted as per the Second Quarter Review of the Monetary Policy Statement were as enumerated below:

- The SLR was restored to 25 per cent with effect from the fortnight beginning 7 November 2009 as SCBs' investment in SLR securities was higher than the stipulated 24 per cent.
- Liabilities of scheduled banks arising from transactions in CBLO (which were earlier exempted from CRR prescription), were brought into the fold for maintenance of CRR with effect from the fortnight beginning 21 November 2009.
- Keeping in view the large increase in credit to the commercial real estate sector, provisioning requirements to the sector classified as "standard assets" were increased from 0.40 to 1 per cent.
- The limit for the export credit refinance facility [under section 17(3A) of the RBI Act], which was raised to 50 per cent of eligible outstanding rupee export credit, was returned to the pre-crisis level of 15 per cent.
- The two non-standard refinance facilities—special refinance facility for SCBs under section 17(3B) of the RBI Act (available up to 31 March 2010), and special term repo facility for SCBs (for funding to mutual funds, non-banking finance companies, and housing finance companies) (available up to 31 March 2010) were discontinued.
- The forex swap facility to banks for tenor up to three months was also discontinued.

In its Third Quarter Review of the Monetary Policy (29 January 2010), the RBI indicated that its stance is shaped by three important considerations: First, the need to shift policy stance from "managing the crisis" to "managing the recovery" which implies reversal from the crisis-driven expansionary stance, thereby recognizing the need for carrying forward the process of exit further. Second, though the inflationary pressures in the domestic economy stem predominantly from the supply side, consolidating recovery increases the risks of these pressures spilling over into a wider inflationary process. Third, strong anti-inflationary measures, while addressing one problem may precipitate another by undermining the recovery, particularly by deterring private investment and consumer spending.

Based on its assessment, the RBI left the bank rate, repo and reverse repo rates and SLR unchanged. However, it raised the CRR by 75 basis points from 5.0 per cent to 5.75 per cent in two stages—the first stage of increase of 50 basis points which became effective the fortnight beginning 13 February 2010, followed by the next stage of increase of 25 basis points effective from the fortnight beginning 27 February 2010. The hike in CRR was estimated to absorb around Rs. 36,000 crore from the system which was witnessing surplus liquidity.

The response of the monetary authority to the changing economic environment was also reflected in the indicative projections for macro-level parameters made by the RBI for 2009-10 in the Annual Policy Statement for the year and subsequent quarterly reviews.

Monetary Policy 2010-11

The annual monetary policy announced by Reserve Bank of India (RBI) in April 2010 increased key policy rates by 25 basis points (bps) to tame rising inflation, sustain economic growth momentum and accommodate the government's borrowing plan. The repo rate was raised by 25 bps to 5.25 per cent and the reverse repo rate by the same amount to 3.75 per cent. RBI also increased the cash reserve ratio (CRR) by 25 bps. The CRR increase took effect from 24 April 2010 and is expected to absorb Rs. 12,500 crore of excess cash from the banking system.

The hike in policy rates was in line with market expectations or in some cases, lower than what the people anticipated. However, the increase in key policy rates is not expected to have any immediate impact on interest rates as there is adequate liquidity in the system. The increase in rates was prompted due to the inflationary pressure spreading from food to other areas of the economy. The central bank was able to turn its attention to dousing inflation as India's economy was, according to RBI Governor D. Subbarao, "firmly on the recovery path", shaking off the effects of the global slump.

The RBI expects inflation to come down to 5.5 per cent by the end of fiscal 2010-11. Despite inflation worries, the central bank is optimistic on the growth front, pegging its forecast for 2010-11 at 8 per cent with an upward bias. The growth expectations are based on the fact that India's exports have been growing and industrial sector recovery has become more broad-based. Gross domestic product (GDP) growth for the fiscal 2009-10 is estimated in the range of 7.2-7.5 per cent.

Most of India's large banks have recorded at least 20 per cent growth in credit in the fiscal year 2009-10, signalling economic revival and growing corporate confidence in fresh investments for capacity expansion. Credit growth has expanded steadily during the second half of the year from its intra-year low of 10.3 per cent in October 2009 to 16.9 per cent by March 2010. The central bank has pegged credit and deposit growth at 20 per cent and 18 per cent respectively.

To ensure continuity of bank finance to the productive sector, in particular the infrastructure sector that needs about Rs. 22.3 trillion by 2012, RBI has proposed to allow banks to classify their investments in non-SLR (statutory liquidity ratio) bonds issued by companies engaged in infrastructure activities and having a minimum residual maturity of seven years under the held-to-maturity category. This is being done as the long-term bonds issued by companies engaged in infrastructure activities are generally held by banks for a long period and not traded and also with a view to incentivizing banks to invest in such bonds.

Additionally, it has also reduced the provisioning requirement for infrastructure loan accounts classified as substandard from 20 to 15 per cent. RBI proposes to set up a working group with representatives from the government, the Securities and Exchange

Board of India, the Insurance Regulatory and Development Authority and the Indian Banks' Association to recommend a road map for the introduction of a holding company structure together with the required legislative amendment.

The rise in food inflation has received unusual interest from unexpected quarters. The inflation numbers received political prominence as the numbers became a major political headache for the ruling UPA. It also received global interest and attention along with India's macroeconomic policies, symbolised by the visit to India by US Treasury Secretary Tim Geithner. The Reserve Bank, as the guardian of price stability, was compelled to take monetary policy actions ahead of the scheduled monetary policy statement. The RBI Governor explained the reasons for the monetary policy actions as the annual headline inflation being outside the announced comfort zone, the fear of inflationary pressures moving from primary articles to manufacturing, asset markets were buoyant, and that the economic recovery was well established.

The art and skill of monetary management is not to react to the past but to look into the future. It requires taking difficult judgments on whether the economy is indeed "overheating", and whether a decisive shift has been made from supply-led to demand-driven inflation. There are several issues as well. First, the world economy remains extremely sluggish outside Asia. Inflation is not a serious concern for the global economy, given the massive, excess physical and human capacity. The Greek tragedy has the potential for additional shocks to European banks which hold that country's debt. On the basis of the Indian economic data available so far, while there is every case for monetary policy to move to whatever RBI considers to be a neutral monetary policy stance, it is too early to judge that the economy is overheating.

Second, balance of payments trends, coupled with sluggish OECD growth and rising commodity prices, make it highly unlikely that net exports will be a strong element on the demand side. Thus, the desired recovery to 9 per cent growth depends crucially on private capital formation (both fixed and inventory) and personal final consumption.

Finally, there is the controversial issue of the role that the nominal exchange rate should play in the monetary policy framework of the "new normal" that lies ahead of RBI.

A fast-growing economy like India can expect to encounter appreciation of the real exchange rate, and guided nominal appreciation is an efficient mechanism to achieve this real appreciation with the least collateral distortion. Of course, greater flexibility by the Chinese on their exchange rate would make this politically much easier. In the circumstances, RBI's best contribution to long-term equitable growth would be through the vigilant and relentless pursuit of low, well-anchored medium-term inflation expectations.

Challenges and Outlook

The concentrated pressure on headline inflation arising from high food prices entails the risk of getting transmitted over time to other non-food items through expectations-driven wage price revisions, which then manifests into a generalized inflation. The sharp increase in food prices during 2009-10 remains a cause of concern. A significant part of this inflation could be explained by supply-side bottlenecks in some of the essential commodities, precipitated by the delayed and sub-normal southwest monsoon as well as drought-like conditions in some parts of the country. However, inflation in some of the commodities, like wheat and rice, in which there is ample stock available, could have been exacerbated due to inflationary expectations. Hence, the real challenge is to make available adequate and timely quantities of these items at different locations by overcoming supply-demand mismatches.

Since a significant proportion of India's requirement of edible oils, pulses and sugar (in years of shortages) is met through import, the country cannot remain immune to global price situations. At the same time, for a large country like India the scope for imports for many commodities is limited. And any decision to import food items raises global prices which impacts domestic prices as well. Therefore, proper and timely assessment of the supply-demand situation and preventive action become the essence of supply-side management.

Another area which needs to be managed is the prices of petroleum products in the domestic market. The international crude oil prices have increased from $ 44/bbl in January-March 2009 to around $ 80/bbl in April 2010. Despite this, the administered prices of petroleum products in the domestic market have been maintained at the same level since July 2009. On the one hand, sustaining current levels of domestic petroleum prices in the scenario of rising international prices may not be viable for long from the fiscal side. On the other hand, increase in prices would have its impact on inflation levels.

Thus, the outlook for inflation is conditioned by supply-side pressures in the near term, possible return of pricing power with stronger recovery in growth, further revival in private demand with improving consumer and business confidence, and possible spurt in global commodity prices in response to recovery in advanced economies.

While the fiscal issues including fiscal rectitude are important, the transmission of the monetary policy stance to the monetary and real sectors is equally critical. So, the policy-framers not only need to address the inflationary expectations but also monitor and ensure that the growth in money supply and credit to productive sectors is at the envisaged levels so that the growth prospects in the near to medium terms are sustained on an even keel, without, at the same time, jeopardizing the price scenario.

Financial Relations between the Centre and the States

6

FINANCIAL RELATIONS UNDER THE CONSTITUTION

Governments are categorized into two types—unitary and federal. Under unitary system whole power of government is conferred by the Constitution upon a single central organ and local governments derive whatever authority they possess from this central organ. This system of government is prevalent in most of Asian countries besides UK, France, Germany and Austria. The other form of government—federal system—provides for a distribution and division of power between the Central Government and the governments of the individual states of which the federation is composed. The general principle of division of power is such that affairs of common interest to the federation as a whole lie with centre and thus the uniformity of regulation is placed under the Central Government, while all local affairs are left to the state governments. Like USA and Canada, India too adopted a federal system of government. In the federal structure, states collect certain taxes as assigned to them, the amount of which is used by the states themselves for running their governments besides for the development of the states. Transfer of resources is main feature of our present financial system in India.

Division of Resources

As per the Constitution of India, a principle is followed for the taxes. Taxes which have an interstate base are levied by the centre while those with a local base are levied by the states.

Following are the taxes levied by the centre as laid down in the list of Seventh Schedule of the Constitution of India:

1. Taxes on income other than income from agriculture; 2. Corporation tax; 3. Customs duties; 4. Excise duties except on alcoholic liquors and narcotics not contained in medical or toilet preparations; 5. Estate and succession duties other than agricultural land; 6. Taxes on the capital value of assets, except agricultural land, of individuals and companies; 7. Rates of stamp duties on financial documents; 8. Taxes other than stamp duties on transactions in stock exchanges and future markets; 9. Taxes on sale or purchase of newspapers and on advertisements therein; 10. Taxes on railway freight and fares; 11. Terminal taxes on goods or passengers carried by railways, sea or air; and 12. Taxes on the sale or purchase of goods in the course of inter-state trade.

List-II of Seventh Schedule of the Constitution of India indicates the undermentioned taxes within the jurisidiction of the states:

1. Land revenue; 2. Taxes on the sale and purchase of goods except newspapers; 3. Taxes on agricultural income; 4. Taxes on land and buildings; 5. Succession and estate duties on agricultural land; 6. Excise on alcoholic liquors and narcotics; 7. Taxes on the entry of goods into a local area; 8. Taxes on mineral rights, subject to any limitations imposed by Parliament; 9. Taxes on the consumption and sale of electricity; 10. Taxes on vehicles, animals and boats; 11. Stamp duties except those in financial documents; 12. Taxes on goods and passengers carried by board or inland waterways; 13. Taxes on luxuries including entertainments, betting and gambling; 14. Taxes on tools; 15. Taxes on professionals, trades, callings and employment; 16. Capitation taxes; and 17. Taxes on advertisements other than those contained in newspapers.

The centre and state governments can mutually decide about the taxes on motor vehicles and stamp duties on non-judicial stamps. Similarly, property of centre is exempted from state taxation and vice versa. Parliament may, however, pass any legislation for any taxes with or without involvement of states and union government is at full liberty to impose any tax not covered by the two lists of Seventh Schedule of Constitution of India.

Moreover, since resources of Central Government yield a substantial surplus whereas state governments normally indicate huge deficits, a provision has been adopted for the transfer of resources from the centre to the states. Article 275 of the Constitution provides for grants-in-aid to the states in need of assistance on the advice of Finance Commission, while according to the provision of Article 282 grants can be fixed by the Central Government on its own discretion.

Distribution and Allocation of Central Revenue

As assigned to states, certain taxes are collected by them whereas the Constitution provides several revenues and taxes in the union list to be allocated in part or entirely to the states. Following are the various provisions of the Constitution in this regard:

(i) Stamp duties and excise duties on medical preparations containing alcohol or narcotics. These are levied by the centre but are collected and appropriated by the states.

(ii) Succession and estate duties, terminal taxes on goods and on the sale and purchase of newspapers and advertisements therein. These are the taxes which are levied and collected by the centre but the entire proceeds of which are assigned to the states, in proportion determined by the Parliament.

(iii) Central tax on income and central excise duties were levied and collected by the centre but were shared by it with the states in a prescribed manner.

(iv) The proceeds of additional excise duties on mill-made textiles, sugar and tobacco which were levied by the centre in 1957 in replacement of states' sales taxes on these commodities are wholly distributed among the states in a manner so as to guarantee their former incomes from the displaced sales taxes.

Grants-in-aid

An important functional feature is assigned to the states that the differences between their revenues and expenditure take and the correction by means of transfer of resources from centre, and the same is done partially through tax sharing. The financial relations between centre and states have a vital role to play pertaining to grants-in-aid by the centre for particular purposes or general aid. Inter-state discrepancies in resources are corrected by the grants besides helping the essential welfare services and development programmes in different states. The grants-in-aid quantum is decided by the Finance Commissions. The First Finance Commission formulated a number of principles for regulating grants-in-aid to states such as budgetary needs, tax efforts, economy in expenditure, standards of special services, special obligations and broad purposes of national importance. In actual transfer of resources, however, the Commission considered mainly the budgetary needs of the states. Subsequent Finance Commissions also gave the concurrence with due importance for above criterion.

Loans

The states are authorised to raise the loans but even then they keep on borrowing substantially from the centre mainly for irrigation, agriculture, industrial housing, river projects or infrastructural development by depositing certain state and local funds with the Central Government. Keeping in view the rapid progress in the past years, the borrowing by the states from the centre has adequately increased.

Resources Transferred to the States

The consistent growing of transfer of resources from the centre to the states has been because of enhanced level of integration between the central and state finances, unavoidable dependence of states on centre besides growing power and interference of the centre in the affairs of the state. During the planning period there has been a remarkable increase in the resources transferred from centre to the states. Precisely, during each successive Five-Year Plan, the resources transferred were twice or even more while comparing with the previous Plan. Evidently, it depicts the helplessness of state governments and their heavy dependence on the centre. The transfer from centre to states largely covers taxes, duties, loans and grants. So as to change the criteria and amount of division between central and state governments, Indian Constitution provides for the appointment of a Finance Commission at the end of every fifth year or earlier, if necessary. The Commission so appointed under the Article 280 of the Constitution is assigned the task of recommending the distribution between centre and states of net proceeds of taxes which are to be or may be divided between them and the allocation between the states of the respective shares of such proceeds, the principles which should govern the grants-in-aid of the revenue of the states out of the Consolidated Fund of India and any other matter referred to the Commission by the President of India in the interests of sound finance.

THE FINANCE COMMISSION AWARDS

Since the inauguration of the Constitution in 1950, twelve Finance Commissions have submitted their reports so far. The thirteenth Finance Commission was constituted by the President of India vide a notification dated November 13, 2007. This Commission is headed by Chairman Mr. Vijay L. Kelkar. The Commission shall make recommendations covering a period of five years commencing on April 10, 2010 related to proposed implementation of goods and services tax (GST), including its impact on country's foreign trade, need to manage ecology and improve the quality of public expenditure. Here we will first discuss the summary of sharing revenues between the centre and states relating to only first ten Finance Commissions.

Distribution of Income Tax

Under Article 270 of Indian Constitution, the personal income tax is imposed as well as collected by Union Government but the net proceeds are shared by the centre and the states. Vertical Division and Horizontal Division are the two points on which the Finance Commissions have to give their award. The Vertical Division relates to the share of the states in the total collection of income tax while Horizontal Division pertains to the principles which should govern the share of each state in the divisible pool.

The share of the states in the net proceeds of income tax varies from 55 per cent as under the First Finance Commission to 85 per cent under Seventh, Eighth and Ninth Finance Commissions. However, Tenth Finance Commission, in its report for the period 1995-2000 recommended that 77.5 per cent of the net proceeds of taxes on income should be assigned to states. The practice adopted by different Finance Commissions has been different about the share of different states.

The First Finance Commission recommended that 80 per cent of the states' share of the divisible pool of income tax should be distributed among the states on the basis of their relative population and 20 per cent on the basis of the relative collections of income tax in different states. The Second Finance Commission determined the share of the states as per rule 90 per cent on the basis of population and 10 per cent based on collection of income tax revenue. The Third Finance Commission reverted to the formula of First Finance Commission and the same was kept intact by the Fourth Finance Commission. The Fifth Commission followed the Second Finance Commission, and allocated 90 per cent based on population and 10 per cent on the basis of collection. The same formula was retained by the Sixth and Seventh Finance Commissions.

Eighth Finance Commission was presided over by Y.B. Chavan with the introduction of new formula giving a weightage of 10 per cent to the factor of contribution in the distribution of the net proceeds of income tax but reduced the weight of population substantially. Instead, it used an information base comprising population and per capita income of the states thereby distributing 90 per cent of the proceeds of income tax as 25 per cent on the basis of population 125 per cent on the basis of inverse of the per capita income of the state, multiplied by population and 50 per cent based on the distance of the per capita income of a state from the highest per capita income state—Punjab and multiplied by the population of the state.

Ninth Finance Commission followed the same formula cited above with the addition of index of poverty and backwardness stating that a larger share of these two components are required to bear substantial expenditure responsibilities. The Tenth Finance Commission mixed both Eighth and Ninth Finance Commissions to draw out a new formula by which the shareable proceeds of income tax were to be distributed among the states. The criteria followed by it are as mentioned below:

(i) 20 per cent based on the population of the year 1971.

(ii) 60 per cent on the basis of distance of per capita income of a state from that of the state having the highest income.

(iii) 5 per cent on the basis of area of a state with certain adjustments at the upper and lower ends.

(iv) 5 per cent based on the index of infrastructure prepared by the Tenth Finance Commission.

(v) 10 per cent on the basis of tax effort measured by ratio of per capita over tax revenue of a state to its per capita income.

Distribution of Excise Duty

The First Finance Commission had taken into account only three commodities—tobacco, vegetable products and matches—for the distribution among states thereby yielding a substantial revenue to the government. It was recommended that 40 per cent of net proceeds of these duties should be allocated and distributed on the basis of population. The Second Finance Commission increased the number of excise duties to be shared from 3 to 8 which was further increased by Third Finance Commission to 35. But the share of states was reduced from 40 per cent to 25 per cent by the Second Commission and was further reduced to 20 per cent by the Third Finance Commission. Fourth Finance Commission widened the list to 45 products retaining share of states of net proceeds at 20 per cent. The Fifth and Sixth Finance Commissions remained silent without making any change whatsoever.

Table 6.1: Recommendations of Finance Commissions on Distribution of Income Tax

Finance Commission	Income tax share of state (per cent)	Income tax distribution to the states on basis of	
		Population and other criteria	Tax contribution
First	55	80	20
Second	60	90	10
Third	65	80	20
Fourth	75	80	20
Fifth	75	90	10
Sixth	80	90	10
Seventh Eighth Ninth	85	90	10
Tenth	77.5	90	10

Source: Finance Commission Reports.

The Seventh Finance Commission increased the share of states to 40 per cent of net proceeds which was further enhanced to 45 per cent by Eighth Commission. Out of this, 40 per cent was distributed on a new formula which was used for distribution of income tax proceeds and balance of 5 per cent to the deficit states. The Ninth Finance Commission made recommendation of distributing the whole amount of 45 per cent without dividing it into two parts. Finally, the Tenth Finance Commission raised the share of the states of the net proceeds of excise duties to 47.5 per cent. This was done to compensate the decline in the share of states in income tax from 85 per cent as recommended by the previous three commissions to 77.5 per cent by the Tenth Finance Commission.

It is interesting to note that the main objective of all Finance Commissions to enhance the share of the states in the proceeds of central excise duties. Over the years, to meet the revenue needs of the states, the Finance Commissions have splendidly done it by virtue of union excise duties. In the beginning the Finance Commissions brought in more and more central excise duties reducing the percentage share of states but later, after the Seventh Finance Commission onwards, raised the share of states

Table 6.2: Recommendations of Finance Commission on Excise Duty

Finance Commissions	States share of excise duty	Distribution of excise duty (per cent)	
		On the basis of population	On the basis of backwardness of states the percentage of the poor in the states, etc.
First	40 per cent of 3 duties	40	60
Second	25 per cent of 8 duties	40	60
Third	20 per cent of 35 duties	40	60
Fourth	20 per cent of 45 duties	80	20
Fifty	20 per cent of 45 duties	80	20
Sixth	20 per cent of 45 duties	75	25
Seventh	40 per cent of all duties	25	75
Eighth	45 per cent of all duties	25	75
Ninth	45 per cent of all duties	25	75
Tenth	45 per cent of all duties	20	80
Eleventh	29.5 per cent of all duties	—	—
Tewlfth	30.5 per cent of all duties	—	—
Thirteenth	50.0 per cent of all duties	—	—

Source: Finance Commission Reports.

from 20 per cent to 40 per cent and then followed finally to 47.5 per cent. The system of distribution favoured populated and backward states. New formula of distribution of excise duties was introduced by Seventh Finance Commission and Eighth Finance Commission followed the same. Ninth Finance Commission with some modifications adopted the following pattern of distribution of excise duties among the states:

(a) 25 per cent based on 1971 population.

(b) 12.5 per cent on the basis of Income Adjusted Total Population.

(c) 12.5 per cent on the basis of index of backwardness.

(d) 33.5 per cent on basis of distance of per capita income of a state from that of the state having the highest per capita income, i.e. Punjab.

(e) The remaining 16.5 per cent should be distributed among the states with deficits after taking into account their shares in income tax, excise duties and other shareable taxes.

The Tenth Finance Commission followed the same pattern with remaining 7.5 per cent distributed among deficit states.

Additional Excise Duties in Lieu of Sales Tax

In December 1956, an agreement was reached by the National Development Council and in pursuance thereof, additional duties of excise are levied by the Central Government. As per the agreement a surcharge on central excise duties on the products like mill-made textiles, tobacco and sugar should replace the sales taxes levied in the states. And the income so derived should be distributed among the states based on the consumption. Accordingly, Second Finance Commission during the period 1956-57 guaranteed the payment to the states equal to their sales tax revenue on these items. Balance amount after having allotted 1 per cent of net proceeds to the union territories and 1.25 per cent to Jammu and Kashmir was distributed among the states on the basis of consumption calculated by population factor. Third, Fourth and Fifth Finance Commissions followed the same pattern. But the Sixth Finance Commission dropped this practice and adopted new pattern of distribution as: 70 per cent was to be distributed on the basis of population, 20 per cent on the basis of State Domestic Product and the remaining 10 per cent on the basis of production of these commodities.

The Eighth Finance Commission made the recommendation that the whole amount of the proceeds of the additional excise duties on sugar, textiles and tobacco after retaining 2.391 per cent for union territories should be distributed among the states on the basis of equal weightage to State Domestic Product and its population. The Ninth Finance Commission came out with new series of comparable work, out of State Domestic Product, taking average of three years, i.e. 1982-83, 1983-84 and 1984-85 along with 1981 census figures of population in determining shares of the states in the next proceeds of additional duties of excise. An amount of 1.903 per cent of the net proceeds was covered by the Central Government for the union territories. The Tenth Finance Commission worked out the share of states in additional excise duties over the period 1995-2000 by giving 50 per cent weightage to the population based on 1991 census, 40 per cent to average of State Domestic Product for three years, i.e. 1987-88, 1988-89 and 1989-90. The remaining 10 per cent was on the basis of the average collection of state sales tax for three years, i.e. 1990-91, 1991-92 and 1992-93. An amount of 2.203 per cent was retained by the Central Government for the union territories.

Grant in Lieu of Tax on Passenger Fares

As per Article 269 of Indian Constitution, Government of India collects taxes on railway fares and freights, the net proceeds of which are to be assigned to the states. This tax was initially imposed in the 1957 and subsequently repeated in 1961. The system of grant was introduced to make up for the loss of revenue of states as the tax on passenger fares was merged with the basic fare. The tax on passenger was revived in 1971 and was again repeated in 1973. Now the Finance Commissions have been given the task to suggest the grants to be made to the states in lieu of the tax.

Confusion prevailed over two points. Firstly, about what should be volume of the grant the centre should transfer to the states in lieu of tax on passenger fares and secondly, about the basis of inter-state sharing of the grant. There have always been differences of opinions between the centre and states. In fact, when the tax on passenger fares was repealed it contributed 10.7 per cent of the non-suburban railway passenger earnings which was insisted by the states as the grant to be, whereas the railways insisted the grant to be fixed at Rs. 23 crores.

The Eighth Finance Commission rejected the argument of railways and raised it to Rs. 95 crores which was in fact 10.7 per cent of the railway passenger earnings at that time. However, the Ninth Finance Commission accepted the railways arguments that the latter could not bear the burden of 10.7 per cent incidence of the grant on non-suburban passenger fares but at the same time the Ninth Finance Commission did not like to peg the quantum of grant of a lump sum of Rs. 150 crores per annum for the Eighth Plan period of 1990-95. The Tenth Finance

Commission too rejected the railways argument but agreed to the views of most states, namely the grants should be equal to 10.7 per cent of the non-suburban passenger earnings. Since the total non-suburban passenger earnings for the latest available year 1992-93 was Rs. 3,540 crores, the Tenth Finance Commission recommended 10.7 per cent of Rs. 3,540, i.e. Rs. 350 crores to be paid to the states annually for the period 1995-2000.

Regarding the inter-state distribution of the grant in lieu of the tax on passenger fares, the Seventh Finance Commission adopted the formula of distribution of the grant in proportion to the non-suburban passenger earnings from traffic originating in each state. As the taxable event was the payment of fare, the states should get the grant on the basis of the fare paid within their boundaries. The Eighth, Ninth and Tenth Finance Commissions accepted the logic and continued to accept the formula propounded by the Seventh Finance Commission. Accordingly, the Tenth Finance Commission fixed the grants for all states.

The Estate Duty

In the year 1953, the estate duty was levied and the proceeds of same were to be distributed among the states. The Second Finance Commission made recommendations such as one per cent of the proceeds be retained for union territories and balance to be apportioned between immovable property and other property in the ratio of the gross value of all such properties brought into assessment in that year, the sum thus apportioned to immovable property be distributed among the states in proportion to the gross value of the immovable property located in each state and the sum apportioned to property other than immovable property be distributed among the states in proportion to their population. The Third Finance Commission followed the same. The Fourth Finance Commission adopted the similar pattern except recommendation of two per cent of the proceeds of estate duty for union territories. Fifth and Sixth Finance Commissions made no changes. The Seventh Finance Commission recommended that the distribution of the net proceeds of estate duty in respect of property other than agricultural land should be in proportion to the gross value of all property located in each state. The Eighth Finance Commission proposed that the net proceeds of estate duty each year should be distributed among the states in proportion to the gross value of the immovable property and property other than immovable property taken together located in each state. For this purpose, the union territories should be taken as one unit and their proceeds will be determined accordingly. The Ninth and Tenth Finance Commissions did not make any recommendations related to distribution of proceeds of estate duty among the states since the Central Government abolished the estate duty w.e.f. 1 April 1985.

Grants-in-aid to the States

As per the Indian Constitution under list II of the Seventh Schedule, the states have been assigned specific functional features as regards their welfare, betterment and development in all respects. But normally the resources provided for such functions are not sufficient, with the result they have to seek grants-in-aid from the centre so as to achieve the desired development. Corresponding to each Five-Year Plan, grants-in-aid are to be decided by the Finance Commissions.

So far the distribution of grants-in-aid is concerned under Article 275 of Indian Constitution, the First Finance Commission formulated several principles for regulating them which include budgetary needs, tax efforts, economy in expenditure, standards of special services, special obligations and broad purposes of national importance. The Second Finance Commission paid attention to the development purposes and special needs of border states. The Third Finance Commission covered non-Plan revenue gap plus 75 per cent of the Plan revenue gap of the states along with tax devolution, besides recommending the distribution of Rs. 36 crores in four years from 1962-63 to 1965-66 among ten states as a special purpose grant pertaining to improvement of communications. The Fourth Finance Commission took care of budgetary deficits while distributing the grants-in-aid to different states. The Fifth Finance

Commission recommended grants-in-aid of Rs. 710.7 crores to states other than Bihar, Gujarat, Haryana, MP, Maharashtra, Punjab and UP which were already having surplus funds.

The Sixth Finance Commission increased the grants-in-aid substantially to Rs. 2,509.6 crores because HP, Manipur, Meghalaya, Nagaland, Tripura and J&K had no resource base of their own. The amount of Rs. 815.84 crores was sanctioned for upgrading and standards of administration. The Seventh Finance Commission recommended grants-in-aid of Rs. 1,173.12 crores to states covering HP, J&K, Manipur, Meghalaya, Nagaland, Orissa, Sikkim and Tripura, besides Rs. 436.79 crores to all states except Gujarat, Haryana, Karnataka, Maharashtra and Punjab for upgradation of standards and services.

The Eighth Finance Commission recommended grant of a little more than Rs. 1,500 crores for the period 1985-90 to cover the deficits. In order to deliver these deficit states the advantage of buoyancy the Commission decided to provide for an annual growth of 5 per cent in respect of amount of grants payable in each year of the forecast period commencing from 1984-85. In addition, the Commission recommended grants amounting to about Rs. 915 crores to sixteen states excluding Gujarat, Harayana, Karnataka, Maharashtra, Punjab and Tamil Nadu for upgrading services. The Ninth Finance Commission granted Rs. 5,017 crores covering deficits on Plan and non-Plan revenue account during 1990-95, besides a special annual grant of Rs. 603 crores for the Calamity Relief Fund as well as a small grant of Rs. 122 crores to Madhya Pradesh for the relief of victims of Bhopal gas leak.

The Tenth Finance Commission recommended the grant of Rs. 7,582.68 crores to cover deficit on revenue account during five year period 1995-2000. In addition to deficit grants, the Tenth Finance Commission also recommended a total sum of Rs. 2,608.50 crores for upgrading standards pertaining to police, fire services, jails, promotion of girls' education, primary schools and drinking water, besides solving special problems of states. Grant of Rs. 4,728.19 crores was made by centre to states for calamity relief. Grant of Rs. 5,380 crores followed for local bodies like panchayats and municipalities. The amount of grants-in-aid recommended by the Tenth Finance Commission was more than Rs. 20,000 crores.

In addition to the above, the Tenth Finance Commission recommended a scheme for general debt relief for all states linked to fiscal performance as well as specific relief for states with high fiscal stress, special category states and states with debt problems warranting special attention. Commission also made recommendations for specific relief for all special category states and three other states, i.e. Orissa, Bihar and Uttar Pradesh which were characterized by high fiscal stress. For these states, the Commission recommended writing off of 5 per cent of repayment due with respect to fresh central loans given during 1989-95 and outstanding on 31 March 1995. The Commission also recommended the waiver of one third of the repayment of principal falling due during 1995-2000 on special term loans to Punjab in view of the special circumstances in which these loans were advanced to fight militancy in the state. This relief amounted to Rs. 490.63 crores. With the above-cited facts, we find that the states due to some or the other reasons are always in need of grants-in-aid for their development and survival. Centre comes to their rescue and provides them grants as per the recommendations of Finance Commissions.

Loans by the Centre to the States

All the states are assigned the task of development in various sectors as per their revenues from different sources. The states normally are hand to mouth keeping in view their expenditure. They always cry for the grants-in-aid from centre and the same are sanctioned every time. So, in absence of any grant from centre they take loan from the centre. Such loans from centre to states are mounting day by day. The Second Finance Commission then was asked to intervene on this issue. Accordingly, the Second Finance Commission should be entitled to only two loans a year, a long-term loan and a medium-term loan at a rate of interest approximately equal to the rate of interest at which the Central Government was borrowing from the market. The Fourth Commission suggested the formation of a competent authority or body to solve the problem but nothing materialized. The Fifth Finance Commission advised the states to spend as per their income from revenues and made the undermentioned recommendations:

(i) Ways and means should not be considered as resources.

(ii) The present position relating to limits of ways and means advances do not call for an immediate change although the Reserve Bank should periodically review the limits.

(iii) The Reserve Bank of India should call upon the states to repay the advances and should stop payment of unauthorised overdrafts.

(iv) The centre should assist the states to clear their overdrafts and achieve fiscal discipline, provided the default was not chronic, and should consider the use of constitutional power in the case of persistent, unauthorised overdrafts. The Sixth Finance Commission recommended spreading out of repayment over 15 to 30 years. Writing off of some loans and rescheduling some of them was recommended by the Finance Commissions. The Ninth Finance Commission was not in favour of such steps and further advised the states to be careful so as to avoid such situations of incurring additional debt.

Finance Commission and Planning Commission

A pointwise comparison of Finance Commission and Planning Commission is provided below:

	Finance Commission	Planning Commission
(i)	It is a statutory body appointed by Presidential proclamation once in five years.	It is a non-statutory permanent body. Its members are full time government employees.
(ii)	It helps to transfer non-Plan resources from centre to states.	It has the discretion to transfer Plan resources from centre to the states.
(iii)	Its recommendations are in the form of awards and Central Government is bound to accept them.	Its transfer of funds is only discretionary.
(iv)	It gets authority from the Constitution. It is not an instrument of the centre.	It is only an instrument of the centre.

Evaluation of the First Ten Finance Commission Awards

For smooth financial relations between the centre and states, the appointment of a Finance Commission every five years has become necessary. No doubt, it has the desired significance for above-cited process. The Finance Commission so appointed also indicates the periodical examination related to the division of resources between the centre and the states, besides the modifications required to be excluded from time to time for which the recommendations are made.

Normally, the Finance Commissions estimate excess of revenue expenditure over their own revenues and adopt certain measures for gap fillings. The Seventh Finance Commission was deeply concerned with the equitable system of transfers and so to say that the devolution award under the Seventh Finance Commission was twice that of Sixth Finance Commission. Similarly, with serious concerns towards backward states, the Eighth Commission's award almost doubled the devolution of the Seventh Finance Commission. The Seventh and Eighth Finance Commissions did not recommend large grants-in-aid to cover the revenue deficit of states because the devolution of tax revenue to the states was too much on the higher side. The Ninth and Tenth Finance Commissions adopted the reverse direction. The huge revenue deficit of the centre was mainly due to large devolutions of revenue suggested by the Eighth Finance Commission.

ELEVENTH FINANCE COMMISSION REPORT FOR 2000-05

Alternative Scheme of Vertical Devolution

The award on the vertical sharing of taxes between the centre and the states as well as the horizontal sharing of the divisible pool between the states was made by the Tenth Finance Commission. Considering it better than the present system of tax sharing, an alternative scheme of vertical sharing between the centre and the states was formulated by the Tenth Finance Commission. Personal income tax and central excise duties are shared with the states as per the current provision of the Indian Constitution. The progress of tax reforms would be largely facilitated in case tax sharing pattern was enlarged according to the Tenth Finance Commission thereby giving more of certainty relating to resources for both the centre and the states. The tax devolution remained constant at 85 per cent for income tax and 45 per cent in central excise duties in the form of awards covered by the Eighth and Ninth Finance Commissions during the period 1985-95 for ten years as pointed out by the Tenth Finance Commission, which means that the Central Government had not shown any interest in income tax as its share was only 15 per cent.

The Tenth Finance Commission further pointed out that all the Finance Commissions always stressed the need to bring corporation tax under the divisible pool and this is the reason why they continuously enhanced the share of states pertaining to income tax from 55 to 85 per cent and their share in central excise duty to 40 per cent. The corporation tax was brought under divisible pool as recommended by the Eighth Finance Commission, supported by the Sarkaria Commission.

The Rajah Chelliah Committee on Tax Reforms (1991) advocated for a re-examination of the constitutional provisions of tax sharing, for in its opinion, "The task of fiscal adjustment at the centre has been rendered more difficult because of the compulsions arising from the formula of tax sharing with the states. At present tax devolution to the states constitutes around 24 per cent of the Gross Central Tax Revenues. With the consent and co-operation of the states, the relevant constitutional provisions could be amended to the effect that 25 per cent of the aggregate revenues of the centre shall be shared with the states. There would be certainty then for the states and the centre regarding what revenues would accrue to their respective budgets and the centre would not have to distort its pattern of taxation by being virtually compelled to raise non-shareable taxes."

Having accepted the above-cited recommendations of Raja Chelliah Committee, Finance Ministry of Government of India made a request to the Tenth Finance Commission to examine the desirability of changing the pattern of tax sharing in such a way that the entire tax revenues of the centre except surcharges and less become shareable. The Tenth Finance Commission paid attention to all these points and accordingly calculated the shares of the states in (a) income tax, (b) central excise duties, (c) revenue from additional excise duties in lieu of central sales tax and (d) grants in lieu of tax on passenger fares for the period 1979-80 to 1994-95. The average of Seventh, Eighth and Ninth Finance Commissions was 27.28 per cent, 25.44 per cent and 27.26 per cent respectively. Hence, the Tenth Finance Commission recommended that the share of grants in the gross receipts of central taxes should be 26 per cent. Besides, the additional excise duties should be merged with basic excise duties and another 3 per cent of the gross tax receipts of the centre should go to the states in lieu of additional excise duties. The Tenth Finance Commission recommended that this arrangement of 26 per cent and 3 per cent of the central tax revenues to be transferred to the states be provided suitably in the Constitution and should be reviewed in 15 years. The Tenth Finance Commission further recommended that the proceeds of taxes under Article 268—taxes levied by the centre but collected by the states and appropriated within the respective areas should be kept out of the pool of central taxes. But the proceeds of the taxes under Article 269 which are levied and collected by the centre but the proceeds of which are wholly assigned to the states should form part of the divisible pool thereby inducing the centre to exploit these tax bases which had remained untapped for a long time. Based on new arrangement, the Tenth Finance Commission described some advantages such as with a fixed share allotted to the states in the aggregate tax revenues, the state would automatically share the buoyancy of central taxes. Besides, the Central Government could pursue tax reforms without the need to consider whether a tax was shareable with the states or not and in case, the taxes under Articles 268 as well as 269 formed part of this arrangement, there was a greater likelihood of their being tapped.

Amendment to the Constitution

The Alternative Scheme of Revolution suggested by the Tenth Finance Commission was accepted by the government. The

Indian Constitution was amended. The 80th Constitutional Amendment Act, 2000 was passed which provided for the following:

(i) All central taxes and duties, except those referred in Articles 268 and 269, surcharges and cesses are to be shared between the centre and the states.

(ii) Only those states in which these taxes and duties are leviable in that year are entitled to a share in these taxes and duties.

(iii) The percentage of net proceeds of those taxes and duties which are assigned to the states in any financial year shall form part of the Consolidated Fund of India.

The Eleventh Finance Commission was appointed in July 1998 with A.M. Khusro as its Chairman. It submitted its report in July 2000 and covered the time period 2000-2005. The Eleventh Finance Commission was asked to make the recommendations on the following matters:

(i) The distribution between the centre and the states of the net proceeds of the taxes which are to be or may be divided between them.

(ii) The principles which should govern the grants-in-aid of the revenues of the states out of the Consolidated Fund of India and the sums to be paid to the states.

(iii) The measures needed to augment the consolidated fund to a state to supplement the resources of the panchayats and the municipalities in the state on the basis of recommendations made by the Finance Commission of the State.

(iv) To review the finances of the centre and the states as well as suggest ways and means by which the governments collectively may bring about a restructuring of the public finances so as to restore budgetary balance and maintain macroeconomic stability.

While making the recommendations, the Eleventh Commission was asked to take into account the following:

(i) the resources of the Central Government and the demands thereon; (ii) revenue resources of the states for the five years commencing on 1 April 2000; (iii) the requirement of the states for meeting the Plan and non-Plan revenue expenditure; (iv) the maintenance and upkeep of capital assets and maintenance expenditure of Plan schemes; (v) the requirements of states for upgradation of standards in non-developmental and social sectors and services; (vi) the need for ensuring reasonable returns on investment by the states in irrigation projects, power projects, state transport understanding, etc.; (vii) provisions for emoluments and terminal benefits of the government employees including teachers and other employees of aided institutions; and (viii) the scope for better fiscal management.

Main Recommendations of the Eleventh Finance Commission

Vertical Devolution

Consequent upon the adoption of the Constitution (80th) Amendment Act, 2000 in June 2000, now all central taxes and duties except those referred in Articles 268 and 269 as well as the surcharges and cesses are to be shared between the centre and the states. The Eleventh Finance Commission recommended that the share of the states in the net proceeds of all the central taxes and dulies be fixed at 28 per cent for each of the five years starting from 2000-01 and ending 2004-05. As a consequence of the Constitution (80th) Amendment Act, 2000, the net proceeds of the additional excise duties now cannot be passed on to the states as Article 272 of the Constitution stands deleted. These now form part of the tax revenue receipts of the Central Government and are shareable with the states. To account for this fact, the Eleventh Finance Commission further recommended that 1.5 per cent of all shareable union taxes and duties be allocated to the states separately, thus totaling 29.5 per cent of the net proceeds of all union taxes and duties.

Grants-in-aid to states facing revenue deficits after devolution, the grants meant for local bodies and grants for calamity relief would amount to another 8 per cent. In overall scheme of transfer of funds, 37.5 per cent of the gross revenue receipts would be the ceiling to be transferred to the states.

Table 6.3: Criteria and Weights for Determining the Relative Share of State

		Tenth Finance Commission	Eleventh Finance Commission
1.	Population	20 per cent	10 per cent
2.	Distance per capita income of the state from that of the state having highest per capita income	60 per cent	62.5 per cent
3.	Area	5 per cent	7.5 per cent
4.	Index of Infrastructure	5 per cent	7.5 per cent
5.	Tax Effort	10 per cent	5 per cent
6.	Fiscal Discipline	—	7.5 per cent
	Total	100 per cent	100 per cent

Horizontal Devolution

The Eleventh Finance Commission amended the formula for sharing the taxes and duties as indicated in above table. The weightage of the population factor was reduced to 10 per cent as against 20 per cent specified by Tenth Finance Commission. Similarly, the weightage to area as well as index of infrastructure was raised from 5 per cent to 7.5 per cent whereas the Tenth Finance Commission made a beginning by using the tax effort of the state in resource mobilization at 10 per cent. The Eleventh Finance Commission used two criteria—tax effort and fiscal discipline—which indicate fiscal efficiency of the state to achieve better fiscal balance, receive a combined weightage of 12.5 per cent in the formula of the Eleventh Finance Commission which measured the improvement of fiscal health of a state not only with reference to tax effort resulting in higher revenues but also in terms of its effort to reduce revenue expenditure.

The most important factor of the share of the states was the distance of per capita income of a particular state from that of the state having the highest per capita income. This measure was raised to 62.5 per cent by the Eleventh Finance Commission as against 60 per cent fixed by the Tenth Finance Commission thereby further helping the poorer states. The Eleventh Finance

Commission recommended a total devolution of Rs. 4,34,905 crores for the five year period 2000-05 in the form of devolution of taxes and grants, out of which 86.5 per cent is the share of taxes and duties whereas that of grants is 13.5 per cent. Out of the total grants-in-aid of Rs. 58,587, a sum of Rs. 35,359 crores goes to meet the revenue deficit of states, a sum of Rs. 4,793 crores was kept for upgradation of administration and special problems associated with certain states. To provide support to local bodies—the panchayat and municipalities at the urban level—the Eleventh Finance Commission recommended a total grant of Rs. 10,000 crores for five year period. Lastly, there was a provision of Rs. 8,256 crores for the relief during calamities such as cyclones, drought, earthquake, fire, flood and hailstorm, etc.

Debt Relief to States

The existing debt relief scheme related to improvements in the ratio of revenue receipts of a state to its total revenue expenditure has been proposed by the Eleventh Finance Commission to continue. Apart from that, the Commission has recommended a moratorium on the payment of installments of debt and interest on the special loan given to Punjab during 1984-94, for contracting insurgency and militancy due for repayment from the state of Punjab during the period 2000-05. Keeping in view the expenditure spent on security, the Commission has further recommended relief to Punjab and Jammu & Kashmir. All the recommendations pertaining to debt relief made by the Eleventh Finance Commission have been accepted by the government.

Measures Suggested by Eleventh Finance Commission to Reduce Budget Deficits

Following are the suggestions and recommendations made by the Eleventh Finance Commission to reduce the budget deficits:

(i) For an enduring solution to the problem of budget deficits, attention needs to be paid to the system of budgeting and budgetary control. The newly constituted

Expenditure Commission is expected to go into the system of budgetary practices and controls for making recommendations for reforms in this direction.

(ii) As service is a fast growing sector of the economy constituting over 50 per cent of the GDP, it should be brought increasingly under the tax net for improving buoyancy in indirect taxes.

(iii) The tax base of the states and the local bodies needs to be widened by better exploitations of land based taxes, better administration of property taxes and other taxes.

(iv) Constitution may be amended to empower the Parliament to revise the ceiling on professional tax.

(v) Massive arrears of assessed but uncollected taxes remain on the account books of both centre and state governments. Effective steps for collection of these arrears in the next few years should be taken.

(vi) User charges should be index-linked to input costs and process of periodic revision should become automatic.

(vii) There should be a regular revision of royalties on minerals. The task of making recommendations on royality rates should be entrusted to an independent body.

(viii) The composition of government expenditure should be restructured in favour of priority areas like elementary education, primary health care, water supply, sanitation and infrastructure like roads and bridges. Expenditure on salaries, pensions, interest payments and subsidies should be strictly controlled.

(ix) There is no need to appoint Pay Commissions at the interval of ten years. As the recommendations of the Central Pay Commission have a bearing on the states, its terms of reference, if and when appointed, should be determined in consultation with the states. The level of salaries and allowances should bear a relationship with the revenue expenditure of the states to be laid down by an expert committee.

(x) Since a larger share of pensions goes to the defence sector, a suitable scheme to absorb the retirees from the armed forces in other government departments may be devised.

(xi) Assessment of excess manpower in the government departments and public enterprises may be made expeditiously and suitable schemes evolved for their redeployment.

Assessment of the Eleventh Finance Commission Report

Whenever anything in any form takes place, it is bound to have positive as well as negative impact which is the thumb rule of nature. Similarly, the Eleventh Finance Commission made some recommendations as regards the sharing of net proceeds of taxes, levies and duties between the centre and the states which were appreciated by same people and at the same time there were a few critics too.

The Eleventh Finance Commission devolved 29.5 per cent of the total central tax revenue to the states as against 29 per cent prevailing earlier. The Commission fixed a ceiling of 37.5 per cent of transfer of centre's gross revenue receipts to the states. In the third instance, the Eleventh Finance Commission was criticised for changing devolution of taxes/duties as per the formula given by the Tenth Finance Commission thereby resulting gain to the backward states and loss to the forward developed states to some extent. The Eleventh Finance Commission had made the suggestions to strengthen infrastructure and acceterate growth in other forms in the poorer states, besides eliminating the prevailing inequalities. A word of appreciation goes to the Eleventh Finance Commission for initiating such an approach. Finally, this Commission had made some recommendations for reducing the budget deficits though same measurers were also suggested by the Central Government.

TWELFTH FINANCE COMMISSION AWARD

After the 80th Amendment Act, 2000 of the Constitution, the Twelfth Finance Commission was appointed by the President under Article 280 of Indian Constitution under

Dr. C. Rangarajan as Chairman. The terms of reference for the Twelfth Finance Commission were as under:

(i) The distribution between the centre and the states of the net proceeds of all taxes and the allocation between the states of the respective shares of such proceeds.

(ii) The principles which should govern:

  (a) The grants-in-aid to the states out of the Consolidated Fund of India; and

  (b) The sums to be paid to those states which are in need of assistance by way of grants-in-aid under Article 275 of the Indian Constitution.

(iii) The measures needed to augment the Consolidated Fund of a state to supplement the resources of the panchayats and municipalities in the states.

(iv) Review the Fiscal Reform Facility introduced by the Central Government on the basis of the recommendations of the Eleventh Finance Commission and suggest measures for effective achievement of its objectives.

(v) Assess the debt position of the states at the end of March 2004 and suggest necessary corrective measures consistent with macroeconomic stability and debt maintainability.

(vi) Review the present arrangements as regards financing of Disaster Management.

(vii) To recommend whether the non-tax income of profit petroleum to the centre, arising out of contractual provisions should be shared with the states from where the mineral oils are produced, and if so, to what extent.

Award of the Twelfth Finance Commission

Vertical Imbalance and Devolution

Keeping in view the above-cited terms of reference, the Twelfth Finance Commission made the recommendations that could retain the growing momentum of development and streamline the transfers from the centre to the states in the form of tax devolutions and grants so as to correct both the vertical and the horizontal imbalances. While giving its award, the main objective of the Twelfth Finance Commission was to recommend a scheme of transfers thereby serving purpose of equity coupled with efficiency. In our country, the centre is enriched with more of revenues, whereas the states are burdened with more and more responsibilities which is the main reason of the vertical imbalance that always exists. So as to correct the vertical imbalance, the transfers from the centre to the state governments becomes inevitable. The Twelfth Finance Commission, while taking into account all the relevant facts of receipts and expenditures of the centre and the states, presented an increase of one per cent of the shareable pool of the states and that too to accommodate the additional excise duty in lieu of sugar, tobacco and textiles. Further, considering the request of Finance Ministry and in view of other factors, the Twelfth Finance Commission fixed the indicative amount of overall transfers to states in central gross revenue at 38 per cent, i.e. 0.7 per cent more than the percentage fixed by the Eleventh Finance Commission.

Horizontal Sharing

It is related to the sharing of the total shareable pool between the states which would become simple if all the states have almost the same per capita income. Various states have different area, population, income, tax base, etc. with the result there are differences in the costs of rendering the required services which needs the correction of horizontal imbalances while distributing central resources among all the states in the country.

On the basis of memoranda submitted by many states, the Twelfth Finance Commission considered recommendations of earlier commissions about the continuation of the use of population as a factor, the use of income distance criteria, continuation of area as a factor and retaining the tax effort as well as index of fiscal discipline criteria. All these points indicate no objective factor in any of above criteria. So far, all the previous Commissions have worked differently to arrive at a reasonable degree of equalization. Every award of Finance Commissions has been criticised by these states which feel that they have been deprived of their large share in the shareable central revenue pool. While looking at and scrutinising the different opinions of different Finance Commissions and different states, the Twelfth Finance Commission adopted the following criteria regarding determination of shares of states:

Criteria	Weightage (per cent)
Population	25
Income Distance	50
Area	10
Tax Effort	7.5
Fiscal Discipline	7.5
Total	100 per cent

Hence, the Twelfth Finance Commission concluded with the note: "We have tried to evolve a formula that balances equity with fiscal efficiency. Equity considerations, however, dominate, as they should, in any scheme of federal transfers trying to implement the equalization principle." Based on this formula, five states, viz. UP, Bihar, Andhra Pradesh, West Bengal and Madhya Pradesh would get the largest share amounting to 51.5 per cent dividing as 19.3 per cent, 11 per cent, 7.4 per cent, 7.19 per cent and 6.7 per cent respectively whereas 23 states would share the balance 48.5 per cent of the shareable pool.

Grants-in-aid

Like other earlier Finance Commissions, the Twelfth Finance Commission, moving on the same lines, recommended non-Plan revenue deficit grants, under Article 275 of the Constitution to be given to 15 states whose total non-Plan revenue deficit was assessed at Rs. 56,856 crores for the period 2005-10, while other grants-in-aid recommended by it are mentioned as under:

Grants for education for 8 states:	Rs. 10,172 crores over the award period, with a minimum of Rs. 20 crores in a year for any eligible state.
Grants for health for 7 states:	Rs. 5,887 crores over the award period with a minimum of Rs. 10 crores in a year for any eligible state.

Grants for maintenance of	Rs. 15,000 crores over the roads and bridges: award period.
(i) public buildings:	Rs. 5,000 crores.
(ii) forests:	Rs. 10,000 crores.
Grants for heritage conservation:	Rs. 625 crores over the award period.
Grants for specific needs:	Rs. 7,100 crores over the award period for state specific needs.
Overall the Twelfth Finance Commission awarded:	Rs. 6,13,112 crores (81 per cent), grants-in-aid Rs. 1,42,640 crores (19 per cent), Total Rs. 7,55,752 (100 per cent)

Local Bodies—Panchayats and Municipalities

The Eleventh Finance Commission had awarded ad hoc annual grant of Rs. 7,000 crores for the panchayats and municipalities for the period 2000-05, but later, considering the views of the states, Ministry of Rural Development as well as Ministry of Urban Development and Poverty Alleviation, the Twelfth Finance Commission recommended a sum of Rs. 25,000 crores as grants-in-aid to supplement the resources of municipalities and panchayats for the period 2005-10 out of which 20 per cent would go to municipalities and 80 per cent to panchayats. Commission had further suggested separate grants for the maintenance of roads and buildings maintained by the municipalities. The criteria and relative weightage for determining the inter-state distribution adopted by the Twelfth Finance Commission is as mentioned below:

	Criteria	Weightage (per cent)
(i)	Population	40
(ii)	Geographical Area	10
(iii)	Distance from highest per capital income	10
(iv)	Index for Deprivation	20
(v)	Revenue Effort	20
	Total	100

Source: Report of the Twelfth Finance Commission (2005-10).

Out of Revenue Effort weightage of 20 per cent, 10 per cent is with respect to own revenue of states and balance 10 per cent is with respect to Gross State Domestic Product. Overall the Twelfth Finance Commission has emphasised that grants allocated to the panchayats should be utilised towards the operations and maintenance of water supply and sanitation.

Financing of Calamity Relief Expenditure

The Twelfth Finance Commission was asked to make suggestions about the financing of relief from damage by natural calamities including landslides, avalanches, cloud bursts, pest attacks, cyclones, droughts, earthquakes, fire, floods and hailstorm as expenditure from National Calamity Relief Fund (CRF) and National Calamity Contingency Fund (NCCF).

After thorough scrutiny of the disaster management, the Twelfth Finance Commission recommended the continuation of the scheme of Calamity Relief Fund with contributions from the centre and the states in the ratio 75:25 as before. The amount of CRF for 2005-10 was worked out of Rs. 21,333.33 crores of which the centre's share would be Rs. 16,000 crores and the balance would be the share of the states. The Twelfth Finance Commission has also agreed to the suggestion made by the states to continue NCCF with a core corpus of Rs. 500 crores besides recommending the outgo from the NCCF to continue to be replenished by way of collection of National Calamity Contingent Duty and levy of special surcharges.

Debt Relief to States

The Twelfth Finance Commission estimated the total outstanding debt of states including short-term borrowings at Rs. 8,65,859 crores at the end of March 2004. The Commission could find that the earlier Finance Commissions had extended the debt relief in several ways such as consolidation of loans on common terms and with reduction in the interest rates in the future, revision in terms of repayment of loans without lowering of interest rates, moratorium on interest payments and repayment of principal due in certain years, write off of loans or repayments falling due during a specified period and introduction of schemes of debt relief linked to fiscal performance, etc.

To provide debt relief to the states and urge the states to reduce and completely remove the revenue deficit, the Twelfth Finance Commission gave the following proposals:

(i) Rescheduling of all central loans outstanding as on end of March 2005 into fresh loans for 20 years carrying 7.5 per cent interest with effect from the year a state enacts the Fiscal Responsibility Legislation.

(ii) A debt write off linked to reduction in revenue deficit by state. The quantum of write off of repayment would be linked to the absolute amount by which the revenue deficit is reduced in each successive year during the award period.

Debt Gross State Domestic Product ratio rose from 21.73 per cent in 1997-98 to 31.15 per cent in 2002-03 which, according to the Twelfth Finance Commission, was the worst for the states in terms of their finances. On the other hand, the combined debt of the centre and the states as a proportion of the GDP rose from 56.5 per cent in 1996-97 to 82.5 per cent in 2004-05.

Sharing of Petroleum Profit

The Twelfth Finance Commission was given the task of deciding the sharing of profit with the states in which mineral oils are produced. As per Articles 294 and 296 of the Constitution of India, the ownership rights of all land and mineral resources located within the territory of a state rest with the state. According to the Petroleum and Natural Gas Rules, 1959 a licence or lease in respect of any land rested in a state should be granted by the State Government though with the agreement of the Central Government. Under the given provisions, royalty in respect of any mineral oil or minerals excavated will have to be paid to the states where the lease has been granted by the states and the centre where the lease has been granted by the centre in the case of off-shore areas.

In the beginning, only two national oil companies were in operation which paid the royalties to the states @ 20 per cent, whereas the New Exploration Licensing Policy (NEPL) reduced the royalties to 12.5 per cent to the new private parties, cancelled cess, exempted imports from customs duties and gave 7 year tax holiday from the date of commencement of commercial production of oil. The terms of NEPL were acceptable to the states while some states like Gujarat, Assam and Madhya Pradesh asked the Central Government for 50 per cent sharing under Production Sharing Contract (PSC) which was not accepted by the Ministry of Law.

Disagreeing with the opinion of Ministry of Law, the Twelfth Finance Commission was convinced that there could be no constitutional or legal objection if the Central Government decided to share petroleum profit under PSCs. While states defending themselves on the basis of the land and mineral resources belonging to them demanded that they should get a share in the petroleum profit under NELP as the royalty has been reduced from 20 to 12.5 per cent. Arguing further, the states desired more profit share while some non-oil producing states suggested that petroleum profit should be shared not only with oil producing states but also with all the states.

In view of above facts, the Twelfth Finance Commission finally made the recommendations as stated below:

(i) The centre should share petroleum profit from NELP areas with the states from where the mineral oil and mineral gas are produced. The share should be in the ratio of 50:50.

(ii) The revenue earned by the Central Government on contracts signed under the coal bed methane policy may also be shared with the producing states in the same manner as petroleum profit.

Conclusion

The government accepted the award of the Twelfth Finance Commission, whereas the Finance Ministry desired that the total share of the states in the Central Government's gross revenue should not exceed 38 per cent. It is painful to learn that in our country, the question of state autonomy is raised mostly to gain political advantages and is not guided by sound economic logic as it should be. In fact, a permanent Finance Commission should be set up instead of one constituted every five years.

THIRTEENTH FINANCE COMMISSION

The Thirteenth Finance Commission (FC-XIII) was constituted on 13 November 2007 to make recommendations for the period 2010-15 under the Chairmanship of Dr. Vijay Kelkar. The Terms of Reference (ToR) of the Commission included making recommendations on the matters concerning the distribution between the Union and the states of the net proceeds of taxes which are to be, or may be, divided between them under Chapter I Part XII of the Constitution and the allocation between the states of the respective shares of such proceeds.

The Commission was also required to make recommendations on the principles which should govern the grants-in-aid of the revenues of the states out of the Consolidated Fund of India and the sums to be paid to the states which are in need of assistance by way of grants-in-aid of their revenues under article 275 of the Constitution. The Commission was required to review the state of the finances of the Union and the states, keeping in view, in particular, the operation of the states' Debt Consolidation and Relief Facility 2005-2010 introduced by the Central Government on the basis of the recommendations of the Twelfth Finance Commission, and suggest measures for maintaining a stable and sustainable fiscal environment consistent with equitable growth.

Visits of the Commission

The Commission visited all the 28 states between June 2008 and July 2009 as part of consultations with the State Governments and other key stakeholders. During state visits, the Commission held discussions with the Chief Ministers, their cabinet colleagues, and other senior officials of the State Governments on the fiscal and financial situation of the states, their funding priorities and requirements. It also held separate meetings with representatives of recognised political parties, representatives of urban and rural local bodies and representatives of trade and industry. The Commission also undertook field visits to get first-hand experience of important developmental issues.

The Commission made a visit to the US and Canada with a view to keep abreast of the latest international developments in fiscal federalism, measures to improve the quality of public expenditure, environmental issues and Goods and Services Tax (GST).

Approach to Fiscal Consolidation

Despite the commendable correction achieved by the centre and states through implementation of the Fiscal Responsibility and Budget Management (FRBM) legislation across the 2005-10 period, the closing debt-GDP ratio for 2009-10 was estimated at 82 per cent, well above the FC-XII target of 75 per cent. FC-XIII proposed a target of 68 per cent for a combined centre and state debt to GDP ratio to be achieved by the year 2014-15 and 45 per cent for the Central Government debt-GDP ratio. It prescribed fiscal consolidation path for the Central Government which entails a decline in the revenue deficit from 4.8 per cent of GDP as projected for the fiscal year 2009-10, to a revenue surplus of 0.5 per cent of GDP by 2014-15. This allows for acceleration in capital expenditure to 3.5 per cent of GDP.

The second round of Fiscal Responsibility Legislation (FRL) by states takes up from where FC-XII left off. The fiscal consolidation path promotes growth-expansionary fiscal consolidation, by incentivising elimination of revenue deficit thereby ensuring that net public borrowing is directed exclusively towards growth enhancing public investment. FC-XIII has projected that revenues of states into 2010-15 will enjoin greater tax effort on the part of states with a poor revenue collection record, thus implicitly rewarding states with higher levels of past achievement.

The Finance Commission has sought to design grants with a view to incentivising improvements in accountability of, transparency in and innovation at, the cutting edge of the public goods delivery process. Further, two game-changing tax reforms, namely GST and the new Direct Tax Code, will give considerable impetus to revenue growth. A major thrust of the proposed expenditure reforms is to improve the supply of public goods which is also inclusive by reducing existing untargeted and regressive subsidies. Other reforms are aimed at improving the productivity of public expenditure. These include:

(i) Performance-linked incentives to states and local bodies.

(ii) Measures to improve transparency and accountability, e.g. stricter audit procedures.

(iii) "Institutional deepening" for better expenditure management, e.g. creation of the local body ombudsman, fiscal council and independent evaluation organizations.

(iv) Promotion of innovations and their diffusion so as to reduce cost as well as to improve quality of public services.

(v) Larger fiscal transfers to the local bodies, to encourage speedier implementation of the 73rd and 74th Constitutional amendments regarding the transfer of functions and functionaries in consonance with the subsidiarity principle.

Principles Governing the Design of Grants

The recommendations of the Finance Commission regarding the principles for disbursement of different grants have a conditionality element, which is informed by three objectives—to ensure additionality of resources, to improve transparency and accountability, and to assist in better monitoring of expenditure. While seeking to incentivise different levels of government to adopt and undertake green policy actions, the approach has been to use the grant instrument to foster such incentives. In addition, the Commission has also sought to discourage policy actions that distract from sustainable development such as the fertilizer subsidy in the case of the centre and power subsidies in the case of the states.

The Commission proposed a forward looking grant that would reward states for their public health efforts towards reduced infant mortality rates—one of the most important MDGs. It also recommended a grant for improving statistical systems at the district and state level, which complements national level initiatives to improve the quality, richness and reliability of national statistical systems. Further, it recommended the creation of a district innovation fund to incentivise and recognise the processes, at the levels of government closest to the ordinary citizen as well as a grant for the establishment of a National Centre for Innovations in Public Systems (CIPS).

State-specific Grants

The Commission recommended the award of state-specific grants following two broad principles. First, even relatively small grants would show discernible results, provided that they are directed towards felt needs, particularly for sectors which do not benefit from centrally sponsored programmes or where there are significant funding gaps. Second, there is a rationale for state-specific grants where these address deprivation, generate significant externalities, especially environmental externalities, meet the needs of the marginal groups or areas and encourage policy innovations.

Review of Central Finances

The review of the fiscal situation revealed that all fiscal indicators, after registering an improvement in the years following the enactment of the FRBMA, had witnessed sharp deterioration in 2008-09 and 2009-10. The Commission revisited the roadmap of fiscal adjustment and suggested a suitably revised roadmap factoring in the need to bring the liabilities of the Central Government on account of oil, food and fertiliser bonds into fiscal accounting as well as the impact of various other obligations on deficit targets with a view to maintaining the gains of fiscal consolidation through 2010-15.

Between 2003-04 and 2007-08, the revenue deficit of the centre declined by 2.46 percentage points of GDP. Much of this decline came from an improvement in tax revenues. The marginal decline in revenue expenditure of the centre was entirely on account of the decline in interest payments following softer interest rates. What also contributed to the reduction in fiscal deficit was compression of capital expenditure. Thus, the fiscal correction at the centre was largely on account of revenue augmentation and partly on account of capital expenditure compression.

The outstanding liabilities of the Central Government, after reaching 63.33 per cent of GDP in 2004-05, started declining consistently as the average nominal interest rate on debt was lower than the nominal GDP growth rate. Despite a sharp increase in the fiscal deficit in the years 2008-09 and 2009-10, a marginal decline in the ratio of outstanding debt to GDP is projected even in these two years. Among the components of outstanding debt, there is an increase in the share of internal debt.

Because of the developments unfolding since the global crisis, the centre increased its net market borrowings sharply, from Rs. 1,31,768 crores in 2007-08 to Rs. 2,61,972 crores in 2008-09 and further to Rs. 3,97,957 crores in the budget estimates for 2009-10. Following the global downturn, the Memorandum of Understanding (MoU) signed with the RBI was amended in February 2009 to allow a part of the amount in the MSS account to be transferred to the Consolidated Fund of India as part of the government's normal market borrowing programme. Following this, an amount of Rs. 12,000 crores was transferred from the MSS account to the Consolidated Fund of the centre in March 2009. A further amount of Rs. 28,000 crores raised through MSS was de-sequestered in May 2009.

To sum up, the following are the main trends in the centre's finances in recent years:

(i) The fiscal correction path, following the enactment of FRBMA was more or less on track till 2007-08, after a pause in 2005-06. A number of developments, particularly the slowdown of the economy and its adverse impact on revenue growth, increasing commodity prices, anti-recessionary measures, farm loan waiver and implementation of the recommendations of the Sixth CPC, have resulted in a worsening, going beyond the reversal of the fiscal correction achieved till 2007-08.

(ii) Despite deterioration in all fiscal indicators in 2008-09 and 2009-10, the debt-GDP ratio remained stable, or even declined marginally. This was because of the growth of nominal GDP remaining higher than the average nominal interest rate.

(iii) Though the tax-GDP ratio has come down in 2008-09, it is still higher than the level reached in 2004-05. The fall in the aggregate tax-GDP ratio in 2008-09 would have been sharper but for buoyant revenues from corporation tax and service tax. There has been a continuous increase in the tax-GDP ratios of these taxes till 2008-09. While the tax-GDP ratio in respect of corporation tax is expected to be maintained even in 2009-10, that of service tax is expected to witness a marginal fall. With buoyant revenues from corporation tax, revenue from direct taxes has, for the first time, overtaken that from indirect taxes in 2007-08.

(iv) Total expenditure of the centre relative to GDP witnessed a significant contraction between 2003-04 and 2006-07, after which it started rising again, despite moderation in capital expenditure. Rising revenue expenditure, particularly in 2008-09 and 2009-10, contributed to growth in total expenditure. Within revenue expenditure there was sharp increase in expenditure on pay and allowances as well as subsidies.

(v) Resumption of the path of fiscal correction is crucial to achieving a sustainable fiscal situation at the centre. Though softening of international oil prices has provided some relief, reverting to the high growth path and a strategy to exit from the expansionary fiscal stance put in place as a countercyclical measure will hold the key to fiscal correction. In recent years, off-budget liabilities of the centre have assumed alarming proportions. In 2008-09, off-budget bonds issued to oil marketing and fertiliser companies amounted to Rs. 95,942 crores or 1.80 per cent of GDP.

Review of State Finances

Improvement in state finances started around 2004-05, aided by a higher rate of growth of the economy and the resultant increase in buoyancy of the states' own tax revenues as well as central transfers. This improvement further received a boost with the FC-XII recommending an increase in the states' share in net central taxes from 29.5 per cent to 30.5 per cent. FC-XII also recommended the Debt Consolidation and Relief Facility (DCRF) comprising consolidation of central loans contracted till March 2004 and outstanding on 31 March 2005, along with debt write offs, linked to reduction of the revenue deficits of states and containment of fiscal deficit at the 2004-05 level. The enactment of FRL brought an element of discipline into budget-making by the states. Another major development having a considerable bearing on improvement of state finances was the introduction of VAT by most states in 2005-06. This has improved the tax base of the states by replacing the single point sales tax previously in place.

The main trends in the aggregate position of state finances can be summarised as follows:

(i) There was considerable improvement in the aggregate finances of states following higher growth of own tax revenues and increased transfers from the centre. The revenue account of states turned surplus in 2006-07 and continued to remain in surplus in 2007-08. This is ahead of the target date of 2008-09 recommended by FC-XII. The process of fiscal consolidation in states was helped by the enactment of FRBMA by most states by bringing in rule based management of public finances.

(ii) There was only a marginal reduction in the revenue expenditure of states. Reduction in interest payments as a proportion of GDP was higher than reduction in revenue expenditure.

(iii) Subsidies by states to power and irrigation sectors, both explicit and implicit, are a big drag on the finances of states. The performance of state level PSUs continues to remain poor.

(iv) One noteworthy development was the increase in the aggregate capital expenditure of states following reduction in revenue expenditure and the surplus on the revenue account.

(v) The expected reduction in the growth of own revenue receipts and central transfers, along with increasing expenditure commitments on account of pay revisions are likely to pose a threat to the fiscal correction achieved so far.

Policy Implications

Putting fiscal correction back on track should be the priority of both the centre and the states. With the moderation in international oil prices, commitments on account of arrears of pay following the recommendations of the Sixth CPC and farm loan waiver having been met and the economy showing signs of recovery, it should be possible to return to the path of fiscal correction at the earliest. There is improvement in the global economic outlook with a number of major economies coming out of recession. There are also indications of the global economic situation improving in the last quarter of 2009 and the improvement continuing through 2010. A calibrated exit strategy from the fiscal expansionary stance of 2008-09 and 2009-10 should be the main agenda for the government in 2010-11. The proposed introduction of GST is expected to reverse the temporary reduction in revenue following rate cuts affected as part of the fiscal stimulus.

The revised roadmap prescribed a combined debt-GDP ratio of 68 per cent for 2014-15. With the target of debt-GDP ratio for the Central Government set at 45 per cent in 2014-15, the target envisaged for all the states by implication is 25 per cent (the state and central ratios do not add up to the combined ratio because of the netting out of central loans to states). The roadmap also targets elimination of revenue deficit by the centre and all the states individually by 2014-15.

Goods and Services Tax

The Commission considered the impact of the proposed implementation of Goods and Services Tax including its impact on the country's foreign trade, while formulating its recommendations. The changeover to the Goods and Service Tax (GST) will be a game-changing tax reform measure which will significantly contribute to the buoyancy of tax revenues and acceleration of growth as well as generate many positive externalities. The Commission supported the implementation of a model GST for the following reasons:

(i) The NCAER study computed the present value of GST-reform induced gains in GDP as the present value of additional income stream based on the discount rate of 3 per cent representing the long-term real rate of interest. The present value of total gain in GDP is estimated as between Rs. 14.69 lakh crores and Rs. 28.81 lakh crores. The corresponding dollar values are US $ 325 billion and $ 637 billion. This represents between 25 and 50 per cent of the 2009-10 GDP gained through this major tax reform. The all-government tax revenue will also increase by about 0.20 per cent of GDP—a significant increment to revenues through implementation of the model GST.

(ii) The Task Force report estimated that such a GST would have a tax base of around Rs. 31,00,000 crores. It further estimated that this would require a revenue-neutral rate of only 12 per cent (5 per cent for the Central GST and 7 per cent for the State GST). This is a substantial decrease from the present 20.5 per cent (8 per cent for CENVAT and 12.5 per cent for VAT). This should be the target.

(iii) Adoption of such a model GST would make India a dynamic common market and also result in generation of positive externalities. Despite lower levels of taxes, the revenue of the Union and the states will be buoyant. Subsumation of all major indirect taxes will result in removal of inefficient taxes. Manufactures will become more competitive and consequently exports will grow.

Provision of seamless input tax credit across all transactions will avoid tax cascading, eliminate double taxation and improve resource allocation. It will foster a common market across the country, reorient supply chains and remove the present bias towards backward integration. Further, it will also inhibit tax induced migration of investment. It will, thus, support the growth of lagging but resource-rich regions. A single rate across all goods and services will eliminate classification disputes and make tax assessment more predictable. The harmonisation of tax assessment, levy and collection procedures across states proposed under the GST will reduce compliance costs, limit evasion, enhance transparency and improve collection efficiency.

(iv) Successful implementation of GST also offers the possibility of strengthening the revenue base of local bodies that form the third tier of government.

(v) The inclusion of real estate in the GST tax base will constrain the parallel economy with consequent positive spillovers into governance and the development of land markets.

(vi) The NCAER model suggests that GST could lead to better environmental outcomes.

The Grand Bargain

The Commission proposed that both the centre and the states conclude a 'Grand Bargain' to implement the model GST. Keeping the experience of the implementation of VAT in mind, it suggested that the six elements of the Grand Bargain comprise: (i) the design of the GST; (ii) its operational modalities; (iii) binding agreement between centre and states with contingencies for change in rates and procedures; (iv) disincentives for non-compliance; (v) the implementation schedule and (vi) the procedure for states to claim compensation.

Any GST model adopted must be consistent with all the elements of the Grand Bargain. To incentivise implementation of the Grand Bargain the Commission recommended the sanction of a grant of Rs. 50,000 crores which would taper down to Rs. 40,000 crores and Rs. 30,000 crores if GST is implemented after 1 April 2013 and 1 April 2014 respectively. The grant would be used for meeting the compensation claims of State Governments for revenue losses on account of GST implemented, consistent with the Grand Bargain, between 2010-11 and 2014-15. Unspent balances in this pool would be distributed on 1 January 2015 amongst all the states as per the devolution formula. In the unlikely event that a consensus to implement all the elements of the Grand Bargain cannot be achieved and the

GST mechanism finally adopted is different from the model GST suggested, the grant of Rs. 50,000 crores shall not be disbursed.

Assessment of Union Revenue and Expenditure

The judgement as to when the process of recovery would become sustained may be critical in assessing Union revenue and expenditure. Hence, the Commission employed a calibrated approach instead of assuming a constant GDP growth rate over its award period. The Commission adopted nominal growth rates of 12.50 per cent in 2010-11, 13 per cent in 2011-12 and 13.5 per cent in each of the years from 2012-13 to 2014-15. The MoF projections are broadly similar, while those of the Planning Commission are higher. The inflation scenario adopted by the Commission was in line with the RBI projections of a rate of 4.5 per cent to 5 per cent. MoF, however, has assumed a lower inflation rate of 3 per cent to 4.5 per cent over the period 2010-15.

In order to project the revenues and expenditures of the centre for the period 2010-15, FC-XIII followed a two-step approach comprising a reassessment of the base year figures and, based on this, their projection for the award period (2010-15). The 2009-10 (BE) figures reflected in the Union Budget presented on 6 July 2009 were, by and large, taken as the base for projections.

Reassessment of Base Year 2009-10

In the case of tax revenues FC-XIII used the 2009-10 (BE) projections made by the Central Government. These reflect decreasing buoyancy relative to the previous years, which is appropriate, given the severity of the economic downturn in 2008-09 and 2009-10 that has affected the direct as well as the indirect tax base. For non-tax revenues FC-XIII used the 2009-10 (BE) projections made by the Central Government in all cases except receipts under economic services.

In the case of economic services, using the BE figure (Rs. 60,039 crores) as the base seemed inappropriate as this figure included receipts from the auction of 3G—a one-time phenomenon which, if included in any growth projections, would significantly overestimate the future non-tax receipts under this head. In view of this consideration, the receipts under other communication services were reassessed at Rs. 23,335 crores as against the BE figure of Rs. 48,335 crores, thereby reducing the overall receipts under economic services to Rs. 35,039 crores. On the non-Plan side too, FC-XIII reassessed some of the items of expenditure.

Projections for the Award Period

With respect to future tax revenue streams, the Commission considered various scenarios. If all taxes grow at the Trend Growth Rate (TGR) for the period 1999-2000 to 2007-08, the implied buoyancy would be 1.43. TGRs for shorter periods yield even higher buoyancies. Assuming such a high buoyancy for the projection period would be unrealistic, given that the 2004-08 period witnessed an unprecedented growth in the direct and service tax base, the Commission decided to moderate the buoyancy estimate and the tax revenues for the period 2010-15 were projected by using an overall buoyancy of 1.33. This was derived by calculating the buoyancy of gross tax revenue, excluding service taxes for the period 1999-2008 (service taxes had a high outlier buoyancy of 4.54 during this period). This was applied on the base year estimates of individual taxes to arrive at year-wise projections for revenue from each tax item. The resultant tax-GDP ratios were 10.95 for 2009-10 BE, 11.35 for 2010-11, 11.78 for 2011-12, 12.24 for 2012-13, 12.72 for 2013-14 and 13.22 for 2014-15. The projections of the Commission were a little lower than the projections of the MoF. However, the potential to improve revenues after the introduction of GST was not factored in the projections.

Under non-tax revenues, interest receipts from State and UT Governments were projected to decline by 2 per cent each year from the base year onwards. This is to take account of the fact that the centre's loan portfolio to states is reducing as past loans are amortised and no new loans are being issued, as per existing policy. Interest receipts from railway capital are projected to remain constant at the base year level of 0.09 per cent of

GDP. Profits from RBI/banks were assumed to grow at the same rate as that of GDP. Receipts from economic services were projected to grow at an annual rate of 18 per cent over the reassessed base year. For all other items, the TGR for the period 1999-2008 was applied on the base year figures to get the annual projections.

With regard to non-Plan expenditure, the Commission concurred with the MoF view that such expenditure is, to a large extent, highly inflexible in the short run, especially for interest payments, defence revenue expenditure, salaries, pensions and transfers to the states and UTs. The Commission was of the view that there exists considerable scope to rationalize expenditures on explicit subsidies.

In making its recommendations on Plan expenditure, the Commission considered, among others, the demands on the resources of the Central Government, especially on account of the projected GBS to the central and state plans. Since projections of GBS were available only for the Eleventh Five-Year Plan period (2007-12) and do not fully cover the award period of the Commission, there was a tendency to project GBS at higher than realizable levels in order to have a larger Plan size. Further, the available projections of GBS were not broken down year-wise and the estimates of each year were arrived at during the finalisation of the annual plans.

The Commission was of the view that there are far too many practical difficulties in taking the GBS for Plan as a demand on the resources of the centre and that the balance of advantage clearly lies in arriving at the GBS residually, as has been the practice in the past. In the context of the recent decision of the Government of India that disinvestment proceeds accruing to the National Investment Fund between April 2009 and March 2012 will be available for utilisation in full on capital expenditure for social sector programmes, the Commission was of the opinion that the policy is unduly restrictive and needs to be liberalised. It recommended that the proceeds should also be utilised for augmenting critical infrastructure and the natural or environmental capital of the economy.

The Commission opined that the increasing investment needs of the social sectors such as education and health to promote inclusive growth and the infrastructure requirements of a growing economy will require greater capital expenditure. This would also "crowd in" private investments in the economy. There are also emerging needs such as environmental protection and growing urbanisation. For instance, the new solar energy programme launched under the National Action Plan on Climate Change will require enormous investment to increase the supply of solar energy in India. Equally, there will be a need for a rapid urban transport system in almost all the major cities. Since these programmes require large investments, the entire proceeds from disinvestment should be utilised to augment the budget resources of the centre to finance the changing requirements of the public capital portfolio.

For the award period, however, the Commission assumed that non-debt capital receipts, including disinvestment, will increase equi-proportionately from 0.5 per cent of GDP in 2010-11 to 1 per cent of GDP in 2014-15. Central Government borrowings were projected keeping in view the FRBM target of achieving a debt-GDP ratio of 45 per cent in 2014-15. The Commission noted with concern that the debt-GDP ratio of the centre has been unsustainably high and felt that this should be reined in. The total capital expenditure was projected at 3, 3.13, 3.75, 3.88 and 4.50 per cent of GDP respectively in each of the years 2010-11 to 2014-15. Plan capital expenditure was arrived at as a residual after providing for the normatively determined non-Plan capital expenditure, i.e. the capital component of defence expenditure; non-Plan loans to states, UTs, public sector enterprises and foreign governments; and other non-Plan loans.

Assessment of State Revenue and Expenditure

The Commission projected non-Plan revenue expenditure (NPRE) of the states in a manner similar to that of the non-tax revenues. Some of the significant items, viz. salaries, pensions, interest payments, food subsidy, committed liabilities and maintenance expenditure for roads and irrigation projects, were projected separately while the remaining items were projected in aggregate. While estimating the NPRE of states, expenditure data for 2001-08 (post-bifurcation of the three states) was used. Some adjustments were made in the 2001-08 data series for NPRE to ensure uniformity in data across states. Expenditure on power, transport and dairy was removed, as in the case of receipts, in order to ensure that states where these sectors are run departmentally are brought on the same footing as the states that have separate boards/corporations/companies providing services in these sectors. Further, in its assessment, FC-XIII did not take into consideration any subsidies in these sectors. Only food subsidy was projected on a normative basis. Expenditure on calamity relief was removed as the needs of states on this account was assessed separately.

Maintenance of roads and bridges was projected for the base year as part of the overall economic services, i.e. expenditure in 2007-08 was projected to grow on the basis of TGR to arrive at the 2009-10 estimates. While doing so, the grants provided by FC-XII, as released in each of the relevant years, was deducted from the expenditure to eliminate their impact on expenditure. The base year amount was projected to grow at 5 per cent for general category states and a higher rate of 7 per cent for special category states.

As regards to food subsidy and other non-Plan expenditure, a normative amount of food subsidy was added to the NPRE of states. Food subsidy was provided at Rs. 20 per capita per year for each of the years in the projection period, calculated on the basis of the population projected for 2008. Other non-Plan revenue expenditures under each service were projected at the respective 2001-08 TGR or 7.5 per cent, whichever is higher, to reach the base year level. Since the line between expenditure booked under different services is becoming blurred and many items of expenditure not being uniformly booked under the same head of account across states and that the practice varies from state to state, the Commission aggregated all the residual items and projected them to grow at a rate of 8 per cent, which is higher than the assumed price rise but less than the nominal GSDP growth rate.

Based on its assessment of revenue and expenditure of states, the Commission worked out pre-devolution non-Plan revenue deficit for each state. The aggregate pre-devolution non-Plan revenue deficit of the states reduced from 0.52 per cent of GSDP in 2010-11 to 0.6 per cent in 2014-15. This was primarily on account of overall improvement in the tax-GSDP ratio and reduction of NPRE as a percentage of GSDP. FC-XIII based its recommendations for grants-in-aid to cover the post-devolution non-Plan revenue deficit.

Power Sector

The deficit in power supply in the country, in terms of peak availability and of total energy availability during 2008-09, was 12 per cent and 11 per cent respectively. The National Electricity Policy envisages the demand for power to be fully met by 2012. Though electricity is in the Concurrent List in the Constitution, the primary responsibility of structuring its availability and distribution is that of the states.

Since one of the fundamental triggers for introduction of market reforms was the bankrupt finances of the State Electricity Boards (SEBs), progress in expansion of power supply and introduction of market reforms needs to be accompanied by corresponding improvements in utility finances to prevent competitive markets from adversely impacting utility finances so as to enable adequate availability of power generation capacity with the utilities.

The impact of power sector performance on the finances of the states is likely to become even more crucial in future with increasing exposure of the sector to market forces. FC-XIII found that subsidies in 2007-08 were of the order of Rs. 16,950 crores, as against enormous financial losses. The key reasons for the large and increasing gap can be summarised as follows:

(i) Inability of the state utilities to enhance operating efficiencies and reduce transmission & distribution (T&D) losses adequately.

(ii) High cost of short-term power purchases. Several utilities have not planned capacity addition in time and are relying on short-term purchases at high rates (an average of Rs. 7.31 per kwh as compared to Rs. 4.52 per kwh in 2007-08). The inability to reduce T&D losses has increased the purchase levels and supply costs.

(iii) Absence of timely tariff increases has increased the gap and has impaired utility operations further. Some states have not raised tariffs for the past eight to nine years in spite of increasing deficits.

Tariff increase requirements to bridge the gap, even in the better performing states, are as much as 7 per cent per annum on an average (considering the 2007-08 subsidy levels). In some of the poorly performing states the increase in requirements is as much as 19 per cent per annum, which is indeed difficult to achieve.

In addition to direct subsidies and subventions, equity investments made in the state utilities by the respective governments amounted to Rs. 71,268 crores as on 31 March 2008. Barring isolated instances, these investments have not been earning financial returns for the State Governments. Similarly, there is considerable debt financing to the power utilities by the states, aggregating to Rs. 70,652 crores as of March 31, 2008. Interest on this is generally adjusted against subsidy and subventions, and is rarely paid for in cash. The states have also been extending very substantial guarantees to state utilities. The overall outstanding guarantees extended by the states to power sector utilities as on 31 March 2008 amounted to Rs. 88,385 crores. Total financial exposure of the states to power utilities as of March 31, 2008 in terms of equity investments was Rs. 71,268 crores, outstanding loans amounted to Rs. 70,652 crores while outstanding guarantees stood at Rs. 88,385 crores.

The huge gap between demand and supply of power in many states, calls for large investments in the sector. Future equity investment requirements of Generation, Transmission and Distribution is estimated at Rs. 19,802 crores for 2010-11, Rs. 21,455 crores for 2011-12, Rs. 20,717 crores for 2012-13, Rs. 19,824 crores for 2013-14 and Rs. 17,739 crores for 2014-15.

Similarly, the total financing requirements of Power Sector is estimated at Rs. 75,880 crores for 2010-11, Rs. 88,529 crores for 2011-12, Rs. 93,604 crores for 2012-13, Rs. 1,01,271 crores for 2013-14 and Rs. 1,15,637 crores for 2014-15. This presents a very large exposure for states, impacting their overall finances. For some of the states, these pose a high risk to the stability of their finances. Urgent measures need to be taken to bring about efficiency in the functioning of utilities in the states.

The Commission recommended that efforts be made towards feeder separation, introduction of High Voltage Distribution Systems (HVDS), metering of distribution transformers and control of supply as per policy. It suggested checking of wastage of large amount of energy in agricultural pumpsets on account of poor equipment efficiency as also wasteful use caused by unmetered tariffs. It favoured consideration by the utilities on a large scale of Distribution franchising and Electricity Services Company (ESCO)-based structures for efficiency improvement.

On the thermal power front, the Commission stressed on the need to locate the projects more efficiently. Several states, which are located far away from the resources and are still focused on developing plants within the state, need to evaluate joint ventures (JVs) in or near the coal-rich states to reduce their costs. The states also need to initiate more competitive procurement processes as well as initiate appropriate demand forecasting and portfolio optimisation exercises. In addition, regulatory institutions need to be strengthened.

The Overall Macro-fiscal Position

The combined liabilities of the Central and State Governments have fallen consistently from 91.7 per cent of Gross Domestic Product (GDP) in 2004-05 to 81.9 per cent by the budget estimates for 2008-09. The combined fiscal deficit also fell from 7.3 per cent in 2004-05 to 5.0 per cent in 2008-09 (BE). Despite the commendable fiscal correction achieved by the centre and states, the closing debt to GDP ratio for 2009-10 is estimated to reach 82 per cent, well above the FC-XII target of 75 per cent, owing largely to the adverse macroeconomic circumstances in 2008-09. Given the imperative of creating an environment favourable to private investment in the Indian economy, it is necessary that the ratio of consolidated liabilities to GDP be reduced, not merely below the level presently estimated for the close of 2009-10, but also that targeted by the previous Finance Commission.

The FC-XIII was of the view that it should be possible to reduce the combined debt of centre and states to around 68 per cent of GDP by 2014-15. This target has been arrived at as the feasible and desirable correction, based on its projections of the medium-term macroeconomic situation during the award period and its assessment of the resource position of the centre and states over this horizon. Accordingly, the fiscal deficit targets prescribed for the centre and states are such as to secure the targeted correction in the combined debt to GDP ratio to around 68 per cent.

Roadmap and Recommendations for Central Government

A long-term and permanent target for the Central Government should be to maintain, at the minimum, a zero revenue deficit. In essence, this target is based on the 'golden rule' which is simply that, in the absence of economic emergencies no economic agent should borrow to finance current consumption. Borrowing should be undertaken for investment purposes only. In the context of the public sector, this requires the government not to use national savings to finance consumption. Thus, all items of consumption expenditure need to be financed from current receipts, a practice which is widely implemented in most countries that have successfully addressed the issue of fiscal responsibility.

While some allowances may be made for revenue deficits during recessionary phases, the medium-term fiscal framework must plan for all current expenditures to be financed entirely out of current revenues. This is an essential requirement for prudent long-term fiscal policy. Thus, FC-XIII was of the view that there is a general consensus on maintenance of the golden rule and on setting the associated revenue deficit target at zero, with surpluses on the revenue account as a desirable goal.

After necessary adjustments, FC-XIII projected Central Government debt at 54.2 per cent of GDP at the conclusion of 2009-10. Taking into account the expected reduction in fuel and fertilizer prices, along with the expected return to the trend growth rate of over 13 per cent from 2011-12, in conjunction with other reforms including reduction of subsidies along a prescribed path, FC-XIII projected a feasible level for outstanding liabilities of the centre at 45 per cent of GDP by 2014-15, while at the same time maintaining adequate resources for public investment.

Roadmap and Recommendations for State Finances

Having specified the medium-term combined debt to GDP ratio target for 2014-15 at 68 per cent and the target Central Government debt at 45 per cent of GDP in 2014-15, implies a target debt to GDP ratio of 25 per cent for all states in the same year (the state and central ratios do not add up to the combined ratio because central loans to the states have to be netted out). This is a feasible target from the perspective of the states. Due to considerable fiscal correction undertaken by the states in the 2005-09 period, their aggregate debt to GDP ratio is not expected to be higher than 30 per cent in 2009-10.

The Government of India has relaxed the borrowing limits for the states to 3.5 per cent and 4 per cent of GSDP for all the states for the years 2008-09 and 2009-10 respectively, as opposed to the 3 per cent target set out in the roadmap of the Government of India for states, following the action taken on the recommendation of FC-XII. It should, therefore, be feasible to undertake a small reduction in the aggregate debt to GDP ratio of the states from about 27 per cent of GDP in 2007-08 to 25 per cent by 2014-15, especially if the Central Government assumes responsibility for all borrowings due to unanticipated shocks and/or parameter changes of a global or national dimension.

However, a long term and permanent target for the states should be to maintain a zero revenue deficit. The arguments advanced in favour of the application of the 'golden rule' to the centre also apply in the case of the states. It is encouraging that most states in the Union are already following this rule. In essence, all that the future fiscal roadmap requires is that they continue to do so and the few states that have not yet reduced revenue deficits to zero, endeavour to do so, by 2014-15. Based on its growth assumptions, FC-XIII was of the view that all states that incurred zero revenue deficit or achieved a revenue surplus in 2007-08 should be able to undertake fiscal corrections to return to a zero revenue deficit by 2011-12. Hence, it recommends that the zero revenue deficit target be attained by all such states from 2011-12 onwards.

Grants-in-Aid

Grants-in-aid are an important component of Finance Commission transfers. The size of the grants has varied from 7.7 per cent of total transfers under FC-VII to 26.1 per cent of total transfers under FC-VI. The Commission suggested several categories of grants-in-aid amounting in aggregate to Rs. 3,18,581 crores which constitutes 18.03 per cent of total transfers.

The first of such grants is the post-devolution Non-plan Revenue Deficit (NPRD) grant. FC-XIII recommended for NPRD grants amounting to 16.26 per cent of the total grants, the lowest ever in FC recommendations. This has been possible due to the sustained efforts of states to adhere to the fiscal reform path laid down by their respective Fiscal Responsibility and Budget Management (FRBM) legislations. Particularly gratifying has been the fact that three special category states, viz. Uttarakhand, Assam and Sikkim, have graduated from NPRD. In recognition of their successful efforts, FC-XIII recommended a performance grant for these three states with the hope that other states would be incentivised to show similar improvements in future.

The second of the Finance Commission grants was recommended in pursuance of the goal of universalisation of elementary education, underpinned by the constitutional right of all children, in the age group 6 to 14, to free and compulsory schooling. This targeted grant is designed to help states overcome their resource constraint in funding this sector, while the national character of the programme is sought to be underscored by ensuring that all states receive a share of this grant.

FC-XIII recommended for the award period, a grant of 15 per cent of the estimated Sarva Siksha Abhiyan (SSA) expenditure of each state. This amount will cover the difference between the targeted state share of 50 per cent by the terminal year of the Eleventh Plan and the contribution required to be made in 2008-09, i.e. 35 per cent of the individual states' SSA share. The recommended grant for elementary education for all states, in aggregate, works out to Rs. 24,068 crores. In order to ensure that these grants do not substitute for the current expenditure of states, FC-XIII stipulated that the expenditure (Plan + non-Plan) under elementary education, exclusive of the grants recommended, should grow by at least 8 per cent, annually, during 2010-15.

Two new considerations in ToR of FC-XIII were the need to improve the quality of public expenditure to obtain better outputs and outcomes and the need to manage ecology, environment and climate change consistent with sustainable development. FC-XIII addressed these issues and recommended the third and fourth sets of grants to enable and incentivise performance for better governance and delivery of public services and for protection of the environment respectively. In doing so, the Commissioned designed some of these grants such as those for promotion of renewable energy, better water sector management and reduction of infant mortality, to be forward looking and linked to attainment of goals in the future.

The forest grant is based on data at a point in time. The formula used is essentially a reward for the present stock. The size of the grant is expected to provide the wherewithal for preservation, so as to halt as well as reverse past declines in the quantum and quality of area under forests. Further, the grant is so configured that, subject to a mandated floor, the funds are not tied to any further expenditure on forests. Beyond the mandated floor, the intent is to provide fiscal resources by which the state can enable alternative economic activities as a substitute for the economic disability imposed by forest cover. The only conditionality is that states develop working plans for each of the several forest zones into which they are divided.

The second of the three environmental grants is a forward looking incentive for generation of grid electricity from renewable sources. The grant is so structured as to reward states for renewable generating capacity that comes on stream into the grid during the first four years of the projection horizon. The third grant provisions is for the purpose of incentivising states to establish an independent regulatory mechanism for the water sector and improved maintenance of irrigation networks. Since many problems in this sector stem from lack of systematic attention by technically qualified people to the issue of the structure and level of user charges, the grant provision is conditional on setting up by states of an independent Water Regulatory Authority by 2011-12.

The fifth grant is for maintenance of roads. A proper road infrastructure is vital, not only for economic development, but also for better delivery of services such as education and health. There is evidence to show that road networks lead to, among other things, improved teacher attendance, quicker medical assistance and a greater number of institutional deliveries. FC-XIII has enhanced provisioning for maintenance, including the focus on the newly created Pradhan Mantri Gram Sadak Yojana (PMGSY) roads, in order to help in sustaining road connectivity.

FC-XIII recommended a substantial increase in the grants to local bodies, linking these grants to a share of the previous year's divisible pool. One of the reasons for this enhanced level of funding is to enable local bodies to address mitigation of environmental risks. There are no usage conditionalities attached to local grants since certification of usage has been found to act as an obstruction to the regular flow to local bodies of funding provisions made by previous Commissions. The considerably enhanced funding for local bodies should address the woefully inadequate sanitary conditions that prevail over the majority of human habitations in the country.

Towards a New Architecture for Federal Finance

The emergence of rural and urban local bodies as key players in bringing about a development transformation has been recognized by the Commission and is supported by a number of measures recommended by it. In order to foster the process, local bodies must be increasingly empowered to fulfill their responsibilities. The Commission was of the view that this would, in the future, involve a fundamental rethink of the Constitutional arrangements regarding inter-governmental allocation as well as devolution of resources to the third tier. To this end, the Commission urged careful thinking about Constitutional changes that would allow the third tier to access resources directly from the divisible pool.

FC-XIII has made a beginning by introducing an environmental dimension into inter-governmental fiscal arrangements. It is envisaged that this dimension will grow in importance in the future as environmental sustainability becomes one of the centrepieces of development policy formulation and the role of incentives in securing such sustainability can be expected to commensurately increase over time. The multidimensional approach to environmental policy within public finance is the need of the hour, looking across different dimensions of environmental sustainability and, especially, those that directly affect the poor and vulnerable in their daily lives like soil quality, water, sanitation, pollution and bio-diversity.

CENTRE-STATE CONFLICT ON FINANCES

It is a thumb rule of nature that whenever a financial dealing occurs, several differences arise out of it. In personal arise the differences do take place thereby spoiling the relations between lender and borrower. In official matters between the centre and the states regarding the finance the differences and so-called the conflicts frequently arise which are normally politically motivated. If the ruling parties of the centre and the states are different then these conflicts are severe.

As per the Constitution of India, the centre has to provide sufficient grants to the states which are facing financial crisis but due to politics, the states are not getting the adequate grants required for their development. The centre has the dominance as regards the grants to the states and sharing of resources. To review the centre-states relations pertaining to finances, many committees have been appointed from time to time apart from Finance Commissions which make their recommendations to the Central Government but on the whole the conflicts on finances between centre and the states always persist. By the time committees so appointed give their reports, the government changes with the result that the implementations of the recommendations linger on.

Responsibility and Resources of the Centre and of the States

As per the Constitution of India, the centre plays an important role in the economic development and growth of the country. The main functional features of the centre are to identify, introduce and implement the viable banking system, railways, ports, establishment of large industries, the exploitation of mineral resources and regulation of foreign trade, besides protecting the nation from wars and aggressions whereas the states have to maintain law and order, apart from providing irrigation, power, road transport facilities as well as promote and develop education, health care, agriculture, fisheries, forests, and small and medium sized industries.

To meet the expenditure, the Constitution has provided different types of financial resources which the centre gets through personal incomes, profits of companies, excise duties and custom duties, etc. while the states generate finance from land, sales tax, state excise duties, electricity taxes and motor vehicle taxes, etc. The centre gets more of revenues as compared to that of states with limited functions to perform while the states have limited resources and the unlimited function to perform. The states, according to their functions, are not getting the adequate grants for their development. In other words, the Constitution of India provides for the existence of a financially strong centre and comparatively weaker states.

Causes of Conflict Listed by the States

There have been conflicts over the question of state's autonomy between centre and states at different times. The various sources of conflict mentioned by the states are as under:

(i) The Constitution of India itself is responsible for a strong centre and weak states which is not accepted by the states who insist that the centre requires equally strong and autonomous states.

(ii) To promote cultural and special conditions of state, the kind of functions to be performed by the states require that the states should be autonomous.

(iii) The performance of the centre since Independence has been such that states have been slaves of the centre. The states are dependent upon the centre.

(iv) The centre creates unnecessary ambiguity in functions to perform which are already handed by the states.

(v) The centre is interfering in law and order affairs of states.

(vi) The centre has more financial resources and limited work to do while the states have limited resources and unlimited performance to carry the functions.

(vii) The states are always dependent upon the centre for their financial requirements with the result that the centre has been dominating the states all the time.

States' Complaint on Financial Arrangements

The centre is strong so far as the financial resources are concerned while states are weak on the same ground. This is not the assumption but the fact for which our Constitution is responsible. This is why the states are always in the financial crisis due to inadequate grants-in-aid they get from the centre because of which states have numerous complaints as regards the finances which are briefly listed hereunder:

(i) Taxes are imposed by centre under Article 269, the proceeds of which go to the states but the centre does not take much interest in the recovery of these taxes.

(ii) Right from the beginning, the corporation tax was not covered in scope of sharing with the states.

(iii) Central excise duties were expanded to include several items taxes on which were earlier levied by the states.

(iv) The sharing pool has been confined to basic duties and additional excise duties. The special and auxiliary duties were excluded from the divisible pool.

(v) The railway passenger tax was substituted by a fixed grant from the centre which was less than the passenger tax.

(vi) The proceeds were not shared with the states for the surcharges on income tax imposed by the Central Government which periodically raised the exemption limit and reduced the divisible pool of income tax.

(vii) More than 60 per cent of states' revenue comes from sales tax which was replaced by value added tax (VAT). Also the centre decided to impose excise duty on electricity, thereby removing the scope of raising electricity tariff by the states.

(viii) The states find it humiliating to make frequent visits to New Delhi for the funds.

(ix) The states do not find the certainty in budgeting. In the absence of any commitment of Central Government as regards the grants, it becomes difficult for the states to decide about the development of various projects.

(x) The states cannot fulfil the electoral promises due to insufficient funds.

(xi) Most of states have resorted to unauthorised overdrafts to finance plan projects.

Regional Imbalances: A Cause of Conflict

There has been a complaint from many states about the imbalance in industrial development which has not so far been corrected by the centre. In the absence of any development of the backward regions, the regional disparities have worsened. It was considered that the Planning Commission would bring about a fine economic integration of the country by means of rapid progress related to agriculture, power, transport and industrialisation, besides enhancement in national income, higher standard of living and reduction of discrimination among the regions. Though some sort of economic development could be seen all around, yet a balanced regional development could not be achieved. Moreover, due to regional imbalances, the states are not able to grow as they are always at the mercy of the centre for the necessary grants required from time to time for completing the projects assigned to them. It is really a pity on the part of the framers of Constitution of India that they could not visualize the financial implications of large scale programmes of planned development. The Constitution itself is accountable for regional imbalances and frequent conflicts arising due to inadequacy of financial resources of the states.

The States' Demand

Following the report of the Rajamannar Committee on Centre-State relations, the West Bengal Memorandum came out with the following recommendations as regards the autonomy of the states.

(i) The powers and functions of the centre and the states should be clearly marked and specified and if necessary, the Constitution should be amended suitably.

(ii) The centre's jurisdiction should be restricted to defence, foreign affairs and foreign trade, communications, currency and economic co-ordination. All other powers should be exclusively reserved for the states. There should be no interference or control by the centre in the exercise of the powers by the states.

(iii) The present instrument of centre's control and interference in the affairs of the states, viz. the Indian Administrative and Police Services, the Central Reserve Police, the Border Security Force, the Industrial Security Force, etc. should be removed forthwith.

(iv) The Planning Commission and the National Development Council which have an important role to play in planning and economic co-ordination should be specifically referred to in the Constitution.

(v) Seventy-five per cent of the central revenues should be automatically transferred by the centre to the divisible pool of the states and only the Finance Commission should have the power to recommend the principles for the distribution of this divisible pool among the states.

Other important suggestions made by the West Bengal Memorandum and the Rajamannar Committee on Centre-State relations included equal representation for all the states in the Rajya Sabha, the maintenance of the special status of Kashmir in the Indian Union, the retention of English as the link language between the centre and the states, the right to use mother tongue at all levels, industrial licensing to be vested with the states except for large companies of national importance, inter-state water disputes to be settled by the Supreme Court, etc.

It has always been seen that the centre and the states have a lot of problems in their financial relations, and the states are increasingly becoming dependent on the centre for their expenditure. The Central Government appointed the Sarkaria Committee with comprehensive terms of reference covering constitutional, legislative, financial and administrative aspects of centre-state relations.

The Sarkaria Commission submitted its report to the government in January 1988. According to the Commission, it was necessary to preserve the unity and integrity of the country, with the result that the Commission rejected the various suggestions made before it either to reduce functions of the centre or modify them. The Commission rejected the suggestion of transfer of subjects like preventive detention, education, labour and electricity to the state list or concurrent list on the ground that it would disturb the basic scheme of the Constitution. The Commission called for a process of consultation by the centre of all concurrent subjects. It also made a strong case for inter-state councils, for the retention of National Development Council (NDC) and for activisation of Zonal Councils.

In the financial sphere, the Sarkaria Commission favoured the amendment of the Constitution to provide for sharing of corporation tax between the centre and the states but rejected all other suggestions for enlarging the divisible pool. The Commission also rejected the suggestion that the devolution of funds from the centre to the states should be automatic. The

Commission recommended the setting up of expert committees to examine taxation reforms and for resource mobilization to study in depth the agricultural income tax and to review the loan grant pattern. The Commission accepted that the present division of functions between the Finance Commissions and the Planning Commission is cordial and that it should continue. However, it suggested that the terms of reference of the Finance Commission should be drawn up in consultation with the State Government. Finally, the Commission recommended legislation to levy consignment tax and constitutional amendment to enable levy of tax on advertisements in broadcasting.

The Central Government did not accept all the recommendations of the Sarkaria Commission. In any case, the Sarkaria Commission's recommendations are not final. However, the states welcomed the recommendations of the Sarkaria Commission regarding centre-states financial relations, viz. the inclusion of corporation tax in the divisible pool which was a long pending demand of the states. But due to its own heavy revenue deficits, the Central Government did not accept this recommendation.

To sum up, most of the conflicts between the centre and the states about the sharing of central taxes were sorted out but still the problems do exist for which the committees would be appointed from time to time to make their suggestions and recommendations to help reach cordial relations.

Government Subsidies in India 7

NIPFP Paper on Subsidies (1997)

In May 1997, the then new Finance Minister P. Chidambaram presented before the Parliament a discussion paper titled "Government Subsidies in India" which he had promised during his budget speech of 1996-97. The subsidies were classified into three categories, viz. (i) public goods, (ii) Merit goods, and (iii) non-Merit goods.

Public goods cover defence of nation, police and general administration. Consumption wise, these services are related to all, and have been defined as non-rivalry and non-excludability goods. These goods are not included while calculating the subsidies with the result same cannot be priced. The second category of goods is Merit goods pertaining to services against infectious diseases, primary education and protection of environment. Externality is an element of these goods benefiting the entire society and justifying subsidies on covering roads, bridges, flood control, space, atomic energy and research of agriculture. Hence, subsidies are justified on them.

For non-Merit goods, the cost of providing service or the commodity is more than the price fixed for extending it to the customer who is benefited in many ways as briefed below:

(i) **Cash Subsidies:** These subsidies aim to provide food or the fertilisers to the consumer at prices lower than those at which they were procured by the government.

(ii) **Interest Subsidies:** They cover the loans extended at interest rates lower than prevailing market rates normally availed by priority sector individuals for buying some vehicle or establishing a small industrial setup. This form of subsidy is also termed as credit subsidy.

(iii) **Tax Subsidies:** They relate to tax exemption on any kind of expenses, e.g. medical expenses, also sometimes postponing the collection of tax arrears.

(iv) **In-kind Subsidies:** They are subsidies pertaining to provisions of equipments to disabled individuals and free medical treatment through hospitals, dispensaries and organizing camps in various parts.

(v) **Procurement Subsidies:** They are exemplified by buying foodgrains at an assured price which is higher than the prevailing market price so that farmers are benefited.

(vi) **Regulatory Subsidies:** They are in the form of prices of steel, coal and other minerals produced by public sector for industrial inputs, which are fixed at a lesser cost besides providing the electricity to the farmers at a rate sufficiently lower than the actual cost of generation.

Estimate of Subsidies

The budget-based subsidies are considered while estimating the budgetary subsidies which are computed as excess of the cost of providing a service over the recoveries from the service. These costs are taken as the sum of revenue expenditure on the concerned service, annual depreciation on cumulative capital expenditure for creation of physical assets in the service and interest costs of the cumulative capital expenditure, equal investment in public enterprises and loans given for the service concerned including those to public enterprises. While calculating subsidies in public enterprises sometimes the recoveries are higher than the costs, thereby generating surplus which has to be deducted from the aggregate of subsidies so as to obtain the net estimate of subsidies.

Table 7.1: Finance Ministry's Estimates of Aggregate Subsidies in India: 1994-95

(Rs. Crores)

	Total cost (1)	Total receipts (2)	Subsidies/Surplus amount (3) = (1 – 2)	(4)	Recovery rate % (5)
1. Centre					
a. Merit Goods/Services	7094	171	6923	—	2.41
b. Non-Merit Goods/Services	41113	4988	36125	38.4	12.13
c. Surplus Sectors	26118	30720	–4602	–4.9	117.62
d. Non-Merit Subsidies (BFC) (Net of Surplus)	67231	35708	31523	33.5	53.11
2. States					
e. Merit Goods/Services	28567	297	28270	—	1.04
f. Non-Merit Goods/Services	72772	6752	66020	70.3	9.28
g. Surplus Sectors	–561	2989	–3550	–3.8	9.28
h. Non-Merit Subsidies (Net of Surplus)	72211	9741	62470	66.5	13.49
3. All India					
i. Merit Goods/Services	35661	468	35193	—	1.31
j. Non-Merit Goods/Services	113885	11740	102145	108.7	10.31
k. Surplus Sectors	25556	33708	–8152	–8.7	131.90
l. Non-Merit Subsidies that of Surplus (J&K)	39441	45448	–6007	100	32.5

Source: Govt. of India, Ministry of Finance, Discussion paper, Government Subsidies in India, May 1997.

In the above table, the estimates of the aggregate budget-based subsidies in India indicate that:

(i) Merit goods/services subsidies, both of centre and state governments for 1994-95 was Rs. 35,193 crores, i.e. Rs. 6,923 crores by the Central Government and Rs. 28,270 crores by the state governments.

(ii) Non-Merit subsidies of the centre and state governments aggregated to Rs. 102,145 crores. Adjusting for the surplus sectors to the tune of Rs. 8,152 crores, non-merit subsidies accounted for Rs. 93,993 crores out of which the share of the Central Government was Rs. 31,523 crores—33.5 per cent of the total and that of state governments was Rs. 62,470 crores—66.5 per cent of the total.

(iii) The recovery rate in case of the centre was 12.1 per cent for non-Merit goods/services and that of state governments was 9.3 per cent. At the aggregate level, the recovery rate was 10.3 per cent.

(iv) Non-Merit subsidies were 10.71 per cent of GDP and merit goods subsidies on all services were 14.40 per cent of GDP.

Table 7.2: Classification of Subsidies: Merit and Non-Merit Categories 2003-04

(Rs. crores)

	Current	Cost capital	Total	Receipts	Subsidy	Recovery rate (%)
Social Services	20619.42	4352.41	24971.82	497.21	24474.61	1.99
Merit I	6062.01	315.25	6377.26	2.65	6374.61	0.04
Merit II	6871.65	2959.82	9831.48	72.02	9759.46	0.73
Total Merit	12933.66	3275.08	16208.73	74.67	16134.06	0.46
Non-Merit	7685.76	1077.33	8763.09	422.54	8340.55	4.82
Economic Services	113128.96	38141.61	151519.42	60169.66	91349.76	39.71
Merit I	397.94	2.72	400.66	0.00	400.66	0.00
Merit II	26500.65	5895.83	32396.48	357.17	32039.31	1.10
Total Merit	26898.60	5898.54	32797.14	357.17	32439.97	1.09
Non-Merit	86230.36	32243.07	118722.28	59812.49	58909.79	50.38
Total Social and Economic Services	133748.37	42494.02	176491.24	60639.14	115824.37	34.37
Merit I	6459.95	317.97	6777.91	2.65	6775.26	0.04
Merit II	33372.31	8855.65	42227.96	429.19	41798.77	1.02
Total Merit	39832.25	9173.62	49005.87	431.84	48574.03	0.88
Non-Merit	93916.12	33320.40	127485.37	60207.31	67250.34	47.25

Source: Controller General of Accounts, Ministry of Finance, Government of India.

The classification of subsidies in Merit and non-Merit categories in 2003-04 is given in Table 7.2. In social services, in Merit I, the total cost during the year was Rs. 6,377 crores, against which the subsidy amounted to Rs. 6,374 crores. In Merit II, the total cost was Rs. 9,831 crores, and the subsidy amounted to Rs. 9,759 crores. In total Merit category, the subsidy amounted to Rs. 16,134 crores against the cost of Rs. 16,209 crores. In the non-Merit category, the total cost was Rs. 8,763 crores and the subsidy Rs. 8,341 crores.

In Indian Services, the cost in Merit I category was just Rs. 401 crores, and the subsidy also amounted to Rs. 401 crores.

However, in Merit II category, the cost was as high as 32,396 crores against which, the subsidy was Rs. 32,039 crores. In non-Merit category under Economic Services, the cost was Rs. 18,722 crores while the subsidy was Rs. 58,910 crores.

In both the services combined, the cost under Merit I was Rs. 6,778 crores and the subsidy Rs. 6,775 crores. In Merit II, the total cost amounted to Rs. 42,228 crores while the subsidy was Rs. 41,799 crores. In Merit, the combined cost was Rs. 49,006 crores while the subsidy amounted to Rs. 48,574 crores. In non-Merit combined, the total cost was Rs. 1,27,485 crores while the subsidy was Rs. 67,250 crores.

The relative share of individual services in total subsidies during 2003-04 is given as per Table 7.3 below:

Table 7.3: Relative Share of Individual Services in Total Subsidies 2003-2004 (Provisional)

Budget code	Service/Heads	Relative share in total subsidies
	Social Services	**18.56**
2202-01	Elementary education	3.84
2211	Family welfare	0.94
2202	General education	9.96
2220-2221	Information and broadcasting	0.83
2230	Labour and employment	0.60
2210-01-05	Medical	1.42
2210	Medical and public health	1.87
2202-80	Other general education	0.25
2250	Other social services	0.02
2210-06	Public health	0.45
2202-02	Secondary education	1.08
2235-2245	Social welfare and nutrition	0.37
2203-2204	Technical education, sports	1.08
2202-03	University and higher education	1.33
2215	Water supply and sanitation	1.00
	Economic Services	**81.44**
2402-2515	Agriculture, rural development and allied activities	36.59
2801-2810	Energy	3.93
3451-3475	General economic services	1.47
2851-2885	Industry and minerals	14.25
2701-2711	Irrigation and flood control	0.31
3201	Postal	0.30
3401-3435	Science technology and environment	4.27

Source (Basic data): Finance Account of the Union Government and National Income Accounts, CSO.

Table 7.3 shows that Social Services which include elementary education, family welfare, general education, information and broadcasting, labour and employment, medical, medical and public health, secondary education and social, welfare and nutrition, technical education and sports, university and higher education amounted to 18.56 per cent. Of these general education was the highest at 9.96 per cent, followed by elementary education at 3.84 per cent. This shows that top priority is being given to education. University and higher education got a share of 1.33 per cent. Besides, secondary education got 1.08 per cent. In total, education got a share of over 16 per cent, accentuating the government's thrust on promoting education.

Medical and public health is also in government's priority, which is evident from the fact that medical got 1.42 per cent share, medical and public health another 1.87 per cent share, public health yet another 0.45 per cent share in subsidy.

Economic Services are comprised of agriculture, rural development and allied activities, energy, general economic services, industry and minerals, irrigation and flood control, postal services, science, technology and environment. While agriculture, rural development and allied activities got the bulk of share in subsidy, i.e. 36.59 per cent, industry and numerals received 14.25 per cent of the share. In total, the share of Economic Services category stood at 81.44 per cent.

TYPES OF SUBSIDY

Food Subsidy

In our country, the food subsidy consists of subsidies to farmers through support prices, to consumers through public distribution and to Food Corporation of India (FCI) in its purchase and maintenance of buffer stock. According to data available during 1997-98 and 2003-04, the central issue price of rice was increased from Rs. 350 per quintal to Rs. 565 per quintal—an increase by 61.4 per cent and that of wheat was increased from Rs. 250 to Rs. 415 per quintal—an increase of 66 per cent, whereas the Consumers Price Index for Agricultural Labourers (CPIAL) increased by only 25.8 per cent during this period. In order to subsidise the farmers keeping foodgrains production at a comfortable level, the issue price was raised at relatively higher rate than the rise in CPIAL.

The buffer stocks in FCI godowns were too much in excess than the prescribed minimum level because FCI purchases foodgrains without any limit with the result that the food stock reached a peak of 63 million tonnes in July 2002 more than 2.5 times the norm of 24 million tonnes. By April 2004, the stocks were brought down to 20 million tonnes by exporting foodgrains at almost BPL prices. The subsidy to FCI covers the cost of handling and carrying costs of foodgrains by the FCI over and above the minimum norm. The subsidy thus is available to the farmers to the states in which FCI has the operations such as Punjab, Haryana, Western UP, Andhra Pradesh and Chhattisgarh. Minimum support Price—(MSP) is limited to only two crops—rice and wheat.

The discussion paper has suggested the following policy reforms:

(i) Minimum Support Price (MSP) should correspond to Commission for Agricultural Costs and Prices (CACP) determined cost which includes all cash costs and the imputed value of family labour.

(ii) Before every sowing season, the food procurement targets should be fixed on the basis of norms and a margin of error of about 10 per cent. FCI should suspend purpose of operations once the targets are achieved.

(iii) A system of price insurance, similar to Farm Income Insurance Program introduced recently on a pilot basis may be developed.

(iv) FCI should include a greater number of states in their price support operations.

(v) In order to enforce efficiency, the reimbursement to FCI should be on the basis of normative unit costs and actually involved quantity, instead of reimbursement on actual basis.

(vi) To improve PDS penetration and reduce leakages, the government can introduce the system of food coupons for the poor. A uniform PDS price will be fixed for APL and BPL facilities but the poor can buy foodgrains partly with coupons and partly with cash. Since the poor cannot afford monthly procurement of foodgrains in one go, the PDS purchases should be allowed on a weekly basis. Restricting monthly bulk purchases of PDS will discourage the not-so-needy from PDS outlets. This will help self-targeting of PDS.

As discussed earlier, with PDS operations confined to five states only, a huge surplus stock of foodgrains was exported barely on BPL prices. Keeping this point in view, it was proposed to extend procurement to more states and also to limit target of procurement right in the beginning of agricultural season. Such proposal does not seem to be viable. On the contrary, the government should continue to procure the foodgrains as due presently and resist further increase in Minimum Support Price beyond the increase in CPIAL. Moreover, procuring surplus foodgrains stock in FCI godowns should provide guarantee of employment to all unemployed with the expansion of provisions of the Employment Guarantee Act, covering the wages to be

Table 7.4: Growth of Food Subsidies in India

Year	Food subsidy* (Rs. crore)	Annual growth (%)	As % of GDP
1990-91	2450	—	0.43
1991-92	2850	16.33	0.44
1992-93	2800	–1.75	0.37
1993-94	5537	97.75	0.64
1994-95	5100	–7.89	0.50
1995-96	5377	5.43	0.45
1996-97	6066	12.81	0.44
1997-98	7900	30.23	0.52
1998-99	9100	15.19	0.52
1999-2000	9434	3.67	0.49
2000-01	12060	27.84	0.58
2001-02	17499	45.10	0.77
2002-03	24176	38.16	0.98
2003-04 (RE)	25800	6.72	0.93

*Other than that on sugar

Source: Budget documents, various issues; *Economic Survey, 2003-04* and CSO.

paid partly in cash and partly in kind in the form of foodgrains. This could be unique method of solving employment problem with the conversion of food subsidy into employment thereby working for the betterment of farmers apart from unemployed population, landless labourers and other semi-literates of weaker sections.

It can be noticed from Table 7.4 above that food subsidies, as a percentage of GDP have nearly doubled since the turn of the century. Since the size of India's GDP itself has grown, the amount of subsidies has become much higher than it was in the 1990s. The quantum jump was made in the initial years of twenty-first century, i.e. from Rs. 9,434 crores in 1999-2000 to Rs. 12,060 crores in 2000-01, Rs. 17,499 crores in 2001-02 and Rs. 24,176 crores in 2002-03.

The major benefits of food subsidies include food security to the citizens particularly the poor, at affordable prices, and incentives to the farmers to keep food grains production at a comfortable level. A key aspect of the system is the Central Issue Price (CIP) and its relativity to the non-PDS price fixed by those who either do not get the benefit of the PDS, or are unable to meet their entire demand from the PDS.

Fertiliser Subsidy

Fertiliser subsidy is the difference between the retention price of fertilisers and the price at which fertilisers are made available to the consumers. The difference is paid to industry as subsidy. From Rs. 6,735 crores in 1995-96, the fertiliser subsidy jumped to Rs. 13,800 crores in 2001-01, i.e. more than double the level during the five year period declining thereafter to Rs. 11,797 crores in 2003-04. Government attempted seriously to reform the Retention Price Scheme (RPS) in order to nationalise fertiliser subsidies having decontrolled the import of phosphorus and potassium fertilisers thereby providing a flat-rate concession on their imports, whereas urea imports continued to be restricted and canalized. On 1 April 2000 Expenditure Reform Commission (ERC) recommended a Group Concession Rate scheme phasing out the unit-wise Retention Price Scheme in stages over a period of six years.

As per data available, the average share of farmers in fertiliser subsidy was 62 per cent and that of industries was 38 per cent. Efficiency of domestic fertiliser industry and the domestic cost of production, besides the international price of urea, are the two factors on which any scheme of rationalisation of fertiliser subsidy depends. Gas-based plants will survive if the fertiliser sector imports are opened whereas others such as naphtha-based plants would die. This forms the reason of naphtha/fuel oil/low sulphur feed stock being more costly as a raw material than the natural gas.

As per the suggestions of the discussion paper, there is a need to reduce the subsidy to farmers as well as industry while the subsidy of short run should be continued. But wherever plenty of natural gas is available, setting up of fertiliser plants may be considered in the long run. Moreover, there is need to increase the farm-gate price of urea at regular intervals. The discussion paper has the opinion that the application of fertilisers is "more dependent on technological and non-price factors than on price or agro-economic variables. These factors include irrigation facilities, cropping pattern, spread of high yielding varieties (HYVs), effective fertiliser distribution and availability of credit. Hence the paper is of the view that increase in urea prices may not translate into lower production. It recommends public investment as "an effective instrument to promote the use of fertilisers". The rationalisation of urea price would bring a salutary impact on balanced application of N (Nitrogen), P (Phosphate) and K (Potash).

Petroleum Subsidies

These are related to two components, viz. subsidy for kerosene for domestic use and LPG subsidy due to difference between the international price and the price at which it is supplied to the consumers. There has been substantial increase in the subsidy bill of Central Government's budget from Rs. 5,225 crores in 2002-03 to Rs. 6,753 crores in 2003-04 because of the unprecedented rise in the international prices of crude and petroleum products. Accordingly, the discussion paper states, "LPG subsidy benefits largely the higher expenditure groups in the urban areas is and may be regressive". The government consequently can legitimately increase the LPG prices to reduce its subsidy bill because of a steep rise in the petroleum crude prices in world market. "With regard to kerosene, on a per capita basis, the urban areas receive a larger subsidy. The limited availability of subsidised kerosene in rural areas is regressive as higher expenditure groups receive more subsidised kerosene than lower expenditure groups.

Oil Bonds

The government issued oil bonds worth over Rs. 80,000 crores in the fiscal year 2008-09. The subsidy for kerosene and LPG is at around Rs. 3,000 crores. So the government suffered a net loss of nearly Rs. 20,000 crores in providing petroleum products to the citizens of India.

For the first quarter of 2008-09, the government had decided to issue bonds worth Rs. 24,500 crores while estimated losses of the Oil Marketing Companies (OMCs) were at Rs. 52,000 crores during the period. Moreover, the government's share of meeting under-recoveries through oil bonds is now 57 per cent compared to the earlier 42.7 per cent of the total under-realisation on fuel sale. Another 33 per cent comes from upstream companies like the ONGC, GAIL and OIL. The remaining losses are borne by the OMCs themselves.

The economists believe that these oil bonds are a very neat short-term solution that pledge our tomorrow for a cosy today. The interest rates of these bonds are estimated at around 8.75 to 9.5 per cent and reports suggest that the RBI has now stopped purchasing them under the Special Market Operations (SMO). Under the SMO, the central bank used to buy the oil bonds directly from the OMCs and pay them the equivalent amount in dollars, allowing them to buy supplies. In 2009-10 the interest burden on the oil bonds is budgeted at Rs. 5,520 crores.

The more prudent mechanism of granting statutory liquidity ratio (SLR) status to the oil bonds has not been accepted by the government. The SLR status gives immediate relief to OMCs by way of liquidity induced by participation of bigger players like banks, gilts and mutual funds, apart from existing pension, provident fund and insurance players that trade less and hold on to the papers till maturity (around 10 years). The SLR bonds are highly secured and liquid in nature as they are sovereign guaranteed. SLR bonds are those issued by the government at market rates to fund its various borrowing activities every year. Banks are required to subscribe to them, as they are mandatory requirement stipulated by the Reserve Bank of India. Currently, banks maintain 25 per cent of their net demand and time liabilities in SLR.

Rising Petroleum Prices and Subsidy Burden

The unprecedented rise in the international prices of crude and petroleum products has led to an increase in the explicit subsidy bill in the Central Government's budget. Moreover, there have been reports of under-recoveries by public sector oil marketing companies leading to demand for greater subsidies.

Retail selling prices of motor spirit and high speed diesel for the consumers are calculated by taking into account the following:

(i) basic price at refinery level on import parity basis,

(ii) marketing cost and margin,

(iii) freight up to depots,

(iv) state-specific irrecoverable levies,

(v) delivery charges from depot to retail pump outlet,

(vi) excise duty,

(vii) sales tax and other local levies, and

(viii) dealers' commission.

The basic selling prices of petrol and high speed diesel are uniform at all refinery locations throughout the country. As per the existing arrangement between the oil marketing companies and refineries, the element at (i) is revised on a fortnightly basis in line with movements in international prices. The marketing costs and margins, dealers' commission, and delivery charges within free delivery zones are also uniform. The prices at various locations vary depending upon the distance from the refinery, rate of sales tax, local levies, etc.

Although the oil marketing companies were granted freedom to fix retail selling prices of motor spirit and high speed diesel on a fortnightly basis, in practice, this arrangement has not appeared to have worked in quite a transparent manner.

In order to mitigate the hardship of oil companies, government worked out a new methodology with effect from August 1, 2004 allowing the oil marketing companies limited freedom to revise the prices of motor spirit and high speed diesel within a price band. Oil companies are permitted to adjust prices on their own within a band of ± 10 per cent of the mean of rolling average import-parity price including cost of freight of the previous 12 months and last quarter. When prices move beyond this band, the oil marketing companies have to approach the government to modulate the excise duty rates.

Policy Options

LPG subsidy benefits largely the higher expenditure groups in the urban areas, and may be regressive. With regard to kerosene, on a per capita basis, the urban areas receive a larger subsidy. The limited availability of subsidized kerosene in rural areas biases its use in favour of lighting rather than cooking. Moreover, the kerosene subsidy in rural areas is regressive as higher expenditure groups receive more subsidized kerosene than lower expenditure groups. Kerosene subsidy is prone to misutilisation as about half the subsidized kerosene supplies are diverted and never reach the intended beneficieries. These arguments suggest that the LPG and kerosene subsidies are ineffective in serving the desired objectives. Therefore, the removal of LPG subsidy in a gradual manner, or at least a substantial reduction in the subsidy element, may be recommended.

Generally, it is assumed that clean fuels like kerosene, that are relatively environment-friendly compared to fuel wood, are not used as they are not affordable because of high prices and low purchasing power of the poor households. However, it is not look of affordability, but non-availability that is restricting the use of clean fuels by poor rural households. Thus, the approach that may be sustainable in the long run for the purposes of expanding access and improving the quality of service is to create an open and competitive market with clearly defined and well-enforced rules and regulations.

Cash transfer to the poor to compensate for the reduction or elimination of subsidy does not appear to be a suitable strategy for inducing a shift toward hydrocarbons for use as cooking fuels. The urban poor and all rural households may use more wood with enhanced incomes from a modest cash transfer. An alternate approach may be to channel all sales of kerosene through the retail markets, and encourage small distributors of fuels.

SUBSIDY REFORMS AND CONCLUDING OBSERVATIONS

There are three main reasons for the increase in the Central Government subsidies in recent years: (i) moving the petroleum sector to a transparent system of budgetary subsidies and delay in the announced phasing out of the subsidies on PDS kerosene and domestic LPG; (ii) increase in explicit budgetary subsidies on food and fertilizer; and (iii) increase in input costs unaccompanied by any improvement in recovery rates resulting in escalation of implicit subsidies on a variety of economic and social services. Besides, operational inefficiency in the case of provision of any public goods or service leads to higher cost of production and greater subsidies. There is a wedge between subsidies that are actually received by the users of the service and subsidies that are borne by the government. Several types of inefficiencies accompany the public provision of services. Apart from direct costs like overstaffing, poor maintenance of assets, and procedural delays, there are systemic inefficiencies.

Subsidy reforms should aim at the following:

(i) reducing their volume relative to revenue receipts;

(ii) limiting these to only Merit I and Merit II categories while eliminating the non-Merit subsidies;

(iii) administering subsidies more directly to the targeted beneficiaries thereby eliminating input subsidies and focusing more on transfers rather than subsidies;

(iv) making these subsidies transparent by showing them explicitly in the budget; and

(v) avoiding multiple subsidies to serve the same policy objective.

Any subsidy restructuring has to address the issue of food subsidy. For foodgrains, support prices should be kept at the C2 level recommended by the CACP. To reduce operational costs, reimbursement of expenses to the FCI should be based on normative unit costs and actual quantities involved. With respect to Public Distribution System (PDS) the system of dual prices encourages leakages. A uniform price policy with a system of food coupons for the BPL families needs serious consideration.

In the case of fertilizers, both farmers and fertilizer industry have been subsidized. There is a need for policy measures to reduce subsidy to both the groups. Fertilizer subsidies should be done away with in their present form. As suggested by the report "Central Government Subsidies in India", urea imports should be de-canalized and a flat rate subsidy system may be introduced with two different rates of subsidy for domestic producers and importers in the short run, and a single rate in the medium term. Further, given the problem of domestic availability of natural gas, which is the cheapest feedstock, the option of setting up fertilizer plants in countries where natural gas is available in plenty may be considered. The fertilizer produced there can be shared between the host country and India as per the agreement reached. Another reason for the increasing burden of fertilizer subsidy is the lack of a mechanism to increase the farm-gate price of urea at regular intervals. A system that provides for such a periodic increase is required.

The domestic LPG and PDS kerosene subsidies has proved ineffective in serving the desired objectives. Therefore, the domestic LPG subsidy may be reduced or at least substantially restricted, while a more cautious approach should be pursued in the reduction of kerosene subsidies. About a half of the rural households use kerosene primarily to light their homes. Only state-owned oil companies are allowed to market subsidized domestic LPG and PDS kerosene. This has stifled competition by curtailing the entry of private retailers. A market environment encouraging fair and healthy competition is the most effective way to expand the supply and availability of competitively-priced kerosene and LPG.

Since social services are associated with strong externalities and scale economies they qualify for large subsidies in comparison to economic services. While human development is legitimately a major concern of the welfare state, it may be necessary to reassess policies in this area at the micro level to temper this concern with the equally legitimate concern for the burgeoning public expenditures.

It has also been suggested that user charges should be linked to costs. Appropriate upward adjustment of these charges would directly reduce the subsidy bill. Services need to be divided into some broad groups, and broad norms for cost recovery need to be established for each of the groups. A concrete plan would require fixing recovery targets in three phases: (i) short-term (immediate increase); (ii) medium-term (in a period of five years); and (iii) long-term (ten or fifteen years). The long-term targets should be determined on the basis of desired or optimum degree of subsidization worked out for broad groups of services. In the short-term, the target should be to recover a specified portion of the variable costs.

High costs of service provision and low or negligible recoveries through user charges are the two critical factors leading to high subsidies. Costs need to be reduced by eliminating producer inefficiencies.

Indian Currency System

8

INDIAN CURRENCY SYSTEM TODAY

Reserve Bank of India splendidly manages the monetary system in India based on the inconvertible paper currency. Rupee coins and currency notes are internal circulation whereas the rupee is convertible into other currencies of the world for external purposes.

Rupee Coins and Small Coins

Based on the decimal system, the monetary unit of India is the rupee, consisting of one hundred paise. Made of nickel, the rupee coin is a token coin having its face value higher than the value of metal. Same is also printed on paper issued by the Ministry of Finance, Government of India. The unlimited legal tenders are the rupee and fifty paise coins whereas the subsidiary coins are only limited legal tender. Reserve Bank of India controls the volume of rupees coins, paise coins and one rupee notes. The total value of rupee coins and small coins circulation amounted to Rs. 390 crores in 1970-71. Thereafter there was substantial increase in the circulation of coins, amount-wise rising to the tune of more than Rs. 6,000 crores in a span of about thirty years. Now there are two-rupee coins, five-rupee coins, and ten-rupee coins issued recently.

Currency Notes in Circulation

Reserve Bank of India, which is wholly owned as well as managed by the Government of India, is authorised to print the currency notes of various denominations ranging from two rupee to thousand rupee notes. Separate Issue Department of RBI looks after currency issue, maintaining reserves against current notes.

Initially, as the proportional system, the assets of the Issue Department consisted of two parts, i.e. (i) At least 40 per cent of total assets consisting of gold coins gold bullion or sterling securities of which the gold part should at least be Rs. 40 crores in value and (ii) 60 per cent of the assets could be in rupee coins, rupee securities of the Government of India, eligible bills of exchange or promissory notes payable in India. These original provisions have been modified many times from time to time and presently, the assets of the Issue Department consist of a minimum of gold and foreign securities to the extent of Rs. 200 crores of which gold should be of the value of Rs. 115 crores and the rest in rupee securities. The present system is termed as the minimum reserve system of note issue. The total Reserve Bank circulation of notes which amounted to Rs. 4,170 crores in 1970-71, has now risen to more than Rs. 3,60,000 crores.

The Volume of Money Supply

The volume of money in circulation, also called the supply of money refers to the volume of money with the people of the country covering the individuals and business houses. The money held by the government in its treasuries as well as the money lying with the commercial banking system is excluded and only the money held and used by the public for the transactions for making payments besides settlement of debt is included:

The quantity of money available in a country at any time or so termed as the supply of money in a spendable form is comprised of two important components, viz.

(i) Currency Component: Which consists of coins and currency notes in circulation issued by RBI; and

(ii) Deposit Component: Consisting of deposits of general public with the banks against which cheques can be issued.

The calculation of money supply in India (M1) is shown in Table 8.1 below:

Table 8.1: Money Supply with Public in India (M1)

(Rs. Crores)

	1990-91	2004-05
A. Currency with the public (a+b+c)–(d)	53050	357420
(a) Notes in circulation	53660	361210
(b) Circulation of rupee coins	940	5980
(c) Circulation of small coins	680	1460
(d) Cash in hand with banks	2230	11230
B. Deposit money with the public (i) + (ii)	39840	303580
(i) Demand deposits of banks	39170	297100
(ii) Other deposits with RBI	670	6480
Money supply (M1) with the public	92890	661000

Source: RBI Bulletin.

We will get a broader idea of money supply (M1) with the public in India from Table 8.1. The currency component of money consists of currency notes and coins in circulation but excluding cash held by banks as this cash is not in circulation. Currency money is the legal tender money with general acceptability used in all transactions as well as settlement of debts, and is also termed as common money or ordinary money. Looking at the above table, we find that the currency with the public covering currency notes and coins was Rs. 53,050 crores as on 31 March 1991 which rose to Rs. 3,57,420 crores at the end of March 2005.

The deposit money with the public is the deposit component of the money supply consisting of demand deposits of the people in banks and other deposits with the Reserve Bank of India. People issue cheques against these deposits. There are certain individuals such as ex-governors of RBI who are permitted to use RBI like any other commercial bank. So RBI has two types of deposits: one is the deposits of above designated individuals and other is the deposits of commercial banks with RBI. Hence, the deposit money covers demand deposits of the people with commercial banks and with RBI, known as the other deposits.

Common money is used for small amount transactions while bank cheques or drafts called the bank money or optional money is used for setting large transactions. It is interesting to note that the bank money refers to bank deposits but not to the bank cheques or drafts. Conventionally, the deposit money covers the general public over which cheques could be issued. In the year 1951, the Indian banks permitted the use of cheque facility against savings deposits too, while since 1978, the general practice of Indian banks is to consider that portion of saving deposits subject to the cheque system as demand deposits, and the portion of savings deposits not subject to the cheque system as time deposits.

As discussed earlier, the ordinary money or common money pertains to the currency with public in India, whereas the bank money refers to the deposit money with Indian public, giving rise to the concept of money supply in India when both are taken together. As indicated in Table 8.1, the money supply in India in 1990-91 was Rs. 92,890 crores, i.e. Rs. 53,050 crores of currency with the public + Rs. 39,840 crores of deposits with the people. The money supply at the end of 1990-91 was Rs. 92,890 crores rising by seven times to the tune of Rs. 6,61,000 crores at the end of 2004-05.

Items Excluded from Narrow Money Supply

Cash, covering coins and currency notes held by the commercial banks also termed as cash reserves of banks, is in fact not held by the public and is therefore excluded from the concept of money supply in India. It is item A(d) indicated in Table 8.1 relating to the cash in hand with banks.

Narrow Money (M1) and Broad Money (M3)

Apart from money supply, M1 discussed above is termed as Narrow Money (M1) consisting of currency plus bank money held by the people. RBI has referred to another concept of money supply known as Broad Money (M3) keeping in view the other liquid resources with the public.

According to Radcliffe Committee, "Spending is not limited by the amount of money in existence but it is related to the amount of money people think they can get hold of." So, not only money but also near-money assets constitute liquid assets in a broad sense that the people can spend at any given time. Savings deposits with post offices and fixed deposits or time deposits with the banking system offices and fixed deposits or time deposits with the banking system are included in near-money assets. Against savings deposits of both banks as well as post offices, the cheques can be issued.

Towards the liquidity of the general public, time deposits or fixed deposits contribute in the undermentioned three ways:

(i) The depositors can borrow from the banks against such time or fixed deposits in case of emergency.

(ii) They can encash their fixed deposits even before their maturity by sacrificing part of the interest.

(iii) They are allowed by some banks to withdraw, even out of their fixed deposits.

Accordingly, after Radcliffe Committee Report, the Reserve Bank of India described two concepts of money supply. Firstly, the conventional money supply M1 and other one being broad money supply designated as M3 which also covers fixed deposits with banks, apart from the conventional money supply.

Money Aggregates in India

In fact, the Reserve Bank of India has categorised four concepts of money supply in India termed as money stock measures or measures of monetary aggregates. Following are the four concepts of money supply in India:

M1 — Currency covering coins and currently notes besides demand deposits of the public. It is called narrow money.

M2 — M1 with the addition of post office savings deposits.

M3 — M1 with the addition of time deposits of public with banks. It is termed as broad money.

M4 — M3 with the addition of total post office deposits which cover fixed deposits of various types with post offices apart from savings deposits.

M2 and M4 do not carry any meanings or significance since Reserve Bank of India has never taken pains to collect up-to-date statistics of post office savings or the total deposits of the public with the post offices.

Table 8.2 shows currency with the public, deposit money of the public, post office savings bank deposits, time deposits with banks and total post office deposits as on 31 March of 2006, 2007 and 2008. Currency with the public includes notes in circulation, coins in circulation and cash in hand with banks. The total amount in this category was Rs. 4,13,119 crores as on 31 March 2006, which rose to Rs. 4,82,906 crores and Rs. 5,67,476 crores as on 31 March 2007 and 2008 respectively.

Deposit money of the public includes demand deposits with banks, and other deposits with Reserve Bank of India. As on 31 March 2006, the total deposit money of the public was Rs. 4,13,256 crores, which rose to Rs. 4,83,183 crores and 5,83,477 as on 31 March 2007 and 2008 respectively. Total currency with public + total deposit money of public shown in columns 6 and 9 respectively of the said Table together constitute M1 shown in column 10. M1 was Rs. 8,26,375 crores as on 31 March 2006, which rose to Rs. 11,50,953 crores as on the said date of 2008—an increase of 38 per cent.

M2 is comprised of M1 + post office savings bank deposits. M2 was Rs. 8,31,416 crores, Rs. 9,71,130 crores and Rs. 11,55,994 crores as on 31 March of 2006, 2007 and 2008 respectively, as shown in column 12 of the said Table.

M3 consists of M2 + time deposits with banks. M3, as shown in column 14 of the said Table, amounted to Rs. 27,29,545 crores, 33,16,093 crores and Rs. 40,06,722 crores as at the end of financial years 2005-06, 2006-07 and 2007-08 respectively. It is pertinent to mention here that bank deposits show the highest figure in money stock measures. These amounted to Rs. 19,03,170 crores as on 31 March 2006, and rose to Rs. 28,55,769 crores as on the same date of 2008, showing an increase of over 33 per cent within a period of two years.

Table 8.2: Money Stock Measures

(Rs. Crores)

March 31/ Reporting Fridays of the month/Last reporting Friday of the month	Currency with the Public					Deposit money of the Public		
	Notes in circulation (1)	Circulation of Rupee Coins (2)	Circulation of Small Coins (2)	Cash in hand with banks	Total (2+3+4-5)	Demand deposits with banks	'Other' deposits with Reserve Bank (3)	Total (7+8)
1	2	3	4	5	6	7	8	9
2005-06	421922	6190	2564	17557	413119	406388	6869	413256
2006-07	495938	6684	1577	21293	482906	475687	7496	483183
2007-08	581577	7656	1668	23425	567476	574408	9069	583477

	Saving bank deposits with banks M1 (6+9)	Post office deposits	Total M2 (10+11)	Time deposits	M3 (10+13)
	10	11	12	13	14
2005-06	826375	5041	831416	1903170	2729545
2006-07	966089	5041	971130	2350004	3316093
2007-08	1150953	5041	1155994	2855769	4006722

Note: Monetary aggregates as at end-March incorporate data on (i) scheduled commercial banks as on last reporting Friday and (ii) the Reserve Bank of India pertaining to the last working day of the fiscal year.

Broad Money (M3)

The Reserve Bank of India, out of four concepts of money supply, considers only two concepts, viz. (M1)—the ordinary money or narrow money and (M3)—the broad money consisting of M1 besides time deposits of the people with the banks. The broad money (M3) is also termed as the aggregate monetary resources of the people.

The treatment of time deposits with banks distinguishes between narrow money (M1) and broad money (M3). Time deposits of the public with the banking system are not included in the narrow money since they are income-earning assets and not liquid as such, while time deposits of the public with the banking system are covered in broad money as part of the total monetary resources of the public. People have come to consider time deposits also as liquid or monetary resources as the banks have been liberalising the rules allowing partial or full convertibility of the time deposits at the request of the deposit holders. As shown in Table 8.2 (M3)—the broad money is calculated as total of narrow money or ordinary money (M1) and time deposits of the people with the banks. While calculating broad money (M3), the Reserve Bank of India takes into account only time deposits of the people with the banking system, whereas the general public have fixed deposits with the Non-Banking Financial Companies (NBFCs) which amazingly, is to the tune of more than 50 per cent of the total time deposits of the whole of organised banking system. It was a great eye-opener to RBI when it came to light at the end of March 1997.

M2 and M4 are two other money stock measures described by Reserve Bank of India. M2 pertains to post office savings bank deposits whereas M4 relates to other deposits with the post offices. People consider these savings and other deposits with the post offices as liquid resources. In fact, this should form a part of aggregate monetary resources of the people in the country, but somehow RBI does not give any importance to these money stock measures with the result that it does not care about updating the figures for the same. For many years, the post office savings have remained static at Rs. 5,040 crores and total post office savings at Rs. 25,970 crores.

SOURCES OF BROAD MONEY (M3): FACTORS AFFECTING MONEY SUPPLY IN INDIA

As per Reserve Bank of India, there are in all five sources contributing to the aggregate monetary resources in the country (M3) as listed below, which we will discuss one by one.

(i) Net bank credit to the government;

(ii) Bank credit to the commercial sector;

(iii) Net foreign exchange assets of the banking sector;

(iv) Government's currency liabilities to the public; and

(v) Non-monetary liabilities of the banking sector.

Net Bank Credit to the Government

There are two types of extending advances called bank credit to the government: (i) RBI's credit to the central and state governments, and (ii) other banks' credit to the central and state governments. In normal course, the Central Government has its own earnings through collection of taxes. If the revenue so gathered is not sufficient, then even the government moves out to borrow the money for its routine expenditure or the specific projects in hand. The effect of reducing the money supply could be seen if the government happens to borrow the money from the general public, with the result that the government borrows money from the Reserve Bank of India by providing government securities against which RBI prints and issues currency notes. So it will have the direct effect of increasing the issue of currency notes in India by every increase in government securities with RBI, resulting in increase of money supply in the country, whereas there occurs direct effect of reducing the money supply when the government repays the loan to the RBI.

The Reserve Bank of India provides credit to the central and state governments against their cash balances as deposits. Accordingly, net RBI credit to the government becomes RBI's claims on government minus the deposits of the governments with RBI. Similarly, when the government borrows money from the other commercial banks, the volume of money supply with the public is increased. So the net bank credit to the government consists of net RBI credit to the government plus other banks' credit to the government.

Bank Credit to the Commercial Sector

Bank credit to the commercial sector is another source affecting money stock in the country. The commercial sector covers the non-governmental activities. The commercial banks extend loan to their customers enabling them to withdraw the loan amount through cheques which come back to the banking system as fresh deposits. It is termed as the credit creation or deposit multiplication. The banks multiply the deposits by providing more of loans which is of significance for the banking system to expand the volume of deposits. Deposits so created by the commercial banks are called a derivative deposits or secondary deposits.

The debt of the commercial banks is acceptable and is money, while the debt of the customers is not generally acceptable and is therefore not money. The bank deposits are no doubt significant because they constitute money and also influence the level of the economic activity in the country. More of bank loans lead to more of investment, more of production, more of trading thereby enhancing the employment opportunities. Accordingly, the bank credit to the commercial sector can be calculated as RBI's credit to the commercial sector and other banks' credit to the commercial sector.

Foreign Exchange Assets

The net foreign exchange assets of the banking system including Reserve Bank of India and other banks constitute the third source of money supply in India. When an exporter exports some commodities, he earns in terms of foreign exchange such as dollars, or currency of that country which received the commodities. The exporter gives that earning in foreign exchange to RBI and in turn RBI makes payment to the exporter in Indian rupees. Hence, whenever exports take place, RBI or some other bank would acquire foreign exchange and equivalent amount of rupees would be distributed in India. Similarly, whenever imports take place, Indian importer pays to foreign suppliers the foreign exchange through RBI. In such case, the foreign exchange with Indian banking system as well as money supply in the country would decline. In other words, the net foreign exchange assets of banking sector are the net foreign exchange assets of RBI plus net foreign exchange assets of other banks.

Government's Currency Liabilities to the Public

The broad money (M3) is the fourth source in terms of government's currency liabilities to the public, affecting the money stock in the country. One rupee notes, rupee coins and small coins printed/minted by the Government of India constitute government's currency liabilities to the public.

Two things, i.e. the volume of money supply with the people and government's currency liabilities to the public increase as and when the government resorts to issuing more currency notes and coins thereby indicating direct and positive relationship between government's currency liabilities to the public as well as the volume of money supply and monetary resources in the country. In order to arrive at the volume of broad money, all the four sources discussed above are added up.

Non-monetary Liabilities of the Banking Sector

While calculating the volume of broad money, one item, i.e. non-monetary liabilities of banking sector, viz. the paid-up capital and reserves, RBI employees' Pension Fund and Provident Fund, etc. are included in the non-monetary liabilities of RBI, whereas the non-monetary liabilities of other banks cover their capital and reserves besides other liabilities like bills payable over other assets such as premises, furniture of banks, etc. Accordingly, the Reserve Bank of India gives the summary indicated below of the factors affecting aggregate monetary resources (M3) which is also called sources of change in money stock (M3).

1. Net bank credit to the government (A+B)
   - (A) RBI's net credit to the government:
     - (i) Claims on government;
     - (ii) Government deposits with RBI.
   - (B) Other banks' credit to government.
2. Bank credit to commercial sector (A+B)
   - (A) RBI's credit to commercial sector;
   - (B) Other banks' credit to commercial sector.

3. Net foreign exchange assets of banking sector (A+B)
   (A) RBI's net foreign exchange assets;
   (B) Other banks' net foreign exchange assets.
4. Governments currency liabilities to the public
5. Net non-monetary liabilities of the banking sector (A+B)
   (A) Net non-monetary liabilities of RBI;
   (B) Net non-monetary liabilities of banks.

Hence, M3 = (1+2+3+4)–5.

THE NEW MONETARY EQUATIONS

Table 8.3: Monetary Aggregates in India

Original aggregates	Revised aggregates	Liquidity aggregates
M1 = currency + demand deposits + other deposits	M1 = currency + demand deposits + other deposits	4 = New M3 + all deposits with post offices savings banks banks (excluding NSCs)
M2 = M1 + savings deposits with post office and banks	M2 = M1 + time liability portion of savings deposits with banks + CDs issued by banks + term deposits maturing within one year	L2 = L1 + term deposits with term lending institutions + term borrowing of RIST CDs issued by FIs
M3 = M1 + time deposits of banks	M3 = M1 + time deposits of banks = M2 + term deposits over one year maturity + call/term borrowings of banks	L3 = L2 + public deposits of NBFCs
M4 = M3 = M3 + total deposits with post office	Abolished	

Earlier, Reserve Bank of India calculated money supply and monetary aggregates with four concepts, i.e. M1, M2, M3 and M4. M2 and M4 were not of significance and in practice, only M1 and M3 were considered, whereas now RBI Working Group on Money Supply has defined its parameters in revised form for measuring money supply. Savings bank deposits of post offices which were previously included in M2 as well as all deposits with post office savings accounts which were covered in M4, have been dropped. Therefore, now only three monetary aggregates M1, M2 and M3 are there as per revised monetary measures and are discussed hereunder:

(a) So far calculation of money supply with the public (M1) remains the same, viz.

M1 = currency (coins + notes)

+ demand deposits

+ other deposits with RBI.

(b) The new or revised M2 comes out to be as follows:

M2 = M1

+ time liabilities portion of savings deposits with banks

+ Certificates of Deposits (CDs) issued by banks

+ term deposits maturing within a year excluding FCNR(B)—Foreign Currency Non-residents Accounts (Banks) Deposits.

Post office savings bank deposits are excluded from new M2 while it includes the short-term deposits of one year maturity and Certificates of Deposits issued by the banks. And if desired, people can convert all these into money.

(c) The new revised M3 has been calculated as under:

M3 = M2

+ term deposits with banks with maturity of over one year + call/short-term borrowing of the banking system.

The new M3 so designated as broad money is a monetary measure of significance.

Moreover, the new concepts of M2 and M3 are the improved forms of corresponding previous concepts. Accordingly,

(a) Post office savings deposits and all other deposits of post office are not included.

(b) Short-term maturity upto one year and long-term maturity above one year are the two options of term deposits held by the public with banks.

(c) Call and short-term borrowing of the banking system gets entry for the first time.

A new concept of liquid resources in India on money supply has been introduced by RBI Working Group, which is:

(i) L1 = New M3

+ all deposits of post office savings banks excluding National Savings Certificates (NSCs).

(ii) L2 = L1

+ term deposits with term lending institutions and refinancing institutions

+ term borrowing by financial institutions (FIs)

+ Certificates of Deposits (CDs) issued by FIs.

(iii) L3 = L2

+ public deposits with Nonbanking Finance Companies (NBFCs).

Revised monetary aggregates M1, M2, and M3 cover only bank deposits and bank borrowings, whereas liquidity aggregates L1, L2 and L3 include also term deposits and term borrowings by financial institutions as well as Certificates of Deposits issued by financial institutions besides public deposits with Nonbanking Financial Companies.

Monetary aggregates as well as liquidity aggregates have also been prepared by Reserve Bank of India but practically only the monetary aggregates are meaningful.

RESERVE MONEY AND MONEY MULTIPLIER

Reserve money (RM) is nothing but the money issued by Reserve Bank of India. Reserve money (RM) is also called government money held by the people and the banks. It consists of the following:

(i) Coins and currency notes (C) held by the general public. This currency with the public in circulation is designated as C which is the total amount of notes and coins issued and circulated by RBI less the amount held by banks as cash in hand.

(ii) Other deposits (OD) of general public with RBI. Deposits of public with RBI are regarded as cashier money.

(iii) Cash reserves (CR) of banks consisting of cash reserves kept by banks with themselves and bankers' deposits with RBI which banks maintain with RBI.

Hence RM = C + OD + CR which indicates that reserve money is held partly by public i.e. OD and partly by banks, CR).

Table 8.4: Reserve Money and its Components

(Rs. Crores)

Outstandings as on March 31/Each Friday/ Last Reporting Friday of the Month	Currency in circulation		'Other' deposits with RBI	Bankers' deposits with RBI	Reserve money (2+4+5)
	Total	o/w cash with banks			
1	2	3	4	5	6
2000-2001	209560	90120	3630	81480	303310
2004-2005	357420	125230	6480	114000	489130
2006-2007	504099	21244	7496	197295	708890
2007-2008	590801	22390	9054	328447	928302
2008-2009	691153	24790	5573	291275	988001

Source: RBI.

From Table 8.4, it is clear that reserve money = total currency in circulation + cash with banks + other deposits with RBI + bankers deposits with RBI.

As on 31 March 2001, the total reserve money (RM) was Rs. 3,03,310 crores, of which the currency in circulation was Rs. 2,09,560 crores, cash with banks was Rs. 90,120 crores, other deposits with banks Rs. 3,630 crores, while bankers deposit with RBI amounted to Rs. 81,480 crores.

The total RM which was Rs. 3,03,310 crores as on 31 March 2001 rose to Rs. 9,88,001 crores as on the said date of 2009, showing a phenomenal threefold increase.

It is interesting to note that cash with banks which rose from Rs. 90,120 crores as on 31 March 2001 to Rs. 1,25,230 crores as on the said date of 2005, showed a drastic decline to Rs. 21,244 crores, Rs. 22,390 crores and Rs. 24,790 crores as on the reporting date of 2007, 2008 and 2009 respectively. This can be attributed to the fact that due to enormous spread of credit card, debit card and ATM system, more and more transactions are being carried through other than cash transactions. Banks have reduced their cash holdings accordingly.

Other deposits with banks constituted the smallest component of RM, and it did not show much increase. From 2001 to 2009 these deposits rose from Rs. 3,630 crores to Rs. 5,573 crores.

Bankers' deposits with RBI showed a steady increase from Rs. 81,480 crores to Rs. 3,28,447 crores from 2001 to 2008. But thereafter, these deposits declined to Rs. 2,91,275 as on 31 March 2009. This was perhaps due to the adverse impact of global recession on the liquidity position of banks.

The currency in circulation is one component that has shown a steady increase over a period of time. It was Rs. 2,09,560 crores as on 31 March 2001, and rose to Rs. 5,04,099 crores and Rs. 6,91,153 crores as on the said date of 2007 and 2009 respectively.

Thus, RM is the government money—the reserve money produced and issued by Reserve Bank of India and held by the general public and the commercial banks. How this reserve money differs from the common money supply (M1) is discussed below.

As discussed earlier common money M1 = C + DD + OD where C stands for the currency with the public, covering notes in circulation, plus rupee coins as well as small coins in circulation minus cash held by banks, DD stands for demand deposits of general public, while OD stands for other deposits with RBI.

Thus, as indicated in above-cited formula, the money supply with the people (M1) at any given time is comprised of (i) net currency notes and coins in the circulation (C) covering the total many issued by RBI minus cash held by the banks themselves with the addition of (ii) demand deposits (DD) with banks, which people consider as their cash with further adding of (iii) other deposits with RBI (OD), also considered as cash by the deposit holders.

Now comparing reserve money with the people (RM) and money supply with the people called M1, we arrive at the following:

$$RM = C + OD + CR, \text{ and}$$

$$M1 = C + DD + OD$$

Looking at above equations, we find that C and OD are common in both the cases. The only difference is that RM consists of cash reserves (CR) while money supply (M1) covers demand deposits of general public (DD).

The difference stated above is of significance since the cash reserve of banks (CR) is the fundamental base for the total demand deposits structure (DD) of the banking system.

Every loan given by a commercial bank gives rise to the bank deposit of equivalent amount which in fact is created with the acquiring an asset in the form of loan extended by the bank. The banks keep on enhancing the total volume of their deposits in the country by giving loans and acquiring other earning assets. Every person who has a savings bank account or a current account can meet the monetary transactions by issuing the cheques. As such, the demand deposits or cash deposits are used as money. Increase or decrease of demand deposits means expansion or contraction of money in the country respectively. So the commercial banks keep on increasing their deposits by enhancing their loans and advances. This course of action is termed as credit creation or multiplication of deposits.

On paper, we can say that banks can just acquire more of assets from the market or extend more of loans to the industrial as well as trading part of commercial activities. But certainly there are limits so far as the volume of credit creation or so-called deposit multiplication is concerned. Fundamentally, the limit is the amount of the cash with the banking system. Cash is required to fulfill the requirements of depositors as and when a demand is made. Against the cash reserve equivalent to 10 per cent of deposits, the bank can increase the volume of deposits to ten times the volume of cash reserves, whereas in case the bank keeps 20 per cent cash reserves against its deposits, then the deposit multiplication or the credit creation would be five times of the cash reserves. Therefore, smaller will be the volume of credit creation and deposit multiplication with the higher percentage of cash reserve. Thus, RM = C + OD + CR which indicates that CR is the actual base for the entire volume of deposits in the banking system. We can further say that RBI can have a bearing on the total volume of bank credit and total volume of bank deposits in the country, with the manipulation of CR.

Here the CR is so prominent that it should have been called as reserve money by RBI as other components of RM such as C and OD are held by the general public having the potential to become CR without the intervention of RBI. For example, the part of their currency holding C into bank deposits can be shifted by the public and similarly part of their deposits can be moved with RBI (OD) into bank deposits. Because of this option the whole of C + OD + CR is termed as reserve money which has the capacity to serve as the reserve base for the creation of bank accounts. It is also regarded as base money or high powered money.

Variations in Money Stock

Broad Money (M3) can be studied from two parameters, viz. components and sources. The components are comprised of currency with the public (C1), aggregate deposits with banks (C2)—which are further divided into (a) demand deposits and (b) time deposits—and other deposits with RBI (C3). Thus, broad money (M3) = C1 + C2 + C3. Table 8.5 shows that as on 31 March 2009, M3 amounted to Rs. 47,64,019 crores, of which C1 was Rs. 6,66,364 crores, C2 Rs. 40,92,083 crores and C3 Rs. 5,573 crores.

Narrow money M1 consists of C1 + C2 (–b) + C3. In other words, we include only demand deposits and not time deposits in M1. As per Table 8.5, narrow money was Rs. 12,53,184 crores i.e. Rs. 47,64,019 crores (M3)—Rs. 35,10,835 crores (time dispatch with banks).

The absolute (new addition) figures of M3 for 2007-08 and

2008-09, i.e. Rs. 7,07,815 crores and Rs. 7,46,136 crores respectively, do not show much variation. However, the variation for the period April-June 2008-09 and 2009-10 at Rs. 89,283 crores and Rs. 1,72,702 crores was most prominent.

Table 8.5 shows the absolute (new additions during the period) figures for C1, C2 (both a and b) and C3. There have been steady additions in C1 and C2 only in (b), i.e. time deposits, during 2007-08 and 2008-09. In C2 (a), the new additions during 2008-09 were just Rs. 2,875 crores as compared to Rs. 1,00,768 crores during 2007-08. New addition in C3, i.e. other deposits with RBI were negative to the tune of Rs. –3,482 crores during 2008-09, which means some of other deposits were withdrawn during this period. This may have been due to liquidity crunch in conditions of global meltdown. In fact, other deposits continued their negative trend in absolute terms during the April-June period of 2009. This incidently was the period when the global downturn continued to impact Indian currency and financial system though not in a big way as compared to most of the advanced countries of Europe and America.

Sources of money stock include the following:

(i) Net bank credit to government (S1):
   (a) Net RBI credit to government;
   (b) Other bank's credit to government.

(ii) Bank credit to commercial sector (S2):
   (a) RBI's credit to commercial sector;
   (b) Other bank's credit to commercial sector.

(iii) Net foreign exchange assets of banking sector (S3):
   (a) RBI's net foreign exchange assets;
   (b) Other bank's net foreign exchange assets.

(iv) Government's currency liabilities to the public (S4); and

(v) Banking sector's net non-monetary liabilities (S5):
   (a) Net non-monetary liabilities of RBI;
   (b) Net non-monetary liabilities of other banks.

Table 8.5: Variations in Money Stock

(Amount in Rupees crore)

Item	Outstanding as on March 31, 2009	Variations							
		Financial Year				April-June			
		2007-08		2008-09		2008-09		2009-10	
		Absolute	Per cent	Absolute	Per cent	Absolute	Per cent	Absolute	Per cent
1	2	3	4	5	6	7	8	9	10
Broad Money (M3)	4764019	707815	21.4	746136	18.6	89283	2.2	172702	3.6
(C.1+C.2+C.3 = S.1+S.2+S.3+S.4-S.5)									
Components									
C.1. Currency with the Public	666364	85556	17.7	97953	17.2	35772	6.3	24449	3.7
C.2. Aggregate Deposits with Banks (a+b)	4092083	620701	22.0	651665	18.9	57621	1.7	142626	3.5
(a) Demand Deposits	581247	100768	21.1	2875	0.5	–79325	–13.7	–33948	–5.8
(b) Time Deposits	3510835	519933	22.2	648790	22.7	136946	4.8	176574	5.0
C.3. 'Other' Deposits with the RBI	5573	1558	20.8	–3482	–38.5	–4110	–45.4	5626	101.0
Narrow Money (M1)[C.1+C.2(a)+C.3]	1253184	187882	19.4	97347	8.4	–47664	–4.1	–3872	–0.3
Sources									
S.1. Net Bank Credit to Government (A+B)	1277199	71891	8.7	377681	42.0	36124	4.0	112756	8.8
A. Net RBI Credit to Government (a+b)	61580	–115632	—	174789	—	–13	—	–11145	—
(a) Net RBI Credit to Central Government	61761	–116772	—	176397	—	1430	—	–11497	—

(Contd....)

1	2	3	4	5	6	7	8	9	10
(b) Net RBI Credit to State Governments	–181	1140	—	–1609	—	–1443	—	352	—
B. Other Banks' Credit to Government	1215619	187523	22.7	202892	20.0	36137	3.6	123902	10.2
S.2. Bank Credit to Commercial Sector (a+b)	3013337	450127	21.1	434347	16.8	30811	1.2	1640	0.1
(a) RBI's Credit to commercial sector	13820	251	—	12032	—	–381	–21.3	–1075	–7.8
(b) Other Banks' Credit to Commercial Sector	2999517	449876	21.1	422315	16.4	31191	1.2	2715	0.1
S.3. Net Foreign Exchange Assets of Banking Sector (a+b)	1352184	381952	41.8	57053	4.4	66858	5.2	–16750	–1.2
(a) RBI's net Foreign Exchange Assets	1280116	369977	42.7	43986	3.6	103932	8.4	–16750	–1.3
(b) Other Banks' net Foreign Exchange Assets	72068	11975	25.5	13067	22.1	–37074	–62.8	0	0.0
S.4. Government's Currency Liabilities to the Public	10054	1063	13.0	831	9.0	225	2.4	157	1.6
S.5. Banking Sector's Net Non-Monetary Liabilities (a+b)	888754	197219	34.7	123775	16.2	44735	5.8	–74899	–8.4
(a) Net Non-Monetary Liabilities of RBI	387927	33202	18.8	177706	84.5	97369	46.3	81	0.0
(b) Net Non-Monetary Liabilities of other Banks (residual)	500828	164016	42.0	–53931	–9.7	–52634	–9.5	–74980	–15.0

Note: Data are provisional.

Source: RBI.

Net bank credit to government as on 31 March 2009 amounted to Rs. 12,77,199 crores, of which RBI's credit to government was only Rs. 61,580 crores while other banks' credit to government was Rs. 12,15,619 crores.

Bank credit to commercial sector amounted to Rs. 30,13,337 crores, while net foreign exchange assets of banking sector was Rs. 13,52,184 crores as on 31 March 2009. Government's currency liabilities to public were just Rs. 10,054 crores, while banking sector's net non-monetary liabilities as on the said date were Rs. 8,88,754 crores. It is pertinent to mention here that during the period April-June 2009-10 the net bank credit to government went down considerably at Rs. 1,12,756 crores while bank credit to commercial sector was just Rs. 1,640 crores.

Net foreign exchange assets of banking sector and banking sector's net non-monetary liabilities showed a negative figure during April-June 2009-10 at Rs. –16,750 crores and Rs. –74,899 crores respectively. This clearly shows the adverse impact of global recession in India's financial system.

EXTERNAL VALUE OF THE RUPEE

The Rate of Exchange of the Rupee

From the external point of view, we find two main changes in value of rupee, one being that its exchange rate has decreased, which means the buying value in terms of foreign currencies has gone down substantially. Secondly, the rupee has become freely convertible which means it is exchangeable with foreign currencies for external transactions. There has been devaluation and depreciation of value of rupee. For example, as on today we pay approx. Rs. 48 for one dollar whereas sometime back we used to pay around Rs. 27 which means that rupee is said to have gone down in value. So to say the foreign currency has become dearer for rupee. Between 1982 and 1990, there was depreciation of rupee by over fifty per cent in terms of four major currencies of the world. Table 8.6 shows the falling rupee-dollar rate from year 1990-91 onwards.

Table 8.6: Rupee-US Dollar Exchange Rate

Year	Per US Dollar
1990-91	Rs. 21
1991-92	Rs. 27
1997-98	Rs. 36
1998-99	Rs. 43
2001-02	Rs. 48
2003-04	Rs. 46
2004-05	Rs. 43
2008-09	Rs. 48
2009-10	Rs. 49

Before 1990-91, the depreciation of rupee with respect to US dollar and other main currencies was because of deficit in India's balance of payments having been worsened by liberal import policy as well as the gulf war which increased the price of oil. The cut in rate of rupee brought about by 1991 devaluation was around 22 per cent in terms of major currencies of the world such as US dollar, UK Pound Sterling, Japanese Yen and French Franc, etc.

There was a continuous depreciation of rupee since 1991-92 in spite of the fact that there has been improvement in India's balance of payments position and foreign exchange reserves. There was no intervention from RBI as the depreciation of rupee was gradual. But there was remarkable speculation in the foreign exchange market and the rupee depreciated tremendously towards the end of 1997.

Serious economic crisis was felt by many Asian countries in the 1990s including Malaysia and Indonesia when their currencies fell by more than 50 per cent against the dollar. Rupee suffered simultaneously. RBI tried to intervene to check foreign exchange market speculation but in vain. Government of India however found its own level of Rs. 48 per dollar in 2002. The rupee later appreciated in value and the rate of exchange was around Rs. 43 per US dollar during the middle of 2005.

Exchange Controls

The rupee should be freely convertible to the currencies of all member countries of International Monetary Fund and this system of multilateral payments was accepted by India being a member of IMF. India in fact had strictly followed the exchange control. Under the Foreign Exchange Regulation Act (FERA), so as to conserve India's foreign exchange resources the Reserve Bank of India had adopted the rigid system of exchange controls thereby prohibiting imports of all unnecessary items and putting curbs on imports. RBI controlled all the authorised dealers through whom all the external payments were routed. So the foreign exchange had to be rationed as per availability. The exporters were paid in rupees in lieu of foreign exchange acquired by them. Indians faced a lot of restrictions as regards the sale and purchase of foreign securities in order to prevent the wrong use of foreign exchange resources as well as utilise them to import machinery and raw materials for the economic growth of our country.

The importers and exporters as well as the public had to face many difficulties and inconveniences with the foreign exchange controls and enforcement of FERA. However, from 1991-92 onwards, we could see relief with the foreign exchange control. Things were relaxed commercially in all respects. Liberalisation of Indian economy could be felt with the end of license raj and controls regime.

Dual Exchange Rate System in 1992-93

The Government of India had introduced a dual exchange rate system during 1992-93 which states as under:

(i) The existence of two exchange rates in the country that is the official rate of exchange which was controlled, and the market rate or the blank market rate of exchange, which was free to move or fluctuate as per market conditions, were accepted by the Government of India.

(ii) The entire foreign exchange remittances into India covering those earned through export of goods or services or through inward remittances were allowed to be converted in the undermentioned manner:

(a) About 60 per cent of the export earnings could be converted at the free market determined rate, and this amount could be used freely for current account transactions and payments, i.e. for import of goods, travel and remittances abroad;

(b) The balance 40 per cent of the earnings should be sold to RBI through authorised dealers at the official rate of exchange. This amount of foreign exchange would be made available by RBI for financing preferred imports, bulk imports, etc.

This system of dual exchange rate of the rupee proved to be a boon for the exporters converting at least 60 per cent of their export earnings at the market rate of exchange thereby substantially promoting exports and enhancing foreign exchange reserves. During 1990-91 to 1994-95 there was a splendid performance of the external sector with foreign exchange reserves superbly zooming from about $6 billion to the tune of more than $25 billion.

Full Convertibility of the Rupee on Current Account

As per the dual exchange rate system introduced by the Government of India during 1992-93 the exporters and the Indians working abroad faced problems as they had to surrender 40 per cent of their earnings at the official rate which was in fact lower than the market rate of exchange. Hence, to overcome this problem, the government announced full convertibility of the rupee on the trade account enabling the Indian exporters as well as Indians working abroad to convert 100 per cent of their foreign exchange earnings at the prevailing market rates.

At the next stage, the government came out with the introduction of the convertibility of rupee on current account so as to liberalise the access to foreign exchange for the current transactions of business covering travel, education and medical expenses, etc. with the aim of eliminating dependence upon illegal channels for such transactions. Considering the remarkable increase in foreign exchange reserves, exports followed by improvement in balance of payments on current account which is the successful achievement in the international sector. Dr. Manmohan Singh, the then Finance Minister, could very well justify his decision for convertibility of the rupee on current account. And, of course, the next course of action was to go for convertibility of the rupee on capital account too.

Tarapore Committee on Capital Account Convertibility (CAC)

So as to extend comprehensive access to global capital and help in better integration of the Indian economy into the world economy, some economists have been advocating full capital account convertibility (CAC) which was supported by the Prime Minister in March 2006. Accordingly, the Reserve Bank of India appointed a committee on capital account convertibility under the chairmanship of former Deputy Governor of RBI S.S. Tarapore. The Committee so constituted submitted its report on capital account convertibility on 31 July 2006 and the same was placed in public domain on 8 September 2006.

The objectives of capital account convertibility are to facilitate the cost of both equity and debt capital, to improve the efficiency of the financial sector through greater competition thereby minimising intermediation costs and to provide opportunities for diversification of investments by residents.

The Tarapore Committee prescribed the following pre-conditions before adopting CAC:

(i) Fiscal deficit should be reduced to 3.5 per cent so as to reduce government debt. A consolidated sinking fund should also be set up.

(ii) The government should fix the annual inflation target between 3 to 5 per cent.

(iii) The financial sector should be strengthened pertaining to interest rates, non-paying assets and cash reserve ratio.

The benefits of CAC as per the committee are:

(i) Availability of large funds to supplement domestic resources and thereby promote economic growth.

(ii) Improved access to international financial markets and reduction in the cost of capital.

(iii) Incentive for Indians to acquire and hold international securities and assets.

(iv) Improvement of the financial system in the context of global competition.

Following are the recommendations made by Tarapore Committee:

(i) Indian companies would be allowed to issue foreign currency denominated bonds to local investors, to invest in such bonds and deposits, to issue global deposit. receipts without government approval, to go for external commercial borrowings within certain limits, etc.

(ii) Indian residents would be permitted to have foreign currency denominated deposits with banks in India, to make financial capital transfers to other countries within certain limits, to take loans from non-relatives and others upto a ceiling of $1 million, etc.

(iii) Indian banks would be allowed to borrow from overseas markets for short term and long term upto certain limits, to invest in overseas money markets, to accept deposits and extend loans denominated in foreign currency. It is also applicable to financial institutions and intermediaries.

(iv) All Indian financial institutions which fulfil certain regulatory and prudential requirements would be allowed to participate in foreign exchange market along with authorised dealers who are at present banks, and later some NBFCs would be included.

(v) Banks and financial institutions would be allowed to operate in domestic and international markets to buy and sell gold freely as well as offer gold denominated deposits and loans.

(vi) The Committee recommended to meet the targets related to fiscal responsibility and budget management, shifting from present measure of fiscal deficit to a measure of public sector borrowing requirement, segregating government debt management and monetary policy operations through the setting up of the Office of Public Debt independent of Reserve Bank of India, imparting greater autonomy and transparency in the conduct of monetary policy.

INDIA'S FOREIGN EXCHANGE RESERVES

According to Reserve Bank of India, the foreign exchange position as on today is comfortable on all norms of adequacy as well. The ratio of foreign exchange reserves to external debt rose from 7 per cent in 1990-91 to 72 per cent in 2002-03 and further to 117 per cent in 2006-07. The ratio of reserves to short-term debt rose from 68.3 per cent in 1990-91 to 75.9 per cent in 2006-07. So far as the money-based indicators are concerned, situation is certainly much better now. The proportion of foreign exchange reserves to broad money rose from 4.3 per cent in 1990-91 to 26.2 per cent in 2006-07. The level of foreign exchange reserves has considerably increased from US$ 5.8 billion at the end of March 1991 to $ 99.2 billion at the end of March 2007 and $ 314 billion at the end of May 2008—a hefty $ 115 billion increase over the end of March 2007. The traditional measure of trade-based indicator of reserve adequacy, i.e. the import cover which shrank to three weeks of imports by the end of December 1990 has improved significantly to about 13 months. Total foreign investment inflows increased from $ 559 million in 1992-93 to $ 26.53 billion at the end of March 2007. Large NRI deposits and FII investments have played a vital role in building up the foreign exchange reserves.

Low Foreign Exchange Reserves and IMF

During the '60s and '70s India had faced severe financial problems, with the result that it approached International Monetary Fund to meet the balance of payments deficits. Earlier, during 1948-49, India had borrowed $ 100 million from IMF which was returned by 1956-57. India had also received help of $ 200 million in 1957 followed by another $ 250 in 1961.

Again with continuing the financial crisis, India's balance of payments position worsened with highly critical stage and accordingly IMF was kind enough to grant a loan under Extended Fund Facility of SDRs 5 billion which was record-breaking being the single largest loan made by IMF to a member country. India of course has utilized the loan facility in a desired manner, having used only SDRs 3.9 billion and surrendered the balance amount to IMF. Thereafter, our country has attained rapid and tremendous progress in all sectors thereby building a good global image.

Foreign Exchange Reserves Crisis, 1991

The fall in the value of the rupee began with its devaluation in July 1991. Devaluation means a deliberate reduction in the external value of the domestic currency in relation to a foreign currency which indicates a policy decision. Such a decision is taken by the government or RBI. Depreciation relates to a fall in the value of the domestic currency caused by the demand for foreign currency exceeding its supply in the market. In such a case, one has to pay more than before to get a unit of foreign currency. This type of fall occurs in the market on its own. Prior to 1991 devaluation, rate of exchange was around Rs. 21 per US dollar (June 1991) whereas in July 1991, after the devaluation, it came to about Rs. 26 per US dollar. In case of Pound Sterling, the rate of exchange was over Rs. 34 prior to devaluation and about Rs. 42 after devaluation.

During the period 1985-1990, a severe financial crisis occurred because of internal fiscal deficits and external balance of payments deficits. India's foreign exchange reserves sharply declined from $7 billion in 1979-80 to merely $750 million in January 1991, reaching a very critical stage having the foreign exchange reserves just of two weeks' import requirements. At that time the rate of exchange of rupee was $ 1 = Rs. 20.

By March 1993 India's foreign debt was $ 90 billion on account of commercial borrowings in the global markets at high rates of interest, putting India into the debt trap with budget deficits and rising inflation. It was also not easy for India to raise loans from international markets in such an adverse situation. So as to find a solution to such economic crisis, Government of India had to take necessary steps.

The government sold about 20 tonnes of confiscated gold in the global markets for $ 200 million equivalent to

Rs. 4,000 crores so as to meet India's international obligations. Simultaneously, India received assistance from Asian Development Bank, Japan, Germany and other countries. World Bank was approached by India for a structural adjustment loan of $ 500 million but it could not be materialized. IMF too prescribed some conditions for giving loan of $ 2.5 billion which were opposed by some Indian political parties.

Dr. Manmohan Singh, the then Finance Minister initiated some steps to speed up the economic reforms since 1990-91 helping India to accumulate large foreign exchange reserves.

Table 8.7: Foreign Exchange Reserves of India

(millions of US dollars)

Year	Gold	SDRs	Foreign currency assets	Total
(1)	(2)	(3)	(4)	(2+3+4)
1970-71	240	150	580	970
1980-81	370	600	5850	6820
1990-91	3,500	100	2230	5830
2000-01	2,730	2	39550	42280
2004-05	4,500	5	135570	144515
2005-06	4,864	21	142308	147193
2006-07	6,784	2	192393	199179
2007-08	10,039	18	299666	309723
2008-09	8,332	3	238014	246349

Note: Reserve tranche position in IMF of $ 1480 million is included in total exchange reserves in 2004-05.

Source: *RBI Bulletin*.

Mounting Forex Reserves

Both domestic as well as international conditions have resulted into enhancement in India's forex reserves. So as to keep a check on the recession and to stabilise its economy, America had cut the interest rate adequately. However, India could fetch NRI investments in spite of cut in relatively higher interest rate in India. There was a booming trend in the stock market especially since May 2003, attracting foreign institutional investors to India, resulting into rise in forex resources. The financial year 2007-08 saw India's foreign excahnge reserves swell by more than 1 billion to US$ 3,09,723. But during the year 2008-09 there was some decline as the reserves were US$ 2,46,349. This was due to global recession.

In fact, so much of rise in forex resources could have increased the money supply in India whereas it pushed up the inflation, increased imports but somehow RBI acted promptly to neutralize the adverse influence of huge inflow of dollars. Dollars were purchased by RBI on one side and simultaneously government securities were sold in order to wipe out liquidity, with the result there was no inflationary pressure.

Some of forex reserves are considered as the hot money which enters India through stock market speculation. Our country does not have to worry with large forex reserves in its pocket. But the question is how the same are to be managed? How much forex reserves should RBI keep to meet sudden withdrawals and what about the balance? As per the suggestion of Planning Commission, RBI should divert the same for the infrastructure development of the country such as the construction of roads, ports, airports and power generation projects, etc.

Investment in infrastructure is of long-term nature and hence an objection came up because large forex reserves have entered through stock market speculation and may be withdrawn at any time with a short notice for which RBI has to be ready all the time. But there is no harm in utilizing the forex reserves partly for the infrastructural development instead of keeping the same idle. There is huge demand for development of infrastructure especially building roads, bridges and food storage godowns.

There was a time when Indian Government used to approach IMF for loan during financial crisis but now with large foreign exchange reserves, India walks proudly among the comity of nations, having been invited by IMF to contribute to its Financial Transactions Plan enabling IMF to extend finance to other member countries to meet their financial obligations.

Management of Reserves

The demands placed on the foreign exchange reserves vary widely depending upon factors including the exchange rate regime adopted the extent of openness of the economy, the size of the external sector in the GDP and the nature of markets operating in the country. Even within this divergent framework most countries have adopted the primary objective of reserve management as preservation of the long-term value of the reserves in terms of purchasing power and the need to minimise risk and volatility in returns. Safety and liquidity constitute the twin objectives of reserve management in India, while return optimisation becomes an embedded strategy within this framework.

Legal Framework and Policies

The Reserve Bank of India Act 1934 provides the legal framework for deployment of the foreign currency assets (FCA) and gold, defining the broad parameters in respect of currencies, instruments, issuers and counterparties. The essential legal framework for reserves management is provided in Subsections 17(6A), 17(12), 17(12A), 17(13) and 33(6) of the above Act. The law broadly permits the following investment categories:

(i) Deposits with other central banks and the Bank for International Settlements (BIS).

(ii) Deposits with foreign commercial banks.

(iii) Debt instruments representing sovereign/sovereign-guaranteed liability with residual maturity for the debt papers not exceeding 10 years.

(iv) Other instruments/institutions as approved by the Central Board of the Reserve Bank in accordance with the provisions of the Act.

(v) Dealing in certain types of derivatives.

The Reserve Bank of India has framed a set guidelines stipulating stringent criteria for issuers/counterparties/investments with a view to enhancing the safety and liquidity aspects of the reserves.

Review of Growth of Reserves Since 1991

India's foreign exchange reserves, which stood at US$ 5.8 billion at end-March 1991 increased gradually to US$ 25.2 billion by end-March 1995. The growth continued in the latter half of the 1990s with the reserves touching the level of US$ 38.0 billion by end-March 2000. Thereafter, the reserves grew fast and rose to US$ 113.0 billion by end-March 2004, US$ 309.7 billion by end-March 2008. Due to global financial crisis, the reserves declined to US$ 252.0 billion by end-March 2009. The reserves increased to US$ 281.3 billion by end-September 2009 which may be taken as a sign of recovery. The yearwise detail is provided in Table 8.8.

Although both US dollar and euro are intervention currencies and the FCA are maintained in major currencies like US dollar, euro, pound sterling and Japanesê yen, the foreign

Table 8.8: Movement in Foreign Exchange Reserves

(US$ million)

Date	FCA	SDR	Gold	RTP	Forex Reserves
31-Mar-06	145108	3 (2)	5755	756	151622
30-Sep-06	158340	1 (1)	6202	762	165305
31-Mar-07	191924	2 (1)	6784	469	199179
30-Sep-07	239954	2 (1)	7367	438	247761
31-Mar-08	299230	18 (11)	10039	436	309723
30-Sep-08	277300	4 (2)	8565	467	286336
31-Mar-09	241426	1 (1)	9577	981	251985
30-Sep-09	264373	5224 (3297)*	10316	1365	281278

Source: RBI.

Notes: 1. FCA (Foreign Currency Assets): FCAs are maintained as a multi-currency portfolio comprising major currencies, such as, US dollar, euro, pound sterling, Japanese yen, etc. and is valued in terms of US dollars.

2. FCA excludes US$ 250.0 million invested in foreign currency denominated bonds issued by IIFC (UK) since March 20, 2009.

3. SDRs (Special Drawing Rights): Values in SDR have been indicated in parentheses.

4. Gold: Physical stock has remained unchanged at approximately 357.75 tonnes as at end-September 2009.

5. RTP refers to the Reserve Tranche Position in the IMF.

* Includes SDRs 3082.5 million (equivalent to US$ 4883 million) allocated under general allocation and SDRs 214.6 million (equivalent to US$ 340 million) allocated under special allocation by the IMF on August 28, 2009 and September 9, 2009 respectively.

exchange reserves are denominated and expressed in US Dollar only. The foreign exchange reserve data prior to 2002-03 do not include the Reserve Tranche Position (RTP) in the International Monetary Fund (IMF). Movements in the FCA occur mainly on account of purchases and sales of foreign exchange by RBI in the foreign exchange market in India. In addition, income arising out of the deployment of foreign exchange reserves is also held in the portfolio of the reserves. External aid receipts of the Central Government also flow into the reserves. The movement of the US dollar against other currencies in which FCA are held also impact the level of reserves in US dollar terms.

Sources of Accretion to the Reserves

The details the major sources of accretion to foreign exchange reserves during the period from March 1991 to end-September 2009 are given in Table 8.9.

Table 8.9: Sources of Accretion to Foreign Exchange Reserves Since 1991

(US$ billion)

		Items	1991-92 to 2009-10 (up to end-September 2009)
A		Reserves as at end-March 1991	5.8
B.I.		Current Account Balance	–97.9
B.II.		Capital Account (net) (a to e)	357.5
	(a)	Foreign Investment	185.7
	Of which:		
		(i) FDI	90.4
		(ii) FII	66.9
	(b)	NRI Deposits	36.9
	(c)	External Assistance	19.2
	(d)	External Commercial Borrowings	68.7
	(e)	Other items in Capital Account*	47.0
B.III.		Valuation Change	15.8
		Reserves as at end-September 2009 (A+BI+BII+BIII)	281.2

Source: RBI.

As can be seen from the table, the major sources of accretion to India's forex reserves since 1991 have been capital account, and foreign investment. Foreign Direct Investment (FDI), Foreign Institutional Investment (FII) and NRI deposits have been the major contributors of foreign investment during the said period.

Sources of Variation in Foreign Exchange Reserves

The foreign exchange reserves increased by US$ 9,533 million during April-September 2009 as against a decline of US$ 2,499 million during April-September 2008. The valuation gain, reflecting the depreciation of the US dollar against the major currencies, accounted for US$ 19,760 million during April-September 2009 as compared with a valuation loss of US$ 20,888 million during April-September 2008. The valuation gain during April-September 2009 accounted for 67.5 per cent of the total increase in foreign exchange reserves. Besides the valuation gain, inflows under foreign investments and NRI deposits and SDR allocations by the IMF contributed to the increase in foreign exchange reserves during April-September 2009. The IMF allocated SDR 3,082.5 million (equivalent to US$ 4,883 million) under general allocation on August 28, 2009 and SDR 214.6 million (equivalent to US$ 340 million) under special allocation on September 9, 2009. The allocations were made by the IMF as a part of the Fund's efforts to provide liquidity to the global economic system by supplementing the Fund's member countries' foreign exchange reserves.

External Liabilities vis-à-vis Foreign Exchange Reserves

The accretion of foreign exchange reserves has to be seen in the light of total external liabilities of the country. India's International Investment Position (IIP), which is a summary record of the stock of country's external financial assets and liabilities, is shown in Table 8.10 below:

Table 8.10: International Investment Position of India

(US$ billion)

Item	September 2009*
A Total Foreign Assets	378.6
1. Direct Investment Abroad	74.1
2. Portfolio Investment	0.8
3. Other Investments	22.4
4. Foreign Exchange Reserves	281.3
B Total Foreign Liabilities	476.4
1. Direct Investment in India	153.8
2. Portfolio Investment	106.0
3. Other Investments	216.6
Net IIP (A–B)	(–) 97.8

* The figures are provisional.
Source: RBI.

Adequacy of Reserves

An important parameter in gauging the ability to absorb external shocks is the adequacy of reserves. With the changing profile of capital flows, the traditional approach of assessing reserve adequacy in terms of import cover has been broadened to include a number of parameters which take into account the size, composition and risk profiles of various types of capital flows and the types of external shocks to which the economy is vulnerable. The High Level Committee on Balance of Payments, which was chaired by Dr. C. Rangarajan, former Governor of the Reserve Bank of India, had suggested that, while determining the adequacy of reserves, due attention should be paid to payment obligations, in addition to the traditional measure of import cover of 3 to 4 months. In 1997, the Report of Committee on Capital Account Convertibility under the chairmanship of Shri S.S. Tarapore, suggested alternative measures of adequacy of reserves which, in addition to trade-based indicators, also included money-based and debt-based indicators. Similar views have been held by the Committee on Fuller Capital Account Convertibility. In the recent period, assessment of reserve adequacy has been influenced by the introduction of new measures. One of the measures requires that the usable foreign exchange reserves should exceed scheduled amortisation of foreign currency debts during the following year, while the another measure is based on a 'Liquidity at Risk' rule that takes into account the foreseeable risks that a country could face. This approach requires that a country's foreign exchange liquidity position could be calculated under a range of possible outcomes for relevant financial variables such as exchange rates, commodity prices, credit spreads, etc.

The traditional trade-based indicator of reserve adequacy, i.e. import cover of reserves, which fell to a low of three weeks of imports at end-December 1990, rose to 11.5 months of imports at end-March 2002 and increased further to 14.2 months of imports or about five years of debt servicing at end-March 2003. At end-March 2004, the import cover of reserves was 16.9 months, which came down to 9.8 months as at end-March 2009. However, the import cover increased to 12.4 months as at end-September 2009. The ratio of short-term debt to the foreign exchange reserves declined from 146.5 per cent at end-March 1991 to 12.5 per cent as at end-March 2005, but increased slightly to 12.9 per cent as at end-March 2006. With expansion in the coverage of short-term debt, the ratio further increased to 14.1 per cent at end-March 2007, to 14.8 per cent at end-March 2008 and then to 17.2 per cent at end-March 2009. The ratio of short-term debt to foreign exchange reserves worked out to 15.1 per cent as at end-September 2009. The ratio of volatile capital flows (defined to include cumulative portfolio inflows and short-term debt) to the reserves declined from 146.6 per cent as at end-March 1991 to 35.0 per cent at end-March 2004. This ratio increased to 48.9 per cent as at end-September 2009 from 47.9 per cent in March 2009.

Management of Gold Reserves

The Reserve Bank held about 357.75 tonnes of gold forming about 3.7 per cent of the total foreign exchange reserves in value terms as at the end of September 2009. Of these, 65.49 tonnes are being held abroad since 1991 in deposits/safe custody with the Bank of England and the Bank for International Settlements.

In November 2009, the Reserve Bank concluded the purchase of 200 metric tonnes of gold from the International Monetary Fund (IMF), under the IMF's limited gold sales programme. The purchase was an official sector transaction and was executed over a two week period during October 19-30, 2009 at market-based prices. As a result of this purchase, the Reserve Bank's gold holdings have increased from 357.75 tonnes to 557.75 tonnes.

Investment Pattern of the Foreign Currency Assets

The foreign currency assets are invested in multi-currency, multi-asset portfolios as per the best international practices followed in this regard. As at end-September 2009, out of the total foreign currency assets of US$ 264.4 billion, an amount of US$ 148.0 billion was invested in securities, US$ 111.3 billion was deposited with other central banks, BIS and the IMF and US$ 5.1 billion was kept in the form of deposits with foreign commercial banks/funds placed with the External Asset Managers (EAMs). A small portion of the reserves has been assigned to the EAMs with the main objective of gaining access to and deriving benefits from their expertise and market research.

The rate of earnings on foreign currency assets and gold, after accounting for depreciation, decreased from 4.82 per cent in July 2007-June 2008 to 4.16 per cent in July 2008-June 2009. This may be attributed to worldwide decrease in interest rates following the global financial crisis. Things are expected to be better in the subsequent periods.

Pre-payment of Foreign Currency Loans

The significant increase in forex reserves gave India the luxury of prepayment of certain high-cost foreign currency loans of the Government of India from the Asian Development Bank (ADB) and the International Bank for Reconstruction and Development (IBRD)/World Bank amounting to US$ 3.03 billion during February 2003. During 2003-04, prepayment of certain high-cost loans to the IBRD and the ADB amounting to US$ 2.6 billion was made by the government. In addition, prepayment of bilateral loans amounting to US$ 1.1 million was also made. Thus, the total quantum of prepayments was of the order of US$ 3.7 billion during 2003-04. During 2004-05, prepayment of bilateral loans to the tune of US$ 30.3 million was made. During 2006-07, there was only one prepayment of US$ 58.7 million in the month of April 2006. There was no prepayment of any debt thereafter till September 30, 2009.

Financial Transaction Plan (FTP) of the IMF

International Monetary Fund designated India as a creditor under its Financial Transaction Plan (FTP) in February 2003. In terms of this arrangement, India participated in the IMF's financial support to Burundi in March-May 2003 with a contribution of SDR 5 million and to Brazil in June-September 2003 with SDR 350 million. In December 2003, SDR 43 million was made available to Indonesia under the FTP. During 2004-05, SDR 61 million was made available under the FTP to countries like Uruguay, Haiti, Dominican Republic and Sri Lanka. During May-June 2005, SDR 34 million was made available to Turkey and Uruguay. During 2008-09, SDR 403 million was made available to Bangladesh, Turkey, Pakistan and Georgia. Further, during April-September 2009, SDR 130 million was made available to Romania and SDR 50 million to Sri Lanka. Thus, the total purchase transactions amounted to SDR 1076 million as at the end of September 2009. There were 21 repurchase transactions during the period from November 2005 to September 2009 totalling SDR 772 million received from 7 countries, viz. Turkey, Algeria, Brazil, Indonesia, Uruguay, Ukraine and Moldova.

Risk Management of Foreign Exchange Reserves

Sound risk management is necessary for efficient foreign exchange reserves management. The strategy for reserves management emphasizes on managing and controlling the exposure to financial and operational risks associated with deployment of reserves. The broad strategy for reserve management including currency composition and investment policy is decided by RBI in consultation with the Government of India. The risk management functions are aimed at ensuring development of sound governance structure in line with the best international practices, improved accountability, a culture of risk awareness across all operations and efficient allocation of resources for development of in-house skills and expertise. The risks attendant on deployment of reserves, i.e. credit risk, market risk, liquidity risk and operational risk and the systems employed to manage these risks are briefly discussed below.

Credit Risk

Credit risk is defined as the potential that a borrower or counterparty will fail to meet its obligation in accordance with agreed terms. RBI has been extremely sensitive to the credit risk it faces on the investment of foreign exchange reserves in the international markets. Investments in bonds/treasury bills, which represent debt obligations of highly rated sovereigns and supranational entities, do not give rise to any substantial credit risk. Placement of deposit with BIS and other central banks is also considered credit risk-free. However, placement of deposits with commercial banks and transactions in foreign exchange and bonds/treasury bills with commercial banks/investment banks and other securities firms give rise to credit risk.

Credit risk has been in focus since the onset of the credit crisis in the US financial markets and its contagion effect on other economies leading to global financial crisis during the second half of 2008 and during 2009. RBI continues to apply stringent credit criteria for selection of counterparties. Credit exposure vis-à-vis sanctioned limit in respect of approved counterparties is monitored continuously. Besides, the financial strength of counterparties is constantly under watch. The basic objective of such an on-going exercise is to assess whether counterparty's credit quality is under potential threat.

Market Risk

Market risk arises on account of exchange rate and interest rate fluctuations. These are analysed under different types of risks, as below.

Currency Risk: Currency risk arises due to uncertainty in exchange rates. Decisions are taken regarding the long-term exposure in different currencies depending on the likely movements in its exchange rate and other considerations in the medium and long-term. The bases on which decisions are taken in this regard include, maintenance of major portion of reserves in the intervention currency, the approximate currency profile of the reserves in line with the changing external trade profile of the country, benefit of diversification, etc. The decision-making process is supported by periodic reviews of the strategy.

Interest Rate Risk: The most important aspect of the management of interest rate risk is to protect the value of the investments as much as possible from the adverse impact of the interest rate movements. The interest rate sensitivity of the reserves portfolio is identified in terms of benchmark duration and the permitted deviation from the benchmark. The focus of the investment strategy revolves around the overwhelming need to keep the interest rate risk of the portfolio reasonably low with a view to minimising losses arising out of adverse interest rate movements, if any.

Liquidity Risk

Liquidity risk involves the risk of not being able to sell an instrument or square a position when required without facing significant costs. The reserves need to maintain a high level of liquidity at all times in order to be able to meet any unforeseen and emergency needs. Since any adverse development has to be met with reserves maintaining a highly liquid portfolio is a necessary constraint in the investment strategy. The choice of instruments determines the liquidity of the portfolio. For example, in some markets, treasury securities could be liquidated in large volumes without much distortion to the price in the market and, thus, can be considered as liquid. With the exception of fixed deposits with the foreign commercial banks and the central banks and securities issued by supranationals, almost all other types of investments are in highly liquid instruments which could be converted into cash at short notice. RBI closely monitors the portion of the reserves which could be converted into cash at a very short notice to meet any contingent needs.

FOREIGN EXCHANGE MANAGEMENT ACT (FEMA)

On 4 August 1998, The Foreign Exchange Management Bill (FEMA) was introduced in the Parliament. The Bill aimed "to consolidate and amend the law relating to foreign exchange with the objective of facilitating external trade and payments and for promoting the orderly development and maintenance of foreign exchange market in India".

So as to regulate the operation of foreign controlled companies in our country, the Government of India enacted the Foreign Exchange Regulation Act 1947 (FERA) after Independence which was later amended in 1973. The main objectives of the same were the conservation of India's precious foreign exchange resources and the issue of guidelines to the foreign investors to invest in India's core sectors employing sophisticated foreign technology.

At a time when almost all the parameters of the economy were sought to be controlled as well as regulated by the government, the FERA 1973 was enacted when India's foreign exchange reserves were less than a billion dollars. As per FERA, all the transactions in foreign exchange and with non-residents were totally prohibited though there were some specific relaxations.

In a similar way, the non-residents were not permitted to have any type of dealings in India. The Foreign Exchange Management Act (FEMA) was introduced in July 1998 in Parliament to repeal FERA 1973 and to consolidate and simplify the law relating to foreign exchange with the aim of facilitating external trade and payments as well as for promoting foreign exchange market in India.

The Salient Features of FEMA

According to Section 3 of FEMA 1998, no person shall deal in or transfer foreign exchange or foreign security to any unauthorised person.

Section 4 provides that no resident in India shall acquire, hold, own, possess or transfer any foreign exchange, foreign security or any immovable property situated outside India, except as otherwise provided in this Act.

Section 5 provides that any person may sell or draw foreign exchange to or from an authorised person if such sale or drawal is a current account transaction, provided that the Central Government may, in public interest and in consultation with RBI, impose such reasonable restrictions for current account transactions as may be prescribed.

Section 6 states that any person may sell or draw foreign exchange to or from an authorised person for a capital account transaction. RBI, in consultation with the Government of India, may specify the class of capital account transactions which are permissible, the limit upto which foreign exchange shall be admissible for such transactions. RBI may prohibit, restrict or regulate the following:

(i) transfer or issue any foreign security by a person resident in India, by a person outside India or by any branch office or agency in India of a person resident outside India.

(ii) Any borrowing or lending in foreign exchange in whatever form or by whatever name called.

(iii) Any borrowing or lending in rupees between a person resident in India and person resident outside India.

(iv) Deposits between persons resident in India and persons resident outside India.

(v) Export, import or holding of currency or currency notes.

(vi) Transfer of immovable property outside India, other than a lease not exceeding five years by a person resident in India. Likewise, acquisition or transfer of immovable property in India other than a lease not exceeding five years by a person resident outside India.

(vii) Giving a guarantee or surety in respect of any debt, obligation or other liability incurred by a person resident in India and owed to a person resident outside India.

Section 6, Subsection 4 provides that a person resident in India may hold, own, transfer or invest in foreign currency, foreign security or any immovable property situated outside India if such currency, security or property was acquired, held or owned by such person when he was resident outside India or inherited from a person who was resident outside India.

Section 6, Subsection 5 applies to persons who reside outside India, i.e. they may hold, own, transfer or invest in Indian currency, security or immovable property situated in India if such currency, security or property was acquired, held or owned by such person when he was resident in India.

Under Subsection 6, RBI may by regulation prohibit, restrict or regulate establishment in India of a branch, office or other place of business by a person resident outside India for carrying on any activity relating to such branch, office or other place of business.

Under FEMA 1998, every exporter of goods shall furnish to RBI, a declaration containing true and correct material particulars including the amount representing the full export value of goods exported for the purpose ensuring the realisation of the full export proceeds by such exporters without any delay.

Further, every exporter of services shall furnish to RBI a declaration containing the true and correct material particulars in relation to payment for such services.

. Where any amount of foreign exchange is due or has accrued to any person resident in India, such person shall take all reasonable steps to realise and repatriate the amount to India within a period and manner specified by RBI. Section 9 refers to certain exemptions from realisation and repatriation of foreign exchange in certain cases.

Contravention and Penalties: If any person contravenes any provision of FEMA 1998 or contravenes any rule, regulation, notification, direction or order issued in exercise of the powers under this Act or contravenes any condition subject to which authorization is issued by RBI, he shall be liable to penalty upto twice the sum involved in such contravention.

The Central Government shall establish an Appellate Tribunal for Foreign Exchange to hear appeals against the orders of the adjudicating authorities under this Act. The jurisdiction to hear Appeal against the judgement of the Appellate Tribunal lies with the High Court.

The Central Government shall establish a Directorate of Enforcement to enforce the provisions of this Act.

Section 40 of the Act gives power to the Central Government to suspend or relax, either indefinitely or for a specific period, the operation of all or any of the provisions of FEMA. The notification issued by the Central Government in this regard will have to be placed before the Parliament and got approved within a specified period.

Evaluation of FEMA

As discussed earlier, some conditions laid down in FERA 1973 do not exit any more thereby departing from FERA. Under FERA it was necessary to obtain Reserve Bank's permission relating to most of the regulations. FEMA brought, change in this regard. So except for Section 3 which relates to dealing in foreign exchange, etc. no other provisions of FEMA stipulate obtaining Reserve Bank's permission. The purpose of FEMA facilitates external trade and payments as well as promotes the orderly development and maintenance of foreign exchange market in India. Unlike in case of FERA, violation of FEMA will not be treated a criminal offence. Thus, FEMA removes the threat of imprisonment.

According to FEMA 1998, the transactions involving foreign exchange and foreign securities are mainly focused. Dealings of non-residents in India have been liberalized. FEMA indicates major departures resulting in two main issues of importance. On one hand, it can be seen as an initial step towards capital account convertibility and on the other, the government seems to have decided to give up even the bare intention of regulating foreign capital in the country, by eliminating FERA from the statute book and thereby replacing it with and FEMA. Such an important change comes at a time when the international institutions under the direction and leadership of developed countries are putting a multilateral investment which would free foreign investors from any restrictions otherwise being imposed by the host countries. India has maintained that it would preserve its sovereign rights for regulating foreign investment. Actual size of the Indian economy in general and also the external transactions in particular have gone up adequately.

THE PREVENTION OF MONEY LAUNDERING ACT 2002

Along with FEMA Bill 1998, the Prevention of Money Laundering Bill 1998 was also introduced simultaneously in the Parliament in July 1998. The same was passed as an Act in the year 2002. Fundamentally, Money Laundering Act aimed to prevent transfer of funds concealing a transaction of dubious nature or illegal origin. The laundering of money derived from specified offences is listed in the Indian Penal Code. The Immoral Traffic (Prevention) Act 1956, the Arms Act 1959, The Narcotic Drugs and Psychotropic Substances Act 1985, and the Prevention of Corruption Act 1988 have served to form the basis for the Prevention of Money Laundering Act 2002. The money laundering is not defined by the Act but it states that a money laundering offence will have the undermentioned ingredients.

(a) A crime should have been committed;
(b) There are proceeds of or gains from the crime; and
(c) There is a transaction in respect of the proceeds of the gains.

Money laundering relates to the cunning act of vesting proceeds of crime with legitimacy which means that whoever acquires, possesses or transfers any proceeds of crime or enters into any transaction related to proceeds of crime directly or indirectly or conceals or aids in the concealment of the proceeds of crime, commits the offence of money laundering.

As per Section 4 of the Act, money laundering is punishable with rigorous imprisonment for a period of not less than three years extendable upto seven years and ten years pertaining to drug related crimes apart from a fine upto Rs. five lac. Section 5 of the Act empowers the Director of Money Laundering to attach the property involved. All the money laundering offences are cognizable non-bailable offences and the onus of proof of innocence is on the accused. The Directorate of Money Laundering has the power to search, seize documents besides attaching the property of the accused after recording their reasons for doing so. The directors or owners of the companies are also liable for prosecution for the offences committed as regards the conduct of their business.

The Act makes it mandatory for all the financial institutions and intermediaries to maintain a record of all transactions which exceed the value of Rs. 25 lac as the money laundering offences can be detected only with the help of financial institutions which are required to furnish the relevant information of such transactions to the Commissioner of Income Tax as per their jurisdiction. The Director of Money Laundering is empowered to call the records maintained by the financial institutions and the intermediaries for the purposes of investigation.

The Act does not state as regards a separate Money Laundering Directorate to be set up but provides for the appointment of Adjudicating Authorities and the setting up of an Appellate Tribunal with benches at Mumbai, Delhi and

Chennai to hear appeals against the decisions of Adjudicating Authorities. Appeals against the decisions of Tribunal will lie with the High Court.

Evaluation of the Money Laundering Act

All the offences by means of which the black money is generated are covered by the Money Laundering Act, though all the tax offences and smuggling are excluded from the definition of money laundering. So the tax evasion is recognized as a money laundering offence even by the Swiss laws which is quite interesting to note. Money Laundering Act overlooks many serious offences such as mis-invoicing rackets, transfer pricing abuses, insider trading and FEMA violations.

Most adverse part of the Act is that any case under this Act is non-bailable which means that if an accused is arrested then he/she may have to wait for a period of six months for the judgement of the appellate authority before the appeal is made to the High Court. As per the Act, the property of the accused is attached with the imprisonment for a minimum period of three years extendable to seven years and ten years in respect of drug-related offences.

For the past more than one and a half decades, many financial crimes such as value based advance licence misuse, excise evasion and bogus exports have been increasing in unmanageable proportion for which Finance Ministry has the justification of imposing stiff penalty. Money Laundering Act considers the provisions of Model Money Laundering Bill prepared by an international body, viz. Financial Action Task Force which works with several countries so as to counter the menace of money laundering.

The association comprising businessmen and industrialists are not satisfied with the Act on the ground that the penal provisions are misused to harass which are more severe than those framed in FERA 1973. In fact, the Act falls short of the requirements for effective legislation in following respects:

(i) Tax evasion and smuggling are excluded.

(ii) Indian banking laws are outmoded and there is no power given to the Income Tax Department or the proposed Money Laundering Directorate to call for statutory reports from banks and financial institutions.

(iii) There is the difficult problem of obtaining information from abroad about the money laundering activities of resident Indians.

(iv) The legal procedure even in this Act is made deliberately lengthy and time consuming. Adjudicating Authority, Appellate Tribunal, High Court and Supreme Court provide good opportunities to lawyers to play with the legislation without punishing anyone.

In our country the laws so made are just an eyewash. The laws are not properly implemented because the same are not applicable to the politicians and corrupt people at high level. Only minor penalty is imposed just for the sake of law that states so. At times the law makers are the law breakers.

Annexure I: Notes and Coins Issued

Year	Small coins	Rupee Notes	Rupee Coins Re. 1	Rupee Coins Rs. 2	Rupee Coins Rs. 5	Notes Rs. 2	Notes Rs. 5	Notes Rs. 10	Notes Rs. 20	Notes Rs. 50	Notes Rs. 100	Notes Rs. 500	Notes Rs. 1000
1	2	3	4	5	6	7	8	9	10	11	12	13	14
1970-71	137	219	43	-	-	69	310	1563	-	-	2210	-	45
1971-72	149	234	43	-	-	66	325	1713	-	-	2482	-	36
1972-73	167	260	45	-	-	70	371	1757	152	-	2848	-	43
1973-74	188	283	46	-	-	83	412	1980	382	-	3216	-	35
1974-75	209	290	46	-	-	56	433	1962	415	-	3285	-	35
1975-76	225	293	53	-	-	116	532	1880	425	86	3422	-	88
1976-77	233	274	75	-	-	127	540	1967	555	734	3726	-	105
1977-78	197	272	96	-	-	148	572	1825	690	995	4302	-	55
1978-79	209	256	110	-	-	174	576	1957	779	1440	5369	-	-
1979-80	225	214	126	-	-	215	588	2123	961	1983	5951	-	-
1980-81	243	207	141	-	-	299	634	2097	1090	2206	7406	-	-
1981-82	263	212	154	-	-	392	692	1991	1214	2724	7829	-	-
1982-83	277	205	172	-	-	431	807	1798	1433	3017	9777	-	-
1983-84	290	198	303	-	-	450	560	1770	1463	3626	11690	-	-
1984-85	307	204	237	-	-	580	1234	2217	1636	3920	13904	-	-
1985-86	366	238	308	-	20	650	1303	2536	1784	4310	15018	-	-
1986-87	439	301	423	-	17	683	1287	2510	1899	5247	17116	-	-
1987-88	498	352	501	-	-	653	1429	2825	2331	7267	19077	180	-
1988-89	539	360	547	-	-	681	1482	2996	2613	9459	21208	230	-
1989-90	640	348	583	-	20	804	1739	3515	3100	12553	23778	1257	-
1990-91	685	335	616	23	-	883	1810	3785	2952	14812	24570	2177	-
1991-92	729	-	-	10	-	942	2400	5202	2743	17719	32266	1854	-
1992-93	780	-	-	37	5	720	2022	4285	2340	22577	32663	4910	-
1993-94	829	328	705	85	58	624	1860	5334	1631	24991	37784	11303	-
1994-95	881	320	795	159	115	602	1765	6943	1120	28537	46457	16882	-
1995-96	940	322	848	226	183	515	1651	9218	718	31659	55105	20873	-
1996-97	991	316	900	286	440	527	1554	11063	703	33623	62600	24270	-
1997-98	1055	319	969	352	672	550	1427	12412	979	34245	70159	27975	-
1998-99	1116	316	1076	497	856	530	1290	12990	899	33316	78197	44827	-
1999-00	1188	308	1260	672	1164	512	1152	13282	1010	33230	85831	57250	-
2000-01	1300	307	1393	814	1544	471	1016	12336	1012	32818	108141	52947	3719
2001-02	1328	308	1547	1062	2025	538	1264	11989	1531	35601	118041	68512	7179
2002-03	1346	305	1692	1210	2419	483	1739	9088	3425	35191	115386	93813	15971
2003-04	1353	299	1757	1255	2535	472	2276	7750	4383	33027	121442	122938	27473
2004-05	1353	299	1790	1290	2619	462	2086	6770	3876	29941	123282	152728	42082
2005-06	1358	299	1894	1365	2735	451	1980	6274	4077	27842	134637	182332	64346
2006-07	1364	301	2029	1488	2880	447	1887	7155	4178	27951	135444	225400	93676
2007-08	1455	300	2214	1907	3249	636	2111	9333	4108	26508	134575	263108	141219
2008-09	1455	300	2396	2236	3570	665	2271	12222	4399	24440	137028	308304	191784

Notes: 1. Notes of Rs. 1000 denomination were demonetised w.e.f. January 16, 1978 and subsequently re-introduced in 2000-01.

2. For the period from 1970-71 to 1974-75, the amount for Re. 1 coins also includes various commemorative Ten Rupee coins.

3. Data for 1986-87 exclude figures from Kolkata.

4. Data from 1980-81 for small coins, include small coins of the denominations 1p, 2p, 3p and Anna Pie coins.

5. Data from 1980-81 onwards for Re. 1 coins Include Mahatma Gandhi Centenary Ten Rupee silver coin, World Food. Agricultural Organisation Commemorative Ten Rupee silver coin and Independence Day Silver Jubliee Ten Rupee coin.

6. Data on Rs. 2 and Rs. 5 coins relates to coins minted.

Annexure II: Components of Money Stock

Year/Month	Currency in circulation	Cash with banks	Currency with public (2-3)	'Other' deposits with the RBI	Bankers' deposits with the RBI	Demand deposits	Time deposits	Reserve money (M0) (2+5+6)	Narrow money (M1) (4+5+7)	Broad money (M3) (8+10)
1	2	3	4	5	6	7	8	9	10	11
2005-06										
April	384319	12436	371884	4486	111859	300965	1654095	500665	677335	2331430
May	389838	12585	377254	4325	96554	287597	1660786	490718	669175	2329960
June	388538	12793	375745	4457	103317	297823	1668561	496312	678026	2346586
July	384337	12931	371406	4955	108186	297669	1684437	497477	674030	2358468
August	384372	12448	371924	4804	115468	305789	1703051	504644	682517	2385567
September	379060	14221	364839	5217	113096	339803	1759796	497373	709859	2469655
October	394282	13553	380729	4635	111995	323389	1762275	510911	708753	2471029
November	401742	13584	388157	4831	117043	324071	1771770	523615	717059	2488829
December	408214	13179	395035	4468	110129	337843	1778219	522811	737345	2515565
January	416161	13386	402776	4581	113127	339655	1775779	533869	747012	2522791
February	423908	13547	410361	4820	112584	355225	1797579	541311	770405	2567984
March	429578	17454	412124	6869	135511	407423	1893104	571958	826415	2719519
2006-07										
April	446376	14649	431727	6644	142207	413383	1911763	595227	851753	2763516
May	451642	15397	436245	6411	130562	373441	1954223	588615	816097	2770320
June	452918	15782	437135	5255	128308	364168	1968024	586480	806558	2774582
July	450244	14857	435388	5760	127058	368157	2018027	583063	809305	2827332
August	453650	15811	437839	5798	130758	380948	2060247	590207	824586	2884833
September	450860	16547	434312	5707	148531	407972	2093696	605098	847991	2941688
October	470842	19241	451600	5535	130375	398978	2080815	606752	856114	2936928
November	468547	16191	452356	5789	139890	398244	2125911	614225	856388	2982300
December	477692	15908	461784	5205	136366	400030	2138840	619264	867020	3005860
January	488261	16275	471987	5588	147830	399578	2190153	641680	877152	3067305
February	498951	16285	482666	4707	165642	437168	2214326	669300	924541	3138867
March	504099	21244	482854	7496	197295	477604	2342113	708890	967955	3310068
2007-08										
April	520898	18160	502738	7016	202508	423120	2373636	730422	932875	3306510
May	522858	18792	504066	5391	197666	413497	2399049	725916	922954	3322003
June	521064	19662	501403	7060	192496	432567	2440143	720621	941030	3381174
July	514638	19031	495607	12352	224980	438478	2509452	751970	946436	3455888
August	506688	20151	486537	5039	234534	440385	2553881	746261	931961	3485842
September	507667	21166	486501	5581	267959	491456	2601498	781208	983538	3585036
October	527022	20942	506079	4857	238095	457286	2647020	769973	968222	3615241
November	547205	22099	525105	4784	240726	482706	2667776	792715	1012595	3680371
December	554449	20343	534105	4762	248590	485115	2681559	807801	1023982	3705541
January	566389	22080	544309	4760	267055	503767	2751524	838204	1052836	3804361
February	575434	21085	554348	5009	270106	509138	2813408	850549	1068495	3881903
March	590801	22390	568410	9054	328447	578372	2862046	928302	1155837	4017883
2008-09										
April	610949	21510	589438	6184	271181	513617	2928370	888314	1109240	4037610
May	625079	22482	602598	6216	280639	505311	2981598	911934	1114124	4095722
June	627660	23477	604182	4944	299115	499047	2998992	931718	1108173	4107165
July	625843	22959	602885	5104	320967	498357	3042676	951914	1106346	4149022
August	611328	24620	586708	5251	330875	521515	3112732	947454	1113474	4226207
September	613144	26998	586146	5459	338334	551818	3140123	956936	1143422	4283545
October	638579	27719	610860	5037	224171	516301	3225770	867787	1132198	4357968
November	645632	26646	618987	4939	224258	494335	3270610	874829	1118260	4388871
December	651421	24870	626550	12503	222561	489661	3315318	886485	1128715	4444033
January	659143	25339	633804	6590	208748	514468	3408651	874480	1154861	4563513
February	675228	25108	650120	5978	206512	530514	3468070	887717	1186612	4654682
March	691153	24790	666364	5573	291275	581247	3510835	988001	1253184	4764019
2009-10										
April	714422	26902	687520	9722	236251	557917	3621289	960395	1255159	4876448
May	724621	29402	695219	4730	228434	568588	3669741	957785	1268537	4938278
June	720748	29935	690813	11199	218611	547300	3687409	950558	1249312	4936721

Note: Data from 2006-07 onwards are provisional.

Annexure III: Sources of Money Stock

Year/Month	Net RBI credit to Central Government	Net RBI credit to State Governments	Other banks' investments in government securities	Net bank credit to government (2+3+4)	RBI credit to commercial sector	Other banks' credit to commercial sector	Bank credit to commercial sector (6+7)
1	2	3	4	5	6	7	8
2005-06							
April	–5850	4651	772916	771717	1390	1301359	1302749
May	–16921	854	777808	761741	1390	1309053	1310443
June	–8658	–41	767910	759210	1390	1333132	1334521
July	–7927	418	770929	763420	1387	1345514	1346901
August	–25656	149	782763	757255	1387	1368525	1369912
September	–33909	–41	788539	754589	1387	1452176	1453563
October	–19853	38	785151	765336	1387	1458658	1460044
November	–8064	193	774633	766761	1387	1479410	1480797
December	–14096	25	763105	749034	1522	1514477	1515999
January	27364	–41	749160	776483	2339	1538012	1540351
February	24796	–41	749194	773949	1741	1576421	1578162
March	5160	1439	752817	759416	1387	1687295	1688681
2006-07							
April	16996	933	781450	799379	1387	1666693	1668080
May	7775	–41	780956	788689	1387	1674443	1675830
June	8230	–41	775447	783637	1387	1701950	1703337
July	–1196	–41	800155	798918	1384	1731740	1733124
August	–1258	6	797804	796552	1384	1767481	1768865
September	10815	201	786478	797493	1472	1846210	1847682
October	10617	115	793165	803898	1384	1841048	1842432
November	3272	155	800203	803629	1384	1870383	1871767
December	–1753	15	785982	784243	1515	1925521	1927036
January	12123	119	792894	805136	1907	1960474	1962381
February	–87	56	805495	805463	1441	2007497	2008938
March	2136	287	825204	827626	1537	2127325	2128862
2007-08							
April	17991	555	842452	860997	1386	2083952	2085338
May	5529	774	848603	854906	1386	2079742	2081128
June	–19690	–41	875001	855271	1386	2095573	2096958
July	21011	873	887505	909389	1383	2119069	2120452
August	–64271	1333	939645	876707	1383	2169486	2170869
September	–75277	852	945792	871366	1383	2243865	2245248
October	–137368	302	985258	848191	1383	2232987	2234370
November	–142103	–19	1003103	860981	1704	2281698	2283403
December	–140355	142	975642	835429	1472	2333530	2335002
January	–155679	–200	993357	837478	1571	2374935	2376506
February	–172281	–41	1029243	856920	1703	2465631	2467334
March	–114636	1427	1012727	899518	1788	2577201	2578990
2008-09							
April	–160915	429	1059820	899335	1383	2536656	2538040
May	–144585	261	1066018	921695	1383	2578467	2579850
June	–113206	–16	1048864	935642	1408	2608393	2609800
July	–59055	–41	1026679	967583	1438	2621669	2623106
August	–89189	–41	1060155	970925	1381	2674102	2675483
September	–61827	–34	1029158	967296	1867	2771071	2772938
October	–109174	264	1099674	990764	1381	2834488	2835868
November	–61503	–3	1110842	1049336	1514	2846296	2847811
December	–31895	263	1128263	1096631	1381	2862173	2863554
January	–47690	738	1218181	1171229	4399	2854812	2859211
February	–39992	201	1236710	1196919	6841	2889535	2896375
March	61761	–181	1215619	1277199	13820	2999517	3013337
2009-10							
April	50460	690	1286112	1337262	13036	2965777	2978813
May	57316	–41	1303833	1361107	12995	2969996	2982991
June	50264	171	1339520	1389955	12745	3002232	3014976

(Rupees crore)

Year/Month	Net foreign exchange assets of the RBI	Net foreign exchange assets of other banks	Net foreign exchange assets of banking sector (9+10)	Government's currency liabilities to public	Net non-monetary liabilities of RBI	Net non-monetary liabilities of other banks	Net non-monetary liabilities of banking sector (13+14)	RBI's gross claims on banks
1	9	10	11	12	13	14	15	16
2005-06								
April	613092	36465	649556	7435	125259	274767	400027	5206
May	602316	36465	638781	7495	111509	276990	388499	7093
June	598196	37682	635877	7832	108819	282036	390855	6413
July	590027	37682	627708	8190	98059	289692	387751	3442
August	617814	37682	655496	8183	100624	304655	405278	3391
September	623018	36921	659939	8741	106370	300808	407178	4546
October	641293	36921	678213	8675	124199	317041	441240	3570
November	644530	36921	681451	8618	127190	321607	448798	4142
December	646759	40881	687640	8641	124552	321198	445750	4513
January	614833	40881	655715	7590	124301	333046	457347	6084
February	624358	40881	665240	7609	123167	333808	456975	6015
March	672983	53211	726194	7656	122463	339966	462429	5795
2006-07								
April	719047	53211	772258	7709	153285	330625	483910	2440
May	741324	53211	794535	7749	170956	325526	496482	1378
June	744829	39452	784281	7792	178377	326087	504464	2660
July	760872	39452	800324	7824	188484	324373	512857	2704
August	765059	39452	804511	7857	184682	308270	492952	1841
September	756221	48256	804477	7900	177193	338672	515865	5682
October	753075	48256	801331	7952	171814	346870	518685	5423
November	772420	48256	820676	7990	174895	346868	521763	3899
December	783471	64166	847638	8027	179716	381368	561084	7704
January	787321	64166	851487	8064	175658	384106	559764	7804
February	830884	64166	895051	8103	174035	404652	578688	2939
March	866153	47026	913179	8161	177019	390742	567761	7635
2007-08								
April	838129	47026	885156	8227	141186	392021	533208	5322
May	830634	47026	877660	8356	125195	374853	500048	4431
June	863408	31826	895234	8427	134206	340510	474717	1337
July	893888	31826	925714	8490	173686	334471	508157	11
August	935470	31826	967296	8615	136361	401284	537645	92
September	982839	30644	1013483	8680	137352	416390	553742	83
October	1035297	30644	1065942	8755	138396	403621	542017	0
November	1075465	30644	1106110	8926	151433	427615	579048	174
December	1077520	30167	1107687	8992	140813	440757	581570	842
January	1117179	30167	1147346	9051	138037	427983	566021	4319
February	1200808	30167	1230975	9137	189573	492890	682463	797
March	1236130	59001	1295131	9224	210221	554759	764980	4590
2008-09								
April	1254862	59001	1313863	9319	217239	505708	722947	474
May	1349895	59001	1408896	9385	304573	519532	824105	166
June	1340062	21928	1361990	9449	307590	502125	809715	1612
July	1311682	21928	1333609	9513	315691	469099	784789	4068
August	1290951	21928	1312878	9624	267360	475344	742704	2089
September	1350398	18862	1369260	9655	349238	486367	835605	6116
October	1285910	18862	1304772	9731	333117	450050	783167	12792
November	1226829	18862	1245691	9787	324871	438884	763755	23075
December	1194068	42731	1236799	9841	298807	463986	762793	11634
January	1214592	42731	1257323	9917	313735	420431	734167	6261
February	1260424	42731	1303156	9984	356854	394898	751753	7113
March	1280116	72068	1352184	10054	387927	500828	888754	10357
2009-10								
April	1261219	72068	1333287	10121	378042	404993	783034	2912
May	1228046	72068	1300114	10212	353101	363044	716146	2360
June	1263366	72068	1335434	10212	388008	425847	813856	1810

Note: Data from 2006-07 onwards are provisional.
Source: http://rbidocs.rbi.org.in/rdocs/publications/PDFs/180T_HB150909.pdf

India's Balance of Payments

9

The strength, resilience and stability of a country's external sector are reflected by various indicators. These include a steady increase in reserves, moderate levels of current account deficit, changing composition of capital inflows, flexibility in exchange rates, sustainable external debt levels with elongated maturity profile and an increase in capital flows. All these, including the net trade balance, all other payments and receipts present a complete picture of economy. A format which presents the development of external sector is called balance of payments. In this chapter, we will discuss India's balance of payments (BoP) to have an overall view of the development in the external sector.

Balance of payments is a periodic statement of the money value of all the transactions that a country has with foreign countries and international institutions. In India, the balance of payments can be classified into two categories: (i) balance of payments on current account, and (ii) balance of payments on capital account. Balance of payments on current account is made up of visible trade including export and import of goods/ commodities or merchandise, and invisible trade, including income and expenditure for services such as banking, insurance, tourism, shipping together with profits and interest on investments and remittances, etc. The capital account comprises items such as inward and outward flow of money for investments, and grants and loans, including loans from governments and international institutions such as the World Bank, the International Monetary Fund, etc. The current account reflects India's balance position, i.e. if India has a favourable balance or deficit balance of payments in any given year. The balance of payments on capital account shows the implications of current transactions for the country's international financial position. For instance, the capital account mirrors the surplus and the deficit of the current account through changes in the foreign exchange reserves of the country, which are indicators of the current strength and weakness of a country's international payments position.

The Reserve Bank of India is responsible for compiling data on the balance of payments for India. It obtains data on the balance of payments primarily as a by-product of the administration of the exchange control. In accordance with the Foreign Exchange Management Act (FEMA) of 1999, all foreign exchange transactions must be channeled through the banking system, and the banks that undertake foreign exchange transactions must submit various periodical returns and supporting documents prescribed under the FEMA. In respect of the transactions that are not routed through banking channels, information is obtained directly from the relevant government agencies, other concerned agencies and departments within the RBI. The information is also supplemented by data collected through various surveys conducted by the RBI. Data are prepared on a quarterly basis and are published in the *RBI Bulletin*.

Recent Trends in Balance of Payments

The trends in various items constituting the balance of payments show an uptrend since 1950. The trend after 1990s is marked by negative feature, i.e. serious deficits in the country's payments' position. The deficits have been inflating continuously, and are large in magnitude. They have a stressful impact on the economy.

The current account has followed an inverted "U" shaped pattern during the period from 2001-02 to 2006-07, rising to a surplus of over 2 per cent of GDP in 2003-04. Thereafter, it has returned close to its post-1990s reform average, with a current account deficit of 1.2 per cent in 2005-06 and 1.1 per cent of GDP in 2006-07. Capital inflows as a proportion of GDP, have been on a clear uptrend during the first decade of the new millennium. They rose to a high of 5.1 per cent of GDP in

2006-07 after a somewhat modest growth of 3.1 per cent in 2005-06. This trend resulted into a gradual rise in reserves which reached 4 per cent of GDP in 2006-07. With capital inflows excluding financing requirements, foreign exchange reserve increase was of the order of US$ 15.1 billion in 2005-06, US$ 36.6 billion in 2006-07. As on 30 September 2009 India's foreign exchange reserves were US$ 281 billion. As a proportion of GDP, external debt was 17.2 per cent and 17.9 per cent in 2005-06 and 2006-07 respectively.

The current account, after being in surplus during the year 2001-02 to 2003-04, reverted to a deficit in 2004-05. This was despite a robust growth in net invisibles account, fuelled by software export, and private transfers. The current account deficit is attributable to the widening trade deficit, primarily contributed by the price in the international prices of petroleum products and gold. Thus, large merchandise deficit coexists with a lower deficit on the goods and services account because of the surplus on non-factor services. Even during the years when there were some surpluses on the current accounts, India had deficit on goods and services account and a relatively larger trade deficit.

Based on the trends in the six months of the 2008-09 financial year and other indicators, we can say that trade deficit would continue to widen during the year, because of a rise in acquisition cost of crude petroleum and prices of other commodities. As such, goods and services balance might also worsen to the extent that the rise in acquisition costs of petroleum are not matched by an increase in non-factor service exports, which had decelerated in the first half of the financial year 2008-09. The rise in the trade deficit may be moderate if the leads and lags in export receipts booked under 'other capital' are taken into account. However, current account deficit is likely to remain at moderate levels given the robust growth in invisible surplus partly compensating for the rising trade deficit. If the delayed export receipts included in 'other flows'—which have suddenly increased this year—are taken into account, then the rise in trade deficit would be moderate. Capital inflows are expected to be robust in the current year, keeping with the accommodative actions of the monetary authorities of the advanced economies to counter the impact of subprime mortgage crisis. Over the next few months this factor could be partly counterbalanced by increasing risk aversion on the part of developed country investors. The outlook for capital inflows in the medium term therefore hinges upon the growth recovery in advanced economies, which in turn depends on how soon the financial market turbulence is overcome.

The rising trend in capital inflows has been accompanied by a change in its composition. The most welcome feature was the rise in gross foreign direct investment inflows of US$ 23.0 billion in 2006-07. With FDI outflows also increasing steadily over the past five years, overall net flows moderated. Portfolio investment in the first half of 2006-07 was lower in comparison because of the initial slump in equity markets. Debt flows, primarily external commercial barrowings, shot up from 0.7 per cent of GDP in 1990-91 to 1.9 per cent in 2006-07.

Current account deficit which mirrors the savings-investment gap in the national income accounts constitutes foreign savings. The challenge before the emerging market economies is to leverage foreign savings to promote domestic growth without having the long-term consequences of external payment imbalances. However, current account deficit by itself need not necessarily enhance the productive capacity and thus overall GDP growth. This would depend upon underlying component factors leading to the current account deficit. The distinction between gross capital inflow and net inflow is useful. As the latter must be equal to the current account deficit. Net use of foreign savings cannot increase without an increase in the current account deficit. The gross inflow can, however, increase to the extent that it is offset by gross outflow in the form of build-up of foreign exchange reserves, reduction in government external debt or outward investment by entrepreneurs. Higher gross inflows have value even for net flows which do not increase to the same extent, as they are likely to improve competition in the financial sector, improve the quality of intermediation and the average productivity of investment, and thus raise the growth rate of the economy. The challenge before the government is to maximize these benefits while minimizing the costs of exchange rate management.

The rise and fall of the current account balance during the period 2000-01 to 2006-07 has been mainly driven by the goods and services balance. The surplus from factor income including remittances which fluctuated between 2 per cent and 3 per cent of GDP has helped moderate the substantial deficit on the trade account. The trade balance of both goods and services and the factor surplus improved between 2000-01 and 2003-04 which led to the improvement of the current account, but thereafter the direction of the two reversed, resulting in a declining trend in the current account. In recent times the current account deficit and factor surplus have averaged 1.2, 3.5 and 2.0 per cent of GDP respectively.

The trends in goods and services trade deficit have been largely driven by the merchandise trade deficit since 2004-05. During 2000-01 to 2003-04, the merchandise trade deficit was around 2 per cent of GDP and the rising non-component of the growth process. As a proportion of GDP, on balance of payments basis, exports rose from 5.8 per cent in 1990 to 14.0 of GDP in 2006-07. The average annual growth rate in the last five years has been at an annual average of 28.2 per cent. As a proportion of GDP, on balance of payments basis, imports during the year 2006-07 were 20.9 per cent of GDP. Thus, trade deficit increased to 6.9 per cent of GDP in 2006-07. This rise in trade deficit was largely due to a hike in prices of petroleum products and non-petroleum products as well.

Thus, the nature of current account deficit is indicated by the contribution of the oil trade deficit and non-oil trade deficit in conjunction with the surpluses on factor and non-factor services.

Arising out of the sharp upward movements in exchange rates and foreign exchange reserves, there is an apprehension about the developments on the BoP front and its consequences in terms of competitive losses and thereby on the growth prospects of exports. BoP data for the first half of financial year 2007-08 shows some deceleration in growth in exports from a level of 24.8 per cent in 2006-07 to 19.9. Simultaneously, growth in imports in the first half of 2007-08 fell to 21.9 per cent from 24.7 per cent in 2006-07 on BoP basis, while merchandise trade deficit reached US$ 42.4 billion in 2007-08 which is 8.1 per cent of GDP. It was US$ 33.8 billion in 2006-07, which was equivalent to 8.3 per cent of GDP. During the same period, there was a decline in software services exports to 15.2 per cent from 37.2 per cent which led to a lower growth in net invisible surpluses. It went down to 17.5 per cent from 35.2 per cent. Receipts from business services actually declined from US$ 8 billion in 2006-07 to US$ 6.4 billion in 2007-08. With a marginal rise, there was a decline of 91 per cent in 2007-08 in net receipts. Thus, goods and services receipts, as a proportion of GDP rose to 5.3 per cent in 2007-08 from 4.7 per cent in 2006-07.

Private transfer receipts, mainly remittances rose sharply by 49.2 per cent in 2007-08 as against 19.2 per cent in the corresponding period of the previous year. Investment income grew by 60 per cent during 2007-08, which reflects the growing foreign exchange reserves. Net invisible surplus grew by 35.2 per cent to reach US$ 31.7 billion in 2007-08. It is 6.1 per cent of GDP. Thus, higher invisible surplus contributed to moderate somewhat the rising deficits on trade account, and current account deficit was placed at US$ 10.7 billion in 2007-08, which was 2 per cent of GDP.

Trends in 1990-91 and Thereafter

For the first time during the last 40 years of planning, net invisibles declined to the tune of Rs. 435 crores to reach negative in 1990-91. This was primarily the result of a net outflow of investment income of the order of Rs. 6,732 crores in 1990-91 as against Rs. 4,875 crores in 1989-91, reflecting an increase of 38 per cent. Thus, the net invisibles, which serve as a cushion to partly neutralize the trade deficit declined.

The situation deteriorated during the second half of 1990 when deficits became massive as a result of eruption of Gulf Crisis which led to a steep rise in oil prices. The value of imports also rose sharply, thus contributing to the rise of deficit. The value of oil imports which was on an average of 499 crores

($ 287 million) per month in June-August 1990 rose hugely to reach Rs. 1221 crores ($ 671 million) per month in the subsequent month. This led to doubling of the BoP deficit from an average of Rs. 619 crores ($ 356 millioln) per month in June-August 1990 to Rs. 1229 crores ($ 679 million) per month in the following six months. The situation took a worst turn when Indian workers in Kuwait had to be airlifted back to India due to the emerging situation there. This caused a heavy loss of remittances to India that ceased to flow from there. Further, the UN trade embargo on Iraq led to the cessation of exports to Iraq and Kuwait. The situation caused a heavy depletion in reserves due to rapidly rising BoP deficits. The government took several measures to curb imports so as to preserve the foreign reserves. The efforts proved successful. The deficit got reduced from Rs. 1412 crores ($ 781 million) per month in October-December 1990 to Rs. 710 crores ($ 382 million) per month in January-March 1991 and further to Rs. 361 crores ($ 172 million) per month in April-June 1991.

However, decline in deficit did not solve the balance of payments crisis. A time came when it appeared that there was complete loss of confidence in the country's ability to manage the crisis. It was speculated that the country would default on its debts, and the rupee would fall heavily in the world market. These speculations were creating longer leads in the payments for imports and lags in the realization of expert proceeds. Many other developments were also contributing to this crisis situation. The short-term credits were drying up and reached from about $ 2 billion in 1989-90 to over half a billion in 1990-91. The interests on these credits too shot up. Commercial borrowings abroad with maturity of over a year as medium-term loans, used by financial institutions and public sector enterprises to finance capital goods imports, also went down from Rs. 5479 crores in 1989-90 to Rs. 3414 crores in 1990-91. The drying up of commercial loans was accompanied by a net outflow of NRI deposits which started in October 1990 and continued till 1991. All these combined to create a horrible situation of crisis of payments of unprecedented dimensions. Its impact was severely felt in financing of current imports and in meeting debt-service obligations. Moreover, the erosion of confidence of short-term tenders and NRI depositors, had a far-reaching impact on the economy.

Certainly, the deficits in the balance of payments are, by all accounts, a big challenge for the economy, as these have adverse serious impact on the economy. This is discussed below.

The reason why the problem was so serious was due to the fact that the imports exceeded exports by a wide margin, being in the range of 8 to 12 per cent of GDP, while the performance of exports was low, ranging as a proportion of GDP from 5 to 8 per cent on an annual basis. It led to the deficit in the trade balance to reach as high as around 3 per cent for most of the years. This is larger than the projections in several plans. But for surpluses, things would have been worse. These surpluses which marked several years, accounted for 1 to 2 per cent of GDP. These helped in reducing the deficit on trade account, and have been less than what they would have been without surpluses on account of invisibles.

Moreover, the large deficit in balance of payments exerted great pressures on foreign exchange reserves of the country. These reserves which are comprised of foreign currency assets of the Reserve Bank of India (RBI), gold holdings of the RBI and special drawing rights (SDR) of the International Monetary Fund, are the maximum that a country can draw upon freely. However, there are limits, beyond which they cannot be drawn and in fact should not be. For example, a sizeable volume of foreign exchange reserves need to be kept to meet normal fluctuations in trade which may occur due to fluctuation in agricultural production caused by various climatic conditions and other factors, and unseen contingencies in India such as trade, failure of crops and drought, a situation which demands the imports of food grains. It is considered prudent on the part of a country to keep an amount of the reserves equivalent of a minimum of three months' merchandise imports to tackle the situation of exigency. Above all, it is to be remembered that sources like SDRs, i.e. loans of special category from the IMF and the drawings from the IMF (technical name for loans granted by the IMF under normal rules), are not self-owned reserves. These are the sources of foreign exchange which a country can tap with cost. In such a situation, the additional demands on foreign exchange should be minimum. But the reality in case of India was different. The balance of payments situation strained the foreign exchange reserves. A time came when the reserves declined so much that it appeared difficult to provide a cushion for a reasonable amount of imports or for meeting payment obligations on current account. For some years, there was little change in reserves. It remained almost the same leading to the emergence of a precarious situation. However, the limitation began to improve after some time and it has improved considerably in recent years as shown in Tables 8.7 and 8.8 in Chapter 8.

The seriousness of the problem was reflected in the large debt the country had to take to meet the deficits in the balance of payments that involved a heavy burden of return of loans and payment of interest. The loans drawn from various sources included external assistance or foreign aid, IMF credits, commercial borrowings and supplier's credit of which external assistance was the major factor. The total external debt which was US$ 23.5 billion in 1980-81 increased four times to reach $ 1,23,204 million in 2005. It further increased to 1,26,391 million in 2006. As a proportion of GDP, it was 14.3 per cent in 1980-81, 17.8 per cent in 2005 and 17.3 in 2006. The burden of the debt service, as indicated by the ratio of total debt service payments to the receipts of current accounts rose to serious proportions. In 1980-81, this ratio was 10.2 per cent which increased as high as 15.9 per cent in 2004-05. It came to 10.2 in 2006. This high level of debt service added to the liability of big magnitude to the economy which already was faced with serious problem. Apart from its size, the debt burden was serious because, unlike internal debt, it has to be repaid in foreign currency, particularly at a time when the foreign reserves were depleting.

The balance of payments crisis, marked by big and continuing deficits shattered the confidence of the foreigners in India's capacity to pay back the debt and its strength to cope with the crisis. The common message that the foreigners drew from the emerging situation was that the country may default on the international debts. In this context, payments due to the country as, for example, for exports, may be delayed. Getting commercial loans on usual market rate may also become difficult. Investors started panicking. In case of India, investors particularly NRIs started withdrawing their deposits. The foreigners insisted on prior payment for imports or some guarantee from a foreign bank regarding payment. All these factors led to evolve a situation of liquidity crisis. Declining imports, delay in receipts of exports, along with no or little commercial credit created a likelihood of disruption in the smooth functioning of various segments of economy. The Indian economy was caught in almost this situation in the middle of 1991.

Thus, it is obvious that the balance of payments deficits is a serious problem for an economy. Often they go beyond the calculated limit, particularly in terms of strain on foreign exchange reserves, debt burden and above all, the erosion in confidence of people in the strength of economy leading to withdrawal of deposits and a decline in the status of the country in the comity of nations. If the situation were allowed to continue, it would have led the country in deeper troubles. However, our government was prompt enough to take effective measures which brought the economy back on track within a period of a few years.

BALANCE OF PAYMENTS POSITION 2008-09 AND 2009-10

The years 2008-09 and 2009-10 have been quite disturbing for the global economy since World War II. The crisis that began in a small corner of the financial system, i.e. the sub-prime mortgage market in the United States engulfed the entire global financial system. The fall of Lehman Brothers in September 2008 made the crisis truly global in terms of outreach, impact and severity for both advanced as well as developing countries.

Countries have, however, been affected by the crisis differently and in varying degrees. Advanced economies as a group have been more severely affected with 3.2 per cent negative growth forecast for 2009 (*World Economic Outlook*, IMF,

January 2010). All rich countries, except Australia, experienced a decline, before a partial upturn in 2010 in most economies.

As emerging economies are ahead on the recovery curve, a major fallout has been large flows of capital from rich countries seeking to benefit from interest rate differentials and a stock market boom. As such outsized inflows are not supported by economic fundamentals, and are contributing to asset price bubbles and appreciation of domestic currency, which may affect the process of recovery.

Under current account of the BoP, transactions are classified into merchandise (exports and imports) and invisibles. Invisible transactions are further classified into three categories, namely

(i) Services-travel, transportation, insurance, government not included elsewhere (GNIE) and miscellaneous, which encompasses communication, construction, financial, software, news agency, royalties, management and business services;

(ii) Income; and

(iii) Transfers (grants, gifts, remittances, etc.) which do not have any quid pro quo.

Capital inflows can be classified by instrument (debt or equity) and maturity (short or long term). The main components of capital account include foreign investment, loans and banking capital. Foreign investment comprising foreign direct investment (FDI) and portfolio investment represents non-debt liabilities, while loans (external assistance, external commercial borrowings and trade credit) and banking capital including non-resident Indian (NRI) deposits are debt liabilities.

India's BoP exhibited considerable resilience during fiscal 2008-09 despite one of the severest external shocks. The current account balance [(–) 2.4 per cent of GDP in 2008-09 vis-à-vis (–) 1.3 per cent in 2007-08] remained within the sustainable limits and there was limited use of foreign exchange reserves, despite massive decline in net capital flows to US$ 7.2 billion in 2008-09 as against US$ 106.6 billion in 2007-08. As per the latest BoP data for fiscal 2009-10, as shown in Table 9.1, exports and imports showed substantial decline during April-September

(H1) of 2009-10 vis-à-vis the corresponding period in 2008-09. There has been improvement in the BoP scenario during H1 of 2009-10 over H1 of 2008-09, reflected in higher net capital inflows and lower trade deficit. However, the invisible surplus declined and current account deficit widened vis-à-vis the corresponding period of previous year.

Table 9.1: Balance of Payments: Summary

Items	2005-06	2006-07	2007-08	2008-09	Apr.-Sep. 2008	Apr.-Sep 2009
Exports	105152	128888	166162	189001	111085	81139
Imports	157056	190670	257629	307651	175483	139356
Trade Balance	–51904	–61782	–91467	–118650	–64398	–58217
Invisibles (net)	42002	52217	75731	89923	48549	39599
Non-factor Services	23170	29469	38853	49631	25110	15371
Income	–5855	–7331	–5068	–4507	–1646	–2353
Private Transfers	24493	29825	41706	44567	25091	26695
Goods and Services Balance	–28734	–32313	–52614	–69019	–39288	–42846
Current Account Balance	–9902	–9565	–15737	–28728	–15849	–18618
External Assistance (net)	1702	1775	2114	2637	869	571
External Commercial Borrowings (net)	2508	16103	22609	7941	3166	745
Non-resident Deposits (net)	2789	4321	179	4290	1072	2864
Foreign Investment (net) of which	15528	14753	43326	3467	8349	32088
(i) FDI (net)	3034	7693	15893	17498	13867	14142
(ii) Portfolio (net)	12494	7060	27433	–14030	–5518	17946
Other Flows (net)	2427	9219	39673	–9687	–106	–8117
Total Capital Account (net) (including errors and omissions)	24954	46171	107901	8648	13350	28151
Reserves [increase (–) / decrease (+)]	(–)15052	(–)36606	(–)92164	(+)20080	(+)2499	(–)9533

Source: RBI.

Current Account

Merchandise (Exports and Imports)

The impact of the global financial crisis was transmitted to India through various external sector transactions, particularly the trade and financial routes. The transmission of external demand shocks was faster and more severe on export growth, which, on a BoP basis, declined from a peak of 57 per cent in the first quarter of 2008-09 to (–)8.4 per cent in the third quarter (October-December 2008) and further to (–)20 per cent in the fourth quarter of 2008-09—a fall for the first time since 2001-02. Import growth, which remained robust till the second quarter of 2008-09, declined by 20.8 per cent in the third quarter over second quarter and 20.1 per cent in the fourth quarter over third quarter, moving in tandem with the slowdown in domestic industrial demand and sharp decline in the price of crude oil and other primary commodities. Thus, trade deficit generally expanded in the first two quarters of 2008-09 due to the combined effect of a high crude oil prices-driven increase in imports and the collapse in external demand. However, in the fourth quarter of 2008-09, with the pace of decline in imports outpacing that in exports, trade deficit narrowed down significantly to US$ 20.2 billion as compared to US$ 25.3 billion in the first quarter, US$ 39.1 billion in the second quarter and US$ 34.0 billion in third quarter. For the full fiscal 2008-09, however, trade deficit witnessed a marked expansion to US$ 118.7 billion (9.7 per cent of GDP) as compared to US$ 91.5 billion (7.4 per cent of GDP) in 2007-08.

India's current account position during the first half of 2009-10 (April-September) continued to reflect the impact of the global economic downturn and deceleration in world trade witnessed since the second half of 2008-09. Growth in exports and imports continued its declining trend during the first half of 2009-10. On a BoP basis, India's merchandise exports, which started falling in October 2008, recorded a decline of 27.0 per cent in the first half of 2009 as against a significant increase of 48.1 per cent during the corresponding period of the previous year.

The declining trend in imports, which began during the third quarter of 2008-09, after a gap of almost seven years, continued during the first half of 2009-10. Import payments, on a BoP basis, registered a decline of 20.6 per cent during the first half of 2009-10 as compared to robust growth of 51.0 per cent in the corresponding period of the previous year.

According to the Directorate General of Commercial Intelligence and Statistics (DGCI & S) data, oil imports recorded a decline of 45.0 per cent in April-September 2009 as against a significant rise of 83.0 per cent during April-September 2008. During the same period, non-oil imports showed a relatively modest decline of 26.3 per cent. In absolute terms, oil imports accounted for about 26 per cent of total imports during April-September 2009. According to the data released by the Gem &

Jewellery Export Promotion Council, total import of gems and jewellery declined by 12 per cent during April-September 2009 as against an increase of 33.6 per cent during the corresponding period of the previous year.

Trade deficit, however, remained lower at US$ 58.2 billion during April-September 2009 as compared to US$ 64.4 billion in April-September 2008 (9.6 per cent decline), mainly on account of the decline in oil imports.

Invisibles

Two components of the current receipts, which remained relatively resilient in the face of the global economic meltdown, were software services and workers' remittances. The invisibles account reflects the combined effects of transactions relating to international trade in services, income associated with non-resident assets and liabilities, labour and property and workers' remittances. India's net invisibles increased by 18.7 per cent in 2008-09, led mainly by receipts under private transfers and software services. The net invisibles surplus increased from US$ 75.7 billion in 2007-08 to US$ 89.9 billion during 2008-09.

Services have shown relative resilience as compared to other components of India's BoP in the face of the global economic slowdown, with the net services surplus expanding from US$ 38.9 billion during 2007-08 to US$ 49.6 billion during 2008-09, led primarily by software services exports. Services exports, however, declined in the last quarter of 2008-09, after a long phase of sustained growth. The impact of the global economic downturn on India's software exports was evident during 2008-09, particularly in the second half of the year. Notwithstanding, software exports during 2008-09 at US$ 43.5 billion recorded a growth of 17.7 per cent (27.2 per cent during 2007-08). Among other major services, travel receipts were adversely affected during 2008-09 as the growth of tourist arrivals in the country significantly decreased. Against the backdrop of slowdown in global trade, business services exports declined marginally in 2008-09.

Reflecting the adverse impact of continuing global financial crisis, invisible receipts, comprising services, current transfers and income, recorded a decline of 11.6 per cent during H1 of 2009-10 as compared to an increase of 32.5 per cent in H1 of 2008-09, mainly attributable to the lower receipts under almost all components of services. However, private transfer receipts, which had marginally declined during the second half of 2008-09, increased by 4.3 per cent in the first half of 2009-10. Private transfers are mainly in the form of the following:

(i) Inward remittances from Indian workers abroad for family maintenance.

(ii) Local withdrawal from NRI rupee deposits.

(iii) Gold and silver brought through passenger baggage.

(iv) Personal gifts/donations to charitable/religious institutions.

Private transfer receipts, comprising mainly remittances from Indians working overseas, increased to US$ 27.5 billion in the first half of 2009 as compared to US$ 26.4 billion in the corresponding period of the previous year. Private transfer receipts constituted 17.6 per cent of current receipts in April-September 2009.

NRI deposits, when withdrawn domestically, form part of private transfers because once withdrawn for local use, these become unilateral transfers and do not have any reciprocal effect. Such local withdrawals/redemptions from NRI deposits cease to exist as liability in the capital account of the BoP and assume the form of private transfers, which are included in the current account of the BoP. Under NRI deposits, both inflows and outflows remained steady. A major part of outflows from NRI deposits is in the form of local withdrawals. These withdrawals, however, are not actually repatriated but are utilized domestically. During April-September 2009, the share of local withdrawals in total outflows from NRI deposits was 63.4 per cent as compared to 64.9 per cent in April-September 2008.

Software receipts at US$ 21.4 billion in April-September 2009 showed a decline of 11.5 per cent as against a growth of 35.3 per cent in April-September 2008. Miscellaneous receipts stood at US$ 7.8 billion in April-September 2009. Receipts under non-software miscellaneous services like business services, construction and royalties, copyrights and licence fees also went down.

The key components of business services receipts and payments were trade-related services, business and management consultancy services, architectural, engineering and services relating to maintenance of offices. Receipts of architectural, engineering and other technical services, maintenance of offices abroad and business and management consultancy services declined while payments related to these services rose moderately, resulting in decline in net exports of these services.

Invisibles payments also showed a decline of 2.6 per cent in April-September 2009. This decline was mainly due to lower payments towards travel, transportation, non-software services and private transfers. Lower transportation payments in April-September of 2009 reflected the lower volume of imports. In addition, lower payments can also be attributed to the lower freight rates on international shipping as compared to the corresponding period of the previous year. Investment income payments, reflecting mainly interest payments on commercial borrowings, external assistance, non-resident deposits and reinvested earnings of FDI enterprises operating in India, amounted to US$ 9.4 billion in April-September 2009 which were higher than that of US$ 8.7 billion during April-September 2008.

Capital Account

There was a sharp turnaround in the capital flows cycle—from a sustained phase of increases in inflows—to large outflows, in the third quarter of 2008-09. The early signs of the impact of the financial crisis on capital inflows were evident in the portfolio outflows that started in February 2008. Following the failure of Lehman Brothers, there was a sudden change in the external environment, marked by a global liquidity crunch and increased risk aversion on the part of international investors. As in the case of other major emerging market economies (EMEs) there was a withdrawal of funds from the domestic equity markets by portfolio investors as part of the global deleveraging process. There was also a significant reduction in the access of Indian corporates to overseas financing.

The deteriorating external financing conditions also made Indian firms' access to external commercial borrowings and trade credits difficult. The resilience shown by FDI inflows during period, however, reflected the continued confidence in the Indian economy as a long-term investment destination.

The adverse impact of the global financial market turmoil was reflected in lower capital inflows during 2008-09. There was a sharp decline in net capital flows from US$ 106.6 billion in 2007-08 to US$ 7.2 billion in 2008-09. The decline was mainly because of net outflows under portfolio investment including foreign institutional investments (FIIs), the US depository receipts (ADRs)/global depository receipts (GDRs) (US$ 14.0 billion), banking capital including NRI deposits (US$ 3.2 billion) and short-term trade credit (US$ 1.9 billion). However, despite these adverse developments, the resilience of FDI inflows reflected the growing perception that India is one of the favourite long-term investment destinations.

The revival in capital flows witnessed during the first quarter of 2009-10 gathered momentum during the second quarter. Net capital flows at US$ 29.6 billion in April-September 2009 remained higher as compared to US$ 12.0 billion in April-September 2008. All the components under net capital flows, except loans and banking capital, showed improvement during April-September 2009 from their levels of the previous year. In banking capital, net inflows under NRI deposits remained higher during April-September 2009 as compared to their previous year's level.

Net inward FDI into India remained buoyant at US$ 21.0 billion during April-September 2009 reflecting the continuing liberalization and better growth performance of the Indian economy. During this period, FDI was channeled mainly into manufacturing (21.4 per cent) followed by communication services (12.8 per cent) and the real estate sector (12.6 per cent). Net outward FDI of India at US$ 6.8 billion in the first half of 2009-10 remained at almost the same level as that of the corresponding period of 2008-09. Due to the large inward FDI, the net FDI was marginally higher at US$ 14.1 billion in April-

September 2009. Portfolio investment consisting mainly of FIIs and ADRs/GDRs witnessed large net inflows (US$ 17.9 billion) in April-September 2009. This was due to large purchases by FIIs in the Indian capital market, reflecting revival in the growth prospects of the economy and improvement in global investors' sentiment. The inflows under ADRs/GDRs increased to US$ 2.7 billion in April-September 2009 as compared to US$ 1.1 billion in April-September 2008.

The net external commercial borrowings (ECBs) inflow remained lower at US$ 0.7 billion in April-September 2009 than the US $ 3.2 billion in April-September 2008. Net banking capital amounted to US$ 1.1 billion in April-September 2009 as compared to US$ 5.0 billion in April-September 2008. Among the components of banking capital, NRI deposits witnessed higher net inflows of US$ 2.9 billion in April-September 2009 as against to US$ 1.1 billion in April-September 2008. Short-term trade credit recorded a net outflow of US$ 0.6 billion during April-September 2009 as compared to a net inflow of US$ 4.9 billion during the same period of the previous year. Other capital including leads and lags in exports, special drawing rights (SDR) allocation, funds held abroad, advances received pending issue of shares under FDI, etc. recorded a lower net outflow of US$ 4.3 billion in April-September 2009 as compared to US$ 10.3 billion in April-September 2008.

Major Causes of BoP Deficits

Since the deficits in the balance of payments pose a serious problem to the economy, it is necessary to identify the factors which are responsible for adverse BoP situation so as to mitigate their negative impacts. The factors are largely related to a big rise in imports, and a small growth in exports. However, other factors like deficits on account of capital transactions also aggravate the problem. Some of these factors are discussed below.

Increase in Imports

One of the major factors leading to big deficits is a rise in imports. Most of these imports have, however, been in the nature of development goods. In the early years of planning, these imports largely consisted of capital goods, i.e. machines, technology, etc. required to implement the industrialization policy of the government as envisaged in the initial Five-Year Plans of this country. In the later stage of planning, these development goods were replaced by maintenance goods required for repairs and replacement, as also intermediate imports. These imports became important soon after the establishment of industries producing machines, tools, etc. This import pattern was replaced with technology and modern equipment for the upgradation of the domestic economy to make it efficient. Large imports have also been made for supplying inputs and modern technology for reducing costs and improving the quality of export products so as to make them internationally competitive.

Other major constituents of imports have been the cereals and edible oils largely arising out of drought or low crop yields. Sometimes, other major items, namely petroleum, oil and lubricants have been swelling our imports. Particularly since the 1970s these imports have been very large indeed—at times about one-third of the total imports.

An increase in the price of imports has been a burdensome factor raising the imports, which was mainly due to the devaluation of the rupee (in 1966 and in 1999) and slow depreciation caused by various factors. Another factor with similar effect has been the rise in the prices of certain imports, in particular, fertilizers, petroleum, etc. The causes such as the deliberate increases in prices by most of the petroleum producing countries and certain situations like Gulf War, etc. have contributed considerably to the rise in the value of import bill. All these and many more factors contributed to the growth of imports.

Slow Rise in Exports

Sharp rise in imports would not have been troublesome, had exports increased simultaneously and substantially. The exports must grow faster if the country wants to avoid a situation of the crisis of balance of payments. There has been, undoubtedly, a rise in exports, but it was not sufficient enough to tone down the rigour or difficulty associated with huge deficits. Not only that these exports have not been rising. In recent times, there have been fluctuations in exports largely caused by the agricultural output arising out of fluctuation in agricultural products. There is nothing unusual for a country largely dependent on agriculture. For example, while bumper agriculture productions during the first Five-Year Plan boosted the economy, a decline in agricultural output in Second Plan brought them down. There has been great improvement in this field. The total contribution of industry in the GDP is rising, which is a good sign.

This was possible because of rising exports of non-traditional items like engineering goods, iron and steel, iron ore, chemical and allied products, etc. Besides, other domestic factors like devaluation in 1966 and also in recent years in 1991, and depreciation of rupee since then have to an extent boosted exports. Recent recessionary conditions occurring in the country also increased the availability of goods for export. Several measures taken by the government to boost the exports resulted in increase in exports. Other external factors have also been helpful to accelerate the pace of growth in exports, particularly during the initial years of planning, for example, the Korean War which coincided with the First Five-Year Plan brought large orders for the Indian exports. In addition, the boom conditions in the Western countries also created large demand for exports. However, there is no sizeable pick-up in export sectors, particularly in recent years. The sluggish growth in the world exports as also the financial crisis in the East Asian countries in the 1990s also reduced the growth of exports.

The earnings of invisibles, which have a great role to play in this field, also did not prove of much help. Though in early years it helped in reducing deficit on trade account in recent years, their contribution declined largely because a major part of earnings is being used to meet rising interest payments on foreign debts. As a consequence, it has led to a decline in the capacity to neutralize the trade deficits. For example, during the Sixth Plan period, net invisibles had offset over 60 per cent of the trade deficit. This ratio which was as high as 72 per cent in 1980-81, came down to 57 per cent in 1984-85 and further to as low as 32 per cent in 1987-88. Further, it declined sharply to reach as low as a per cent in 1992-93. Under the new policy regime, the offsetting impact of the net invisibles has been steadily rising and has been on the average 72 per cent per annum during 1997-2004.

Deficits on Capital Transactions

The growing deficit on account of capital transaction has been a major contributory factor in recent years. Of its different constituents, namely private capital transactions, amortization payments, purchase of rupees from IMF, and banking capital, the rising obligations to meet amortization payments have been the major sources of deficits. The transitions involved large sums on the return of loans which were due, and the large interest payments thereon. During the eighties, this has been one of the largest contributors. In certain years, capital transactions on government account, as also on banking account have added to this deficit. Capital transactions, however, showed surpluses during the eighties.

The composition of capital flows is changing. Among the components of capital inflows, foreign investment has been a relatively stable component, broadly fluctuating between 1 and 2 per cent of GDP during this decade. However, it seems to have shifted to a higher plane from 2003-04 with the average for 2003-04 to 2006-07 roughly double that during 2000-01 to 2002-03. The relative stability of investment flow is primarily due to steadily rising FDI. In contrast, debt flows have fluctuated much more, with net outflows in three years to 2003-04. The variations in debt flows have been primarily due to humpy repayments on government guaranteed ECB. The ratio of debt flows to GDP was on a downtrend till 2003-04 and a rising trend from 2004-05. Debt flows, primarily external commercial borrowings, shot up on a net basis in 2006-07 to a level of US$ 16.2 billion. The trend in net capital flows since 2003-04, seems to be broadly driven by the rising ratio of debt flows.

Certainly, both national and international factors have contributed to crisis of situation of a balance of payments in recent years in 1997-98 which is reflected in the rise of current account deficits to 1.6 per cent of GDP and trade deficit rising to 4.9 per cent of GDP in 2004-05. The situation further deteriorated and trade deficit reached US$ 9.2 billion in 1998-99 as per GDCI 85. This is due to a decline in export from US$ 35.6 billion in 1997-98 to US$ 34.3 billion in 1998-99. The trade deficit reached on unprecedented level of US$ 7.9 billion in 1998-99. This indicates that "the fundamentals of economy are not sound and all measures of export promotion have not produced the desired effect". To meet this deficit the larger inflow from the Resurgent India Bond during 1998-99 from NRIs or larger inflow of foreign direct investment and external commercial borrowings only show our dependency on FDI and NRI inflows. It is marked as dependency syndrome. It shows that the internal resistance of the economy is still weak and it needs to be strengthened against US dollar about 7.1 per cent from 38.50 per US dollar in March 1998 to Rs. 45.68 per US dollar in 2000-01. The situation has further worsened to Rs. 48 per US dollar in the subsequent period. Hence, more cautious approach needs to be taken while admitting large inflows of external commercial borrowings, portfolio investment by foreigners and also larger contribution from NRIs in the form of bonds.

However, during 2006-07 and 2007-08, there was an appreciation in the exchange rate of the rupee vis-à-vis the US dollar. The exchange rate declined from Rs. 44.27 in 2005-06 to Rs. 42.25 in 2006-07. This declining trend continued and reached 39.44 per US dollar in November 2007. It affected exports while imports saw a rise leading to a further increase in trade deficit. This situation called for measures to promote exports-import measures such as incentives for exporters and modification in export duties.

The excess of capital inflows over the current account deficit has been a clear uptrend since 2003-04. It rose to 7.72 per cent of GDP in the first half of 2007-08. It declined slightly in 2004-05 and 2005-06 because of special conditions, i.e. a reversion of deficit on the current account and the maturing and repayment of IMD bonds. Such high levels of reserve change were due to various factors which included the strong growth performance and potential together with high returns on equity, robust financial markets, interest differential, and rising expectation including on the value of the rupee.

Crisis Management

The measures taken in the early years of the 1990s largely aimed at bringing immediate impact on the BoP situation. There were a few steps which constituted the part of this category of measure. First, gold was used for acquiring foreign currency to meet the payment obligations which had become due. Twenty tonnes of gold out of the confiscated gold lying under the ownership of government was sold to a bank in Switzerland in May 1991, with the condition that it would be repurchased after six months. Another about forty-seven tonnes of gold, which was the assets of the Reserve Bank of India, was shopped to the bank of England in July 1991. The government had to do so to raise foreign currency from England and Japan.

Secondly, the government took to downward adjustment of the exchange rate of rupee which popularly came to be known as devaluation. This devaluation was done to the extent of 18 to 20 per cent in terms of major currencies like the US dollar, UK pound sterling, German deutsche mark, Japanese yen and French franc. It was affected in two stages on July 1 and July 3, 1991. This step was intended to boost exports and to discourage imports. This gave the message that Indian economy is strong enough to cope with the situation and that it would not default on the payments due to foreign investors.

As a third step to the crisis management, the government took steps to curb the imports which were rising to drain the foreign exchange. In October 1990, RBI imposed a cash margin of 50 per cent on imports other than those of capital goods. This cash margin was subsequently raised to 133.3 per cent in March 1991 and 200 per cent in April 1991. As for capital goods, these were allowed only against foreign sources of credit. In December 1990, a surcharge of 25 per cent was imposed on the prices of petroleum products except domestic gas. The auxiliary customs duties were also raised as a part of corrective measure. In May 1991, the RBI imposed a 25 per cent surcharge on interest on bank credit for interests.

Further, steps were taken to get foreign exchange to meet the immediate and the future BoP needs as also to relax the curbs on imports. Multilateral financial institutions with the IMF, the World Bank and the Asian Development Bank were approached to get foreign exchange. Besides, government formulated two schemes, which were introduced in October 1991. The schemes—the India Bond Scheme and the Immunity Scheme—were initiated to encourage the inflow of capital funds from abroad.

Reforms in Policy

The government's main attempt is to have a long-term solution to the BoP, and take certain measures to restructure the economy so as to make it efficient and competitive. As for the external sector, the government tried to ensure a broad-based, rapid and sustained growth of exports, at the same time taking measures for efficient import substitution. Various radical policy changes were introduced in different sectors of the economy. In terms of public finance, several measures were taken to contain growth in expenditure and for raising revenues so as to reduce the fiscal deficit. In addition, a contractionary monetary policy was adopted to curb the rate of inflation. It largely aimed to reduce the demand for imports so as to boost the economy. It was also sought as a measure to align the domestic prices with the international prices.

A new trade policy was started in 1991, with the objective to promote exports, by easing the process involved. The new policy was focused to liberalize the economy. As a part of policy, rupee was fully convertible on trade account from March 1993 and on current account from March 1994—a new mechanism for self-balancing of trade. Giving rationale for the new policy, the Commerce Minister noted as under:

> For several decades, trade policy in India has been formulated in a system of administrative controls and licenses. As a result, we have a bewildering number and variety of lists, appendices and licenses. This system has led to delays, waste, efficiency and corruption. Human

intervention—described as discretion—at every stage, has shifted enterprise and spawned arbitrariness.

It was decided by the government that while all essential imports like POL, fertilizer and edible oil should be protected, all other imports should be linked to exports by enlarging and liberalizing the replenishment licence system. For this, government announced major trade reforms which included the following:

(i) Rep will become the principal instrument for export-related imports.

(ii) The new Rep scheme gave maximum incentive to exporters whose import intensity was low. For instance, in agriculture sector, the replenishment rate was as low as five or 10 per cent. This sector was to gain considerably from the policy.

(iii) All exports now will have a uniform Rep rate of 30 per cent of the f.o.b. value. This was a substantial increase from the present Rep rates which vary between five per cent and 20 per cent of f.o.b. value.

(iv) All additional licenses granted to export houses shall stand abolished.

(v) All supplementary licenses shall stand abolished except in the case of small scale sector and for producers of life saving drugs/equipments.

(vi) The goal of the government was to decanalize all items except those that are essential.

(vii) All items, now listed in the Committed Permissible List (OGL Items), would hereafter be imported through the Rep route.

(viii) The Exim policy contained a category known as Unlisted OGL. This category stands abolished and all items falling under this category may be imported only through the Rep scheme.

(ix) Advance licensing has been an alternative to the Rep route for obtaining imports for exporters. It was expected that many exporters would find the Rep route more attractive now. However, for exporters who wish to go through advance licensing, this route would remain open.

(x) In the light of the substantial liberalization of the trade regime, and also the recent changes in exchange rates (after devaluation), Cash Compensatory Scheme (CCS) was abolished from July 3, 1991.

In fact, this industrial policy was introduced as a complement to the policy reforms in the spheres of public finances, trade and exchange. It was aimed at making the domestic industry more competitive. For this, licensing system was liberalized. Moreover, in most of the industries, industrial licensing has been done away with. Area reserved for the public sector was brought down and participation of private sector was promoted in care and basic sector. Measures were also taken to attract foreign direct investment. Significant changes were also introduced in public sector enterprises to make them more efficient, competitive and self-reliant in terms of their resource-need.

Certainly, these measures proved effective. The situation began to improve over a period of time. There is an increase in the reserves of foreign exchange. Much assistance has also been extended by the international financial institutions and some countries as well. Gold sold and mortgaged has been brought back. However, the position cannot be said to be very satisfactory. It is still fragile as large positions of foreign reserves consist of loans. The real solution lies in the improvement of export performance of the country.

Suggested Measures

Since BoP is serious and long-standing problem for the country, it is of great importance to take a comprehensive view of the situation so as to draw out strategy for a satisfactory and lasting solution to this problem, consistent with the objectives of accelerated growth and greater self-reliance. Following corrective measures can be taken in this regard:

Change in Import Structure

An important aspect of this solution in concerned with the imports of the country. A substantial reduction in imports is one of the major alternatives. In terms of developmental activities and progress as well as the quantum of imports, there remains little scope for the reductions in imports. As there is increase in development activities and rise in domestic product there is bound to be further increase in imports. Thus, any reduction in the quantum of imports as a solution to this problem is not possible. Though there is limited scope for reduction in imports particularly foodgrains, certain other agricultural products may be eliminated so as to contain the quantum of imports. Other than agriculture and agricultural products there is not much possibility of keeping imports at low level. But, considering a sharp rise in the prices of food items during 2008-09 and 2009-10 due to increase in demand and shortage of supply, it does not appear possible to cut down inputs of agriculture items. What is practical and desirable is the need to bring about a change in the structure of imports, which involve replacement of certain imports, partly or wholly, by domestic production, encouragement of imports of certain items which directly or indirectly help in domestic exports industries and promoting the imports of goods which help in achieving the rapid growth of the country such as advanced technology. These changes have a far-reaching impact on the overall growth of the economy. Besides, it will also help in earning foreign exchange.

Promotion of Export

The other significant aspect of the solution was with the export. It would not be wrong to say that export constitutes the centre of policy concerning the solution to the problem of deficits. It involves various factors such as the need to maintain and increase traditional exports in absolute terms, promotion of the export of non-traditional items on a large scale with particular emphasis on selected items like engineering goods, and an attempt at checking domestic consumption of certain items which have great export potential so as to ensure a surplus stock available for the exports. To evolve such a situation it is necessary to adopt measures which help in the production of goods with such quality and cost that they may sustain in international markets. Above all, there should be a properly conceived system of export incentives.

Improving Quality

To export and to find an import substitution, it is very important that the cost and efficiency of the product should be in tune with the international market. This will cause competition among the domestic industry leading to efficiency. This has a far-reaching impact on the demand of Indian products and will serve as a stimulus for export. It involves use of latest techniques and tools in the production so as to cut the production cost and maintain the price level in tune with the international price level so that Indian goods are not priced out of the world market. In other words, it means keeping under check inflationary tendencies. Above all, it is very important to maintain the tempo of export promotion, otherwise the efforts made in this regard will not help much in checking the financial deficits. Besides, various other measures such as a suitable exchange rate policy, including the devaluation of the rupee will serve as a supplementary measure.

Increasing Earnings from Invisibles

Services sector holds tremendous potential to bring foreign reserves. In recent years we have witnessed consistent growth in this sector. This is a good sign for the economy. This growth tendency needs to be maintained. For quite many years these have recorded surpluses. To a large extent, these have been helpful in reducing the deficits in balance of trade. In this sector, tourism is expanding fast as a good source for foreign exchange earnings. The potential for tourism earnings is indeed very great since the country is abundantly rich in attractions for tourists of all tastes and shades. In recent years, consultancy services are also gaining importance in India's exports. This needs to be promoted and given further boost. Another big component of this sector is transfer payments largely on private account, in the form of remittances from abroad, though a big portion of these remittances depends on the tempo of economic activities in foreign countries. Hence, nothing can be said about it. There is rather uncertainty in this sphere. Hence, all our efforts need to be focused on exploring and exploiting the potentiality in services like tourism, shipping, banking, etc.

Developing Counter Trade Mechanism

If counter trade mechanism is developed, it can help in overcoming the balance of payments crisis. Since it implies reciprocity, it can ensure that the country from whom we import, undertakes to accept an equivalent exports. This type of trade is common in developing countries. In a sense, this principle is followed in bilateral trade agreements with different countries of the world. Besides these agreements, the trading in respect of a number of products can be placed on this basis. This will ensure simultaneous balancing of trade for a part of the balance of payments. However, it is to be noted that this type of trade practice can be a short-term solution, not a long-term measure as it goes against the sound principle of multilateral trading wherein deficits/surpluses between two countries are offset through surpluses/deficits with the third and other countries. In the present scenario, counter trade can be justified in view of balance of payments difficulties. Such trade practice has become necessary, particularly in view of the present difficulties in trade with the developed countries, which often resort to nesting practices like protectionism. It can serve as an alternative to the best solution since it is better to have little trade than no trade.

Thus, we see that there are many ways to tackle the problem of exports, but there is no doubt that the biggest solution lies with the growth in exports. With imports rising, it is necessary that exports expand, and there is expansion in absorption of imports, as inputs. To be on the rising curve of exports and imports and with little or no deficits, the trade policies have to be conceived and formulated in terms of both the domestic needs and capabilities as also the global requirements. India needs to reach the stage of positive trade balance, rather than develop an economy with rising trade deficits. In other words, Indian economy will have to be an outward looking economy.

Rangarajan Panel on Balance of Payments

A high level committee was constituted to assess the balance of payments situation under the chairmanship of Dr. C. Rangarajan (former Governor, Reserve Bank of India) who submitted its report on June 4, 1993. The Committee suggested some measures which are as follows:

(i) The Committee emphasized the need for a proper integration of a realistic exchange rate and a gradual relaxation of restrictions on current account transactions.

(ii) The Committee suggested that the current account deficit of 1.6 per cent of GDP should be treated as ceiling rather than target.

(iii) The Committee also suggested a number of measures related to foreign borrowings, foreign investment and external debt management, some of which are enumerated given below:

(a) The government should adopt a continuous approach while extending concessions or facilities to foreign investors which are more favourable than what are offered to domestic investors and also against enhancing external debt to supplement equity;

(b) A deliberate policy to prioritize the use of external debt should be pursued and approval should be accorded for any commercial loan with a maturity of less than five years;

(c) The Committee recommended that efforts should be made to replace debt flows with equity flows. However, it recognized that direct foreign investment would contain both debt and equity and the system of approval is applicable to all external debt. Hence, as an operational guideline, the approval of debt linked to equity should be limited to the ratio of 1:2.

(iv) The Committee suggested that a minimum foreign exchange reserves target should be fixed at such a level that the reserves are sufficient enough to accommodate imports of three months.

A close study of the recommendations made by the Committee on balance of payments reveals that it aimed to contain the process of indiscriminate permissions to the inflow of foreign reserves in the name of foreign investments in any sphere of economic activity. Besides, it suggested the need to prioritize the sectors in which the debt is to be used. The recommendations aimed to make the government efficient in the management of external debt so as to ensure the best use of the debt in the largest interest of the economy.

Balance of Payments during Various First Plan Periods

First Plan Period

During the First Plan period the country faced balance of payments crisis due to some external and internal factors as well. External factors included Korean War and American recession of 1953, while at home uncertain monsoon, and old methods of farming accounted for low agricultural production. The industrial output was poor.

India had the experience of persistent trade deficits, while generally it had a surplus in net invisibles. Hence, the adverse balance of payments of the country was to the tune of Rs. 42 crores. The overall position of balance of payments during the First Plan period was however stated to be satisfactory.

Second Plan Period

The Second Plan period is marked by heavy deficit in the balance of trade which shot up to reach Rs. 2,339 crores. This unprecedented rise in the balance of payments in the Second Plan was the consequence of various factors which include: (a) a surge in imports of capital goods to develop heavy and basic industries; (b) decline in agricultural production leading to the failure to meet the growing demand for food for a rapidly growing population and raw materials for expanding industry; (c) the inability of the economy to increase exports; and (d) the necessity of making minimum maintenance imports for a developing economy like India. It is important to note that earnings on account of invisibles and donations from friendly countries aggregated Rs. 614 crores.

Due to these factors the foreign exchange reserves sharply declined. The only way left for the country was to contain imports and boost exports.

Third Plan and Annual Plans Period

The balance on current account was not favourable during the Third Plan period. Major factors contributing to the situation included: (a) a sharp increase in imports due to rising demand in defence and developmental activities and foodgrains shortages; and (b) lack of proportional rise in exports. The resulting imbalance in the current account was over Rs. 1,957 crores which was financed by loans from foreign countries, i.e. a PL-480 and PL-665, loans from the World Bank and withdrawal from IMF. Despite all these, there was a depletion in the foreign exchange reserves of the country. The situation of adverse balance of payments which started in the Second Plan continued during the Third Plan and even Annual Plans.

It is important to note that trade deficits inflated during the Annual Plans. This was largely caused by heavy imports of foodgrains because of droughts in different parts of India and sluggish pace of exports due to economic recession. Besides, the devaluation of the rupee was also a major factor which, instead of reducing the trade balance deficit, further aggravated the problem. A worrisome development witnessed during the period was that net invisibles which used to be positive and helped in reducing the trade deficits, also declined significantly. In fact, India had to pay heavy amounts as interest payments on loans, contracted earlier. This brought down the surplus available on invisible account. The influence of net invisible in bringing down the balance of payments deficit was however, considered negligible.

Fourth Plan Period

The main thrust of the Fourth Plan was on self-reliance by import substitution of certain commodities, which may help Indian economy through exports promotion. Accordingly, the government took measures to reduce import and to promote exports. The imports could be restricted because of the good crops in 1968-69 and 1970-71, and consequent significant reduction of imports of foodgrains. Exports also boosted as a result of measures taken by the government.

The abnormal favourableness in the invisibles account in 1973-74 was due to the receipt of Rs. 1,680 crores from the USA on the disposition of PL-480 and other rupee funds. The trade deficit during the Fourth Plan was Rs. 1,564 crores and the surplus in the net invisible accounted for Rs. 1,664 crores. The net result was a surplus in the balance of payments. It was for the first time that there was a surplus in the balance of payments, though a nominal amount of Rs. 1000 crores.

Fifth Plan Period

During the Fifth Plan, trade balance was mainly affected by the two major factors: (i) the value of imports was rising due to hike in oil prices, and (ii) the value of exports also increased under the impact of the promotional measures taken by the government. The two factors were reflected in the gradual decline in the deficit in the trade balance and the appearance of a surplus in the trade balance in 1976-77. This rise in imports accompanied with inadequate expansion in exports led to the revival of deficit trade balance in the last two years of the Fifth Plan period. Besides, net invisibles receipt rose sharply during 1975-76 to 1978-79. In fact, the significant increase in the invisible receipts was due to: (a) measures taken against smuggling and illegal payment transactions; (b) the relative stability in the external value of the rupee, particularly at a time when major currencies of the world were experiencing great fluctuations; (c) increase in earnings from tourism; (d) growth in earnings in service sector, particularly from technical, consultancy and contracting services; and (e) larger remittances sent by those Indians who went abroad in search of employments. Duing this period, India had huge surplus balance of payments of 3,082 crores. Since the beginning of planning, it was for the first time that the country was in a comfortable position in its external accounts.

Sixth Plan Period

The balance of payments position witnessed a sea change since 1979-80. The position of surplus balance of payments as experienced during the Fifth Plan period began to show downward trend from 1979-80 onwards as the gap between India's exports and imports also increased considerably. The dismal picture in the balance of payments was mainly attributed to tremendous growth in the rate of imports vis-à-vis lower rate of growth of exports since 1979-80. The trade deficit which was more than offset by the flow of funds under net invisibles during the Fifth Plan period but it could no longer remain the same since 1979-80. The adverse position in balance of payments increased to the tune of 4,384 crores during the Sixth Plan. India had to meet this huge deficit in the current account through withdrawals of SDRs and borrowing from IMF, apart from net external assistance.

Seventh Plan Period

The total trade deficit rose to the tune of 54,204 crores during the Seventh Plan period. After adjustments for the positive balance on invisible account, the deficit in balance of payments on current account was Rs. 41,047 crores. The adverse position in balance of payments was a cause of serious concern.

Eighth Plan Period

Exports during the Eight Plan period (1992-97) shot up to reach a record level of Rs. 52,561 crores from Rs. 16,934 crores in 1990-91—a high threefold increase. During the period invisibles neutralized the trade deficit to the extent of about 58 per cent. It was really a good achievement. However, the developing trend in the balance of payments continued throughout the Eighth Plan period.

Ninth Plan Period

During 1997-98, the current account deficit reached a record level of Rs. 20,883 crores and during 1998-99 declined to Rs. 16,789 crores. In 1999-2000, it again went back to 20,331 crores. This was mainly due to high trade deficit of Rs. 77,359 crores which could not be neutralized though net invisible earned a surplus of Rs. 57,028 crores. This situation improved in 2000-01 when the current account deficit declined to Rs. 16,426 crores.

During 2001-02, the heavy receipts on account of invisibles, which were to the tune of Rs. 71,381 crores, helped in bringing down balance of payments from 77,359 crores in 1999-2000 to 54,955 crores. Moreover, they also created or surplus in current account balance of the order of 16,929 crores. In the entire Ninth Plan period (1997-02) trade deficit was wiped out to the extent of 82 per cent by invisible account surplus. As a result, the total deficit in current account balance fell to reach to the tune of 53,175 crores.

Tenth Plan Period

During the first two years of the Tenth Plan in 2002-03, the current account balance which was to the extent of Rs. 30,660 was satisfactory. It increased to 63,983 crores during 2003-04. This was the result of a heavy surplus on invisibles account which not only wiped out the trade deficit, but also yielded a net positive balance on current account. The trade balance which showed a massive deficit for a period of three years from 2001-02 to 2003-04, resulted in a positive balance on current account because of heavy inflow of net invisibles.

However, trade deficit shot up to Rs. 1,51,765 crores largely due to unprecedented rise in our imports, though exports also showed a good increase. It is to be noted that our invisibles showed a record positive balance of Rs. 1,39,591 in 2004-05. But this could wipe out the trade balance only to the extent of 92 per cent. As a consequence, there was a deficit of 12,174 crores in current account in 2004-05. This was not good for economy. But it continued to worsen in subsequent Plans due to recklessly pursuing a policy of trade liberalization. The current account deficit increased to the extent of Rs. 43,737 crores in 2004-05 and Rs. 45,343 crores in 2006-07. In the entire period of Tenth Plan (2002-03 to 2006-07), the total current account deficit was of the order of Rs. 6,611 crores. The trade deficit in the Tenth Plan was wiped out by the surplus from invisibles to the tune of 99.2 per cent.

Eleventh Plan Period

The Eleventh Plan period (2007-12) saw a serious global financial crisis during 2007-08 and 2008-09, and partial recovery during 2009-10. Emerging market economies like India were not significantly affected by the global financial crisis in the initial stages, which had set in around August 2007. In fact, the initial effect of the global financial crisis was positive, as India received huge Foreign Institutional Investment (FII) inflows of US$ 22.5 billion during September 2007 to January 2008, as against US$ 11.8 billion during April-July 2007. This contributed to the debate on "decoupling", where it was believed that the emerging economies might remain largely insulated from the crisis and provide an alternative engine of growth to the world economy.

The argument was proved unfounded as the global financial crisis intensified and spread to emerging economies through capital and current account routes of the balance of payments (BoP). The global crisis began to impact emerging market economies through slowing down and reversal of capital flows. The portfolio flows to India (net) turned negative due to sale of equity stakes by Foreign Institutional Investors (FIIs) to replenish overseas cash balances. This had knock-on effect on the stock market and the exchange rates through creating a supply-demand imbalance in the foreign exchange market.

The current account was also affected after September 2008 through slowdown in exports. The exports of US$ 36.7 billion in the third quarter (October-December, Q3) of the 2008-09 indicated 10.4 per cent decline over the third quarter of 2007-08 as against an increase of 33.0 per cent in Q3 of 2007-08 over Q3 of 2006-07. During 2008-09 (April-December 2008), the current account deficit was 4.1 per cent and capital account surplus 1.8 per cent of GDP, leading to decline in foreign exchange reserves (excluding valuation) of US$ 20.4 billion, as against an accretion to reserves of US$ 67.2 billion in April-December 2007.

Developing countries are likely to grow by 6.0 per cent in 2010, led by India and China, which remained the most resilient to the crisis. The impact on the emerging world was through reversal of capital flows, fall in stock markets, depreciation of local currency, decline in exports and general risk aversion, which affected consumption and investment. The social impact of the crisis, though, has been more severe for the emerging economies, as they have fewer cushions against shocks.

The response to the crisis, however, has been equally swift, with concerted and coordinated efforts by governments and monetary authorities, through conventional and non-conventional fiscal and monetary instruments. As a result, there are signs of recovery in the global economy with the US, Euro Zone and Japan already out of recession.

Risks however remain, with rich countries continuing to be more vulnerable to double-dip recession. Firstly, levels of unemployment remains high despite expansionary policies. Secondly, the extensive use of fiscal policy has meant a sizeable increase in fiscal deficit with the gross public debt to gross domestic product (GDP) ratio in advanced economies likely to rise from 75 to 115 per cent during 2008-2014. Thirdly, the timing of exit is important. An early exit could increase the risk of another recession, while late exit could worsen public debt ratios, crowd out private investment and fuel inflationary expectations. Finally, return of recession could cause havoc. With most policy toolkits already exhausted, public debt ratios skyrocketing and the balance sheets of central banks stretched, little ammunition remains for dealing with another crisis.

As emerging economies are ahead on the recovery curve, a major fallout has been large flows of capital from rich countries seeking to benefit from interest rate differentials and a stock market boom. As such outsized inflows are not supported by economic fundamentals, they are contributing to asset price bubbles and appreciation of domestic currency, which may affect the process of recovery.

The Indian economy was initially affected through a reversal of capital flows, rupee depreciation and stock market decline. Thereafter, especially after the collapse of Lehman Brothers, the real sector was affected through a fall in exports and general risk aversion. The decline, however, was partly offset by the resilience of the rural economy due to improvement in the agricultural terms of trade because of higher support prices for agricultural produce, income generated through the National Rural Employment Guarantee Scheme, agriculture loan waivers, building up of rural infrastructure under the Bharat Nirman programme and increasing awareness through media and mobile phone penetration. Together with the fact that it is largely domestic demand driven (merchandise exports account for 15 per cent of the GDP), the Indian economy has exhibited considerable resilience in the face of the crisis.

Export-Import Policy

The main thrust of the important policy in the post-Independence period was to boost the growth so as to be able to achieve the ultimate objective of self-reliance.

Export-Import Policy during First and the Second Five Year Plans

To attain the objective of mass industrialization as envisaged in the Second Five-Year Plan, the government adopted a liberal import policy. Consequently, import rose sharply both in private and public sector. The schemes of modernization in exports was met as per the plan. This caused a heavy depletion in the foreign reserves of the country as India had to use them to pay off its adverse balance. In fact, this led to the emergence of a crisis situation in the Second Five-Year Plan as the country had to suffer from a serious shortage of foreign exchange. This necessitated a reversal of import policy and drastic restrictions were placed on imports.

During the Second Plan period it was felt that earnings from exports could not be increased unless there was mass industrialization. This was pronounced in the Second Plan in these words:

> India's export earnings are derived from a few commodities. Three of them, namely tea, jute and cotton account for nearly one-half of the quota. These major exports are meeting increasing competition from abroad. This limits the scope for any substantial increase in exports

in the short run. While every effort has to be made to promote exports of new items and to develop and diversify the markets of country's major exports. It has to be recognized that it is only after industrialization has proceeded some way that increased production at home will be reflected in large export earnings.

Export-oriented Export-Import Policy

Since 1975-76, the Government of India has been following a liberalized import policy with emphasis on increasing the production, especially export production. It was mainly oriented towards enhancing maintenance imports so as to ensure the optimum capacity utilization. Since the primary focus of the import policy was to push up exports, it is characterized as export-oriented import policy.

Exim-Import (EXIM) Policy (1985)

The EXIM Policy was announced on 12 April 1985 by Mr. Vishwanath Pratap Singh, the then Commerce Minister. It was for the first time that the policy was announced on a three-year basis. The main objective of the policy was to facilitate production through easier and quicker access to imported inputs, import continuity and stability of Exim Policy. In addition, strengthening the export production base, facilitating technological upgradation and affecting all possible savings in imports were adopted to accelerate the pace of production.

Export-Import Policy (1990)

A new Export-Import Policy was announced on April 30, 1990 for a period of another three years. The main objectives of the Plan were made clear in the policy statement in these words: "Improvement in our balance of payments can be achieved not so much through import curtailment as through promotion of exports". Thus, the new policy focused on liberalization and added momentum to the ongoing process of liberalization. The main thrust was to strengthen the impulses of industrial and export growth. The salient features of the policy are enumerated below.

(i) List of items imported under Open General Licence (OGL) was expanded to ensure easy accessibility to import of items which are not available in the country.

(ii) The number of capital goods items permitted under OGL was raised from 1,261 to 1,343.

(iii) A scheme of automatic licensing was introduced which provided for the import of up to 10 per cent of the value of the previous year's licence.

(iv) Imports of raw material like petroleum products, fertilizers, oils/oilseeds, feature films, video films, ammonia, phosphoric acids, cereals, newsprints, etc. were canalized through public sector agencies in view of the distinctive character of these products. However, with the objective of promoting exports, trading houses and star trading houses were also permitted to import canalized items.

(v) The concept of net foreign exchange earnings was made a guiding criterion for issuing licenses thereunder to registered exporters. The changes made in this regard are mentioned below:

(a) Replenishment licensing (REP) scheme was expended and simplified;

(b) Services like computer software, overseas management and consultancy services contracts as well as advertising jobs would qualify for import replenishments;

(c) A scheme of star trading houses was introduced for exporters with an average annual net foreign exchange earnings of Rs. 75 crores in the preceding three licensing years of the base period;

(d) Under the scheme of registration of export houses, and trading houses, for determining eligibility, the annual average of net foreign exchange earnings in the base period should not be less than Rs. 5 crores for an export house and Rs. 20 crores for trading houses. These houses would be eligible for additional licences for import of raw materials, components, consumables and tools and capital goods allowed under OGL, besides other permissible and canalized items;

(e) Blanket Advance Licensing was introduced under the Duty Exemption Scheme for manufacturer-exporters having a minimum net foreign exchange earnings of Rs. 10 crores during the preceding three years.

Export-Import (EXIM) Policy (2002-2007)

The EXIM policy was announced by Union Commerce and Industry Minister Murasoli Maran on March 31, 2002 for the five-year period. The major thrust of the policy was to boost India's exports. Several measures were taken to augment exports, particularly of farm goods, small scale sector, textiles, electronic hardware, gems and jewelries, etc. In addition, a number of measures were also taken to reduce transaction cost, and procedures were also simplified for the purpose.

The salient features of EXIM Policy are:

(i) Growth-oriented

(a) *Neutralising fuel cost*: Fuel costs were to be rebated for all export products. This aimed at enhancing the cost competitiveness of our export products;

(b) *Diversification of market*: Several initiatives were taken to diversify the markets.

Focus LAC (Latin American Countries) was launched in November 1997 in order to accelerate trade with these countries. The initiatives helped to increase the exports with these countries by 40 per cent. It was further extended up to March 2003.

Focus Africa was launched in April 2002 as the region was said to contain tremendous potential for trade, particularly with sub-Saharan Africa.

The status-holders would be eligible for hundred per cent retention of foreign exchange in exchange earners foreign currency account.

(ii) Employment-oriented

A number of measures were taken with an objective to bring about employment orientation, some of which are mentioned below:

(a) EXIM Policy removed all quantitative restrictions on all agricultural products except for a few items like jute and onions;

(b) To promote cottage sector exports coming under KVIC, an amount of Rs. 5 crores under market access initiative (MAI) were earmarked. The provisions also include handicrafts units which can access for funds under MAI. These units would be entitled to the benefit of Export House status on achieving lower average export performance of Rs. 5 crores as against Rs. 15 crores for others while the handicrafts units would be entitled to duty-free imports of many items up to 3 per cent of f.o.b. value of their exports. Under the Export Promotion Capital Goods (EPCG) scheme, these units would not be required to maintain an average level of exports, while calculating export obligation;

(c) Several initiatives were taken to promote development of centres of economic and export excellence such as Tripura for hosiery, woollen blankets in Panipat, and woollen knitwear in Ludhiana. A number of measures were taken to provide benefits to this sector. The benefits are that common service providers in these areas would be entitled to the facilities of EPCG scheme, while there will be entitlement for export house status at Rs. 5 crores instead of Rs. 15 crores for others.

(iii) Special Economic Zones

Indian banks were allowed to set up offshore banking units in Special Economic Zones. These units would work to attract foreign direct investment. These offshore units would be foreign branches of Indian banks, located in India. These units would be exempted from cash reserve ratio (CRR) and statutory liquidity ratio (SLR) and would provide access to international finance rates to SEZ developers and various SEZ units. This aimed to make Special Economic Zones internationally competitive.

Assessment of EXIM Policy

In this policy, several measures like providing tax concessions, streamlining certain procedures and removing quantitative restrictions were taken so as to push exports. A distinctive feature of the EXIM Policy was that it focused on Africa which holds tremendous potential for Indian exporters. Certainly, it was intended to help the Indian exporters to explore this fast growing market which has remained unexplored so far.

A major initiative of the policy was to permit offshore banking units in Special Economic Zones. It aimed to help Indian banks in developing foreign branches so as to make international finance available to them at international rates. This would help to cut down the cost of credit to our exporters. This measure directed towards Special Economic Zones was one of the positive features of EXIM Policy.

However, the Policy was criticized on several grounds. EXIM Policy took measures to boost the export of agriculture. Accordingly, wheat was sold in international market as cattle feed at throwaway prices, thus reducing the mounting buffer stocks of foodgrains which were as high as 58 million tonnes in January 2002. This is really distressing and speaks volumes about the current state of affairs in the FCI. It indicates that the quality of wheat procured by the FCI is poor, particularly in a situation when the government continues to raise the support price of wheat for the farmers every year. The government had the option either to sell the surplus stock in international market at good price or to use the stock in food for work programmes, thus creating employment in public work programme, but it failed to do so. The Policy is also criticized on the ground this situation points to the failure of the Central Government in persuading the State Governments to lift foodgrains from FCI godowns, which is evident from the fact that as against an allocation of

28.55 million tonnes in 2000-01 in case of rice and wheat, the offtake was merely 11.72 million tonnes which was only 41 per cent of the allocation. This was largely due to irrational policy of fixing the issue price of foodgrains quite high. As a result, public preferred to buy foodgrains from the open market. If the government wants to boost the exports, it should resort to such policy which helps in improving the quality of rice and wheat procured so that they can compete in the international markets.

The EXIM Policy has focused on Special Economic Zones, which are modified forms of Export Promotion Zones (EPZs) and Export Oriented Units (EOUs) promoted earlier. But the experience of the government has not been good in these two areas. They together account for only 12 per cent of total exports. Besides, there were several procedural hurdles which also served as constraints in export promotion. So, it is the need of the hour that such bureaucratic hurdles as experienced earlier should be avoided in case of Special Economic Zones, so that they may capture the export markets. India needs to learn from China where Special Economic Zones account for over 40 per cent of the country's total exports. Hence, it should take initiatives which help in improving the performance of the Special Economic Zones.

The Policy also made some concessions to help the small and cottage industry which accounts for 35 per cent of the country's exports. But it is ironical that no attention was paid to increase the credit facility to this sector of economy without which much still remains to achieve.

The Policy made the imports of rough diamonds duty-free. But when we assess them in terms of statistics, its imports declined from 60.1 per cent in 1995-96 to 28 per cent in 1999-2000, which improved slightly in 2004-05 with a rise to 31.4 per cent. This underlines the fact that merely making them duty-free does not serve the purpose, nor fulfill the much-needed elasticity required for exports.

However, it may be noted that Commerce and Industry Ministry alone cannot create an environment to push up exports. Various sectors of economy need to work in proper coordination and are required to be made more efficient towards achieving the objectives envisaged in the Policy. Besides, Centre and State Governments must also coordinate with each other to boost exports. This requires proper credit facility, infrastructure development and improvement in technology in exports.

Foreign Trade Policy (2004-09)

Foreign Trade Policy was announced on 31 August 2004 by Union Commerce and Industry Minister Mr. Kamal Nath for the five-year period. It aimed at doubling India's percentage share in global merchandise trade from 0.7 per cent in 2003 to 1.5 per cent in 2009. India's merchandise exports which were valued at US$ 111 billion in April-December 2007 registered a growth of 21.6 per cent from 2003-04. India's merchandise exports amounted to $ 61.8 billion which accounted for about 0.7 per cent of world's exports. For doubling the target of the Foreign Trade Policy, the country's exports were aimed to reach $ 195 billion by 2009. It implies that a 10 per cent compound annual growth rate in world trade was necessary, and India's exports should grow at the annual average growth rate of 26 per cent. Besides, the service sector should increase its share in export of invisibles to more than $ 120 billion. Together, the two sectors were aimed to achieve the target of US$ 300 billion by 2009.

The Foreign Trade Policy has mainly two objectives:

(i) To double India's percentage share in global merchandise trade from 0.7 per cent in 2003 to 1.5 per cent in 2009; and

(ii) To act as an effective tool of economic growth by focusing on employment generation, especially in semi-urban and rural area.

Key strategies drawn to achieve these targets include:

(a) Creating an atmosphere of trust, confidence and transparency;

(b) Removing controls;

(c) Adopting fundamental principle that duties and levies should not be imposed;

(d) Simplifying procedures to facilitate the tasks of economic growth and reducing transactions cost; and

(e) Identifying some focus areas and develop them to facilitate the growth of the country to make it a global hub for manufacturing, trading and services.

In addition, a number of other initiatives were also taken which are discussed briefly below.

Package for Agriculture

A new scheme called Vishesh Krishi Upaj Yojana was initiated to push up the exports of fruits, vegetables, flowers, minor forest produce and their value-added products. Export of these products shall be entitled to duty-free credit equivalent to 5 per cent of f.o.b. value of exports.

Handicrafts

Duty-free import of handlooms and handicrafts sector was raised to 5 per cent of f.o.b. value of exports.

Gems and Jewellery

Imports of gold of 18 carat and above were to be allowed under the replenishment scheme.

Export Promotion Scheme

A new scheme called "Target Plus" was started to accelerate the pace of growth of exports. Duty-free credit facilities based on incremental exports substantially higher than the general export target were provided to the exporters. Duty-free credit would be 5 per cent, 10 per cent, 15 per cent and 100 per cent respectively of f.o.b. value of incremental exports.

Service Exports

A scheme called "Served from India" which received instant international recognition was introduced for services exports. Under the scheme, individual service providers earning foreign exchange of Rs. 10 lakh would be eligible for duty-free credit entitlement of 10 per cent of total foreign exchange earned of them.

Special Focus Area

Sector having significant export prospects and enough employment generation potential in semi-urban and rural areas have been identified as thrust areas. These include agriculture, handicrafts, handlooms, gems and jewellery, leather and footwear sectors.

Duty-free Import under EPCG

Under Export Promotion Capital Goods (UPLG), the import of capital goods was made duty-free. Capital goods imported under EPCG for agriculture would be permitted to be installed anywhere in an agro-export zone (AEZ).

EOUs

Export Oriented Units (EOUs) shall be exempted from service tax in proportion to their goods and services.

Free Trade and Warehousing Zones

A new scheme was introduced to establish Free Trade and Warehousing Zones (FTWZs) to create and develop trade-related infrastructure with an objective to promote the export and import of goods and services and to carry out transaction in free currency. This was aimed at making India's position strong as a global trading nation.

(i) FDI up to 100 per cent would be permitted in the development and establishment of these zones and the infrastructure facilities related to them.

(ii) A minimum attorney of Rs. 100 crores and five lakh sq. mt. built-up area was scheduled for each zone.

(iii) FTWZs units would be entitled to all other benefits as applicable in for SEZQ units.

Biotechnology Parks

Biotechnology parks to be established would be granted facilities of 100 per cent EOUs.

Import of Second Hand Capital Goods

There would be no restriction on the imports of second hand goods and without any age restriction.

Assessment of Foreign Trade Policy

The Foreign Trade Policy announced by the Commerce Minister Kamal Nath breathes the essence of the Common Minimum Programme of the UPA Government. Its centre of focus was to double the percentage share of India's exports from 0.7 per cent in 2003-04 to 1.5 per cent in 2008-09 along with a major thrust on employment generation in semi-urban and rural areas. One of the basic features of the Foreign Trade Policy is that instead of emphasizing only removal of quantitative restrictions. It moved away from it and concentrated on initiating measures to promote exports in major thrust areas identified which *inter alia* include agriculture, handicrafts, handlooms, gems and jewellery, leather and footwear sectors. Since these areas were largely dominated by small and medium enterprises, the thrust provided to SMEs was likely to boost export and generate more employment. In this sense, the policy direction can be said to be good as it attempted to reach much larger number of small business units and smaller business houses rather than focused to star export houses.

The policy rationalized star export houses from one star to five star export houses which will provide incentives for the small exporters from low category of star export houses to the position of higher star export houses. The incentives will create competition among the smaller units to rise and grow to avail the benefits of the status. This diversification and extension of outreach to more and more units is certainly a great move.

The 'Target Plus Scheme' provides incentives which are linked to the performance. The better the performance, the greater the duty-free entitlement of the units. This is likely to create an environment of healthy competition among the units to improve performance in the export sector of the economy and is good for promoting exports.

Since the focus of study of the Foreign Trade Policy is to push up the exports, several initiatives were proposed to help achieve the target envisioned in FTP. "Served from India" is one of such welcome moves taken to push forward India's image in foreign markets. In addition, the proposed plan to set up

Services Expert Promotion Council was also an initiative to deal with the issues related to developing market access as well as brand building, which can prove very effective in realizing the targets of FTP.

A major initiative of exempting all exported goods and services from service tax was in accordance with the fundamental principal that heavy duties and levies should not be imposed. It helped Indian exporters to improve their competitive strength in the international markets.

A significant initiative taken in FTP to set up Free Trade and Warehousing was largely intended to improve infrastructural facilities in the foreign trade sector. For this, 100 per cent FDI was permitted. It is pointed out that FDI can help to develop world class infrastructure, but it is apprehended that FDI inflows may not be adequate enough for infrastructural development. In such case, this sector can never be ignored because it may prove detrimental to India's export growth. So, the government should do it on its own. Once the country succeeds in this front FDI inflows are bound to increase.

An important issue which calls for our attention was to reduce the transaction cost, particularly when the thrust was on SMEs the margins of which are not very high. The exemption from furnishing bank guarantee by exporters whose minimum turnover was Rs. 5 crores, measuring the validity of all licenses the entitlement to a uniform 24 months, and removal of service tax from all goods and services exports are all aimed at reducing transaction cost.

Certainly the initiatives and measures taken in FTP are all welcome steps taken in right direction. But the success of the FTP will depend on the implementation. It is known to all that bureaucracy in India is a big hurdle in the way of implementing the plans and policies. A big challenge that lies before the government is to facilitate the SMEs and other major exporters to achieve the targets of new FTP of taking the merchandise export to US$ 195 billion and together with service sector to take up the earning to $ 300 billion in terms of foreign exchange by 2009. The target fixed in the FTP is very heartening and good but it requires 25 per cent average annual growth in exports which is not very easy since export growth is much influenced by various external factors operating in world trade. However, every work demands efforts, if efforts are put in right earnest, they are bound to make a difference.

All the above policies announced helped India's merchandise exports to grow at more than 20 per cent during the first nine months of the fiscal 2008-09, despite appreciation of Indian rupee.

Conclusion

Efforts were made to reduce trade deficit by boosting exports. But global economic slowdown during 2008-09 made things difficult as India's exports went down sharply while high prices of oil in international markets kept the country's import bill high. As of March 2010, the trade deficit continues to be high. More efforts are required to bring this deficit down.

The Parallel Economy in India 10

BLACK MONEY IN INDIA

The term 'parallel' has connotation of functioning an unsanctioned sector of economy running quite parallel to the economy but having objectives quite contrary to social objectives. It is based on the unaccounted money. It is variously known as 'black money', 'unaccounted economy', 'illegal economy', 'subterranean economy' or 'unsanctioned economy'. It is a big menace to Indian economy and cause of confrontation between the legitimate and the illegitimate sectors. It creates roadblocks in the path of achieving the social objectives of establishing a welfare state as enshrined in the Constitution of India. It is a challenge for the goals of planned development which aim at promoting greater social welfare. The principal function of the state committed to implement the ideals of Constitution, i.e. establishing a socialist democratic society, is to ensure that state policies and controls are so geared that the progressive forces dominate and anti-social forces, which attempt to frustrate the efforts of the state, should be subjugated, so as to create a social order based on equality and social justice.

The history of the emergence of the black money goes back to the Second World War when controls and rationing had to be introduced due to shortages of certain essential goods. It was expected that the phenomena would end with the Second World War, but they continued even after the end of the Second World War. In the concept of mixed economy there were the provisions of co-existence of public sector and private sector. The advent of era of planning opened up avenues for investment in a large number of industries. The public sector was mainly concerned with the social cause, hence it concentrated on the development of infrastructure such as roads, railways, ports, irrigation facilities and hydroelectric works, apart from the development of heavy, basic industries, education and health care among others.

The remaining sphere of economy was left to be developed by the private sector. This provided space to those having black money to carry on their business.

As the economic activities grew and expanded during the post-Independence period, this unsanctioned sector of economy also grew and expanded to such an extent that it began to play a dominant role in moulding the state policies. The operators of black money grew so strong that they established a parallel economy. This development contributed towards widening the economic inequalities in society. It also led to the breeding of a new class of rich having abundance of unaccounted wealth. For a better understanding of the problem of black money, it is important to have an estimate of black income.

Various Estimates of Black Money

According to one estimate, over a trillion dollars (roughly the size of our GDP) may be lying in undisclosed, offshore bank accounts held by Indians, and taxing a slice of this pool could substantially lower the fiscal deficit. "There are various estimates doing the rounds. Nevertheless, we are talking about a significant part of capital that could be used for productive purposes. The advantages are manifold—there will be incremental capital at zero cost and it will also have favourable macroeconomic implications both from the BoP and fiscal perspective", said Hemant Mishr, Standard Chartered Bank's head of global markets in India. It's a tempting thought and possibly worth a try.

According to IMF survey on the unaccounted sector of the economy (1982-83), the estimated black money in India stands at 50 per cent of Gross National Product (GNP), which was Rs. 1,45,141 crores at that time. On this calculation India's unaccounted sector was of the order of Rs. 72,000 crores in 1982-83. As Indian economy is growing at nearly 6 per cent rate, its underground economy or black economy is thriving well. Quoting various studies done in the past, the Indira Gandhi National Institute of Development estimates that black money in India is around 18-21 per cent of GDP. As India's GDP is now estimated at Rs. 17,70,000 crores, as per the Centre for Monitoring Indian Economy, the unaccounted black money circulating in the system works out to a whopping Rs. 3,54,000 crores. In total, India has about $50 billion of black money as of June 2008. This means 2 trillion rupees.

In 2006, the most recent Global Financial Integrity study showed that the average amount stashed away from India annually during 2002-06 is $ 27.3 billion (about Rs. 1,36,466 crores). It means that during the five year period the amount stashed away constitutes 136.5 billion (about Rs. 6,92,328 crores). The well-known economist Professor Arun Kumar also estimates black money generations in India to be currently 50 per cent of the GDP. The growth of black money has shown proportional alarming increase in recent years from 20 per cent in the 1980s to 45-50 per cent at the turn of the century. Preliminary investigations to analyze the Swiss banking chain and to assess Indian wealth in that single country suggests that the number is much larger than the US$ 1.4 trillion figure and is more likely to be near US$ 3 trillion. The larger figure can be derived from the deposits in vaults of gold, diamonds and other precious gems alongside assets managed out of Switzerland in other tax havens.

Surprisingly, India still regarded as a poor country by many, has US$ 1.5 trillion in Swiss banks, which is more black money than in the rest of the world combined. This is thought to be unaccounted money earned in India by inappropriate means as otherwise any Indian citizen or corporation wishing to open a bank account abroad has to take permission from the Reserve Bank of India and records do not show any such permissions granted for deposits in Switzerland. A 2006 report of the Swiss Banking Association claims Indians are the biggest depositors of black money in banks located in Switzerland.

With private account deposits of US$ 1.5 trillion in foreign reserve which have been misappropriated, an amount 10 times larger than India's foreign debt, i.e. more than US$ 155 billion, one needs to rethink if India is a poor country. Many Indians regard this money as public loot. However, the biggest question is "Can we bring back our money?" It is argued that once this huge amount of black money and property comes back to India, the entire foreign debt can be repaid immediately, still leaving a huge surplus amount of foreign exchange reserves in India.

Experts point out that the new investment environment of the last two decades which shows state intervention and favoured massive deregulation, contributed to this phenomenon. The retreat of the nation state ensured that the restraint exercised on capital to keep its greed in check was diluted and some amount of the money went into the process of being legalized. They point out that in a free market environment takeovers were much easier. Those who possess black money tried to buy legal businesses to gain legitimacy for their shadow wealth.

If the growth of the black money has been the same as the white economy so that black income forms roughly 20 per cent of GDP, tapping even 10 per cent of this income through better tax compliance will fetch the government two per cent of GDP.

Impact of Black Money

The growing proliferations of black money in every sector of economy has very serious impact on the economy as well as social system of the country. The same is described below.

First of all, black money causes great loss to the state exchequer. It adversely affects the direction and momentum of valuable national resources. A major portion of black money is kept in such forms which contribute little to the productive activities. It is used for tax evasion—directly or indirectly. Moreover, tax evasion does not include loss of revenue resulting from unreported production or illegal economic activities. Since the government finds it difficult to plug the leakage of tax evasion, it has to resort to other avenues for raising funds. To compensate for this, the government has to resort to other measures such as by imposing more taxes on commodities or by raising the existing rates of taxation on commodities. This led to the developing of a regressive tax structure in India. In this connection Direct Taxes Enquiry Committee stated: "Black money and tax evasion, which go hand in hand, have also the effect of seriously undermining the equity concept of taxation and warping its progressiveness. Together they throw a greater burden on the honest tax-payer and lead to economic inequality and concentration of wealth in the hands of the unscrupulous few in the country." It is the salaried person who has to suffer as he cannot escape taxation, but the dishonest people get away from paying tax. They splurge the money on their lavish lifestyle which. The major portion of the money is used to buy real estate, gold, diamonds, etc. which are mainly unproductive assets.

Black money has widened the gap of economic inequality, which has an adverse impact on the fabric of the society. The salaried class finds itself ever being pushed to the lower rung of the income ladder. They have to pay taxes. Capitalists and big businessmen have larger amount of money at their disposal. Easy money as it is obtained, finds ready outlets in non-essential items of conspicuous consumption. This has an adverse impact on the consumption pattern of society which is tilted in favour of the rich and the elite. This also affects the production pattern. The items of luxuries and those which are used by this class of society are produced in large amount at the cost of the production of articles of mass consumption. This has led to the development of a consumerist culture where larger portion of the income is consumed and very little is saved. This rise in consumption leaves less resources for investment in priority areas. It is not good for the development of the country. This distortion in productions pattern caused by the consumption pattern has affects the society adversely and defeats the very objective of planning.

Black money creates disparity in income. Many high placed officials and employees have much less money than an average small shopkeepers in big cities like Mumbai and Delhi have. The unorganized wage earners are already at the bottom rung of the income ladder. All this contributes to create a very unfair situation.

The huge unaccounted money is a big problem for the policymakers as they fail to make a correct analysis of the situation. For instance, it is not possible to calculate accurately the vital indicators of progress like saving-income ratio, sectoral composition of income, national income, etc. It is also a big hurdle in monitoring the developments of economy with precision and accuracy. Much of these are based on guesswork. Hence, it is a big constraint in formulating proper policies in the absence of correct data.

Black money has caused erosion in the value system of the country. Black money is mostly acquired from illegal means. Hence, it is spent in undesirable and very often an illegitimate manner. Such money gives rise to a tendency of ostentation among the people. This contributes to the spread of corruption. A well placed official who is honest and lives by his means finds himself nowhere near those who spend more for show-off. Black money promotes malpractices in society. It is used to get the works done through bribing, etc., which are not good for society. Power-centres, based on money power rather than on the laws of the land, exercise a hold over many activities of the society. People who own black money believe that the "money can do anything". Hence, the people use black money to get their illegal work done and give a wrong message to society at large.

Black money leads to the accumulation of abundance of liquidity as a major portion of it is kept as cash, gold, silver, property, assets, etc. These are unproductive assets which are not used for the welfare of society. Thus, all attempts of government to control excess demand with the help of measures of credit control or rationing meet with no success as huge liquidity is provided by black money. Since this liquidity results in heavy inventory build-up, it becomes a challenge to establish price stability.

A big portion of black money is transferred to foreign countries through clandestine channels. For this, foreign exchange regulations are violated through under-invoicing of exports and over-invoicing of imports. This leads to the emergence of a paradoxical situation where capital, particularly foreign exchange reserves are scarce but the country becomes a *de facto* lender of aid and capital to those who are economically advanced and already have much more at their disposal. This situation has deteriorated over the years.

An international study entitled "Secret Money—The Shadow World of Tax Evasion and Capital Fight by Fraud", conducted by Iago Walter estimates that during 1975 to 1983 over US$ 120 billion (Rs. 1,55,000 crores) was transferred by residents of developing countries into clandestine assets abroad. In this context, S. Gurumurty states in the *Financial Express*, "India is no exception the buccaneers of the private sectors would no doubt lead in number and in volume. That the public sector is no different is not a secret either. Dr. Raja Chelliah and colleagues have confirmed with the help of retired government officials and public sector executives that foreign suppliers usually provide a 'cushion' of three per cent to five per cent on imports of the public sector. Where does this cushion go? Its destination is predictably clandestine Indian assets abroad." It is because of the secrecy guaranteed by the foreign banks that people find it safe to keep their money with these banks. At the same time it is difficult for the government to pin down and prove these bribes. Besides, they are not paid directly, but are routed through "agents fees" to independent third parties acting on behalf of the payer.

Prof. J.D. Agarwal, Director, Indian Institute of Finance, Delhi estimated that capital flight from India to USA for the three year period—1993, 1994 and 1995 to be to the tune of US$ 15.8 billion (Rs. 57,000 crores) at USA/world average prices. This capital flight through abnormal trade pricing has adversely affected foreign exchange reserves of India, and to a great extent, it contributed to the trade deficit of US$ 13.115 billion during 1993-95. If this flight of capital could be checked, the country would have sufficient reserves of foreign exchange which would have helped the country in repaying its external debts. It would have lessened the debt burden of the country. In addition, this money laundering sent wrong signals to those interested in investing in India. This also discouraged MNCs and FIIs from making investment in India. A part of the money kept abroad, generated through abnormal trade pricing is brought back to the country through Hawala route. This leads to distortion in exchange rate. Though the government has declared convertibility on current account, difference between official and non-official exchange rate still continues. The use of capital flight is considered to be the best way to convert black money into white money. However, there are a number of reasons behind such massive flight of capital which include political uncertainty, craze for foreign exchange, tax evasion, use of foreign exchange as a hedge for business transactions and for other transaction such as shopping, travel, medical expenses and studying abroad.

Black money contributes to the emergence and spread of anti-social elements like musclemen, touts, and brokers who are required to protect the black money. They are used to fight against the forces of law and order. Besides, there are contact men, chartered accountants, income tax advisors who also work for the black money operators. They negotiate with the government machinery to win favour for the black money operators. This has provided a favourable atmosphere for the flourishing of a black money culture in the country. At the same time it has vitiated the work culture. Black money is used as an instrument to get things done expeditiously, if there are difficulties and delays. This sort of dealings are common and frequent.

Black money has helped to develop a nexus between politician and black money operators. This nexus acts as a shield against them. They manipulate this relation in their favour. At the time of election, politicians, ministers and party functionaries approach the business tycoons for funds. From local to national level this is done openly. In fact, when Indira Gandhi Government banned the company donations in 1968, the disastrous impact of black money even penetrated deeper into the political system. Now this practice seems to have gained social acceptance. This relation even interferes with the policy matters. Under the pressure of black money, national policies have a tilt in favour of big business houses. The political leadership who has a relation with them acts as a mouthpiece of big businessmen to justify the abolition of controls or introduction of a dual system of prices in the name of productivity or rational interests. Election Commissioner, S.Y. Quraishi, expressed his concern in these words: "Role of black money in elections is the biggest problem.

We admit that we have failed to curb it." The Wanchoo Committee put this relationship in these words: "It is, therefore, no exaggeration to say that black money is like a cancerous growth in the country's economy which, if not checked in time, is sure to lead its ruination."

Why is Black Money Generated?

The evil of black money is big indeed with disastrous consequences for the economy. A major question is why is it generated? What are the factors which help it? It is certain that various political and economic factors contribute to its generation and growth. Principal factors responsible for the genesis, growth and expansion of black money are discussed below.

A Consequence of Permits, Quotas and Licenses

A group of economists is of the view that there is a close relation between the system of controls, quotas, permits and licenses with the mal-distribution of commodities in short supply, which results in the generation of black money. The Wanchoo Committee, explaining it as a source of black money observed, "In spite of the vigilance exercised by the Government, controls and regulations came to be used by the unscrupulous for amassing money for themselves. Since considerable discretionary powers lay in the hands of those who administered controls, this provided them with a scope of corruption—'speed money' for turning a blind eye to the violation of controls. All this gave rise to trading in permits, quotas and licenses, malpractices distribution and in the process, it generated sizeable sums of black money."

A regime of controls, quotas and permits contributed a lot to the spread of black money. Parallely runs the psychology of making easy money. Its results were twofold: (i) In the first place it provided ground for corruption. Big money was issued to secure permits, quotas, licenses, etc. Even the public undertakings did not escape this evil net. The National Institute of Public Policy in its study found that "for most substantial public sector contracts, whether at home or abroad, significant cuts and kickbacks to key decision-makers have become the rule rather than the exceptions". (ii) Secondly, these controls created shortages, sometimes artificial shortages. This had adverse effect on a large variety of goods, manufactures or raw materials, imported or domestically produced. The prices paid or received on controlled goods were much above the official prices. These excess prices contributed to the growth and expansion of black money.

Dagli Committee also observed price controls and subsidies as causes responsible for the genesis of black money in these words: "Price and distribution controls have in the past led to the generation of black money on a significant scale. Any price control without any adequate machinery of distribution and speedy arrangement for increasing supplies is potentially a source of black money generation." The Committee also pointed out that rent control led to the emergence of *pugree* system, and this became another source of black money. Similarly, the system of licenses requires large number of inspectors for completing various formalties. A large amount of black money is used to get the work done. Where controls are not implementable, they have led to harassment and generation of black money.

Donations to Political Parties

With the ban of donations to political parties in 1968, the businessmen took to other route to impress the political parties. They started funding the political parties, particularly the ruling party with their black money. Theoretically, the decision to ban the donations was taken to reduce the influence of the corporate sector on the election process of the country, but in practice, what happened was quite the opposite. Businessmen everywhere have the impression that they should pay a certain portion of their black money to the political parties so as to carry on their business smoothly and win some favours from them. Big business in the process, has been able to tame the political leadership and thus the latter has started obliging the former as per their desire.

Black Money in Public Sector

In every Five-Year Plan government announces a larger size of fund for expansion, upgradation and renovation. The projects to be undertaken by the government are monitored by the bureaucrats and officials of the public sector undertakings. Tenders are invited for the purpose and these tenders are awarded in consultation with the politicians. There is a nexus between the politicians, bureaucracy and contractors. While awarding the tenders, this relation along with various other devices are at work. These underhand practices contribute to the generation of black money. Political instability also helps in furthering the momentum of this process. The rapid change, drop and reshuffling of the ministers add to the dimension of this problem. This instability in their career makes them think of taking optimum advantages of the time they are in power. They begin to misuse their power and position. The large numbers of scandals that are unearthed by the opposition only support the contention that huge investment in the public sector serves as potential source of black money generation.

Gap between the Acceptable Net Rate of Return and Legally Permissible Rate of Return

A group of economists holds the view that a wide gap between the expectation and actual situation in terms of rate of return is a major factor which contributes to the generation of black money. Individuals expect a higher net rate of return than what is legally permitted. In this connection, higher marginal rates of taxes assume special importance. The Federation of Indian Chambers of Commerce and Industry (FICCI) is of the opinion that very high rates of taxation on incomes above a certain limit are in fact expropriatory in nature. For example, at one time, the marginal rate of income tax was as high or 97.5 per cent and this was tantamount to near nationalization of all incomes beyond a certain level. Many experts on public finance, describing the situation, put this view that we are "the most highly taxed nation". However, government realized the implications and these high rates were gradually brought down to 40 per cent by the then finance minister Dr. Manmohan Singh by 1996. This continued even during the time of P. Chidambaram who further cut down the rate in 1997-98 to 30 per cent for individual and 35 per cent for corporations.

Another group of experts, influenced by Left, believes that the argument of high marginal tax rates is overplayed. They assert that actually paid rates on declared incomes are not as high as determined by the officially prescribed marginal rates of taxation. Consequently, a reduction in rates of taxation would not result in reduction in tax evasion, but it only grants more relief to those who evade tax. K.N. Kabra, a renowned economist writes, "In a regime which induces reduction in tax evasion by a method 'soft' on tax evaders (like cut in tax rates) rather than by 'harder' method which enhances the costs and risks of tax evasion, it would be difficult to expect a better tax compliance through 'soft-methods'."

However, tax evasion accounts for only a part of the black economy. The IGIDR study says black income is generated from illegal activities that are harmful to society such as smuggling, trafficking in illicit drugs, pornography and gambling. But there are other apparently harmless illegal activities too such as "moonlighting (e.g. private tuition by salaried teachers and private practices by publicly employed doctors)". "While amnesty schemes provided an opportunity to cover black income into white in the case of tax-evaded income, there are in general several other possible means of money laundering," it said.

Certainly, defects in tax structure have a significant role to play in the black income generation. For instance, we can take direct taxation. Till recently, tax on income and wealth was very high, which led to tax evasion. The rate of income tax was as high as 75 per cent to those who came under the high income groups. When combined with the tax on wealth, it was all the higher. For instance, a person having net wealth of Rs. 12 lakhs, the combined tax rate was as high as 95 per cent. Again a person whose net wealth exceeded 18 lakhs, the marginal rate of tax was very high during the pre-reforms period. The corporate tax too was very high. In such a situation, people try to find ways for tax evasion.

The situation was not very different in indirect tax. To some extent it was worse than the direct tax as the revenues from these taxes constitute a big portion of all the tax revenues. For example, in case of government, revenue from customs and central excise duties has been as much as 80 per cent of the total tax revenue. Hence, a small fraction of the evaded tax runs into crores of rupees of black money. According to the National Institute of Public Finance and Policy, the excise tax evasion was rampant particularly in cotton fabrics and plastics industries. The Institute pointed out that the tax evasion through the underestimation of production and sales is most pronounced in manufacturing, trade, hotels and restaurants.

Illegal Estate Transactions

An important factor of considerable importance is illegal real estate transactions in urban, real estate in various forms such as renting, buying and selling of land, buildings, transfers of ownership deeds, etc. These transactions have taken on several forms. Black income is widely used from the time of construction till the allotment of buildings.

The evil practice of black money is prevalent even in case of rented house. The operation of rent control is such as has led to the phenomenon of *pugree*, i.e. the scarcity premium, with rent remaining the same. In the sale and purchase of real estate, both the parties involve, in transaction find substantial advantages in declaring the lower price, while the remaining amount is settled in cash. Such a practice provides ample scope for the growth of black incomes. The seller does so to evade capital gains tax. The buyer is benefitted by evading stamp duty for registration of the property and house property tax.

Increase in Public Expenditure

An unprecedented increase in public expenditure is a significant factor that helps in the growth and expansion of black money. This aspect of black money was also pointed out in the Black Money Committee Report of the National Institute of Public Finance and Policy. This factor fuelled the growth of black money during the early seventies when government took certain measures to remove poverty, supply foodgrains to the needy and start large plans, etc. But the huge spending, which these measures necessitated, has neither been efficiently administered, nor properly targeted. It resulted into huge leakage of funds into the stream of unaccounted income.

APPROACH OF GOVERNMENT TOWARDS BLACK MONEY

A huge amount of black money is stashed away in several foreign banks. According to international reports, wealth stashed away by Indians in offshore banks could be $ 1-1.5 trillion. Tax Justice Network, an organization that works towards fair tax treatments, says the wealth concealed in tax havens across the world stands at between US$ 11-12 trillion. According to the organization, Indian income tax laws have sufficient provisions to prosecute a tax-payer who refuses to pay tax after a crystallized tax demand. Mahesh Jethmalani, senior advocate says that the prospect of prosecution could be the most effective way of bringing such money back to India.

But the country is not very keen to bring black money back. Transparency International says, India has maintained "a stoic silence over the issue and has not approached the German Government to receive the data". Hundreds of rich Indians have black money parked in Liechtenstein which could be made available to the authorities by the German Government. Liechtenstein is a small land-locked country situated between Austria and Switzerland. It provides tax havens.

Suspecting that the government's soft stand could stem from fears that influential politicians and industrialists might be compromised on the Liechenstein data, Transparency International has, in a statement, said, "It is alleged that this money belongs to rich and powerful politicians, industrialists and stock brokers and that is why the reluctance on the part of government of India to get details from Germany."

Expressing concern over the Indian Government's apparently lackadaisical attitude in getting after offenders who have cheated the tax authorities of millions of dollars is quite surprising and the Indian Charter of Transparency International (TI)—an organization campaigning to reduce corruption—has urged the government to take all necessary steps to seek the data.

Admiral R.H. Tahilani, Chairman of TI India and former navy chief, said. "This money belongs to the people of India and it is possible that it has been tucked away in this distant country by those who have acquired it illegally and are now evading taxes."

"There should be complete transparency and accountability about this money and it is for the government to find this out and inform people", Admiral Tahilani said, referring to the black money stashed away abroad.

However, tax experts and senior income-tax officials opine that there are roadblocks on the way to accessing accounts in LGT bank because of the limitation period that bars the IT department to take up cases older than six years. Experts say the existing law on limitation needs to be altered. But to be effective, the law should have retrospective effect.

Corruption: A Big Challenge

Corruption is a big challenge in India. It is a big constraint to the development of the country. In the Corruption Perception Index prepared by Transparency International, India ranked 71 among 102 countries surveyed in 2002 while it was 88 among 158 countries surveyed in 2005. Its score was 2.9 in 1998, which declined to 2.7 in 2007. It again rose to 2.9 in 2005 and further to 3.5 in 2007.

Table 10.1: India's Rank in Corruption Perception Index (CPI)

Year	No. of countries	Corruption Perception Index (CPI)	Rank
1995	41	2.8	35
1996	54	2.6	46
1997	52	2.7	45
1998	85	2.9	66
1999	99	2.9	72
2000	90	2.8	69
2001	91	2.7	71
2002	102	2.7	71
2005	158	2.9	88
2006	163	3.3	70
2007	180	3.5	72
2008	180	3.4	85
2009	180	3.4	84

Source: Transparency International, Berlin.

It is clear from the Table that India has been ranked as a highly corrupt country where no serious efforts have been made by the government to improve the situation. K.R. Narayanan, the then President of India, also expressed his concern in his address to the Lok Sabha in 1997 saying, "Sheer opportunism and valueless power politics have taken over the place of principles and idealism, relationship between peoples groups and parties...and corruption is corroding the vitals of politics and our society."

Transparency International in its report has estimated that from people by way of corruption, a sum of Rs. 26,768 crores is extracted from people by officials in India in various sectors which include education, power, health care, telephone, railways, land and building, administration, judiciary and public distribution system.

Corruption Perceptions Index 2009

India's score on Transparency International's Corruption Perception Index (CPI) remained unchanged at 3.4 out of 10 in the 2009 list. However, it inched up one place to 84 in the anti-corruption watchdog's annual list of 180 countries and territories around the world. The scores and rankings were based on 13 different expert and business surveys.

The CPI highlights that the vast majority of the 180 countries included in the 2009 index score below five on a scale from 0 (perceived to be highly corrupt) to 10 (perceived to have low level of corruption). The top spots were retained by New Zealand at 9.4, Denmark at 9.3, Singapore and Sweden tied at 9.2 and Switzerland at 9.0. The report attributed their formidable performance to the "political stability, long-established conflict of interest regulations and solid, functioning public institutions" in these nations.

At the bottom of the index, war-ravaged Somalia remains the world's most corrupt country, followed by Afghanistan, Myanmar, Sudan and Iraq. Barring Bhutan, which has a score of 5.0, India is still at the top of South Asian countries. Till 2005, India performed poorly with a CPI score of less than 3 but has since picked up. China is just a few notches above India with a score of 3.6 and a ranking of 79. Nearly half of the 180 countries scored 3 or lower.

Table 10.2 shows the rank of some important countries in the Corruption Perceptions Index (CPI), giving each country's ranking and score, the number of surveys used to determine the score, and the confidence range of the scoring. The rank shows how one country compares to others included in the index. The CPI score indicates the perceived level of public sector corruption in a country/territory. The CPI is based on 13 independent surveys. However, not all surveys include all countries. The surveys used column indicates how many surveys were relied upon to determine the score for that country. The confidence range indicates the reliability of the CPI scores and tells us that allowing for a margin of error, we can be 90 per cent confident that the true score for this country lies within this range.

Table 10.2: Rank of Important Countries in Corruption Perception Index (CPI) 2009

Rank	Country/Territory	CPI 2009 score	Surveys used	Confidence range
1	New Zealand	9.4	6	9.1 — 9.5
2	Denmark	9.3	6	9.1 — 9.5
3	Singapore	9.2	9	9.0 — 9.4
12	Hong Kong	8.2	8	7.9 — 8.5
14	Germany	8	6	7.7 — 8.3
17	Japan	7.7	8	7.4 — 8.0
17	United Kingdom	7.7	6	7.3 — 8.2
19	United States	7.5	8	6.9 — 8.0
22	Qatar	7	6	5.8 — 8.1
24	France	6.9	6	6.5 — 7.3
30	United Arab Emirates	6.5	5	5.5 — 7.5
32	Israel	6.1	6	5.4 — 6.7
37	Taiwan	5.6	9	5.4 — 5.9
39	Korea (South)	5.5	9	5.3 — 5.7
42	Mauritius	5.4	6	5.0 — 5.9
46	Bahrain	5.1	5	4.2 — 5.8
46	Hungary	5.1	8	4.6 — 5.7
49	Bhutan	5	4	4.3 — 5.6
55	South Africa	4.7	8	4.3 — 4.9
56	Malaysia	4.5	9	4.0 — 5.1
63	Saudi Arabia	4.3	5	3.1 — 5.3
66	Kuwait	4.1	5	3.2 — 5.1
75	Brazil	3.7	7	3.3 — 4.3

Contd...

79	China	3.6	9	3.0 — 4.2
84	India	3.4	10	3.2 — 3.6
84	Thailand	3.4	9	3.0 — 3.8
89	Mexico	3.3	7	3.2 — 3.5
97	Sri Lanka	3.1	7	2.8 — 3.4
106	Argentina	2.9	7	2.6 — 3.1
111	Egypt	2.8	6	2.6 — 3.1
111	Indonesia	2.8	9	2.4 — 3.2
120	Kazakhstan	2.7	7	2.1 — 3.3
120	Vietnam	2.7	9	2.4 — 3.1
126	Syria	2.6	5	2.2 — 2.9
130	Libya	2.5	6	2.2 — 2.8
130	Nigeria	2.5	7	2.2 — 2.7
139	Bangladesh	2.4	7	2.0 — 2.8
139	Pakistan	2.4	7	2.1 — 2.7
139	Philippines	2.4	9	2.1 — 2.7
143	Nepal	2.3	6	2.0 — 2.6
146	Kenya	2.2	7	1.9 — 2.5
146	Russia	2.2	8	1.9 — 2.4
146	Ukraine	2.2	8	2.0 — 2.6
154	Yemen	2.1	4	1.6 — 2.5
168	Haiti	1.8	3	1.4 — 2.3
168	Iran	1.8	3	1.7 — 1.9
176	Iraq	1.5	3	1.2 — 1.8
178	Myanmar	1.4	3	0.9 — 1.8
179	Afghanistan	1.3	4	1.0 — 1.5
180	Somalia	1.1	3	0.9 — 1.4

Source: Transparency International.

Fortunately, the situation has slightly improved in the post-reforms period as a result of the dismantling of the system of controls and quotas, and the level of corruption has declined. The demand for transparency facilitated by the Right to Information Act is also contributing in bringing down the level of corruption. But still much remains to be done to reach the levels of least corrupt countries.

Causes of Corruption

Corruption has been widely studied by experts. They have found various reasons behind the spread of corruption. The reasons so far revealed in the studies include the following:

(i) A situation of scarcity of goods and services leads to the growth of corruption. First a scarcity is created then the scarce goods are made available to the needy at much higher costs.

(ii) The system of quotas, licenses and permits which was prevalent in India upto mid-1990s, provided opportunities to bureaucracy to make money. In this system people were forced to pay hush money to get their work done. In the post-Independence period it was a major cause of corruption.

(iii) Certain sanctions and approvals involve complex procedures which provide the bureaucracy ample scope for harnessing money as they harass the public so much that they are forced to pay the officials to get their work done.

(iv) Low salaries of government employees particularly at lower level were one of the causes of corruption. This led to the development of a culture of bribery, which is used as an incentive to get the file cleared.

(v) A nexus between politicians and bureaucracy helps in the growth of corruption. Bribery of politicians helps to buy the influence which is utilized to exploit some situation. At the same time the influence gained with the help of money helps the politicians win vote bank for them.

(vi) High ranking officials in bureaucracy, who act as intermediaries, get kickbacks from the public and share them with the politicians. Thus, this malpractice continues to thrive under the safe patronage of politicians.

(vii) In cities, where there are illegal constructions, the regularization of colonies, exoneration of violation of building by laws, political protection given to slum dwellers to use water, electricity, without any charge provide suitable environment for flourishing corruption —both by officials and politicians.

(viii) High costs of election campaigning and contesting election are also responsible for the growth of corruption in India. The corporate sector funds the politicians during elections to contest election. In turn they are granted various sorts of favours.

(ix) A rising tendency of show off in society is a significant factor behind the growth of corruption. People spend huge amount of money on a small family function. Marriages are getting costlier. This leads people to look for other sources of income resulting in corruption.

(x) Increasing tolerance in society about corruption contributes to the growth of corruption. It appears that corruption has gained social acceptance. People no longer take it as a social evil. It is taken as a way of life. Such mindset perpetuates the growth of corruption. Society seems to have failed to create institutional structure to tackle cases of corruption, particularly at high places. It creates a feeling of helplessness about corruption among the masses.

In brief, corruption breeds inefficiency, leading to the production of inferior quality of goods like roads, railways, substandard houses, etc. It raises the cost of developments. It also reduces the realization in the form of tax revenue to the government. Corruption creates a parallel economy of black money, which uses various ways and means to perpetuate corruption.

Corruption is a big constraint to the development of a healthy society. It is important that corruption should be eliminated or reduced to the extent that the phenomenon of black money does not destroy the vitals of society. However, much more important is that the factors responsible for the growth of corruption should be identified and necessary measures are taken to correct the situation.

Measures to Control Black Money

Economists have a divided opinion on how to control the growth of black economy. One school of experts believes that within the framework of the mixed economy as in India, the expansion of black money can be brought within manageable limits so that it may interfere with the very objectives of national economic policies, while the other group of economists holds the view that mixed economy is only an euphemism for capitalist system and there is no way of controlling black money in the existing framework of the mixed economy that is present in India.

However differences may be there in their viewpoints, black money is a big evil, it calls for certain measures to get rid of it and make the economy function in a healthy manner. Following concrete measures suggested can be of great help in controlling the parallel economy of black money in India:

Rationalization of Tax Structure

The economists have a unanimous opinion regarding the rationalization of tax structure since tax evasion is basic to the phenomenon of black money generation. Efforts need to be made to devise such taxes that curb or prevent taxable income, goods and services from escaping the tax net. Steps need to be taken to discourage undervaluation of assets to reduce tax. It is equally important to reduce these tax rates. For instance, it has been argued that marginal tax rates on higher income should be reduced. Besides, tax laws should be liberalized regarding depreciation and writing off of capital. There should be complete exemption of savings from taxation. Direct taxes should be linked to the cost of living, etc. In this connection, it appears relevant to mention that abolition of estate duty, i.e. the tax payable at the time of inheriting property/wealth can be much of help in this regard. The tax net should be expanded to cover new tax-payers. Government machinery needs to be made sincere and stern at implementing all measures taken. Merely direct tax regime is not going to make big difference in the present scenario. Furthermore, the structure of indirect taxes needs to be rationalized so as to expand it to cover those goods and services which are not in the tax net. The introduction of MODVAT, for example, is the best example in which tax is levied on the final commodity, instead of a number of taxes levied at different stages of production\distribution. Introduction of a full-fledged VAT can be a welcome move in this regard. In addition, the proposed GST (Goods & Services Tax) system is a welcome decision taken in right direction.

The GST system has worked well for countries with a federal or central tax administration mechanism where the levy and collection of tax was made by the union government. When applied as a single federal levy to a large tax base at a low and uniform rate, GST emerged as a highly successful mechanism of indirect taxation. Subsequently, such a federal levy was found to be impractical in countries that had their fiscal powers apportioned between the federal and provincial governments. Countries like Canada and Brazil grappled with the situation and addressed the same by suitably modifying GST model, and thus evolved the ingenious system of a dual GST.

In the Indian context, present indications are that a dual GST structure has been finalized whereby the central and state governments would concurrently levy the tax. It is expected that the proposed concurrent dual GST system would preserve and protect the fiscal powers and at the same time rationalize the indirect tax structure by subsuming a plethora of central and local taxes into a consolidated levy.

Worldwide experience shows that if structured and implemented uniformly, on a pan-national basis, GST is likely to emerge as an efficient system of taxation that works to the benefit of the industry, consumer as well the government. It would, therefore, be imperative to arrive at some conclusion to smoothen India's transition into the GST regime.

The greatest challenge is how to curb the tendency of tax evasion among the people particularly those who come in the high income groups and indulge in evasion of tax on a massive scale. It is this aspect which needs to be attended to. For this, the state needs to have a strict attitude so as to ensure the realization of tax revenue from persons who come under the tax net. Certainly, this requires to make tax administration more efficient to ensure better tax compliance.

Tax Reforms

Another major step includes reforms in tax structure. This calls for efforts to bring down tax rates. The argument in its favour is that reduction in tax rates will dampen the urge for concealing income to evade taxes. Large tax revenue following tax reductions in direct taxes means that larger amounts of incomes have been declared. Besides, simplification of tax laws and tax procedures will also help in this regard.

Removal of Unnecessary Controls

A group of economists does support the controls and licensing procedures. They believe that these are not good for the productivity and create hindrances for the market forces. They think that these controls are unnecessary and hence should be withdrawn.

In pursuance of this logic, government lifted control on cement and introduced a dual system of pricing. Even the prices of levy cement were raised. The cement manufacturers fixed a little high price for the open market. But it resulted in a rise in the prices of cement. The cement which was sold at Rs. 65 per bag the open market is being sold at Rs. 240 per bag at present. Now, checking the further hike in the cement prices is a big challenge for the government. The abolition of controls helped to remove shortage of cement, and at the same time, it saw an unprecedented rise in its prices. The main objective behind abolishing controls over the cement prices was that it would result in competition and that the forces of competition in course of time would bring the prices of cement down. But this did not happen. The benefits of liberalization went the manufacturers rather than consumers.

It is believed that the ineffective use of controls results in such a situation. The absence of controls gives the businessmen opportunities to exploit the consumers by creating artificial scarcity which helps in the generation of black money. Dagli Committee on controls and subsidies stated in this regard, "Price and distribution controls in the past led to the generation of black money on a significant scale. Any price control without any adequate machinery of distribution and speedy arrangement for increasing supplies is potentially a source of black money generation. It is not the abolition of price control, rather rationalization of them...with an effective system of distribution that can be of much help in this regard. The abolition of controls in order to speed up the growth rate of economy is not likely to bring the desired result."

The basic remedy lies in uprooting the source of black transactions. In this connection, stringent measures can be taken against those who indulge in the reported transactions, which fall within the tax net. More importantly, opportunities for the growth of corruption should be eliminated. This requires an efficient machinery which should be sincere and committed enough to carry on the objectives of economic equality as enshrined in the Constitution of India. At the same time proper remuneration should be paid to the administrative functionaries so as to eliminate any temptation for the same. People also need to change their mindset. We should have zero tolerance in terms of corruption. The present situation has degenerated to such a low level that businesses see much advantages in dealing in cash, and no stigma is attached to tax evasion and black transactions. Nothing is considered immoral. This marks a decline in our social morals and values. People need to be made aware of the evils of black money.

A significant aspect of black income relates to transactions in real estate in urban areas. Speculation is rampant in real estate business, namely renting, buying and selling of land/ building, transfers of ownership deeds, etc. These transactions are carried on in several other forms. The investment in various transactions of real estate brings very high capital gains. A large portion of black income is invested in real estate with an objective to gain more money. Besides, black income is widely used to grease the palm of the authorities concerned so as to making the rules and procedures easier in their favour like rationing of plans, grant of completion certificates, allotment of building materials, etc. When the real estate is sold and bought, both the parties involved find substantial advantage in declaring lower prices while settling the remaining payments in cash. This helps the parties involved in transactions in tax saving. One of the important ways for tackling the evils of black money is to appropriate the gains from property speculation. The growth of the black income has been the same as the white economy so that black income forms roughly 20 per cent of GDP. Tapping even 10 per cent of this income through better tax compliance will fetch the government two per cent of GDP.

Organisation of Rural Credit in India

11

Rural Credit Cooperatives in India

India is essentially a rural India, and rural India is virtually a cultivator, the village handicraftsman and agricultural labourer. About 70 per cent of all Indians live in rural areas. However, rural India is increasingly becoming a diversified market with a strong demand for credit for agriculture like buying inputs like seeds, pesticides, farm implements, etc. and non-agricultural, purposes, like health, insurance and money-transfers among others.

In the development strategy adopted by independent India, the primary form was growth with equity. Given an understanding of the seasonally credit requirements of farm operations, institutional credit was preceded fairly early in the development process as a powerful tool for enhancing productivity to achieve the objectives of production and productivity. The stance of policy towards rural credit was to ensure provision of sufficient and timely credit at reasonable rates of interest to as large a segment of the rural population as possible. The strategy drawn for the purpose rested on three pillars: (i) expansion of the institutional structure, (ii) direct lending to disadvantaged borrowers and sectors, and (iii) lower interest rates.

The institutional vehicles chosen for the task include cooperatives, commercial banks and regional rural banks (RRBs). During the period 1950-69, the emphasis was on the promotion of cooperatives, which shifted to commercial banks during the post-nationalisation period to establish branches in the rural areas and the creation of new institutional structures—RRBs in

1970s, NABARD in the 1980s and Local Area Banks in the late 1990s.

How to make the credit available at concessional rates was one of the key elements of the strategy to be deployed for rural credit. The justification for offering credit at concessional rates to certain categories of borrowers was based on the argument that farm-based activity in the short run does not yield enough return to enable regular servicing of loans. As concessional lending impacted the profitability of rural financial institutions, a policy of cross subsidization and refinance from the RBI and later NABARD was introduced.

The strategies items adopted under this policy helped to build a broad-based institutional infrastructure for the delivery and deployment of credit and ensured a wider accessibility of financial services to the poor. The following indicators show the growth of credit during 1970-95 which in real terms at 7 per cent was greater than:

- The annual growth in GDP,
- Real public agricultural capital formation at 3 per cent,
- Real private agricultural capital formation at 4 per cent,
- Real agricultural input spending at 6 per cent.

As a consequence, a much greater number of rural households have accessibility to credit from these multiple formal institutions which was less than 10 per cent in the early 1950s.

Need for Credit for Farmers

The farmers constitute a dominant section of our rural masses. The credit requirement of most of the villagers particularly farmers are met by cooperative societies. The financial requirements of Indian farmers can be classified into three types as enumerated below, based on the period and purpose for which the credits are sought.

1. Indian farmers generally require financial assistance for a period of less than 15 months, either for cultivation or for meeting domestic expenses. They want to buy seeds, fertilizers, fodder for their cattle, etc. There may be some financial requirements in the family in the years when there have been

crops failure or crops production has not been sufficient enough to meet their requirements. Generally, these type of loans are paid back after the harvest.

2. The farmers also require funds for medium term, ranging from 15 months to 5 years. This type of funds are required to buy cattle, agricultural implements and for making improvement on land. In terms of quantity, they are larger than the short-terms loans. They are repaid over a longer period of time.

3. The farmers require finances for purchasing land, for making improvement of land, to pay off old debt and also to purchase agricultural implements and machinery. These loans are for longer periods of more than five years.

Types of Credit

The credit requirements of the farmers can be classified into two groups—productive and unproductive groups. Productive loans are those used to buy seeds, fertilizers, implements, etc. so as to improve the production and productivity. These type of loans are also used to improve the quality of lands, which includes digging and deepening of wells, fencing of land, etc.

The farmers also have to take loans to meet some family obligations such as marriages, births and death, etc. Sometimes they are entangled in litigation, hence they have to take loan to meet litigation expenses. Such loans are used in unproductive purposes. They are not used in occupational activities, but they are raised at high rates of interest.

Sources of Rural Credit

The sources of rural credit can be broadly divided into two categories—institutional and private. Institutional credit refers to the credit provided to the farmers by commercial banks, cooperative societies, cooperative banks, including regional rural banks. Private and non-institutional sources include money-lenders, traders, commission agents, relatives and landlords.

During the early years of Independence, non-institutional sources were the major sources of money lending, accounting for nearly 93 per cent of the total credit requirements of which the institutional sources, including the government had only

7 per cent of the total credit. According to the All India Debt and Investment Survey, the share of non-institutional lending declined to about 37 per cent. In 1981, the moneylender's share was barely 16 per cent, but the share of institutional credit rose to 63 per cent, with cooperatives contributing 30 per cent, while the share of commercial banks was about 29 per cent.

Importance of Credit Delivery Mechanism in Rural Finance

Since Independence, the government has been taking a multi-agency approach so as to provide cheaper and adequate credit to the farmers as well as providing them with security against the exploitation of the moneylenders and commission agents who force the farmers to sell their produce at low price while they charge a heavy commission for their dealings. The approach comprises making credit available through cooperatives, commercial banks and regional rural banks, widely known as institutional credit. The major thrust of the policy has been to ensure adequate and timely flow of credit to promote development in undeveloped and neglected areas.

Main objectives of the government policy include the following:

(a) To reduce and gradually eliminate the moneylenders from the rural supply system.

(b) To ensure timely and adequate supply of credit to the farming community who have to depend on the non-institutional sector for their credit requirements.

(c) To ensure credit availability even in the backward areas of the country thereby reducing regional imbalances.

(d) To provide larger credit support to areas covered by special programmes focused on increasing agricultural produce, namely Special Rice Production Programme, Pulses Development Programme, National Oilseeds Development Project, etc.

Rural Credit Cooperatives have existed in India for a long time. There has always been a shortage of supply of rural credit in India. To meet the demand for short- and long-term rural credit the Cooperative Credit Structure was set up. While the short-term credit is supplied by the State Cooperative Banks (SCB), District Central Cooperative Banks (DCCB) and Primary Agricultural Credit Societies (PACS), long-term credit is supplied by the Primary Cooperative Agriculture and Rural Development Bank.

Rural Credit Cooperatives were started in India long back, some of them even before India's Independence in 1947. During the post-Independence period rural credit cooperative system was developed. Besides, rural banks were set up. However, despite the measures and initiatives, credit needs of rural people could not be met effectively. Supply of credit even for agriculture was not proportionate to the demand. The cooperative credit movement failed to meet the demand of the people though much was expected from the credit movement as it was led by the farmers themselves. A survey of rural credit in 1950-51 showed that the cooperatives could meet barely 3.3 per cent of the total credit requirements of the farmers, while the moneylenders accounted for 93 per cent of the credit needs of the farmers. In this context, the All India Rural Credit Survey Committee (1954) stated, "Cooperation has failed but it must succeed". The Royal Committee on Agriculture stated, "If the cooperatives fail, this will be a failure for best hope of India". It was therefore that the planners of post-Independence era gave thrust to the cooperative movement, and the first Prime Minister of free India, Pandit Jawaharlal Nehru, emphasized the need to promote the cooperative movement.

To realize this vision, All India Rural Credit Survey Committee (1969) recommended the adoption of multi-agency approach to finance the rural sector. It was for the first time that the government accepted that the rural credit could not be met by cooperative societies alone. Hence, there was a need for a role of the commercial banks in the rural sector.

On the recommendations of this committee, RBI took several measures with the objective of strengthening the cooperative movement. The State Bank of India was set up in 1955 after nationalizing the Imperial Bank of India to show a special concern for agricultural credit.

In 1969, 14 leading banks were nationalized. Later, Regional Rural Banks (RRBs) were set up, followed by many more banks. Thus, the multi-agency approach of institutional credit to agriculture was evolved over a number of years.

While RBI was helping the cooperative sector directly, the need for an institution for multi-agency approach to rural finance was felt to help and coordinate the institutions specializing in rural finance. It was for this reason that NABARD was set up as the apex bank for rural finance in India.

In India, cooperative movement was basically organized against the exploitation of unscrupulous moneylenders to lift the farming community from poverty and indebtedness. The government took several measures to improve the conditions of the farming sector and as such promoted Cooperative Credit Societies.

Cooperative movement in its modern form was started in 1904 with the introduction of Co-operative Credit Societies Act on 25 March 1904. Thus, cooperative movement enjoys a glorious existence of more than hundred years. The movement has been acknowledged as a powerful instrument towards achieving socio-economic transformation of Indian society with a particular focus on rural society. Cooperation since inception has been strived hard to usher socio-economic development of our country.

Today, cooperative movement in India is one of the largest movements in the world. Initially, it was started with a limited spectrum of activities. However, dispensation of rural credit has not entered all fields of economic activity with social content. Today, the movement has covered 100 per cent villages and 75 per cent rural households and functioning over 545 thousand cooperatives of various levels with membership coverage of 236 million and working capital of Rs. 34,00,555 million. It has been playing a significant role in disbursing agricultural credit, distribution of agricultural inputs, providing market support among other things.

Today, agricultural credit disbursed by the cooperatives constitutes 46.15 per cent of total agricultural credit. Cooperatives have contributed in every walk of life.

This shows that modern cooperative movement has made tremendous progress in every walk of activities and occupies a major place in the share of Indian economy.

Growth of Institutional Credit in India

As a result of government initiative there is a wide network of well-developed institutional framework which is providing credit facilities to the farmers.

Table 11.1: Flow of Institutional Credit to Agriculture and Allied Activities

Rs. Crores

Institutional credit from	2004-05	2005-06	2006-07	2007-08	2008-09	2009-10*
Cooperative banks	31424	39786	42480	48258	36762	45000
Commercial banks	81481	125477	166485	181087	223663	250000
RRBs	12404	15223	20435	25312	26724	30000
Total	125309	180486	229400	254657	287149	325000

Source: RBI.

* Provisional estimate.

To accelerate the flow of credit to agriculture and allied activities, the government is implementing a comprehensive Farm Credit Package since June 2004. The package inter-alia envisaged doubling of agriculture credit flow in next three years beginning from 2004-05 taking 2003-04 as base year. The credit package also envisaged to finance 50 lakhs new farmers each year by Commercial Banks including RRBs and Debt Relief Measures for farmers in distress and farmers in arrears, One Time Settlement (OTS) scheme for small and marginal farmers and relief to farmers indebted to non-institutional lenders such as money lenders.

From kharif 2006-07, farmers are receiving crop loans up to a principal amount of Rs. 3 lakhs at 7 per cent rate of interest and the government is providing necessary interest subvention to banks for this purpose. Additional subvention of 1 per cent is also being paid, as incentive to those farmers who repay short-term crop loans on schedule. The government is also implementing revival package for Short-term Rural Cooperative Credit Structure involving financial outlay of Rs. 13,596 crores.

Twenty-five State Governments have signed the MoU with Government of India and NABARD covering more than 96 per cent of the STCCS units in the country as on October 2009.

Besides making farm loan up to Rs. 50,000 collateral/security free, the government has implemented the Agricultural Debt Waiver and Debt Relief Scheme, 2008 under which about 3.68 crores farmers have been benefited from the scheme involving debt waiver and debt relief of Rs. 65,318 crores. Under One Time Settlement component of the scheme, farmers were required to pay the dues in three installments by 30 June 2009. However, the government has given further extension in time to farmers having more than two hectares of land to pay 75 per cent of their overdue under Debt Waiver and Debt Relief Scheme from 30 June 2009 to 31 December 2009.

A Task Force has been constituted by the government to look into the issue of a large number of farmers, who had taken loans from private moneylenders in the country. Initiative has been taken by Ministry of Agriculture to provide Kisan Credit Card (KCC) to all the eligible and willing farmers in a time bound manner. To achieve this, the State Governments have been advised to launch an intensive branch/village level campaign. As a result, 8.53 crore KCCs were issued by July 2009.

The Reserve Bank of India vide its circular dated 1 July 2009 has issued detailed guidelines to the banks for undertaking relief measures by banks in areas affected by natural calamities. The guidelines inter-alia includes restructuring of existing loans, conversion of loans, sanction of consumption loan, grant of fresh loans, etc.

Currently, the government is implementing a Rehabilitation Package for 31 suicide prone districts in the states of Andhra Pradesh, Karnataka, Kerala and Maharashtra involving financial outlay of Rs. 16,979 crores.

Institutional Credit and their Defects

During the early years after achieving Independence, private moneylenders were dominant in the field of credit supply to rural masses. Their share was as high as 97 per cent while institutional sources met only 3 per cent of the credit requirements of the rural masses. This situation took a reverse turn when during the Five-Year Plans there was progressive institutionalization of agriculture credit. As a consequence, the contribution of credit institutions reached over 60 per cent of the required short-term production credit such as cooperatives, commercial banks and RRBs.

The significant increase in the credit flow from institutional services brought forth a strong sense of expectation from the public sector banks. However, this expectation could not be sustained and the emphasis throughout was on achieving certain quantitative targets. As a consequence, adequate attention was not paid to the qualitative aspects of lending, resulting in loan defaults and erosion of repayment ethics, to greater or lesser extent by all categories of borrowers. It led to a disturbing growth in overdues. It not only affected the recycling of search resources of banks, but also affected profitability and viability of financial institutions. Besides, rural credit appears to have failed to improve the condition of poverty and provide adequate credit supply to 70 per cent of rural masses. The major reasons behind this state of affairs are enumerated below:

(a) Many new institutions created by the government and the extended facilities of rural finance provided by these institution have generally been given by the top 30 per cent of middle and well-off farmers in the country.
(b) The credit facilities exclusively created for marginal and small farmers and economically weaker sections of society did not reach the targeted groups and were misappropriated by big affluent sections of farmers with the connivance of some corrupt officials and politicians.
(c) Very little was done for the weaker sections of rural population constituting 25 to 30 per cent of the total rural population, which include bonded labourers, landless agricultural labourers, tribals, scheduled castes and scheduled tribes, etc. They still continue to be exploited by the moneylenders, landlords and commission agents, etc.

The resultant effect has been widespread discontent and despair among the rural poor, sometimes leading to extreme action like suicides by farmers, particularly in states like Andhra Pradesh, Maharashtra, Karnataka and Gujarat.

Shortcomings of Multi-agency Approach

It was viewed by the government that multi-agency approach to rural credit was the real solution to the problems of farmers who were in the clutches of moneylenders and landlords for their credit requirements. But the Working Group under the chairmanship of C.E. Kamath found the following drawbacks in the multi-agency approach:

(i) There has been a steady decline in the share of cooperative banks in the flow of institutional credit which slipped to 40 per cent in 1999-2000 from 55 per cent in 1984-85. It further declined to 28 per cent in 2004-05. Hence, there is a need for restructuring and reforming these banks.

(ii) Different agencies adopted different procedures and policies in terms of credit disbursement and recovery, thus leading to fierce competition among different agencies, even though there were guidelines from the RBI in this regard.

(iii) Lack of coordination between different agencies working in the same area resulting in difference in financing and overfinancing in some areas, while in other areas there was the problem of underfinancing.

(iv) Despite the introduction of Lead Bank Scheme and District Credit Plan, the agencies involved in the rural credit failed to formulate and develop meaningful agricultural credit programmes.

(v) There were problems in recovery of loans when different agencies had lent to the same person against the same securities. This resulted in heavy overdues.

The Service Area Approach (SAA) introduced in 1989 in the banks and other credit institutions has definitely brought some improvement in the credit delivery system, but it does not do away with the problems of multi-agency approach.

The major problems faced by the credit institutions particularly the cooperatives include accepting deposits at higher rate for depositors, huge expenses on administration, lack of management skill, lack of training and education to the employees, poor performance in recovery, allotment of loans without proper security. Certainly the biggest among these problems the unsatisfactory level of overdues. The ratio of overdues to demand is around 40 to 42 per cent in case of cooperatives while it stood for 47 per cent in case of Regional Rural Banks. Accordingly, the position of agriculture credit institutions—cooperatives and RRBs—was not good in several parts of the country. The Planning Commission has this to say in this regard:

> Willful default and overdues are mounting in a number of states including some cooperatively progressive states like Maharashtra and Gujarat. By writing off agricultural loans and providing subsidies out of the state exchequer, some of the states have set example to the entire country. If this trend is not reversed and if banks are reduced to institutions providing grants rather than recycling scarce resources to get the maximum benefits for the country as a whole, the banking system will be unable to provide more credit to meet the growing needs of the farmers.

New Initiatives for the Agricultural Sector

To strengthen the rural credit delivery system for facilitating smooth credit flow to the rural sector in general and to agriculture in particular, a number of steps have been taken by the Reserve Bank and the Government of India. Some of the steps taken in recent years are Special Agricultural Credit Plan (SACP), measures for doubling of flow of credit to agriculture sector, Kisan Credit Card (KCC), interest subvention relief to farmers, agricultural debt waiver and debt relief scheme, 2008, the National Agricultural Insurance Scheme (NAIS), the Weather Based Crop Insurance Scheme (WBCIS) and several micro finance schemes.

As against the target of Rs. 2,80,000 crores (provisional) for agricultural credit in 2008-09, the banking system disbursed credit of Rs. 2,92,437 crores to the agricultural sector thereby exceeding the target by around 4 per cent. Commercial banks and regional rural ranks (RRBs) together extended credit to 81.02 lakhs new farmers during 2008-09. In addition to this, cooperative banks provided loans to 13.88 lakhs new farmers during the period, thus taking the total number of farmers financed by the banking system to 94.90 lakhs. The total credit flow to agriculture during 2009-10 up to October 31, 2009 by commercial banks, cooperative banks and RRBs was of the order of Rs. 1,65,439.37 crores, amounting to 51 per cent of the annual target of Rs. 3,25,000 crores.

Kisan Credit Card Scheme (KCC)

The KCC scheme was introduced in 1998-99 to enable the farmers to purchase agricultural inputs and draw cash for their production needs. This scheme has become a widely accepted mechanism for delivery of credit to farmers. The banking system has issued 878.30 lakh KCCs as on November 30, 2009. The scheme now also covers borrowers of the long-term cooperative credit structure. The KCC has thus become a single window for a comprehensive credit product.

Personal Accident Insurance Scheme (PAIS)

In order to safeguard the interests of KCC holders, NABARD has allowed banks the discretion to opt for any insurance company of their choice. The banks have, however, to keep in mind the guiding principles of PAIS, especially the premium-sharing formula, and coverage while negotiating with insurance companies.

Enlargement of the Scope of KCC

With a view to making it more user-friendly, NABARD has enlarged the scope of the KCC scheme to cover term loans for agriculture and allied activities, including a reasonable component for consumption needs, besides the existing facility of providing crop loan limit.

Crop Insurance on KCC

Crop loans disbursed under the KCC Scheme for notified crops are covered under the Rashtriya Krishi Bima Yojana (National Crop Insurance Scheme), introduced to protect the interests of the farmer against crop loss caused by natural calamities, pest attacks, etc. This scheme is in addition to the National Agricultural Insurance Scheme (NAIS) for crops implemented from rabi 1999-2000 season with the objective of providing a comprehensive insurance solution to the farmers in the event of failure of any of the notified crops as a result of natural calamities, pests and diseases.

Microfinance

In February 2000, the RBI issued comprehensive guidelines to banks for mainstreaming micro credit and enhancing the outreach of micro credit providers. However, no particular model was prescribed for micro finance and banks were given freedom to formulate their own model(s) or choose any conduit/ intermediary for extending micro credit. Banks have also been advised that micro credit should cover not only consumption and production loans for various farm and non-farm activities of the poor, but also include their other credit needs such as housing and shelter improvements. Subsequently in April 2008, banks were also advised to meet the entire credit requirements like (i) income generation activities, (ii) social needs like housing, education, marriage, etc. and (iii) debt swapping.

Self-Help Groups (SHGs)

In an effort to mainstream micro credit and increase its outreach, the RBI had issued comprehensive guidelines in February 2000 stipulating that micro credit extended by banks to individual borrowers directly or through any intermediary would henceforth be reckoned part of their priority-sector lending. The SHG-Bank Linkage Programme implemented by commercial banks, RRBs and cooperative banks has emerged as the major micro-finance programme in the country. Under which, as on March 31, 2009, 61,21,147 SHGs held savings bank accounts with total savings of Rs. 5,546 crores as against

50,09,794 SHGs with savings of Rs. 3,785 crores as on March 31, 2008. Thus, more than 8.06 crore poor households were associated with banking agencies under the SHG-Bank Linkage Programme in 2008-09.

As on March 31, 2009, commercial banks had the maximum share of SHG savings with savings of 35,49,509 SHGs (58 per cent) amounting to Rs. 2,773 crores (50 per cent) followed by RRBs with savings bank accounts of 16,28,588 SHGs (26.6 per cent) and savings amount of Rs. 1,990 crores (35.9 per cent) and cooperative banks with savings bank accounts of 9,43,050 SHGs (15.4 per cent) and savings amount of Rs. 782.88 crores (14.1 per cent).

The share of the Swarnajayanti Gram Swarozgar Yojana (SGSY) in SHG savings accounts was 15,05,581 SHGs, forming 25 per cent of the total SHGs having savings accounts in banks. During 2008-09, the average savings per SHG with all banks increased from Rs. 7,556 as on March 31, 2008 to Rs. 9,060 as on March 31, 2009, varying between a high of Rs. 12,218 per SHG with RRBs and a low of Rs. 7,812 per SHG with commercial banks. As on March 31, 2009, the share of women SHGs in total SHGs with savings bank accounts was 48,63,921, accounting for 79.46 per cent as compared to the previous year's share of 79.56 per cent.

Pursuant of the announcement made in the Reserve Bank's Annual Policy Statement for the year 2007-08, all Regional Offices (ROs) of the Reserve Bank undertook an evaluation of the SHG-Bank Linkage Programme to ascertain the degree of transparency in maintaining accounts by SHGs and their adherence to best practices. The evaluation revealed that there was scope for improvement in the area of maintenance of books of accounts. It also brought out that rotation of group leaders was generally not followed by SHGs. However, other best practices like strict adherence to attendance of group meetings, recording minutes of the meetings and prompt repayment of bank loans were being followed.

The momentum of growth in the microfinance sector has brought into focus the importance of regulating the sector to function in an efficient and orderly manner. There would be need for greater transparency in their functioning and for facilitating their reach to un-banked population of the country.

Plight of Small and Marginal Farmers

The farmers all over the country are dissatisfied and full of anger and resentment due to not having accessibility to the falling rates of interest of banks and on being forced to borrow at high interest rates from the moneylenders. This resentment is manifested in the sudden spurt in the incidence of suicides among the farmers in different parts of the country particularly in Andhra Pradesh, Maharashtra, Karnataka, Punjab, etc., particularly in the initial years of the new millennium. This is said to be one of major causes of the fall of NDA government in 2004.

The UPA government which succeeded the NDA announced a slew of measures in consultation with the RBI, NABARD, and commercial banks for the benefit of farming community. Some of the measures announced include:

(i) Increasing agricultural credit from all lending institutions including cooperative banks, RRBs and commercial banks from about 85,000 crores to Rs. 1,05,000 crores, which is an increase of 30 per cent. This would continue from year after year.

Following the policy of farm credit package of the UPA government which was 1,25,000 crores in 2004-05 increased to 1,80,480 crores in 2005-06 and 2,04,000 in 2006-07. It is ironical that on the one hand there was an increase in the farm credit and on the other the cases of farm suicide also increased. The biggest question is why farmers commit suicide. Perheps the credit package failed to reach the targeted people. Only the well-to-do farmers benefitted from the farm credit package.

(ii) The branches of the commercial banks and RRBs would be intensified particularly in rural areas to increase the flow of agricultural credit.

(iii) Under special agricultural credit plan, each rural and semi-urban plan would finance at least 100 new farmers each year.

(iv) Financing of at least 2 to 3 new investment projects by each branch in plantation and horticulture, fisheries, organic farming, etc.

(v) Providing credit facilities to tenant farmers and oral lessees.

(vi) Debt restructuring instead of debt writing off so as to benefit the following:

(a) Relief to farmers in distress by rescheduling their loans and making them eligible for fresh loans; and

(b) One-time settlement for small and marginal farmers and consider them eligible for fresh loans.

All these proposals failed to achieve the targets. The farmers could not get the benefits as proposed. Non-institutional credit system continued to remain the stronghold of agricultural credit of which the moneylenders dominated the scene, particularly for poor and marginal farmers the moneylenders were still the main source of credit.

National Policy on Cooperatives

Lack of proper policy support combined with internal and structural weaknesses contributed to widen the regional imbalances, neutralizing the positive impact of cooperative. The need for a clear-cut national policy on cooperatives was felt. Thus, a comprehensive National Policy on Cooperatives was announced by Government of India in April 2002. The salient features of this policy are as follows:

- Cooperatives would be provided necessary support, encouragement and assistance so as to ensure that they work as autonomous, self-reliant and democratic institutions having accountability to their members and make a significant contribution to the national economy.
- The policy recognizes the cooperatives as autonomous associations of persons, united voluntarily to meet their

common economic, social and democratically controlled enterprise, at the same time upholding the values of principles of cooperation.

- It recognizes cooperatives as a distinct economic sector and an integral component of the socio-economic system of the country and an effective instrument of socio-economic development.
- It accepts the need to phase out its share holdings/equity participation in the cooperatives. The cooperative shall be enabled to set up holding companies subsidiaries, enter into strategic partnership, venture into futuristic areas like insurance, food processing and information technology, etc. and shall be independent to take the financial decisions in the interest of the members and the advancement of their stand.
- The policy recognizes the role of the government in ensuring that the benefits of liberalization and globalization in the emerging special provision in the Cooperative Societies Act regarding banking, housing, real estate development, accessing, manufacturers cooperatives, infrastructural development, etc. reach the targeted beneficiaries.
- It undertakes to devise and execute suitable programmes and schemes to build and develop cooperative institutions in those states and regions where cooperatives are not well developed, particularly in 'North-Eastern states including Sikkim'.
- It recognizes the importance of cooperative movement in developing human resources, cooperative education and training, appropriate technologies and infrastructural facilities to promote professional management in cooperatives.
- It undertakes to initiate structural reforms to improve the functioning of the cooperatives at different levels to ensure greater efficiency and viability.

Globalization Regime: Problems and Prospects of the Cooperative Movement in India

Indian policymakers considered cooperation as a tool of economic development, particularly the disadvantaged sections of society in rural areas. It was seen as a system to safeguard the interests of the deprived sections against the exploitation of moneylenders and commission agents and also to help the farmers to come out from the clutches of poverty and indebtedness. The basic idea behind this was to improve the condition of this section of people. The non-exploitative character of cooperatives, voluntary nature of membership, the decentralized decision making and self-imposed curbs on profits eminently qualified them as an instrument of development. Thus, the movement which was started 100 years ago, largely with an objective to provide funds for agricultural operations at low rates of interest, and at the same time protecting the farming community from the clutches of the moneylenders turned out to be an important plank of socio-economic development in India.

Cooperatives have extended all over the country. At present, there are an estimated 230 million members nation-wide. The credit cooperatives system in India has the largest network in the world. These cooperatives have advanced more credit in the Indian agricultural sector than the commercial banks. The village cooperative societies provide strategic inputs for the agricultural sector. Various types of development activities are now being carried on through cooperatives. Cooperative societies are not helping in building up of storage godowns, cold storages, rural roads besides providing facilities like irrigation, electricity, transport and health. The Indian Farmers Fertilizers Cooperative (IFFCO) commands over 35 per cent of the marketing in production and distribution of fertilizers. The market share of cooperativeness in the production of sugar is over 58 per cent while in the distribution and marketing of cotton, they have a share of 60 per cent. The cooperative sector accounts for 55 per cent of the looms in the hand weaving sector. Dairy cooperatives operating under the leadership of the National Dairy Development Board with the help of 15 state cooperative milk marketing federations has now become the largest producer of milk in the world. With the passage of Insurance Act, cooperatives have been allowed entry into the insurance business, as immense potential of cooperatives in this field still remains untapped.

It is now increasingly recognized that the cooperative system in India has the capacity and potentiality to neutralize the adverse effects of the process of globalization. After economic liberalization under the new economic environment, cooperatives at every level of activities are making efforts to reorient their functions according to the market demands. Privatization has failed to bring about significant changes in rural areas. Thus, great hopes lie with the cooperatives. Quite contrary to the past, cooperatives are now given great importance. The government is committed to cooperative development. Cooperatives are considered efficient in tackling the problems of poverty alleviation, food security and employment generation. They are seen to have immense potentiality in delivering goods and services in areas where public and private sector have not been found successful. In recent times, cooperative movement has made tremendous progress in India in every level its various activities.

Types of Cooperatives

The cooperative movement in India was started with the main objective of safeguarding the interest of the farmers by providing them credit facilities so as to free them from the clutches of the moneylenders. The rural credit societies were formed as per the Cooperative Credit Societies Act 1904. Within a short period it was realized that the Act had some shortcomings, hence a more comprehensive act, known as the Cooperative Societies Act 1912 was enacted, which recognized non-credit societies also.

Primary Agriculture Credit/Service Societies

A cooperative credit society, commonly known as the primary agriculture credit society, may be started with ten or more persons, normally belonging to a village. The value of each share is nominal so that even the poorest of the farmers can join the movement. Primary agriculture credit/service societies are the grassroots level units of the short-term credit structure as the society directly deal with farmer-borrowers.

The agricultural cooperative credit structure deals with the short-term, medium-term and long-term credit. The credit delivery structure of cooperative is based on a three-tier system, i.e. the apex cooperative bank at the state level, the central cooperative bank at the district/tehsil level and primary agriculture societies at the village level. The major objectives of the primary agricultural credit/service societies are to supply agricultural credit to meet the requirements for funds for agricultural production, the distribution of essential commodities, the provision of storage and marketing facilities and for buying agricultural implements and machinery.

Long-term cooperative credit holds great significance in terms of development of land and agriculture. The primary agricultural credit society is the foundation stone on which the whole edifice of cooperatives is erected. These societies dominate the cooperative picture even today.

An elected body consisting of President, Secretary and Treasurer is responsible for the management of society. All the positions are honorary except the accountants. But a whole-time paid accountant is required only if the society is large. Loans are given normally for a short period of one year for carrying out agricultural operations. The rate of interest is low. Profits are not distributed among the shareholders but are utilized for the development of the villagers such as for constructing of a well, or maintenance of the village school and so on.

The utility of the primary agriculture credit society is constantly on the increase. In 1950-51, the loan advancements of the society were just Rs. 23 crores which rose to Rs. 200 crores in 1960-61. They further rose to become 34,520 crores in 2000-01. The loans have been advanced mainly to the weaker sections of society. This progress has been quite significant but not satisfactory, particularly when there exists a wide gap between credit demand and credit supply. However, the primary credit societies continue to remain significant links in the entire cooperative structure.

In the past few decades, considerable attention has been given to strengthen this institution of credit so as to extend its coverage in rural areas. One such programme was introduced by the government and RBI to reorganize and revitalize the primary agricultural societies. It was successfully completed in a few states, namely Rajasthan, Orissa, Madhya Pradesh, Kerala, Tamil Nadu and Gujarat. In other states, it failed to make significant progress.

The number of primary agricultural credit societies had declined from 2,12,000 in 1960 to 1,62,000 in 1970-71 and 1,06,380 at the end of March 2006 having estimated membership of more than 10 crore farmers all over the country.

Most of the primary agricultural credit societies depend on the finance provided by central cooperatives. In case the central cooperative banks are weak, the primary agricultural credit society has to face the problems of finances which further affect the efficient functioning of credit supply of the society.

To make the primary agricultural credit societies more efficient and viable and to ensure adequate and timely flow of cooperative credit, a number of steps are being taken by the Reserve Bank of India in collaboration with state governments to reduce regional imbalance in cooperative development. These efforts are being intensified by providing larger funds to those societies which are weak so as to write off their losses, bad debts and overdues.

The cooperative credit system since being at the grassroots level is an important medium to provide credit supply to the farmers. But it is financially and organizationally weak. Hence, in practice, its ability to support credit to the agricultural sector is considerably limited. Besides, there are other drawbacks, some of which are mentioned below:

(i) The extent and coverage of credit cooperative institutions have been limited forming a small portion of the borrowings of the farmers.

(ii) Most of the primary credit societies are financially weak and are not able to completely meet the demand for credit for production.

(iii) Primary credit cooperative societies failed to completely satisfy the needs of tenants and small farmers.

(iv) Alarmingly, increasing overdues at all levels indicate the failure of cooperative credit institutions.

(v) Primary credit cooperative societies have failed to ensure adequate and timely credit supply for the borrowing farmers.

District Central Cooperative Banks

These are federations of primary credit societies in specified areas, normally extending to a whole district. Hence, they are often called district cooperative banks. Their major objective is to lend to village primary societies. These banks are provided with finance and management by a few private individuals who are shareholders of these banks. Many of these banks act as intermediaries between the state cooperative bank and the village primary cooperative societies. The central banks supervise the functioning of the primary societies of a district and offer financial assistance to them. Their capital is drawn from public deposits, share capitals and loans from other sources. Since they draw money from a variety of sources, they act as a 'link between cooperative societies and the money market'. They function as balancing centres by diverting surplus funds of societies to useful channels. They perform ordinary bank function as well. The Reserve Bank and NABARD have formulated a scheme for rehabilitation of weak central cooperative banks. NABARD is providing liberal financial assistance to the state governments to contribute to the share capital of the weak central cooperative banks selected for the purpose.

State Cooperative Banks

There are over 30 state cooperative banks—each having several branches—operating in the country. They are at the apex of the cooperative credit structure in each state. They control the working of central banks and provide finance to them. They serve as a link between Reserve Bank of India, which is the source of their finances, and the central banks and the primary societies. They control and guide the cooperative movement in the state. They control the working of central banks and provide finance to them. Their sources of capital are share capital, public deposits and loans and advances from the state and the Reserve Bank of India, and now NABARD. As a matter of fact, NABARD is the major source which constitutes about 50-90 per cent of the working capital of state cooperative banks in the country. The state cooperative banks are not only contributing in the rural cooperative credit movement but also in other cooperative ventures.

All these institutions of cooperative largely serve the short- and medium-term credit demands of the people. Long-term loans are given by Land Development Banks, which have a unitary structure with their branches at different places. Their sources of finances are share capital, reserves, deposits, bonds and debentures. However, the major portion of their resource is drawn from the floating of ordinary debentures in the market. The main investors in these debentures are: Life Insurance Corporation of India, commercial banks, cooperative banks, central and state governments and the Reserve Bank of India.

Cooperatives in the Changing Scenario

Cooperatives have made substantial contribution to the economy of the country. Despite their phenomenal growth and popularity, the progress is not very satisfactory. Cooperatives are beset with several issues and confront with challenges in an era of liberalization and globalization, which have been discussed below:

WTO and Cooperatives: One of the biggest challenges that the WTO is faced within the new millennium is related to WTO Agreement on Agriculture. Since cooperatives are closely related to agriculture, there is a growing concern among the cooperative members that the implementation of various provisions of Agreement on Agriculture are likely to affect the farming community in terms of their income and standard of living. This is of particular importance to India as more than three-fourths of its population depends on agriculture and related activities for their livelihood, while merely four per cent population in developed countries is dependent on agriculture and allied activities.

We need to ensure that food security in terms of providing foodgrains for various sections of Indian population does not get adversely affected by the WTO Agreement on Agriculture. This makes it all the more necessary to provide a separate "Food Security Box" under WTO provision with greater emphasis on encouraging food production and per hectare productivity of various crops. In the emerging scenario, various segments of cooperative movement need to be encouraged for improving their operational efficiency so as to promote cost effectiveness and to ensure that quality standards remain viable in an age of stiff challenges and high competition.

Insufficient Participation of Women: It is agreed that there should be greater participation of women in cooperative, particularly in areas where they have a natural advantage. With growing awareness and rising literacy, it is felt that women participation should be increased at all levels. Central and state governments are also extending concessions to promote education and awareness among women. Despite these efforts and developments, a majority of women in our country are still illiterate and have no access to various resources including various credit supply systems.

To realize this objective, Self-Help Groups were formed which is in tune with the cooperatives. This goes a long way in the improvement of women in view of a vibrating democratic structure of the cooperatives. Promoting micro finance through SHGs by involving more and more women is likely to make great difference in this regard. SHGs have empowered women by enhancing their contribution to household income, increasing the value of their assets and generally by giving them better control over decisions that affect their lives.

Lack of Professionalization of Cooperatives: The cooperative societies need to be evolved as independent, self-reliant, autonomous and member-driven institutions. But cooperatives have lost their democratic character and have become government-controlled organizations. Capoor Committee on

Cooperatives has recommended, besides professionalization, human resource development, business diversification, recovery management fund mechanism and setting up of a cooperative rehabilitation and development fund. The Committee also warned against excessive control and regulation.

Central government along with state governments are taking initiatives to strengthen infrastructure facilities and develop the professional skills and efficiency in the cooperatives.

Besides, the National Cooperative Union of India and National Council for Cooperative Training and Junior Level Cooperative Training Centre are also implementing various cooperative education and training programmes so as to ensure greater efficiency and skills. However, lack of professionalism is widely felt everywhere. The cooperatives professionals need to redefine their roles in the fast emerging knowledge society. Besides, they need to be made conversant with the use of technology. In an age of Information Technology, people and system need to be well equipped with the technology. In this context, the use of i-business, e-commerce, e-governance, etc. needs to be promoted. This is likely to make the cooperatives more efficient and help them to be compatible in the present era of fast economic development.

Cooperative Law Reforms

The recommendations of Chowdhury Brahma Perkash Committee provide scope for cooperators to develop self-reliant cooperatives with greater autonomy and participation in democratic management. Accordingly, State Cooperative Law/ Self-Reliant Cooperatives was first evicted in Andhra Pradesh in 1995. It was followed by Madhya Pradesh, Chhattisgarh, Karnataka, Orissa, Bihar, Jharkhand, Jammu & Kashmir and Uttarakhand. This change in cooperatives reflects the flexible and adjusting nature of cooperatives in India. The changes are attempts to keep pace with the reforms sweeping across the cooperatives sector all over the world. Self-Reliant Cooperatives seek to the cooperatives do not ensure that depend on the government equity and share. This attempts to make the cooperatives more member-driven and hence, cooperative law reforms have been brought to materialize the goal.

In this regard, the amendment of Multi-State Cooperative Societies Act 2002, the fifth legislation, which is a central legislation on cooperatives is another landmark. It attempts to remove the restrictive provisions of Multi-State Cooperative Societies Act 1984. This amendment has cut government's power to give directions and suppression of Board of those societies in which the government's holding is 51 per cent or more. The societies will be free to raise resources by receiving deposits, getting loans and grants. The federal cooperatives will have more responsibilities and the disputes would be settled through arbitration at the discretion of society.

Besides, the NCDC Amendment Bill was passed in 2002 which provides that now NCDC shall be financing more activities allied to agriculture, like animal husbandry products, including meat, milk, skin, wool, etc. so as to augment the earnings in rural areas. Similarly, service sector and industrial cooperatives, including goods produced by the cottage and village industries will come within the purview of the NCDC. The NCDC would also be able to undertake direct financing of cooperatives against reasonable security, without any guarantee from central and state governments.

Thus, the cooperatives in the 21st century need to remain on vanguard in providing the required lead to the millions of producers involved with them. This calls for efficient management of cooperative sector to make it more and more people-oriented. There should be minimum interference in the smooth functioning of the cooperatives. Cooperatives need to be managed and equipped in such a way that they withstand the challenges of competitive business environment where excellence, efficiency and high productivity are the parameters of success. However, we need to focus on the improvement in the cooperative governance through the process of restructuring and rejuvenation.

NABARD AND ITS ROLE IN RURAL CREDIT

Since the very beginning, RBI has been very concerned for agriculture credit and hence was maintaining a separate department for the purpose. Short-term and long-term credit to agriculture was extended through state level cooperative banks and land development banks.

At the same time, Agricultural Refinance Development Cooperation (ARDC) was set up by RBI to provide refinance support to the banks to promote programmes of agricultural development, particularly term credit. As the role of bank credit expanded from agriculture to rural development, the need for a broad-based organization at the apex level was felt so as to extend support and guidance to various credit institutions in matters related to formulation and implementation of rural development programmes. Therefore, a National Bank for Agriculture and Rural Development (NABARD) was set up in July 1982, by an Act of Parliament as a substitute to ARDC to undertake refinancing functions of RBI, related to cooperative banks and RRBs. NABARD is organically linked with the RBI as the latter contributes half of its share capital, while the remaining half is contributed by the Government of India. Besides, RBI nominates three of its Central Board Directors on the board of NABARD. In addition, a Deputy Governor of RBI is also appointed as Chairman of NABARD. NABARD has its head office at Mumbai and 16 regional offices throughout the country.

NABARD is a landmark in the evolution of agricultural finance and is an all-India refinance apex agency. It has replaced the Agricultural Refinance and Development Corporation, largely concerned with the long-term finance and two credit related constituents of RBI—Agriculture Credit Development and Rural Planning, and Credit Cell. It was largely formed with the objective of strengthening the credit delivery mechanism, particularly those institutions which are at the forefront of credit delivery mechanism such as cooperatives, commercial banks and regional small banks. The main concern of NABARD is credit, but it also performs the complementary work of directing, inspecting and supervising the credit flows for agricultural and rural development. For arranging capital it depends upon many sources; for short-term finance it depends on RBI and for long-term capital needs, it has access to World Bank, money market and can also take bilateral credit from other countries.

Functions of NABARD

As an apex institution, NABARD has to shoulder many responsibilities, attend to many problems and address the shortcomings in the credit delivery system of the country. In fact, NABARD has inherited its apex role from RBI, i.e. it is performing all the functions relating to agriculture credit, which were earlier performed by RBI. NABARD has taken over the functions of ARDC and thus provides refinance facilities to all banks and financial institutions leading to agriculture and rural development.

NABARD serves as a "single window" from where all types of credit is made available. NABARD promotes integrated rural development and extends refinancing for all kinds of production and investment credit to agriculture, small-scale industries, cottage and village industries, handicrafts and rural crafts and real artisans and other allied economic activities.

NABARD provides short-term, medium-term and long-term credits to various lending institutions such as state cooperative banks, RRBs, LDBs and other financial institutions approved by RBI. NABARD has the responsibility to inspect RRBs and cooperative banks, other than primary cooperative societies.

NABARD is responsible for coordination in various activities of central and state governments, the Planning Commission and many state and national level institutions entrusted with the development of small scale industries, village and cottage industries and other rural-based sectors of economy.

NABARD extends long-term loans to any institution approved by the Central Government or contributes to the share capital or invests in securities of any institution concerned with agriculture and rural development.

NABARD attempts to create an environment for the promotion of the generation of repayment ethics so as to find a solution to the return of large and long overdues that rural people owe to credit institutions. NABARD has constituted an organization named Vikas Volunteer Vahini (VVV), consisting of successful farmers (those who have developed themselves through credit), scientists—retired and in service, technologists to educate the farmers how to succeed with the credit. The most important function of NABARD is to have a novel approach to banking with poor which is aimed at promoting micro finance. This involves participation of potential beneficiaries of rural credit in the credit delivery mechanisms through constituting institutions like Self-Help Groups, Non-Government Organizations, Credit Unions, etc. This approach is mainly aimed at promoting credit supplies to the poor.

NABARD maintains a research and development fund with an objective to promote research in agriculture and rural development, to formulate and design projects and programmes as per the requirements of different areas and at the same time catering to particular needs and activities.

NABARD is making serious attempts for the promotion of investment in agriculture sector particularly backward states or under-banked states like Uttar Pradesh, Bihar, Madhya Pradesh, etc.

NABARD is playing a significant role in strengthening and reorganizing the cooperative credit structure in the country. Its programme of restructuring of Primary Agricultural Credit Societies, with the objective of building a strong and viable structure at grass-roots level in the cooperative credit system, is almost complete in all states in India. NABARD has formulated guidelines for the planning of the future development of reorganized societies. It is working to coordinate difference co-operative societies and is also involved in the monitoring of implementation of its various programmes. It is constantly reviewing the rehabilitation programme of those central cooperative banks which have been identified as weak and are being helped to rehabilitate themselves. NABARD is also contributing in the rehabilitation of State Agriculture and Rural Development Banks and Agricultural Rural Land Development Banks, apart from improving the organizational and managerial efficiency of these institutions. Thus, NABARD is doing a remarkable service in channalising the bank credit in rural sectors.

Causes of Slow Progress in India

The cooperative movement in India has made tremendous progress during the last hundred years since its beginning in 1904. It occupies a major place in the share of the national economy. Its extent and coverage have increased substantially. Its activities have been diversified so as to make it more people-oriented. Despite rapid growth, the overall progress of the movement has not been satisfactory. Hence, it calls for the analysis of the factors responsible for the poor performance of the movement so as to draw out adequate measures for faster growth of cooperative movement in India. The major causes of slow progress in India are discussed below.

Corruption and Manipulation

The cooperative movement gives the farmers the status of shareholders and assures them agricultural, educational and medical facilities. The relationship between the shareholder farmer and the cooperative is simple and committed to the growth of cooperative and the farmers as well. In fact, the strength of the movement lies in more and more involvement of farmers regardless of the size of their holdings. But over the years, this truly democratic idea has got spoiled, and the farmers have grown more powerful. In practice, this has brought a negative impact on the power structure of the cooperatives. There was a manipulation in the election of high ranking officials. Money has become such a powerful tool that generally the posts of chairman and vice-chairman have gone to the richest farmers even though the majority of members are farmers with small or medium sized holdings. This undemocratic practice has had an adverse effect on the popularity of the movement. The movement is neither properly managed nor it has found the right type of leadership. Evils like favouratism, nepotism, etc. have emerged, particularly in terms of the distributions of its resources. The management of these institutions often passes into the hands of big landlords who use them for their personal gains.

Interference of Government

The cooperative movement in India was initiated in 1904 under the auspices of British Government. Right from the beginning the cooperative institutions were not treated separately. They were taken as an integral part of the government machinery. In its every decision government's interference became an essential element. This caused a decline in the popularity of the movement. The independent entity of the movement was lost. Its independence and self-reliance were confined to papers only. The cooperatives which had emerged as a result of voluntary associations of individuals, failed to become full-fledged movement of people. The organization voluntarily formed for furtherance of predetermined economic and non-economic objectives, lost its popularity and now the cooperatives are imposed upon the people. People have not developed much faith in the movement. They still regard it as a government agency for the grant of loans and other services. Though in terms of members, the movement grew substantially, yet the spirit of cooperation could not be maintained. Its growth has quite slow, and that too haphazard.

Restricted Coverage

Restricted coverage of the movement was one of the major constraints of the movement. The size of the cooperative societies has been very small, just extending to one or two villages. Consequently, their resources remained limited. They did not grow much. Besides, there was a lack of efficiency on the part of the people involved with movement. It is evident from the fact that very often the loan advanced by the Reserve Bank of India are not fully utilized. The societies have been found deficient in their working. Besides, most of the societies have been single purpose societies. They have not much to show in the field of non-credit spheres. They remained preoccupied with the supply of credit. In this connection, the tardy growth of cooperatives is pointed in the field of processing of agricultural produce, marketing, distribution of consumer products, etc. For this reason these societies are unable to take a total view of the persons seeking help, nor can they analyse and solve problems from different angles. Thus, the help rendered by these societies cannot be adequate. This confined approach of the societies affected their operational efficiency. Many weaker sections of the populations such as Scheduled Castes and Scheduled Tribes continue to suffer from the gross inadequacies of cooperatives.

Functional Weakness

The cooperative movement suffered from inadequacy of trained personnel. The movement does not have institutions for proper training. Due to the unsatisfactory working of cooperative institutions, efficient personnel did not feel attracted towards this movement. Even the functioning of the societies is beset with problems. For instance, some of these societies are taking no care of the need of credit seekers or their repaying capacity at the time of granting loans, making no adequate provisions for the return of loans. Besides, there are other weaknesses like lack of proper maintenance of accounts, politics at management level, lack of proper coordination among various divisions of the cooperative structure, lack of proper and timely auditing, etc. Such weaknesses prevented them from making worthwhile progress.

Lack of Enthusiasm Among People

People were not well informed of the objectives of the cooperative movement, its role and its rules and regulations. No efforts were made to educate people and to make them aware in this regard. People looked upon them as a medium through which they could obtain facilitates and concessions from the government. When these aspirations of the people failed to come true they lost interest in them. Lack of proper education, dirty politics of the villages, unfair elections, too much government intervention, bureaucratic attitudes of the government officials at the lower level acted as major constraints in spreading the current information about the role of cooperatives in rural society.

Lack of Proper Planning

Right from the beginning, the government did not have a planned approach towards the movement. It was not given a proper placing in the economy. For example, the cooperative movement was never taken as a part of the bigger plan of economy, rather it was taken as another institution through which the government could function. In fact, the movement attempted to reach the masses. But it failed to win the heart of the people as there was no plan nor strategy for its growth.

Lack of Sufficient Funds

A major weakness of the movement was the lack of funds. The cooperative was instituted with the vision that the members themselves should save and deposit their savings and thus contribute to the working capital of the societies. The central and state cooperative societies failed to attract as much credit as was anticipated. This situation continues to remain the same even today. The Reserve Bank of India was eager to extend loan facilities to the cooperatives at concessional rates of interest, but the cooperatives did not respond enthusiastically.

Confined Approach

The cooperative movement took a very confined approach of providing only credit to the farmers without any provision of helping them in any other way. Thus, the movement failed to appreciate the connection between various other aspects of farming such as credit, marketing and processing. In certain areas different societies were started with different purposes. This was rather a complex situation for the farming community. What was really needed was a cooperative society which would meet all the needs of the farmers and be accessible and eager for extending any facility whatsoever required by them throughout the year. Its failure to provide credit, marketing, processing, better farming, etc. to the farmers proved to a major weakness of the movement in India.

Conservation in Rural Society

Rural society in India is largely an agrarian society which is suffering from backwardness and illiteracy. Most of our farmers are not educated. Hence, they could not understand the role and importance of cooperatives in India. In addition, rural society is riddled with castes, ethnic feelings and many other such issues which are not considered good for the socio-economic growth of society. This did not favour the growth of cooperative spirit. This situation continues to prevail even now in rural areas and there is little progress.

Loans for Productive Purposes Only

The cooperative credit societies provided loan for agricultural activities only. Credit facilities were not available for other requirements of the farmers while they required loans to meet their personal requirements as well like social functions, treatment of serious illnesses, etc. As a result, the farmers have to depend on other sources such as moneylenders, commission agents, etc. for their loan requirements. This was a major constraint in the growth of cooperative movement in India. Due to this, the cooperatives failed to win the confidence of the rural masses in India.

Thus, the cooperative societies in India are playing multifunctional roles, both in urban and rural area. Various development activities in agriculture, small industry marketing and processing, distribution and supplies are now being carried on through cooperatives. The cooperatives in India have made an all-around progress, particularly in the field of agriculture, though not to the expected or required level.

The following statements of the UN Research Institute for Development serve as the best concluding remarks of the cooperative movement in India:

> The cooperatives have not really helped members to improve their position or fought against those who exploit the peasants and restrained their development.
>
> The cooperatives are marginal institutions that survive as instruments of government or because they reinforce existing structures.

Achievement of Cooperatives

The criticism regarding the slow growth or total failure of the movement seems to be rather exaggerated as it ignores the overall growth and performance of the movement. Despite several shortcomings and weaknesses, the movement has produced a beneficial impact on the rural society. Its significant achievements are mentioned below.

Economic Gains

One of the biggest achievements of the cooperative movement is that it has led to sufficient credit flow at low rate of interests to the farmers. The credit advancement by cooperative societies and land development banks is definitely cheaper than that given by moneylenders, commission agents and other non-institutional sources. The cooperative movement has faced the moneylenders and other non-institutional financers to bring down their rates of interests. Thus, credit has started being available at lower rates of interest in the villages. Certainly, it has to some extent, provided relief to the farmers from the exploitation of local lenders of credit and the farmers are reducing their dependence on them. It promoted in the farmers the habit to save and use the banking media for ordinary transactions among the people in general and among rural people in particular. The money saved in banks was thus utilized for productive purposes. Cooperative societies have offered the farmers opportunities in respect of marketing of agricultural produce, purchases of agricultural inputs, supply of irrigation facilities, etc.

The cooperative societies have improved the practices in agriculture leading to the use of improved seeds, manuring, etc. The marketing and processing societies have helped members to buy their requirements cheaply and sell their agricultural produce at good price. The storage facilities provided to the farmers have proved immensely beneficial.

To sum up, this can be said, the cooperative movement has not been a complete success. In certain respect the cooperative movement has achieved success, but the movement has developed certain weaknesses. Thus, its performance has not been satisfactory. The picture that emanates from the situation is that achievements of cooperative movement have been limited. There is no denial of the fact that this formal institution of credit needs revamping to improve the efficiency of the credit delivery system in rural India.

Credit societies have brought a change in rural areas. They have improved the life of the rural masses. They have educated the farmers so that the latter could give up many of their bad habits like gambling, drinking, etc. They have also attempted to remove undesirable social customs like reckless spending on marriages, religious ceremonies, etc. They attempted to settle disputes on local level thereby discouraging unnecessary wastages of money and time in costly litigation.

In addition, the non-credit societies like the housing credit societies, the consumers' cooperative societies, etc. have been helping in bringing about a change in the life of their members. They have also helped to save them from the exploitation of various powerful groups. For example, consumer cooperatives have done great service to the community by helping to distribute goods in short supply and in settling them at reasonable prices. In many places they have played a significant role in preventing the shopkeepers from taking the advantages of supply shortages. In urban areas, the housing cooperatives have enabled middle income groups to secure plots of land and construct their own houses.

Besides, the non-agricultural sector craftsmen engaged in small and cottage industries, small producers and consumers have greatly benefited from this movement. However, it can be said with certainly that as compared to the agricultural sector, the progress made by the cooperative movement in the non-agricultural sector is rather limited.

Social Gains

Cooperative movement has brought about a great change in the social life of the people, particularly in rural India. It has helped in curbing the habit of wasteful expenditure of people furthering a habit of keeping expenditure within the limits of their income. Besides, cooperative movements have been actively involved in various welfare activities in rural India such as providing drinking water, hospitals, drainage facilities, entertainments, etc. However, there are benefits which cannot be put into statistics, like moral, political and educative benefits. For instance, a member seeking enrolment in the cooperatives is required to be a man of good moral character, bearing no bad reputation, and having a cooperative attitude of taking care of others' interest.

Further, the provision of regular elections to the offices of the cooperatives helped in creating political awareness among the masses. The working with the cooperative institutions has the educative value of knowing how strength emanates from cooperation among members. It promotes among people a sense of cooperation. During recent few months some significant changes have taken place in the cooperative movement. The government is taking measures to make the cooperatives autonomous and democratic, providing them opportunities for diversification so as to give the movement a wider coverage. It has been a long overdue demand that the Central Government should introduce democratic reforms in the regulation, supervision and functioning of cooperatives. In view of the consistent demand and persistent efforts of the National Cooperative Union of India, the government has recently passed the Multi-State Cooperatives Societies Act, apart from formulating a national cooperative policy that provides greater autonomy to cooperatives.

Besides, more and more educated people are being employed to make the movement efficient and mass-oriented. These people are being entrusted with responsibilities for ensuring the accessibility of different commodities to people. The government is even attempting to involve the movement in the greater task of procuring foodgrains. Modifications have been made in the laws relating to cooperative movement to make it qualitatively stronger. The Reserve Bank of India now contributes a lot for the promotion and growth of cooperative movement through its various activities which include supervision, research, training facilities, etc. This has led to greater cooperation and coordination among different constituents of the cooperative structure. The broad approach of the government towards the cooperatives includes the following:

(i) The cooperative movement is perceived as a powerful tool of economic growth.

(ii) The scope of cooperatives has been extended and diversified.

(iii) Emphasis is given on multi-purpose societies.

(iv) The size of the societies is extended on the basis of scientific principle.

(v) More and more societies are now run on the basis of the limited liabilities.

At present the Government of India is in the process of formulating of National Policy on Cooperatives with the primary aim of upholding the values and principles of cooperation, recognizing its autonomous character and attaching priority to professionalism, human resource development so as to make at a preferred instrument of the execution of public policy, particularly in rural areas and in those sectors where their performance has been efficient and satisfactory. Moreover, management initiative, cost reduction initiative and total quality control initiatives are also being taken to add to their competitiveness. It is now increasingly recognized that the cooperative system in India has the potentiality to neutralize the adverse effects of globalization and liberalization and in employment generation and poverty alleviation, though cooperatives are not an instrument of employment generation. They do effectively create and maintain employment in urban and rural areas as well. Of course, they have the capacity to provide a source of income to both members and employees in the forms of shares of surplus income, wages and salaries as profits, depending on the type of cooperatives.

The recent initiatives being taken by the government are likely to have a positive impact on the growth of agro-processing sector, export of fruits and vegetables and value-added produce from agriculture and the development of retail chain management, as the sector will be able to source the requirement of their produce directly from the farmers. This will also have a favourable impact on large private investment coming into agricultural sector, development of infrastructure like pre-cooling units, cold storages, cold chain for transportation of perishable produce, putting up of the processing industries, etc. This will improve the situation of employment generation in agriculture and allied sectors. It is envisaged that these changes will boost the growth of the economy. The farmers will also get better returns on their produce. All these will improve the quality of life of the farmers.

Future Prospects: How to Make the Movement Efficient

The cooperative movement has made a tremendous progress in various spheres of its activities and occupies a major place in the national economy. But it has failed to turn out as a people's movement. Hence, the situation calls for reforms to overcome its shortcomings and consolidate its strengths. An expert group was constituted by the government in 1990 which gave its recommendation as follows:

- To facilitate building up of integrated cooperative structure.
- To make the cooperative organizations responsive towards their members.
- To minimize government interference and control in the functioning of cooperatives.
- To eliminate politicization in the cooperative sector.

However, the movement needs to be reformed in a way so that it performs in a satisfactory manner. To make it more efficient and consolidate its strengths the following measures need to be taken.

Reorganizing the Primary Societies

The first major improvement required is to reorganize the primary societies. For this, the weak and inefficient societies should be wound-up and merged with strong and efficient societies. This will reduce the number of societies which are inefficient and weak. It will help to win the confidence of the people in the movement. In addition, the merger of small societies, leading to the formation of big societies, will bring large amount of resources at their disposal. These societies can avail certain facilities. For instance, these societies can afford to engage highly trained and competent personnel and thus conduct their business efficiently. Since small societies have meager resources, they cannot work efficiently, nor are they able to do much for their members. The size should not be too large, as it will become difficult to keep proper control over the functioning of the society. In the changing scenario, multi-purpose societies are considered more efficient instead of single purpose societies as the former have a balanced view about the needs of its members and can meet them accordingly. This will help in efficient utilization of the resources of such societies. At the same time, the members will derive the greatest possible advantages from the resources that lie at their disposal. Experience of the last few years shows that the cooperative movement has gained much from the formation of such multi-purpose societies.

Efficiency in Functioning

The second most important thing is to ensure efficiency in the functioning of the cooperative institutions. Some important measures are necessary to be taken in this regard which include the following: (i) The loans from credit societies should be granted in such a manner and under such conditions that these are used for productive purposes. It will ensure efficient use of resources and then repayment will be ensured as well. Besides, it is necessary to maintain close coordination among different constituents of the cooperative structure. Their coordination should be institutional so that they work together, in mutual cooperation. (ii) There should be close integration among cooperative institutions, Reserve Bank of India, State Bank of India, commercial banks and National Bank of Agriculture and Rural Development and the government. For the promotion of cooperative movement, collaboration and coordination is of great importance. (iii) More and more trained and skilled persons should be involved in the movement so as to impart efficiency to its working. It is equally important that the functioning of the cooperatives should be made simple, straight and convenient.

The movement needs to be turned into a people's movement. Involvement of people should be promoted. Government intervention should be minimized. People should be made aware and educated about the advantages of the movement. The use of mass media can be of great help in this regard. The government should extend a helping hand to the movement without any intervention in the smooth functioning of the movement. Cooperative movement should be developed as a part of national economy. It should be treated as a separate sector along with private and public sector. Appropriate concessions and facilities should be extended to those societies which promote the involvement of the weaker and the vulnerable groups such as SCs and STs, so as to make them free from the clutches of the middlemen. The cooperative movement will thus help in rapid rural development of the country.

List of Important Tables on Indian Economy

Table 1: Key Indicators of Indian Economy

	Data Categories and Components	Units	2004-05	2005-06	2006-07	2007-08	2008-09	2009-10
1	**GDP and Related Indicators**							
	GDP (current market prices)	Rs. crore	3239224	3706473	4283979	4947857	5574449[QE]	6164178 [AE]
	Growth Rate	%	—	14.4	15.6	15.5	12.7	10.6
	GDP (factor cost 2004-05 prices)	Rs. crore	2967599	3249130	3564627	3893457	4154973[QE]	4453064 [AE]
	Growth Rate	%	–	9.5	9.7	9.2	6.7	7.2
	Savings Rate	% of GDP	32.2	33.1	34.4	36.4	32.5	na
	Capital Formation (rate)	% of GDP	32.7	34.3	35.5	37.7	34.9	na
	Per Cap. Net National Income (factor cost at current prices)	Rs.	24095	27183	31080	35430	40141	43749
2	**Production**							
	Foodgrains	Mn tonnes	198.4	208.6	217.3	230.8	233.9[a]	na
	Index of Industrial Production (growth)	Per cent	8.4	8.2	11.6	8.5	2.6	na
	Electricity Generation (growth)	Per cent	5.1	5.2	7.3	6.3	2.7	na
3	**Prices**							
	Inflation (WPI) (52-week average)	% change	6.5	4.4	5.4	4.7	8.4	1.6[b]
	Inflation CPI (IW) (average)	% change	3.8	4.4	6.7	6.2	9.1	11.4[b]

(Contd...)

Data Categories and Components	Units	2004-05	2005-06	2006-07	2007-08	2008-09	2009-10
4 External Sector							
Export Growth (US$)	% change	30.8	23.4	22.6	29.0	13.6	-20.3[c]
Import Growth (US$)	% change	42.7	33.8	24.5	35.5	20.7	-23.6[c]
Current Account Balance (CAB)/GDIP	Per cent	-0.4	-1.2	-1.0	-1.3	-2.4	-3.3[d]
Foreign Exchange Reserves	US$ Bn.	141.5	151.6	199.2	309.7	252	283.5[e]
Average Exchange Rate	Rs/US$	44.93	44.27	45.25	40.26	45.99	47.94[f]
5 Money and Credit							
Broad Money (M_3) (annual)	% change	12.0	16.9	21.7	21.4	18.6	16.5[g]
Scheduled Commercial Bank Credit (growth)	% change	27.0	30.8	28.1	22.3	17.5	13.9[g]
6 Fiscal Indicators (Centre)							
Gross Fiscal Deficit	% of GDP	3.9	4.0	3.3	2.6	5.9[h]	6.5[j]
Revenue Deficit[i]	% of GDP	2.4	2.5	1.9	1.1	4.4[h]	4.6[j]
Primary Deficit	% of GDP	0.0	0.4	-0.2	-0.9	2.5[h]	2.8[j]
7 Population	Million	1089	1106	1122	1138	1154	1170

[AE] advance estimates; [QE] quick estimates

[a] for 2008-09 the figures are the 4th advance estimates as on July 21, 2009.

[b] Average Apr.-Dec. 2009.

[c] Apr.-Dec. 2009.

[d] CAB to GDP ratio for 2009-10 is for the period Apr.-Sept. 2009.

[e] as of December 31, 2009.

[f] Average exchange rate for 2009-10 (Apr.-Dec. 2009).

[g] As on January 15, 2010.

[h] fiscal indicators for 2008-09 are based on the provisional actuals for 2008-09.

[i] fiscal indicators are as per revised GDP at current market prices based on National Accounts 2004-05 series.

[j] fiscal deficit, revenue deficit and primary deficit were envisaged at 6.8, 4.8 and 3.0 per cent of GDP respectively at the time of presentation of the 2009-10 Budget.

Source: Economic Survey 2009-10.

Table 2: Selected Indicators: 1950-51 to 2008-09

	1950-51	1960-61	1970-71	1980-81	1990-91	2000-01	2004-05	2005-06	2006-07	2007-08	2008-09
1	2	3	4	5	6	7	8	9	10	11	12
Economic Indicators											
GDP at factor cost: at current prices Rs. Cr.	9719	16512	42981	132520	515032	1925017	2877701	3282385	3779384	4320892Q	4933183R
GDP at factor cost: at constant prices Rs. Cr.	224786	329825	474131	641921	1083572	1864300	2388768	2616101	2871120	3129717Q	3339374R
Per capita Net National Product at constant prices Rs.	5708	7121	8091	8594	11535	16172	19331	20868	22580	24295Q	25494R
Gross Domestic Capital Formation as percentage to GDP at current market prices	8.4	14.0	15.1	19.9	26.0	24.3	32.1	35.5	36.9	39.1Q	na
Gross domestic savings as percentage to GDP at current market prices	8.6	11.2	14.2	18.5	22.8	23.7	31.7	34.2	35.7	37.7Q	na
Index of agricultural production (Base: triennium ending 1981-82)	46.2	68.8	85.9	102.1	148.4	165.7	177.3	191.9	200.7	207.1	188.7
Index of industrial production[a] (Base:1993-94=100)	7.9[b]	15.6	28.1	43.1	91.6	162.6	204.8	221.5	247.1	268.0	274.3
Wholesale Price Index average (Base 1993-94=100)	6.8	7.9	14.3	36.8	73.7	155.7	187.3	195.6	206.2	215.8	234.0
Consumer Price Index for Industrial Workers[c] average (Base 1982=100)	17.0	21.0	38.0	81.0	193.0	444.0	520.0	542.0	125	133	145
Output											
(a) Foodgrains (million tonnes)	50.8	82.0	108.4	129.6	176.4	196.8	198.4	208.6	217.3	230.8	229.9[d]
(b) Finished Steel[e] (million tonnes)	1.0	2.4	4.6	6.8	13.5	31.2	41.3	44.4	50.2	53.3	53.5
(c) Cement (million tonnes)	2.7	8.0	14.3	18.6	48.8	99.2	125.3	140.5	154.7	167.6	181.4
(d) Coal and lignite[f] (million tonnes)	32.3	55.2	76.3	119.0	225.5	332.6	413.0	437.1	462.1	491.1	na
(e) Crude oil (million tonnes)	0.3	0.5	6.8	10.5	32.2	32.4	34.0	32.2	34.0	34.1	33.5
(f) Electricity generated (utilities only) (Billion KWH)	5	17	56	111	264	499	587	617	663	704	724
Plan outlay (Rs. Crore)	260[g]	1117	2524	15023	58369	185737	193114	247178	244230	292336	375486

(Contd...)

	1950-51	1960-61	1970-71	1980-81	1990-91	2000-01	2004-05	2005-06	2006-07	2007-08	2008-09
1	2	3	4	5	6	7	8	9	10	11	12
Foreign Trade											
(i) Exports											
Rs. Crore	606	642	1535	6711	32553	203571	375340	456418	571779	655864	766935
US $ million	1269	1346	2031	8486	18143	44560	83535	103092	126361	162904	168704
(ii) Imports											
Rs. crore	608	1122	1634	12549	43198	230873	501065	660409	840506	1012312	1305503
US $ million	1273	2353	2162	15869	24075	50536	111516	149167	185749	251439	287759
Foreign exchange reserves[h] (excluding gold, SDRs and Reserve Tranche Position at IMF):											
Rs. crore	911	186	438	4822	4388	184482	593121	647327	836597	1196023	1230066
US $ million	1914	390	584	5850	2236	39554	135571	145108	191924	299230	241426
Social Indicators											
Population (Million)[i]	359.0	434.0	541.0	679.0	839.0	1019	1089	1106	1122	1138	1154
Birth Rate[j] (per 1000)	39.9	41.7	36.9	33.9	29.5	25.4	23.8	23.5	23.1	na	na
Death Rate[j] (per 1000)	27.4	22.8	14.9	12.5	9.8	8.4	7.6	7.5	7.4	na	na
Life Expectancy at Birth[k] (in Years)	32.1	41.3	45.6	50.4	58.7	62.5	na	na	63.5	na	na
(a) Male	32.5	41.9	46.4	50.9	58.6	61.6	na	na	62.6	na	na
(b) Female	31.7	40.6	44.7	50.0	59.0	63.3	na	na	64.2	na	na
Education: Literacy Rate[l] (%)	18.3	28.3	34.4	43.6	52.2	64.8	na	67.6	na	na	na
(a) Male	27.2	40.4	46.0	56.4	64.1	75.3	na	na	na	na	na
(b) Female	8.9	15.4	22.0	29.8	39.3	53.7	na	na	na	na	na

(Contd...)

	1950-51	1960-61	1970-71	1980-81	1990-91	2000-01	2004-05	2005-06	2006-07	2007-08	2008-09
1	2	3	4	5	6	7	8	9	10	11	12
Health & Family Welfare											
Registered Medical Practitioner (RMP) (Allopathy) (Thousand) on 31st Dec	61.8	83.7	151.1	268.7	393.6	577.1	660.8	na	na	na	na
RMP per 10,000 population	1.7	1.9	2.8	3.9	4.7	5.6	6.0	na	na	na	na
Beds (All Types)[m] per 10,000	3.2	5.7	6.4	8.3	9.5	na	na	na	na	na	na

R Revised estimates. Q Quick estimates.

na: Not available.

a The Index of Industrial Production has been revised since 1993-94.

b Relates to the calender year 1950.

c Data until 2005-06 is at base 1982=100, since January, 2006 new series of CPI (IW) has been introduced with base 2001=100. The conversion factor for deriving the data at base 1982=100 is 4.63.

d 3rd Advance Estimates.

e Including secondary producers.

f Coal output includes Meghalaya Coal from 2001-02 onwards.

g Relates to 1951-52.

h As on end-March.

i Relate to mid-financial year (as on October 1) based on population figures of C.S.O.

j For calendar year. Figure shown against 1990-91 is for calendar year 1991 and so on. Source : Office of R.G.I.

k Data for 1950-51, 1960-61, 1970-71 and 1980-81 relate to the decades 1941-50, 1951-60, 1961-70 and 1971-80 respectively, centred at midpoints of the decade, i.e., 1946, 1956, 1966 and 1976. The estimates for 1990-91 and 1991-92 refer to the periods 1988-92 and 1989-93 respectively. The estimates for 2006-07 refers to the period 2002-06.

l Data for 1950-51, 1960-61, 1970-71, 1980-81, 1990-91 and 2000-01 are as per Census of India 1951, 1961, 1971, 1981, 1991 and 2001. The figures for 1951, 1961 and 1971 relate to population aged 5 years and above and those for 1981, 1991 and 2001 to population aged 7 years and above. All India literacy rates exclude Assam for 1981 and J&K for 1991. For 2005-06, data is based on National Family Health Survey (2005-06) (+ 6 years).

m Includes beds in hospitals, dispensaries, P.H.Cs, clinics, sanatoriums, etc.

Source: Economic Survey 2008-09.

Table 3: Macroeconomic Aggregates
(at Current Prices)

(Rupees crore)

Year	Population @(million)	GDP at Factor Cost	Consumption of Fixed Capital	NDP at Factor Cost	Indirect Taxes less Subsidies	GDP at Market Prices	NDP at Market Prices	Net Factor Income from Abroad
1	2	3	4	5	6	7	8	9
			New Series (Base: 1999-2000)					
1950-51	359	9719	526	9193	366	10085	9559	-41
1951-52	365	10262	591	9670	460	10721	10130	-35
1952-53	372	10120	634	9486	402	10522	9888	-25
1953-54	379	11019	647	10372	433	11452	10805	-19
1954-55	386	10351	677	9674	482	10834	10157	-29
1955-56	393	10518	481	10037	512	11030	10548	-10
1956-57	401	12556	546	12011	584	13140	12594	-17
1957-58	409	12837	621	12215	699	13536	12914	-20
1958-59	418	14360	685	13674	726	15086	14401	-35
1959-60	426	15083	765	14318	812	15895	15130	-57
1960-61	434	16512	847	15665	896	17407	16560	-72
1961-62	444	17424	945	16479	1021	18445	17501	-98
1962-63	454	18631	1046	17585	1196	19826	18780	-108
1963-64	464	21293	1049	20244	1481	22774	21725	-112
1964-65	474	24876	1205	23670	1687	26563	25358	-145
1965-66	485	26047	1404	24643	1969	28016	26612	-164
1966-67	495	29647	1652	27995	2064	31711	30058	-230
1967-68	506	34840	1896	32944	2293	37133	35237	-258
1968-69	518	36741	1935	34807	2583	39324	37390	-255
1969-70	529	40405	2218	38188	2893	43298	41081	-271
1970-71	541	42981	2562	40419	3268	46249	43687	-284
1971-72	554	45731	2919	42811	3792	49523	46603	-291
1972-73	567	50304	3348	46956	4286	54591	51243	-302
1973-74	580	61649	4059	57591	4779	66428	62370	-325
1974-75	593	72566	5276	67289	5860	78426	73149	-291
1975-76	607	77071	6080	70991	7150	84221	78141	-255
1976-77	620	82845	6554	76291	7905	90751	84196	-233
1977-78	634	94552	7231	87321	8244	102796	95565	-233
1978-79	648	101619	8200	93419	9751	111371	103171	-156
1979-80	664	110887	10013	100874	11268	122155	112142	153
1980-81	679	132520	11736	120784	12850	145370	133634	345
1981-82	692	155158	14085	141073	15647	170805	156720	40
1982-83	708	173337	16305	157032	17722	191059	174754	-634
1983-84	723	202750	18533	184217	19735	222485	203952	-944
1984-85	739	227694	21397	206297	21574	249268	227870	-1424
1985-86	755	254427	25295	229132	26903	281330	256035	-1429
1986-87	771	283681	28935	254746	31135	314816	285881	-1805
1987-88	788	321589	32979	288611	36272	357861	324883	-2619
1988-89	805	383790	38634	345156	40742	424531	385897	-4496
1989-90	822	442134	45567	396568	45549	487684	442117	-5731
1990-91	839	515032	51078	463954	54592	569624	518546	-7545
1991-92	856	594168	61971	532197	60561	654729	592759	-10077
1992-93	872	681517	72129	609389	71074	752591	680462	-11645
1993-94	892	792150	80882	711268	73655	865805	784923	-12080
1994-95	910	925239	93822	831417	90525	1015764	921942	-13083
1995-96	928	1083289	111126	972163	108523	1191813	1080686	-13484
1996-97	946	1260710	128391	1132320	117906	1378617	1250226	-13082
1997-98	964	1401934	143749	1258185	125224	1527158	1383409	-13205
1998-99	983	1616082	162202	1453881	135116	1751199	1588997	-14968
1999-00	1001	1786525	181422	1605103	165510	1952035	1770613	-15431
2000-01	1019	1925017	201817	1723200	177297	2102314	1900497	-22733
2001-02	1040	2097726	228298	1869428	181226	2278952	2050654	-20068
2002-03	1056	2261415	250477	2010938	193146	2454561	2204084	-16690
2003-04	1072	2538171	279982	2258189	216450	2754621	2474639	-18250
2004-05	1089	2877706	328923	2548783	271706	3149412	2820489	-22375
2005-06 P	1106	3275670	378804	2896866	304674	3580344	3201540	-26116
2006-07 QE	1122	3790063	434468	3355595	355747	4145810	3711342	-29778
2007-08 RE	1138	4303654	492313	3811341	409494	4713148	4220835	-21859

(Contd...)

(Rupees crore)

Year	GNP at Factor Cost	NNP at Factor Cost	GNP at Market Prices	NNP at Market Prices	PFCE	PFCE in Domestic Market	GFCE	GDP of Public Sector	NDP of Public Sector
	10	11	12	13	14	15	16	17	18
			New Series (Base : 1999-2000)						
1950-51	9678	9152	10044	9518	8990	9643	580	.	.
1951-52	10227	9635	10686	10095	9864	10581	609	.	.
1952-53	10095	9461	10497	9863	9841	10556	630	.	.
1953-54	11000	10353	11433	10786	10708	11486	665	.	.
1954-55	10322	9645	10805	10128	9966	10690	694	.	.
1955-56	10508	10027	11020	10538	9968	10692	744	.	.
1956-57	12539	11994	13123	12577	11757	12611	820	.	.
1957-58	12817	12195	13516	12894	11926	12793	959	.	.
1958-59	14325	13639	15051	14366	13539	14522	1028	.	.
1959-60	15026	14261	15838	15073	14074	15097	1083	.	.
1960-61	16440	15593	17335	16488	15207	16312	1182	1638	1352
1961-62	17326	16381	18347	17403	15902	17057	1313	1846	1520
1962-63	18523	17477	19718	18672	16747	17964	1593	2128	1758
1963-64	21181	20132	22662	21613	18593	19944	2047	2458	2038
1964-65	24731	23525	26418	25213	21889	23479	2206	2768	2271
1965-66	25883	24479	27852	26448	23105	24783	2541	3175	2586
1966-67	29417	27765	31481	29828	26908	28863	2785	3583	2882
1967-68	34582	32686	36875	34979	32067	34396	3114	4068	3268
1968-69	36486	34552	39069	37135	32082	34412	3409	4610	3859
1969-70	40134	37917	43027	40810	34704	37225	3822	5252	4397
1970-71	42697	40135	45965	43403	36819	39493	4271	5907	4909
1971-72	45440	42520	49232	46312	39711	42595	4944	6599	5458
1972-73	50002	46654	54289	50941	43768	46947	5258	7300	5979
1973-74	61324	57266	66103	62045	52762	56595	5764	8613	6995
1974-75	72275	66998	78135	72858	63925	68568	6994	11105	9027
1975-76	76816	70736	83966	77886	65374	70123	8244	13170	10735
1976-77	82612	76058	90518	83963	67968	72905	9156	15363	12661
1977-78	94319	87088	102563	95332	78268	83953	9769	16975	13930
1978-79	101463	93263	111215	103015	85122	91305	10845	18869	15408
1979-80	111040	101027	122308	112295	92433	99147	12467	21730	17491
1980-81	132865	121129	145715	133979	111961	120094	14474	25409	20472
1981-82	155198	141113	170845	156760	128598	138385	16959	31413	25436
1982-83	172703	156398	190425	174120	141608	149022	20046	38412	31315
1983-84	201806	183273	221541	203008	166542	176019	23159	45173	36976
1984-85	226270	204873	247844	226446	184216	193517	26630	51719	42119
1985-86	252998	227703	279901	254606	201783	212371	31712	60561	49013
1986-87	281876	252941	313011	284076	226596	235409	37496	71469	58154
1987-88	318970	285992	355242	322264	253924	263036	44016	82773	67571
1988-89	379294	340660	420035	381401	293708	302738	50805	98454	80550
1989-90	436403	390837	481953	436386	328875	343011	58164	114637	93380
1990-91	507487	456409	562079	511001	376943	392142	66296	130202	105835
1991-92	584091	522120	644652	582682	435723	451815	74814	155420	125983
1992-93	669872	597744	740946	668817	490823	506915	84720	177302	143386
1993-94	780070	699188	853725	772843	562932	581447	98279	201758	164453
1994-95	912156	818334	1002681	908859	651951	669124	109346	234913	191718
1995-96	1069805	958679	1178329	1067202	751734	769542	129572	276342	226628
1996-97	1247628	1119238	1365535	1237144	886559	905672	146933	302074	245414
1997-98	1388729	1244980	1513953	1370204	965339	981262	173780	354856	292533
1998-99	1601114	1438913	1736231	1574029	1121595	1130216	215232	405955	337584
1999-00	1771094	1589672	1936604	1755182	1253643	1257541	252744	457006	383305
2000-01	1902284	1700467	2079581	1877764	1339274	1345583	265088	480952	403526
2001-02	2077658	1849360	2258884	2030586	1467195	1470301	281786	523781	439414
2002-03	2244725	1994248	2437871	2187394	1551365	1552618	290978	576210	486584
2003-04	2519921	2239939	2736371	2456389	1699486	1703547	310297	613897	517139
2004-05	2855331	2526408	3127037	2798114	1840406	1848490	338052	669335	560533
2005-06 P	3249554	2870750	3554228	3175424	2055387	2062222	373076	712447	592346
2006-07 QE	3760285	3325817	4116032	3681564	2312105	2324109	427007	812315	681371
2007-08 RE	4281795	3789482	4691289	4198976	2607584	.	477697	.	.

(Contd...)

(Rupees crore)

Year	Personal Disposable Income #	GDCF	NDCF	GDS	NDS	Per Capita GNP at Factor Cost (Rupees)	Per Capita NNP at Factor Cost (Rupees)
	19	20	21	22	23	24	25
			New Series (Base : 1999-2000)				
1950-51	8858	850	324	871	345	270	255
1951-52	9298	1152	561	969	378	280	264
1952-53	9237	811	177	845	211	271	254
1953-54	10125	862	215	875	228	290	273
1954-55	9392	1004	327	988	311	267	250
1955-56	9794	1395	914	1356	875	267	255
1956-57	11692	1921	1375	1561	1015	313	299
1957-58	11933	1829	1208	1356	735	313	298
1958-59	13362	1755	1070	1379	694	343	326
1959-60	13971	1951	1186	1720	955	353	335
1960-61	14983	2433	1586	1952	1105	379	359
1961-62	15719	2419	1474	2074	1129	390	369
1962-63	16698	2880	1834	2440	1394	408	385
1963-64	19077	3143	2094	2703	1654	456	434
1964-65	22515	3677	2472	3077	1872	522	496
1965-66	23569	4432	3028	3833	2429	534	505
1966-67	26957	5251	3599	4328	2676	594	561
1967-68	31931	5130	3234	4293	2397	683	646
1968-69	33692	5073	3138	4657	2722	704	667
1969-70	36797	6285	4067	6044	3826	759	717
1970-71	38898	6965	4403	6571	4009	789	742
1971-72	41151	7759	4840	7281	4362	820	768
1972-73	45523	8085	4737	7788	4440	882	823
1973-74	55923	11304	7245	10912	6853	1057	987
1974-75	64968	12951	7675	12298	7022	1219	1130
1975-76	69233	14079	7999	14196	8116	1265	1165
1976-77	73824	16011	9457	17320	10766	1332	1227
1977-78	85267	18530	11299	19995	12764	1488	1374
1978-79	91507	23729	15529	23601	15401	1566	1439
1979-80	99632	24793	14780	24213	14200	1672	1521
1980-81	123067	28975	17239	26881	15145	1957	1784
1981-82	142181	33507	19422	30896	16811	2243	2039
1982-83	157291	36353	20048	33787	17482	2439	2209
1983-84	185749	40608	22075	38091	19558	2791	2535
1984-85	207491	48745	27348	45453	24056	3062	2772
1985-86	229527	59623	34328	53389	28094	3351	3016
1986-87	256413	64391	35456	58036	29101	3656	3281
1987-88	291585	79089	46110	72264	39285	4048	3629
1988-89	345011	99470	60836	87166	48532	4712	4232
1989-90	395239	118371	72804	106092	60525	5309	4755
1990-91	465097	148206	97128	130010	78932	6049	5440
1991-92	531515	144466	82495	141089	79118	6823	6100
1992-93	618587	173498	101369	159682	87553	7682	6855
1993-94	716964	194724	113842	189933	109050	8745	7838
1994-95	842261	259355	165533	247462	153640	10024	8993
1995-96	959733	311782	200656	291002	179876	11528	10331
1996-97	1145206	330806	202415	313068	184677	13188	11831
1997-98	1263982	385808	242059	363506	219757	14406	12915
1998-99	1474404	408109	245907	389747	227545	16288	14638
1999-00	1617964	506244	324823	484256	302835	17693	15881
2000-01	1773251	511787	309970	499033	297215	18668	16688
2001-02	1954838	520656	292358	534885	306588	19977	17782
2002-03	2069144	619484	369008	647970	397493	21257	18885
2003-04	2296323	775647	495667	821027	541047	23507	20895
2004-05	2500193	1013762	684838	1000424	671501	26220	23199
2005-06 P	2805199	1271952	893149	1227348	848544	29381	25956
2006-07 QE	3217237	1487785	1053319	1441423	1006956	33514	29642
2007-08 RE	-	-	-	-	-	37457	33299

P: Provisional. QE: Quick Estimates. RE: Revised Estimates. @: Relates to mid-financial year.

#: Separate data on fees, fines, etc., paid by producers are not available and to that extent, personal disposable income is underestimated.

Source: Central Statistical Organisation.

Table 4: Key Deficit Indicators of the Central Government

(Rupees crore)

Year	Gross Fiscal Deficit	Net Fiscal Deficit	Gross Primary Deficit	Net Primary Deficit	Revenue Deficit	Primary Revenue Deficit*	Drawdown of Cash Balances#	Net RBI Credit@
1	2	3	4	5	6	7	8	9
1970-71	1408	780	803	749	-163	-769	285	223
1971-72	1727	1217	1057	1146	100	-570	519	583
1972-73	2179	990	1403	927	15	-761	870	1211
1973-74	1733	772	851	626	-237	-1119	328	630
1974-75	2302	865	1301	640	-765	-1766	720	528
1975-76	3029	1364	1802	1070	-886	-2114	367	-288
1976-77	3802	1572	2314	1189	-298	-1786	131	816
1977-78	3680	1813	2034	1608	-430	-2076	932	-260
1978-79	5710	2126	3726	1569	-292	-2276	1506	2191
1979-80	6392	3133	4100	2201	694	-1598	2433	2650
1980-81	8299	5110	5695	4301	2037	-567	2477	3551
1981-82	8666	4591	5471	3611	392	-2803	1400	3207
1982-83	10627	5973	6689	4887	1308	-2630	1656	3368
1983-84	13030	7770	8235	5643	2540	-2255	1417	3949
1984-85	17416	10972	11442	8961	4225	-1749	3745	6055
1985-86	21858	13544	14346	10627	5889	-1623	5316	6190
1986-87	26342	17036	17096	13143	7777	-1469	8261	7091
1987-88	27044	18431	15793	12935	9137	-2114	5816	6559
1988-89	30923	20770	16645	13473	10515	-3763	5642	6503
1989-90	35632	23722	17875	14439	11914	-5843	10592	13813
1990-91	44632	30692	23134	17924	18562	-2936	11347	14746
1991-92	36325	24622	9729	8961	16261	-10335	6855	5508
1992-93	40173	30232	9098	11644	18574	-12501	12312	4257
1993-94	60257	45994	23516	24331	32716	-4025	10960	260
1994-95	57703	40313	13644	12050	31029	-13031	961	2130
1995-96	60243	42432	10198	10806	29731	-20314	9807	19855
1996-97	66733	46394	7255	9022	32654	-26824	13184	1934
1997-98	88937	63062	23300	22748	46449	-19188	-910	12914
1998-99	113349	79944	35466	32138	66976	-10906	-209	11800
1999-00	104716	89910	14467	33556	67596	-22653	864	-5588
2000-01	118816	107854	19502	41351	85234	-14080	-1197	6705
2001-02	140955	123074	33495	51152	100162	-7298	-1496	-5150
2002-03	145072	133829	27268	53647	107879	-9925	1883	-28399
2003-04	123273	115558	-815	30008	98261	-25827	-3942	-76065
2004-05	125794	126252	-1140	31705	78338	-48596	-8130	-60177
2005-06	146435	145743	13805	35145	92299	-40331	-20888	28417
2006-07	142573	151245	-7699	23497	80222	-70050	4518	-3024
2007-08 RE	143653	137158	-28318	-17349	63488	-108483	-18184	-116772
2008-09 BE	133287	129542	-57520	-42130	55184	-135623	7225	-

RE: Revised Estimates. BE: Budget Estimates.

*: Revenue deficit net of interest payments.

#: Represents conventional budget deficit prior to 1997-98. With discontinuation of the ad hoc treasury bills and 91-day tap Treasury bills, the concept of conventional budget deficit has lost its relevance since April 1,1997.

@: Variation over end-March, as per RBI records, after closure of Government accounts.

Note: 1. Negative (-) sign indicates surplus.

2. Since 1999-00, gross fiscal deficit excludes States' share in small savings as per the new system of accounting.

Source: Budget documents of the Government of India.

Table 5: Combined Deficits of the Central and State Governments

(Rupees crore)

Year	Gross Fiscal Deficit	Gross Primary Deficit	Revenue Deficit
1	2	3	4
1980-81	10780	7818	551
1981-82	10608	6849	-987
1982-83	11116	6482	420
1983-84	15971	10441	2330
1984-85	22013	15150	5148
1985-86	22174	13551	5235
1986-87	30789	20148	7607
1987-88	32432	19427	10225
1988-89	35887	19431	12322
1989-90	43135	22603	15596
1990-91	53580	28585	23871
1991-92	45850	14858	21912
1992-93	52404	15936	23688
1993-94	70952	27938	36529
1994-95	71639	19313	37185
1995-96	77671	18598	37932
1996-97	87244	17156	48768
1997-98	110743	32466	62782
1998-99	157053	63956	110618
1999-00	184826	74375	121393
2000-01	199852	75035	138803
2001-02	226425	84039	159350
2002-03	234987	75927	162990
2003-04	234501	56928	159408
2004-05	234721	42409	114761
2005-06	239560	35583	99312
2006-07	230432	-399	55366
2007-08 RE	247831	-15905	40959
2008-09 BE	244460	-43017	26758

RE: Revised Estimates. BE: Budget Estimates.

Note: Negative (-) sign indicates surplus.

Source: Budget documents of the Government of India and the State Governments.

Table 6: Select Macro-Economic Aggregates—Growth Rate, Saving Rate and Investment Rate (at Current Prices)

(Per cent)

Year	Annual Growth Rate					Rate of GDS $	Rate of NDS $$	Rate of GDCF $	Rate of NDCF $$
	GDP at Factor Cost	NDP at Factor Cost	GNP at Factor Cost	NNP at Factor Cost	Per Capita NNP				
1	2	3	4	5	6	7	8	9	10
			New Series (Base : 1999-2000)						
1950-51	-	-	-	-	-	8.6	3.6	8.4	3.4
1951-52	5.6	5.2	5.7	5.3	3.5	9.0	3.7	10.7	5.5
1952-53	-1.4	-1.9	-1.3	-1.8	-3.7	8.0	2.1	7.7	1.8
1953-54	8.9	9.3	9.0	9.4	7.4	7.6	2.1	7.5	2.0
1954-55	-6.1	-6.7	-6.2	-6.8	-8.5	9.1	3.1	9.3	3.2
1955-56	1.6	3.7	1.8	4.0	2.1	12.3	8.3	12.6	8.7
1956-57	19.4	19.7	19.3	19.6	17.2	11.9	8.1	14.6	10.9
1957-58	2.2	1.7	2.2	1.7	-0.3	10	5.7	13.5	9.4
1958-59	11.9	11.9	11.8	11.8	9.4	9.1	4.8	11.6	7.4
1959-60	5.0	4.7	4.9	4.6	2.6	10.8	6.3	12.3	7.8
1960-61	9.5	9.4	9.4	9.3	7.3	11.2	6.7	14.0	9.6
1961-62	5.5	5.2	5.4	5.1	2.7	11.2	6.5	13.1	8.4
1962-63	6.9	6.7	6.9	6.7	4.3	12.3	7.4	14.5	9.8
1963-64	14.3	15.1	14.3	15.2	12.7	11.9	7.6	13.8	9.6
1964-65	16.8	16.9	16.8	16.9	14.4	11.6	7.4	13.8	9.7
1965-66	4.7	4.1	4.7	4.1	1.7	13.7	9.1	15.8	11.4
1966-67	13.8	13.6	13.7	13.4	11.1	13.6	8.9	16.6	12.0
1967-68	17.5	17.7	17.6	17.7	15.2	11.6	6.8	13.8	9.2
1968-69	5.5	5.7	5.5	5.7	3.3	11.8	7.3	12.9	8.4
1969-70	10.0	9.7	10.0	9.7	7.5	14.0	9.3	14.5	9.9
1970-71	6.4	5.8	6.4	5.9	3.5	14.2	9.2	15.1	10.1
1971-72	6.4	5.9	6.4	5.9	3.5	14.7	9.4	15.7	10.4
1972-73	10.0	9.7	10.0	9.7	7.2	14.3	8.7	14.8	9.2
1973-74	22.6	22.6	22.6	22.7	20.0	16.4	11.0	17.0	11.6
1974-75	17.7	16.8	17.9	17.0	14.4	15.7	9.6	16.5	10.5
1975-76	6.2	5.5	6.3	5.6	3.1	16.9	10.4	16.7	10.2
1976-77	7.5	7.5	7.5	7.5	5.3	19.1	12.8	17.6	11.2
1977-78	14.1	14.5	14.2	14.5	12.0	19.5	13.4	18.0	11.8
1978-79	7.5	7.0	7.6	7.1	4.8	21.2	14.9	21.3	15.1
1979-80	9.1	8.0	9.4	8.3	5.7	19.8	12.7	20.3	13.2
1980-81	19.5	19.7	19.7	19.9	17.2	18.5	11.3	19.9	12.9
1981-82	17.1	16.8	16.8	16.5	14.3	18.1	10.7	19.6	12.4
1982-83	11.7	11.3	11.3	10.8	8.3	17.7	10.0	19.0	11.5
1983-84	17.0	17.3	16.9	17.2	14.8	17.1	9.6	18.3	10.8
1984-85	12.3	12.0	12.1	11.8	9.4	18.2	10.6	19.6	12.0
1985-86	11.7	11.1	11.8	11.1	8.8	19.0	11.0	21.2	13.4
1986-87	11.5	11.2	11.4	11.1	8.8	18.4	10.2	20.5	12.4
1987-88	13.4	13.3	13.2	13.1	10.6	20.2	12.1	22.1	14.2
1988-89	19.3	19.6	18.9	19.1	16.6	20.5	12.6	23.4	15.8
1989-90	15.2	14.9	15.1	14.7	12.4	21.8	13.7	24.3	16.5
1990-91	16.5	17.0	16.3	16.8	14.4	22.8	15.2	26.0	18.7
1991-92	15.4	14.7	15.1	14.4	12.1	21.5	13.3	22.1	13.9
1992-93	14.7	14.5	14.7	14.5	12.4	21.2	12.9	23.1	14.9
1993-94	16.2	16.7	16.5	17.0	14.3	21.9	13.9	22.5	14.5

(Contd...)

Year	Annual Growth Rate					Rate of GDS $	Rate of NDS $$	Rate of GDCF $	Rate of NDCF $$
	GDP at Factor Cost	NDP at Factor Cost	GNP at Factor Cost	NNP at Factor Cost	Per Capita NNP				
1	2	3	4	5	6	7	8	9	10
1994-95	16.8	16.9	16.9	17.0	14.7	24.4	16.7	25.5	18.0
1995-96	17.1	16.9	17.3	17.2	14.9	24.4	16.6	26.2	18.6
1996-97	16.4	16.5	16.6	16.7	14.5	22.7	14.8	24.0	16.2
1997-98	11.2	11.1	11.3	11.2	9.2	23.8	15.9	25.3	17.5
1998-99	15.3	15.6	15.3	15.6	13.3	22.3	14.3	23.3	15.5
1999-00	10.5	10.4	10.6	10.5	8.5	24.8	17.1	25.9	18.3
2000-01	7.8	7.4	7.4	7.0	5.1	23.7	15.6	24.3	16.3
2001-02	9.0	8.5	9.2	8.8	6.6	23.5	15	22.8	14.3
2002-03	7.8	7.6	8.0	7.8	6.2	26.4	18	25.2	16.7
2003-04	12.2	12.3	12.3	12.3	10.6	29.8	21.9	28.2	20.0
2004-05	13.4	12.9	13.3	12.8	11.0	31.8	23.8	32.2	24.3
2005-06 P	13.8	13.7	13.8	13.6	11.9	34.3	26.5	35.5	27.9
2006-07 QE	15.7	15.8	15.7	15.9	14.2	34.8	27.1	35.9	28.4
2007-08 RE	13.6	13.6	13.9	13.9	12.3	-	-	-	-

P: Provisional. QE : Quick Estimates. RE: Revised Estimates.
$: GDS and GDCF rates are percentages to GDP at current market prices.
$$: NDS and NDCF rates are percentages to NDP at current market prices.
Source: Central Statistical Organisation.

Table 7: Ratio of Savings and Investment to GDP
(% at Current Market Prices)

	2004-05	2005-06	2006-07	2007-08	2008-09
Gross Domestic Saving	32.2	33.1	34.4	36.4	32.5
Public Sector	2.3	2.4	3.6	5.0	1.4
Private Sector	29.9	30.7	30.9	31.4	31.1
Household Sector	23.3	23.2	22.9	22.6	22.6
Financial Saving	9.8	11.4	10.9	11.2	10.4
Saving in Physical Assets	13.5	11.8	11.9	11.5	12.2
Private Corporate Sector	6.6	7.5	8.0	8.7	8.4
Gross Capital Formation (Investment)	32.7	34.3	35.5	37.7	34.9
Public Sector	7.4	7.9	8.4	8.9	9.4
Private Sector	23.8	25.3	26.4	27.6	24.9
Corporate Sector	10.3	13.5	14.5	16.1	12.7
Household Sector	13.5	11.8	11.9	11.5	12.2
Gross fixed Capital Formation	28.8	30.4	31.4	33.0	33.0
Stocks	2.5	2.8	3.4	3.5	1.3
Valuables	1.3	1.1	1.2	1.1	1.3
Saving-investment Gap					
Public Sector	-5.1	-5.5	-4.8	-3.9	-8.0
Private Sector	6.1	5.4	4.4	3.8	6.2

Note: Totals may not tally due to adjustment for errors and omissions.

Source: Central Statistical Organisation.

Table 8: Annual Growth Rate of Gross National Product and Net National Product

(Per cent)

Year	Gross National Product at Factor Cost		Net National Product at Factor Cost		Per Capita Net National Product	
	At Current Prices	At 1999-00 Prices	At Current Prices	At 1999-00 Prices	At Current Prices	At 1999-00 Prices
1	2	3	4	5	6	7
1951-52	5.7	2.5	5.3	2.3	3.5	0.6
1952-53	-1.3	2.9	-1.8	2.8	-3.7	0.9
1953-54	9.0	6.1	9.4	6.4	7.4	4.4
1954-55	-6.2	4.2	-6.8	4.2	-8.5	2.3
1955-56	1.8	2.7	4.0	6.5	2.1	4.6
1956-57	19.3	5.7	19.6	5.5	17.2	3.4
1957-58	2.2	-1.3	1.7	-1.8	-0.3	-3.7
1958-59	11.8	7.5	11.8	7.6	9.4	5.3
1959-60	4.9	2.0	4.6	1.7	2.6	-0.2
1960-61	9.4	7.0	9.3	7.2	7.3	5.2
1961-62	5.4	3.0	5.1	2.7	2.7	0.4
1962-63	6.9	2.0	6.7	1.8	4.3	-0.5
1963-64	14.3	5.1	15.2	5.7	12.7	3.4
1964-65	16.8	7.5	16.9	7.4	14.4	5.1
1965-66	4.7	-3.7	4.1	-4.5	1.7	-6.6
1966-67	13.7	1.0	13.4	0.6	11.1	-1.5
1967-68	17.6	8.0	17.7	8.0	15.2	5.7
1968-69	5.5	2.7	5.7	3.1	3.3	0.7
1969-70	10.0	6.5	9.7	6.4	7.5	4.2
1970-71	6.4	5.0	5.9	4.9	3.5	2.6
1971-72	6.4	1.0	5.9	0.6	3.5	-1.8
1972-73	10.0	-0.3	9.7	-0.8	7.2	-3.1
1973-74	22.6	4.7	22.7	4.5	20.0	2.2
1974-75	17.9	1.3	17.0	0.9	14.4	-1.3
1975-76	6.3	9.1	5.6	9.5	3.1	6.9
1976-77	7.5	1.3	7.5	0.9	5.3	-1.2
1977-78	14.2	7.6	14.5	7.7	12.0	5.3
1978-79	7.6	5.5	7.1	5.5	4.8	3.2
1979-80	9.4	-5.0	8.3	-6.0	5.7	-8.2
1980-81	19.7	7.2	19.9	7.4	17.2	5.0
1981-82	16.8	5.5	16.5	5.5	14.3	3.5
1982-83	11.3	2.6	10.8	2.3	8.3	-0.1
1983-84	16.9	7.8	17.2	8.1	14.8	5.8
1984-85	12.1	3.8	11.8	3.6	9.4	1.3
1985-86	11.8	4.2	11.1	4.0	8.8	1.8
1986-87	11.4	4.3	11.1	4.1	8.8	2.0
1987-88	13.2	3.3	13.1	3.0	10.6	0.8
1988-89	18.9	9.8	19.1	10.3	16.6	7.9
1989-90	15.1	6.1	14.7	6.1	12.4	3.9
1990-91	16.3	5.0	16.8	5.2	14.4	3.1
1991-92	15.1	1.4	14.4	0.9	12.1	-1.1
1992-93	14.7	5.4	14.5	5.4	12.4	3.4
1993-94	16.5	5.9	17.0	5.9	14.3	3.5

(Contd...)

Year	Gross National Product at Factor Cost		Net National Product at Factor Cost		Per Capita Net National Product	
	At Current Prices	At 1999-00 Prices	At Current Prices	At 1999-00 Prices	At Current Prices	At 1999-00 Prices
1	2	3	4	5	6	7
1994-95	16.9	6.5	17.0	6.5	14.7	4.4
1995-96	17.3	7.3	17.2	7.3	14.9	5.2
1996-97	16.6	8.1	16.7	8.2	14.5	6.2
1997-98	11.3	4.5	11.2	4.3	9.2	2.3
1998-99	15.3	6.7	15.6	6.6	13.3	4.6
1999-00	10.6	6.4	10.5	6.2	8.5	4.3
2000-01	7.4	4.0	7.0	3.7	5.1	1.8
2001-02	9.2	6.0	8.8	5.8	6.6	3.7
2002-03	8.0	4.0	7.8	3.6	6.2	2.0
2003-04	12.2	8.5	12.2	8.6	10.5	7.0
2004-05	13.4	7.5	12.9	7.3	11.1	5.6
2005-06	14.0	9.6	13.8	9.6	12.1	7.9
2006-07	15.2	9.8	15.2	9.8	13.5	8.2
2007-08[Q]	14.6	9.3	14.3	9.1	12.7	7.6
Annual Average Growth Rates						
First Plan (1951-56)	1.8	3.7	2.0	4.4	0.2	2.6
Second Plan (1956-61)	9.5	4.2	9.4	4.0	7.2	2.0
Third Plan (1961-66)	9.6	2.8	9.6	2.6	7.2	0.4
Three Annual Plans (1966-69)	12.3	3.9	12.3	3.9	9.9	1.6
Fourth Plan (1969-74)	11.1	3.4	10.8	3.1	8.3	0.8
Fifth Plan (1974-79)	10.7	5.0	10.3	4.9	7.9	2.6
Annual Plan (1979-80)	9.4	-5.0	8.3	-6.0	5.7	-8.2
Sixth Plan (1980-85)	15.4	5.4	15.2	5.4	12.8	3.1
Seventh Plan (1985-90)	14.1	5.5	13.8	5.5	11.4	3.3
Two Annual Plans (1990-92)	15.7	3.2	15.6	3.1	13.3	1.0
Eighth Plan (1992-97)	16.4	6.6	16.5	6.7	14.2	4.5
Ninth Plan (1997-2002)	10.8	5.5	10.6	5.3	8.5	3.3
Tenth Plan (2002-2007)	12.6	7.9	12.4	7.8	10.7	6.1

Q: Quick estimates.

Note: Growth rates from 2000-01 based on New Series with base year 1999-2000.

Source: Economy Survey, 2008-09.

Table 9: Components of Net State Domestic Product at Factor Cost by Industry of Origin (at Current Prices) (Base: 1999-2000)

(Rupees crore)

State/Union Territory/Year	Agriculture and Allied Activities				Industry			
	Agriculture	Forestry and Logging	Fishing	Total (2+3+4)	Mining and Quarrying	Manufacturing		
						Registered	Unregistered	Sub Total (7+8)
1	2	3	4	5	6	7	8	9
Andhra Pradesh								
1999-00	31425.4	1366	2874.4	35665.7	3047	12368.2	8295.3	4072.9
2000-01	36421.1	1416.4	3732.9	41570.4	3335.1	12297.3	7897.5	4399.8
2001-02	36746.7	1377.7	4503.2	42627.6	3752.6	13623.3	9309.1	4314.2
2002-03	34028.5	1447.0	5644.6	41120.1	4357.5	15514.1	10680.2	4833.9
2003-04	41787.4	1504.3	5838.4	49130.2	4573.6	17878.2	12264.5	5613.8
2004-05	44532.2	1580.7	5211.3	51324.2	5307.9	19472.5	13641.3	5831.2
2005-06	50260.1	1645.1	5487.0	57392.2	6243.1	21588.9	15290.3	6298.6
2006-07	54459.8	1744.4	5893.8	62098.0	8352.7	24674.8	17639.5	7035.3
Arunachal Pradesh								
1999-00	424.3	66.9	13.2	504.5	32.0	46.9	0.0	46.9
2000-01	517.7	82.9	13.7	614.3	28.7	54.9	0.0	54.9
2001-02	529.7	67.4	15.1	612.2	27.1	50.6	0.0	50.6
2002-03	550.3	62.2	14.9	627.4	51.6	54.9	0.0	54.9
2003-04	610.1	50.1	15.0	675.2	42.6	53.6	0.0	53.6
2004-05	601.7	51.4	17.5	670.5	71.6	60.0	0.0	60.0
2005-06	618.6	58.2	20.7	697.5	94.6	69.8	0.0	69.8
Assam								
1999-00	10998.1	457.6	515.3	11971.0	1450.4	2275.3	1746.2	529.0
2000-01	11052.1	443.6	517.4	12013.1	1856.0	1965.0	1411.5	553.6
2001-02	11161.4	526.8	533.5	12221.7	1776.5	2345.7	1816.8	529.0
2002-03	11198.7	539.4	613.2	12351.2	2973.0	3317.2	2728.1	589.1
2003-04	11639.7	548.9	731.0	12919.7	2736.7	4109.4	3438.9	670.5
2004-05	12839.5	508.1	675.7	14023.3	3075.7	4651.8	3886.5	765.4
2005-06	13894.5	570.3	852.1	15316.9	3321.2	5229.7	4397.9	831.8
2006-07	15595.4	598.4	1051.7	17245.4	4052.2	5826.2	4944.9	881.2
Bihar								
1999-00	14308.4	875.7	627.1	74.8	1577.6	3144.7	997.1	2147.5
2000-01	18714.6	970.4	735.9	87.3	1793.6	2937.9	696.7	2241.2
2001-02	16503.6	1043.5	900.5	131.6	2075.7	2647.2	553.8	2093.3
2002-03	19877.5	1106.6	973.5	42.8	2122.9	3040.2	814.7	2225.4
2003-04	17652.0	1194.2	1011.4	37.1	2242.7	2979.7	505.1	2474.7
2004-05	18130.8	1296.1	939.6	34.0	2269.7	3403.0	847.5	2555.5
2005-06	17898.9	1402.1	952.1	39.2	2393.4	4948.7	2107.1	2841.6
2006-07	23741.0	1516.3	1035.7	45.2	2597.2	5427.0	2392.4	3034.7

(Contd...)

State/Union Territory/Year	Industry		Services							
	Electricity, Gas and Water Supply	Total (6+9+10)	Construction	Transport, Storage and Communication	Trade, Hotels and Restaurants	Banking and Insurance	Real Estate, Ownership of Dwelling and Business Services	Public Administration	Other Services	Total (12 to 18)
	10	11	12	13	14	15	16	17	18	19
Andhra Pradesh										
1999-00	2061.2	9181.1	7464.7	7298.8	16492.2	5450.5	9412.9	5548.2	12156.4	63823.8
2000-01	2130.1	9864.9	8381.1	8033.0	18898.4	5811.5	10907.5	6276.8	13481.4	71780.7
2001-02	2188.7	10255.4	9368.1	9509.4	20508.1	7466.9	12227.8	6554.1	14771.5	80405.8
2002-03	2642.0	11833.3	10265.1	10623.6	21912.0	8526.3	13647.0	7167.0	16291.0	88432.0
2003-04	2464.6	12652.0	11293.0	12398.5	25206.2	9401.5	15360.6	7652.8	17915.6	99228.0
2004-05	2557.9	13697.0	12637.6	14770.3	27994.8	9798.7	16650.4	8105.2	20235.2	110192.1
2005-06	2753.0	15294.8	14684.5	17001.9	31311.7	10282.6	18182.3	8798.9	22533.4	122795.3
2006-07	3080.5	18468.6	17601.5	20103.6	36861.4	11346.0	21412.8	9513.4	25216.1	142054.9
Arunachal Pradesh										
1999-00	13.0	91.9	218.1	80.4	95.4	38.3	47.7	213.4	214.0	907.4
2000-01	13.2	96.7	211.5	84.0	115.2	47.1	53.4	251.6	212.1	974.9
2001-02	11.1	88.8	477.8	88.7	115.5	51.3	55.5	266.2	230.0	1285.1
2002-03	28.8	135.3	337.1	96.9	121.9	61.4	58.1	285.5	230.8	1191.6
2003-04	125.7	221.9	399.8	105.7	128.6	63.6	62.4	310.7	268.8	1339.6
2004-05	203.3	334.9	576.2	108.3	134.0	52.5	67.0	354.8	291.7	1584.6
2005-06	208.5	372.9	600.1	116.1	152.4	56.4	72.9	367.2	331.0	1696.1
Assam										
1999-00	171.5	2151.0	1391.5	1631.9	3881.8	1117.4	986.3	1928.4	5205.3	16142.5
2000-01	207.3	2616.9	1720.8	1490.2	4221.0	1161.3	1145.5	2110.5	5869.1	17718.3
2001-02	123.4	2428.8	1882.1	1633.4	4436.9	1328.7	1185.1	2156.1	6004.4	18626.6
2002-03	340.8	3902.9	1949.7	1849.0	5368.9	1586.2	1135.7	2180.2	6342.1	20411.8
2003-04	365.5	3772.7	2454.1	2088.9	5940.8	1627.6	1331.7	2403.6	6949.3	22796.0
2004-05	572.8	4413.9	2733.7	2323.0	7250.0	1538.3	1274.2	2715.4	7673.2	25507.7
2005-06	514.7	4667.6	2948.8	2463.6	7755.5	1602.2	1369.7	2775.8	8615.1	27530.8
2006-07	622.0	5555.5	3238.2	2593.5	8119.4	1704.7	1396.4	3777.4	9697.3	30526.8
Bihar										
1999-00	407.7	4132.8	1889.4	2902.3	7426.7	1766.4	1341.4	3228.4	7924.4	26479.0
2000-01	569.0	4603.7	1884.9	3099.1	8481.4	1988.3	1476.0	3445.7	7972.8	28348.1
2001-02	323.3	4492.4	2167.5	3202.7	9453.1	2649.7	1487.5	3776.7	8010.6	30747.8
2002-03	385.4	4733.8	2620.0	3410.1	11801.6	2645.1	1626.9	3385.6	8362.3	33851.6
2003-04	472.7	5190.0	2688.8	3665.6	12608.7	2807.4	1917.1	4047.8	9152.9	36888.3
2004-05	568.7	5393.9	3323.2	3989.8	15894.3	2815.8	1943.6	4453.0	9409.7	41829.4
2005-06	712.0	5947.0	3717.9	4152.7	16414.8	2940.0	2070.6	4733.1	11024.2	45053.1
2006-07	921.7	6553.6	5489.7	4493.6	17502.9	3069.6	2191.5	5963.3	13028.5	51739.0

(Contd...)

State/Union Territory/Year	Agriculture and Allied Activities				Industry			
	Agriculture	Forestry and Logging	Fishing	Total (2+3+4)	Mining and Quarrying	Manufacturing		
						Registered	Unregistered	Sub Total (7+8)
1	2	3	4	5	6	7	8	9
Chattisgarh								
1999-00	5575.8	695.1	260.1	6531.1	2699.9	2028.5	938.1	2966.6
2000-01	4074.3	765.4	338.0	5177.7	2682.0	1827.9	976.9	2804.7
2001-02	6277.7	951.9	350.3	7580.0	2645.5	1641.4	962.2	2603.5
2002-03	4830.1	957.1	373.6	6160.8	3415.4	2682.8	1045.1	3727.9
2003-04	7778.6	1129.1	420.9	9328.6	3396.7	4429.6	1217.4	5647.0
2004-05	6517.3	1253.2	477.4	8247.9	4576.3	7594.6	1343.9	8938.5
2005-06	8376.6	1357.0	542.1	10275.6	4049.3	9421.9	1534.0	10955.9
Goa								
1999-00	532.7	8.7	117.4	658.8	209.2	1185.2	235.8	1421.0
2000-01	400.5	6.4	175.6	582.4	194.9	1359.8	261.1	1620.9
2001-02	442.2	10.0	159.7	611.9	222.8	1493.0	265.7	1758.7
2002-03	455.4	12.5	169.0	636.9	276.3	1710.6	292.2	2002.9
2003-04	513.0	10.8	211.8	735.7	366.9	2175.3	333.2	2508.5
2004-05	559.2	14.7	206.0	779.9	520.7	2842.3	385.6	3227.9
2005-06	539.7	14.9	345.1	899.6	520.0	3300.1	384.7	3684.8
Gujarat								
1999-00	14920.0	250.0	1187.0	16357.0	2206.0	17253.0	7227.0	24480.0
2000-01	13659.0	339.0	1074.0	15072.0	2542.0	14125.0	8028.0	22153.0
2001-02	17046.0	406.0	1244.0	18696.0	2661.0	14036.0	7915.0	21951.0
2002-03	16866.0	403.0	1396.0	18665.0	4613.0	19865.0	8505.0	28370.0
2003-04	26318.0	465.0	1194.0	27977.0	4393.0	25055.0	9524.0	34579.0
2004-05	23303.0	519.0	1200.0	25022.0	6212.0	31168.0	11059.0	42227.0
2005-06	32204.0	558.0	1779.0	34541.0	6796.0	35739.0	12514.0	48253.0
Haryana								
1999-00	15402.0	372.6	60.7	15835.4	124.7	6190.1	2410.2	8600.4
2000-01	16625.7	345.1	66.3	17037.1	152.3	6977.4	2573.8	9551.1
2001-02	16773.4	438.7	67.9	17279.9	195.7	8295.3	2734.8	11030.2
2002-03	17221.9	379.5	71.1	17672.5	146.3	9537.2	3002.3	12539.5
2003-04	19268.4	484.9	84.0	19837.3	162.3	10821.6	3352.9	14174.5
2004-05	19982.3	542.7	94.5	20619.5	165.8	12685.9	3686.9	16372.7
2005-06	20336.0	669.5	107.4	21112.8	326.6	14329.0	4103.3	18432.3
2006-07	24795.2	983.3	134.3	25912.8	322.3	16597.9	4800.1	21398.0

(Contd...)

State/Union Territory/Year	Industry		Services							
	Electricity, Gas and Water Supply	Total (6+9+10)	Construction	Transport, Storage and Communication	Trade, Hotels and Restaurants	Banking and Insurance	Real Estate, Ownership of Dwelling and Business Services	Public Administration	Other Services	Total (12 to 18)
	10	11	12	13	14	15	16	17	18	19
Chattisgarh										
1999-00	877.1	6543.6	1001.2	1247.4	3048.2	666.3	1469.2	845.8	2757.0	11035.0
2000-01	774.2	6260.9	1035.0	1337.0	2765.4	730.5	1569.6	877.2	2086.8	11301.4
2001-02	594.9	6844.0	1187.7	1415.1	3157.9	820.3	1691.7	1578.4	2730.3	12581.3
2002-03	1243.8	8387.0	1519.0	1610.1	3361.1	988.8	1784.1	1524.8	2795.3	13583.2
2003-04	1115.3	10159.0	1781.3	1914.4	4227.7	1076.9	1857.2	1221.1	3528.1	15606.6
2004-05	1014.0	14528.8	1851.0	2271.5	5051.4	1103.1	1914.3	1362.4	3961.6	17515.3
2005-06	994.0	15999.1	2087.0	2568.2	6041.3	1244.9	2102.6	1446.5	3978.0	19468.4
Goa										
1999-00	57.7	1687.9	342.3	522.6	946.4	521.1	331.5	284.6	275.3	3223.7
2000-01	55.8	1871.6	392.4	612.7	1080.6	415.6	385.8	296.7	292.8	3476.5
2001-02	49.3	2030.8	424.2	664.7	875.7	477.8	420.6	311.3	340.8	3515.0
2002-03	144.5	2423.7	502.5	666.9	931.7	723.9	458.9	334.0	329.9	3947.7
2003-04	142.7	3018.1	608.0	869.1	860.2	765.0	509.6	357.6	326.8	4296.4
2004-05	138.6	3887.3	737.4	1082.9	1388.4	784.7	575.8	359.4	443.6	5372.2
2005-06	146.5	4351.3	804.2	1086.4	1473.2	854.9	643.7	375.2	462.9	5700.6
Gujarat										
1999-00	1927.0	28613.0	6171.0	4800.0	13008.0	7076.0	5647.0	4321.0	6548.0	47571.0
2000-01	2650.0	27345.0	6153.0	5497.0	14394.0	5959.0	6346.0	4214.0	7294.0	49857.0
2001-02	3783.0	28395.0	5012.0	6602.0	16854.0	7325.0	6789.0	4288.0	7829.0	54699.0
2002-03	3692.0	36675.0	6833.0	6983.0	20421.0	8940.0	6964.0	4370.0	8279.0	62790.0
2003-04	3631.0	42603.0	9271.0	7994.0	24898.0	9525.0	7075.0	4646.0	8545.0	71954.0
2004-05	4166.0	52605.0	11386.0	8947.0	29795.0	9865.0	7169.0	4711.0	9031.0	80904.0
2005-06	5204.0	60253.0	13695.0	10155.0	35064.0	11133.0	7266.0	4830.0	9705.0	91848.0
Haryana										
1999-00	397.7	9122.7	3360.8	2868.0	6707.6	1855.6	2367.2	1463.4	3542.3	22164.9
2000-01	472.1	10175.5	3470.7	3322.5	8705.0	1989.9	3354.1	1478.9	3776.8	26097.8
2001-02	565.0	11790.9	4455.2	3992.2	10115.5	2276.8	4256.9	1572.9	4290.7	30960.3
2002-03	963.8	13649.6	5175.8	4453.3	11371.0	2646.9	5117.6	1674.5	4578.9	35017.9
2003-04	965.0	15301.9	6478.5	5279.7	12686.7	2856.6	6191.6	1889.2	5005.7	40388.0
2004-05	732.5	17270.9	8348.7	6214.5	15239.7	2992.0	7130.4	2116.8	5555.6	47597.7
2005-06	1265.7	20024.6	10074.2	7092.0	17856.0	3225.6	9224.9	2365.0	6186.0	56023.7
2006-07	1246.2	22966.5	12062.6	8200.0	21658.1	3428.8	11818.4	2567.9	6963.7	66699.4

(*Contd...*)

State/Union Territory/Year	Agriculture and Allied Activities				Industry			
	Agriculture	Forestry and Logging	Fishing	Total (2+3+4)	Mining and Quarrying	Manufacturing		
						Registered	Unregistered	Sub Total (7+8)
1	2	3	4	5	6	7	8	9
Himachal Pradesh								
1999-00	2608.7	482.8	26.1	3117.5	67.0	992.8	237.6	1230.5
2000-01	3216.3	570.4	26.1	3812.8	48.0	1140.1	254.7	1394.8
2001-02	3598.0	654.0	27.4	4279.3	58.4	1167.4	254.8	1422.2
2002-03	3708.9	762.0	27.6	4498.5	50.5	1300.4	275.1	1575.4
2003-04	4186.3	800.6	25.5	5012.4	59.8	1432.0	316.3	1748.3
2004-05	4739.7	831.5	30.3	5601.5	61.5	1602.4	330.7	1933.1
2005-06	4955.5	922.3	32.0	5909.7	64.9	1781.0	347.6	2128.6
2006-07	5192.3	1007.1	33.8	6233.2	68.4	1970.2	379.9	2350.1
Jammu and Kashmir								
1999-00	4057.9	393.5	104.4	4555.8	25.3	207.0	307.1	514.1
2000-01	4222.0	384.5	103.1	4709.6	19.9	160.7	316.4	477.0
2001-02	4525.4	441.1	110.8	5077.3	22.0	170.8	290.2	461.0
2002-03	5169.7	490.3	118.7	5778.7	18.4	186.4	298.9	485.3
2003-04	5795.4	463.1	139.3	6397.8	19.4	219.6	313.6	533.2
2004-05	6042.2	483.0	154.2	6679.5	24.8	576.6	362.4	939.0
Jharkhand								
1999-00	4721.1	410.6	288.8	5420.5	3380.4	6847.3	671.7	7518.9
2000-01	4608.0	482.7	65.6	5156.4	3699.2	3176.0	703.2	3879.2
2001-02	6350.2	575.1	40.9	6966.1	3539.4	2409.8	663.6	3073.4
2002-03	5109.5	681.6	74.4	5865.6	4522.5	5596.9	710.8	6307.8
2003-04	5431.3	809.9	19.6	6260.7	4627.1	6693.5	777.4	7471.0
2004-05	6680.5	836.9	45.7	7563.1	5608.8	14811.6	805.2	15616.8
2005-06	6764.9	966.0	58.4	7789.2	6186.9	17269.7	944.2	18213.9
2006-07	6849.0	1114.9	64.0	8027.9	6818.8	20131.3	993.3	21124.5
Karnataka								
1999-00	23196.6	1514.1	542.7	25253.4	404.8	6663.5	3719.0	10382.5
2000-01	24361.7	1590.1	532.7	26484.5	461.2	6595.5	4057.8	10653.3
2001-02	19916.0	1682.0	497.4	22095.4	557.2	7787.2	4222.2	12009.3
2002-03	19396.0	1615.9	600.4	21612.3	628.6	9858.2	4856.0	14714.2
2003-04	17465.9	1719.1	498.3	19683.2	952.2	11972.9	5240.2	17213.2
2004-05	22729.0	1930.6	544.8	25204.3	1624.9	13509.8	5590.6	19100.4
2005-06	27261.4	2047.3	736.1	30044.9	1660.0	14949.6	6101.7	21051.3

(Contd...)

State/Union Territory/Year	Industry		Services							
	Electricity, Gas and Water Supply	Total (6+9+10)	Construction	Transport, Storage and Communication	Trade, Hotels and Restaurants	Banking and Insurance	Real Estate, Ownership of Dwelling and Business Services	Public Administration	Other Services	Total (12 to 18)
	10	11	12	13	14	15	16	17	18	19
Himachal Pradesh										
1999-00	529.6	1827.1	2609.6	286.5	1189.9	531.2	482.6	036.0	1405.9	7522.4
2000-01	622.8	2065.5	2707.4	352.1	1391.3	573.9	505.4	899.6	1544.4	7974.2
2001-02	635.7	2116.4	3115.6	383.1	1574.7	668.2	564.9	892.1	1621.2	8819.6
2002-03	722.0	2347.9	3542.2	462.8	1863.7	730.1	604.2	970.6	1731.4	9904.9
2003-04	865.8	2673.8	3712.4	519.3	1910.3	783.8	662.3	1045.9	1807.0	10441.0
2004-05	1036.9	3031.6	4100.4	581.5	2167.6	798.3	735.0	1263.7	1982.7	11629.2
2005-06	1281.4	3474.9	4824.8	665.3	2266.4	850.3	808.7	1370.5	2219.3	13005.3
2006-07	1435.5	3854.0	5322.9	755.3	2536.9	1101.3	888.8	1665.0	2440.9	14711.1
Jammu and Kashmir										
1999-00	612.8	1152.2	1569.6	388.3	1164.7	566.9	786.8	1996.4	1352.4	7825.0
2000-01	830.9	1327.8	1606.6	429.3	1175.6	626.6	832.2	2099.5	1521.3	8291.0
2001-02	866.7	1349.7	2022.6	483.3	1276.9	723.3	846.3	2110.3	1566.8	9029.5
2002-03	867.8	1371.4	2245.7	542.2	1401.5	869.7	849.4	2455.0	1886.3	10249.7
2003-04	884.6	1437.2	2555.6	580.5	1543.0	940.7	885.5	2508.0	2143.4	11156.7
2004-05	767.9	1731.7	3268.2	659.5	1737.7	938.9	924.3	2474.5	2309.7	12312.7
Jharkhand										
1999-00	280.7	11180.1	2115.2	2039.1	3371.9	640.0	1183.1	878.2	3100.8	13328.2
2000-01	367.7	7946.1	2118.3	2108.2	3017.6	720.4	1342.6	1526.1	3569.1	14402.3
2001-02	358.1	6970.9	2669.5	2185.9	3272.1	960.1	1465.6	1951.8	3479.8	15984.6
2002-03	494.7	11324.9	2345.0	2366.0	3714.9	958.4	1611.6	1301.6	3421.8	15719.3
2003-04	546.4	12644.5	2981.7	2561.4	4061.8	1017.2	1907.5	2277.7	2788.4	17595.7
2004-05	431.1	21656.7	2982.2	2890.8	5718.0	1020.3	2125.2	2111.6	4075.3	20923.3
2005-06	416.4	24817.2	3193.8	3091.9	6355.0	1065.2	2385.3	2511.6	4303.6	22906.5
2006-07	397.5	28340.9	3420.1	3313.7	7063.0	1159.4	2675.7	2985.7	4544.5	25162.2
Karnataka										
1999-00	1375.4	12162.7	6556.1	4207.2	11108.0	5305.8	9508.5	3806.2	7971.0	48462.8
2000-01	1819.0	12933.5	6261.3	4801.6	12077.7	5755.9	11323.6	3937.5	8319.6	52477.0
2001-02	1793.8	14360.3	7265.5	5924.6	13185.6	6710.6	12838.4	4250.4	8938.4	59113.4
2002-03	1744.1	17087.0	7893.8	6406.9	14930.6	8151.0	14303.5	4430.4	9550.4	65666.5
2003-04	1711.0	19876.4	8825.3	7296.6	17571.7	9109.7	16367.3	4784.2	10713.9	74668.6
2004-05	1682.8	22408.1	9982.2	7770.0	20712.6	9329.8	19704.1	5155.5	11676.7	84330.8
2005-06	2088.3	24799.5	11734.8	9309.3	23693.2	10528.7	23151.7	5637.3	12841.9	96896.9

(*Contd...*)

State/Union Territory/Year	Agriculture and Allied Activities: Agriculture	Forestry and Logging	Fishing	Total (2+3+4)	Industry: Mining and Quarrying	Manufacturing: Registered	Unregistered	Sub Total (7+8)
1	2	3	4	5	6	7	8	9
Kerala								
1999-00	10055.2	1177.6	1373.5	12606.3	113.1	3328.4	2208.4	5536.8
2000-01	8664.5	1195.5	1384.3	11244.3	158.9	3337.4	2413.3	5750.7
2001-02	9129.5	1308.5	1412.5	11850.5	152.6	3047.2	2357.6	5404.8
2002-03	10313.6	1244.4	1269.5	12827.5	166.1	3206.9	2579.5	5786.4
2003-04	11047.8	1386.7	1266.3	13700.8	171.5	3559.2	2866.3	6425.5
2004-05	12044.4	1210.1	1539.9	14794.4	178.5	3581.2	3453.4	7034.6
2005-06	13225.0	1210.1	2106.7	16541.9	178.5	3847.0	4020.4	7867.4
2006-07	14579.3	1191.4	2244.3	18015.1	182.1	4064.8	4758.7	8823.5
Madhya Pradesh								
1999-00	21542.6	1166.1	169.7	22878.4	2284.3	5026.3	2572.6	7598.9
2000-01	17061.2	1297.3	183.0	18541.4	2188.0	4992.7	2410.6	7403.3
2001-02	21021.1	1562.4	182.5	22766.0	2764.4	4690.1	2410.9	7101.0
2002-03	18306.0	1509.0	156.0	19971.1	2804.8	3854.4	2414.6	6269.1
2003-04	27672.3	1638.6	186.1	29497.0	3769.1	3782.8	2719.4	6502.2
2004-05	25341.0	1653.0	229.7	27223.7	4613.9	4181.1	3162.4	7343.5
2005-06	27917.1	1839.3	221.5	29977.9	4645.7	4156.3	3240.6	7396.9
2006-07	31680.1	1919.6	265.9	33865.6	4880.9	4528.4	3483.3	8011.7
Maharashtra								
1999-00	34428.5	1744.8	829.0	37002.3	1578.0	31178.5	8807.4	39985.9
2000-01	33243.2	2031.9	815.1	36090.2	1786.9	27203.8	9844.0	37047.8
2001-02	36997.9	2226.1	891.8	40115.8	1931.6	26321.8	9537.9	35859.7
2002-03	37626.9	2219.0	954.7	40800.5	2109.2	31528.0	10707.0	42235.0
2003-04	41610.5	2246.4	1114.3	44971.2	2452.7	37522.7	12204.6	49727.3
2004-05	41430.1	2294.8	1220.4	44945.4	2621.7	39531.4	13859.1	53390.5
2005-06	47110.5	2557.7	1364.1	51032.2	2842.9	46107.1	15178.0	61285.1
Manipur								
1999-00	714.4	53.1	62.3	829.8	0.0	1.3	173.5	174.8
2000-01	737.4	52.9	78.2	868.5	0.0	1.9	186.8	188.7
2001-02	776.3	51.7	82.7	910.8	0.0	2.8	177.1	179.9
2002-03	814.1	53.3	85.8	953.2	0.0	4.4	188.0	192.4
2003-04	962.6	57.9	92.4	1112.9	0.0	3.3	207.6	210.9
2004-05	1083.5	56.6	100.8	1240.9	0.0	6.1	225.2	231.3
2005-06	1117.3	65.0	102.7	1285.1	0.0	6.9	244.3	251.2
2006-07	1170.6	74.4	104.6	1349.6	0.0	7.4	257.7	265.1

(Contd...)

State/Union Territory/Year	Industry		Services							
	Electricity, Gas and Water Supply	Total (6+9+10)	Construction	Transport, Storage and Communication	Trade, Hotels and Restaurants	Banking and Insurance	Real Estate, Ownership of Dwelling and Business Services	Public Administration	Other Services	Total (12 to 18)
	10	11	12	13	14	15	16	17	18	19
Kerala										
1999-00	627.0	6276.9	6370.8	4724.7	14556.6	3104.8	4051.9	2850.7	6100.7	41760.2
2000-01	910.9	6820.5	6844.3	5391.6	15042.9	3372.4	5045.6	2847.2	6524.8	45068.8
2001-02	938.6	6496.0	7625.6	5927.8	16022.4	4147.9	5637.0	2887.8	6689.7	48938.2
2002-03	1014.3	6966.8	8746.6	6319.6	18192.7	5349.5	6335.7	3159.3	7191.7	55295.3
2003-04	1167.8	7764.9	10036.3	7486.2	20800.7	5776.9	7124.4	3635.4	7562.6	62422.5
2004-05	1054.6	8267.7	11462.9	8968.5	21770.1	5842.6	8075.1	4179.2	8791.4	69089.9
2005-06	988.9	9034.8	13122.7	10390.3	23286.4	6659.3	9414.6	4550.0	9508.3	76931.5
2006-07	816.1	9821.7	15005.4	12246.3	24639.9	7162.6	10823.5	5092.2	10668.4	85638.4
Madhya Pradesh										
1999-00	1229.9	11113.1	4516.1	3891.3	11969.3	2659.6	4461.1	3155.6	8011.0	38663.9
2000-01	1735.1	11326.4	4898.8	4025.2	12847.3	2904.8	4750.7	3208.6	8507.5	41142.8
2001-02	1778.7	11644.1	5057.4	4617.3	13277.9	3268.2	5068.8	3281.2	8541.0	43111.7
2002-03	1771.3	10845.2	5605.7	4818.3	13810.3	3941.7	5300.2	3460.5	8908.6	45845.3
2003-04	1362.5	11633.8	6539.9	5397.0	15172.0	4303.4	5471.7	3320.0	9535.9	49739.8
2004-05	1594.3	13551.7	7465.1	5907.9	15454.5	4167.0	5416.3	4294.9	10208.7	52914.5
2005-06	1799.7	13842.3	8089.0	6608.5	16752.0	4443.9	5672.1	4521.3	10960.0	57046.9
2006-07	2151.4	15044.0	8612.0	7246.7	18262.7	4720.9	6100.8	5158.9	12213.3	62315.2
Maharashtra										
1999-00	4805.2	46369.1	12992.8	16182.2	33862.1	27153.8	19664.0	10242.8	16835.1	136932.7
2000-01	2946.7	41781.4	11868.8	17780.9	35368.8	25664.4	24072.7	10403.6	18078.2	143237.5
2001-02	3750.9	41542.2	13218.8	18977.7	37668.6	30947.2	27128.4	10594.6	19238.6	157773.8
2002-03	4369.3	48713.4	15235.6	18355.1	43504.1	35486.0	30619.5	11399.8	21175.7	175775.8
2003-04	4849.3	57029.3	18921.8	21172.4	48750.5	39473.8	35279.0	12103.5	22874.4	198575.3
2004-05	4379.5	60391.6	23661.4	24592.4	63626.8	40763.9	41391.2	13762.8	25118.5	232917.0
2005-06	4925.6	69053.5	28997.5	28422.3	73476.8	46002.8	45918.9	15860.9	27475.8	266154.9
Manipur										
1999-00	75.5	250.3	381.7	83.9	259.8	44.4	80.5	534.5	489.1	1874.0
2000-01	78.6	267.3	304.1	85.7	264.6	55.8	90.8	414.3	462.5	1677.8
2001-02	76.2	256.0	357.9	87.5	267.2	58.6	102.5	483.4	490.3	1847.3
2002-03	79.7	272.1	439.6	99.6	276.9	78.3	105.5	459.3	457.4	1916.5
2003-04	95.2	306.1	576.3	100.1	320.6	83.1	124.1	493.9	447.3	2145.3
2004-05	103.8	335.1	1239.1	108.2	367.0	95.8	129.1	541.2	484.3	2964.6
2005-06	130.1	381.2	1537.5	120.1	388.8	100.1	148.2	627.1	532.5	3454.2
2006-07	138.8	403.9	1917.3	133.3	411.8	115.2	171.0	695.5	581.9	4025.9

(Contd...)

State/Union Territory/Year	Agriculture and Allied Activities				Industry			
	Agriculture	Forestry and Logging	Fishing	Total (2+3+4)	Mining and Quarrying	Manufacturing		
						Registered	Unregistered	Sub Total (7+8)
1	2	3	4	5	6	7	8	9
Meghalaya								
1999-00	706.4	41.7	20.1	768.2	312.0	20.8	29.2	50.0
2000-01	782.6	47.0	27.9	857.5	382.3	22.4	29.7	52.1
2001-02	873.0	54.4	24.2	951.6	549.9	24.8	27.8	52.6
2002-03	925.6	58.6	28.7	1012.9	477.6	59.0	28.4	87.4
2003-04	954.4	70.3	27.9	1052.7	645.6	74.6	30.7	105.3
2004-05	965.4	74.8	32.3	1072.4	661.2	112.3	29.0	141.4
2005-06	1058.2	84.1	34.2	1176.5	703.1	119.0	31.7	150.7
2006-07	1131.9	94.5	37.4	1263.8	747.7	139.6	34.3	173.9
Mizoram								
1999-00	307.0	14.0	14.6	335.6	6.2	5.4	9.3	14.6
2000-01	303.9	15.6	15.9	335.5	2.0	6.0	9.1	15.0
2001-02	357.4	16.5	22.6	396.5	3.8	6.9	7.5	14.4
2002-03	362.9	20.4	23.0	406.3	2.0	7.0	7.0	13.9
2003-04	375.4	18.7	25.7	419.8	7.7	7.0	7.9	15.0
2004-05	376.9	20.7	24.9	422.5	8.0	7.5	8.3	15.7
2005-06	389.7	21.5	24.3	435.4	7.9	8.2	9.9	18.2
2006-07	398.7	23.0	23.4	445.2	7.9	8.8	9.8	18.6
2007-08	407.6	24.7	22.5	454.8	8.0	9.5	9.4	18.9
Nagaland								
1999-00	661.3	90.0	20.7	772.0	0.4	6.7	32.4	39.1
2000-01	942.3	98.0	20.8	1061.1	0.9	7.4	34.2	41.6
2001-02	1161.6	102.1	22.4	1286.0	1.8	11.4	36.9	48.2
2002-03	1354.7	106.1	23.4	1484.1	2.6	13.4	42.4	55.8
2003-04	1435.8	116.5	16.1	1568.4	3.1	15.4	46.0	61.4
2004-05	1562.5	124.4	19.1	1705.9	3.4	13.2	55.5	68.7
Orissa								
1999-00	10739.3	1061.6	609.3	12410.2	1599.3	2214.9	911.7	3126.6
2000-01	9318.1	1134.2	771.9	11224.2	1862.1	1884.9	931.4	2816.2
2001-02	10837.2	1149.6	815.2	12802.0	1977.3	1479.4	880.7	2360.1
2002-03	10908.5	1024.6	825.4	12758.5	2508.4	2015.2	955.3	2970.5
2003-04	14702.6	1390.9	873.5	16966.9	3572.7	2840.7	1089.7	3930.4
2004-05	14743.6	1277.4	868.5	16889.5	4959.7	5511.2	1109.7	6620.9
2005-06	15754.6	1329.8	949.6	18034.0	5169.8	6461.2	1284.0	7745.2
2006-07	17818.0	1702.0	967.2	20487.3	6362.6	9040.6	1521.2	10561.8

(Contd...)

State/Union Territory/Year	Industry		Services							
	Electricity, Gas and Water Supply	Total (6+9+10)	Construction	Transport, Storage and Communication	Trade, Hotels and Restaurants	Banking and Insurance	Real Estate, Ownership of Dwelling and Business Services	Public Administration	Other Services	Total (12 to 18)
	10	11	12	13	14	15	16	17	18	19
Meghalaya										
1999-00	50.2	412.2	323.6	202.4	336.4	95.7	352.0	443.0	335.2	2088.2
2000-01	68.4	502.9	405.9	220.5	368.3	113.5	399.4	478.9	348.3	2334.6
2001-02	66.4	669.0	422.5	244.4	458.7	125.3	460.1	500.4	388.4	2599.7
2002-03	68.8	633.8	454.7	268.1	483.9	150.2	506.2	539.7	390.2	2792.9
2003-04	64.1	815.0	500.2	292.3	578.6	170.7	544.2	591.6	423.7	3101.2
2004-05	77.5	880.2	551.3	346.2	611.4	174.1	568.6	680.7	434.0	3366.3
2005-06	79.6	933.4	637.7	387.6	655.3	196.1	609.4	684.0	476.6	3646.8
2006-07	82.0	1003.7	693.2	447.4	704.7	218.8	651.3	745.6	526.4	3987.5
Mizoram										
1999-00	36.7	57.5	148.1	25.2	146.5	37.6	209.4	229.1	220.6	1016.4
2000-01	46.0	63.0	155.0	28.1	140.6	43.8	260.7	296.3	244.4	1168.9
2001-02	37.5	55.7	191.3	30.9	164.7	43.9	291.1	331.3	246.6	1299.8
2002-03	53.1	69.0	219.3	32.9	164.7	70.3	327.6	401.3	241.3	1457.4
2003-04	42.8	65.5	261.4	39.3	178.1	78.6	385.6	400.6	254.7	1598.2
2004-05	42.9	66.5	251.4	45.2	167.6	81.2	454.9	417.9	273.9	1692.2
2005-06	42.3	68.4	282.7	48.5	181.9	91.6	536.3	471.3	268.9	1881.2
2006-07	41.2	67.7	319.0	53.7	191.8	103.3	632.9	531.5	283.1	2115.3
2007-08	39.5	66.3	340.2	60.6	202.3	116.5	747.9	599.3	292.4	2359.2
Nagaland										
1999-00	10.3	49.7	271.1	416.6	142.8	29.0	296.0	362.1	216.8	1734.5
2000-01	22.6	65.2	334.8	563.4	182.9	46.1	367.2	427.4	237.8	2159.8
2001-02	24.5	74.6	417.7	620.3	220.9	55.8	401.0	487.1	310.9	2513.7
2002-03	29.0	87.5	517.6	672.6	241.7	60.2	442.4	549.0	326.9	2810.3
2003-04	26.9	91.4	534.0	725.2	249.9	70.8	556.9	564.7	337.5	3038.9
2004-05	32.0	104.0	547.2	750.0	253.4	71.4	610.5	579.5	358.5	3170.4
Orissa										
1999-00	800.4	5526.3	2729.2	2372.3	3732.1	1324.4	2329.3	2130.5	5645.7	20263.5
2000-01	832.6	5510.9	2830.6	2579.1	4132.4	1470.0	2541.1	2216.3	5774.4	21543.8
2001-02	879.1	5216.6	2735.6	2904.7	4543.6	1800.9	2825.5	2302.1	5934.3	23046.7
2002-03	702.3	6181.2	3167.2	3203.5	4924.6	2164.1	3060.6	2251.3	6496.9	25268.1
2003-04	1364.7	8867.9	2852.6	3922.5	6177.3	2347.9	3345.5	2516.5	7050.2	28212.6
2004-05	1742.9	13323.5	3423.2	4689.8	8000.4	2392.7	3505.4	2711.5	7561.1	32284.0
2005-06	1089.5	14004.5	3691.9	5439.7	9616.4	2530.8	3784.6	2708.2	8485.0	36256.6
2006-07	1003.6	17928.0	4427.6	6107.7	10802.7	2819.1	4231.4	3103.1	9523.2	41014.7

(Contd...)

State/Union Territory/Year	Agriculture and Allied Activities				Industry			
	Agriculture	Forestry and Logging	Fishing	Total (2+3+4)	Mining and Quarrying	Manufacturing		
						Registered	Unregistered	Sub Total (7+8)
1	2	3	4	5	6	7	8	9
Punjab								
1999-00	24037.7	208.4	152.1	24398.2	4.3	4953.7	3296.0	8249.6
2000-01	25596.3	170.6	166.2	25933.0	3.5	5241.9	3516.8	8758.7
2001-02	26440.1	213.4	181.5	26835.0	11.9	4723.9	3447.7	8171.6
2002-03	25553.6	201.8	211.9	25967.3	26.1	5141.5	3820.2	8961.8
2003-04	27853.1	198.4	254.6	28306.1	28.1	5208.2	4361.2	9569.3
2004-05	29152.3	322.9	227.7	29702.9	26.4	5830.9	4829.6	10660.4
2005-06	31656.3	325.2	276.2	32257.7	29.0	6712.3	5505.5	12217.8
2006-07	36172.3	371.0	309.0	36852.4	30.3	7337.2	6189.8	13527.0
Rajasthan								
1999-00	22319.4	1160.6	49.5	23529.5	1534.5	4869.8	3146.3	8016.1
2000-01	20066.0	1277.1	48.6	21391.7	1532.5	4229.5	3429.3	7658.8
2001-02	24300.8	1406.9	58.5	25766.2	1541.5	3633.5	3379.7	7013.1
2002-03	17803.2	1605.3	54.7	19463.3	1838.3	3317.2	3750.1	7067.3
2003-04	30479.1	1752.2	58.8	32290.0	1984.0	3509.1	4280.9	7790.0
2004-05	27703.5	1859.1	70.2	29632.9	2433.6	4426.2	4696.1	9122.3
2005-06	28589.4	2062.3	78.7	30730.4	2902.5	4521.7	5051.8	9573.5
2006-07	33543.4	2398.4	101.2	36043.0	3326.7	4944.7	5524.9	10469.6
Sikkim								
1999-00	161.5	11.6	0.6	173.7	0.8	11.8	19.8	31.6
2000-01	181.5	12.3	0.6	194.5	0.9	12.1	21.0	33.1
2001-02	203.3	13.5	0.6	217.5	1.0	13.3	21.2	34.5
2002-03	226.4	14.1	0.6	241.1	1.1	14.3	22.7	37.0
2003-04	255.3	14.6	0.7	270.6	1.2	15.8	25.1	41.0
2004-05	279.2	15.0	0.7	294.9	1.3	17.6	27.6	45.2
2005-06	301.9	15.7	0.7	318.2	1.5	19.6	30.8	50.4
2006-07	327.6	16.3	0.7	344.6	1.6	21.8	34.3	56.1
Tamil Nadu								
1999-00	19047.0	596.9	1734.3	21378.2	503.9	13257.5	7605.0	20862.5
2000-01	20310.4	580.4	1799.0	22689.8	673.3	14655.4	8380.7	23036.1
2001-02	19889.5	497.5	1875.4	22262.4	766.2	12034.1	8088.3	20122.4
2002-03	15755.2	682.1	1819.4	18256.7	957.7	12570.9	8737.5	21308.4
2003-04	16110.4	606.1	1787.2	18503.7	1226.5	16004.0	9614.7	25618.7
2004-05	21183.7	742.4	1508.3	23434.3	1432.6	18119.6	10730.8	28850.4
2005-06	24400.2	911.0	2420.3	27731.5	1452.9	20456.5	11907.5	32364.0
2006-07	25510.1	901.1	2252.2	28663.3	1525.7	23442.0	13645.4	37087.4

(Contd...)

State/Union Territory/Year	Industry		Services							
	Electricity, Gas and Water Supply	Total (6+9+10)	Construction	Transport, Storage and Communication	Trade, Hotels and Restaurants	Banking and Insurance	Real Estate, Ownership of Dwelling and Business Services	Public Administration	Other Services	Total (12 to 18)
	10	11	12	13	14	15	16	17	18	19
Punjab										
1999-00	1296.0	9549.9	2861.8	2488.5	7984.6	2897.6	2429.2	2759.6	5724.2	27145.4
2000-01	1517.4	10279.7	3493.1	2835.8	10521.8	3091.4	2502.4	2891.6	6190.1	31526.2
2001-02	1872.0	10055.5	3861.8	3405.0	11611.9	3513.3	2517.3	3040.3	6434.3	34383.9
2002-03	1775.5	10763.4	3579.2	3681.8	12677.9	4078.3	2612.1	3418.5	6734.6	36782.4
2003-04	2081.1	11678.5	4389.2	4164.2	13323.3	4410.2	2698.0	3668.5	7001.8	39655.2
2004-05	1467.2	12154.0	5525.6	4554.2	15013.8	4710.1	2799.9	3881.5	7908.5	44393.6
2005-06	1882.3	14129.1	7033.9	5194.9	17918.3	5106.7	2846.2	4258.4	8640.8	50999.2
2006-07	2011.1	15568.3	8811.4	5775.2	20136.6	5495.3	2923.6	4588.8	9307.8	57038.8
Rajasthan										
1999-00	2022.5	11573.1	6998.1	3397.7	11394.4	2425.9	4680.5	3072.0	7102.9	39071.2
2000-01	1930.3	11121.7	6718.8	3683.6	11285.5	2639.7	5130.2	3298.6	7496.4	40252.9
2001-02	2037.0	10591.7	7624.7	4219.9	12465.2	3154.8	5588.0	3459.8	8009.5	44521.9
2002-03	2517.1	11422.7	8250.3	4518.1	11535.4	3846.5	5914.3	3573.3	8080.7	45718.6
2003-04	2239.0	12013.0	11042.4	5212.1	14594.4	4229.2	6150.9	3986.3	8717.5	53932.9
2004-05	1950.2	13506.1	11672.8	5853.4	15514.8	4279.4	6175.0	4179.1	9382.2	57056.6
2005-06	1902.6	14378.7	13042.6	6608.9	17097.1	4531.3	6413.7	4345.7	9833.8	61873.1
2006-07	2050.7	15847.0	15370.0	7901.0	19550.8	5433.0	6960.3	4525.3	11198.4	70938.7
Sikkim										
1999-00	22.9	55.3	90.9	13.4	48.4	18.7	64.1	139.9	161.0	536.4
2000-01	44.9	78.8	112.3	14.2	53.8	23.1	71.1	144.1	163.4	582.0
2001-02	47.8	83.3	150.4	15.4	59.5	28.6	77.6	156.4	167.7	655.5
2002-03	46.9	85.1	195.8	17.1	65.5	37.7	83.9	171.8	180.4	752.1
2003-04	48.6	90.7	235.7	19.9	72.8	44.3	89.6	194.2	191.5	847.8
2004-05	53.7	100.3	286.3	22.7	78.7	52.1	94.3	218.4	208.6	960.9
2005-06	57.9	109.8	352.4	26.2	85.2	61.2	101.3	244.6	227.8	1098.6
2006-07	62.8	120.6	437.9	30.3	92.3	71.8	108.8	274.2	249.5	1264.8
Tamil Nadu										
1999-00	9150.8	30517.1	2094.0	9626.5	20107.6	9342.4	7524.8	6284.7	12491.9	67471.9
2000-01	9786.0	33495.4	2477.9	10562.5	22085.3	9224.0	9100.8	6799.4	13694.5	73944.3
2001-02	10368.6	31257.1	1127.7	11366.8	22763.4	10600.7	10329.5	7072.8	14500.5	77761.4
2002-03	11886.7	34152.8	2403.8	11710.4	24244.9	12838.1	11420.3	6877.8	16240.3	85735.6
2003-04	13585.9	40431.0	1724.8	13513.3	28887.8	14737.0	12625.2	7305.0	16269.1	95062.2
2004-05	16063.4	46346.4	1684.6	14929.8	33969.8	13951.4	14207.6	7706.4	18573.7	105023.2
2005-06	17825.6	51642.4	1674.1	16673.8	36862.3	14967.8	16127.6	8775.7	20072.8	115154.2
2006-07	19688.9	58301.9	1532.2	18171.8	40014.5	15823.1	18091.1	10402.0	23186.9	127221.5

(Contd...)

State/Union Territory/Year	Agriculture and Allied Activities				Industry			
	Agriculture	Forestry and Logging	Fishing	Total (2+3+4)	Mining and Quarrying	Manufacturing		
						Registered	Unregistered	Sub Total (7+8)
1	2	3	4	5	6	7	8	9
Tripura								
1999-00	1258.5	56.1	50.5	1365.1	44.6	24.3	66.8	91.0
2000-01	1162.0	58.2	54.2	1274.4	44.8	129.6	72.1	201.7
2001-02	1506.4	66.8	54.6	1627.8	50.5	76.3	75.0	151.3
2002-03	1466.3	71.8	69.4	1607.5	59.2	47.2	81.3	128.5
2003-04	1624.2	72.8	80.6	1777.6	67.5	69.4	91.8	161.2
2004-05	1716.2	74.5	90.7	1881.4	80.1	77.8	94.7	172.5
2005-06	1824.5	79.2	96.4	2000.1	85.1	82.0	99.7	181.6
Uttar Pradesh								
1999-00	55633.3	1454.3	540.4	57628.0	1454.4	8931.2	8347.4	17278.7
2000-01	56584.7	1742.1	601.5	58928.3	1667.3	7812.6	8984.7	16797.3
2001-02	58880.2	994.6	652.1	60526.9	1746.6	7631.8	8720.3	16352.2
2002-03	61512.2	1619.1	717.5	63848.8	2157.1	8630.9	9445.4	18076.3
2003-04	66573.9	1784.0	794.4	69152.2	1940.6	9400.3	10372.7	19773.0
2004-05	69040.1	2015.1	812.2	71867.4	2333.7	10409.4	11445.7	21855.2
2005-06	77300.7	2720.9	877.7	80899.3	2591.1	12143.0	12707.6	24850.6
2006-07	84860.1	3176.3	933.6	88970.0	2662.5	13721.5	13719.2	27440.7
Uttarakhand								
1999-00	3226.4	333.6	6.5	3566.4	114.2	482.7	481.0	963.7
2000-01	3680.9	280.8	6.9	3968.6	94.3	927.8	515.1	1442.9
2001-02	3549.6	297.2	7.0	3853.8	110.1	820.8	500.7	1321.6
2002-03	3951.5	353.0	7.4	4311.9	148.6	1339.6	561.5	1901.1
2003-04	4307.6	360.6	7.8	4676.1	321.9	1487.7	652.9	2140.7
2004-05	4573.1	467.6	7.6	5048.3	280.1	1638.9	692.3	2331.2
2005-06	4619.8	569.2	8.4	5197.5	450.1	1963.1	761.2	2724.3
2006-07	4928.6	602.5	9.1	5540.2	500.2	2429.1	849.5	3278.5
West Bengal								
1999-00	34341.1	973.6	4383.7	39698.5	1298.0	4887.7	5797.2	10684.8
2000-01	33350.2	1089.9	5307.8	39747.8	1581.5	4758.5	6709.8	11468.3
2001-02	35658.3	1107.4	5090.5	41856.1	1904.4	5142.4	6881.0	12023.3
2002-03	35773.6	1185.0	5492.1	42450.6	1821.0	6075.5	7825.8	13901.3
2003-04	40095.7	1236.7	5924.3	47256.7	2020.3	6507.5	8793.3	15300.7
2004-05	40475.5	1356.7	6148.7	47980.9	2459.3	8684.3	9493.8	18178.2
2005-06	43833.1	1537.6	6740.9	52111.6	2734.2	10333.0	10411.8	20744.8

(Contd...)

State/Union Territory/Year	Industry		Services							
	Electricity, Gas and Water Supply	Total (6+9+10)	Construction	Transport, Storage and Communication	Trade, Hotels and Restaurants	Banking and Insurance	Real Estate, Owner ship of Dwelling and Business Services	Public Administration	Other Services	Total (12 to 18)
	10	11	12	13	14	15	16	17	18	19
Tripura										
1999-00	83.2	218.9	421.2	163.1	746.8	97.2	142.8	569.1	771.4	2911.6
2000-01	72.0	318.5	782.6	163.4	852.4	111.0	168.3	587.2	856.9	3521.6
2001-02	93.6	295.4	855.8	176.1	922.0	125.9	187.8	721.0	978.0	3965.5
2002-03	120.6	308.3	955.0	209.7	957.1	160.5	246.4	787.7	990.5	4306.9
2003-04	108.3	337.0	1182.6	213.1	1009.7	167.0	296.2	822.6	1184.7	4875.8
2004-05	107.4	359.9	1249.0	234.1	1103.2	168.7	357.1	1010.6	1284.1	5406.6
2005-06	113.0	379.7	1314.9	263.5	1242.0	189.9	402.0	1137.7	1445.7	5995.6
Uttar Pradesh										
1999-00	3766.8	22499.8	8212.5	9916.9	22124.7	5604.6	9511.9	7445.6	13387.2	76203.5
2000-01	3182.3	21646.9	8993.7	10673.4	23146.2	6099.9	10443.9	7714.5	13643.1	80714.7
2001-02	2529.8	20628.5	9318.3	11489.6	24373.1	7107.0	11714.6	8077.1	14877.4	86957.0
2002-03	3075.4	23308.8	10215.9	12405.1	26285.7	8511.5	12833.4	9319.8	15646.8	95218.2
2003-04	2804.3	24518.0	11901.6	14063.0	29651.9	9235.6	13717.9	10949.9	16691.3	106211.2
2004-05	645.5	24834.3	14738.2	15682.0	32631.9	9666.7	14521.0	12326.4	18238.3	117804.6
2005-06	341.4	27783.1	18517.9	17780.6	37115.1	10251.4	15938.8	13619.9	20275.1	133498.8
2006-07	803.3	30906.5	22733.1	20306.1	41067.6	10871.5	17542.2	15745.5	24015.5	152281.5
Uttarakhand										
1999-00	157.8	1235.7	911.9	619.2	2004.3	435.5	671.7	639.4	1232.6	6514.5
2000-01	127.5	1664.7	1149.0	650.2	2421.4	473.9	751.5	667.8	1297.8	7411.6
2001-02	181.6	1613.2	1519.2	782.8	2534.7	552.2	853.7	757.7	1607.4	8607.7
2002-03	376.4	2426.1	1779.9	848.8	2813.2	661.3	950.3	823.6	1792.9	9670.1
2003-04	292.3	2754.9	1870.9	994.9	3231.8	717.6	1024.9	956.7	1965.0	10761.6
2004-05	198.0	2809.3	2431.1	1069.7	3591.2	751.1	1090.0	1076.7	2047.4	12057.2
2005-06	216.6	3391.0	2949.5	1212.7	4167.0	796.5	1216.1	1300.4	2289.1	13931.2
2006-07	403.5	4182.2	3740.5	1396.2	4738.6	847.5	1458.9	1498.9	2538.8	16219.5
West Bengal										
1999-00	1224.3	13207.1	6240.9	8407.3	19767.1	9225.9	9050.8	6395.9	12814.8	71902.7
2000-01	1517.3	14567.1	6944.3	8880.9	21304.2	9242.0	10963.4	6933.4	13319.6	77587.8
2001-02	1294.4	15222.1	7898.4	10236.5	24103.3	10367.5	12143.6	7433.7	14644.2	86827.2
2002-03	1600.7	17323.0	8744.2	10649.6	25142.9	10988.7	14320.8	7629.8	16330.6	93806.4
2003-04	2038.7	19359.7	11374.7	12050.1	28195.3	12100.2	16627.9	7591.0	17995.7	105935.0
2004-05	2150.5	22787.9	13356.5	13443.8	31473.0	12252.0	19539.7	8892.5	19236.1	118193.7
2005-06	2169.9	25648.8	17572.1	15134.9	36094.8	13105.4	23386.6	9971.8	20971.7	136237.2

(Contd...)

State/Union Territory/Year	Agriculture and Allied Activities				Industry			
	Agriculture	Forestry and Logging	Fishing	Total (2+3+4)	Mining and Quarrying	Manufacturing		
						Registered	Unregistered	Sub Total (7+8)
1	2	3	4	5	6	7	8	9
Andaman & Nicobar Islands								
1999-00	188.2	21.9	66.4	276.5	3.0	13.6	16.8	30.4
2000-01	208.8	32.4	77.8	319.0	5.1	5.5	17.5	23.0
2001-02	248.8	7.0	77.4	333.2	14.6	3.4	16.1	19.5
2002-03	293.0	5.2	85.6	383.7	10.0	2.0	17.1	19.1
2003-04	282.9	5.2	86.1	374.1	8.7	12.7	19.2	31.8
2004-05	247.2	0.8	48.0	296.0	3.7	6.3	20.5	26.8
2005-06	272.1	0.7	50.8	323.6	5.1	6.2	21.1	27.3
Chandigarh								
1999-00	50.2	0.9	0.0	51.2	0.0	142.7	230.1	372.8
2000-01	50.5	0.9	0.0	51.5	0.0	130.0	256.1	386.1
2001-02	53.0	0.9	0.2	54.1	0.0	98.7	260.2	358.9
2002-03	54.9	0.9	0.3	56.1	0.0	115.9	288.8	404.8
2003-04	59.8	1.0	0.3	61.1	0.0	119.9	338.2	458.2
2004-05	57.1	1.1	0.3	58.5	0.0	125.9	415.0	540.9
2005-06	61.2	1.0	0.3	62.5	0.0	131.0	504.4	635.4
Delhi								
1999-00	830.9	1.3	19.9	852.0	1.5	2486.5	2880.7	5367.2
2000-01	794.7	1.4	18.2	814.4	6.9	2803.5	3371.4	6174.9
2001-02	813.8	1.6	12.7	828.1	3.3	2909.0	3494.6	6403.5
2002-03	838.2	2.0	9.2	849.4	3.5	3189.6	3714.9	6904.5
2003-04	859.8	2.5	9.9	872.2	8.9	3629.3	4111.3	7740.6
2004-05	867.5	2.6	6.8	876.9	4.2	4275.1	4980.5	9255.6
2005-06	850.7	3.0	3.7	857.4	0.0	4871.3	5716.6	10587.9
Puducherry								
1999-00	142.7	12.0	66.2	220.8	0.0	897.7	155.9	1053.6
2000-01	140.2	12.1	68.5	220.8	0.0	1262.6	178.5	1441.1
2001-02	135.0	12.1	72.2	219.2	0.0	1498.6	188.2	1686.8
2002-03	133.4	12.1	74.2	219.7	0.0	1775.0	208.6	1983.6
2003-04	149.8	12.2	74.2	236.2	0.0	1971.9	237.1	2209.0
2004-05	162.3	13.1	58.4	233.7	0.0	1423.9	273.4	1697.3
2005-06	171.9	13.3	77.3	262.5	0.0	1534.4	305.9	1840.3
2006-07	186.1	13.6	79.4	279.1	0.0	1718.2	340.7	2059.0

(Contd...)

State/Union Territory/Year	Industry		Services							
	Electricity, Gas and Water Supply	Total (6+9+10)	Construction	Transport, Storage and Communication	Trade, Hotels and Restaurants	Banking and Insurance	Real Estate, Owner ship of Dwelling and Business Services	Public Administration	Other Services	Total (12 to 18)
	10	11	12	13	14	15	16	17	18	19
Andaman & Nicobar Islands										
1999-00	-5.2	28.2	57.3	98.2	62.4	21.5	37.1	125.2	121.9	523.5
2000-01	-1.3	26.8	58.4	97.4	65.9	23.9	42.1	136.2	121.6	545.5
2001-02	-2.4	31.6	78.6	110.0	74.2	28.2	45.7	141.0	130.2	608.5
2002-03	4.0	25.1	126.5	219.4	102.8	28.7	47.4	144.7	141.9	811.3
2003-04	5.9	46.4	207.5	243.8	113.7	30.3	48.6	173.3	151.8	968.9
2004-05	13.0	43.4	221.5	217.9	92.5	32.7	67.0	159.9	198.2	989.7
2005-06	7.5	39.8	337.5	251.4	116.8	35.4	71.2	172.2	207.9	1192.3
Chandigarh										
1999-00	56.5	429.3	110.4	142.3	812.8	501.4	829.1	438.9	359.8	3194.6
2000-01	60.9	446.9	167.3	168.8	1088.1	643.1	908.1	427.4	386.9	3789.6
2001-02	50.9	409.9	251.1	204.3	1391.5	788.6	1018.1	443.6	415.4	4512.7
2002-03	63.5	468.3	281.6	218.3	1716.5	975.5	1165.7	446.8	448.7	5253.0
2003-04	61.0	519.2	441.1	242.3	2122.8	1050.1	1367.4	430.4	529.7	6184.0
2004-05	65.1	606.0	592.1	258.7	2644.4	1061.8	1618.5	492.7	576.6	7244.6
2005-06	67.9	703.3	726.6	277.4	3416.7	1130.0	1931.6	550.0	627.1	8659.4
Delhi										
1999-00	410.0	5778.7	3626.1	4398.7	11302.8	11228.7	5514.9	2737.9	5245.6	44054.8
2000-01	427.5	6609.3	5120.0	4929.7	12947.3	10425.6	6857.6	2829.8	5752.5	48862.6
2001-02	563.1	6969.9	5110.1	5249.4	14394.1	11954.9	7803.4	2949.5	6084.7	53546.1
2002-03	330.6	7238.6	6102.2	5276.4	15079.9	13103.9	8745.1	3051.5	6476.5	57835.5
2003-04	545.3	8294.7	6877.5	6152.1	17592.9	14450.4	10069.1	3249.9	6880.6	65272.3
2004-05	715.6	9975.4	8254.1	7019.7	19888.3	14961.7	12285.1	3657.5	8073.5	74140.0
2005-06	769.6	11357.4	9990.0	8153.9	22841.9	16884.9	13925.0	4304.2	9527.6	85627.5
Puducherry										
1999-00	22.5	1076.1	185.3	49.2	635.6	95.9	266.3	148.5	250.7	1631.6
2000-01	22.8	1463.8	197.7	53.9	714.5	110.0	321.1	157.6	261.9	1816.7
2001-02	26.2	1713.0	233.4	61.1	715.2	121.0	362.7	156.2	273.2	1922.8
2002-03	32.8	2016.4	269.8	71.0	944.9	155.4	391.4	149.9	288.6	2270.9
2003-04	27.6	2236.5	315.3	77.0	1004.5	172.4	425.7	163.8	333.5	2492.2
2004-05	53.2	1750.5	364.0	77.4	1055.2	183.9	462.0	191.4	361.3	2695.1
2005-06	67.1	1907.4	419.1	84.6	1167.6	199.9	515.8	201.3	388.6	2976.9
2006-07	82.2	2141.1	487.0	92.9	1288.4	215.2	567.4	205.5	421.2	3277.5

Note: Owing to differences in methodology of compilation, data for different states/union territories are not strictly comparable.
Source: Central Statistical Organisation (CSO) website as on 28-2-2008.

Table 10: Gross Domestic Saving and Gross Domestic Capital Formation

(As per cent of GDP at current market prices)

Year	Gross Domestic Saving				Gross Fixed Capital Formation		
	House-hold Sector	Private Corporate Sector	Public Sector	Total (2+3+4)	Public Sector	Private Sector	Total (6+7)
1	2	3	4	5	6	7	8
			(1999-2000 series)				
1950-51	5.7	0.9	2.0	8.6	2.6	6.1	8.7
1951-52	5.1	1.3	2.7	9.0	2.8	6.2	9.0
1952-53	5.7	0.6	1.7	8.0	3.1	5.4	8.5
1953-54	5.4	0.8	1.5	7.6	3.2	4.6	7.8
1954-55	6.2	1.1	1.8	9.1	4.1	5.4	9.5
1955-56	9.0	1.2	2.1	12.3	5.4	6.3	11.7
1956-57	8.4	1.2	2.3	11.9	5.2	7.2	12.5
1957-58	6.8	0.9	2.3	10.0	5.3	7.4	12.7
1958-59	6.2	0.9	2.0	9.1	5.2	6.2	11.4
1959-60	7.6	1.2	2.1	10.8	6.2	5.7	11.9
1960-61	6.5	1.6	3.1	11.2	6.7	5.8	12.5
1961-62	6.2	1.7	3.3	11.2	6.7	6.5	13.2
1962-63	7.0	1.7	3.5	12.3	7.3	6.3	13.6
1963-64	6.3	1.7	3.8	11.9	7.6	6.4	14.0
1964-65	6.3	1.5	3.8	11.6	7.6	6.4	14.0
1965-66	8.6	1.4	3.6	13.7	8.1	6.9	14.9
1966-67	9.5	1.3	2.8	13.6	7.2	7.5	14.7
1967-68	8.1	1.1	2.4	11.6	6.1	7.8	13.8
1968-69	7.9	1.1	2.8	11.8	6.0	7.8	13.8
1969-70	9.7	1.3	3.0	14.0	5.7	8.1	13.8
1970-71	9.5	1.5	3.3	14.2	5.8	7.9	13.8
1971-72	9.9	1.6	3.2	14.7	6.3	8.1	14.5
1972-73	9.6	1.5	3.1	14.3	7.4	7.7	15.1
1973-74	11.4	1.6	3.4	16.4	6.7	7.1	13.9
1974-75	9.8	1.9	4.0	15.7	6.1	8.1	14.3
1975-76	10.9	1.3	4.7	16.9	7.4	8.6	16.1
1976-77	12.4	1.3	5.4	19.1	8.6	8.5	17.1
1977-78	13.2	1.4	4.8	19.5	8.3	8.7	17.0
1978-79	14.6	1.5	5.1	21.2	8.3	8.9	17.2
1979-80	13.0	2.0	4.9	19.8	9.0	8.7	17.7
1980-81	12.9	1.6	4.0	18.5	8.9	9.5	18.4
1981-82	11.5	1.5	5.1	18.1	9.4	9.3	18.8
1982-83	11.1	1.6	5.0	17.7	10.7	8.4	19.0
1983-84	11.7	1.5	3.9	17.1	10.1	8.6	18.7
1984-85	13.1	1.6	3.5	18.2	10.3	9.1	19.4
1985-86	13.1	1.9	3.9	19.0	10.7	9.7	20.4
1986-87	13.2	1.7	3.5	18.4	11.6	9.4	20.9
1987-88	15.6	1.7	2.9	20.2	10.6	10.8	21.3
1988-89	15.8	2.0	2.8	20.5	10.3	11.3	21.6
1989-90	17.0	2.4	2.4	21.8	9.8	12.6	22.5
1990-91	18.4	2.7	1.8	22.8	9.6	13.4	23.0
1991-92	15.8	3.1	2.6	21.5	9.8	12.3	22.1
1992-93	16.4	2.7	2.2	21.2	8.8	13.7	22.4
1993-94	17.3	3.4	1.2	21.9	8.5	12.9	21.4
1994-95	18.6	3.5	2.3	24.4	9.4	12.7	22.1
1995-96	16.9	5.0	2.6	24.4	8.3	16.2	24.4
1996-97	16.0	4.5	2.2	22.7	7.3	15.8	23.1
1997-98	17.7	4.3	1.8	23.8	6.8	16.2	23.0
1998-99	18.8	3.9	-0.5	22.3	6.9	15.9	22.8
1999-2000	21.1	4.5	-0.8	24.8	6.6	16.8	23.4
2000-01	21.6	3.9	-1.8	23.7	6.5	16.3	22.7
2001-02	22.1	3.4	-2.0	23.5	6.5	17.1	23.6
2002-03	22.9	4.0	-0.6	26.3	6.3	17.6	23.8
2003-04	24.1	4.6	1.1	29.8	6.5	18.5	25.0
			(2004-2005 series)				
2004-05	23.3	6.6	2.3	32.2	6.9	21.8	28.8
2005-06	23.2	7.5	2.4	33.1	7.3	23.1	30.4
2006-07	22.9	8.0	3.6	34.4	8.0	23.4	31.4
2007-08	22.6	8.7	5.0	36.4	8.1	24.9	33.0
2008-09[Q]	22.6	8.4	1.4	32.5	8.6	24.4	33.0

Q: Quick estimates

(Contd...)

Change in Stocks			Gross Fixed Capital Formation						
Public Sector	Private Sector	Total (9+10)	Public Sector	Private Sector	Valuables	Total (12+13)	Errors & Omissions	Adjusted Total (14+15)	Year
9	10	11	12	13	14	15	16	17	18
				(1999-2000 series)					
0.3	1.2	1.6	2.9	7.4	na	10.3	-1.9	8.4	1950-51
0.4	1.2	1.6	3.2	7.4	na	10.6	0.1	10.7	1951-52
-0.2	0.4	0.2	2.8	5.9	na	8.7	-1.0	7.7	1952-53
-0.3	-0.3	-0.6	2.9	4.3	na	7.2	0.3	7.5	1953-54
0.6	-0.3	0.3	4.7	5.1	na	9.8	-0.5	9.3	1954-55
-0.3	0.9	0.6	5.1	7.2	na	12.3	0.3	12.6	1955-56
0.4	1.4	1.8	5.6	8.7	na	14.3	0.3	14.6	1956-57
1.4	0.4	1.8	6.7	7.8	na	14.5	-1.0	13.5	1957-58
0.8	-0.7	0.1	6.0	5.5	na	11.5	0.1	11.6	1958-59
0.1	1.2	1.3	6.3	6.9	na	13.2	-0.9	12.3	1959-60
0.5	1.4	1.9	7.2	7.2	na	14.4	-0.5	14.0	1960-61
0.2	1.3	1.5	6.9	7.9	na	14.7	-1.6	13.1	1961-62
0.7	1.2	1.8	8.0	7.4	na	15.5	-0.9	14.5	1962-63
0.5	0.7	1.3	8.1	7.2	na	15.3	-1.5	13.8	1963-64
0.5	0.9	1.4	8.1	7.3	na	15.4	-1.5	13.8	1964-65
0.6	0.6	1.2	8.7	7.4	na	16.1	-0.3	15.8	1965-66
0.3	1.4	1.7	7.5	8.9	na	16.4	0.2	16.6	1966-67
0.9	0.3	1.2	6.9	8.1	na	15.0	-1.2	13.8	1967-68
0.1	0.2	0.4	6.2	8.0	na	14.2	-1.3	12.9	1968-69
0.2	1.2	1.4	5.8	9.3	na	15.1	-0.6	14.5	1969-70
0.9	0.9	1.8	6.7	8.9	na	15.6	-0.5	15.1	1970-71
1.0	1.3	2.2	7.3	9.4	na	16.7	-1.0	15.7	1971-72
0.2	0.7	0.9	7.6	8.4	na	16.0	-1.2	14.8	1972-73
1.1	1.5	2.6	7.8	8.6	na	16.5	0.5	17.0	1973-74
1.6	2.2	3.9	7.8	10.4	na	18.1	-1.6	16.5	1974-75
2.4	0.4	2.7	9.8	9.0	na	18.8	-2.1	16.7	1975-76
1.7	0.1	1.8	10.3	8.6	na	18.9	-1.3	17.6	1976-77
0.1	1.4	1.5	8.5	10.0	na	18.5	-0.4	18.0	1977-78
1.4	2.0	3.3	9.7	10.8	na	20.5	0.8	21.3	1978-79
1.5	2.0	3.5	10.6	10.7	na	21.2	-0.9	20.3	1979-80
0.1	0.1	0.2	8.9	9.6	na	18.5	1.4	19.9	1980-81
1.2	2.3	3.4	10.6	11.6	na	22.2	-2.6	19.6	1981-82
0.6	1.8	2.4	11.3	10.1	na	21.4	-2.4	19.0	1982-83
0.2	0.7	0.8	10.3	9.2	na	19.5	-1.2	18.3	1983-84
0.7	1.3	2.0	11.0	10.4	na	21.4	-1.8	19.6	1984-85
0.7	2.3	3.0	11.4	12.1	na	23.5	-2.3	21.2	1985-86
0.3	1.8	2.1	11.8	11.2	na	23.0	-2.6	20.5	1986-87
-0.4	1.1	0.7	10.2	11.8	na	22.0	0.1	22.1	1987-88
-0.1	2.1	2.0	10.2	13.5	na	23.6	-0.2	23.4	1988-89
0.3	0.9	1.3	10.2	13.5	na	23.7	0.5	24.3	1989-90
0.3	0.8	1.1	10.0	14.2	na	24.2	1.9	26.0	1990-91
-0.3	0.2	-0.1	9.5	12.5	na	22.0	0.1	22.1	1991-92
0.4	1.0	1.3	9.1	14.7	na	23.8	-0.7	23.1	1992-93
0.2	-0.4	-0.2	8.8	12.5	na	21.2	1.3	22.5	1993-94
-0.1	1.5	1.4	9.3	14.2	na	23.5	2.0	25.5	1994-95
-0.1	2.2	2.2	8.2	18.4	na	26.6	-0.4	26.2	1995-96
0.1	-1.2	-1.0	7.5	14.6	na	22.1	1.9	24.0	1996-97
0.2	0.6	0.9	7.1	16.8	na	23.9	1.4	25.3	1997-98
0.1	-0.2	-0.1	7.0	15.6	na	22.6	0.7	23.3	1998-99
0.8	1.1	1.9	7.4	17.9	0.8	26.1	-0.2	25.9	1999-2000
0.4	0.3	0.7	6.9	16.6	0.7	24.2	0.2	24.3	2000-01
0.4	-0.4	-0.1	6.9	16.7	0.6	24.2	-1.3	22.8	2001-02
-0.2	1.0	0.8	6.1	18.6	0.6	25.2	0.0	25.2	2002-03
-0.1	1.0	0.9	6.3	19.6	0.9	26.8	0.8	27.6	2003-04
				(2004-2005 series)					
0.5	1.9	2.5	7.4	23.8	1.3	32.5	0.2	32.7	2004-05
0.6	2.2	2.8	7.9	25.3	1.1	34.3	0.0	34.3	2005-06
0.4	3.0	3.4	8.4	26.4	1.2	36.0	-0.5	35.5	2006-07
0.8	2.7	3.5	8.9	27.6	1.1	37.6	0.1	37.7	2007-08
0.8	0.5	1.3	9.4	24.9	1.3	35.6	-0.7	34.9	2008-09[Q]

Source: Central Statistical Organisation.

Table 11: Receipts and Expenditure of the Central Government

	2004-05	2005-06	2006-07	2007-08#	2008-09 (B.E.)	2008-09 (Prov.)	2009-10 (R.E.)
			(Rs. crore)				
1. **Revenue Receipts (a+b)**	3,05,991	3,47,077	4,34,387	5,41,864	6,02,935	5,44,651	6,14,497
(a) Tax Revenue (Net of States' Share)	2,24,798	2,70,264	3,51,182	4,39,547	5,07,150	4,47,726	4,74,218
(b) Non-tax Revenue	81,193	76,813	83,205	1,02,317	95,785	96,925	1,40,279
2. **Revenue Expenditure** *of which:*	3,84,329	4,39,376	5,14,609	5,94,433	6,58,118	7,91,697	8,97,232
(a) Interest Payments	1,26,934	1,32,630	1,50,272	1,71,030	1,90,807	1,90,485	2,25,511
(b) Major Subsidies	44,753	44,480	53,495	67,498	67,037	1,23,640	1,06,004
(c) Defence Expenditure	43,862	48,211	51,682	54,219	57,593	72,836	86,879
3. **Revenue Deficit (2-1)**	78,338	92,299	80,222	52,569	55,183	2,47,046	2,82,735
4. **Capital Receipts**	1,92,261	1,58,661	1,49,000	1,70,807	1,47,949	3,36,818	4,06,341
of which:							
(a) Recovery of Loans*	62,043	10,645	5,893	5,100	4,497	6,158	4,225
(b) Other Receipt	4,424	1,581	534	38,795	10,165	546	1,120
(Mainly PSU Disinvestment)							
(c) Borrowings and Other Liabilities $	1,25,794	1,46,435	1,42,573	1,26,912	1,33,287	3,30,114	4,00,996
5. **Capital Expenditure****	1,13,923	66,362	68,778	1,18,238	92,766	89,772	1,23,606
6. **Total Expenditure [2+5=6(a)+6(b)]**	4,98,252	5,05,738	5,83,387	7,12,671	7,50,884	8,81,469	10,20,838
of which:							
(a) Plan Expenditure	1,32,292	1,40,638	1,69,860	2,05,082	2,43,386	2,75,450	3,25,149
(b) Non-Plan Expenditure	3,65,960	3,65,100	4,13,527	5,07,589	5,07,498	6,06,019	6,95,689
7. **Fiscal Deficit [6-1-4(a)-4(b)]**	1,25,794	1,46,435	1,42,573	1,26,912	1,33,287	3,30,114	4,00,996
8. **Primary Deficit [7-2(a)]**	-1140	13,805	-7,699	-44,118	-57,520	1,39,629	1,75,485
			(As per cent of GDP)				
1. **Revenue Receipts (a+b)**	9.4	9.4	10.1	11.0	11.4	9.8	10.0
(a) Tax Revenue (Net of States' Share)	6.9	7.3	8.2	8.9	9.6	8.0	7.7
(b) Non-tax Revenue	2.5	2.1	1.9	2.1	1.8	1.7	2.3
2. **Revenue Expenditure**							
of which:	11.9	11.9	12.0	12.0	12.4	14.2	14.6
(a) Interest Payments	3.9	3.6	3.5	3.5	3.6	3.4	3.7
(b) Major Subsidies	1.4	1.2	1.2	1.4	1.3	2.2	1.7
(c) Defence Expenditure	1.4	1.3	1.2	1.1	1.1	1.3	1.4

(Contd...)

	2004-05	2005-06	2006-07	2007-08#	2008-09 (B.E.)	2008-09 (Prov.)	2009-10 (R.E.)
				(Rs. crore)			
3. Revenue Deficit (2-1)	2.4	2.5	1.9	1.1	1.0	4.4	4.6
4. Capital Receipts *of which:*	5.9	4.3	3.5	3.5	2.8	6.0	6.6
(a) Recovery of Loans*	1.9	0.3	0.1	0.1	0.1	0.1	0.1
(b) Other Receipts (Mainly PSU Disinvestment)	0.1	0.0	0.0	0.8	0.2	0.0	0.0
(c) Borrowings and Other Liabilities $	3.9	4.0	3.3	2.6	2.5	5.9	6.5
5. Capital Expenditure**	3.5	1.8	1.6	2.4	1.7	1.6	2.0
6. Total Expenditure [2+5=6(a)+6(b)]							
of which:	15.4	13.6	13.6	14.4	14.2	15.8	16.6
(a) Plan Expenditure	4.1	3.8	4.0	4.1	4.6	4.9	5.3
(b) Non-Plan Expenditure	11.3	9.9	9.7	10.3	9.6	10.9	11.3
7. Fiscal Deficit [6-1-4(a)-4(b)]	3.9	4.0	3.3	2.6	2.5	5.9	6.5
8. Primary Deficit [7-2(a)]	0.0	0.4	-0.2	-0.9	-1.1	2.5	2.8
Memorandum Items				(Rs. crore)			
(a) Interest Receipts	32,387	22,032	22,524	21,060	19,135	20,556	19,174
(b) Dividend and Profit	15,934	18,549	18,969	21,531	24,758	20,653	19,340
(c) Non-Plan Revenue Expenditure	2,96,835	3,27,518	3,72,191	4,20,861	4,48,351	5,56,521	6,18,834

Based on Provisional Actuals for 2007-08.

* Includes receipts from States on account of Debt Swap Scheme for 2004-05.

** Includes repayment to National Small Savings Fund for 2004-05.

$ Does not include receipts in respect of Market Stabilization Scheme, which will remain in the cash balance of the Central Government and will not be used for expenditure.

Notes: 1. The ratios to GDP at current market prices are based on CSO's National Accounts 2004-05 series.

2. The figures may not add up to the total due to rounding/approximations.

Source: Union Budget documents.

Table 12: Sources of Tax Revenue

	2004-05	2005-06	2006-07	2007-08	2008-09 (BE)	2008-09 (Prov.)@	2009-10 (BE)
			(Rs. crore)				
Direct Taxes (a)	1,32,181	1,57,557	2,19,722	2,95,938	3,65,000	3,38,213	3,70,000
Personal Income Tax	49,268	55,985	75,093	1,02,644	1,38,314	1,24,014	1,12,850
Corporate Tax	82,680	1,01,277	1,44,318	1,92,911	2,26,361	2,13,812	2,56,725
Indirect Taxes (b)	1,70,936	1,99,348	2,41,538	2,78,845	3,21,264	2,69,454	2,69,477
Customs	57,611	65,067	86,327	1,04,119	1,18,930	99,848	98,000
Excise	99,125	1,11,226	1,17,613	1,23,425	1,37,874	1,08,740	1,06,477
Service Tax	14,200	23,055	37,598	51,301	64,460	60,866	65,000
Gross Tax Revenue #	3,04,958	3,66,151	4,73,512	5,93,147	6,87,715	6,09,705	6,41,079
		Tax revenue as a proportion of gross tax revenue (in per cent)					
Direct Taxes (a)	43.3	43.0	46.4	49.9	53.1	55.5	57.7
Personal Income tax	16.2	15.3	15.9	17.3	20.1	20.3	17.6
Corporate Tax	27.1	27.7	30.5	32.5	32.9	35.1	40.0
Indirect Taxes (b)	56.1	54.4	51.0	47.0	46.7	44.2	42.0
Customs	18.9	17.8	18.2	17.6	17.3	16.4	15.3
Excise	32.5	30.4	24.8	20.8	20.0	17.8	16.6
Service Tax	4.7	6.3	7.9	8.6	9.4	10.0	10.1
		Tax revenue as a proportion of gross domestic product* (in per cent)					
Direct Taxes (a)	4.1	4.3	5.1	6.0	6.9	6.1	6.0
Personal Income Tax	1.5	1.5	1.8	2.1	2.6	2.2	1.8
Corporate Tax	2.6	2.7	3.4	3.9	4.3	3.8	4.2
Indirect Taxes (b)	5.3	5.4	5.6	5.6	6.1	4.8	4.4
Customs	1.8	1.8	2.0	2.1	2.2	1.8	1.6
Excise	3.1	3.0	2.7	2.5	2.6	2.0	1.7
Service Tax	0.4	0.6	0.9	1.0	1.2	1.1	1.1
Gross Tax Revenue #	9.4	9.9	11.1	12.0	13.0	10.9	10.4

@ Provisional and unaudited as reported by Controller General of Accounts, Department of Expenditure, Ministry of Finance.

\# includes taxes referred to in (a) & (b) and taxes of Union Territories and "other" taxes.

* Refers to GDP at current market prices.

Notes: 1. Direct taxes also include taxes pertaining to expenditure, interest, wealth, gift and estate duty.

2. The ratios to GDP at current market prices are based on the CSO's National Accounts 2004-05 series.

Source: Union Budget documents.

Table 13: Total Expenditure and Capital Formation of the Central Government

(As per economic and functional classification of the Central Government budget)

	2004-05	2005-06	2006-07	2007-08	2008-09 (RE)	2009-10 (BE)
			(Rs. crore)			
I. Total Expenditure	4,63,831	5,01,083	5,70,185	6,88,908	8,87,032	10,00,019
II. Gross Capital Formation out of Budgetary Resources of the Central Government	92,855	84,757	87,885	14,3892	1,40,085	1,52,119
(i) Gross Capital Formation by the Central Government	27,396	34,450	36,487	43,652	55,973	63,364
(ii) Financial Assistance for Capital Formation in the Rest of the Economy	65,459	50,307	51,398	1,00,240	84,112	88,755
III. Gross Savings of the Central Government	-60,378	-61,431	-33,918	13,674	-1,64,293	-2,07,747
IV. Gap(II-III)	1,53,233	1,46,188	1,21,803	1,30,218	3,04,378	3,59,866
Financed by						
a. Draft on other Sectors of the Domestic Economy	1,35,918	1,09,799	1,10,801	1,18,180	2,82,424	3,41,683
(i) Domestic Capital Receipts	2,08,259	1,30,687	1,06,284	1,45,351	2,52,440	3,41,683
(ii) Budgetary Deficit/Draw Down of Cash Balance	-72,341	-20,888	4,517	-27,171	29,984	0
b. Draft on Foreign Savings	17,315	36,389	11,002	12,038	21,954	18,183
			(As per cent of GDP)			
I. Total Expenditure	14.3	13.5	13.3	13.9	15.9	16.2
II. Gross Capital Formation out of Budgetary Resources of Central Government	2.9	2.3	2.1	2.9	2.5	2.5
(i) Gross Capital Formation by the Central Government	0.8	0.9	0.9	0.9	1.0	1.0
(ii) Financial Assistance for Capital Formation in the Rest of the Economy	2.0	1.4	1.2	2.0	1.5	1.4
III. Gross Savings of the Central Government	-1.9	-1.7	-0.8	0.3	-2.9	-3.4
IV. Gap(II-III)	4.7	3.9	2.8	2.6	5.5	5.8
Financed by						
a. Draft on Other Sectors of Domestic Economy	4.2	3.0	2.6	2.4	5.1	5.5
(i) Domestic Capital Receipts	6.4	3.5	2.5	2.9	4.5	5.5
(ii) Budgetary Deficit/Draw Down of Cash Balance	-2.2	-0.6	0.1	-0.5	0.5	0.0
b. Draft on Foreign Savings	0.5	1.0	0.3	0.2	0.4	0.3
			(increase over previous year)			
I. Gross Capital Formation out of Budgetary Resources of the Central Government	12.5	-8.7	3.7	63.7	-2.6	8.6
Memorandum Items				(Rs. crore)		
1. Consumption Expenditure	1,05,692	1,16,305	1,21,609	1,31,396	1,72,637	2,19,553
2. Current Transfers	2,59,529	2,97,267	3,56,560	4,08,676	5,55,958	5,98,836
				(As per cent of GDP)		
1. Consumption Expenditure	3.3	3.1	2.8	2.7	3.1	3.6
2. Current Transfers	8.0	8.0	8.3	8.3	10.0	9.7

Notes: (i) Gross capital formation includes loans given for capital formation on a gross basis. Consequently domestic capital receipts include loan repayments to the Central Government.

(ii) Consumption expenditure is the expenditure on wages and salaries and commodities and services for current use.

(iii) Interest payments, subsidies, pension, etc. are treated as current transfers.

(iv) Gross capital formation and total expenditure are exclusive of loans to States/UTs against States'/UTs' share in the small savings collection.

(v) The figures of total expenditure of the Central Government as per economic and functional classification do not tally with figures given in the Budget documents. In the economic and functional classification, interest transferred to Departmental Commercial Undertakings, loans written off, etc. are excluded from the current account. In the capital account, expenditure financed out of Railways, Posts & Telecommunications' own funds, etc, is included.

(vi) The ratios to GDP at current market prices are based on the CSO's National Accounts 2004-05 series.

Source: Ministry of Finance, An Economic and Functional classification of the Central Government Budget—various issues.

Table 14: Annual Inflation Rate Average Based WPI (%)

Year	Primary Articles	Fuel, Power, Light & Lubri.	Manufactured Products	All Commodities
Weights (%)	22.02	14.23	63.75	100.00
2000-01	2.8	28.5	3.3	7.2
2001-02	3.6	8.9	1.8	3.6
2002-03	3.3	5.5	2.6	3.4
2003-04	4.3	6.4	5.7	5.5
2004-05	3.7	10.1	6.3	6.5
2005-06	2.9	9.5	3.1	4.4
2006-07	7.9	5.6	4.4	5.4
2007-08	7.6	0.9	5.0	4.7
2008-09	10.1	7.5	8.1	8.4
2008-09(Apr.-Dec.)	10.93	11.32	9.47	10.20
2009-10(Apr.-Dec.)[P]	8.78	-6.35	1.77	1.63

[P]: Provisional.
Source: Department of Industrial Policy & Promotion.

Table 15: Annual Average Inflation by Major Heads in WPI (%)

Commodities	Weight (%)	2004-05	2005-06	2006-07	2007-08	2008-09	2008-09 (Apr.-Dec.)	2009-10 (Apr.-Dec.)[P]
All Commodities	100.00	6.48	4.43	5.42	4.66	8.39	10.20	1.63
I. Primary Articles	22.03	3.69	2.87	7.85	7.61	10.06	10.93	8.78
A. Food Articles	15.40	2.70	4.83	7.78	5.46	8.02	7.57	13.31
B. Non-Food Articles	6.14	0.70	-4.48	5.14	12.64	11.17	14.24	0.43
C Minerals	0.48	110.31	26.54	28.13	13.20	34.90	45.53	-5.51
II. Fuel, Power, Light & Lubricants	14.23	10.14	9.49	5.61	0.93	7.46	11.32	-6.35
A. Coal Mining	1.75	15.34	3.72	0.00	2.68	6.60	9.08	-0.91
B. Minerals Oils	6.99	15.17	13.93	7.87	0.95	11.08	17.17	-10.12
C. Electricity	5.48	1.73	4.07	3.15	0.48	1.06	1.40	-0.08
III. Manufactured Products	63.75	6.26	3.07	4.43	4.97	8.09	9.47	1.77
A. Food Products	11.54	4.98	1.09	3.22	4.27	10.04	10.59	15.49
B. Beverages, Tobacco & its Products	1.34	5.26	4.85	7.36	10.27	9.50	9.53	5.25
C. Textiles	9.80	3.04	-4.50	2.16	-0.98	5.95	4.96	4.18
D. Wood & Wood Products	0.17	0.06	8.41	6.01	4.65	8.34	8.30	1.62
E. Paper & Paper Products	2.04	0.75	2.23	6.83	1.84	4.38	4.23	1.04
F. Leather & Leather Products	1.02	5.99	7.13	-4.38	4.14	1.08	0.83	-0.99
G. Rubber & Plastic Products	2.39	-0.37	3.42	6.61	7.15	4.66	5.47	1.79
H. Chemicals & their Products	11.93	2.54	3.58	3.03	5.57	7.23	8.85	3.20
I. Non-Metallic Mineral Products	2.52	6.34	7.80	12.82	8.86	3.74	4.32	3.27
J. Basic Metal Alloys & Products	8.34	21.16	7.43	6.82	6.86	14.44	19.65	-12.67
K. Machinery & Machine Tools	8.36	5.65	5.14	5.56	7.07	4.74	5.44	-1.34
L. Transport Equipment & Parts	4.29	4.68	3.63	1.56	2.71	5.22	6.09	0.05

[P]: Provisional.
Source: Department of Industrial Policy & Promotion.

Table 16: Weighted Contribution and Inflation in WPI (%)

	Weight (%)	Weighted Contribution			Inflation		
		Oct-09	Nov-09P	Dec-09P	Oct-09	Nov-09P	Dec-09P
All Commodities	100.00	100.00	100.00	100.00	1.46	4.78	7.31
Primary Articles	22.02	137.15	58.39	48.23	8.67	11.84	14.88
Food combined	25.43	232.53	90.68	66.56	14.24	17.78	19.77
Food Articles	15.40	140.38	56.52	42.54	12.99	16.71	19.17
Food MP	10.03	92.14	34.16	24.02	16.68	19.88	20.93
Essential Commodities	17.63	209.39	75.00	51.88	18.53	21.15	21.89
Rice	2.45	21.48	6.19	3.99	14.29	12.95	12.33
Wheat	1.38	8.78	3.74	2.39	9.31	12.66	12.04
Pulses	0.60	11.44	5.04	3.95	25.08	35.22	41.58
Vegetables	1.46	7.67	5.98	7.28	7.06	16.92	39.22
Potatoes	0.26	17.60	5.60	3.70	98.60	101.58	123.85
Onions	0.09	2.03	0.70	0.42	33.10	32.41	27.41
Fruits	1.46	7.21	3.96	2.43	5.90	10.64	9.83
Milk	4.37	28.70	10.33	8.06	10.03	11.49	13.36
Eggs, Meat & Fish	2.21	36.96	14.55	9.03	23.37	29.75	27.16
Tea	0.16	0.29	0.43	0.37	2.96	15.30	21.45
Fuel and Power	14.23	-100.02	-3.94	12.03	-6.66	-0.89	4.29
Rest mineral oils	1.55	-66.59	6.46	13.77	-21.96	9.53	38.18
Manufactured Products	63.75	60.11	46.10	39.46	1.60	3.99	5.17
Food Products	11.54	117.69	51.30	36.33	17.33	24.70	26.40
Sugar	3.62	76.82	27.95	18.72	46.26	53.76	53.98
Gur	0.06	1.40	0.37	0.28	40.02	32.60	37.23
Oil Cakes	1.42	25.52	17.14	12.31	21.14	50.39	56.87

P: Provisional.

Source: Department of Industrial Policy & Promotion.

Table 17: Annual Inflation as per Different Price Indices (%)

Month	WPI		CPI-IW		CPI-UNME		CPI-AL		CPI-RL	
	2008-09	2009-10	2008-9	2009-10	2008-09	2009-10	2008-09	2009-10	2008-09	2009-10
April	8.0	1.3	7.8	8.7	7.0	8.8	8.9	9.1	8.6	9.1
May	8.9	1.4	7.8	8.6	6.8	9.7	9.1	10.2	8.8	10.2
June	11.8	-1.0	7.7	9.3	7.3	9.6	8.8	11.5	8.7	11.3
July	12.4	-0.5	8.3	11.9	7.4	13.0	9.4	12.9	9.4	12.7
August	12.8	-0.2	9.0	11.7	8.5	12.9	10.3	12.9	10.3	12.7
September	12.3	0.5	9.8	11.6	9.5	12.4	11.0	13.2	11.0	13.0
October	11.1	1.5	10.4	11.5	10.4	12.0	11.1	13.7	11.1	13.5
November	8.5	4.8 P	10.4	13.5	10.8	13.9	11.1	15.7	11.1	15.7
December	6.1	7.3 P	9.7	15.0	9.8	-	11.1	17.2	11.1	17.0
January	5.0		10.4		10.4		11.6		11.4	
February	3.5		9.6		9.9		10.8		10.8	
March	1.2		8.0		9.3		9.5		9.7	
Average	**8.4**		**9.1**		**8.9**		**10.2**		**10.2**	

P: Provisional.

IW: Industrial Workers, UNME: Urban Non-Manual Employees, AL: Agricultural Labourer, RL: Rural Labour.

Source: Department of Industrial Policy and Promotion, Labour Bureau and Central Statistical Organization (CSO).

Table 18: Wholesale Price Index—Annual Average

Year	Index (Average of Weeks)					
	AC	PA	*of which*		FPL&L	MP
			FA	NF		
1	2	3	4	5	6	7
			(Base : 1970-71 = 100)			
1970-71	100.0	100.0	100.0	100.0	100.0	100.0
1971-72	105.6	100.9	101.1	98.6	105.9	109.5
1972-73	116.2	110.7	111.3	107.5	110.1	121.9
1973-74	139.7	141.8	136.6	146.6	130.6	139.5
1974-75	174.9	177.5	172.1	163.7	198.3	168.8
1975-76	173.0	165.8	163.6	139.8	219.2	171.2
1976-77	176.6	167.2	155.3	167.4	230.8	175.2
1977-78	185.8	183.8	173.6	178.0	234.3	179.2
1978-79	185.8	181.4	172.4	170.4	244.7	179.5
1979-80	217.6	206.5	186.6	194.6	283.1	215.8
1980-81	257.3	237.5	207.9	217.7	354.3	257.3
1981-82	281.3	264.4	235.1	240.5	427.5	270.6
			(Base : 1981-82 = 100)			
1981-82	100.0	100.0	100.0	100.0	100.0	100.0
1982-83	104.9	106.7	111.1	100.8	106.5	103.5
1983-84	112.8	118.2	126.5	112.4	112.5	109.8
1984-85	120.1	125.5	131.8	124.6	117.3	117.5
1985-86	125.4	125.7	134.1	120.4	129.8	124.5
1986-87	132.7	137.1	147.8	134.1	138.6	129.2
1987-88	143.5	152.6	161.1	163.0	143.3	138.5
1988-89	154.2	160.1	177.1	160.2	151.2	151.5
1989-90	165.7	163.6	179.3	166.0	156.6	168.6
1990-91	182.7	184.9	200.6	194.2	175.8	182.8
1991-92	207.8	218.3	241.1	229.2	199.0	203.4
1992-93	228.7	234.6	271.0	228.7	227.1	225.6
1993-94	247.8	250.9	284.4	249.1	262.4	243.2
			(Base : 1993-94 = 100)			
1993-94	100.0	100.0	100.0	100.0	100.0	100.0
1994-95	112.6	115.8	112.8	124.2	108.9	112.3
1995-96	121.6	125.3	122.2	135.4	114.5	121.9
1996-97	127.2	135.8	137.3	134.2	126.4	124.4
1997-98	132.8	139.4	141.4	137.5	143.8	128.0
1998-99	140.7	156.2	159.4	151.8	148.5	133.6
1999-00	145.3	158.0	165.5	143.0	162.0	137.2
2000-01	155.7	162.5	170.5	146.5	208.1	141.7
2001-02	161.3	168.4	176.1	152.9	226.7	144.3
2002-03	166.8	174.0	179.2	165.4	239.2	148.1
2003-04	175.9	181.5	181.5	186.3	254.5	156.5
2004-05	187.3	188.1	186.3	187.6	280.2	166.3
2005-06	195.5	193.6	195.3	179.2	306.7	171.4
2006-07	206.1	208.6	210.3	188.2	323.9	179.0
2007-08	215.9	224.8	222.1	212.2	327.2	188.0

AC: All commodities PA: Primary articles
FA : Food articles NF: Non-food articles
FPL&L: Fuel, power, light & lubricants MP: Manufactured products.
Source: Office of the Economic Adviser, Ministry of Commerce and Industry, Government of India.

Table 19: WPI Based Domestic Year-on-year Inflation (%)

Period	Energy	Non-energy Commodities	Agriculture	Beverages	Food	Fats and Oils	Grains	Other Food	Raw Materials	Timber	Other Raw Materials	Fertilizers	Metals and Minerals
Jan. 2009	-1.70	6.81	9.79	8.91	9.37	0.60	11.25	32.73	9.98	10.05	0.19	8.38	9.54
Feb. 2009	-3.40	5.41	7.32	10.08	9.32	-3.01	13.14	25.52	1.76	7.69	-2.69	8.54	1.88
Mar. 2009	-6.00	3.17	5.14	9.34	8.07	-6.96	11.61	20.37	0.56	7.74	-12.90	5.43	-7.47
Apr. 2009	-5.69	3.21	6.71	5.88	10.14	-4.05	11.92	15.66	2.55	10.05	-16.35	4.03	-12.11
May 2009	-6.14	3.43	6.91	5.60	10.62	-2.14	14.14	36.27	1.86	3.57	-15.77	-0.60	-12.19
Jun. 2009	-12.53	2.32	7.74	5.99	11.13	-7.85	14.39	26.50	-2.20	0.25	-18.08	-1.46	-13.95
Jul. 2009	-10.37	2.29	9.03	5.45	12.36	-9.38	13.90	18.88	-5.18	0.25	-18.69	-3.19	-15.03
Aug. 2009	-9.26	2.44	9.08	5.14	12.98	-7.29	14.19	13.90	-4.22	0.25	-17.04	-3.03	-13.46
Sep. 2009	-8.18	2.91	9.08	4.75	13.75	-5.59	16.10	7.19	-3.57	0.25	-16.76	-2.68	-12.74
Oct. 2009	-6.66	3.75	9.35	4.75	14.67	-3.93	14.75	4.83	-0.66	0.25	-14.47	-2.28	-11.68
Nov. 2009[P]	-0.89	6.30	12.61	4.47	19.75	-1.38	16.46	12.50	1.17	0.25	-6.18	-2.03	-8.28
Dec. 2009[P]	4.29	8.09	16.01	5.29	21.94	0.18	16.86	16.30	5.62	0.25	-2.31	-3.52	-6.93

[P]: Provisional.

Source: Department of Industrial Policy and Promotion.

Table 20: Credit Flow from Scheduled Commercial Banks

(Rs. crore)

Credit Flow from	Outstanding as on March 27, 2009	Variations (year-on-year)			
		As on March 28, 2008		As on March 27, 2009	
		Amount	Per Cent	Amount	Per Cent
Public Sector Banks	20,11,591	3,07,310	22.5	3,41,442	20.4
Foreign Banks	1,69,350	36,116	28.5	6,483	4.0
Private Banks	5,23,038	78,301	19.9	51,559	10.9
All Scheduled Commercial Banks*	27,70,012	4,30,724	22.3	4,08,099	17.3

* Includes Regional Rural Banks.

Note: Data are provisional.

Source: RBI.

Table 21: Deployment of Gross Bank Credit by Major Sectors

(Rs. crore)

Sector	Outstanding as on 27-Mar 2009	Annual Variation 2007-08* Absolute	2007-08* %	2008-09** Absolute	2008-09** %
Non-food gross bank credit (1 to 4)	2,602,290	401,650	22.3	399,400	18.1
1. Agriculture & Allied Activities	338,656	44,966	19.5	63,313	23.0
2. Industry (Small, Medium & Large)	1,054,390	169,536	24.3	187,515	21.6
of which, Small Enterprises	257,027	76,932	65.2	62,185	31.9
3. Personal Loans	562,479	54,730	12.1	54,991	10.8
Housing	276,957	26,802	11.6	19,165	7.4
Advances against Fixed Deposits	48,676	4,170	10.2	3,671	8.2
Credit Card Outstanding	28,000	8,094	44.2	1,607	6.1
Education	28,579	5,324	35.0	8,047	39.2
Consumer Durables	8,187	-390	-4.2	-612	-7.0
4. Services	646,765	132,419	31.5	93,580	16.9
Transport Operators	39,302	9,486	33.5	1,484	3.9
Professional and Other Services	45,373	3,201	13.4	18,240	67.2
Trade	144,377	17,059	16.0	20,656	16.7
Real Estate Loans	91,575	19,235	43.6	28,261	44.6
Non-Banking Financial Companies	98,853	30,094	61.5	19,835	25.1
Priority Sector	915,886	111,414	17.5	168,506	22.5
INDUSTRY (Small, Medium and Large Scale)	1,054,390	169,536	24.3	187,515	21.6
Food Processing	53,779	9,371	23.4	4,397	8.9
Textiles	102,695	17,483	22.1	6,206	6.4
Paper & Paper Products	15,983	1,874	16.2	2,521	18.7
Petróleum, Coal Products and Nuclear Fuels	68,147	5,715	15.9	26,546	63.8
Chemicals and Chemical Products	75,555	6,560	11.7	13,095	21.0
Rubber, Plastic & their Products	13,587	1,898	20.5	2,439	21.9
Iron and Steel.	99,159	18,858	29.6	16,557	20.0
Other Metal and Metal Products	29,604	4,906	24.5	4,705	18.9
Engineering	65,807	10,690	24.4	11,355	20.9
Vehicles, Vehicle Parts and Transport Equipments	34,642	8,366	40.1	5,421	18.6
Gems & Jewellery	28,537	1,233	5.2	3,454	13.8
Construction	38,505	7,952	39.8	10,556	37.8
Infrastructure	269,972	61,745	43.1	64,852	31.6

* March 28, 2008/March 31, 2007 ** March 27, 2009/March 28, 2008

Note: Data are provisional and relate to select scheduled commercial banks.

Source: RBI.

Table 22: Flow of Institutional Credit to Agriculture and Allied Activities

(Rs. crore)

Institutional Credit from	2002-03	2003-04	2004-05	2005-06	2006-07	2007-08	2008-09*
Cooperative banks	23716	26959	31424	39786	42480	48258	35747
RRBs	6070	7581	12404	15223	20435	25312	25852
Commercial banks	39774	52441	81481	125477	166485	181087	202856
Grand Total	69560	86981	125309	180486	229400	254657	264455

* Provisional.

Source: NABARD.

Table 23: Fact Sheet on Foreign Direct Investment (FDI)

(From August 1991 to November 2008)

1. FDI EQUITY INFLOWS:

A. CUMULATIVE FDI EQUITY INFLOWS *(equity capital components only):*

1.	Cumulative amount of FDI inflows *(from August 1991 to November 2008)*	Rs. 4,16,427 crore	US$ 99,005 million

B. FDI EQUITY INFLOWS (WITH COMPANY-WISE DETAILS) AVAILABLE 2000-08:

1.	Cumulative amount of FDI inflows *(from April 2000 to March 2008)*	Rs. 2,70,100 crore	US$ 62,509 million
2.	Amount of FDI inflows during 2008-09 *(from April 2008 to November 2008)*	Rs. 85,700 crore	US$ 19,790 million
3.	Cumulative amount of FDI inflows *(updated upto November 2008)*	Rs. 3,55,800 crore	US$ 82,299 million

Note: FDI inflows include amount received on account of advances pending for issue of shares for the years 1999 to 2004.

C. FDI EQUITY INFLOWS DURING FINANCIAL YEAR 2008-09:

	Financial Year 2008-09 (April-March)	Amount of FDI inflows (In Rs. crore)	(In US$ mn)
1.	April 2008	15,005	3,749
2.	May 2008	16,563	3,932
3.	June 2008	10,244	2,392
4.	July 2008	9,627	2,247
5.	August 2008	9,995	2,328
6.	September 2008	11,676	2,562
7.	October 2008	7,284	1,497
8.	November 2008	5,305	1,083
2008-09 (up to November 2008)		85,700	19,790
2007-08 (up to November 2007)		45,098	11,142
%age growth over last year		(+) 90 %	(+) 78 %

D. FDI EQUITY INFLOWS DURING CURRENT CALENDAR YEAR 2008:

	Calendar Year 2008 (Jan.-Dec.)	Amount of FDI inflows (In Rs. Crore)	(In US$ mn)
1.	January 2008	6,960	1,767
2.	February 2008	22,529	5,670
3.	March 2008	17,932	4,443
4.	April 2008	15,005	3,749
5.	May 2008	16,563	3,932
6.	June 2008	10,244	2,392
7.	July 2008	9,627	2,247
8.	August 2008	9,995	2,328
9.	September 2008	11,676	2,562
10.	October 2008	7,284	1,497
11.	November 2008	5,305	1,083
Year 2008 (up to November 2008)		128,541	31,671
Year 2007 (up to November 2007)		73,590	17,598
%age growth over last year		(+) 75 %	(+) 80 %

Note: * Figures are provisional, subject to reconciliation with RBI, Mumbai.

E. SHARE OF TOP INVESTING COUNTRIES FDI EQUITY INFLOWS *(Financial year-wise):*

Amount Rupees in crores (US$ in million)

Ranks	Country	2005-06 (April-March)	2006-07 (April-March)	2007-08 (April-March)	2008-09 (April–Nov.08)	Cumulative Inflows (April '00 to Nov. '08	%age to Total Inflows (in terms of rupees)
1.	MAURITIUS	11,441 (2,570)	28,759 (6,363)	44,483 (11,096)	35,172 (8,064)	145,545 (33,699)	44 %
2.	SINGAPORE	1,218 (275)	2,662 (578)	12,319 (3,073)	8,512 (1,983)	26,638 (6,340)	8 %
3.	U.S.A.	2,210 (502)	3,861 (856)	4,377 (1,089)	5,506 (1,294)	25,463 (5,826)	8 %
4.	U.K.	1,164 (266)	8,389 (1,878)	4,690 (1,176)	3,191 (732)	22,255 (5,095)	7 %
5.	NETHERLANDS	340 (76)	2,905 (644)	2,780 (695)	3,344 (766)	15,266 (3,471)	5 %
6.	JAPAN	925 (208)	382 (85)	3,336 (815)	989 (227)	10,325 (2,353)	3 %
7.	GERMANY	1,345 (303)	540 (120)	2,075 (514)	2,331 (544)	9,070 (2,088)	3 %
8.	CYPRUS	310 (70)	266 (58)	3,385 (834)	4,486 (988)	8,553 (1,973)	3 %
9.	FRANCE	82 (18)	528 (117)	583 (145)	1,804 (409)	5,188 (1,169)	2 %
10.	U.A.E.	219 (49)	1,174 (260)	1,039 (258)	938 (218)	3,810 (881)	1 %
TOTAL FDI INFLOWS *		24,613 (5,546)	70,630 (15,726)	98,664 (24,579)	85,700 (19,791)	331,758 (76,915)	-

Note: (i) *Includes inflows under NRI Schemes of RBI, stock swapped and advances pending for issue of shares. (ii) Cumulative country-wise FDI inflows (from April 2000 to November 2008) – Annex-'A'. (iii) %age worked out in rupees terms & FDI inflows received through FIPB/SIA+ RBI's Automatic Route+ acquisition of existing shares only.

F. SECTORS ATTRACTING HIGHEST FDI EQUITY INFLOWS:

Amount Rupees in crores (US$ in million)

Ranks	Sector	2005-06 (April-March)	2006-07 (April-March)	2007-08 (April-March)	2008-09 (April-Nov.08)	Cumulative Inflows (April '00 to Nov. '08	%age to Total Inflows (in terms of rupees)
1.	SERVICES SECTOR (financial & non-financial)	2,399 (543)	21,047 (4,664)	26,589 (6,615)	15,919 (3,600)	71,616 (16,658)	22 %
2.	COMPUTER SOFTWARE & HARDWARE	6,172 (1,375)	11,786 (2,614)	5,623 (1,410)	6,670 (1,543)	38,837 (8,820)	12 %
3.	TELECOMMUNICATIONS (radio paging, cellular mobile, basic telephone services)	2,776 (624)	2,155 (478)	5,103 (1,261)	9,231 (2,052)	25,978 (5,894)	8 %
4.	CONSTRUCTION ACTIVITIES (including roads & highways)	667 (151)	4,424 (985)	6,989 (1,743)	7,490 (1,767)	20,875 (4,930)	6 %
5.	HOUSING & REAL ESTATE	171 (38)	2,121 (467)	8,749 (2,179)	8,353 (1,941)	19,515 (4,652)	6 %
6.	AUTOMOBILE INDUSTRY	630 (143)	1,254 (276)	2,697 (675)	3,401 (782)	13,257 (3,019)	4 %
7.	POWER	386 (87)	713 (157)	3,875 (967)	2,467 (594)	12,097 (2,800)	4 %
8.	METALLURGICAL INDUSTRIES	6,540 (147)	7,866 (173)	4,686 (1,177)	3,420 (812)	10,769 (2,574)	3 %
9.	PETROLEUM & NATURAL GAS	64 (14)	401 (89)	5,729 (1,427)	947 (212)	9,193 (2,193)	3 %
10.	CEHMICALS (other than fertilizers)	1,731 (390)	930 (205)	920 (229)	1,991 (462)	8,132 (1,847)	2 %

Note: Cumulative Sector-wise FDI inflows (from April 2000 to November 2008)—Annex-'B'.

Source: Central Statistical Organisation.

Table 24: Foreign Investment Inflows

Year	A. Direct Investment		B. Portfolio Investment		Total (A+B)	
	Rs. Crore	US $ million	Rs. Crore	US $ million	Rs. crore	US $ million
1	2	3	4	5	6	7
1990-91	174	97	11	6	185	103
1991-92	316	129	10	4	326	133
1992-93	965	315	748	244	1713	559
1993-94	1838	586	11188	3567	13026	4153
1994-95	4126	1314	12007	3824	16133	5138
1995-96*	7172	2144	9192	2748	16364	4892
1996-97*	10015	2821	11758	3312	21773	6133
1997-98*	13220	3557	6794	1828	20014	5385
1998-99*	10358	2462	-257	-61	10101	2401
1999-00*	9338	2155	13112	3026	22450	5181
2000-01*	18406	4029	12609	2760	31015	6789
2001-02*	29235	6130	9639	2021	38874	8151
2002-03*	24367	5035	4738	979	29105	6014
2003-04*	19860	4322	52279	11377	72139	15699
2004-05*	27188	6051	41854	9315	69042	15366
2005-06*	39674	8961	55307	12492	94981	21453
2006-07*P	99985	22079	31713	7003	131698	29082
2007-08*P	130522	32435	118288	29395	248810	61830

P: Provisional.

*: Includes acquisition of shares of Indian companies by non-residents under Section 6 of FEMA, 1999. Data on such acquisitions are included as part of FDI since January 1996.

Notes: 1. Data on FDI have been revised since 2000-01 with expanded coverage to approach international best practices. Data from 2000-01 onwards are not comparable with FDI data for earlier years.

2. Negative (-) sign indicates outflow.

3. Direct Investment data for 2006-07 include swap of shares of 3.1 billion.

Source: Reserve Bank of India.

Table 25: Non-resident Deposits Under Different Schemes

(US$ million)

Part A: Outstanding Balances Under Different Schemes

	As at the end of March							
Scheme	2003	2004	2005	2006	2007	2008	Dec 2007	Dec 2008
Foreign currency non-resident (banks) FCNR (B)	10199	10961	11452	13064	15129	14168	14758	12936
Non-resident (external) rupee account (NR(E)RA)	14923	20559	21291	22070	24495	26716	26078	23226
Non-resident (non-repatriable) rupee deposits (NR(NR)RD)	3407	1746	232	-	-	-	-	-
Non-resident ordinary rupee account (NRO)	-	-	-	1148	1616	2788	2198	4134
Total	28529	33266	32975	36282	41240	43672	43034	40296

(US$ million)

Part B: Net Flows Under Non-Resident Deposits

Scheme	2003-04	2004-05	2005-06	2006-07	2007-08	2007-08	2008-09
						April-December	
Foreign currency non-resident (banks) FCNR (B)	762	492	1612	2065	-960	-371	-1232
Non-resident (external) rupee Account (NR(E)RA	4695	84	1177	1830	109	-960	1383
Non-resident (non-repatriable) rupee deposits (NR(NR)RD)	-1816	-1538	-	-	-	-	-
Non-resident ordinary rupee account (NRO)	-	-	930	426	1030	400	1963
Total	3641	-962	3719	4321	179	-931	2114

Source: RBI.

Table 26: Composition of Exports by Major Markets

	Percentage Share			CAGR	Growth Rate[a]		
	2000-01 (Apr-Mar)	2007-08 (Apr-Mar)	2008-09 (Apr-Feb)	2000-01 to 2005-06	2006-07	2007-08	2008-09 (Apr-Feb)
I Primary products							
World	16.0	16.6	14.6	17.3	19.8	41.9	-2.3
USA	9.4	5.9	6.6	6.1	-3.1	7.4	10.5
EU	13.1	8.9	7.8	8.9	17.0	21.5	-1.2
others	19.8	21.1	18.4	20.9	22.5	47.7	-3.2
(a) Agri & allied products							
World	14.0	11.6	10.6	11.0	23.5	44.9	-0.5
USA	9.0	5.6	6.3	5.8	-1.7	6.8	11.5
EU	11.9	7.8	7.1	7.4	17.8	25.1	3.0
others	16.8	13.9	12.5	13.0	28.6	53.4	-2.1
(b) Ores and minerals							
World	2.0	5.0	4.0	42.7	12.6	35.3	-6.6
USA	0.4	0.3	0.3	12.2	-25.3	19.5	-8.3
EU	1.3	1.1	0.7	19.9	12.5	0.6	-29.8
others	3.0	7.2	5.8	46.5	13.1	37.8	-5.3
II Manufactured goods							
World	78.8	64.4	68.3	16.1	16.9	21.0	10.4
USA	90.6	89.9	92.1	12.9	12.0	7.6	0.7
EU	86.8	78.5	80.5	14.8	18.7	22.8	12.5
others	70.9	55.0	59.8	18.2	18.0	25.0	12.6
(a) Textiles incl. RMG							
World	23.6	10.9	10.7	7.3	5.7	11.8	2.9
USA	27.2	19.2	18.5	9.4	1.5	-1.2	-4.6
EU	33.5	31.1	31.8	12.3	3.5	12.2	0.9
others	45.7	21.2	20.8	2.3	10.9	20.1	8.7
(b) Gems & jewellery							
World	16.6	12.1	11.2	16.0	2.9	23.2	-3.7
USA	29.3	24.0	20.2	9.9	8.8	4.6	-18.5
EU	11.5	7.6	6.7	10.1	1.7	28.5	-4.3
others	13.9	11.2	11.1	21.8	0.3	31.6	2.7
(c) Engineering goods							
World	15.7	20.7	23.9	25.0	38.1	14.5	23.0
USA	13.4	21.0	25.2	21.9	12.9	14.7	20.2
EU	14.0	22.9	26.8	25.3	30.6	31.1	30.4
others	17.2	19.9	22.6	25.8	47.0	9.4	20.8
(d) Chemical & related products							
World	10.4	10.7	11.0	20.9	19.1	22.1	11.3
USA	5.7	11.3	13.2	22.7	24.1	28.1	19.2
EU	9.7	11.0	11.1	17.9	25.7	27.1	14.7
others	12.5	10.4	10.5	21.5	16.2	19.4	8.5
(e) Leather & leather mnfrs.							
World	4.4	2.1	2.1	6.6	12.1	12.6	3.2
USA	3.7	1.4	1.7	-2.0	-4.2	-0.8	14.3
EU	11.4	6.4	6.2	6.5	11.0	19.5	3.8
others	1.6	0.8	0.8	12.8	21.7	2.5	-1.8
(f) Handicrafts including carpet handmade							
World	2.8	0.9	0.6	0.9	4.1	7.2	-26.4
USA	6.0	2.4	1.8	-0.8	-3.1	-4.7	-31.3
EU	4.4	1.6	1.2	2.7	7.1	-6.8	-17.0
others	0.8	0.4	0.3	1.2	15.2	65.6	-32.4
III Petroleum, crude & products							
World	4.3	17.8	16.8	43.8	59.3	53.6	3.5
USA	0.0	3.3	0.9	273.5	-60.8	138.8	-76.3
EU	0.0	11.8	11.5	377.4	-19.4	103.4	16.0
others	7.9	22.5	21.5	35.0	91.9	46.1	4.1
Total exports							
World	100.0	100.0	100.0	18.3	22.6	28.9	6.6
USA	100.0	100.0	100.0	13.3	8.7	9.8	-1.6
EU	100.0	100.0	100.0	16.7	15.6	28.5	11.5
others	100.0	100.0	100.0	20.6	29.0	33.5	6.6

[a]: Growth rate in US dollar terms.

Source: Calculated on the basis of data from DGCI&S, Kolkata.

Table 27: Commodity Composition of Imports

Commodity Group	Share				CAGR	Growth Rate (per cent)[a]		
	2001-02	2006-07	2007-08	2008-09 (Apr-Feb)	2001-02 to 2005-06	2006-07	2007-08	2008-09 (Apr-Feb)
I. Food and allied products, of which	4.7	2.9	2.3	2.2	11.5	42.4	8.3	7.2
1. Cereals	0.0	0.7	0.3	0.0	18.8	3589.7	-46.8	-93.9
2. Pulses	1.3	0.5	0.5	0.4	-4.2	53.8	55.2	-4.6
3. Edible oils	2.6	1.1	1.0	1.2	10.5	4.2	21.4	32.8
II. Fuel, of which	29.5	33.2	34.2	36.4	33.3	29.0	39.4	25.3
4. POL	27.2	30.8	31.7	32.8	33.1	30.0	39.4	22.4
III. Fertilizers	1.2	1.6	2.0	4.8	33.8	52.4	66.2	164.2
IV. Capital goods, of which	11.4	15.4	18.7	13.4	41.4	21.8	63.8	11.8
5. Machinery except electrical & machine tool	6.2	7.5	7.9	7.3	36.8	24.9	43.3	7.1
6. Electrical machinery	1.2	1.1	1.2	1.1	26.1	30.3	53.3	12.7
7. Transport equipment	2.2	5.1	8.0	2.8	66.5	6.8	113.1	-1.8
V. Others, of which	48.5	43.8	38.9	39.0	27.2	24.6	20.2	15.2
8. Chemicals	6.8	5.2	4.9	5.3	25.1	14.1	25.9	24.3
9. Pearls, precious & semiprecious stones	9.0	4.0	3.2	4.9	18.6	-18.0	6.5	76.5
10. Gold & silver	8.9	7.9	7.1	6.8	25.4	29.4	22.0	10.1
11. Electronic goods	7.4	8.6	8.2	7.4	36.8	20.6	29.3	6.4
Total Imports	100.0	100.0	100.0	100.0	30.5	24.5	35.4	21.8

[a]: Growth rate in US dollar terms.

Source: Calculated from DGCI&S data.

Table 28: India's External Debt Outstanding

(Rs. crore)

	As at End-March											End-June	End-Sept.
	1991	2000	2001	2002	2003	2004 R	2005 R	2006 R	2007 R	2008 R	2009 PR	2009 PR	2009 QE
1. MULTILATERAL	40,386	137,132	145,105	155,633	142,683	131,105	138,897	145,503	154,053	157,901	201,425	197,437	203,458
A. Government Borrowing	38,429	120,321	127,886	138,023	129,727	120,073	127,782	133,800	141,746	144,627	181,997	177,451	181,886
(i) Concessional	25,849	84,051	89,008	96,177	102,559	101,490	105,114	105,852	108,448	107,395	127,771	124,045	127,956
(a) IDA	25,221	82,721	87,753	94,848	101,122	100,065	103,671	104,457	107,019	105,947	126,127	122,428	126,296
(b) Others	628	1,330	1,255	1,329	1,437	1,425	1,443	1,395	1,429	1,448	1,644	1,617	1,660
(ii) Non-concessional	12,580	36,270	38,878	41,846	27,168	18,683	22,668	27,940	33,298	37,232	54,226	53,406	53,930
(a) IBRD	12,161	25,343	26,376	28,012	19,069	14,074	16,500	19,626	21,864	22,631	29,948	29,304	28,970
(b) Others	419	10,927	12,502	13,834	8,099	4,509	6,168	8,322	11,434	14,601	24,278	24,102	24,960
B. Non-Government Borrowing	1,957	16,811	17,219	17,610	12,956	11,032	11,115	11,703	12,307	13,274	19,428	19,986	21,572
(i) Concessional	0	0	0	0	0	0	0	0	0	0	0	0	0
(ii) Non-concessional	1,957	16,811	17,219	17,610	12,956	11,032	11,115	11,703	12,307	13,274	19,428	19,986	21,572
(a) Public Sector	303	12,183	12,386	12,729	9,255	7,916	8,000	8,510	9,315	10,352	14,298	14,323	15,092
(i) IBRD	303	6,931	7,114	7,298	4,378	4,402	4,462	4,594	4,550	4,690	7,105	7,302	7,971
(ii) Others	0	5,252	5,272	5,431	4,877	3,514	3,538	3,916	4,765	5,662	7,193	7,021	7,121
(b) Financial Institutions	1,270	3,099	3,368	3,736	3,177	2,902	2,789	2,628	2,414	2,350	3,721	3,797	4,439
(i) IBRD	872	999	1,017	1,049	525	381	252	630	655	593	744	714	1,084
(ii) Others	398	2,100	2,351	2,687	2,652	2,521	2,537	1,998	1,759	1,757	2,977	3,083	3,355
(c) Private Sector	384	1,529	1,465	1,145	524	214	326	565	578	572	1,409	1,866	2,041
(i) IBRD	330	1,173	1,148	929	298	0	0	0	0	0	0	0	0
(ii) Others	54	356	317	216	226	214	326	565	578	572	1,409	1,866	2,041
II. BILATERAL	27,378	79,278	74,519	74,762	79,921	77,084	74,530	70,302	70,034	78,779	104,973	102,299	105,989
A. Government borrowing	23,065	60,920	56,802	56,302	60,243	58,121	57,458	54,593	53,810	59,391	74,662	72,630	75,382
(i) Concessional	23,065	59,380	55,504	55,418	59,688	57,742	57,207	54,468	53,810	59,391	74,662	72,630	75,382
(ii) Non-concessional	0	1,540	1,298	884	555	379	251	125	0	0	0	0	0
B. Non-Government borrowing	4,313	18,358	17,717	18,460	19,678	18,963	17,072	15,709	16,224	19,388	30,311	29,669	30,607
(i) Concessional	514	4,022	5,579	6,885	8,013	8,876	7,471	6,949	1,727	1,737	3,262	3,300	3,434
(a) Public Sector	0	1,488	2,962	4,278	5,152	5,759	5,653	5,285	1,241	1,226	1,156	1,138	1,188
(b) Financial Institutions	514	2,534	2,617	2,607	2,861	3,117	1,818	1,664	486	511	2,106	2,162	2,246
(c) Private Sector	0	0	0	0	0	0	0	0	0	0	0	0	0
(ii) Non-concessional	3,799	14,336	12,138	11,575	11,665	10,087	9,601	8,760	14,497	17,651	27,049	26,369	27,173
(a) Public Sector	2,957	4,752	3,715	4,822	5,116	4,851	4,353	3,628	7,420	10,097	15,076	14,393	14,556
(b) Financial Institutions	527	4,151	3,568	3,708	3,571	3,119	2,847	2,386	3,828	3,735	4,311	4,142	4,056
(c) Private Sector	315	5,433	4,855	3,045	2,978	2,117	2,401	2,746	3,249	3,819	7,662	7,834	8,561
III. IMF[a]	5,132	113	0	0	0	4,381	4,503	4,378	4,484	4,479	5,188	5,063	30,288
IV. EXPORT CREDIT	8,374	29,564	27,625	26,110	23,750	20,553	21,976	24,175	31,237	41,422	74,204	71,505	73,823
(a) Buyers' credit	2,230	18,734	17,336	16,147	13,421	11,061	13,040	16,088	23,617	33,131	64,034	61,805	63,767
(b) Suppliers' credit	933	5,582	5,401	5,144	5,139	4,471	3,961	3,351	2,941	3,127	3,678	3,384	3,501
(c) Export credit component of bilateral credit	1,390	5,165	4,828	4,819	5,190	5,021	4,975	4,736	4,679	5,164	6,492	6,316	6,555
(d) Export credit for defence purchases	3,821	83	60	0	0	0	0	0	0	0	0	0	0

(Contd...)

	As at End-March											End-June	End-Sept.
	1991	2000	2001	2002	2003	2004 R	2005 R	2006 R	2007 R	2008 R	2009 PR	2009 PR	2009 QE
V. COMMERCIAL BORROWINGS	19,727	86,963	113,839	113,908	106,843	95,611	115,533	117,991	180,669	249,164	318,022	301,612	320,841
(a) Commercial bank loans[b]	13,200	44,015	46,169	48,683	46,929	50,346	62,896	73,508	107,145	160,839	220,276	209,140	223,818
(b) Securitized borrowings[c]	5,840	39,564	64,769	62,714	57,495	41,567	48,992	41,112	68,020	82,291	90,723	85,915	91,153
(c) Loans/securitized borrowings etc., with multilateral/bilateral guarantee + IFC(W)	687	3,271	2,901	2,511	2,419	3,698	3,645	3,371	5,504	6,034	7,023	6,557	5,870
(d) Self-Liguidating Loans	0	113	0	0	0	0	0	0	0	0	0	0	0
VI. NRI & FC(B&O) DEPOSITS (Above one year maturity)	20,030	59,120	77,273	83,712	110,022	135,618	143,267	161,834	179,786	174,623	210,118	216,229	220,551
(a) NRI deposits[d]	19,843	59,120	77,273	83,712	110,022	135,618	143,267	161,834	179,786	174,623	210,118	216,229	220,551
(b) FC (B&O) Deposits[e]	187	0	0	0	0	0	0	0	0	0	0	0	0
VII. RUPEE DEBTf	25,199	19,218	17,345	14,807	13,405	11,856	10,071	9,184	8,508	8,065	7,780	7,695	7,690
(a) Defence	22,875	17,290	15,573	13,198	11,946	10,539	8,887	8,112	7,533	7,172	6,955	6,896	6,892
(b) Civilian	2,324	1,928	1,772	1,609	1,459	1,317	1,184	1,072	975	893	825	799	798
VIII. TOTAL LONG TERM DEBT (1 TO VII)	146,226	411,388	455,706	468,932	476,624	476,208	508,777	533,367	628,771	714,433	921,710	901,840	962,640
IX. SHORT-TERM DEBT	16,775	17,162	16,919	13,396	22,180	19,251	77,528	87,155	122,631	182,881	220,908	201,234	203,577
(a) NRI deposits (up to one year maturity)[g]	7,018	5,983	4,463	4,724	9,320	1,321	0	0	0	0	0	0	0
(b) FC(B&O) Deposits (up to one-year maturity)[g]	328	0	0	0	0	0	0	0	0	0	0	0	0
(c) Trade-Related Credits													
(1) Above 6 Months	9,429	11,179	12,456	8,672	12,860	17,930	71,173	86,531	113,256	167,540	203,597	184,342	189,018
(2) Upto 6 Months	4,976	11,179	12,456	8,672	12,860	17,930	32,922	38,788	52,188	91,502	118,936	114,346	116,035
(d) FII Investment in Govt. Treasury Bills and	4,453	0	0	0	0	0	38,251	47,743	61,068	76,038	84,661	69,996	72,983
other instruments	0	0	0	0	0	0	6,355	624	1,732	2,603	10,522	10,288	8,457
(e) Investment in Treasury Bills by foreign central banks and international institutions etc.	0	0	0	0	0	0	0	0	712	620	534	498	370
(f) External Debt Liabilities of:	0	0	0	0	0	0	0	0	6,931	12,118	6,255	6,106	5,732
(1) Central Bank	0	0	0	0	0	0	0	0	2,185	4,458	3,892	3,681	3,371
(2) Commercial banks	0	0	0	0	0	0	0	0	4,746	7,660	2,363	2,425	2,361
X. GRAND TOTAL (VIII+IX)	**163,001**	**428,550**	**472,625**	**482,328**	**498,804**	**495,459**	**586,305**	**620,522**	**751,402**	**897,314**	**1,142,618**	**1,103,074**	**1,166,217**

R Revised PR Partially Revised QE Quick Estimates

IFC(W): International Finance Corporation, Washington D.C. FC (B&O) Deposits : Foreign Currency (Banks & Others) Deposits FII : Foreign Institutional Investors

[a] Relates to SDR allocations from March, 2004 onwards. [b] includes Financial Lease since 1996. [c] Also includes India Development Bonds (IDBs), Resurgent India Bonds (RIBs), India Millenium Deposits (IMDs), also includes Foreign Currency Convertible Bonds (FCCBs) and net investment by 100% FII debt funds. FCCB debt has been adjusted since End-March, 1998 after netting out conversion into equity. [d] Figures include accrued interest. [e] The Scheme was discontinued in July, 1993. [f] Rupee denominated debt owed to Russia and payable through exports. [g] Special Short-term credits under Banker's Acceptance Facility.

Note: NRO Deposits are included under NRI Deposits from the quarter ended June 2005. Supplier's Credits upto 180 days and FII investment in short-term debt instruments are included under short-term debt from the quarter ended March 2005. Vostro balances/Nostro overdrafts of commercial banks, balances of foreign central banks/international institutions with RBI and invsetment in T-bills/securities by foreign central banks/ international institutions have been included in external debt from the quarter ended March 2007.

Source: Ministry of Finance (Department of Economic Affairs), Ministry of Defence, Reserve Bank of India, Securities & Exchange Board of India.

Table 29: Currency Composition of India's External Debt
(as per cent of total external debt)

Sl. No. Currency	As at End-March						As at End of		
	2003	2004	2005	2006	2007	2008 R	June 2008 PR	Sept. 2008 PR	Dec. 2008 QE
1. US dollar	46.6	40.5	48.0	49.2	51.4	54.4	56.5	54.0	53.1
2. SDR	15.2	15.5	14.2	13.7	11.9	10.0	10.0	9.6	9.3
3. Indian rupee	17.3	22.7	19.6	18.9	18.6	17.5	16.4	16.0	15.8
4. Japanese yen	10.7	11.6	10.5	10.9	11.5	12.0	11.3	14.3	15.9
5. Euro	6.2	5.8	4.6	4.4	3.9	3.6	3.5	4.0	3.8
6. Pound sterling	3.0	3.4	2.6	2.6	2.4	2.2	2.0	1.9	1.8
7. Others	1.0	0.5	0.5	0.3	0.3	0.3	0.3	0.2	0.3
Total	100.0	100.0	100.0	100.0	100.0	100.0	100.0	100.0	100.0

R: Revised PR: Partially Revised. QE Quick Estimates

Source: Ministry of Finance, Deptt. of Economic Affairs, Economic Division.

Table 30: India's Key External Debt Indicators (per cent)

Year	External Debt (US$ billion)	Ratio of Total External Debt to GDP	Debt-service Ratio	Ratio of Foreign Exchange Reserves to Total External Debt	Ratio of Concessional Debt to Total External Debt	Ratio of Short-term Debt to Foreign Exchange Reserves	Ratio of Short-Term Debt to Total Debt
1990-91	83.8	28.7	35.3	7.0	45.9	146.5	10.2
1995-96	93.7	27.0	26.2	23.1	44.7	23.2	5.4
2001-02	98.8	21.1	13.7	54.7	35.9	5.1	2.8
2005-06	138.1	17.2	10.1#	109.8	28.6	12.9	14.1
2006-07 PR	171.3	18.1	4.8	116.2	23.1	13.2	16.4
2007-08 PR	224.8	19.0	5.4	137.8	19.7	15.2	20.9
End-June 08 PR	223.8	-	-	139.5	19.1	15.6	21.7
End-Sept. 08 PR	224.6	-	-	127.5	18.5	17.7	22.6
End-Dec. 08 QE	230.8	-	-	110.9	18.7	18.5	20.6

PR: Partially Revised; QE: Quick Estimates.- Not worked out for the broken period

\# Works out to 6.3 per cent, with the exclusion of India Millennium Deposits (IMDs) repayments of US$ 7.1 billion and prepayment of US$ 23.5 million.

Note: Debt-service ratio is the proportion of gross debt service payments to external current receipts (net of official transfers).

Source: Ministry of Finance, Deptt. of Economic Affairs, Economic Division.

Table 31: Agriculture Sector—Key Indicators

Item	2007-08	2008-09
1. GDP-share and growth (per cent at 1999-00 prices)		
Growth in GDP in agriculture & allied sectors	4.9	1.6
Share in GDP-Agriculture and allied sectors	17.8	17.1
Agriculture	16.3	-
Forestry and logging	0.7	-
Fishing	0.8	-
2. Share in total gross capital formation in the country (per cent at 1999-00 prices)		
Share of agriculture & allied sectors in total gross capital	6.7	-
Agriculture	5.7	-
Forestry and logging	0.1	-
Fishing	0.9	-
3. Agricultural imports & exports (per cent at current prices)		
Agricultural imports to national imports	3.1	-
Agricultural exports to national exports	12.2	-
4. Employment in the agriculture sector as share of total employment in 2004-05 as per Current Daily Status (per cent)	52.1	-

Source: Central Statistical Organisation & Dept of Agriculture and Cooperation.

Table 32: Irrigated Area Under Different Crops

(Million hectares)

	1970-71	1980-81	1990-91	1995-96(P)	1996-97(P)	1997-98(P)	1998-99(P)	1999-2000(P)	2000-01(P)
1	2	3	4	5	6	7	8	9	10
Rice	14.3	16.4	19.4	21.5	22.2	22.1	23.4	24.5	24.0
	(38.4)	(40.8)	(45.5)	(49.9)	(51.0)	(50.7)	(52.1)	(54.0)	(53.6)
Jowar	0.6	0.8	0.8	0.8	0.8	0.8	0.8	0.8	0.8
	(3.6)	(4.7)	(5.6)	(6.8)	(7.0)	(7.3)	(8.1)	(7.8)	(8.0)
Bajra	0.5	0.6	0.5	0.6	0.5	0.6	0.7	0.7	0.8
	(4.0)	(5.5)	(5.1)	(6.2)	(4.9)	(6.1)	(7.4)	(7.7)	(8.0)
Maize	0.9	1.2	1.2	1.4	1.3	1.3	1.4	1.5	1.5
	(15.9)	(20.1)	(19.7)	(22.6)	(20.3)	(20.3)	(22.2)	(21.2)	(22.1)
Wheat	9.9	15.6	19.5	21.6	22.4	22.9	23.7	24.2	22.8
	(54.3)	(70.0)	(81.1)	(85.8)	(86.2)	(85.8)	(86.2)	(87.7)	(88.0)
Barley	1.3	0.9	0.5	0.5	0.5	0.5	0.5	0.4	0.5
	(52.0)	(50.6)	(54.5)	(60.3)	(62.5)	(55.6)	(62.5)	(57.1)	(62.5)
Total Cereals	28.1	35.8	42.3	46.5	47.9	48.5	51.6	52.4	50.7
	(27.6)	(34.1)	(41.0)	(46.6)	(47.0)	(47.7)	(50.4)	(50.8)	(49.2)
Total Pulses	2.0	2.0	2.6	3.0	3.0	2.7	3.0	2.9	2.7
	(8.8)	(9.0)	(10.5)	(12.9)	(12.9)	(11.3)	(12.3)	(13.1)	(12.7)
Total Foodgrains	30.1	37.8	44.9	49.5	50.8	51.2	53.6	55.3	53.4
	(24.1)	(29.7)	(35.1)	(40.1)	(40.6)	(40.8)	(42.3)	(44.2)	(43.4)
Oilseeds	1.1	2.3	5.8	7.3	7.4	6.8	6.6	6.7	5.8
	(7.4)	(14.5)	(22.9)	(26.0)	(26.2)	(24.4)	(23.2)	(25.0)	(22.9)
Cotton	1.4	2.1	2.5	3.2	3.3	3.3	3.3	3.1	3.0
	(17.3)	(27.3)	(32.9)	(35.0)	(35.9)	(37.1)	(34.7)	(34.4)	(34.1)
Sugarcane	1.9	2.4	3.4	3.9	3.9	3.8	4.1	4.1	4.2
	(72.4)	(81.3)	(86.9)	(87.4)	(88.6)	(90.5)	(93.2)	(91.1)	(91.3)

(P): Provisional.

Notes: 1. Figures in parentheses represent percentages of irrigated area to total area under the crop.

2. Irrigated area under oilseeds denotes the area under groundnut, rapeseed & mustard, linseed, sesamum and others.

Source: Directorate of Economics & Statistics, Department of Agriculture & Cooperation.

Table 33: Foodgrain Production (million tonnes)

Crop	2007-08 Final	2008-09 Targets	2008-09 3rd Advance Estimates	Percentage Increase (+) Decrease(-) Over final 2007-08	Percentage Increase (+) Decrease (-) vis-à-vis target for 2008-09
1 Rice	96.69	97.00	99.37	2.8	2.4
2 Wheat	78.57	78.50	77.63	-1.2	-1.1
3 Coarse cereals	40.76	42.00	38.67	-5.1	-7.9
4 Cereals	216.02	217.50	215.67	-0.2	-0.8
5 Total pulses	14.76	15.50	14.18	-3.9	-8.5
6 Total food grains	230.78	233.00	229.85	-0.4	-1.4

Source: Department of Food & Public Distribution.

Table 34: Growth of Food Subsidies in India

Year	Food subsidy* (Rs. crore)	Annual growth (per cent)
1998-99	8700	16.0
1999-00	9200	5.8
2000-01	12010	30.5
2001-02	17494	45.7
2002-03	24176	38.2
2003-04	25160	4.1
2004-05	25746	2.3
2005-06	23071	-10.4
2006-07	23828	3.3
2007-08	31260	31.2
2008-09 (Prov)	43668	40.0

*The subsidy amount above is in respect of wheat and rice only.

Source: Department of Food & Public Distribution.

Table 35: Population 1901-2001

Census Years	Population	Decadal Growth		Change in Decadal Annual Growth		Progressive Exponential Growth Rate (per cent)	Average Growth Rate Over 1901 (per cent)
		Absolute	Per Cent	Absolute	Per Cent		
1	2	3	4	5	6	7	8
1901	23,83,96,327	–	–	–	–	–	–
1911	25,20,93,390	1,36,97,063	5.75	–	–	0.56	5.75
1921	25,13,21,213	–7,72,177	– 0.31	– 1,44,69,240	– 6.05	– 0.03	5.42
1931	27,89,77,238	2,76,56,025	11.00	2,84,28,202	11.31	1.04	17.02
1941	31,86,60,580	3,96,83,342	14.22	1,20,27,317	3.22	1.33	33.67
1951[1]	36,10,88,090	4,24,27,510	13.31	27,44,168	– 0.91	1.25	51.47
1961[1]	43,92,34,771	7,81,46,681	21.64	3,57,19,171	8.33	1.96	84.25
1971	54,81,59,652	10,89,24,881	24.80	3,07,78,200	3.16	2.22	129.94
1981[2]	68,33,29,097	13,51,69,445	24.66	2,62,44,564	– 0.14	2.20	186.64
1991[3]	84,64,21,039	16,30,91,942	23.87	2,79,22,497	– 0.79	2.14	255.05
2001[4]	1,02,87,37,436	18,23,16,397	21.54	1,92,24,455	– 2.33	1.95	331.47

Notes:

1. In working out 'Decadal Growth' and 'Percentage Decadal Growth' for India 1941-51 and 1951-61, the population of Tuensang district for 1951 (7,025) and the population of Tuensang (83,501) and Mon (5,774) districts for 1961 Census of Nagaland state have not been taken into account as the areas went in for census for the first time in 1951 and the same are not comparable.
2. The 1981 Census could not be held owing to disturbances in Assam. Hence, the population figures for 1981 of Assam have been worked out by 'interpolation.'
3. The 1991 Census could not be held owing to disturbances in Jammu and Kashmir. Hence the population figures for 1991 of Jammu and Kashmir have been worked out by 'interpolation' on the basis of 2001 final population.
4. The population figures of 2001 are final and include estimated figures for those of the three sub-divisions, *viz.* Mao Maram, Paomata and Pural of Senapati district of Manipur as population Census 2001 in these three sub-divisions was cancelled due to technical and administrative reasons although a population census was carried out in these sub-divisions aiso as per schedule.

Source: Census of India, 2001.

Table 36: Distribution of Population by Workers and Non-workers by Sex

State Code	India/State/UT	Total Population			Total Workers			Total Non-workers		
		Persons	Males	Females	Persons	Males	Females	Persons	Males	Females
1	2	3	4	5	6	7	8	9	10	11
	India@	1,028,610,328	532,156,772	496,453,556	402,234,724	275,014,476	127,220,248	626,375,604	257,142,296	369,233,308
01	Jammu & Kashmir	10,143,700	5,360,926	4,782,774	3,753,815	2,679,941	1,073,874	6,389,885	2,680,985	3,708,900
02	Himachal Pradesh	6,077,900	3,087,940	2,989,960	2,992,461	1,686,658	1,305,803	3,085,439	1,401,282	1,684,157
03	Punjab	24,358,999	12,985,045	11,373,954	9,127,474	6,960,213	2,167,261	15,231,525	6,024,832	9,206,693
04	Chandigarh	900,635	506,938	393,697	340,422	284,419	56,003	560,213	222,519	337,694
05	Uttaranchal	8,489,349	4,325,924	4,163,425	3,134,036	1,996,177	1,137,859	5,355,313	2,329,747	3,025,566
06	Haryana	21,144,564	11,363,953	9,780,611	8,377,466	5,715,526	2,661,940	12,767,098	5,648,427	7,118,671
07	Delhi	13,850,507	7,607,234	6,243,273	4,545,234	3,960,101	585,133	9,305,273	3,647,133	5,658,140
08	Rajasthan	56,507,188	29,420,011	27,087,177	23,766,655	14,695,802	9,070,853	32,740,533	14,724,209	18,016,324
09	Uttar Pradesh	166,197,921	87,565,369	78,632,552	53,983,824	40,981,558	13,002,266	112,214,097	46,583,811	65,630,286
10	Bihar	82,998,509	43,243,795	39,754,714	27,974,606	20,483,003	7,491,603	55,023,903	22,760,792	32,263,111
11	Sikkim	540,851	288,484	252,367	263,043	165,716	97,327	277,808	122,768	155,040
12	Arunachal Pradesh	1,097,968	579,941	518,027	482,902	293,612	189,290	615,066	286,329	328,737
13	Nagaland	1,990,036	1,047,141	942,895	847,796	488,968	358,828	1,142,240	558,173	584,067
14	Manipur@	2,166,788	1,095,634	1,071,154	945,213	527,216	417,997	1,221,575	568,418	653,157
15	Mizoram	888,573	459,109	429,464	467,159	263,008	204,151	421,414	196,101	225,313
16	Tripura	3,199,203	1,642,225	1,556,978	1,159,561	831,346	328,215	2,039,642	810,879	1,228,763
17	Meghalaya	2,318,822	1,176,087	1,142,735	970,146	568,491	401,655	1,348,676	607,596	741,080
18	Assam	26,655,528	13,777,037	12,878,491	9,538,591	6,870,960	2,667,631	17,116,937	6,906,077	10,210,860
19	West Bengal	80,176,197	41,465,985	38,710,212	29,481,690	22,388,044	7,093,646	50,694,507	19,077,941	31,616,566
20	Jharkhand	26,945,829	13,885,037	13,060,792	10,109,030	6,659,856	3,449,174	16,836,799	7,225,181	9,611,618

(Contd...)

State Code	India/State/UT	Total Population			Total Workers			Total Non-workers		
		Persons	Males	Females	Persons	Males	Females	Persons	Males	Females
1	2	3	4	5	6	7	8	9	10	11
21	Orissa	36,804,660	18,660,570	18,144,090	14,276,488	9,802,006	4,474,482	22,528,172	8,858,564	13,669,608
22	Chhattisgarh	20,833,803	10,474,218	10,359,585	9,679,871	5,531,859	4,148,012	11,153,932	4,942,359	6,211,573
23	Madhya Pradesh	60,348,023	31,443,652	28,904,371	25,793,519	16,194,368	9,599,151	34,554,504	15,249,284	19,305,220
24	Gujarat	50,671,017	26,385,577	24,285,440	21,255,521	14,477,286	6,778,235	29,415,496	11,908,291	17,507,205
25	Daman & Diu	158,204	92,512	65,692	72,791	60,569	12,222	85,413	31,943	53,470
26	Dadra & Nagar Haveli	220,490	121,666	98,824	114,122	75,835	38,287	106,368	45,831	60,537
27	Maharashtra	96,878,627	50,400,596	46,478,031	41,173,351	26,852,095	14,321,256	55,705,276	23,548,501	32,156,775
28	Andhra Pradesh	76,210,007	38,527,413	37,682,594	34,893,859	21,662,192	13,231,667	41,316,148	16,865,221	24,450,927
29	Karnataka	52,850,562	26,898,918	25,951,644	23,534,791	15,235,355	8,299,436	29,315,771	11,663,563	17,652,208
30	Goa	1,347,668	687,248	660,420	522,855	375,218	147,637	824,813	312,030	512,783
31	Lakshadweep	60,650	31,131	29,519	15,354	13,204	2,150	45,296	17,927	27,369
32	Kerala	31,841,374	15,468,614	16,372,760	10,283,887	7,765,645	2,518,242	21,557,487	7,702,969	13,854,518
33	Tamil Nadu	62,405,679	31,400,909	31,004,770	27,878,282	18,100,397	9,777,885	34,527,397	13,300,512	21,226,885
34	Pondicherry	974,345	486,961	487,384	342,655	258,670	83,985	631,690	228,291	403,399
35	Andaman & Nicobar Islands	356,152	192,972	163,180	136,254	109,162	27,092	219,898	83,810	136,088

Note: @ – Excludes Mao-Maram, Paomata and Purul sub-divisions of Senapati district of Manipur.

Source: Primary Census Abstract : Census of India 2001.

Table 37: Distribution of Workers by Category of Workers

(e.g., Cultivators, Agricultural Labourers, Household Industry Workers and Other Workers by Sex)

State Code	India/State/UT		Total Workers	Cultivators		Agricultural Labourers		Household Industry Workers		Other Workers	
				Number	%	Number	%	Number	%	Number	%
1	2	3	4	5	6	7	8	9	10	11	12
00	India@										
		Persons	402,234,724	127,312,851	31.7	106,775,330	26.5	16,956,942	4.2	151,189,601	37.6
		Males	275,014,476	85,416,498	31.1	57,329,100	20.8	8,744,183	3.2	123,524,695	44.9
		Females	127,220,248	41,896,353	32.9	49,446,230	38.9	8,212,759	6.5	27,664,906	21.7
01	Jammu & Kashmir										
		Persons	3,753,815	1,591,514	42.4	246,421	6.6	234,472	6.2	1,681,408	44.8
		Males	2,679,941	1,004,535	37.5	190,339	7.1	126,262	4.7	1,358,805	50.7
		Females	1,073,874	586,979	54.7	56,082	5.2	108,210	10.1	322,603	30.0
02	Himachal Pradesh										
		Persons	2,992,461	1,954,870	65.3	94,171	3.1	52,519	1.8	890,901	29.8
		Males	1,686,658	834,312	49.5	55,658	3.3	34,034	2.0	762,654	45.2
		Females	1,305,803	1,120,558	85.8	38,513	2.9	18,485	1.4	128,247	9.8
03	Punjab										
		Persons	9,127,474	2,065,067	22.6	1,489,861	16.3	333,770	3.7	5,238,776	57.4
		Males	6,960,213	1,762,869	25.3	1,104,140	15.9	178,798	2.6	3,914,406	56.2
		Females	2,167,261	302,198	13.9	385,721	17.8	154,972	7.2	1,324,370	61.1
04	Chandigarh										
		Persons	340,422	2,141	0.6	563	0.2	3,880	1.1	333,838	98.1
		Males	284,419	1,687	0.6	461	0.2	2,504	0.9	279,767	98.4
		Females	56,003	454	0.8	102	0.2	1,376	2.5	54,071	96.6
05	Uttarakhand										
		Persons	3,134,036	1,570,116	50.1	259,683	8.3	72,448	2.3	1,231,789	39.3
		Males	1,99-6,177	684,422	34.3	190,494	9.5	43,744	2.2	1,077,517	54.0
		Females	1,137,859	885,694	77.8	69,189	6.1	28,704	2.5	154,272	13.6

(Contd...)

State Code	India/State/UT		Total Workers	Cultivators		Agricultural Labourers		Household Industry Workers		Other Workers	
				Number	%	Number	%	Number	%	Number	%
1	2	3	4	5	6	7	8	9	10	11	12
00	India@										
06	Haryana										
		Persons	8,377,466	3,018,014	36.0	1,278,821	15.3	214,755	2.6	3,865,876	46.1
		Males	5,715,526	1,855,547	32.5	717,133	12.5	132,069	2.3	3,010,777	52.7
		Females	2,661,940	1,162,467	43.7	561,688	21.1	82,686	3.1	855,099	32.1
07	Delhi										
		Persons	4,545,234	37,431	0.8	15,773	0.3	140,032	3.1	4,351,998	95.7
		Males	3,960,101	26,840	0.7	11,224	0.3	112,522	2.8	3,809,515	96.2
		Females	585,133	10,591	1.8	4,549	0.8	27,510	4.7	542,483	92.7
08	Rajasthan										
		Persons	23,766,655	13,140,066	55.3	2,523,719	10.6	677,991	2.9	7,424,879	31.2
		Males	14,695,802	7,062,726	48.1	1,055,332	7.2	419,528	2.9	6,158,216	41.9
		Females	9,070,853	6,077,340	67.0	1,468,387	16.2	258,463	2.8	1,266,663	14.0
09	Uttar Pradesh										
		Persons	53,983,824	22,167,562	41.1	13,400,911	24.8	3,031,164	5.6	15,384,187	28.5
		Males	40,981,558	17,479,887	42.7	8,245,599	20.1	1,946,545	4.7	13,309,527	32.5
		Females	13,002,266	4,687,675	36.1	5,155,312	39.6	1,084,619	8.3	2,074,660	16.0
10	Bihar										
		Persons	27,974,606	8,193,621	29.3	13,417,744	48.0	1,100,424	3.9	5,262,817	18.8
		Males	20,483,003	6,457,265	31.5	8,730,251	42.6	656,662	3.2	4,638,825	22.6
		Females	7,491,603	1,736,356	23.2	4,687,493	62.6	443,762	5.9	623,992	8.3
11	Sikkim										
		Persons	263,043	131,258	49.9	17,000	6.5	4,219	1.6	110,566	42.0
		Males	165,716	70,107	42.3	8,762	5.3	2,849	1.7	83,998	50.7
		Females	97,327	61,151	62.8	8,238	8.5	1,370	1.4	26,568	27.3

(Contd...)

State Code	India/State/UT		Total Workers	Cultivators		Agricultural Labourers		Household Industry Workers		Other Workers	
				Number	%	Number	%	Number	%	Number	%
1	2	3	4	5	6	7	8	9	10	11	12
12	Arunachal Pradesh										
		Persons	482,902	279,300	57.8	18,840	3.9	6,043	1.3	178,719	37.0
		Males	293,612	136,336	46.4	10,329	3.5	3,177	1.1	143,770	49.0
		Females	189,290	142,964	75.5	8,511	4.5	2,866	1.5	34,949	18.5
13	Nagaland										
		Persons	847,796	548,845	64.7	30,907	3.6	21,873	2.6	246,171	29.0
		Males	488,968	270,927	55.4	15,985	3.3	9,193	1.9	192,863	39.4
		Females	358,828	277,918	77.5	14,922	4.2	12,680	3.5	53,308	14.9
14	Manipur@										
		Persons	945,213	379,705	40.2	113,630	12.0	96,920	10.3	354,958	37.6
		Males	527,216	214,282	40.6	49,928	9.5	20,547	3.9	242,459	46.0
		Females	417,997	165,423	39.6	63,702	15.2	76,373	18.3	112,499	26.9
15	Mizoram										
		Persons	467,159	256,332	54.9	26,783	5.7	7,100	1.5	176,944	37.9
		Males	263,008	130,497	49.6	12,775	4.9	3,476	1.3	116,260	44.2
		Females	204,151	125,835	61.6	14,008	6.9	3,624	1.8	60,684	29.7
16	Tripura										
		Persons	1,159,561	313,300	27.0	276,132	23.8	35,292	3.0	534,837	46.1
		Males	831,346	220,962	26.6	162,640	19.6	14,830	1.8	432,914	52.1
		Females	328,215	92,338	28.1	113,492	34.6	20,462	6.2	101,923	31.1
17	Meghalaya										
		Persons	970,146	467,010	48.1	171,694	17.7	21,225	2.2	310,217	32.0
		Males	568,491	255,018	44.9	90,888	16.0	9,358	1.6	213,227	37.5
		Females	401,655	211,992	52.8	80,806	20.1	11,867	3.0	96,990	24.1

(Contd...)

State Code	India/State/UT		Total Workers	Cultivators		Agricultural Labourers		Household Industry Workers		Other Workers	
				Number	%	Number	%	Number	%	Number	%
1	2	3	4	5	6	7	8	9	10	11	12
18	Assam										
		Persons	9,538,591	3,730,773	39.1	1,263,532	13.2	344,912	3.6	4,199,374	44.0
		Males	6,870,960	2,634,068	38.3	832,508	12.1	133,902	1.9	3,270,482	47.6
		Females	2,667,631	1,096,705	41.1	431,024	16.2	211,010	7.9	928,892	34.8
19	West Bengal										
		Persons	29,481,690	5,653,922	19.2	7,362,957	25.0	2,172,070	7.4	14,292,741	48.5
		Males	22,388,044	4,655,210	20.8	5,080,236	22.7	917,180	4.1	11,735,418	52.4
		Females	7,093,646	998,712	14.1	2,282,721	32.2	1,254,890	17.7	2,557,323	36.1
20	Jharkhand										
		Persons	10,109,030	3,889,506	38.5	2,851,297	28.2	430,965	4.3	2,937,262	29.1
		Males	6,659,856	2,405,371	36.1	1,485,322	22.3	237,466	3.6	2,531,697	38.0
		Females	3,449,174	1,484,135	43.0	1,365,975	39.6	193,499	5.6	405,565	11.8
21	Orissa										
		Persons	14,276,488	4,247,661	29.8	4,999,104	35.0	701,563	4.9	4,328,160	30.3
		Males	9,802,006	3,347,691	34.2	2,587,196	26.4	320,011	3.3	3,547,108	36.2
		Females	4,474,482	899,970	20.1	2,411,908	53.9	381,552	8.5	781,052	17.5
22	Chhattisgarh										
		Persons	9,679,871	4,311,131	44.5	3,091,358	31.9	198,691	2.1	2,078,691	21.5
		Males	5,531,859	2,466,477	44.6	1,262,559	22.8	115,860	2.1	1,686,963	30.5
		Females	4,148,012	1,844,654	44.5	1,828,799	44.1	82,831	2.0	391,728	9.4
23	Madhya Pradesh										
		Persons	25,793,519	11,037,906	42.8	7,400,670	28.7	1,033,313	4.0	6,321,630	24.5
		Males	16,194,368	6,882,776	42.5	3,518,368	21.7	519,127	3.2	5,274,097	32.6
		Females	9,599,151	4,155,130	43.3	3,882,302	40.4	514,186	5.4	1,047,533	10.9

(Contd...)

State Code	India/State/UT		Total Workers	Cultivators		Agricultural Labourers		Household Industry Workers		Other Workers	
				Number	%	Number	%	Number	%	Number	%
1	2	3	4	5	6	7	8	9	10	11	12
24	Gujarat										
		Persons	21,255,521	5,802,681	27.3	5,161,658	24.3	429,682	2.0	9,861,500	46.4
		Males	14,477,286	3,906,697	27.0	2,509,651	17.3	243,835	1.7	7,817,103	54.0
		Females	6,778,235	1,895,984	28.0	2,662,007	39.1	185,847	2.7	2,044,397	30.2
25	Daman & Diu										
		Persons	72,791	4,034	5.5	1,323	1.8	1,180	1.6	66,254	91.0
		Males	60,569	2,008	3.3	347	0.6	381	0.6	57,833	95.5
		Females	12,222	2,026	16.6	976	8.0	799	6.5	8,421	68.9
26	D. & N. Haveli										
		Persons	114,122	39,470	34.6	14,715	12.9	850	0.7	59,087	51.8
		Males	75,835	18,072	23.8	5,429	7.2	492	0.6	51,842	68.4
		Females	38,287	21,398	55.9	9,286	24.3	358	0.9	7,245	18.9
27	Maharashtra										
		Persons	41,173,351	11,813,275	28.7	10,815,262	26.3	1,089,318	2.6	17,455,496	42.4
		Males	26,852,095	6,680,696	24.9	4,924,034	18.3	566,861	2.1	14,680,504	54.7
		Females	14,321,256	5,132,579	35.8	5,891,228	41.1	522,457	3.6	2,774,992	19.4
28	Andhra Pradesh										
		Persons	34,893,859	7,859,534	22.5	13,832,152	39.6	1,642,105	4.7	11,560,068	33.1
		Males	21,662,192	5,201,564	24.0	6,453,741	29.8	710,222	3.3	9,296,665	42.9
		Females	13,231,667	2,657,970	20.1	7,378,411	55.8	931,883	7.0	2,263,403	17.1
29	Karnataka										
		Persons	23,534,791	6,883,856	29.2	6,226,942	26.5	959,665	4.1	9,464,328	40.2
		Males	15,235,355	4,832,840	31.7	2,620,927	17.2	405,091	2.7	7,376,497	48.4
		Females	8,299,436	2,051,016	24.7	3,606,015	43.4	554,574	6.7	2,087,831	25.2

(Contd...)

State Code	India/State/UT		Total Workers	Cultivators		Agricultural Labourers		Household Industry Workers		Other Workers	
				Number	%	Number	%	Number	%	Number	%
1	2	3	4	5	6	7	8	9	10	11	12
30	Goa										
		Persons	522,855	50,395	9.6	35,806	6.8	14,746	2.8	421,908	80.7
		Males	375,218	25,708	6.9	15,970	4.3	8,991	2.4	324,549	86.5
		Females	147,637	24,687	16.7	19,836	13.4	5,755	3.9	97,359	65.9
31	Lakshadweep										
		Persons	15,354	0	0	0	0	902	5.9	14,452	94.1
		Males	13,204	0	0	0	0	537	4.1	12,667	95.9
		Females	2,150	0	0	0	0	365	17.0	1,785	83.0
32	Kerala										
		Persons	10,283,887	724,155	7.0	1,620,851	15.8	369,667	3.6	7,569,214	73.6
		Males	7,765,645	602,038	7.8	1,078,354	13.9	191,637	2.5	5,893,616	75.9
		Females	2,518,242	122,117	4.8	542,497	21.5	178,030	7.1	1,675,598	66.5
33	Tamil Nadu										
		Persons	27,878,282	5,116,039	18.4	8,637,630	31.0	1,499,761	5.4	12,624,852	45.3
		Males	18,100,397	3,262,489	18.0	4,256,360	23.5	648,589	3.6	9,932,959	54.9
		Females	9,777,885	1,853,550	19.0	4,381,270	44.8	851,172	8.7	2,691,893	27.5
34	Pondicherry										
		Persons	342,655	10,900	3.2	72,251	21.1	6,339	1.8	253,165	73.9
		Males	258,670	9,637	3.7	42,117	16.3	3,248	1.3	203,668	78.7
		Females	83,985	1,263	1.5	30,134	35.9	3,091	3.7	49,497	58.9
35	A & N Islands										
		Persons	136,254	21,461	15.8	5,169	3.8	7,086	5.2	102,538	75.3
		Males	109,162	14,937	13.7	4,043	3.7	4,655	4.3	85,527	78.3
		Females	27,092	6,524	24.1	1,126	4.2	2,431	9.0	17,011	62.8

Note: @ – Excludes Mao-Maram, Paomata and Purul sub-divisions of Senapati district of Manipur.

Source: Primary Census Abstract: Census of India 2001.

Table 38: Employment in Organised Sectors—Public and Private

(Lakh persons as on 31st March)

	1991	1995	1996	1997	1998	1999	2000	2001	2002	2003	2004	2005	2006	2007
1	2	3	4	5	6	7	8	9	10	11	12	13	14	15
PUBLIC SECTOR														
A. By branch														
1. Central Government	34.11	33.95	33.66	32.95	32.53	33.13	32.73	32.61	31.95	31.33	30.27	29.38	28.60	28.00
2. State Governments	71.12	73.55	74.14	74.85	74.58	74.58	74.60	74.25	73.84	73.67	72.22	72.02	73.00	72.09
3. Quasi-Governments	62.22	65.20	64.58	65.35	64.61	63.85	63.26	61.92	60.20	59.01	58.22	57.48	59.09	58.61
4. Local bodios	23.13	21.97	21.92	22.44	22.46	22.59	22.55	22.61	21.75	21.79	21.26	21.18	21.18	21.32
Total	**190.58**	**194.66**	**194.29**	**195.59**	**194.18**	**194.15**	**193.14**	**191.38**	**187.73**	**185.8**	**181.97**	**180.07**	**181.88**	**180.02**
B. By industry														
1. Agriculture, hunting etc.	5.56	5.39	5.40	5.33	5.30	5.15	5.14	5.02	4.83	5.06	4.93	4.96	4.69	4.75
2. Mining and quarrying	9.99	10.16	9.93	9.78	9.37	9.26	9.24	8.75	8.61	8.47	10.30	10.14	11.46	11.37
3. Manufacturing	18.52	17.56	17.38	16.61	16.16	15.69	15.31	14.30	13.50	12.60	11.89	11.30	10.92	10.87
4. Electricity, gas and water	9.05	9.35	9.46	9.56	9.54	9.62	9.46	9.35	9.23	9.13	8.74	8.60	8.49	8.49
5. Construction	11.49	11.64	11.59	11.34	11.09	11.07	10.92	10.81	10.26	9.48	9.32	9.11	8.94	8.66
6. Wholesale and retail trade	1.50	1.62	1.62	1.64	1.64	1.63	1.63	1.63	1.57	1.82	1.81	1.84	1.82	1.78
7. Transport, storage & communications	30.26	31.06	30.92	30.92	30.84	30.84	30.77	30.42	30.09	29.39	28.15	27.51	26.75	26.37
8. Finance, insurance, real estate etc.	11.94	12.83	12.80	12.94	12.88	12.95	12.96	12.81	12.30	13.77	14.08	14.08	13.90	13.69
9. Community, Social & personal services	92.27	95.04	95.20	97.47	97.37	97.94	97.71	98.30	97.35	96.09	92.76	92.52	91.76	90.90
Total	**190.58**	**194.66**	**194.29**	**195.59**	**194.18**	**194.15**	**193.14**	**191.38**	**187.73**	**185.80**	**181.97**	**180.07**	**178.73**	**176.88**
PRIVATE SECTOR														
1. Agriculture, hunting etc.	8.91	8.94	9.19	9.12	9.04	8.71	9.04	9.31	8.55	8.95	9.17	9.83	10.28	9.50
2. Mining and quarrying	1.00	1.03	1.07	0.92	0.91	0.87	0.81	0.79	0.68	0.66	0.65	0.79	0.95	1.00
3. Manufacturing	44.81	47.06	50.49	52.39	52.33	51.78	50.85	50.13	48.67	47.44	44.89	44.89	45.49	47.50
4. Electricity, gas and water	0.40	0.40	0.42	0.41	0.42	0.41	0.41	0.52	0.42	0.50	0.47	0.49	0.40	0.50
5. Construction	0.73	0.53	0.53	0.54	0.74	0.71	0.57	0.57	0.56	0.44	0.45	0.49	0.55	0.70
6. Wholesale and retail trade	3.00	3.08	3.17	3.17	3.21	3.23	3.30	3.39	3.35	3.60	3.51	3.75	3.87	4.10
7. Transport, storage & communications	0.53	0.58	0.60	0.63	0.65	0.69	0.70	0.76	0.76	0.79	0.81	0.85	0.87	1.00

(Contd...)

	1991	1995	1996	1997	1998	1999	2000	2001	2002	2003	2004	2005	2006	2007
1	2	3	4	5	6	7	8	9	10	11	12	13	14	15
8. Finance, insurance,real estate etc.	2.54	2.93	3.06	3.22	3.41	3.58	3.58	3.70	3.91	4.26	4.58	5.23	6.52	8.80
9. Community, social & personal services	14.85	16.03	16.58	16.44	16.77	17.00	17.23	17.34	17.42	17.56	17.92	18.20	18.78	19.50
Total	**76.77**	**80.59**	**85.12**	**86.86**	**87.48**	**86.98**	**86.46**	**86.52**	**84.32**	**84.21**	**82.46**	**84.52**	**87.71**	**92.40**
BY SEX														
PUBLIC SECTOR														
Male	167.10	168.66	167.94	168.31	166.55	166.04	164.57	162.79	158.86	156.75	153.07	150.86	151.85	149.84
Female	23.47	26.00	26.35	27.28	27.63	28.11	28.57	28.59	28.87	29.05	28.90	29.21	30.03	30.18
Total	190.57	194.66	194.29	195.59	194.18	194.15	193.14	191.38	187.73	185.80	181.97	180.07	181.88	180.02
PRIVATE SECTOR														
Male	62.42	64.31	67.20	67.77	67.37	66.80	65.80	65.62	63.83	63.57	62.02	63.57	66.87	69.80
Female	14.34	16.28	17.92	19.09	20.11	20.18	20.66	20.90	20.49	20.64	20.44	20.95	21.18	22.94
Total	**76.76**	**80.59**	**85.12**	**86.86**	**87.48**	**86.98**	**86.46**	**86.52**	**84.32**	**84.21**	**82.46**	**84.52**	**88.05**	**92.74**
PUBLIC AND PRIVATE SECTOR														
Male	229.52	232.97	235.14	236.08	233.92	232.84	230.37	228.40	222.71	220.32	215.09	214.42	218.72	219.64
Female	37.81	42.28	44.26	46.37	47.74	48.29	49.23	49.49	49.35	49.68	49.34	50.16	51.21	53.12
Total	**267.33**	**275.25**	**279.41**	**282.45**	**281.66**	**281.13**	**279.60**	**277.89**	**272.06**	**270.00**	**264.43**	**264.58**	**269.93**	**272.76**

Notes: 1. Coverage in construction, particularly on private account, is known to be inadequate.

2. Employment in private sector relates to non-agriculture establishments in private sector employing 10 or more persons. Employment in public sector relate to all estalishments irrespective of size.

3. Excludes Sikkim, Arunachal Pradesh, Dadra & Nagar Haveli and Lakshadweep as these are not yet covered under the programme.

4. Due to non-availability of data as per NIC 1998, information in respect of J&K, Meghalaya, Mizoram, Daman & Diu not included in totals.

Source: Ministry of Labour & Employment, Director General of Employment and Training.

Table 39: Employment in the Public and Organised Private Sectors

(In million)

Year	Public Sector (End-March)	Private Sector (End-March)	Number of Persons on the Live Register (End-December)
1	2	3	4
1970-71	11.10	6.73	5.10
1971-72	11.69	6.96	6.90
1972-73	12.40	6.72	8.22
1973-74	12.73	6.75	8.43
1974-75	13.13	6.79	9.33
1975-76	13.63	6.79	9.78
1976-77	14.18	6.95	10.92
1977-78	14.73	7.11	12.68
1978-79	15.58	7.23	14.33
1979-80	15.12	7.24	16.20
1980-81	15.48	7.40	17.84
1981-82	16.28	7.53	19.75
1982-83	16.75	7.39	21.95
1983-84	17.22	7.36	23.55
1984-85	17.58	7.43	26.27
1985-86	17.68	7.37	30.13
1986-87	18.24	7.39	30.25
1987-88	18.32	7.39	30.05
1988-89	18.51	7.45	32.78
1989-90	18.77	7.58	34.63
1990-91@	19.06	7.68	36.30
1991-92@	19.21	7.85	36.76
1992-93@	19.33	7.85	36.28
1993-94@	19.45	7.93	36.69
1994-95@	19.47	8.06	36.74
1995-96@	19.43	8.51	37.43
1996-97@	19.56	8.69	39.14
1997-98@	19.42	8.75	40.09
1998-99@	19.41	8.70	40.37
1999-00	19.31	8.65	41.34
2000-01	19.14	8.65	42.00
2001-02	18.77	8.43	41.17
2002-03@	18.58	8.42	41.39
2003-04@	18.20	8.25	40.46
2004-05@	18.01	8.45	39.35
2005-06@	-	-	41.47

@: Data are based on Quarterly Employment Review.

Also see Notes on Tables.

Source: Directorate General of Employment and Training, Ministry of Labour & Employment, Government of India.

Table 40: Number and Percentage of Population Below Poverty Line—1973-74

State/Union Territory	Rural			Urban			Combined	
	No. of Persons (Lakh)	% of Persons	Poverty Line (Rs.)	No. of Persons (Lakh)	% of Persons	Poverty Line (Rs.)	No. of Persons (Lakh)	% of Persons
1	2	3	4	5	6	7	8	9
Andhra Pradesh	178.21	48.41	41.71	47.48	50.61	53.96	225.69	48.86
Arunachal Pradesh	2.57	52.67	-	0.09	36.92	-	2.66	51.93
Assam	76.37	52.67	49.82	5.46	36.92	50.26	81.83	51.21
Bihar	336.52	62.99	57.68	34.05	52.96	61.27	370.57	61.91
Goa	3.16	46.85	50.47	1.00	37.69	59.48	4.16	44.26
Gujarat	94.61	46.35	47.10	43.81	52.57	62.17	138.42	48.15
Haryana	30.08	34.23	49.95	8.24	40.18	52.42	38.32	35.36
Himachal Pradesh	9.38	27.42	49.95	0.35	13.17	51.93	9.73	26.39
Jammu & Kashmir	18.41	45.51	46.59	2.07	21.32	37.17	20.48	40.83
Karnataka	128.4	55. 14	47.24	42.27	52.53	58.22	170.67	54.47
Kerala	111.36	59.19	51.68	24.16	62.74	62.78	135.52	59.79
Madhya Pradesh	231.21	62.66	50.20	45.09	57.65	63.02	276.30	61.78
Maharashtra	210.84	57.71	50.47	76.58	43.87	59.48	287.42	53.24
Manipur	5.11	52.67	-	0.75	36.92	-	5.86	49.96
Meghalaya	4.88	52.67	-	0.64	36.92	-	5.52	50.20
Mizoram	1.62	52.67	-	0.20	36.92	-	1.82	50.32
Nagaland	2.65	52.67	-	0.25	36.92	-	2.90	50.81
Orissa	142.24	67.28	46.87	12.23	55.62	59.34	154.47	66.18
Punjab	30.47	28.21	49.95	10.02	27.96	51.93	40.49	28.15
Rajasthan	101.41	44.76	50.96	27.10	52.13	59.99	128.51	46.14
Sikkim	1.09	52.67	-	0.10	36.92	-	1.19	50.86
Tamil Nadu	172.6	57.43	45.09	66.92	49.40	51.54	239.52	54.94
Tripura	7.88	52.67	-	0.66	36.92	-	8.54	51.00
Uttar Pradesh	449.99	56.53	48.92	85.74	60.09	57.37	535.73	57.07
West Bengal	257.96	73. 16	54.49	41.34	34.67	54.81	299.3	63.43
Andaman & Nicobar Islands	0.59	57.43	-	0.15	49.40	-	0.74	55.56
Chandigarh	0.07	27.96	-	0.77	27.96	-	0.84	27.96
Dadra & Nagar Haveli	0.37	46.85	50.47	0.01	37.69	59.48	0.38	46.55
Daman & Diu	-	-	-	-	-	-	-	-
Delhi	1.06	24.44	49.95	21.78	52.23	67.95	22.84	49.61
Lakshadweep	0.18	59.19	-	0.03	62.74	-	0.21	59.68
Puducherry	1.61	57.43	-	1.13	49.40	-	2.74	53.82
All India	**2612.9**	**56.44**	**49.63**	**600.46**	**49.01**	**56.64**	**3213.36**	**54.88**

(Contd...)

Table 40: Number and Percentage of Population Below Poverty Line—1983-84 (Contd.)

State/Union Territory	Rural			Urban			Combined	
	No. of Persons (Lakh)	% of Persons	Poverty Line (Rs.)	No. of Persons (Lakh)	% of Persons	Poverty Line (Rs.)	No. of Persons (Lakh)	% of Persons
1	2	3	4	5	6	7	8	9
Andhra Pradesh	114.34	26.53	72.66	50.24	36.3	106.43	164.58	28.91
Arunachal Pradesh	2.7	42.6	98.32	0.12	21.73	97.51	2.82	40.88
Assam	73.43	42.6	98.32	4.26	21.73	97.51	77.69	40.47
Bihar	417.7	64.37	97.48	44.35	47.33	111.8	462.05	62.22
Goa	1.16	14.81	88.24	1.07	27.00	126.47	2.23	18.90
Gujarat	72.88	29.8	83.29	45.04	39.14	123.22	117.92	32.79
Haryana	22.03	20.56	88.57	7.57	24.15	103.48	29.6	21.37
Himachal Pradesh	7.07	17.00	88.57	0.34	9.43	102.26	7.41	16.40
Jammu & Kashmir	13.11	26.04	91.75	2.49	17.76	99.62	15.60	24.24
Karnataka	100.5	36.33	83.31	49.31	42.82	120.19	149.81	38.24
Kerala	81.62	39.03	99.35	25.15	45.68	122.64	106.77	40.42
Madhya Pradesh	215.48	48.9	83.59	62.49	53.06	122.82	277.97	49.78
Maharashtra	193.75	45.23	88.24	97.14	40.26	126.47	290.89	43.44
Manipur	4.76	42.6	98.32	0.89	21.73	97.51	5.65	37.02
Meghalaya	5.04	42.6	98.32	0.57	21.73	97.51	5.62	38.81
Mizoram	1.58	42.6	98.32	0.37	21.73	97.51	1.96	36.00
Nagaland	3.19	42.6	98.32	0.31	21.73	97.51	3.50	39.25
Orissa	164.65	67.53	106.28	16.66	49.15	124.81	181.31	65.29
Punjab	16.79	13.2	88.57	11.85	23.79	101.03	28.64	16.18
Rajasthan	96.77	33.5	80.24	30.06	37.94	1 13.55	126.83	34.46
Sikkim	1.24	42.6	98.32	0.10	21.73	97.51	1.35	39.71
Tamil Nadu	181.61	53.99	96.15	78.46	46.96	120.30	260.07	51.66
Tripura	8.35	42.6	98.32	0.6	21.73	97.51	8.95	40.03
Uttar Pradesh	448.03	46.45	83.85	108.71	49.82	1 10.23	556.74	47.07
West Bengal	268.6	63.05	105.55	50.09	32.32	105.91	318.69	54.85
Andaman & Nicobar Islands	0.84	53.99	96.15	0.26	46.96	120.30	1.11	52.13
Chandigarh	0.09	23.79	101.03	1.10	23.79	101.03	1.19	23.79
Dadra & Nagar Haveli	0.16	14.81	88.24	0.02	27.00	126.47	0.18	15.67
Daman & Diu	-	-	-	-	-	-	-	-
Delhi	0.44	7.66	88.57	17.95	27.89	123.29	18.39	26.22
Lakshadweep	0.09	39.03	99.35	0.10	45.68	122.64	0.19	42.36
Puducherry	1.56	53.99	96.15	1.72	46.96	120.30	3.28	50.06
All India	**2519.57**	**45.65**	**89.5**	**709.4**	**40.79**	**115.65**	**3228.97**	**44.48**

(Contd...)

Table 40: Number and Percentage of Population Below Poverty Line—1993-94 (Contd.)

State/Union Territory	Rural			Urban			Combined	
	No. of Persons (Lakh)	% of Persons	Poverty Line (Rs.)	No. of Persons (Lakh)	% of Persons	Poverty Line (Rs.)	No. of Persons (Lakh)	% of Persons
1	2	3	4	5	6	7	8	9
Andhra Pradesh	74.49	15.92	163.02	74.47	38.33	278.14	153.97	22.19
Arunachal Pradesh	3.62	45.01	232.05	0.11	7.73	212.42	3.73	39.35
Assam	94.33	45.01	232.05	2.03	7.73	212.42	96.36	40.86
Bihar	450.86	58.21	212.16	42.49	34.50	238.49	493.35	54.96
Goa	0.38	5.34	194.94	1.53	27.03	328.56	1.91	14.92
Gujarat	62.16	22.18	202.11	43.02	27.89	297.22	105.19	24.21
Haryana	36.56	28.02	233.79	7.31	16.38	258.23	43.88	25.05
Himachal Pradesh	15.40	30.34	233.79	0.46	9.18	253.61	15.86	28.44
Jammu & Kashmir	19.05	30.34	233.79	1.86	9.18	253.61	20.92	25.17
Karnataka	95.99	29.88	186.63	60.46	40.14	302.89	156.46	33.16
Kerala	55.95	25.76	243.84	20.46	24.55	280.54	76.41	25.43
Madhya Pradesh	216.19	40.64	193. 10	82.33	48.38	317.16	298.52	42.52
Maharashtra	193.33	37.93	194.94	111.90	35.15	328.56	305.22	36.86
Manipur	6.33	45.01	232.05	0.47	7.73	212.42	6.8	33.78
Meghalaya	7.09	45.01	232.05	0.29	7.73	212.42	7.38	37.92
Mizoram	1.64	45.01	232.05	0.30	7.73	212.42	1.94	25.66
Nagaland	4.85	45.01	232.05	0.20	7.73	212.42	5.05	37.92
Orissa	140.90	49.72	194.03	19.70	41.64	298.22	160.60	48.56
Punjab	17.76	11.95	233.79	7.35	11.35	253.61	25.11	11.77
Rajasthan	94.68	26.46	215.89	33.82	30.49	280.85	128.50	27.41
Sikkim	1.81	45.01	232.05	0.03	7.73	212.42	1.84	41.43
Tamil Nadu	121.70	32.48	196.53	80.4	39.77	296.63	202.10	35.03
Tripura	11.41	45.01	232.05	0.38	7.73	212.42	11.79	39.01
Uttar Pradesh	496.17	42.28	213.01	108.28	35.39	258.65	604.46	40.85
West Bengal	209.9	40.80	220.74	44.66	22.41	247.53	254.56	35.66
Andaman & Nicobar Islands	0.73	32.48	196.53	0.33	39.77	296.63	1.06	34.47
Chandigarh	0.07	11.35	253.61	0.73	11.35	253.61	0.80	11.35
Dadra & Nagar Haveli	0.72	51.95	194.94	0.06	39.93	328.56	0.77	50.84
Daman & Diu	0.03	5.34	194.94	0.15	27.03	328.56	0.18	15.80
Delhi	0.19	1.90	233.79	15.32	16.03	309.48	15.51	14.69
Lakshadweep	0.06	25.76	243.84	0.08	24.55	280.54	0.14	25.04
Puducherry	0.93	32.48	196.53	2.38	39.77	296.63	3.31	37.40
All India	**2440.31**	**37.27**	**205.84**	**763.37**	**32.36**	**281.35**	**3203.67**	**35.97**

(Contd...)

Table 40: Number and Percentage of Population Below Poverty Line—1999-2000 (30 Day Recall Period (Contd.)

State/Union Territory	Rural			Urban			Combined	
	No. of Persons (Lakh)	% of Persons	Poverty Line (Rs.)	No. of Persons (Lakh)	% of Persons	Poverty Line (Rs.)	No. of Persons (Lakh)	% of Persons
1	2	3	4	5	6	7	8	9
Andhra Pradesh	58.13	11.05	262.94	60.88	26.63	457.4	119.01	15.77
Arunachal Pradesh	3.80	40.04	365.43	0.18	7.47	343.99	3.98	33.47
Assam	92.17	40.04	365.43	2.38	7.47	343.99	94.55	36.09
Bihar	376.51	44.30	333.07	49.13	32.91	379.78	425.64	42.60
Goa	0.11	1.35	318.63	0.59	7.52	539.71	0.70	4.4
Gujarat	39.80	13.17	318.94	28.09	15.59	474.41	67.89	14.07
Haryana	11.94	8.27	362.81	5.39	9.99	420.20	17.34	8.74
Himachal Pradesh	4.84	7.94	367.45	0.29	4.63	420.20	5.12	7.63
Jammu & Kashmir	2.97	3.97	367.45	0.49	1.98	420.20	3.46	3.48
Karnataka	59.91	17.38	309.59	44.49	25.25	511.44	104.40	20.04
Kerala	20.97	9.38	374.79	20.07	20.27	477.06	41.04	12.72
Madhya Pradesh	217.32	37.06	311.34	81.22	38.44	481.65	298.54	37.43
Maharashtra	125.12	23.72	318.63	102.87	26.81	539.71	227.99	25.02
Manipur	6.53	40.04	365.43	0.66	7.47	343.99	7.19	28.54
Meghalaya	7.89	40.04	365.43	0.34	7.47	343.99	8.23	33.87
Mizoram	1.40	40.04	365.43	0.45	7.47	343.99	1.85	19.47
Nagaland	5.21	40.04	365.43	0.28	7.47	343.99	5.49	32.67
Orissa	143.69	48.01	323.92	25.40	42.83	473.12	169.09	47.15
Punjab	10.20	6.35	362.68	4.29	5.75	388.15	14.49	6.16
Rajasthan	55.06	13.74	344.03	26.78	19.85	465.92	81.83	15.28
Sikkim	2.00	40.04	365.43	0.04	7.47	343.99	2.05	36.55
Tamil Nadu	30.51	20.55	307.64	49.97	22.11	475.60	130.48	21.12
Tripura	12.53	40.04	365.43	0.49	7.47	343.99	13.02	34.44
Uttar Pradesh	412.01	31.22	336.88	117.88	30.89	416.29	529.89	31.15
West Bengal	180.11	31.85	350.17	33.38	14.86	409.22	213.49	27.02
Andaman & Nicobar Islands	0.58	20.55	307.64	0.24	22.11	475.6	0.82	20.99
Chandigarh	0.06	5.75	388. 15	0.45	5.75	388.15	0.51	5.75
Dadra & Nagar Haveli	0.30	17.57	318.63	0.03	13.52	539.71	0.33	17.14
Daman & Diu	0.01	1.35	318.63	0.05	7.52	539.71	0.06	4.44
Delhi	0.07	0.40	362.68	11.42	9.42	505.45	11.49	8.23
Lakshadweep	0.03	9.38	374.79	0.08	20.27	477.06	0.11	15.6
Puducherry	0.64	20.55	307.64	1.77	22.11	475.6	2.41	21.67
All India	**1932.43**	**27.09**	**327.56**	**670.07**	**23.62**	**454.11**	**2602.5**	**26.1**

(*Contd...*)

Table 40: Number and Percentage of Population Below Poverty Line—2004-05 (Based on URP$ Consumption) (Contd.)

State/Union Territory	Rural			Urban			Combined	
	No. of Persons (Lakh)	% of Persons	Poverty Line (Rs.)	No. of Persons (Lakh)	% of Persons	Poverty Line (Rs.)	No. of Persons (Lakh)	% of Persons
1	2	3	4	5	6	7	8	9
Andhra Pradesh	64.70	11.20	292.95	61.40	28.00	542.89	126.10	15.80
Arunachal Pradesh	1.94	22.30	387.64	0.09	3.30	378.84	2.03	17.60
Assam	54.50	22.30	387.64	1.28	3.30	378.84	55.77	19.70
Bihar	336.72	42.10	354.36	32.42	34.60	435.00	369.15	41.40
Chhattisgarh	71.50	40.80	322.41	19.47	41.20	560.00	90.96	40.90
Goa	0.36	5.40	362.25	1.64	21.30	665.90	2.01	13.80
Gujarat	63.49	19.10	353.93	27.19	13.00	541.16	90.69	16.80
Haryana	21.49	13.60	414.76	10.60	15.10	504.49	32.10	14.00
Himachal Pradesh	6.14	10.70	394.28	0.22	3.40	504.49	6.36	10.00
Jammu & Kashmir	3.66	4.60	391.26	2.19	7.90	553.77	5.85	5.40
Jharkhand	103.19	46.30	366.56	13.20	20.20	451.24	116.39	40.30
Karnataka	75.05	20.80	324.17	63.83	32.60	599.66	138.89	25.00
Kerala	32.43	13.20	430.12	17.17	20.20	559.39	49.60	15.00
Madhya Pradesh	175.65	36.90	327.78	74.03	42.10	570.15	249.68	38.30
Maharashtra	171.13	29.60	362.25	146.25	32.20	665.90	317.38	30.70
Manipur	3.76	22.30	387.64	0.20	3.30	378.84	3.95	17.30
Meghalaya	4.36	22.30	387.64	0.16	3.30	378.84	4.52	18.50
Mizoram	1.02	22.30	387.64	0.16	3.30	378.84	1.18	12.60
Nagaland	3.87	22.30	387.64	0.12	3.30	378.84	3.99	19.00
Orissa	151.75	46.80	325.79	26.74	44.30	528.49	178.49	46.40
Punjab	15.12	9.10	410.38	6.50	7.10	466.16	21.63	8.40
Rajasthan	87.38	18.70	374.57	47.51	32.90	559.63	134.89	22.10
Sikkim	1.12	22.30	387.64	0.02	3.30	378.84	1.14	20.10
Tamil Nadu	76.5	22.80	351.86	69.13	22.20	547.42	145.62	22.50
Tripura	6.18	22.30	387.64	0.20	3.30	378.84	6.38	18.90
Uttar Pradesh	473.0	33.40	365.84	117.03	30.60	483.26	590.03	32.80
Uttarakhand	27.11	40.80	478.02	8.85	36.50	637.67	35.96	39.60
West Bengal	173.22	28.60	382.82	35.14	14.80	449.32	208.36	24.70
Andaman & Nicobar Islands	0.60	22.90	351.86	0.32	22.20	547.42	0.92	22.60
Chandigarh	0.08	7.10	410.38	0.67	7.10	466.16	0.74	7.10
Dadra & Nagar Haveli	0.68	39.80	362.25	0.15	19.10	665.90	0.84	33.20
Daman & Diu	0.07	5.40	362.25	0.14	21.20	665.90	0.21	10.50
Delhi	0.63	6.90	410.38	22.30	15.20	612.91	22.93	14.70
Lakshadweep	0.06	13.30	430.12	0.06	20.20	559.39	0.11	16.00
Puducherry	0.78	22.90	351.86	1.59	22.20	547.42	2.37	22.40
All India	**2209.24**	**28.30**	**356.30**	**807.96**	**25.70**	**538.60**	**3017.20**	**27.5**

$: URP: Uniform Recall Period.

(Contd...)

Table 40: Number and Percentage of Population Below Poverty Line (Based on MRP[$] Consumption) (Concld.)

State/Union Territory	Rural			Urban			Combined	
	No. of Persons (Lakh)	% of Persons	Poverty Line (Rs.)	No. of Persons (Lakh)	% of Persons	Poverty Line (Rs.)	No. of Persons (Lakh)	% of Persons
1	2	3	4	5	6	7	8	9
Andhra Pradesh	43.21	7.50	292.95	45.50	20.70	542.89	88.71	11.10
Arunachal Pradesh	1.47	17.00	387.64	0.07	2.40	378.84	1.54	13.40
Assam	41.46	17.00	387.64	0.93	2.40	378.84	42.39	15.00
Bihar	262.92	32.90	354.36	27.09	28.90	435.00	290.01	32.50
Chhattisgarh	54.72	31.20	322.41	16.39	34.70	560.00	71.11	32.00
Goa	0.13	1.90	362.25	1.62	20.90	665.90	1.74	12.00
Gujarat	46.25	13.90	353.93	21.18	10.10	541.16	67.43	12.50
Haryana	14.57	9.20	414.76	7.99	11.30	504.49	22.56	9.90
Himachal Pradesh	4.10	7.20	394.28	0.17	2.60	504.49	4.27	6.70
Jammu & Kashmir	2.20	2.70	391.26	2.34	8.50	553.77	4.54	4.20
Jharkhand	89.76	40.20	366.56	10.63	16.30	451.24	100.39	34.80
Karnataka	43.33	12.00	324.17	53.28	27.20	599.66	96.60	17.40
Kerala	23.59	9.60	430.12	13.92	16.40	559.39	37.51	11.40
Madhya Pradesh	141.99	29.80	327.78	66.97	39.30	570.15	210.97	32.40
Maharashtra	128.43	22.20	362.25	131.40	29.00	665.90	259.83	25.20
Manipur	2.86	17.00	387.64	0.14	2.40	378.84	3.00	13.20
Meghalaya	3.32	17.00	387.64	0.12	2.40	378.84	3.43	14.10
Mizoram	0.78	17.00	387.64	0.11	2.40	378.84	0.89	9.50
Nagaland	2.94	17.00	387.64	0.09	2.40	378.84	3.03	14.50
Orissa	129.29	39.80	325.79	24.30	40.30	528.49	153.59	39.90
Punjab	9.78	5.90	410.38	3.52	3.80	466.16	13.30	5.20
Rajasthan	66.69	14.30	374.57	40.50	28.10	559.63	107.18	17.50
Sikkim	0.85	17.00	387.64	0.02	2.40	378.84	0.87	15.20
Tamil Nadu	56.51	16.90	351.86	58.59	18.80	547.42	115.10	17.80
Tripura	4.70	17.00	387.64	0.14	2.40	378.84	4.85	14.40
Uttar Pradesh	357.68	25.30	365.84	100.47	26.30	483.26	458.15	25.50
Uttarakhand	21.11	31.70	478.02	7.75	32.00	637.67	28.86	31.80
West Bengal	146.59	24.20	382.82	26.64	11.20	449.32	173.23	20.60
Andaman & Nicobar Islands	0.44	16.90	351.86	0.27	18.80	547.42	0.71	17.60
Chandigarh	0.04	3.80	410.38	0.36	3.80	466.16	0.40	3.80
Dadra & Nagar Haveli	0.62	36.00	362.25	0.16	19.20	665.90	0.77	30.60
Daman & Diu	0.03	1.90	362.25	0.14	20.80	665.90	0.16	8.00
Delhi	0.01	0.10	410.38	15.83	10.80	612.91	15.83	10.20
Lakshadweep	0.04	9.60	430.12	0.05	16.40	559.39	0.09	12.30
Puducherry	0.58	16.90	351.86	1.34	18.80	547.42	1.92	18.20
All India	**1702.99**	**21.80**	**356.30**	**682.00**	**21.70**	**538.60**	**2384.99**	**21.80**

$: MRP: Mixed Recall Period.

Also see Notes on Tables.

Source: Planning Commission, Government of India.

Table 41: Incidence of Poverty (per cent)

Sl. No.	Category	1993-94	2004-05
	By Uniform Recall Period (URP) Method		
1	Rural	37.3	28.3
2.	Urban	32.4	25.7
3.	All-India	36.0	27.5
	By Mixed Recall Period (MRP) Method		
		1999-2000	2004-05
4	Rural	27.1	21.8
5	Urban	23.6	21.7
6	All-India	26.1	21.8

Source: Planning Commission.

Table 42: Average Price of Gold and Silver in Domestic and Foreign Markets

Year	Gold				Silver			
	Mumbai	London		Spread in	Mumbai	New York		Spread in
	Rupees per 10 gms.	$ per troy oz.	Rupees per 10 gms.	Rupees (2-4)	Rupees per kg.	Cents per troy oz.	Rupees per kg.	Rupees (6-8)
1	2	3	4	5	6	7	8	9
1970-71	184.96	36.81	89.44	95.52	536.08	170.80	415.02	121.06
1971-72	200.16	43.01	103.33	96.83	561.35	151.30	363.51	197.84
1972-73	242.57	64.86	160.31	82.26	554.24	185.54	458.89	95.35
1973-74	369.33	115.77	291.17	78.16	799.01	320.08	809.59	-10.58
1974-75	519.19	166.37	424.73	94.46	1122.40	458.83	1170.86	-48.46
1975-76	545.21	149.49	415.79	129.42	1171.64	437.36	1220.06	-48.42
1976-77	549.82	126.64	369.59	180.22	1247.89	447.58	1291.78	-43.90
1977-78	637.93	157.56	433.83	204.09	1240.54	473.46	1305.77	-65.24
1978-79	791.22	208.29	550.12	241.10	1500.94	589.92	1559.13	-58.19
1979-80	1158.75	405.38	1052.88	105.87	2301.30	1748.88	4532.00	-2230.70
1980-81	1522.44	584.92	1484.67	37.76	2617.61	1585.14	4020.30	-1402.69
1981-82	1719.17	420.95	1209.94	509.23	2636.06	914.52	2617.36	18.70
1982-83	1722.54	401.43	1250.38	472.16	2798.34	906.49	2829.46	-31.11
1983-84	1858.47	404.15	1342.06	516.41	3505.80	1060.64	3516.66	-10.87
1984-85	1983.92	340.01	1293.78	690.13	3593.59	740.98	2810.19	783.40

(*Contd....*)

1	2	3	4	5	6	7	8	9
1985-86	2125.47	327.75	1289.76	835.71	3918.38	609.00	2396.35	1522.02
1986-87	2323.49	383.33	1577.02	746.46	4247.10	539.87	2220.03	2027.08
1987-88	3082.43	458.84	1912.54	1169.89	5538.83	721.49	3016.70	2522.12
1988-89	3175.22	422.01	1960.38	1214.84	6366.76	639.65	2971 .52	3395.24
1989-90	3229.33	384.79	2063.01	1166.32	6841.91	531.61	2846.31	3995.61
1990-91	3451.52	374.65	2164.26	1287.26	6760.79	449.86	2579.21	4181.58
1991-92	4297.63	357.40	2841.07	1456.55	7332.41	409.34	3269.89	4062.52
1992-93	4103.66	338.35	3332.95	770.71	7078.39	381.97	3749.87	3328.52
1993-94	4531.87	373.42	3766.28	765.58	6348.12	469.98	4741.09	1607.03
1994-95	4667.24	382.79	3864.15	803.09	6692.31	513.91	5187.33	1504.98
1995-96	4957.60	389.36	4188.58	769.03	7220.50	540.18	5811.03	1409.48
1996-97	5070.71	375.52	4283.94	786.77	7165.07	505.21	5762.65	1402.42
1997-98	4347.07	316.94	3775.92	571.15	7352.27	521.38	6153.96	1198.31
1998-99	4268.00	292 32	3952.00	316.00	7855.00	529.00	7144.00	712.00
1999-00	4393.56	279 65	3896.66	496.90	8066.94	523.16	7286.51	780.43
2000-01	4473.60	272.12	4007.79	465.81	7868.39	483.16	7110.18	758.20
2001-02	4579.12	277.74	4260.24	318.88	7447.19	437.47	6708.71	738.49
2002-03	5332.36	325.49	5062.11	270.25	7990.53	467.11	7268.46	722.07
2003-04	5718.95	377.65	5573.53	145.41	8721.90	541.35	7982.49	739.40
2004-05	6145.38	413.95	5976.14	169.24	10680.82	676.64	9766.58	914.24
2005-06	6900.56	476.58	6790.26	110.30	11828.81	801.23	11417.37	411.45
2006-07	9240.32	628.41	9137.79	102.53	19056.57	1248.02	18133.96	922.61
2007-08	9995.62	765.78	9897.12	98.50	19427.45	1447.36	18661.40	766.05

Notes: 1. The data source for this table for the period 1970-71 to 2000-01 are Bombay Bullion Association and Press Trust of India. For the period 2001-02 onwards, the data sources are (i) Economic Times, Mumbai for gold price in Mumbai and London and silver price in Mumbai and (ii) Thomson datastream for silver price in New York.

2. Data provided in this Table for the period 1970-71 to 2000-01 and 2001-02 to 2006-07 may not be strictly comparable due to different sources of information.

Sources: 1. Bombay Bullion Association Ltd.

2. Economic Times, Mumbai.

3. Press Trust of India.

4. Thomson Financial Ltd.

Table 43 (A): Foreign Exchange Reserves

(Rs. crore)

End of	Reserves							Transactions with IMF		
	Gold		RTP Rs. crore	SDRs		Foreign Currency Assets Rs. crore	Total Rs. crore (3+4+6+7)	Drawals	Repur-chases[g]	Outstanding Repurchase Obligations
	Tonnes	Rs. crore		Million	Rs. crore					
1	2	3	4	5	6	7	8	9	10	11
1950-51	220	118	...	...	...	911	1029	...	...	48
1951-52	220	118	...	...	...	747	865	...	...	48
1952-53	220	118	...	...	...	763	881	...	...	48
1953-54	220	118	...	...	...	792	910	...	17	30
1954-55	220	118	...	...	...	774	892	...	17	13
1955-56	220	118	...	...	...	785	903	...	7	6
1956-57	220	118	...	...	...	563	681	61	6	61
1957-58	220	118	...	...	...	303	421	35	...	95
1958-59	220	118	...	...	...	261	379	...	...	95
1959-60	220	118	...	...	...	245	363	...	24	71
1960-61	220	118	...	...	...	186	304	...	11	61
1961-62	220	118	...	...	...	180	298	119	61	119
1962-63	220	118	...	...	...	177	295	12	...	131
1963-64	220	118	...	...	...	188	306	...	24	107
1964-65	250	134	...	...	...	116	250	48	48	107
1965-66	216	116	...	...	...	182	298	65	36	137
1966-67	216	183	...	...	...	296	479	89	43	313
1967-68	216	183	...	...	...	356	539	68	43	338
1968-69	216	183	...	...	...	391	574	...	59	279
1969-70	217	183	...	123	92	546	821	...	125	154
1970-71	216	183	...	149	112	438	733	...	154	...
1971-72	216	183	...	248	194	480	857	...	...	...
1972-73	216	183	...	247	226	479	888	...	...	...
1973-74	216	183	...	245	230	581	994	62	...	59
1974-75	216	183	...	235	229	611	1023	485	...	557
1975-76	216	183	...	203	211	1492	1886	207	...	804
1976-77	223	188	...	187	192	2863	3243	...	303	492
1977-78	229	193	...	162	170	4500	4863	...	249	210
1978-79	260	220	...	365	381	5220	5821	...	207	...
1979-80	266	225	...	529	545	5164	5934	...	55 [e]	...
1980-81	267	226	...	491	497	4822	5545	274 [a]	5 [f]	268
1981-82	267	226	...	425	444	3355	4025	637 [b]	...	901
1982-83	267	226	...	270	291	4265	4782	1893 [b]	...	2867
1983-84	267	226	...	216	248	5498	5972	1414 [b]	72 [h]	4444
1984-85	291	246	...	147	181	6817	7244	219 [b]	156 [i]	4888
1985-86	325	274	...	115	161	7384	7819	...	253 [j]	5285
1986-87	325	274	...	139	232	7645	8151	...	672 [k]	5548
1987-88	325	274	...	70	125	7287	7686	...	1209 [l]	4732
1988-89	325	274	...	80	161	6605	7040	...	1547 [m]	3696
1989-90	333	281	...	82	184	5787	6252	3334 [c]	1460 [n]	2572
1990-91	333	6828	...	76	200	4388	11416	3205 [d]	1156 [o]	5132
1991-92	351	9039	...	66	233	14578	23850	4231	1127 [p]	8934
1992-93	354	10549	...	13	55	20140	30744	1007	868 [q]	14986
1993-94	367	12794	...	77	339	47287	60420	...	420 [r]	15812
1994-95	396	13752	...	5	23	66006	79781	...	3585 [s]	13545
1995-96	398	15658	...	56	280	58446	74384	...	5749 [t]	8152
1996-97	398	14557	...	1	7	80368	94932	...	3461 [u]	4714
1997-98	396	13394	...	1	4	102507	115905	...	2286 [v]	2624
1998-99	357	12559	...	6	34	125412	138005	...	1652 [w]	1220
1999-00	358	12973	...	3	16	152924	165913	...	...	...

(Contd...)

1	2	3	4	5	6	7	8	9	10	11
2000-01	358	12711	...	2	11	184482	197204	...	...	...
2001-02	358	14868	...	8	50	249118	264036	...	...	...
2002-03	358	16785	3190	3	19	341476	361470	...	...	...
2003-04	358	18216	5688	2	10	466215	490129	...	...	...
2004-05	358	19686	6289	3	20	593121	619116	...	...	...
2005-06	358	25674	3374	2	12	647327	676387	...	...	...
2006-07	358	29573	2044	1	8	836597	868222	...	...	...
2007-08	358	40124	1744	11	74	1196023	1237965	...	...	...
2008-09	358	48793	5000	1	6	1230066	1283865	...	...	...
2009-10										
April	358	46357	4938	1	6	1212747	1264048	...	...	...
May	358	45417	5886	...	2	1189136	1240441	...	...	...
June	358	46914	5974	...	2	1216345	1269235	...	...	...
July	358	46576	6444	...	3	1255197	1308220	...	...	...
Aug.	358	48041	6595	3083	23597	1276976	1355209	...	...	...
Sept.	358	49556	6557	3297	25096	1270049	1351258	...	...	...
Oct.	358	50718	7426	3297	24618	1252740	1335502			
Nov.	558	84508	6806	3297	24676	1223313	1339303			
Dec.	558	85387	6655	3297	24128	1207065	1323235			

SDRs: Special Drawing Rights, RTP : Reserve Tranche Position in IMF, ... : Negligible

[a] Excludes Rs. 544.53 crore drawn under Trust Fund. [b] Drawals under Extended Fund Facility (EFF). [c] Drawals of Rs.1883.6 crore under Compensatory and Contingency Financing Facility and Rs.1450.2 crore under First Credit Tranche of Stand-by Arrangement. [d] Drawals of Rs 2217.2 crore under Compensatory and Contingency Financing Facility and Rs 987.5 crore under First Credit Tranche of Stand-by Arrangement. [e] Includes voluntary repurchases of Rupees (Rs.199 crore) and sales of Rupees (Rs.35.2 crore) by the IMF under its General Resources Account. [f] Sales of Rupees by the IMF. [g] Additionally, SDR 59.9 million in May 1979, SDR 7.3 million in July 1980 and SDR 34.5 million in March 1982 were used for voluntary repurchases of Rupees. [h] SDR 66.50 million were used for repurchases of drawals under Compensatory Financing Facility. [i] SDR 33.25 million and Rs. 117.85 crore in foreign currencies were used for repurchases of drawals under CFF. [j] SDR 66.5 million and SDRs 131.25 million were used for repurchases of drawals under CFF and EFF, respectively. [k] SDR 431.25 million were used for repurchases of drawals under EFF. [l] SDR 704.17 million were used for repurchases of drawals under EFF. [m] SDR 804.18 million were used for repurchases of drawals under EFF. [n] SDR 681.25 million were used for repurchases of drawals under EFF. [o] SDR 468.75 million were used for repurchases of drawals under EFF [p] SDR 337.49 million were used for repurchases of drawals under EFF. [q] SDR 237.49 million were used for repurchases of drawals under EFF. [r] SDR 95.84 million were used for repurchases of drawals under EFF. [s] SDR 812.77 million were used for repurchases of drawals under EFF. [t] SDR 1130.48 million were used for repurchases of drawals under EFF. [u] SDR 678.38 million were used for repurchases of drawals under EFF. [v] SDR 449.29 million were used for repurchases of drawals under EFF. [w] SDR 212.46 million were used for repurchases of drawals under EFF.

Notes: (1) Figures after 1965-66 are not comparable with those of the earlier years owing to devaluation of the Rupee in June 1966. (2) Also figures for July 1991 onwards are not comparable with those of earlier periods due to the downward adjustment of the Rupee effected on July 1,1991 and July 3, 1991. (3) Drawals, Repurchase and outstanding repurchase obligations are calculated at the ruling rates of exchange. (4) Gold is valued at Rs. 53.58 per 10 grams up to May 1966 and at Rs. 84.39 per 10 grams up to September 1990 and closer to international market price w.e.f. October 17,1990. (5) Foreign exchange includes (a) foreign assets of the Reserve Bank of India and (b) Government balances held abroad upto 1955-56. (6) While reserves pertain to end period, repurchases are for the relevant periods. (7) FCA excludes US$ 250.00 million (as also its equivalent value in Indian Rupees) invested in foreign currency denominated bonds issued by IIFC (UK) since March 20, 2009. (8) Includes Rs. 31463 Crore (US$ 6699 million) reflecting the purchase of 200 metric tonnes of gold from IMF on November 3, 2009. (9) Includes SDRs 3082.5 million allocated under general allocation and SDRs 214.6 million allocated under special allocation by the IMF done on August 28, 2009 and September 9, 2009 respectively. (10) Totals may not tally due to rounding off.

Source: Reserve Bank of India.

Table 43 (B): Foreign Exchange Reserves

(US $ million)

End of	Reserves					Transactions with IMF		
	Gold	RTP	SDRs	Foreign Currency Assets	Total (2+3+4+5)	Drawals	Repurchases[g]	Outstanding repurchase obligations
1	2	3	4	5	6	7	8	9
1950-51	247	...	...	1914	2161	...	..	100
1951-52	247	..	..	1568	1815	...	..	100
1952-53	247	..	..	1603	1850	...	..	100
1953-54	247	..	..	1664	1911	...	36	64
1954-55	247	..	..	1626	1873	...	36	28
1955-56	247	..	..	1648	1895	...	15	13
1956-57	247	..	..	1184	1431	126	12	128
1957-58	247	..	..	637	884	72	...	200
1958-59	247	..	..	548	795	...	...	200
1959-60	247	..	..	515	762	...	50	150
1960-61	247	..	..	390	637	...	23	128
1961-62	247	..	..	377	624	249	127	250
1962-63	247	..	..	372	619	25	...	275
1963-64	247	..	..	395	642	...	50	225
1964-65	281	..	..	243	524	99	100	225
1965-66	243	..	..	383	626	137	75	288
1966-67	243	..	..	395	638	126	57	418
1967-68	243	..	..	475	718	89	58	450
1968-69	243	..	..	526	769	...	78	372
1969-70	243	...	123	728	1094	...	167	205
1970-71	243	...	148	584	975	...	205	...
1971-72	264	...	269	661	1194	...	...	...
1972-73	293	...	297	629	1219	...	...	...
1973-74	293	...	296	736	1325	79	...	75
1974-75	304	...	293	782	1379	608	...	715
1975-76	281	...	234	1657	2172	239	...	896
1976-77	290	...	217	3240	3747	...	336	559
1977-78	319	...	200	5305	5824	...	333	249
1978-79	377	...	470	6421	7268	...	256	...
1979-80	375	...	662	6324	7361	...	145	...
1980-81	370	...	603	5850	6823	342	16	327
1981-82	335	...	473	3582	4390	692	40	964
1982-83	324	...	291	4281	4896	1968	...	2876
1983-84	320	...	230	5099	5649	1376	70	4150
1984-85	325	...	145	5482	5952	201	134	3932
1985-86	417	...	131	5972	6520	...	209	4290
1986-87	471	...	179	5924	6574	...	521	4291
1987-88	508	...	97	5618	6223	...	930	3653
1988-89	473	...	103	4226	4802	...	1070	2365
1989-90	487	...	107	3368	3962	...	873	1493
1990-91	3496	...	102	2236	5834	1858	644	2623
1991-92	3499	...	90	5631	9220	1240	460	3451
1992-93	3380	...	18	6434	9832	1623	335	4799
1993-94	...	...	...	...	19254	...	...	...
1994-95	4370	...	7	20809	25186	...	1146	4300

(Contd...)

1	2	3	4	5	6	7	8	9
1995-96	4561		82	17044	21687		1710	2374
1996-97	4054	...	2	22367	26423	...	977	1313
1997-98	3391	...	1	25975	29367	...	615	664
1998-99	2960	...	8	29522	32490	...	102	287
1999-00	2974	...	4	35058	38036	...	...	...
2000-01	2725	...	2	39554	42281	...	...	...
2001-02	3047	...	10	51049	54106	...	26	...
2002-03	3534	672	4	71890	76100	...	..	..
2003-04	4198	1311	2	107448	112959	...	..	..
2004-05	4500	1433	5	135571	141514	...	..	..
2005-06	5755	756	3	145108	151622	...	..	..
2006-07	6784	469	2	191924	199179	...	..	..
2007-08	10039	436	18	299230	309723	...	..	..
2008-09	9577	981	1	241426	251985	...	..	..
2009-10								
April	9231	983	1	241487	251702	...	..	..
May	9604	1245	1	251456	262306	...	..	..
June	9800	1243	1	254093	265142	...	..	..
July	9671	1333	1	260631	271641	...	..	..
Aug.	9828	1349	4828	261247	277252	...	..	..
Sept.	10316	1365	5224	264373	281278	...	..	..
Oct.	10800	1581	5242	266768	284391	...	..	..
Nov.	18182	1464	5309	263191	288146	...	..	..
Dec.	18292	1423	5169	258583	283469	...	..	..

Notes: 1. For compiling figures in US dollars, gold is valued at SDR 35 per troy ounce as in the International Financial Statistics of the IMF upto October 16, 1990. Thereafter gold has been valued close to international market price.

2. Conversion of foreign currency assets and SDR in US dollars is done at exchange rates supplied by the IMF.

3. Transactions with IMF are converted at respective SDR/$ rate.

4. While reserves pertain to end period, repurchases are for the relevant periods.

5. FCA excludes US$ 250.00 million (as also its equivalent value in Indian Rupees) invested in foreign currency denominated bonds issued by IIFC (UK) since March 20, 2009.

6. Includes Rs. 31463 crore (US$ 6699 million) reflecting the purchase of 200 metric tonnes of gold from IMF on November 3, 2009.

7. Includes SDRs 3082.5 million allocated under general allocation and SDRs 214.6 million allocated under special allocation by the IMF done on August 28, 2009 and September 9, 2009 respectively.

8. Totals may not tally due to rounding off.

Source: Reserve Bank of India.

Table 44: Sources of Accretion to Foreign Exchange Reserves (US$ billion)

Sl. No.	Items	April-December 2006-07	2007-08	2007-08	2008-09
I	Current account balance	-9.6	-17.0	-15.5	-36.5
II	Capital account (net) (A to F)	46.2	109.2	82.7	16.1
	A External assistance	1.8	2.1	1.3	1.9
	B External commercial borrowing	16.1	22.6	17.4	7.1
	C Foreign investment	14.8	44.9	40.2	4
	D Short-term credit	6.6	17.2	10.7	0.5
	E Banking capital	1.9	11.8	5.9	-0.1
	Of which: NRI deposits	*4.3*	*0.2*	*-0.9*	*2.1*
	F Other items in capital account	4.2	9.5	7.1	2.7
III	Valuation change	10.9	18.4	8.9	-33.4
	Total (I+II+III)	47.5	110.6	76.1	-53.8

Source: Reserve Bank of India.

Table 45: Balance of Payments

Item	1990-91 Rs. Crore	1990-91 U.S. $ Million	2000-01 Rs. Crore	2000-01 U.S. $ Million	2004-05 Rs. Crore	2004-05 U.S. $ Million	2005-06 Rs. Crore	2005-06 U.S. $ Million
1	2	3	4	5	6	7	8	9
1. Imports (c.i.f.)	50086	27915	264589	57912	533550	118908	695412	157056
2. Exports (f.o.b.)	33153	18477	207852	45452	381785	85206	465748	105152
3. Trade balance (2-1)	-16934	-9438	-56737	-12460	-151765	-33702	-229664	-51904
4. Invisibles								
(a) Receipts	13396	7464	147778	32267	311550	69533	397660	89687
(b) Payments	13829	7706	102639	22473	171959	38301	211733	47685
(of which: Interest & Service payments on loans and credits)	(4958)	(2763)	(21948)	(4801)	(17087)	(3803)	(24293)	(5487)
(c) Net	-433	-242	45139	9794	139591	31232	185927	42002
5. Current account (net)	-17366	-9680	-11598	-2666	-12174	-2470	-43737	-9902
6. Capital Account								
I. Foreign Investment	183	103	26744	5862	58057	13000	68782	15528
(a) Inflow	202	113	80824	17720	210205	46934	342778	77298
(b) Out flow	19	10	54080	11858	152148	33934	273996	61770
(c) Net	183	103	26744	5862	58057	13000	68782	15528
II. Loans[a]	9929	5533	24459	5264	48595	10909	34397	7909
(i) External Assistance								
(a) Inflow	6095	3397	13521	2941	16988	3809	16133	3631
(b) Out flow	2140	1193	11519	2531	8463	1886	8541	1929
(c) Net	3955	2204	2002	410	8525	1923	7592	1702
(ii) Commercial Borrowings[b]								
(a) Inflow	10829	6035	95750	20865	118697	26478	158596	35848
(b) Out flow	4855	2706	73293	16011	78627	17492	131791	29641
(c) Net	5974	3329	22457	4854	40070	8986	26805	6207

(Contd...)

Item	1990-91		2000-01		2004-05		2005-06	
	Rs. Crore	U.S. $ Million	Rs. Crore	U.S. $ Million	Rs. Crore	U.S. $ Million	Rs. Crore	U.S. $ Million
1	2	3	4	5	6	7	8	9
III. Banking								
(a) Receipts	18133	10106	44448	9744	65278	14581	95988	21658
(b) Payments	16908	9424	53592	11705	48238	10707	90193	20285
(c) Net	1225	682	-9144	-1961	17040	3874	5795	1373
IV. Rupee Debt Service	-2140	-1193	-2760	-617	-1858	-417	-2557	-572
V. Other Capital								
(a) Receipts	5593	3117	12948	2856	30507	6737	26451	5941
(b) Payments	2129	1186	11637	2564	26974	6081	20903	4709
(c) Net	3464	1931	1311	292	3533	656	5548	1232
VI. Errors & omissions	234	132	-1369	-305	2714	607	-2332	-516
7. Total Capital (I to VI of 6)	12895	7188	39241	8535	128081	28629	109633	24954
8. Overall Balance (5 + 7)	-4471	-2492	27643	5868	115907	26159	65896	15052
9. Monetary Movement								
(a) IMF Transactions								
(i) Purchases	3334	1858						
(ii) Repurchases	1156	644	115	26				
(iii) Net	2178	1214	-115	-26				
(b) Increase (-)/decrease (+) in Reserves	2293	1278	-27528	-5868	-115907	-26159	-65896	-15052
10. Total Reserve movement (9a(iii)+9b) [(-)Increase/ (+) decrease]	4471	2492	-27643	-5842	-115907	-26159	-65896	-15052

Item	2006-07		2007-08		2008-09[PR]		2009-10 (Apr.-Sep.)[P]	
	Rs. Crore	U.S. $ Million	Rs. Crore	U.S. $ Million	Rs. Crore	U.S. $ Million	Rs. Crore	U.S. $ Million
1	10	11	12	13	14	15	16	17
1. Imports (c.i.f.)	862833	190670	1035672	257629	1401118	307651	677133	139356
2. Exports (f.o.b.)	582871	128888	668008	166162	857960	189001	394295	81139
3. Trade balance (2-1)	-279962	-61782	-367664	-91467	-543158	-118650	-282838	-58217
4. Invisibles								
(a) Receipts	517146	114558	598088	148875	750333	163534	366268	75368
(b) Payments	281567	62341	293902	73144	338789	73612	173798	35770
(of) which: Interest & Service payments on loans and credits)	(24742)	(5468)	(24742)	(5468)	(26600)	(6607)	(22237)	(4971)
(c) Net	235579	52217	304185	75731	411544	89923	192470	39599
5. Current account (net)	-44383	-9565	-63479	-15737	-131614	-28728	-90368	-18618
6. Capital Account[a]								
I. Foreign Investment[b]	66791	14753	174395	43326	11786	3467	155929	32088
(a) Inflow	600951	133210	1086530	271122	743513	164915	506539	104248
(b) Out flow	534160	118457	912135	227796	731726	161448	350610	72160
(c) Net	66791	14753	174395	43326	11786	3467	155929	32088

(Contd...)

1	10	11	12	13	14	15	16	17
II. Loans[a]	110434	24490	163491	40653	36388	8669	3311	698
(i) External Assistance								
(a) Inflow	16978	3767	17019	4241	23532	5041	9992	2057
(b) Out flow	9005	1992	8553	2126	11102	2405	7223	1486
(c) Net	7973	1775	8466	2114	12430	2637	2769	571
(ii) Commercial Borrowings[b]								
(a) Inflow	229547	50875	313312	77951	261395	57085	130501	26860
(b) Out flow	127086	28160	158287	39413	237436	51053	129958	26734
(c) Net	102461	22715	155025	38538	23959	6032	543	126
III. Banking								
(a) Receipts	167494	37209	223979	55814	295408	65207	156098	32121
(b) Payments	159017	35296	176824	44055	314613	68453	151104	31063
(c) Net	8477	1913	47155	11759	-19205	-3245	4994	1057
IV. Rupee Debt Service	-725	-162	-492	-122	-472	-100	-114	-23
V. Other Capital								
(a) Receipts	36797	8230	117094	29229	93704	20179	48654	10047
(b) Payments	18101	4021	73716	18261	93712	21723	69392	14298
(c) Net	18696	4209	43377	10968	-8	-1545	-20738	-4251
VI. Errors & omissions	4344	968	5241	1316	6009	1402	-6854	-1417
7. Total Capital (I to VI of 6)	208017	46171	433167	107901	34499	8648	136528	28151
8. Overall Balance (5 + 7)	163634	36606	369689	92164	-97115	-20080	46161	9533
9. Monetary Movement								
(a) IMF Transactions								
(i) Purchases	...	...	...	...	...	...	...	...
(ii) Repurchases	...	...	...	...	...	...	...	...
(iii) Net	...	...	...	...	...	...	...	...
(b) Increase (-)/decrease (+) in Reserves	-163634	-36606	-369689	-92164	97115	20080	-46161	-9533
10. Total Reserve movement (9a(iii)+9b) [(-) Increase/ (+) decrease]	-163634	-36606	-369689	-92164	97115	20080	-46161	-9533

PR Partially Revised. P Preliminary

a: Amounts are net of foreign investments and loan operation by Indian abroad.

b: Commercial borrowings include short-term credit.

Notes: 1. The rupee equivalent of all foreign currency transactions has been arrived at by applying the par/central rates upto June 1972 and thereafter on the basis of the average of RBI's spot buying and selling rate for sterling and the monthly averages of cross-rates based on London market for non-sterling currencies. Effective March 1993, conversion is made by crossing average spot buying and selling rate for US Dollar in the forex market and the monthly averages of cross rates of non-dollar currencies based on London market. 2. Grants received are covered under item 4(a). 3. Estimated interest accrued and credited to NRI deposits during the year has been treated as notional outflow under invisible payments and added as reinvestment in NRI deposits under banking capital. 4. Balance of payments data from the year 1990-91 are presented in a format in which in the year of imports, the value of defence-related imports are recorded under imports with credits financing such imports shown in the capital account. Interest payments on defence debt owed to the General Currency Area (GCA) (as and when they are made) are recorded under investment income payments in the invisible account and principal repayments under commercial borrowings (as outflows) in the capital account. In the case of the Rupee Payment Area (RPA), interest payment on and principal repayment of debt is clubbed together and shown separately under the item 'Rupee Debt Service' in the capital account. This is in line with the recommendation of the High Level Committee on Balance of Payments (Chairman : Dr. C. Rangarajan). 5. In accordance with the recommendations of Report of the Technical Group on Reconciling of Balance of Payments and DGCI&S Data on Merchandise data on gold brought out by the Indians returning from abroad have been included under Import payments with contra entry under Private Transfer Receipts. Data has, therefore, been revised from 1992-93 i.e. since the inception of the scheme. 6. In accordance with the provision of IMF's Balance of Payments Manual (5th Edition), gold purchased from the Government of India by the RBI has been excluded from the BOP statistics. Data for the earlier years has, therefore, been amended by making suitable adjustments in "Other Capital-Receipts and Foreign Exchange Reserves". 7. With effect from 1996-97, private transfer receipts include redemption in rupees of both principal and interest under Non-Resident External (Rupee) Account [NRE(R)A] and Non-Resident Non-Repatriable Rupee Deposit [NR(NR)RD] schemes. This marks an improvement in data reporting. 8. The presentation of balance of payments statistics in the above table differs from the adjusted balance of payments statistics published in the previous issues of the Economic Survey. 9. Totals may not tally due to rounding off.

Source: Reserve Bank of India.

Table 46: India's Overall Balance of Payments—Rupees

(Rupees crore)

Item/Year	1990-91			1991-92			1992-93		
	Credit	Debit	Net	Credit	Debit	Net	Credit	Debit	Net
1	2	3	4	5	6	7	8	9	10
A. Current Account									
1. Merchandise	33153	50086	16933	44023	51417	-6494	54701	72000	-17239
2. Invisibles (a+b+c)	13396	13829	-433	23449	19190	4259	27042	22567	4475
a) Services	8169	6408	1761	12347	9214	3133	13721	11023	2698
i) Travel	2613	703	1910	4892	1112	3780	6061	1177	4884
ii) Transportation	1765	1961	-196	2308	3190	-882	2851	4548	-1697
iii) Insurance	199	159	40	265	307	-42	460	450	10
iv) G.n.i.e.	27	310	-283	42	292	-250	220	306	-86
v) Miscellaneous	3565	3275	290	4840	4313	527	4129	4542	-413
b) Transfers	4567	28	4539	10560	38	10522	12317	37	12280
i) Official	830	3	827	1141	1	1140	1056	2	1054
ii) Private	3737	25	3712	9419	37	9382	11261	35	11226
c) Income	660	7393	-6733	542	9938	-9396	1004	11507	-10503
Total Current Account (1+2)	46549	63915	-17366	68372	70607	-2235	81803	94567	-12764
B. Capital Account									
1. Foreign Investment (a+b)	202	19	183	385	46	339	1797	98	1699
a) In India	202	19	183	385	46	339	1797	98	1699
i) Direct	191	19	172	375	46	329	1051	92	959
ii) Portfolio	0	0	0	10	0	10	746	6	740
iii) Others	11	0	11	0	0	0	0	0	0
b) Abroad	0	0	0	0	0	0	0	0	0

(Contd...)

Item/Year	1990-91			1991-92			1992-93		
	Credit	Debit	Net	Credit	Debit	Net	Credit	Debit	Net
1	2	3	4	5	6	7	8	9	10
2. Loans (a+b+c)	16924	6995	9929	23220	13293	9927	26640	25195	1445
a) External assistance	6095	2140	3955	10715	3334	7381	10172	4435	5737
i) By India	0	11	-11	0	14	-14	0	11	-11
ii) To India	6095	2129	3966	10715	3320	7395	10172	4424	5748
b) Commercial borrowings (MT & LT)	7684	3639	4045	7896	4074	3822	3621	4740	-1119
i) By India	54	44	10	45	29	16	38	62	-24
ii) To India	7630	3595	4035	7851	4045	3806	3583	4678	-1095
c) Short-term to India	3145	1216	1929	4609	5885	-1276	12847	16020	-3173
3. Banking Capital (a+b)	18133	16908	1225	26771	25422	1349	34257	22099	12158
a) Commercial banks	14282	12659	1623	22451	21849	602	29684	20727	8957
i) Assets	763	1415	-652	3397	2838	559	3783	485	3298
ii) Liabilities	13519	11244	2275	19054	19011	43	25901	20242	5659
of which Non-resident deposits	13184	10427	2757	18972	17965	1007	25191	19094	6097
b) Others	3851	4249	-398	4320	3573	747	4573	1372	3201
4. Rupee Debt Service	0	2140	-2140	0	2785	-2785	0	2335	-2335
5. Other Capital	5593	2129	3464	6923	5944	979	3351	4191	-840
Total Capital Account (1 to 5)	40852	28191	12661	57299	47490	9809	66045	53918	12127
C. Errors & Omissions	234	0	234	0	300	-300	0	244	-244
D. Overall Balance (A+B+C)	87635	92106	-4471	125671	118397	7274	147848	148729	-881
E. Monetary Movements (i+ii)	5627	1156	4471	3205	10479	-7274	4231	3350	881
i) I.M.F.	3334	1156	2178	3205	1128	2077	4231	869	3362
ii) Foreign exchange reserves (Increase - / Decrease +)	2293	0	2293	0	9351	-9351	0	2481	-2481

(Contd...)

Item/Year	1993-94			1994-95			1995-96			1996-97		
	Credit	Debit	Net	Credit	Debit	Net	Credit	Debit	Net	Credit	Debit	Net
1	11	12	13	14	15	16	17	18	19	20	21	22
A. Current Account												
1. Merchandise	71147	83870	-12723	84329	112748	-28419	108482	146543	-38061	121193	173754	-52561
2. Invisibles (a+b+c)	35501	26412	9089	48839	31003	17836	59443	41028	18415	76093	39814	36279
a) Services	16510	14833	1677	19260	17377	1883	24748	25450	-702	26565	23944	2621
i) Travel	6971	1559	5412	7424	2570	4854	9150	3909	5241	10232	3049	7183
ii) Tranoportation	4404	5537	-1043	5320	5852	-524	6764	7280	-516	6942	8497	-1555
iii) Insurance	388	611	-223	476	567	-91	600	478	122	771	543	228
iv) G.n.i.e.	94	481	-387	28	519	-491	44	724	-680	257	636	-379
v) Miscellaneous	4563	6645	-2082	6004	7869	-1865	8190	13059	-4869	8363	11219	-2856
b) Transfers	17753	83	17670	26797	71	26726	29963	130	29833	45716	291	45425
i) Official	1171	15	1156	1323	14	1309	1194	21	1173	1507	51	1456
ii) Private	16582	68	16514	25474	57	25417	28769	109	28660	44209	240	43969
c) Income	1238	11496	-10258	2782	13555	-10773	4732	15448	-10716	3812	15579	-11767
Total Current Account (1+2)	106648	110282	-3634	133168	143751	-10583	167925	187571	-19646	197286	213568	-16282
B. Capital Account												
1. Foreign Investment (a+b)	14461	1180	13281	18087	2999	15088	19082	3420	15662	27784	6622	21162
a) In India	14461	1179	13282	18059	2609	15450	19034	2722	16312	27751	5923	21828
i) Direct	2041	204	1837	4241	25	4216	7317	101	7216	10170	77	10093
ii) Portfolio	12420	975	11445	13818	2584	11234	11717	2621	9096	17581	5846	11735
b) Abroad	0	1	-1	28	390	-362	48	698	-650	33	699	-666

(Contd...)

Item/Year	1993-94			1994-95			1995-96			1996-97		
	Credit	Debit	Net	Credit	Debit	Net	Credit	Debit	Net	Credit	Debit	Net
1	11	12	13	14	15	16	17	18	19	20	21	22
2. Loans (a+b+c)	31276	25592	5684	34330	24787	9543	38397	30421	7976	62990	46010	16980
a) External assistance	10903	4955	5948	10031	5257	4774	10102	6799	3303	10893	6924	3969
i) By India	0	15	-15	5	30	-25	0	54	-54	0	28	-28
ii) To India	10903	4940	5963	10026	5227	4799	10102	6745	3357	10893	6896	3997
b) Commercial borrowings (MT & LT)	9458	7309	2149	13347	9813	3534	14472	9892	4580	26896	16864	10032
i) By India	321	76	245	306	11	295	31	0	31	29	0	29
ii) To India	9137	7233	1904	13041	9802	3239	14441	9892	4549	26867	16864	10003
c) Short-term to India	10915	13328	-2413	10952	9717	1235	13823	13730	93	25201	22222	2979
3. Banking Capital (a+b)	36072	28974	7098	22034	23092	-1058	21692	19246	2446	28395	20504	7891
a) Commercial banks	33290	28094	5196	20244	22215	-1971	20787	17703	3084	27053	19146	7907
i) Assets	864	3514	-2650	756	3779	-3023	2845	4320	-1475	2651	5738	-3087
ii) Liabilities	32426	24580	7846	19488	18436	1052	17942	13383	4559	24402	13408	10994
of which:												
Non-resident deposits	27760	23980	3780	18225	17686	539	16671	12849	3822	24039	12145	11894
b) Others	2782	880	1902	1790	877	913	905	1543	-638	1342	1358	-16
4. Rupee Debt Service	0	3302	-3302	0	3090	-3090	0	3105	-3105	0	2542	-2542
5. Other Capital	9014	3872	5142	6912	701	6211	2474	11141	-8667	9390	10267	-877
Total Capital Account (1 to 5)	90823	62920	27903	81363	54669	26694	81645	67333	14312	128559	85945	42614
C. Errors & Omissions	2512	0	2512	2049	0	2049	1284	0	1284	0	2112	-2112
D. Overall Balance (A+B+C)	199983	173202	26781	216580	198420	18160	250854	254904	-4050	325845	301625	24220
E. Monetary Movements (i+ii)	1007	27788	-26781	0	18160	-18160	9799	5749	4050	0	24220	-24220
i) I.M.F.	1007	420	587	0	3585	-3585	0	5749	-5749	0	3460	-3460
ii) Foreign exchange reserves (Increase - / Decrease +)	0	27368	-27368	0	14575	-14575	9799	0	9799	0	20760	-20760

(*Contd...*)

Item/Year	1997-98			1998-99			1999-2000		
	Credit	Debit	Net	Credit	Debit	Net	Credit	Debit	Net
1	23	24	25	26	27	28	29	30	31
A. Current Account									
1. Merchandise	132703	190508	-57805	144436	199914	-55478	162753	240112	-77359
2. Invisibles (a+b+c)	86245	49323	36922	108459	69770	38689	131449	74421	57028
a) Services	35102	30159	4943	55527	46413	9114	68137	50467	17670
i) Travel	10880	5339	5541	12603	7326	5277	13166	9268	3898
ii) Transportation	6805	9353	-2548	8109	11266	-3157	7400	10450	-3050
iii) Insurance	890	680	210	945	472	473	1004	525	479
iv) G.n.i.e.	1038	594	444	2520	1360	1160	2523	1167	1356
v) Miscellaneous	15489	14193	1296	31350	25989	5361	44044	29057	14987
b) Transfers	45348	165	45183	44799	257	44542	54939	150	54789
i) Official	1418	0	1418	1305	5	1300	1659	2	1657
ii) Private	43930	165	43765	43494	252	43242	53280	148	53132
c) Income	5795	18999	-13204	8133	23100	-14967	8373	23804	-15431
i) Investment income	5795	18764	-12969	7953	23032	-15079	7727	23747	-16020
ii) Compensation of employees	0	235	-235	180	68	112	646	57	589
Total Current Account (1+2)	218948	239831	-20883	252895	269684	-16789	294202	314533	-20331
B. Capital Account									
1. Foreign Investment (a+b)	34444	14612	19832	24825	15088	9737	53125	30941	22184
a) In India	34075	14114	19961	24210	14041	10169	52607	30106	22501
i) Direct	13317	124	13193	10550	162	10388	9409	13	9396
ii) Portfolio	20758	13990	6768	13660	13879	-219	43198	30093	13105
b) Abroad	369	498	-129	615	1047	-432	518	835	-317

(*Contd...*)

Item/Year	1997-98			1998-99			1999-2000		
	Credit	Debit	Net	Credit	Debit	Net	Credit	Debit	Net
1	23	24	25	26	27	28	29	30	31
2. Loans (a+b+c)	64144	46687	17457	61872	43008	18864	56646	49695	6951
a) External assistance	10827	7441	3386	11508	8107	3401	13342	9471	3871
i) By India	0	77	-77	2	85	-83	3	47	-44
ii) To India	10827	7364	3463	11506	8022	3484	13339	9424	3915
b) Commercial borrowings (MT & LT)	27254	12653	14601	30646	12067	18579	13910	12463	1447
i) By India	43	0	43	22	0	22	87	0	87
ii) To India	27211	12653	14558	30624	12067	18557	13823	12463	1360
c) Short-term to India	26063	26593	-530	19718	22834	-3116	29394	27761	1633
3. Banking Capital (a+b)	33056	36243	-3187	37524	34396	3128	46212	36995	9217
a) Commercial banks	30328	34838	-4510	31506	33194	-1688	44496	34486	10010
i) Assets	2093	10214	-8121	5713	11421	-5708	11486	8079	3407
ii) Liabilities	28235	24624	3611	25793	21773	4020	33010	26407	6603
of which:									
Non-resident deposits	28041	23716	4325	25266	21207	4059	32133	25424	6709
b) Others	2728	1405	1323	6018	1202	4816	1716	2509	-793
4. Rupee Debt Service	0	2784	-2784	0	3308	-3308	0	3059	-3059
5. Other Capital	14458	9171	5287	19339	11879	7460	19839	9804	10035
Total Capital Account (1 to 5)	146102	109497	36605	143560	107679	35881	175822	130494	45328
C. Errors & Omissions	931	0	931	0	847	-847	2773	0	2773
D. Overall Balance (A+B+C)	365981	349328	16653	396455	378210	18245	472797	445027	27770
E. Monetary Movements (i+ii)	0	16653	-16653	0	18245	-18245	0	27770	-27770
i) I.M.F.	0	2286	-2286	0	1652	-1652	0	1122	-1122
ii) Foreign exchange reserves (Increase - / Decrease +)	0	14367	-14367	0	16593	-16593	0	26648	-26648

(Contd...)

Item/Year	2000-01			2001-02			2002-03			2003-04		
	Credit	Debit	Net	Credit	Debit	Net	Credit	Debit	Net	Credit	Debit	Net
1	32	33	34	35	36	37	38	39	40	41	42	43
A. Current Account												
1. Merchandise	207852	264589	-56737	213345	268300	-54955	260079	311776	-51697	303915	367301	-63386
2. Invisibles (a+b+c)	147778	102639	45139	175108	103727	71381	202757	120400	82357	245413	118044	127369
a) Services	74555	66650	7905	81739	65850	15889	100419	82775	17644	123175	76794	46381
i) Travel	16064	12741	3323	14975	14336	639	15991	16155	-164	23054	16534	6520
ii) Transportation	9364	16172	-6808	10326	16486	-6160	12261	15828	3567	11711	10688	4026
iii) Insurance	1234	1004	230	1374	1339	35	1783	1687	96	1922	1672	250
iv) G.n.i.e.	2986	1460	1526	2467	1349	1118	1417	1105	312	1105	976	129
v) Miscellaneous	44907	35273	9634	52597	32340	20257	68967	48000	20967	82380	46924	35456
of which: Software services	29013	2705	26308	36038	3202	32836	46424	3565	42859	58781	2175	56606
b) Transfers	60948	981	59967	77289	1729	75560	85289	3886	81403	104329	2633	101696
i) Official	1156	0	1156	2197	0	2197	2174	0	2174	2531	0	2531
ii) Private	59792	981	58811	75092	1729	73363	83115	3886	79229	101798	2633	99165
c) Income	12275	35008	-22733	16080	36148	-20068	17049	33739	-16690	17909	38617	-20708
i) Investment income	11690	32885	-21195	15487	33830	-18343	16484	33647	-17163	17314	34586	-17272
ii) Compensation of employees	585	2123	-1538	593	2318	-1725	565	92	473	595	4031	-3436
Total Current Account (1+2)	355630	367228	-11598	388453	372027	16426	462836	432176	30660	549328	485345	63983
B. Capital Account												
1. Foreign Investment (a+b)	80824	54080	26744	73907	41987	31920	67756	47658	20098	149465	86623	62842
a) Foreign direct Investment (i+ii)	18727	3803	14924	29741	7111	22630	25036	9442	15594	20484	9540	10944
i) In India	18404	0	18404	29269	24	29245	24681	284	24397	19830	0	19830
Equity	10948	0	10948	19570	24	19546	13699	284	13415	10213	0	10213
Reinvested earnings	6177	0	6177	7841	0	7841	8866	0	8866	6710	0	6710
Other capital	1279	0	1279	1858	0	1858	2116	0	2116	2907	0	2907
ii) Abroad	323	3803	-3480	472	7087	-6615	355	9158	-8803	654	9540	-8886
Equity	323	1906	-1583	472	3176	-2704	355	3314	-2959	654	5809	-5155
Reinvested earnings	0	1553	-1553	0	3339	-3339	0	5342	-5342	0	2536	-2536
Other capital	0	344	-344	0	572	-572	0	502	-502	0	1195	-1195

(Contd...)

Item/Year	2000-01			2001-02			2002-03			2003-04		
	Credit	Debit	Net	Credit	Debit	Net	Credit	Debit	Net	Credit	Debit	Net
1	32	33	34	35	36	37	38	39	40	41	42	43
b) Portfolio investment	62097	50277	11820	44166	34876	9290	42720	38216	4504	128981	77083	51898
In India	62097	49485	12612	44166	34550	9616	42720	38045	4675	128981	77083	51898
Abroad	0	792	-792	0	326	-326	0	171	-171	0	0	0
2. Loans (a+b+c)	109271	84812	24459	55418	61302	-5884	55899	74469	-18570	90303	109916	-19613
a) External assistance	13521	11519	2002	16070	10661	5409	13902	28922	-15020	15311	28343	-13032
i) By India	0	78	-78	0	410	-410	0	157	-157	110	589	-479
ii) To India	13521	11441	2080	16070	10251	5819	13902	28765	-14863	15201	27754	-12553
b) Commercial borrowings (MT & LT)	44455	24284	20171	12845	20373	-7528	16976	25196	-8220	23979	37239	-13260
i) By India	0	23	-23	15	0	15	43	0	43	14	0	14
ii) To India	44455	24261	20194	12830	20373	-7543	16933	25196	-8263	23965	37239	-13274
c) Short-term to India	51295	49009	2286	26503	30268	-3765	25021	20351	4670	51013	44334	6679
3. Banking Capital (a+b)	44448	53592	-9144	66113	52335	13778	91681	41348	50333	88321	60539	27782
a) Commercial banks	43020	51753	-8733	63830	50998	12832	89057	40157	48900	86767	56833	29934
i) Assets	954	20137	-19183	6121	8046	-1925	29443	4777	24666	4345	733	3612
ii) Liabilities	42066	31616	10450	57709	42952	14757	59614	35380	24234	82422	56100	26322
of which:												
Non-resident deposits	41022	30461	10561	54464	41337	13127	49439	35015	14424	65739	48870	16869
b) Others	1428	1839	-411	2283	1337	946	2624	1191	1433	1554	3706	-2152
4. Rupee Debt Service	0	2760	-2760	0	2457	-2457	0	2306	-2306	0	1756	-1756
5. Other Capital	12948	11637	1311	10966	7243	3723	8901	6090	2811	19885	11913	7972
Total Capital Account (1 to 5)	247491	206881	40610	206404	165324	41080	224237	171871	52366	347974	270747	77227
C. Errors & Omissions	0	1369	-1369	0	913	-913	0	989	-989	2783	0	2783
D. Overall Balance (A+B+C)	603121	575478	27643	594857	538264	56593	687073	605036	82037	900085	756092	143993
E. Monetary Movements (i+ii)	6442	34085	-27643	0	56593	-56593	0	82037	-82037	0	143993	-143993
i) I.M.F.	0	115	-115	0	0	0	0	0	0	0	0	0
ii) Foreign exchange reserves (Increase - / Decrease +)	6442	33970	-27528	0	56593	-56593	0	82037	-82037	0	143993	-143993

(Contd...)

Item/Year	2004-05			2005-06			2006-07 PR			2007-08 P		
	Credit	Debit	Net	Credit	Debit	Net	Credit	Debit	Net	Credit	Debit	Net
1	44	45	46	47	48	49	50	51	52	53	54	55
A. Current Account												
1. Merchandise	381785	533550	-151765	465748	695412	-229664	579128	865404	-286276	637190	999286	-362096
2. Invisibles (a+b+c)	311550	171959	139591	397660	211733	185927	519425	278492	240933	583424	291685	291739
a) Services	193711	124880	68831	255668	153057	102611	343895	200291	143604	352315	201392	150923
i) Travel	29858	23671	6287	34871	29432	5439	41127	30253	10874	45524	37083	8441
ii) Transportation	21021	20363	658	28023	36928	-8905	36394	36504	-110	38156	46665	-8509
iii) Insurance	3913	3249	664	4694	4965	-271	5434	2903	2531	6371	4186	2185
iv) G.n.i.e.	1797	1843	-46	1396	2343	-947	1130	1825	-695	1334	1544	-210
v) Miscellaneous	137122	75854	61268	186684	79389	107295	259810	128806	131004	260930	111914	149016
of which :	79404	3579	75825	104632	5954	98678	141356	10212	131144	161968	13081	148887
Software services												
Business Services	23067	32807	-9740	41356	34428	6928	86928	76929	9999	66878	66923	-45
Financial Services	2279	3735	-1456	5355	4265	1090	13062	9352	3710	12392	11438	954
Communication Services	6191	3298	2893	7000	1285	5715	9506	2980	6526	9797	3368	6429
b) Transfers	97201	4066	93135	113566	4134	109432	133530	6423	127107	173995	9334	164661
i) Official	2762	1598	1164	2970	2103	867	2877	1858	1019	3029	2077	952
ii) Private	94439	2468	91971	110596	2031	108565	130653	4565	126088	170966	7257	163709
c) Income	20638	43013	-22375	28426	54542	-26116	42000	71778	-29778	57114	80959	-23845
i) Investment income	18538	36947	-18409	27633	51112	-23479	40218	67483	-27265	55397	76543	-21146
ii) Compensation of employees	2100	6066	-3966	793	3430	-2637	1782	4295	-2513	1717	4416	-2699
Total Current Account (1+2)	693335	705509	-12174	863408	907145	-43737	1098553	1143896	-45343	1220614	1290971	-70357

(Contd...)

Item/Year	2004-05			2005-06			2006-07 PR			2007-08 P		
	Credit	Debit	Net	Credit	Debit	Net	Credit	Debit	Net	Credit	Debit	Net
1	44	45	46	47	48	49	50	51	52	53	54	55
B. Capital Account												
1. Foreign Investment (a + b)	210205	152148	58057	342778	273996	68782	598106	527663	70443	1084072	903920	180152
a) Foreign direct Investment (i+ii)	27392	10647	16745	40690	27265	13425	103610	65057	38553	140240	77901	62339
i) In India	27234	287	26947	39730	273	39457	99646	385	99261	130252	506	129746
Equity	17028	287	16741	26512	273	26239	74354	385	73969	101215	438	100777
Reinvested earnings	8555	0	8555	12220	0	12220	23029	0	23029	27714	0	27714
Other capital	1651	0	1651	998	0	998	2263	0	2263	1323	68	1255
ii) Abroad	158	10360	-10202	960	26992	-26032	3964	64672	-60708	9988	77395	-67407
Equity	158	7517	-7359	960	17678	-16718	3964	54634	-50670	9988	60167	-50179
Reinvested earnings	0	1114	-1114	0	4834	-4834	0	4868	-4868	0	4363	-4363
Other capital	0	1729	-1729	0	4480	-4480	0	5170	-5170	0	12865	-12865
b) Portfolio investment	182813	141501	41312	302088	246731	55357	494496	462606	31890	943832	826019	117813
In India	182813	141394	41419	302088	246731	55357	494102	462472	31630	942872	825718	117154
Abroad	0	107	-107	0	0	0	394	134	260	960	301	659
2. Loans (a+b+c)	135685	87090	48595	174729	140332	34397	246908	136279	110629	335471	166843	168628
a) External assistance	16988	8463	8525	16133	8541	7592	16961	9024	7937	17022	8557	8465
i) By India	108	576	-468	106	390	-284	73	163	-90	97	113	-16
ii) To India	16880	7887	8993	16027	8151	7876	16888	8861	8027	16925	8444	8481
b) Commercial borrowings (MT & LT)	40679	17566	23113	63476	52971	10505	94332	21736	72596	120173	30856	89317
i) By India	0	1036	-1036	0	1105	-1105	2936	4290	-1354	6245	6303	-58
ii) To India	40679	16530	24149	63476	51866	11610	91396	17446	73950	113928	24553	89375

(Contd...)

Item/Year	2004-05			2005-06			2006-07 PR			2007-08 P		
	Credit	Debit	Net	Credit	Debit	Net	Credit	Debit	Net	Credit	Debit	Net
1	44	45	46	47	48	49	50	51	52	53	54	55
b) Commercial borrowings (MT & LT)	40679	17566	23113	63476	52971	10505	94332	21736	72596	120173	30856	89317
i) By India	0	1036	-1036	0	1105	-1105	2936	4290	-1354	6245	6303	-58
ii) To India	40679	16530	24149	63476	51866	11610	91396	17446	73950	113928	24553	89375
c) Short-term to India	78018	61061	16957	95120	78820	16300	135615	105519	30096	198276	127430	70846
i) Suppliers' Credit >180 days & buyers' Credit	78018	61061	16957	85766	78114	7652	115125	100196	14929	171182	127430	43752
ii) Suppliers' Credit up to 180 days	0	0	0	9354	706	8648	20490	5323	15167	27094	0	27094
3. Banking Capital (a+b)	65278	48238	17040	95988	90193	5795	167494	159017	8477	223654	176507	47147
a) Commercial banks	64038	46532	17506	91200	89569	1631	165656	158660	6996	223338	174793	48545
i) Assets	2276	2481	-205	3369	17711	-14342	64972	80726	-15754	78365	50733	27632
ii) Liabilities	61762	44051	17711	87831	71858	15973	100684	77934	22750	144973	124060	20913
of which:												
Non-resident deposits	36225	40664	-4439	79190	66733	12457	89950	70376	19574	117757	117051	706
b) Others	1240	1706	-466	4788	624	4164	1838	357	1481	316	1714	-1398
4. Rupee Debt Service	0	1858	-1858	0	2557	-2557	0	725	-725	0	488	-488
5. Other Capital	30507	26974	3533	26451	20903	5548	34540	16975	17565	75956	37492	38464
Total Capital Account (1 to 5)	441675	316308	125367	639946	527981	111965	1047048	840659	206389	1719153	1285250	433903
C. Errors & Omissions	2714	0	2714	0	2332	-2332	2588	0	2588	6143	0	6143
D. Overall Balance (A+B+C)	1137724	1021817	115907	1503354	1437458	65896	2148189	1984555	163634	2945910	2576221	369689
E. Monetary Movements (i+ii)	0	115907	-115907	0	65896	-65896	0	163634	-163634	0	369689	-369689
i) I.M.F.	0	0	0	0	0	0	0	0	0	0	0	0
ii) Foreign exchange reserves (Increase - / Decrease +)	0	115907	-115907	0	65896	-65896	0	163634	-163634	0	369689	-369689

PR : Partially Revised. P : Preliminary. G.n.i.e: Government not included elsewhere.

Source: Reserve Bank of India.

Table 47: Principal Imports

Quantity : Thousand tonne
Value : Rs. Crore & US $ Million

		1960-61			1970-71			1980-81		
		Qty.	Rs. cr	$ million	Qty.	Rs. cr	$ million	Qty.	Rs. cr	$ million
1	2	3	4	5	6	7	8	9	10	11
I.	**Food and live animals chiefly for food (excl. cashew raw) of which:**	...	214	449	...	242	321	...	380	481
I.1	Cereals and cereal preparations	3747.7	181	380	3343.2	213	282	400.8	100	127
II.	**Raw materials and intermediate manufactures**	...	527	1105	...	889	1176	...	9760	12341
II.1	Cashewnuts (unprocessed)	na	...	...	169.4	29	39	25	9	11
II.2	Crude rubber (including synthetic and reclaimed)	36.2	11	23	7.8	4	5	26.2	32	40
II.3	Fibres of which:	...	101	212	...	127	168	...	164	208
II.3.1	Synthetic and regenerated fibres (man-made fibres)	0.2	...	...	15.8	9	12	68.8	97	122
II.3.2	Raw wool	1.9	1	2	19	15	20	18.8	43	55
II.3.3	Raw cotton	237.1	82	172	139.1	99	131	na		
II.3.4	Raw jute	100.4	8	17	0.7	...	0	8	1	1
II.4	Petroleum, oil and lubricants	800	69	145	12767	136	180	23537	5264	6656
II.5	Animal and vegetable oils and fats of which:	...	5	10	...	39	51		709	896
II.5.1	Edible oils	31.1	4	8	84.7	23	31	1633.3	677	857
II.6	Fertilizers and chemical products of which:	...	88	185	...	217	286	...	1490	1884
II.6.1	Fertilizers and fertilizer mfg	307	13	27	2392.7	86	113	5560.2	818	1034
II.6.2	Chemical elements and compounds	...	39	82	...	68	90	...	358	453
II.6.3	Dyeing, tanning and colouring material	...	1	2	...	9	12	...	21	26
II.6.4	Medicinal and pharmaceutical products	...	10	21	...	24	32	...	85	107
II.6.5	Plastic material, regenerated cellulose and artificial resins	...	9	19	...	8	11	...	121	154
II.7	Pulp and waste paper	80.3	7	15	71.7	12	16	36.9	18	23
II.8	Paper, paper board and manufactures thereof	55.6	12	25	159	25	33	371.4	187	236
II.9	Non-metallic mineral manufactures of which:	...	6	13	...	33	44	...	555	702
II.9.1	Pearls, precious and semiprecious stones, unworked or worked	...	1	2	...	25	33	...	417	527
II.10	Iron and steel	1325.2	123	258	683.4	147	194	2031.1	852	1078
II.11	Non-ferrous metals		47	99		119	158	...	477	604
III.	**Capital goods**[a]		356	747	...	404	534	...	1910	2416
III.1	Manufactures of metals		23	48	...	9	12	...	90	113
III.2	Non-electrical machinery apparatus and appliances including machine tools[b]	...	203	426	...	258	341	...	1089	1377
III.3	Electrical machinery, apparatus and appliances[b]		57	120	...	70	93	...	260	328
III.4	Transport equipment		72	151	...	67	88	...	472	597
IV.	**TOTAL IMPORTS**	**...**	**1122**	**2353**	**...**	**1634**	**2162**	**...**	**12549**	**15869**

(Contd...)

		1990-91			2000-01			2007-08		
		Qty.	Rs. cr	$ million	Qty.	Rs. cr	$ million	Qty.	Rs. cr	$ million
1	2	12	13	14	15	16	17	18	19	20
I.	**Food and live animals chiefly for food (excl. cashew raw) of which:**	...	...	...	...	...	...	...	...	...
I.1	Cereals and cereal preparations	308.3	182	102	69.9	90	20	1848	2839	705
II.	**Raw materials and intermediate manufactures**	...	...	...	...	...	...	...	...	...
II.	Cashewnuts (unprocessed)	82.6	134	75	249.7	962	211	592	1715	426
II.2	Crude rubber (including synthetic and reclaimed)	105.1	226	126	119.1	695	152	339	3163	786
II.3	Fibres of which:	...	...	...	...	...	...	...	...	...
II.3.1	Synthetic and regenerated fibres (man-made fibres)	21.2	56	31	42.6	275	60	44	446	111
II.3.2	Raw wool	29.4	182	102	53.7	458	100	93	1090	271
II.3.3	Raw cotton	0.2	1	0	212.3	1185	259	137	912	227
II.3.4	Raw jute	32.1	20	11	67.3	84	18	136	148	37
II.4	Petroleum, oil and lubricants	29359	10816	6028	...	71497	15650	...	320654	79645
II.5	Animal and vegetable oils and fats of which:	...	...	...	...	...	...	...	...	...
II.5.1	Edible oils	525.8	326	182	4267.9	6093	1334	4903	10301	2559
II.6	Fertilizers and chemical products of which:	...	...	...	...	...	...	...	...	...
II.6.1	Fertilizers and fertilizer mfg	7560.3	1766	984	7423.4	3034	664	18532	20307	5044
II.6.2	Chemical elements and compounds	...	2289	1276	...	1542	338	...	46388	11522
II.6.3	Dyeing, tanning and colouring material	...	168	94	...	874	191	...	2999	745
II.6.4	Medicinal and pharmaceutical products	...	468	261	...	1723	377	...	6730	1672
II.6.5	Plastic material, regenerated cellulose and artificial resins	...	1095	610	...	2551	558	...	14837	3685
II.7	Pulp and waste paper	678.2	458	255	1050.9	1290	282	2238	3132	778
II.8	Paper, paper board and manufactures thereof	286.4	456	254	585.6	2005	439	1513	5736	1425
II.9	Non-metallic mineral manufactures of which:	...	na	na	...	797	174	...	...	...
II.9.1	Pearls, precious and semiprecious stones, unworked or worked	...	3738	2083	...	22101	4838	...	32094	7972
II.10	Iron and steel	1920.5	2113	1178	1613.6	3569	781	7958	34981	8689
II.11	Non-ferrous metals	...	1102	614	...	2462	539	...	86046	21372
III.	**Capital goods**[a]		10466	5833	...	25281	5534	...	197305	49007
III.1	Manufactures of metals		302	168	...	1786	391	...	10720	2663
III.2	Non-electrical machinery apparatus and appliances including machine tools[b]	...	4240	2363	...	16915	3703	...	88849	22068
III.3	Electrical machinery, apparatus and appliances[b]	...	1702	949	...	2227	487	...	11557	2871
III.4	Transport equipment	...	1670	931	...	4353	953	...	80971	20112
IV.	**TOTAL IMPORTS**	**...**	**43198**	**24075**	**...**	**230873**	**50536**	**...**	**1012312**	**251654**

(Contd...)

		2008-09			2008 (April-Sep.)			2009 (April-Sep.)		
		Qty.	Rs. cr	$ million	Qty.	Rs. cr	$ million	Qty.	Rs. cr	$ million
1	2	21	22	23	24	25	26	27	28	29
I.	**Food and live animals chiefly for food (excl. cashew raw) of which:**	...	...	...	...	...	...	...	...	...
I.1	Cereals and cereal preparations	50	216	47	20	96	22	25	102	21
II.	**Raw materials and intermediate**	...	...	...	...	...	...	...	...	...
	Cashewnuts (unprocessed)	614	2671	581	425	1748	409	471	1753	361
II.2	Crude rubber (including synthetic and reclaimed)	302	3959	861	184	2433	570	283	2328	479
II.3	Fibres of which:									
II.3.1	Synthetic and regenerated fibres (man-made fibres)	55	632	137	31	357	84	33	364	75
II.3.2	Raw wool	66	1033	225	41	655	153	32	457	94
II.3.3	Raw cotton	212	1690	368	102	834	195	90	537	110
II.3.4	Raw jute	52	71	15	33	35	8	35	86	18
II.4	Petroleum, oil and lubricants	...	419946	91316	...	270534	63337	...	181431	37338
II.5	Animal and vegetable oils and fats of which:									
II.5.1	Edible oils	6714	15819	3440	2870	6226	1458	3875	11871	2443
II.6	Fertilizers and chemical products of which:									
II.6.1	Fertilizers and fertilizer mfg	21615	59569	12953	11021	32339	7571	9408	14922	3071
II.6.2	Chemical elements and compounds	...	9614	2090	...	37833	8857	...	32687	6727
II.6.3	Dyeing, tanning and colouring material	...	3782	822	...	2127	498	...	2186	450
II.6.4	Medicinal and pharmaceutical products	...	8649	1881	...	4361	1021	...	4787	985
II.6.5	Plastic material, regenerated cellulose and artificial resins	...	18109	3938	...	...	...	...	11444	2355
II.7	Pulp and waste paper	2402	3681	800	1152	1929	452	1393	1777	366
II.8	Paper, paper board and manufactures thereof	1607	8141	1770	927	4212	986	730	3402	700
II.9	Non-metallic mineral manufactures of which:									
II.9.1	Pearls, precious and semiprecious stones, unworked or worked	...	76130	16554	...	44657	10455	...	26394	5432
II.10	Iron and steel	7135	43531	9466	3660	21905	5128	4475	18815	3872
II.11	Non-ferrous metals	...	126669	27544		86151	20169	...	63456	13059
III.	**Capital goods**[a]	...	216511	47080		108541	25411	...	86223	17744
III.1	Manufactures of metals	...	14903	3241		7143	1672	...	5555	1143
III.2	Non-electrical machinery apparatus and appliances including machine tools[b]	...	109275	23762	...	57530	13469	...	49584	10204
III.3	Electrical machinery, apparatus and appliances[b]	...	16862	3667	...	9144	2141	...	7376	1518
III.4	Transport equipment	...	60803	13222	...	28227	6608	...	13709	2821
IV.	**TOTAL IMPORTS**	**...**	**1374436**	**303696**	**...**	**790616**	**184996**	**...**	**603206**	**124194**

na: Not available.

[a]: From the year 1987-88 onwards, Capital Goods include Project Goods.

[b]: From the year 1991-92 onwards, Items III.2 & III.3 exclude electronic goods.

Source: DGCI&S, Kolkata.

Table 48: Principal Exports

Quantity : Thousand tonne
Value : Rs. Crore & US $ Million

		1960-61			1970-71			1980-81		
		Qty.	**Rs. cr**	**$ million**	**Qty.**	**Rs. cr**	**$ million**	**Qty.**	**Rs. cr**	**$ million**
1	2	3	4	5	6	7	8	9	10	11
I.	**Agricultural and allied products of which:**	...	284	596	...	487	644	...	2057	2601
I.1	Coffee	19.7	7	15	32.2	25	33	87.3	214	271
I.2	Tea and mate	199.2	124	260	199.1	148	196	229.2	426	538
I.3	Oil cakes	433.8	14	29	878.5	55	73	886	125	158
I.4	Tobacco	47.5	16	34	49.8	33	43	91.3	141	178
I.5	Cashew kernels	43.6	19	40	60.6	57	76	32.3	140	177
I.6	Spices	47.2	17	36	46.9	39	51	84.2	11	14
I.7	Sugar and molasses	99.6	30	60	473	29	39	97	40	50
I.8	Raw cotton	32.6	12	25	32.1	14	19	131.6	165	209
I.9	Rice	...	...	...	32.8	5	7	726.7	224	283
I.10	Fish and fish preparations	19.9	5	10	32.6	31	40	69.4	217	274
I.11	Meat and meat preparations	...	1	2		3	4	...	56	70
I.12	Fruits, vegetables and pulses (excl. cashew kernels, processed fruits & juices)	...	6	13	...	12	16	...	80	101
I.13	Miscellaneous processed foods (incl. processed fruits and juices)	...	1	2	...	4	6	...	36	45
II.	**Ores and minerals (excl. coal) of which**	...	52	109	...	164	217	...	414	523
II.1	Mica	28.4	...	...	26.7	16	21	16.7	18	22
II.2	Iron ore (million tonne)	3.2	17	36	21.2	117	155	22.4	303	384
III.	**Manufactured goods of which**	...	291	610	...	772	1021	...	3747	4738
III.1	Textile fabrics & manufactures (excl. carpets hand-made) of which	..	73	153	...	145	192	...	933	1179
III.1.1	Cotton yarn,fabrics, made-ups etc.	...	65	136	...	142	188	...	408	516
III.1.2	Readymade garments of all textile materials	...	1	2	...	29	39	...	550	696
III.2	Coir yarn and manufactures	...	6	13	...	13	17	...	17	22
III.3	Jute manufactures incl.twist & yarn	790	135	283	560	190	252	660	330	417
III.4	Leather & leather manufactures incl. leather footwear,leather travel goods & leather garments	...	28	59	...	80	106	...	390	493
III.5	Handicrafts (incl. carpets hand-made)[c] of which:	...	11	23	...	73	96	...	952	1204
III.5.1	Gems and jewellery	...	1	2	...	45	59	...	618	782
III.6	Chemicals and allied products[a]	...	7	15	...	29	39	...	225	284
III.7	Machinery, transport & metal manufactures including iron and steel[b]	...	22	46	...	198	261	...	827	1045
IV.	**Mineral fuels and lubricants (incl. coal)[d]**	...	7	15	...	13	17	...	28	35
V.	**Total Exports**	**...**	**642**	**1346**	**...**	**1535**	**2031**	**...**	**6711**	**8486**

(Contd...)

		1990-91			2000-01			2007-08		
		Qty.	Rs. cr	$ million	Qty.	Rs. cr	$ million	Qty.	Rs. cr	$ million
1	2	12	13	14	15	16	17	18	19	20
I.	**Agricultural and allied products of which:**	...	6317	3521	...	28582	6256	...	65230	16202
I.1	Coffee	86.5	252	141	184.9	1185	259	178	1872	465
I.2	Tea and mate	199.1	1070	596	202.4	1976	433	197	2034	505
I.3	Oil cakes	2447.8	609	339	2417.8	2045	448	6909	8141	2022
I.4	Tobacco	87.1	263	147	108.3	871	191	173	1932	480
I.5	Cashew kernels	55.5	447	249	83.8	1883	412	126	2235	555
I.6	Spices	103.3	239	133	244.9	1619	354	615	4315	1072
I. 7	Sugar and molasses	191	38	21	769	511	112	5582	5663	1407
I.8	Raw cotton	374.4	846	471	30.2	224	49	1558	8865	2202
I.9	Rice	505	462	257	1534.4	2943	644	6469	11755	2920
I.10	Fish and fish preparations	158.9	960	535	502.6	6367	1394		6927	1721
I.11	Meat and meat preparations	...	140	78	...	1470	322	...	3749	931
I.12	Fruits, vegetables and pulses (excl.cashew kernels, processed fruits & juices)	...	216	120	...	1609	352	...	4053	1007
I.13	Miscellaneous processed foods (incl. processed fruits and juices)	...	213	119	...	1094	239	...	2135	530
II.	**Ores and minerals (excl. coal) of which**	...	1497	834	...	4139	906	...	36440	9051
II.1	Mica	42	35	19	63.2	64	14	...	88	22
II.2	Iron ore (million tonne)	32.5	1049	585	20161.4	1634	358	...	23400	5812
III.	**Manufactured goods of which**	...	23736	13229	...	160723	35181	...	421200	104618
III.1	Textile fabrics & manufactures (excl. carpets hand-made) of which	...	6832	3807	...	...	...	...	...	...
III.1.1	Cotton yarn, fabrics, made-ups etc.		2100	1170	...	16030	3509	...	18734	4653
III.1.2	Readymade garments of all textile materials	...	4012	2236	...	25478	5577	...	39002	9687
III.2	Coir yarn and manufactures	...	48	27	...	221	48	...	645	160
III.3	Jute manufactures incl. twist & yarn	220	298	166	...	932	204	...	1319	328
III.4	Leather & leather manufactures incl. leather footwear, leather travel goods & leather garments	...	2600	1449	...	8914	1951	...	13674	3396
III.5	Handicrafts (incl. carpets hand-made)[c]	...	6167	3437	...	5097	1116	...	5772	1434
III.5.1	Gems and jewellery	...	5247	2924	...	33734	7384	...	79228	19679
III.6	Chemicals and allied products[a]	...	2111	1176	...	22851	5002	...	69937	17371
III.7	Machinery, transport & metal manufactures including iron and steel[b]	...	3872	2158	...	31870	6976	...	149849	37220
IV.	**Mineral fuels and lubricants (incl.coal)[d]**	...	948	528	...	8822	1931	...	116878	29030
V.	**Total Exports**	**...**	**32553**	**18143**	**...**	**203571**	**44560**	**...**	**655864**	**163132**

(Contd...)

		2008-2009			2008 (April-Sept.)			2009 (April-Sept.)		
		Qty.	Rs. cr	$ million	Qty.	Rs. cr	$ million	Qty.	Rs. cr	$ million
1	2	21	22	23	24	25	26	27	28	29
I.	**Agricultural & allied products of which**	...	77783	16914	...	42523	9955	...	33421	6878
I.1	Coffee	174	2256	491	97	1254	294	74	937	193
I.2	Tea & mate	208	2689	585	109	1361	319	86	1260	259
I.3	Oil cakes	6743	10269	2233	3138	4782	1120	1900	3210	661
I.4	Tobacco	208	3461	753	118	1666	390	117	2206	454
I.5	Cashew Kernels	137	2931	637	73	1607	376	59	1356	279
I.6	Spices	674	6338	1378	375	3300	773	320	2755	567
I.7	Sugar & molasses	3504	4532	985	3245	4155	973	46	65	13
I.8	Raw cotton	458	2866	623	264	1653	387	214	1255	258
I.9	Rice	2488.2	11164	2428	1541	6038	1414	1151	6461	1330
I.10	Fish & fish preparations	...	7066	1536	...	3312	775	...	3642	750
I.11	Meat & meat preparations	...	5371	1168	...	2667	624	...	2464	507
I.12	Fruits,vegetables & pulses (excl.cashew kernels, processed fruits & juices)	...	5650	1229	...	2511	588	...	2816	580
I.13	Miscellaneous processed foods (incl. Processed fruits & juices)	...	3176	691	...	1563	366	...	1515	312
II.	**Ores & Minerals (excl. coal) of which**	...	35529	7726	...	18913	4428	...	13854	2851
II.1	Mica	...	136	30		68	16	...	57	12
II.2	Iron Ore (million tonne)	...	21725	4724	...	10712	2508	...	8187	1685
III.	**Manufactured goods of which**	...	566156	123110	...	301383	70559	...	257380	52967
III.1	Textile fabrics & manufactures (excl.carpets hand-made) of which									
III.1.1	Cotton yarn,fabrics,made-ups etc	...	18930	4116	...	10050	2353	...	7425	1528
III.1.2	Readymade garments of all textile materials	...	50294	10936	...	23103	5409	...	23626	4862
III.2	Coir yarn and manufactures	...	681	148	...	344	81	...	380	78
III.3	Jute manufactures incl. twist & yarn	...	1377	299	...	792	185	...	534	110
III.4	Leather & Leather manufactures incl. leather footwear, leather travel goods and leather garments	...	15931	3464	...	8610	2016	...	7429	1529
III.5	Handicrafts (incl. carpets hand-made)[c] of which	...	4890	1063	...	2562	600	...	1932	398
III.5.1	Gems & Jewellery	...	128575	27958	...	74194	17370	...	66064	13596
III.6	Chemicals and allied products[a]	...	85697	18635	...	43729	10238	...	40552	8345
III.7	Machinery, transport & metal manufactures incl. Iron & Steel[b]	...	216856	47155	...	115403	27018	...	88627	18239
IV.	Mineral fuels and lubricants (incl.coal[d]	...	127324	27686	...	82851	19397	...	52764	10859
VI	**Total Exports**	**...**	**840755**	**185295**	**...**	**464450**	**108907**	**...**	**372096**	**76589**

[a] Chemicals and allied products figrues relate to "Basic Chemicals" and "Plastic Linoleum products".

[b] Also includes electronic goods and computer software.

[c] Gems and Jewellery excluded from Handicarafts and reported as individual item since 1997-98.

[d] During 1990-91 and 2000-01 Crude oil exports amount to Nil.

Source: DGCI&S, Kolkata.

Table 49: Real GDP Growth Rates for Some Emerging Economies

No.	Country	1970	1971	1972	1973	1974	1975	1976	1977	1978	1979	1980	1981	1982	1983	1984
1.	Argentina	0.0	6.7	6.3	5.9	5.6	-1.3	-3.3	4.9	-3.4	7.1	0.7	-5.7	-3.1	3.7	2.0
2.	Brazil	2.6	12.2	10.9	13.5	9.8	4.2	9.8	4.6	5.0	6.8	9.2	-4.4	0.6	-3.4	5.3
3.	Bulgaria	7.0	6.9	7.7	8.1	7.6	8.8	6.5	6.3	5.6	6.6	5.7	5.3	4.2	3.0	4.6
4.	Chile	1.4	9.0	-1.2	-5.6	1.0	-12.9	3.5	9.9	8.2	8.3	7.9	6.2	-13.6	-2.8	5.9
5.	China,P.R.: Mainland	16.2	6.9	4.6	12.8	4.0	6.8	-2.7	8.0	7.7	7.0	7.9	4.7	9.1	10.9	15.2
6.	China,P.R.:Hong Kong	9.4	7.3	11.0	12.7	2.2	0.2	17.1	12.5	9.5	11.7	10.2	9.2	2.8	5.8	10.0
7.	Colombia	9.3	6.0	7.7	6.7	5.8	2.3	4.7	4.2	8.9	4.9	4.4	2.3	0.9	1.6	3.4
8.	Costa Rica	7.5	6.8	8.2	7.7	5.5	2.1	5.5	8.9	6.3	4.9	0.8	-2.3	-7.3	4.2	8.0
9.	Egypt	1.8	4.9	3.9	-1.3	5.1	14.3	7.2	9.1	8.6	2.3	3.4	2.2	7.3	8.9	8.0
10.	Hungary	16.0	6.2	6.1	6.9	5.9	6.2	3.6	7.6	4.5	2.7	0.2	2.9	2.8	0.7	2.7
11.	India	5.8	2.3	-0.7	3.6	0.2	9.8	1.5	5.9	5.9	-2.5	3.6	6.4	4.3	6.2	4.8
12.	Indonesia	6.5	7.0	9.4	11.3	7.6	5.0	6.9	8.9	8.5	5.5	9.9	7.6	2.2	4.2	7.0
13.	Israel	8.0	11.1	11.9	5.1	4.1	3.5	1.4	1.0	3.7	4.8	3.6	4.7	1.4	2.6	2.2
14.	Kenya	7.4	6.9	16.1	5.9	2.1	1.5	4.6	10.1	8.0	5.5	5.6	4.1	5.1	1.6	1.6
15.	Lebanon	6.6	9.2	12.2	4.7	2.4	-30.3	-57.0	67.7	-2.6	2.4	1.5	0.6	-36.8	22.7	44.5
16.	Malaysia	5.0	7.1	9.4	11.7	8.3	0.8	11.6	7.8	6.7	9.4	7.4	6.9	5.9	6.3	7.8
17.	Mexico	6.9	4.2	8.5	8.4	6.1	5.7	4.4	3.4	9.0	9.7	9.5	8.5	-0.5	-3.5	3.4
18.	Nigeria	29.8	18.4	7.3	9.5	5.9	0.2	10.8	-6.7	-6.7	2.6	2.9	20.8	-1.1	-5.1	-2.0
19.	Pakistan	-2.4	0.7	0.4	6.9	5.6	4.5	4.6	3.8	6.4	6.8	8.5	6.8	6.5	6.8	5.1
20.	Paraguay	3.9	5.4	6.5	7.2	8.2	6.3	7.0	14.0	12.2	9.8	11.7	9.2	-1.4	-3.0	2.8
21.	Philippines	4.6	4.9	4.8	9.2	5.0	6.4	8.0	6.2	5.6	6.9	5.1	3.4	3.6	1.9	-7.3
22.	Poland	6.1	7.4	4.7	4.2	7.1	5.9	7.9	7.1	5.4	3.9	-6.0	-10.0	-4.8	5.6	-0.4
23.	Romania	3.8	5.4	2.3	1.6	5.7	5.4	14.2	4.6	8.0	6.6	3.3	0.1	3.9	6.0	6.0
24.	Singapore	13.7	12.5	13.4	11.5	6.4	4.1	8.4	7.8	8.6	9.3	9.7	9.7	7.1	8.5	8.3
25.	South Africa	5.3	5.2	2.0	3.9	7.1	2.2	1.5	0.0	2.9	3.8	6.6	5.4	-0.4	-1.8	5.1
26.	Taiwan Prov. of China	11.3	12.8	13.3	12.9	1.2	4.9	13.9	10.2	13.6	8.2	7.4	6.2	3.5	8.3	10.7
27.	Thailand	6.5	4.7	4.8	9.4	5.4	7.1	8.7	7.2	10.1	6.1	4.6	5.9	5.4	5.6	5.8
28.	Turkey	4.9	9.1	6.6	4.4	8.5	8.9	8.5	7.5	2.8	-0.9	-0.8	4.4	3.4	4.8	6.8
29.	Ukraine	n.a.	n.a.	n.a.	n.a.	n.a.	n.a.	n.a.	n.a.	n.a.	n.a.	n/a	n/a	n/a	n/a	n/a
30.	Uruguay	4.8	1.7	-1.6	0.4	3.1	5.9	4.0	1.2	5.3	6.2	6.0	1.9	-9.3	-3.3	-1.1
31.	Venezuela, Rep. Bol.	8.8	3.0	2.7	6.3	6.1	6.1	8.8	6.7	2.1	1.3	-1.9	-0.4	0.7	-5.5	1.2
	Average	7.3	7.1	6.6	6.9	5.3	3.2	4.4	8.3	5.9	5.6	5.0	4.1	0.1	3.4	5.9
	Average 1/	7.0	7.1	6.7	6.6	5.3	3.0	4.6	8.4	5.8	5.5	4.9	4.1	-0.2	3.1	5.6
	Average 2/	7.0	7.2	7.0	6.8	5.5	2.8	4.7	8.4	5.8	5.8	4.9	4.0	-0.4	3.0	5.6

1/ Average excluding China

2/ Average excluding India and China

(Contd...)

No.	Country	1985	1986	1987	1988	1989	1990	1991	1992	1993	1994	1995	1996	1997	1998	1999
1.	Argentina	-7.0	7.1	2.5	-2.0	-7.0	-1.3	10.5	10.3	6.3	5.8	-2.8	5.5	8.1	3.9	-3.4
2.	Brazil	7.9	7.5	3.6	0.3	3.2	-4.2	1.0	-0.5	4.9	5.9	4.2	2.2	3.4	0.0	0.3
3.	Bulgaria	1.8	5.3	4.7	2.4	-0.5	-9.1	-10.8	-8.4	-11.6	-3.7	-1.6	-8.0	-5.6	4.0	2.3
4.	Chile	2.0	5.6	6.6	7.3	10.6	3.7	8.0	12.3	7.0	5.7	10.6	7.4	6.7	3.3	-0.4
5.	China,P.R.: Mainland	13.5	8.8	11.6	11.3	4.1	3.8	9.2	14.2	14.0	13.1	10.9	10.0	9.3	7.8	7.6
6.	China,P.R.:Hong Kong	0.5	2.4	13.4	8.4	2.2	3.9	5.7	6.1	6.0	6.0	2.3	4.2	5.1	-6.0	2.6
7.	Colombia	3.1	5.8	5.4	4.1	3.4	4.3	2.4	4.4	5.7	5.1	5.2	2.1	3.4	0.6	-4.2
8.	Costa Rica	0.7	5.5	4.8	3.4	5.7	3.6	2.3	9.2	7.4	4.7	3.9	0.9	5.6	8.4	8.2
9.	Egypt	7.4	4.8	4.3	4.0	3.0	2.4	2.1	0.3	2.9	4.2	4.5	4.9	5.9	7.5	6.1
10.	Hungary	-0.3	1.5	4.1	-0.1	0.7	-3.5	-11.9	-3.1	-0.6	2.9	3.4	1.3	4.6	4.9	4.2
11.	India	5.3	5.0	4.4	8.5	7.2	6.1	2.1	4.4	4.9	6.2	7.4	7.6	4.7	6.0	7.1
12.	Indonesia	2.5	5.9	4.9	5.8	7.5	7.2	7.0	6.5	6.8	7.5	8.2	7.8	4.7	-13.1	0.8
13.	Israel	4.5	3.6	7.5	3.6	1.4	6.6	4.6	7.2	3.8	7.0	7.8	5.4	2.8	4.2	2.9
14.	Kenya	4.1	7.0	5.8	6.1	4.6	4.1	1.3	-1.1	-0.1	2.5	4.3	4.0	0.2	3.3	2.4
15.	Lebanon	24.3	-6.8	16.7	-28.2	-42.2	-13.4	38.2	4.5	7.0	8.0	6.5	4.0	4.0	2.6	-0.8
16.	Malaysia	-0.9	1.2	5.4	9.9	9.1	9.0	9.5	8.9	9.9	9.2	9.8	10.0	7.3	-7.4	6.1
17.	Mexico	2.2	-3.1	1.7	1.2	4.2	5.1	4.2	3.6	2.0	4.4	-6.2	5.2	6.8	5.0	3.8
18.	Nigeria	8.3	-8.8	-10.8	7.5	6.5	12.8	-0.6	0.4	2.1	0.9	-0.3	5.0	2.8	2.7	0.5
19.	Pakistan	7.6	5.5	6.5	7.6	5.0	4.5	5.5	7.8	1.3	3.7	5.0	4.8	1.0	2.6	3.7
20.	Paraguay	3.9	0.3	4.1	5.9	5.8	2.9	2.5	3.4	3.9	3.7	5.5	0.4	3.0	0.6	-1.5
21.	Philippines	-7.3	3.4	4.3	6.8	6.2	3.0	-0.6	0.3	2.1	4.4	4.7	5.8	5.2	-0.6	3.4
22.	Poland	3.9	3.5	2.3	3.3	3.8	-7.2	-7.0	2.0	4.3	5.2	6.7	6.2	7.1	5.0	4.5
23.	Romania	-0.1	2.4	0.8	-0.5	-5.8	-5.6	-12.9	-8.8	1.5	3.9	7.1	3.9	-6.1	-4.8	-1.2
24.	Singapore	-1.4	2.1	9.8	11.5	10.0	9.2	6.6	6.3	11.7	11.6	8.2	7.8	8.3	-1.4	7.2
25.	South Africa	-1.2	0.0	2.1	4.2	2.4	-0.3	-1.0	-2.1	1.2	3.2	3.1	4.3	2.6	0.5	2.4
26.	Taiwan Prov. of China	5.0	11.5	12.7	8.0	8.5	5.7	7.6	7.8	6.9	7.4	6.5	6.3	6.6	4.5	5.7
27.	Thailand	4.6	5.5	9.5	13.3	12.2	11.6	8.1	8.1	8.3	9.0	9.2	5.9	-1.4	-10.5	4.4
28.	Turkey	4.3	6.9	10.0	2.1	0.3	9.3	0.9	6.0	8.0	-5.5	7.2	7.0	7.5	3.1	-3.4
29.	Ukraine	n/a	n/a	n/a	n/a	n/a	n/a	n/a	n/a	-14.2	-22.9	-12.2	-10.0	-3.0	-1.9	-0.2
30.	Uruguay	1.5	8.9	7.9	1.5	1.1	0.3	3.5	7.9	2.7	7.3	-1.4	5.6	5.0	4.5	-2.8
31.	Venezuela, Rep. Bol.	0.2	6.5	3.6	5.8	-8.6	6.5	9.7	6.1	0.3	-2.4	4.0	-0.2	6.4	0.3	-6.0
	Average	3.4	3.8	5.7	4.1	2.1	2.7	3.6	4.1	3.8	4.0	4.2	4.1	3.9	1.3	2.0
	Average 1/	3.0	3.7	5.5	3.9	2.1	2.7	3.4	3.8	3.4	3.7	4.0	3.9	3.8	1.1	1.8
	Average 2/	2.9	3.6	5.5	3.7	1.9	2.5	3.4	3.8	3.4	3.6	3.9	3.8	3.7	0.9	1.6

1/ Average excluding China

2/ Average excluding India and China

(*Contd...*)

No.	Country	2000	2001	2002	2003	2004	2005	2006	2007	2008 Estimates	2009 Estimates	Average 10 Years 1970-79	Average 10 Years 1980-89	Average 10 years 1990-99	Average 9 years 2000-08	Average 39 Years 1970-2008
1.	Argentina	-0.8	-4.4	-10.9	8.8	9.0	9.2	8.5	8.7	6.50	3.60	2.84	-0.87	4.28	3.84	2.49
2.	Brazil	4.3	1.3	2.7	1.1	5.7	3.2	3.8	5.4	5.23	3.50	7.94	2.98	1.71	3.63	4.08
3.	Bulgaria	5.4	4.1	4.5	5.0	6.6	6.2	6.3	6.2	6.25	4.25	7.11	3.65	-5.25	5.62	2.71
4.	Chile	4.5	3.5	2.2	4.0	6.0	5.6	4.3	5.1	4.46	3.80	2.15	3.57	6.43	4.40	4.13
5.	China,P.R.: Mainland	8.4	8.3	9.1	10.0	10.1	10.4	11.6	11.9	9.74	9.25	7.13	9.71	9.99	9.95	9.18
6.	China,P.R.: Hong Kong	8.0	0.5	1.8	3.0	8.5	7.1	7.0	6.4	4.09	3.47	9.36	6.50	3.58	5.15	6.17
7.	Colombia	2.9	2.2	2.5	4.6	4.7	5.7	6.8	7.7	4.00	3.50	6.04	3.44	2.89	4.56	4.22
8.	Costa Rica	1.8	1.1	2.9	6.4	4.3	5.9	8.8	7.3	4.00	3.50	6.34	2.35	5.42	4.72	4.71
9.	Egypt	5.4	3.5	3.2	3.2	4.1	4.5	6.8	7.1	7.23	6.00	5.59	5.32	4.08	5.00	5.00
10.	Hungary	5.2	4.1	4.4	4.2	4.8	4.1	3.9	1.3	1.90	2.30	6.56	1.53	0.23	3.76	3.00
11.	India	5.7	3.9	4.6	6.9	7.9	9.1	9.8	9.3	7.93	6.94	3.17	5.58	5.64	7.23	5.36
12.	Indonesia	5.4	3.6	4.5	4.8	5.0	5.7	5.5	6.3	6.08	5.51	7.66	5.74	4.34	5.21	5.75
13.	Israel	8.9	-0.3	-0.6	1.8	5.0	5.1	5.2	5.4	4.32	2.78	5.46	3.50	5.23	3.88	4.54
14.	Kenya	0.6	4.7	0.3	2.8	4.6	5.9	6.4	7.0	3.26	6.43	6.80	4.54	2.11	3.95	4.36
15.	Lebanon	1.7	4.5	3.3	4.1	7.5	1.1	0.0	4.0	6.00	5.00	1.53	-0.37	6.06	3.57	2.68
16.	Malaysia	8.7	0.5	5.4	5.8	6.8	5.3	5.8	6.3	5.75	4.75	7.76	5.90	7.25	5.60	6.65
17.	Mexico	6.6	-0.2	0.8	1.7	4.0	3.1	4.9	3.2	2.05	1.80	6.63	2.36	3.38	2.92	3.85
18.	Nigeria	5.3	8.2	21.2	10.3	10.6	5.4	6.2	5.9	6.21	8.11	7.11	1.84	2.63	8.81	5.00
19.	Pakistan	4.3	2.0	3.2	4.8	7.4	7.7	6.9	6.4	5.80	3.50	3.74	6.59	3.98	5.38	4.91
20.	Paraguay	-3.3	2.1	-0.0	3.8	4.1	2.9	4.3	6.8	5.50	4.20	8.05	3.92	2.44	2.90	4.36
21.	Philippines	6.0	1.8	4.4	4.9	6.4	5.0	5.4	7.2	4.40	3.80	6.16	2.01	2.78	5.05	3.97
22.	Poland	4.3	1.2	1.4	3.9	5.3	3.6	6.2	6.6	5.24	3.76	5.97	0.11	2.69	4.20	3.22
23.	Romania	2.1	5.7	5.1	5.2	8.5	4.2	7.9	6.0	8.60	4.80	5.75	1.61	-2.28	5.93	2.67
24.	Singapore	10.1	-2.4	4.2	3.5	9.0	7.3	8.2	7.7	3.62	3.45	9.56	7.54	7.55	5.68	7.63
25.	South Africa	4.2	2.7	3.7	3.1	4.9	5.0	5.4	5.1	3.83	3.31	3.40	2.24	1.39	4.21	2.77
26.	Taiwan Prov. of China	5.8	-2.2	4.6	3.5	6.2	4.2	4.9	5.7	3.83	2.50	10.21	8.18	6.51	4.05	7.32
27.	Thailand	4.8	2.2	5.3	7.1	6.3	4.5	5.1	4.8	4.74	4.53	7.00	7.24	5.28	4.98	6.15
28.	Turkey	6.8	-5.7	6.2	5.3	9.4	8.4	6.9	4.6	3.50	3.00	6.02	4.22	4.02	5.03	4.82
29.	Ukraine	5.9	9.2	5.2	9.6	12.1	2.7	7.3	7.6	6.39	2.50	n.a.	n.a.	-9.22	7.32	0.08
30.	Uruguay	-1.4	-3.4	-11.0	2.2	11.8	6.6	7.0	7.4	6.50	5.50	3.09	1.50	3.26	2.84	2.67
31.	Venezuela, Rep. Bol.	3.7	3.4	-8.9	-7.8	18.3	10.3	10.3	8.4	6.00	2.00	5.18	0.16	2.46	4.87	3.12
	Average	4.5	2.1	2.7	4.4	7.3	5.6	6.4	6.4	5.26	4.24	6.04	3.75	3.38	4.98	4.53
	Average 1/	4.4	1.9	2.5	4.3	7.2	5.5	6.2	6.2	5.11	4.07	6.01	3.55	3.15	4.81	4.37
	Average 2/	4.4	1.8	2.5	4.2	7.1	5.4	6.1	6.1	5.01	3.97	6.11	3.47	3.07	4.73	4.33

1/ Average excluding China

2/ Average excluding India and China

(Contd...)

No. Country	1970	1971	1972	1973	1974	1975	1976	1977	1978	1979	1980	1981	1982	1983	1984
1. World	5.2	4.6	5.4	6.9	2.8	1.9	5.2	4.4	4.6	3.8	2.2	2.2	1.1	3.0	4.6
2. Developing Asia	8.6	4.1	2.8	8.3	3.8	6.9	2.1	6.9	6.9	4.0	5.8	5.7	5.8	7.1	8.0
3. Central & Eastern Europe	4.9	3.3	4.4	6.1	2.1	-0.9	4.6	2.8	3.0	3.7	0.1	-0.6	1.0	3.8	3.7
4. Developing Countries	7.0	6.2	6.0	7.8	6.1	4.5	5.1	5.4	4.9	4.2	4.1	2.8	2.6	3.2	4.5
5. Middle East	7.9	9.6	11.8	8.6	9.1	4.2	10.5	7.4	3.5	1.3	-2.0	3.9	1.0	3.4	3.9
6. Western Hemisphere	4.5	7.2	7.4	8.5	7.0	3.0	5.5	4.7	4.6	6.6	6.6	0.5	-0.8	-2.1	3.7
7. India	5.8	2.3	-0.7	3.6	0.2	9.8	1.5	5.9	5.9	-2.5	3.6	6.4	4.3	6.2	4.8
8. EME Average	7.3	7.1	6.6	6.9	5.3	3.2	4.4	8.3	5.9	5.6	5.0	4.1	0.1	3.4	5.9
9. EME Average excluding China	7.0	7.1	6.7	6.6	5.3	3.0	4.6	8.4	5.8	5.5	4.9	4.1	-0.2	3.1	5.6
10. EME Average excluding India & China	7.0	7.2	7.0	6.8	5.5	2.8	4.7	8.4	5.8	5.8	4.9	4.0	-0.4	3.0	5.6

No. Country	1985	1986	1987	1988	1989	1990	1991	1992	1993	1994	1995	1996	1997	1998	1999
1. World	3.6	3.5	3.7	4.5	3.7	2.9	1.5	2.0	2.0	3.4	3.3	3.7	4.0	2.5	3.5
2. Developing Asia	7.0	6.2	7.4	9.2	6.2	5.5	6.1	8.9	9.0	9.4	8.9	8.4	6.4	3.6	6.3
3. Central & Eastern Europe	2.5	3.9	3.9	1.8	1.1	-0.8	-7.3	-1.5	2.4	0.6	6.0	5.1	4.4	2.8	0.6
4. Developing Countries	3.6	3.8	3.9	4.2	3.3	2.8	1.5	1.7	3.1	3.3	4.1	5.1	5.0	2.5	3.5
5. Middle East	2.3	-1.4	0.5	-1.1	3.9	8.3	7.7	6.1	2.5	2.2	2.5	4.8	4.2	3.7	1.7
6. Western Hemisphere	3.2	4.4	3.3	0.9	1.4	0.5	3.9	3.3	3.9	4.9	1.4	3.4	5.3	2.3	0.3
7. India	5.3	5.0	4.4	8.5	7.2	6.1	2.1	4.4	4.9	6.2	7.4	7.6	4.7	6.0	7.1
8. EME Average	3.4	3.8	5.7	4.1	2.1	2.7	3.6	4.1	3.8	4.0	4.2	4.1	3.9	1.3	2.0
9. EME Average excluding China	3.0	3.7	5.5	3.9	2.1	2.7	3.4	3.8	3.4	3.7	4.0	3.9	3.8	1.1	1.8
10. EME Average excluding India & China	2.9	3.6	5.5	3.7	1.9	2.5	3.4	3.8	3.4	3.6	3.9	3.8	3.7	0.9	1.6

No. Country	2000	2001	2002	2003	2004	2005	2006	2007	2008 Estimates	Average 10 Years 1970-79	Average 10 Years 1980-89	Average 10 years 1990-99	Average 9 years 2000-08	Average 39 Years 1970-2008	Average last 5 years 2004-2008
1. World	4.2	1.5	1.9	2.7	4.0	3.4	3.9	3.7	2.7	4.5	3.2	2.9	3.10	3.43	3.54
2. Developing Asia	6.9	5.8	6.9	8.1	8.6	9.0	9.6	9.7	8.2	5.4	6.8	7.3	8.08	6.87	9.01
3. Central & Eastern Europe	4.9	0.4	4.2	4.8	6.9	6.1	6.6	5.8	4.4	3.4	2.1	1.2	4.90	2.87	5.98
4. Developing Countries	5.9	3.8	4.7	6.2	7.5	7.1	7.8	7.9	6.7	5.7	3.6	3.3	6.40	4.70	7.38
5. Middle East	5.4	3.0	4.0	6.6	5.6	5.4	5.6	5.9	5.9	7.4	1.4	4.4	5.27	4.60	5.68
6. Western Hemisphere	4.1	0.7	0.4	2.1	6.2	4.6	5.5	5.6	4.4	5.9	2.1	2.9	3.72	3.66	5.24
7. India	5.7	3.9	4.6	6.9	7.9	9.1	9.8	9.3	7.9	3.2	5.6	5.6	7.23	5.36	8.82
8. EME Average	4.5	2.1	2.7	4.4	7.3	5.6	6.3	6.3	5.0	6.0	3.8	3.4	4.92	4.51	6.11
9. EME Average excluding China	4.4	1.9	2.5	4.2	7.2	5.4	6.2	6.2	4.9	6.0	3.5	3.2	4.76	4.36	5.96
10. EME Average excluding India & China	4.4	1.8	2.4	4.1	7.1	5.3	6.0	6.1	4.8	6.1	3.5	3.1	4.68	4.32	5.86

Source: International Monetary Fund, World Economic Outlook (WEO) Database, October, 2008.

Table 50: Overview of the *World Economic Outlook* Projections

(Percent change, unless otherwise noted)

	Year over Year						Q4 over Q4		
					Difference from November				
			Projections		2008 WEO Projections		Estimates	Projections	
	2007	2008	2009	2010	2009	2010	2008	2009	2010
World output[1]	5.2	3.4	0.5	3.0	-1.7	-0.8	1.1	1.2	3.4
Advanced economies	2.7	1.0	-2.0	1.1	-1.7	-0.5	-1.1	-0.5	1.6
United States	2.0	1.1	-1.6	1.6	-0.9	0.1	-0.7	—	2.0
Euro area	2.6	1.0	-2.0	0.2	-1.5	-0.7	-0.7	-1.4	0.9
Germany	2.5	1.3	-2.5	0.1	-1.7	-0.4	-1.2	-1.0	0.4
France	2.2	0.8	-1.9	0.7	-1.4	-0.8	-0.5	-1.8	2.2
Italy	1.5	-0.6	-2.1	-0.1	-1.5	-0.1	-1.5	-1.3	0.8
Spain	3.7	1.2	-1.7	-0.1	-1.0	-0.9	-0.4	-1.5	0.5
Japan	2.4	-0.3	-2.6	0.6	-2.4	-0.5	-3.0	-0.2	0.8
United Kingdom	3.0	0.7	-2.8	0.2	-1.5	-0.9	-1.8	-1.5	0.8
Canada	2.7	0.6	-1.2	1.6	-1.5	-1.4	-0.4	-0.4	2.0
Other advanced economies	4.6	1.9	-2.4	2.2	-3.9	-1.0	-1.6	0.1	2.7
Newly industrialized Asian economies	5.6	2.1	-3.9	3.1	-6.0	-1.1	-3.4	0.6	3.3
Emerging and developing economies[2]	8.3	6.3	3.3	5.0	-1.8	-1.2	4.5	3.5	5.8
Africa	6.2	5.2	3.4	4.9	-1.4	-0.5	...	...	...
Central and eastern Europe	5.4	3.2	-0.4	2.5	-2.6	-1.3	...	...	...
Russia	8.1	6.2	-0.7	1.3	-4.2	-3.2	2.7	-1.3	1.9
Excluding Russia	9.7	5.4	0.3	4.4	-1.3	-0.3	...	...	...
Developing Asia	10.6	7.8	5.5	6.9	-1.6	-1.1	...	...	...
China	13.0	9.0	6.7	8.0	-1.8	-1.5	6.8	7.5	8.1
India	9.3	7.3	5.1	6.5	-1.2	-0.3	5.1	5.3	7.1
ASEAN-5	6.3	5.4	2.7	4.1	-1.5	-1.3	4.1	3.1	4.5
Middle East	6.4	6.1	3.9	4.7	-1.5	-0.6	...	...	...
Memorandum									
European Union	3.1	1.3	-1.8	0.5	-1.6	-0.8	...	...	...
World growth based on market exchange rates	3.8	2.2	-0.6	2.1	-1.7	-0.7	...	...	...
World trade volume (goods and services)	7.2	4.1	-2.8	3.2	-4.8	-2.5	...	...	...
Imports									
Advanced economies	4.5	1.5	-3.1	1.9	-3.0	-1.8	...	...	...
Emerging and developing economies	14.5	10.4	-2.2	5.8	-7.0	-3.6	...	...	...
Exports									
Advanced economies	5.9	3.1	-3.7	2.1	-5.0	-1.8	...	...	...
Emerging and developing economies	9.6	5.6	-0.8	5.4	-5.8	-3.5	...	...	...
Commodity prices (U.S. dollars)									
Oil[3]	10.7	36.4	-48.5	20.0	-16.7	9.7	...	...	...
Nonfuel (average based on world commodity export weights)	14.1	7.4	-29.1	7.3	-10.4	6.3	...	...	...
Consumer Prices									
Advanced economies	2.1	3.5	0.3	0.8	-1.1	-0.8	2.6	0.3	0.9
Emerging and developing economies[2]	6.4	9.2	5.8	5.0	-1.3	-0.5	7.6	4.7	4.2
London interbank offered rate (per cent)[4]									
On U.S. dollar deposits	5.3	3.0	1.3	2.9	-0.7	-1.4	...	...	...
On euro deposits	4.3	4.6	2.2	2.7	-0.8	-0.8	...	...	...
On Japanese yen deposits	0.9	1.0	1.0	0.4	—	-0.3	...	...	...

Notes: Real effective exchange rates are assumed to remain constant at the levels prevailing during December 08, 2008-January 05, 2009. Country weights used to construct aggregate growth rates for groups of countries were revised.

1 The quarterly estimates and projections account for 90 per cent of the world purchasing-power-parity weights.

2 The quarterly estimates and projections account for approximately 76 per cent of the emerging and developing economies.

3 Simple average of prices of U.K. Brent, Dubai, and West Texas Intermediate crude oil. The average price of oil in U.S. dollars a barrel was $97.03 in 2008; the assumed price based on future markets is $50.00 in 2009 and $60.00 in 2010.

4 Six-month rate for the United States and Japan. Three-month rate for the euro area.

Source: WEO Database, 29 January 2009.

Table 51: Purchasing-Power-Parity (PPP)—GDP Projections for Some Countries

	PPP GDP 2007 (billions US $)	Estimated Projection for (billion US $)					
		2008	2009	2010	2011	2012	2013
USA	13,808	14,334	14,571	15,092	15,859	16,605	17,310
China	7,035	7,890	8,758	9,760	10,938	12,264	13,751
Japan	4,292	4,405	4,490	4,640	4,859	5,083	5,280
India	2,997	3,305	3,591	3,927	4,319	4,753	5,231
Germany	2,812	2,920	2,962	3,051	3,156	3,273	3,400
UK	2,168	2,231	2,261	2,358	2,490	2,625	2,765
France	2,068	2,125	2,159	2,238	2,350	2,467	2,589
Italy	1,788	1,821	1,843	1,887	1,943	2,004	2,074
Mexico	1,486	1,550	1,603	1,687	1,799	1,921	2,044
Spain	1,352	1,400	1,419	1,466	1,531	1,609	1,693
Canada	1,270	1,307	1,344	1,402	1,483	1,564	1,640
Korea	1,202	1,279	1,345	1,436	1,536	1,642	1,752

Source: IMF, World Economic Outlook Database, October 2008.

Table 52: GDP Projections for Some Countries

	2007 GDP (billions of US $)	Estimated Projection for (billion US $)					
		2008	2009	2010	2011	2012	2013
USA	13,808	14,334	14,571	15,092	15,859	16,605	17,310
Japan	4,382	4,844	4,803	4,908	5,107	5,287	5,439
Germany	3,321	3,818	3,773	3,897	4,035	4,195	4,376
China	3,280	4,222	4,772	5,350	6,005	6,739	7,562
UK	2,804	2,787	2,734	2,888	3,076	3,279	3,491
France	2,594	2,978	3,011	3,135	3,297	3,467	3,647
Italy	2,105	2,399	2,407	2,475	2,555	2,643	2,743
Spain	1,440	1,683	1,703	1,780	1,878	1,996	2,132
Canada	1,436	1,564	1,570	1,647	1,744	1,842	1,933
India	1,101	1,237	1,350	1,483	1,632	1,796	1,978
Mexico	1,023	1,143	1,192	1,268	1,354	1,445	1,539
Korea	970	953	1,019	1,103	1,191	1,283	1,379

Source: IMF, World Economic Outlook Database, October 2008.